THE

HISTORY

OF

NOTTINGHAM

BY

CHARLES DEERING, M.D.

Together with an Index

By R. C. Chicken, F.R.C.S., ENG.,

AND

A new Foreword

By Miss L. I. EDWARDS

REPUBLISHED BY S.R. PUBLISHERS LTD. 1970

FIRST PUBLISHED NOTTINGHAM, 1751

(INDEX FIRST PUBLISHED NOTTINGHAM, 1899)

BIBLIOGRAPHIC NOTE

The *History* is reprinted in original sequence, ending at page 370. The reprint of the *Index* follows this, its original pagination being retained. The only adjustment made in reprinting the Index is in the List of Plates, where alternative page numbers are omitted, so that the list corresponds with the reprinted History.

The Plates *face* the pages noted in the Index.

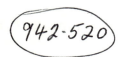

Reprinted in England by

The Scolar Press Ltd., Menston,
Yorkshire, U.K.

Foreword

Charles Deering, M.D., (circa 1695-1749), was born in Saxony and educated at Hamburg and Leyden. He came to England in 1713, first as secretary to Baron Schach, Russian envoy to Queen Anne, then as tutor in Sir John Cope's household. In 1718 he contracted an unhappy marriage, which together with ill-health soured his disposition for the rest of his life. He obtained his doctor's degree at Rheims in December, 1718, following this with medical courses in Paris. It seems strange that so little is known of the subsequent career of a man so well endowed with knowledge and experience. He returned to London in 1719 and practised there but without prosperity. Probably in the hope of bettering himself he moved to Nottingham in 1735 and remained there for the rest of his life. In 1736 he published a treatise on smallpox, which had a chilly reception among the local medical people. Disappointedly turning his attention to botany, a subject which had long interested him, he published in 1738 *Catalogus Stirpium*, or catalogue of . . . plants growing in the Nottingham area. By 1740 he had already begun to write his history of Nottingham. Although he had almost completed it by 1743, he was beginning to despair of it ever being published. He died, a poor man, in 1749, two years before its publication.

The value of Deering's History today lies not so much in its account of Nottingham's early history, but in the major part of the work which so vividly describes the contemporary scene. For this reason alone it ranks with the history of the county by that other great historian Dr. Robert Thoroton.

The index compiled by R. C. Chicken was first published in 1899 as a separate volume, and is now published with the History for the first time.

MISS L. I. EDWARDS

(v)

NOTTINGHAMIA VETUS ET NOVA

OR AN

HISTORICAL ACCOUNT

OF THE

ANCIENT AND PRESENT STATE

OF THE TOWN OF

NOTTINGHAM.

GATHER'D

From the REMAINS of ANTIQUITY and Collected from Authentic
MANUSCRIPTS and Ancient as well as Modern HISTORIANS.

ADORN'D

With beautiful COPPER-PLATES

WITH

An APPENDIX,

CONTAINING

Besides Extracts of WILLS and DEEDS relating to CHARITIES,
Diverse other CURIOUS PAPERS.

By *CHARLES DEERING*, M.D.

NOTTINGHAM:

Printed by and for, GEORGE AYSCOUGH, & THOMAS WILLINGTON.
MDCCLI.

To the READER.

Candid READER,

THE *Title and Table of Contents informing the Reader in a great Measure what to expect in the following Sheets, I shall not trouble him with a long Preface, only thus much I have thought necessary to acquaint him with, That the Author is neither a Native of the Town of Nottingham nor born in the County and therefore cannot be supposed to have that Prepossession which Men too commonly have in favour of the spot which has given them Birth : That his real Motives for undertaking this Task, were, The Antiquity of the Place, its extremely inviting natural as well as acquired Beauties ; its Importance in ancient Times and its flourishing State in our Days.*

He hopes therefore to be credited when he declares that whatever is contained in this Book is delivered with the utmost impartiality.

To the MOST NOBLE

THOMAS HOLLES,

DUKE of *NEWCASTLE*,

MARQUIS and EARL of CLARE,

VISCOUNT HAUGHTON,

BARON PELHAM of *Laughton*,

Lord Lieutenant and Cuftos Rotulorum of the Counties of *Nottingham* and *Middlefex*,

Lord Warden of the Foreft of SHERWOOD,

Knight of the Moft Noble Order of the GARTER,

One of the LORDS of his MAJESTY's Moft Honourable PRIVY-COUNCIL,

Principal SECRETARY of STATE,

Lord Lieutenant, Cuftos Rotulorum and Recorder of the Town and County of the Town of *Nottingham*,

This Book is with all Humility infcribed, by your GRACE's

Moft obedient and moft

humble Servants

The EDITORS.

GEORGE AYSCOUGH,
THO. WILLINGTON.

To the Most Noble

THOMAS HOLLES,

DUKE of *NEWCASTLE*,

Marquis and Earl of CLARE,

Viscount HAUGHTON,

Baron PELHAM of *Laughton*,

May it please your Grace,

ENCOURAGED by a well grounded Confidence that my Subject will plead in Favour of its Author, I humbly offer this Historical Essay to Your Grace's Powerful Patronage.

It is an Account of the former and present State of the ancient Town of *Nottingham* ; a Town, which not only Your great Ancestors but yourself have taken under your special Protection, and which you have honoured with condescending to be their Recorder.

This Town has long since experienced in a particular Manner and still daily feels the valuable Effects
of

of your Grace's more than paternal Care for its well being, at the same Time that the whole Nation in general is throughly sensible of Your Grace's Greatness of Mind, Generosity and disinterested Love for your Country. Qualities rarely to be met with, and which to represent in their due Lustre, require one of the ablest Pens. Whilst I in Silence admiring what I dare not aspire to celebrate, only crave leave to say, that To have filled up some of the most eminent Posts in the Kingdom, for a long Series of Years *un-envied*, to the *entire Satisfaction of Your* PRINCE and the *Universal Applause* of all the thinking part of Mankind, be-speaks in Your Grace all that is Great and Good. And that Heaven would long continue the Blessing this Your Native Country enjoys in Your Grace, with increase of Days, in Health and Vigour shall ever be the fervent Prayer of

Your Grace's

Most obedient

Most humble Servant

Charles Deering.

The INTRODUCTION.

An INTRODUCTORY ACCOUNT of the Antiquity of the Town of *Nottingham.*

IT is too common an Obfervation that Writers of the Hiftory of particular Places as well as whole Kingdoms, are fond of the *Marvellous,* and think they do not fufficient Juftice to their Subject, without tracing the Original of their Kings, or the firft Foundation of their Cities and Towns, fo far back, as to be obliged either to have Recourfe to the Fertility of their own Brains, for fome romantic Beginning of them, or elfe to be beholden to fabulous Authors who have done the Bufinefs to their Hands.

OUR Englifh Hiftory can fhew the Truth of my Affertion, if we only give ourfelves the Trouble to look into fome of the Monkifh Authors of it. (*a*)

WHEREAS nothing can be a real Advantage to the Subject an Author treats upon, which does not carry along with it fuch Evidence either pofitive or circumftantial, as is fufficient to gain the Credit of the difcerning Readers.

A confiftent Account gathered from well attefted Facts, and drawn from a curious and judicious occular Infpection, after having duly compared Things with Things, like a Reading Glafs which only clears up the Letters but neither magnifies or diminifhes them, ferves the Reader to fee the Truth in a proper Light ; but as fuch a Glafs the farther the Object is removed from its true Focus, reprefents the fame the more and more dim : So the farther an Author retires into the dark Receffes of Antiquity, the more he clouds his Subject, and too often renders his Veracity in other particulars fufpected.

JOHN ROWSE, a Monk of *Warwick,* and Canon of *Ofney,* in his Hiftory written to King HENRY VII. fhews himfelf one of this Clafs : He there places the Antiquity of the Town of *Nottingham,* 980

*
Years

(*a*) *David Tavenfis, Radulphus Aga, Geoffry ap Arthur, Matthew of Weftminfter, John Rowfe,* &c.

Years before Christ. He says that King EBRANC did build this Town upon *Trent*, on a dolorous Hill, so called from the grief of the *Britains*, of whom King HUMBER made a very great Slaughter in the Reign of ALBANACT.

THIS remarkable Hill methinks, might have afforded the *Britains* a Name for this Town, but our Author gives us none.

THE Improbability of this Tale will manifest itself, if we cast an Eye on the State and Condition of the *Britains* even in *Cæsar's* Time, but a few Years before CHRIST. They were then a People not unlike the present *American Indians*, or some of the Hords of the *Tartars* in the North-East parts of *Europe* and *Asia*, and the more inland they were the more Savage and unpolished, having no Commerce with other Nations, not to speak of their Nakedness, and that in the South parts only they used to cover themselves, and that in a very careless manner with the Skins of Wild Beasts, more to avoid giving Offence to Strangers who came to Trade with them, than for any other Reason : Their Habitations consisted according to *Cæsar*, of a confused parcel of Huts, generally placed in the midst of Woods, at a little Distance from each other, without any distinction of Streets ; the Avenues of these little Colonies or Villages of theirs, were defended by slight Ramparts or Banks of Earth, or with Trees which they had felled to clear the Ground : The whole Country was divided into many small States, of which each had their Chief, and in the Time of War they chose one for their Generalissimo, such was *Cassibilan* Chief of the *Tribonantes* in *Cæsar's* Time, such *Caractacus* Chief of the *Sileurs* in the Time of *Claudius*.

AFTER this View of the State of the *Britains*, in the beginning of the Roman Monarchy, will any one presume that these People were more civilized, and better acquainted with the manner of Building Towns above 900 Years before, than they were when *Cæsar* first visited this Island ? I can hardly think so.

THE most then that may be supposed with some Appearance of Truth is : That considering the convenient Situation of that part of the Forest of *Shirwood*, on or near which the present Town of *Nottingham* stands, it is not unlikely that several Colonies of *Britains* had planted themselves hereabout, where they were sheltered from the Injuries of the North and East Winds and cherished by a warm Southern Air, as well as plentifully provided with Water. Nay it is highly probable, that as soon as these People were provided with Tools for the Purpose, finding in these parts a yeilding Rock, they might improve their Habitations by making their way into the main Rock and framing to themselves convenient Appartments in it, and that perhaps long before the Romans

came

came into this Neighbourhood. I am the rather induced to favour this Conjecture of mine, by a late difcovery the Right Honourable the Lord MIDDLETON's Goodnefs to this Town has furnifhed me with. His Lordfhip like his Noble Ancefters (who have always witneffed a more than common Affection for *Nottingham*, as will appear in proper Places) did offer, in the Spring of 1740, to the Corporation, to level a deep and narrow Hollow-way, between the two Hills called the Sand-Hills, the only way to this Town from the *Derby* Road, and make the Avenue to *Chapel-Bar*, (the fole ancient Gate, lately ftill in being,) both fpacious and pleafant, and upon their Acceptance of His Offer, has generoufly performed the fame, at his own Coft and Charge. When the Workmen had removed a good deal of the Sandy part of the Hills, they met here and there with fome folid Rock, which (upon clearing away the Sand from it,) appeared to be partition Walls of feveral Rooms, of which fome were higher and fome lower, all cut out of the firm Rock. Thefe having no Mark of Roman Contrivance nor any thing being found there to give Room to fuppofe it, I take to be *Britifh*, which Opinion of mine I endeavour to fupport thus :

IN the firft Place, the Sandy part of thefe Hills is indifputably adventitious, and confequently muft be brought from fome other Place, and whence could it be brought but from *Nottingham* ? the whole Rock on which it is built being fo undermin'd and hollow'd, that it is almoft a queftion, whether the folid Contents of what is erected on the Top, would fill up the Cavities under Ground.

IN the fecond Place, when this *Nottingham* Sand was carried thither, thefe Concamerations muft then have been in a ruinous Condition and confequently much older than the Excavations of the *Nottingham* Rock, therefore they muft be *Britifh*.

THIRDLY, there are more Sand-Hills of this kind about the Town, where the like has been obferved, which has given room for a Tradition that the Town of *Nottingham* did once ftand farther North.

FOURTHLY, that thefe ftraggling Habitations were no part of the Town of *Nottingham* in the Saxon Times is plain, in that they are a pretty way without the Confines of that ancient Wall, with which EDWARD the *Elder* fortified this Town, and whereof there remain ftill fome Traces.

SOME to prove the great Antiquity of the Town of *Nottingham* affirm

** **

firm that (*a*) *Coilus* a Britiſh King was buried in it, A. M. 3832. Suppoſe we grant that it is not at all incredible that theſe Colonies of *Britains* might be under the Government of a Chief of that Name, who might have choſen to be buried hereabout ; yet to conclude from ſuch a looſe Aſſertion, that the Foundation of the Town of *Nottingham* was laid near a Thouſand Years before the Chriſtian Æra, is as ridiculous as if an Author ſhould write the Hiſtory of *New-York* or *Philadelphia,* and ſhould affirm that one of theſe Places was of a thouſand, the other of fifteen hundred Years ſtanding, becauſe ſo long ago ſome *Indian* Hutts had ſtood upon the very Spots, where now theſe Cities are built. Here we leave the *Britains,* and in the next Place enquire whether the *Romans* were the Founders of this Place.

THE Reverend DR. *Thomas Gale,* late Dean of *York,* a very learned Antiquary, in his Latin Commentaries upon *Antoninus's* Imperial Itinerary through *Britain,* takes Notice of *Nottingham,* viz. (*b*) in the 5th Journey

---

(*a*) *Hollinſhed* makes mention of two Britiſh Kings of the Name of *Coilus,* viz. in his Hiſtory of *Scotland,* p. 9. he tells us, that in the Reign of *Ferguſius,* the firſt King of *Scots.* between A. M. 3640 & 50, *Coilus* a Britiſh King, invaded *Scotland,* that the *Britains* were beaten and *Coilus* ſlain, and according to his Eſtate, ſolemnly buried at *Troinovantum* the ancient Name for *London.* The ſame Author in his Hiſtory of *England* takes no Notice of this *Coilus,* but in p. 73 mentions one of that Name, who A C. 125. ſucceeded his Father *Marius,* otherwiſe called *Meurig,* and died at *York* 165, leaving *Lucius* his Succeſſor. This laſt is out of the Queſtion, whilſt the firſt is ſaid to be buried at *London,* and if he had been interred at *Nottingham,* A. M. 3832, he muſt be near two hundred Years old, if *Hollinſhed's* Chronology be true ; ſo confuſed and contradictory to each other are our Hiſtorians when they look back beyond the Romans.

(*b*) Cauſennas itaq; lego, per illas autem intelligo *Nottingham.* De illa *Cambdenus* : " *A præruptis Saxis in auſtrali parte fluviolum Linum de ſpectat et Caſtrum ſublime in rupe ſurgit.* Nec dubito quin operoſæ illæ cryptæ, concamerationes, cavernæ ſubterraneæ è vivo Saxo exciſæ, romanam loquantur magnificentiam, uti ut illæ aliæ quæ *Devæ* et *Iſcæ Silurum* celebrantur eoſdem Authores habuerint, adde his ſupputationem diſtantiæ, à Cauſennis ad Durobrivas (*Nottingham* et *Bridgcaſterton*) pulchrè cum numeris *Antonini* concordare, uti etiam cum illis quos inter Cauſennas at Lindum locat. Cauſennis aliter Gauſennis rectius Goſennis vel Govennis. *Ceven* et Govennæ et Covennæ ſunt rupes conglomeratæ. In Comitatu *Eboracenſi* rupes prope *Ottely* dicuntur *the Cheven.* In illo Cantii, oppidum *Savennoc i. e. Chevennoc* ita dicitur â vicinis collibus. Gevennus eſt tum mons tum fluvius in agro *Monmouthenſi* unde Gobanium *Antonino.* Saxonibus fuit oppidum hoc *Snottengham* Speluncarum Domus. Britannis in antiquis *Kaff* vel *Kaou* Caverna. Si itaq; minus arrideat conjectura noſtra quæ Gauvennas a Ceven deduxit, originem iſtius dictionis â *Kaff* vel *Kaou* petas licet quod non minus noſtram confirmabit Sententiam de ſitu hujus Stationis. Iter Britanniarum Commentariis illuſtratum. 1709. p. 95, 96.

Journey of *Antoninus* from *Gormanchester* to *Littleburgh*, the Emperor mentions the following Places :

> *Duroliponte*
> *Durobrivis* — 35 M.
> *Caufennis* — 30 —
> *Lindum* — — 26 —
> *Agelocum* — 14 —

Total 105 M.

Of thefe Dr. *Gale*, makes Durobrivas *Brigcaftern*, and Caufennas *Nottingham*.

But another Antiquary of great Fame, Mr. *William Baxter*, 'who has wrote fince, will have Durobrivas to be *Cafter*, and Caufennas *Grantham*. Their Names and Diftances ftand thus :

	GALE.			BAXTER.	
From	*Gormanchefter* to *Brigcafterton* — 35 M.		From	*Gormanchefter* to *Cafter* — — 22 M.	
	Nottingham — 30 —			*Grantham* — 24 —	
	Lincoln — — 26 —			*Lincoln* — 24 —	
	Littleburgh — 14 —			*Littleburgh* — 15 —	
	Total 105.			Total 85.	

Here the Reader may obferve that Dr. *Gale's* Diftances exactly anfwers the Diftances of the Imperial Traveller, whilft Mr. *Baxter* is 20 Miles fhort in the total Diftance : Befides this great Difference in the Number of Miles, there is no Appearance of any old Roman Road from *Huntington* or *Gormanchefter* to *Grantham*. (a) The Dean farther fupports his Opinion by the

Derivation

(a) Dr. *Stukeley* in his *Itinerarium curiofum* is of Mr. *Baxter's* Mind, that *Durobrivæ* is *Cafter*, tho' he himfelf in his 5th Iter p. 112. lays it down as a Rule, that Diftances, ought to be moft regarded. He there places *Noviomagus*, with Mr. *Somner*, about *Weftend* or *Crayford*, on Account of the refpective Diftances on each fide, notwithftanding no marks of Roman Antiquity are there obferved, he brings Authority and fays : " Dr. *Plot* fettles *Pennocrucium* at *Stretton* in *Staffordfhire*, " becaufe it is upon this fame *Watlingftreet* and Anfwers the Diftances, tho' no " Roman Antiquities are difcovered there, and the like muft we do in other " Places." Surely he had forgot that in the fame Iter he had been fo lavifh as to fling out ten Miles (or a decimal as he Terms it) in favour of *Cafter*, when at the fame Time *Brigcafterton*, which he we would fain have a Station, is of the exact Diftance of the Itinerary of *Antoninus*. Antiquaries fhould have fome Standard to go by, they fhould either infift upon Diftances and Marks of Antiquity together, or fhould at leaft hold to Diftances.

The INTRODUCTION.

Derivation of the Name *Caufennæ* which he alters into *Gofennæ* or *Govennæ*, and fays that fignifies a Clufter of Hills, or elfe (which to me feems rather more probable) from the old British Words *Kaff* or *Kaou* fignifying a *Cavern* or *Cave*, which anfwers the Signification of the Name which the Saxons afterwards gave to this Town. The Doctor will befides have it, that the Caves and Rock Holes, &c. which have been, and are in part ftill obferved about *Nottingham*, are Remains of the *Roman* Grandeur, to which I cannot agree for feveral Reafons. *Firft*, nothing appears in any of them now to be feen that befpeaks the Roman Tafte, and thofe fubteraneous Structures which upon digging for Foundations have been difcovered within the Memory of Man, and have fhewn the moft curious Workmanfhip of any, will by and by appear to be of a much later Date. *Secondly*, if we allow with Dr. *Gale*, that *Caufennæ* is the Place where *Nottingham* now ftands, this Name is derived from the British, whence the Romans ufually borrowed their Names of Places which they met with in their Way, hence it follows that thefe cavernous Dwelling Places were in being before their Time, elfe they would have called them by a Name of their own. The Romans were the firft that took Notice of the Bath in *Somerfetfhire*, whence *Antoninus* calls it *Aquæ folis* which Name has no Affinity with any British Word, fo the *Pharos* at *Dover*, a true Monument of the Roman Magnificence, derives its Name from the Ifland of *Pharo*, where Queen *Cleopatra* had formerly caufed fuch an high Tower to be erected, furnifhed with Lights for the Service of Mariners. Of this kind many more Inftances might be brought, which to avoid too great Prolixity I omit. Thus what the Reverend Antiquary has advanced in fome Meafure proves, that, at or very near the Place where *Nottingham* is built, there was a Roman Station, but it does not make out that there was either a *British* or *Roman* Town, built on the top of *John Roufe's* dolorous Hill. For my part if I confider that the Foffe way is on the South of the River *Trent*, and that the *Romans* always made their *Vallum* on the South-fide and where the Ground was rifing, I can hardly forbear thinking that there was a Station in that Neighbourhood, where now *Weft-Bridgeford* ftands, (almoft directly over-againft *Nottingham*,) a little Town not built till many Ages after, and that from the remarkablenefs of the many Caves in the oppofite Rock they might give the Station the Name of *Caufennæ* or *Caufennæ*, and what feems to add to my Conjecture, is what Dr. *Stukeley* informs us of, that one Mr. *Cooper*, a Man of 72 Years of Age, told him, that there was found at *Wilford* a Pot of Roman Coins, a Town which lies on the fame fide of the River, and at a very little Diftance from *Bridgeford*, the High-Road only, parting the Parifhes. A learned Gentleman, Native of this Town, who has been fo kind as to fend me fome Remarks of his own, relating to a Roman Station hereabout, feems rather to favour Mr. *Baxter's* Opinion, the which with my Anfwer to them the curious will find in the *Appendix*.—I have done with the Romans.

THE SAXONS who were the next Poffeffors of *Britain*, afford us a more satisfactory Account concerning our Town, and tho' History does not furnish us with the Name of the Founder, or the exact Year it was begun to be built in ; yet all our best Historians agree, that it was a considerable Place in the 8th Century, provided with a strong Tower, that it was called by the Saxons in the Time of the Heptarchy *Snoden-gaham* as Dr. *Thoroton* has it, or rather *Snottengaham* from *Snottenga* Caves, and *Ham* Home or Dwelling Place. *Camden* and others gives us a British Translation of it, *viz. Tui ogo bauc*, or more rightly as Mr. *Baxter* has it, *Din ogo vaiic* or *Din ogoloco* which however none pretends to be the ancient British Name. This *Saxon* Name was doubtless given to it by that People, from the Condition they found the Neighbourhood in, before they themselves made Improvements by Building. It belonged to the Kingdom of *Mercia*, and a part of that Kingdom took afterwards in King *Alfred's* Reign, its Name from this Town *Snottengaham-Scyre* now *Nottinghamshire.*

BEFORE I proceed to the Time of the *Saxon* Kings of all *England*, I must take Notice that in several parts of *Nottingham*, Structures of a very considerable Extent, arched in a regular manner, and supported by Columns with carved Capitals, &c. framed for Places of Worship, hewn out of the Rock, have been discovered by Workmen when digging for Foundations, with very obscure Entrances, hardly to be suspected, and also other Apartments for lodging Places, such were observed under diverse Houses on the Row, on the South-side of the Great Market-Place called *Timber-Hill,* and one *Edward Goddard*, a Bricklayer yet living, assures me, that when he was an Apprentice being at work on the East-side of the *Weekday-Cross*, he there got into one of these subterraneous Fabricks, which he found supported and adorned with Pillars as has been mentioned, and that he made his way from one spacious Place to another till he came as far as the upper End of *Pilchergate*, and under a small Close at present the Property of *John Sherwin*, Esq; one of his Majesty's Justices of the Peace for the County of *Nottingham* at large, and opposite to his Dwelling House : He the said *Goddard* says, that in one of these Places, he found a Wooden Cup and a Wooden Cann, which seemed to be found and whole, but that when he took hold of them, they mouldered into Dust. These Places being of the *Gothic* Order, I conjecture to have been contrived in the Time of the Heptarchy, when the *Danes* who were Pagans, made frequent Inroads into the Kingdom of *Mercia*, where they in a more extraordinary manner exercised their Cruelty upon Nuns and Friers, and indeed Christian Priests of all kinds. To these they might in Time of Danger betake themselves as Places of Refuge, and were they might Exercise their Religious Functions, without being exposed to the Fury of those persecuting Idolaters.

EDWARD SENIOR, between 919 and 924 according to *Marianus Scotus*

did

did build a Bridge over the *Trent* and on the other Side a little Town overgainst the old Town of *Nottingham*, now call'd *Bridgeford*. (*a*)

IN EDWARD the *Confeſſor's* Time, who properly was the laſt of the Royal Saxon Race, *Snottengaham* was a very conſiderable Borough, of which in *Doomſday-Book* there is the following Account.

" IN the Time of *Edward* the *Confeſſor* in the Borough of *Nottingham*,
" were One hundred and ſeventy three Burgeſſes and nineteen *Villains* (or
" Husbandmen) : To this Borough lay ſix Carucats (*b*) of Land to or for
" the King's Geld (or Tax), and one Meadow and ſmall Wood, ſix Qua-
" rentens (*c*) long and five broad, this Land was parted between thirty-
" eight Burgeſſes, and of the Rate or Rent (Cenſu) of the Land and of the
" Works of the Burgeſſes yielded 75 *s*. 7 *d*. and of two Mints (Mone-
" tariis) 40 *s*. Within it had Earl *Toſti* one Carucat of Land of the *Soc*
" (*d*) of which the King was to have 2 *d*. and the Earl himſelf the 3 *d*. At-
terwards

(*a*) *Thoroton*, p. 62. ſeems to be ſomewhat too haſty in taking up Mr. *Camden* for ſaying it was *Bridgeford* which *Edward* the *Elder* built over againſt *Nottingham*; — his Words are theſe : " That might likely enough be, if that was not miſtaken " for ſome Buildings, which may have been within *Nottingham* on the South-ſide " of *Trent*, where there is Ground enough within the Limits of it, near the Bridge- " End for ſuch a Purpoſe ; and I rather ſuſpect it, becauſe before the Saxon Go- " vernment was changed, I find *Bridgeford* a Member of *Clifton* Soc and not of " *Nottingham*, &c." *Stow* is expreſs that *Edward* the Elder, built a *New-Town* over-againſt the *Old-Town* of *Nottingham*, and a Bridge over the *Trent*, between the two Towns. A few ſtragling Houſes which only may have been, cannot with any Colour be called a Town, and a Town being built oppoſite to *Nottingham*, does no ways infer that it muſt needs belong to *Nottingham*, beſides *Nottingham* has not Ground enough to build a Town upon near the End of the *Trent-Bridge*.
(*b*) *Carucat* with the *Normans* is the ſame as *Family-Manſe* or *Hide* of the *Saxons*, it is at a Medium computed an hundred Acres, ſix ſcore to the hundred, of arable Land, together with Paſture and Meadow, with Barnes, Stables and Dwellings, for ſuch a Number of Men and Beaſts, as were neceſſary to manage ſo much Land. But as ſome Soil is lighter and ſome ſtiffer, ſo the Quantity may be more or leſs, and therefore by it is generally underſtood as much Land as with one Plough and Beaſts ſufficient, could be tilled in one Year.
(*c*) *Quarenten* is a Furlong of 40 Perches : Theſe alſo differed in divers Places, and were from 16 to 20 Feet each Perch, and even the Feet in ſome Places were 12, in ſome 18 Inches.
(*d*) *Soc* and *Sac* are two Saxon Words importing : The firſt not only the Circuit or Territory wherein any Power is lodged, but the Power, Authority or Liberty to adminiſter Juſtice and execute Laws. The other the Priviledge to hear and Judge Cauſes and levy Forfeitures and Amerciaments ariſing among the People reſident within ſuch Circuit or Territory, Part whereof was ever as well by the King in his

" terwards, when King *William* the *Conqueror* survey'd it, *Hugh* the
" Sheriff the son of *Baldric* found 156 Men dwelling there. When
" *Doomsday-Book* was made towards the latter end of his Reign there
" were 16 less. Yet that *Hugh* himself made 13 Dwellings or Man-
" sions in the Land of the Earl in the New-Borough which were not
" there before, putting them in the *Cense* or Rate of the old Borough."

" In *Snottingham* in the Demesne of the King was one Church, in which
" were three Mansions of the Borough and five Bovats of Land, of
" the above-said six Carucats with *Sac* and *Soc*, and to the same Church
" five Acres of Land and a half, of which the King had *Sac* and *Soc*.
" The Burgesses had six Carucats to plough, and twenty Borders, and
" 14 Carucats (Ploughs, Carts, Draughts, Teams, or Plough-Lands.)
" They were wont to Fish in the Water of *Trent*, and at that Time
" made Complaint that they were prohibited to fish "

" In the Time of *Edward* the *Confessor*, *Snottingham* yielded Rent
" 18 *l*. when *Doomsday-Book* was made 30 *l*. and 10 *l*. of the Mint (de
" *Moneta*.)

" Roger *de* Bushly had in *Snottingham* three Mansions, in which
" were seated eleven Houses. The Rent 4 *s*. 7 *d*.

" William Peverel had forty eight Merchant's-Houses or (Trades
" men's.) The Rent 36 *s*. and 13 Houses of Knights (or Horsemen)
[*Equitum*] and eight Borders. (*a*)

**

RALPH

---

his as other Lords in theirs, kept in his or their own respective Hands and Tenancies, for the support and sustenance of his or their particular Family there, which
is now called Demesne.

(*a*) *Borders* are the same as our Cottages, which had but very little Land layd to
their Houses, yet with this difference, that the modern Cottagers pay a certain
Rent and are Freemen, but the Borders were Bondsmen, and (except their Lives)
entirely at the Disposal of their Lords, and when they worked at the Lord's, or
where they were ordered, they had also their Diet, from whence proceeds the
Name *Border*

As this State and Condition of Nottingham *is taken out of* Doomsday-Book, *it may
perhaps not be displeasing to some of the Readers if I give them the following short
Account of that famous Book, according to* St. Dunelm. Hoved. Ingulph. &c.

" In the Year 1080, *William* the 1st. ordered an exact Survey to be taken of the
" Lands, Goods, and Chattels of all his Subjects. This Survey contained the
" Number of Acres in each Man's Estate, what he was wont to pay in the *Saxon*
" Times, how much he had been Taxed of late Years since the Revolution. ——
" Moreover

" RALPH *de* BURUN had thirteen Houses of Knights, in one of these
" dwelt one Merchant.

" GULBERT four Houses.

" RALPH Son of (or FITZ) HUBERT had eleven Houses, in these re-
" mained (or dwelt) three Merchants Tradesmen or Shopkeepers.)

" GOISFRID *de* ALSELINE had twenty one Houses.

" ACADUS the Priest (*Presbyter*) two Houses.

" IN the Croft of the Priest were 65 Houses and in these the King
" had *Sac* and *Soc*.

" THE Church with all things belonging to it was 100 *s*. p. *Ann*. Value.

" RICHARD TRESLE, had four Houses.

" IN the (*fossata*) Ditch of the Borough were 17 Houses, and other
" six Houses.

" THE King granted to *William Peverel* ten Acres of Land to make
" an Orchard.

" THE Water of *Trent*, the Ditch and the Road to *York* are taken
" care of by *Snottingeham*, insomuch, that if any one should hinder the
" Passage of Vessels, and if any one should Plough or dig an Hole
" within two Perches of the King's Highway shall pay a fine of 8 *l*.

Of these Proprietors in the Borough besides *William Peverel* of whom
mention is made in the 9th Section, and Earl *Tosti*, I find four among
the ancient Barons, viz. *Ralph de Burun*, *Ralph Fitz-Hubert*, *Goisfrid de
Alselyn*, and *Roger de Busly*.

TOSTY

" Moreover what Stock each had of Horses, Cattle, Sheep, &c. how much ready
" Money he had in his House, what he owed, and what was owing to him, all this
" was set down in great Order in a Book called *Doomsday-Book*, that is the Book
" of the Day of Judgement, apparently to denote that the Means of the *English*
" were sifted in that Book, as the Actions of Men will be at the great Day. This
" general Register which some Term the great Terror or Land Book of *England*,
" was laid up in the Exchequer or King's Treasury, to be consulted upon Occasi-
" on. This Book was compleated in the Year 1086.

Tosty was second Son of Earl *Goodwin*, the Chief Minister of *Edward the Confessor* and Father to the Queen, *Harold*, who after the Death of *Edward* was for a while King of *England*, was his Brother. This Man, was by King *Edward* made Earl of *Northumberland*, he was by common consent of all our Historians a Person in all Respects of the vilest Character. He governed the *Northumbrians* in a most tyrannical manner for ten Years. As Instances of his Cruelty I will just mention, 1st. His causing several Noblemen of that Country to be murthered in his own Chamber, when he had allured them thither on Pretence of easing their Grievances. 2d. " His flaying all his Brother's Servants at *Hereford*, " and sending their Limbs potted to the King, with a Message *That he* " *should find the Meat well poudered*, and this upon falling out with his " Brother *Harold* in the Presence of the King.

This cruel Behaviour at last turned the Hearts of the *Northumbrians* against him, who rose with one accord and drove him out of the Country. (*b*)

Ralph *de* Burun besides his Possessions in the Town of *Nottingham*, held eight Lordships in *Nottinghamshire* and five in *Derbyshire*, (*c*) of this ancient Stock there is still remaining an eminent Branch, I mean the Right Honourable the Lord *Buron* or *Byron* in this County.

Ralph Fitz-Hubert held in *William the Conqueror's* Time 49 Lordships in *England*. He sided with King *Stephen* against the Empress *Maud*, surprized and plundered several places, but was at length surprized himself and taken, and for refusing to deliver the Castle of the *Devizes* again, was hanged like a Thief says the *Peerage* Vol. II. *part* 2. *p*. 113.

Goisfrid Alselyn or Hanselyn possessed in the *Conqueror's* Time 30 Lordships (*d*) in several Counties, but made *Shelford* in *Nottinghamshire* the Chief Seat of his Barony.

Roger *de* Busly had at the Time of the Survey many Lordships in *England* and his principal Residence was at *Tikhill* in Com. *Ebor*. But this Barony terminated in his Son *John*, whose Daughter married *Robert de Vipont*, a great Baron mentioned in *Sect*. IX.

AND

(*b*) See more of him in *Drake's* Antiquity of *York* p. 82. *seq*. —— (*c*) Peerage Vol. I. p. 84. —— (*d*) Peerage, Vol. II. part II. p. 85.

AND now with the End of the *Saxon* Government in *England*, ended also the *Saxon* Name of this Town, being thenceforth called *Nottingham* *i. e.* from the Time of *William Peverel*, Natural Son of *William* I. was made Lord of it, who in his Foundation Deed of the Priory of *Lenton* calls it by that Name, (*e*) where he gives to that Monastery among other Things of greater Importance the Tythe of the Fish of the fishing of *Nottingham*. Some will have the Alteration of the Name of this Town, taken from the vast Quantity of Haffels growing about and near this Place, *q. d. Nuttingham*, nor does it seem very improbable, since we have a like Instance in a neighbouring Seat of Sir *Charles Sedley*, situate d about three Miles North-West of this Town, which upon that Account, bears the Name of *Nuthall*.

THUS we have fixed the Antiquity of the Town of *Nottingham* upon good and firm Grounds to the beginning of the 8th Century, a Time, when the Kingdom of *Mercia* was no longer inhabited by Savages, but a civilized People, and one that had received the Light of the Gospel near 200 Years before. (*f*)

WHAT if I have cut off a considerable number of chimerical Ages, during which this Town is supposed to have had its pretended being; yet dare I be confident, that no Person of Understanding will dissent from me when I say : That a nameless Town, said to be built at a certain Time, and of which not the least mention is made by any Historian for above 1600 Years after, may be looked upon with the same Eye, as if no such Place had ever been.

THIS Town notwithstanding the Hardships it has undergone from Time to Time by the Inroads and Ravages of the *Danes*, appeared at the *Norman Conquest* so considerable as the Reader has just now observed. And here we will stop our Course of Enquiry for a while, reserving the farther Progress of the Town of *Nottingham* to the sequel of our History, only this may be added before we conclude, that about sixteen Cities claim a seniority of *Nottingham*, among which, one, (I mean the famous City of *Oxford*) were the fabulous Tales' curtailed would hardly dare to claim an Equality of Age ; for till King *Alfred* the great took Notice of it, it was only supported by a Legend of a pretended Miracle wrought by St. *Frideswide*. (*g*)

THE

(*e*) *Thoroton*, p. 490. —— (*f*) A. C. 644. The Christian Religion was first introduced into the Kingdom of *Mercia* by *Peda* the Son of *Penda* King of *Mercia*, who on marrying the Daughter of *Oswy* King of *Northumberland*, was baptised.
—— (*g*) Part of the Legend is as follows : St. *Frideswide* a Virgin of high Esteem
for

THE
HISTORY
OF
NOTTINGHAM.

****

SECT. I.

*A Defcription of the advantageous Situation and prefent Appearance of the Town of
Nottingham, with the Footfteps of former Times yet remaining, together with
the Extent of its Jurifdiction as a County. An Alphabetical Lift of the Names of
Streets and the Number of Houfes in each, as well as, that of the Inhabitants, Publick-Buildings, as Courts of Judicature, Town Halls, Goals, &c.*

H A T part of the *Britains* which by the Romans were called *Coritani*, and which afterwards in the Time of the Saxons became a part of the Kingdom of *Mercia*, * is the very
fame large Tract of Land, which in this our Time is divided
into the Counties of *Northampton, Leicefter, Rutland, Lincoln, Derby* and *Nottingham*, the Capital of this laft and
whence it has received its Name, is the Town of *Nottingham*,
the healthful, advantageous and delightful Situation of which,
defervedly gives it the Pre-eminence above moft inland
Towns in the Kingdom of *England*. It lies almoft in the Middle, equidiftant from
Berwick upon *Tweed* Northward, and *Southampton* Southward, nor is there any great
difference in the Diftance of our Town from *Bofton* Eaftward, and from *Chefter* Weftward.

I T is placed in the Southweft Corner of that ancient and famous Foreft of *Shirwood*, built upon a foft Rock the Surface of which is a Sandy Soil. On the Eaft, Weft
and North Sides it is encompaffed with divers Ridges of Hills of an eafy Affent, of
which the remoteft are the higheft ; thefe Hills protect it from the Inclemency of the

---

* *The* Mercians *were divided by the River* Trent *into the Southern and Northern,
the Southern Mercians lived in* Lincolnfhire *and* Northamptonfhire, *and (which was
formerly a part of it)* Rutlandfhire, Huntingdonfhire, *the northern part of* Bedford-
fhire *and* Hertfordfhire, Buckinghamfhire, Oxfordfhire, Gloucefterfhire, Warwickfhire, Worcefterfhire, Herefordfhire, Staffordfhire *and* Shropfhire : *The Northern*
Mercians *inhabited* Chefhire, Derbyfhire *and* Nottinghamfhire. — Ufher's Primord.
Ecclef.

rigid

rigid Seasons of the Year, whilst on the South Side it receives the enlivening Beams of a Meridian Sun, and is at the same Time fanned by the refreshing Breezes of a Southerly Wind.

HERE from an high perpendicular Rock it not only overlooks a large Plain of rich Meadows of its own; but commands a Horizon of the Compass of many Miles including that fertile Vale of *Belvoir*, which so plentifully furnishes it with the best of Barley whereof the Inhabitants make great Advantage. This Rock is so high, that many of the Bases of the Houses built on the Edge of it, are at least one third higher then the Tops of some Houses in the *Narrowmarsh*, a street just under the Rock. On this Side the Town in the Middle, adorned with many stately new Buildings, the Castle on the left, and *Sneinton* and *Colwick* Hills on the right, present the Travellers coming from the South with a surprisingly grand and magnificent Prospect, in the framing of which (it is hard to say) whether Art or Nature has the greatest Share; a Prospect which puts even a Person the most acquainted with all the Parts of *England* to a stand, to Name its equal. Near the Foot of this steep Rock, glides along a small River, which besides the great use it is of, to several Trades, who live near it, furnishes the Town with a sufficient Quantity of Water, for cleanliness and all other Uses. At a little Mile's Distance farther South there runs a navigable River, abounding in variety of Fish, this yearly overflows its Banks, and impregnates the Meadows, which are happily placed between the two Currents.

NOR is the South Side only blessed with all the Advantages, for on the North, North-west and South-west Sides, are spacious Fields belonging to the Town, of which in former Times some used annually to be sown with Corn, when the Fertility of the Soil was observed such, that the Ground which had born one Year a plentiful Crop of Corn, would yield the next a good Crop of Hay, * these are now almost all enclosed and very luxuriant on Account of the Plenty of Manure this Town affords.

SOMEWHAT farther North of these Fields there are two large Coppices appertaining to *Nottingham*, and thence called *Nottingham Coppices*, which formerly were well stored with Oaks and Underwood, one of these, *viz.* the upper Coppice is cleared and turned into Pasture Land, the lower Coppice is still tolerably well provided with Underwood, neither is it altogether destitute of Timber.

ON the North side of the Town are two Springs, one arises almost at the Foot of the last mentioned Coppice, it is walled in and covered with a Tiled Roof, the waste of it runs in a small Channel through the midst of the Fields, of this more hereafter. The other springs forth about half-way between the Town and the former, it is not quite so large, is also walled about and an Iron Dish used to hang by a Chain for Passengers to drink at, the Waste of this, first runs into a Stone Trough, and thence in a small Trench proceeds and falls into the Channel of the former, thus forming one Current they make their way by the side of the Town and cast themselves into the *Leen*. These Springs are of the same use to the Cattle on the North, as the Rivers are on the South side, the other parts of the Fields which are somewhat remote from both, are mostly provided with Wells.

THUS were a Naturalist in Quest of an exquisite Spot to build a Town or City upon, could he meet with one that would better Answer his Wishes?

* *Anonym. MSS.*

H A-

A WEST VIEW OF CHAPEL BAR

SECT. I.

HAVING now taken a View of the happy Situation in general, we will proceed to the Examination of the Town itself, which even fo early as the Heptarchy was famed for a ftrong Tower, wherein the Danes once fuffer'd a Blockade for fome Time.

EDWWARD the Elder for the better Security and Defence of this Place, incircled it with a ftrong Wall, about the Year of Chrift 910. And William I in the fecond Year of his Reign did build a Caftle on the fame Rock where the old Tower ftood. The Wall of the Town did join the outer Wall of the Caftle and thence ran Northward to Chappel-Bar. Of this are manifeft Footfteps remaining. About the Midway between the Caftle and Chappel-Bar in part of the Ditch where now a Refervoir is made, (of which in another Place) are fome Ruins ftill to be feen of a Poftern which was erected in Obedience to a Precept of Henry III. dated *October* 18. 56 Henry III. * whereby he commands " *his Bailiffs and Burgeffes of Nottingham* " *without Delay to make a Poftern in the Wall of the faid Town, near the Caftle to-* " *wards Lenton, of fuch a Breadth and Height that two armed Horfemen carrying two* " *Lances on their Shoulders might go in and out, where* William *Archbifhop of* York " *had appointed it, who made the King underftand that it was expedient for him and* " *his Heirs, and for the Caftle and Town.*" From this Poftern a Bridge went over the Town Ditch, which Place though now filled up as well as the whole Ditch between this and Chappel-Bar, bears to this Day the Name of *Bofton-Bridge* a Corruption of *Poftern-Bridge.* The Ditch itfelf is now converted into Kitchen Gardens, and is called at this Time × *Butt-Dyke*, from fome neighbouring Butts where the Townfmen ufed to exercife themfelves, in fhooting at a Mark with Bows and Arrows.

CHAPPEL-BAR was the only ancient Gate which had efcaped the Injuries of Time, and was preferved entire 'till the Year 1743, when it was pulled down; under it on each Side was an arched Room of a Pentagonal Figure, of which that which had a Door opening under the Middle of the Gate was a Guard-Room, the other, the Door of which faced the Eaft, was a Chappel for the Conveniency of the Guard, this had given the Gate the Name of Chappel-Bar; it was long fince turned into a Brewhoufe, late in the Tenure of Mr. *Thomas Hawkfley*, once an Alderman, and for fome Time Mayor of *Nottingham*, to whofe own Houfe it was contiguous. In-fomuch that where feveral Altars ftood, Coppers, Mafh-Tubs and other Utenfils fill up the Room, which has given Occafion to the following Lines:

> Here Priefts of old turned Wafers into God,
> And gave poor Laymen Bread, for Flefh and Blood,
> But now a Liquid Myft'ry's here fet up,
> Where Prieft and Layman both, partake the Cup.

On the Top of this Gate at the Eaft End, exactly in the middle, did grow one of the greater fort of Maples, vulgarly called a Sycamore Tree, part of the Branches of which covered an Arbour where fix People might conveniently regale themfelves. The North half of this Top was very neatly difpofed into Beds of various Figures and turned into a pleafant Garden, where befides many different kinds of Flowers, a beautiful variety of Tulips has formetly from on high challenged all the Gardens in Nottingham. Had the other half which was in different Hands and did lie

* *Thoroton* p. 490.

B 2

un-

uncultivated, been managed in like manner, both would have made a Garden of a confiderable Extent, and given a pretty lively Idea of the Babylonian hanging Gardens.

FROM *Chappel-Bar* farther North and round to the Eaft, the true ancient Wall is not to be traced above Ground, however, there are very old Perfons ftill living, who being Labourers have within thefe 20 Years, met when digging, with that old Wall in different Places, and by what they have fhewn me, I may reafonably Conjecture that from the Bar it went flanting through a Clofe called *Roper's* Clofe and the next to it, thence croffing the *Mansfield* Road, along behind the North of the *Back-fide*, crofs *Boot-Lane* by or under a Summer-houfe called Dr. *Greave's* Summer-houfe, through a Clofe called *Pannier* Clofe crofs the North Road and Back-fide excluding the Houfe of Correction, along part of *Coalpit-lane* and through a Cherry Orchard at prefent the Property of *John Sherwin* Efq; and on the outfide of two Clofes belonging to the fame Gentleman, where a Ditch is obferved to run towards the *New-ark* Road, thence it mounted again and croffing at the End of *Cartergate*, extending Weftward along the Rock by the Coal-yard to the *Hollow-ftone*, where a Portion of the Wall was lately vifible. The *Hollow-ftone* being a narrow Paffage cut out of the Rock, the South Entrance into the Town, was fecured by a ftrong Port-cullice, of which not long ago there were plain Marks to be feen; within this Gate on the Left hand going up to the Town, juft turning the Elbow of the Hollow-ftone, there was a Cavity cut into the Rock, able to hold about 20 Men, with a Fire-place in it and Benches fixed, befides a Stair-Cafe cut out of of the fame Rock; this had been a Guard-houfe, and the Stair-Cafe leading up to the Top of the Rock, was for Centinels to Spy the Enemy at a Diftance; this no doubt was of good Service to the Parliament Party during the Civil War, if it was not contrived by them. A little farther up the Hollow-ftone, againft and upon the Rock there ftood an Houfe the Property of his Grace the Duke of *Kingfton*, who upon Application made to him, has given Leave to the Corporation to pull it down, being generoufly willing to forward their Defign of making the *Hollow-ftone* * a more gradual Defcent and enlarging the South Entrance into the Town, fo that two or more Carriages may conveniently pafs each other, to which Purpofe Men were fet to Work on Tuefday the 17th of *December* 1740, and this ufeful and pleafant Way into the Town was compleated in a few Weeks. On the Top of the Rocks on the left fide of the Paffage into *Nottingham* Town, the Workmen met with a Portion of the Town-Wall, the Stones of which were fo well cemented, that the Mortar exceeded them in Hardnefs. Hence the Wall extended itfelf along *Short-Hill* and the *High-Pavement*, at the lower End of which it runs down a Hill called *Brightmore-Hill*, and at the Bottom forms an Acute Angle, and runs again up *Mont-lane*, in a kind of a Curve to the *Week-day-Crofs*; both thefe Paffages are open, and it is difficult to guefs how they were formerly fecured, or whether they are of a more modern date, as well as the Long-ftairs by *Malin-hill*. The Wall continued along behind the Houfes of the *Middle-Pavement* & over againft *Bridlefmith-gate*, there ftood an ancient Poftern, 'till within thefe 10 Years, on the Eaft fide of which, where now the *Bull's-head* is, was a Gatehoufe, where a Guard was kept, as is to this Day plainly to be feen; on the Weft fide ftood an Houfe formerly called *Vout-Hall*, ‡ once

the

---

* *See Sect.* VIII.   ‡ *It had its name from very large Vaults which were under it, where in the Time of the Staple of Calais, great Quantities of Wool ufed to be lodged. In one of thefe Vaults, in the Reign of King* CHARLES II. *the*

De-the Mansion House of the Family of the *Plumptre's*, after in the Possession of Alderman *Drury*, whose eldest Son Mr. *William Drury*, sold it to Mr. *Gawthorn*, the present Proprietor. From this Gate the Wall goes to *Lister-gate* the bottom of the *Low-Pavement*, where tho' built upon, it is still visible in divers Places. Here, I mean at the End of *Lister-gate*, over against *Peter-lane*, in the Remembrance of some old Persons were to be seen the Marks of a Stone Gate leading towards the River *Leen*. From hence the Wall on Account of the Buildings in *Castle-gate* is quite hid, but it seems more then probable that it went along the South Side of *Castle-gate*, including St. *Nicholas's* Church-yard and so run upon the Rock West to join the Castle near *Brewhouse-yard*. Insomuch that *Cartergate*, *Fishergate*, the *Narrow* and *Broad-Marsh*, and all other Streets and Buildings, between the Meadows and the South Rock of the Town, made a Suburb. And this is what I have been able to gather concerning the ancient Wall of this Town, which was built so long ago as 830 Years. But I should not forget to take Notice of a Wall of less Antiquity which runs from *Chappel-Bar* in a straight Line Northward to *Coalpit-lane* and excluded part of the Ground between *Chappel-Bar* and *Broad-lane*. This Wall is plainly discernable, it serving for a Foundation to many Houses between the Gate and *Cow-lane*, and where now a Middle Row of Houses is built at the End of *Cow-lane*, there stood a Gate facing the North, and the Town Wall is still to be seen in the Cellars of these Houses. Probably this Wall was erected in *Henry* II. Reign, after *Robert* Duke of *Gloucester* had demolished it, in the War between King *Stephen* and Empress *Maud*.

THE Houses in this Town, as well as all the Kingdom over, (if we except Churches and some other Public Buildings,) the King's and Nobleman's Castles and Royal Palaces with some few private Gentlemen's Seats, were from the Time of the Saxons to the Reign of King *Henry* VIII, * generally Wood and Plaister, and tho' History informs us that *Alfred* the Great was the first Introducer of Brick and Stone Buildings in the Year of Christ 886, yet did they not become common 'till many Ages after. The Roofs were mostly thatched with Straw or Reeds; And the first Tiled House in *Nottingham* appears that of Mr. *Stanton* on the *Long-Row* late the *Unicorn* Inn, in whose Writings it is expressed, that this House was built in the Year 1503, the first that was Tiled and the last on the *Long-Row*. The Floors commonly were Plaister, and even

---

Dissenters privately met for the Exercise of their Religion, as they did after the Act of Toleration publickly, in a House at the upper End of Pilchergate, *which is since pulled down and a new one built in its Room, the Property and present Mansion House of* John Sherwin, Esq; *This Place on Account of Mr.* Whitlock's *and* Reinold's *(displaced Minister of St.* Mary's) *officiating in it obtained the By-Name of* Little St. Mary's

Holinshed *who lived still later in the Reign of Queen* Elizabeth, *in his Description of* Britain, *fol.* 84. *gives us this Account of the Buildings in his Time, which compleatly Answers those of* Nottingham: *viz.* " *The greatest part of our Building*
" *in the Cities and good Towns of* England, *consists only of Timber, for as yet few of the*
" *Houses of the Commonalty, (except here and there in the West Country Towns) are made*
" *of Stone. --- In the Wooddy Countries our Houses are commonly well timbred, so that*
" *in many Places there are not above six or nine Inches between Stud and Stud. ----*
" *where plenty of Wood is, they cover their Houses with Tiles, otherwise with*
" *Straw, Sedge or Reed, (except where some Quarry of Slate be near.)*

at

at this Day thefe fort Floors are here ftill much in Ufe.   It is perhaps peculiar to this
Town and Neighbourhood, that the Inhabitants did put a great deal more Timber into their Buildings than in many other Towns, and that on Account of the great Plenty
of good Oak which the Foreft of Shirwood afforded them, they were grown fo lavifh
as to make the Steps of their Stair-cafes not of Boards but folid blocks of Timber, the
Truth of this (tho' very few of thefe ancient Houfes are now remaining) may be feen
in the laft Houfe in St. *Peters* Church-yard near *Peter-gate*, and alfo in the Friers in
Moothall-gate, commonly called *Fryar-lane* : Nay farther, on the Foreft it has been
obferved, that the firft Floor has been made of folid Summer Trees, fquared and
clofely joined together.   The Date of the oldeft Brick Houfe I meet with, is that of
the *Green-Dragon*, a Public Houfe on the *Long-Row* 1615 ; the Window Frames of
this are Stone, the manner of Building in King *James* I. and *Charles* 1fts. Reign.
Many Houfes were afterwards built of Brick during the Civil War, when this Town
happened to be on the ftrongeft and moft fortunate Side, and foon after the Reftoration *Nottingham* put on quite a new Face, fince which Time many of the Inhabitants
have taken to new Fronting their Houfes after the neweft Fafhion, fome with Parapet
Walls, following the Example of *William Toplady*, [Son of an Alderman of that Name
who was remarkable for being in 1682, the firft Mayor by King *Charles* II's new
Charter] a confiderable Number of handfome Houfes have of late been built by
Wealthy Tradefmen, and more are daily building, a manifeft Proof of the increafe of
Riches among the Inhabitants, owing chiefly to a beneficial Manufactury, which as it
had its *Punctum Saliens*, not above five Miles from this Town, fo the greateft Advan-
tage of it feems of late Years to center here.

  AND tho' Towns of confiderable Bufinefs and a flourifhing Trade, feldom give
Gentlemen great-Encouragement to be fond of fettling in them, yet this muft be faid
for our Town, that the healthful Air, the pleafant Site, and the plenty of all forts of
Neceffaries as well as Conveniencies of Life, maugre all other Objections, has even
very lately induced fome Gentlemen to build themfelves Manfion Houfes in it, the
laft of thefe are Sir *William Parfons*, who built a very convenient Habitation on the
Short-hill, next to a well finifhed Houfe of the late *John Bury* Efq; and *Rothwell
Willoughby* Efq; Brother to the Right Honourable the Lord *Middleton*, on the upper
End of the *Low-pavement*, has adorned that Place, and enriched the South Profpect
of the Town with a beautiful Fabric ; befides all thefe,✝ *Thurland-Hall* otherwife
Clare-Hall belonging to his Grace the Duke of *Newcaftle*, and the Houfe of the Ho-
nourable *William Pierepont* Efq; * now the Property of *John Plumptre* Efq; tho'
fomewhat altered are yet ftanding ; And here I muft not pafs over in Silence the
ftately Houfes of thofe Genlemen whofe Families have for a long feries of Years inhabited this our Town ; as Mr. *Plumptre's* on St. *Mary's* Hill, the Grand Stuko'd
Front of which (being built in the Italian Tafte and facing the Eaft) makes a great
Addition to the beauty of the Profpect of *Nottingham* from the *Newark* Road, Mr. *Gregory's* on *Swine-green*, Mr. *Sherwin's* at the upper Corner of *Pilcher-gate*, being
built upon the higheft Spot in the Town, the late Mr. *Bennet's* and Mrs. *Newdigate's*‡
                                                                                        both

---

* *This Houfe was built by* Francis Pierepont, 3d *Son of* Robert *Earl of* Kingfton.
  He died January 30, 1657. *Collins's Peerage* Vol. 1, p. 389.
‡ *In this Houfe Marfhal* Tallard *refided* [*who was taken by the Duke of* Marlborough
  at the Battle of Blenheim] *during his Captivity, and made very fine Gardens.*
                                                                            There

both in *Castle-gate*, with the Houses of several Gentlemen of the Law, and others too tedious to mention particularly.

THE West Entrance into *Nottingham* offers to the Travellers View a Market Place in spaciousness superior to most; inferior to very few * (if any) in the Kingdom, graced with many beautiful Buildings. This Place has since the Year 1711, received great Additions ; here the grand Saturday Market and all the Fairs are kept. It was formerly divided lengthways in two by a Wall Breast-high, which had openings at proper Distances to pass from one side to the other. On the North side, *i. e.* by the *Long-Row*, was kept the great Market of Corn and Malt, Oat-Meal and Salt, and and many Stalls and Booths tented for Milliners, Pedlars, Sale-shops, Hardware Men, &c. with Bakers, Turners, Brasiers, Tinmen, Chandlers, Collar-makers, Gardiners, &c. On the South side between the Wall and a large hanging Bank was the Horse-Market, not paved, called the Sands ; on the East End of the just mention ed Bank all sorts of sawn Timber, as Boards, Planks, Quarters, Pannels, and all kinds of Stuff, for Carpenters, Joyners, and Coopers was sold, which has given an handsome Row of Houses built along this Bank, the Name of *Timber-hill*. On the remaining part of this Bank, were every Saturday placed Sheep folds for the use of the Country People, who bring Sheep to sell. West of the Horse-Market under *Fryar-Row* and *Angel-Row* was kept the Beast-Market, this extended as far as the Market Wall reached *i. e.* to the End of *Bearward-lane* and at the skirt of this between Frier-Row and the Sheepfolds, was the Swine Market. At the East End of the Market-Place between the *Long-Row* and *Cuck-stool-Row* are two large Shambles called the old and new Shambles. In the old are 24 several Butcher's Stalls, over them is a Room of a considerable Length and Breadth floored over with a strong Plaister Floor, at the West End of which was an open, Breast-high, whence the whole Market might be view'd, here formerly the Fairs, &c. used to be proclaimed. In the South-West Corner of them was a Square Room wainscotted and seated about, where the Mayor, Sheriffs and other Officers used to meet in order to walk the Saturday Market, (a Custom now left off) in this Room also used to sit the Steward or his Deputy all Day long, on the Market Day, to enter Actions, take Bail, &c. all which he now does at his own House. In the Remainder of this large Place on both Sides were Shops of divers Tradesmen with a large Passage between. At the West End of the South side of this Room used to stand some Haberdashers of Hats, over against them on the North side stood Country Grocers and Mercers, as the People used to call them, coming from *Mansfield*, *Loughborough*, *Mount-Sorrel*, &c. whence this Room was called the *Spice-Chamber*, a Name it bears to this Day, all the rest of the Shops on both Sides were occupied by Leathersellers, and Glovers, these 'till the Year 1747, took up almost the whole Place. ‡

There were also taken at the same Time, and sent Prisoners to Nottingham, *the* Marquis de Montperroux *General of Horse,* Compte de Blanzac *Lieutenant General,* Marquis de Hautefeuille *General of Dragoons,* Marquis de Valseme, Marquis de Seppeville, Marquis de Silly, Chevalier de Crovssy, Marquis de Valliere, *Major Generals,* Monf. de St. Second *Brigadier,* Marquis de Vassey, *Colonel of Dragoons, and* Compte de Horne.
* *The Area of it is* 4 *Acres and* 26 *Perches.*   ‡ *In the Year* 1747, *the* Spice-Chamber *and* Old Shambles, *were pulled down, enlarged and rebuilt, in a very commodious manner.*

ON

ON the North and outſide of theſe Shambles uſed to ſtand Fiſhmongers and Fiſhermen.

THE New-Shambles which contain 26 Stalls for Butchers, adjoin to the old ones; on the South-ſide over theſe is likewiſe a long Room where in Time paſt the Tanners after they had done buying raw Hides uſed to ſtand the Remainder of the Day to ſell bend Leather. South of the New-Shambles are two Rows of Building with a paved Paſſage between, call'd the *Shoemaker-Booths*, where on a Saturday the Men of that Trade keep Market, but all the Week beſide they are ſhut up. South of theſe over againſt Peck-Lane, uſed to ſtand all the Rope-makers. On the Weſt End of Shoemaker-Booths, did ſtand ſuch as ſold Northern Cloths, Hampſhire and Burton-Kerſeys, and near them was to be had great Store of Houſewives Cloth both Linnen and Woollen.

IN this great Market-Place uſed to be two Croſſes, the firſt on the Weſt End of the Long-Row near *Sheep-Lane* ſeated about ten Steps high with a Pillar in the Middle, called the *Malt-Croſs*, becauſe near it the Malt uſed to be ſold; here all Proclamations are read as alſo Declarations of War in the Face of a Full Market. The ſecond ſtood on the Eaſt End of the Market Place, oppoſite to the firſt, near the Shambles called the *Butter-Croſs*, this had large Seats about it of four Heights and was covered with a large tiled Roof ſupported by ſix Pillars, here thoſe ſat who dealt in Butter, Eggs, Bacon, &c. near it was the Fruit-Market plentifully provided with all kinds of Fruit in Seaſon.

SUCH was the Face of the Market Place till within theſe Forty Years, ſince which Time the Market-Wall has been removed, as well as the Butter-Croſs and the whole Place well paved, the Malt-Croſs has likewiſe been altered, is now but four Steps high, has a raiſed tiled Roof (the Top of which is adorned and rendered uſeful by ſix Sun-Dials and a Fane) reſts upon ſix Pillars; under this Roof and about this Croſs ſit ſuch as ſell Earthern Ware both courſe and fine. The Sheep-folds are removed to a Place not far diſtant from this Market Place, and where the Butter-Croſs ſtood, or rather between that and the Shambles, which looked before very bare, there is ſince erected a Brick-Building 123 Feet in length, the Front of which is ſupported by Ten Stone Pillars, in the middle of this Front are three Niches of Stone, deſigned for placing of the Statues of King *George* the 1ſt, and the Prince and Princeſs of *Wales* in them, but they remain ſtill empty; above theſe is a Dial with an Hour Hand, and on the Top of all the Building is placed the Statue of *Juſtice*; between the Pillars and ſome Shops and the Shambles is an open Walk, in the middle of which a broad Stair Caſe leads up into the long Room where the Tanners were wont to ſell their Leather, this has now a boarded Floor and two Chimneys in it; here the Mayor and Sheriffs give their Michaelmas Entertainments &c. on the the left Hand a few ſteps higher is the Court were the Aſſizes and Seſſions were held for the Town, which formerly uſed to be done in the old Town Hall, and whither, ſince the late reparation, (new Fronting and otherwiſe beautifying of it) they are again removed. This Building is called the *New-Change*; it coſt the Corporation 2400 *l*. Notwithſtanding all theſe Alterations the ſeveral Dealers or Market People keep to the ſame Spots or as near to them as they can, where they uſed to vend their different Commodities, except, that Timber is not now brought to Market, but ſold on Wharfs and in Yards, neither do the Rope-makers at this Time ſtand in the Market, and thoſe who ſell Fiſh have at preſent their ſtands before the *New-Change*,

THE NEW CHANGE. P.ϕ

THE HOUSE OF THE HON.ᴮᴸᴱ JOHN PLUMPTRE ESQ.ᴿ

The TOWN HALL

I Cox del et Sc 1750

Change, and the Gardiners who are mightily encreafed fince the Year 1705, have a Row of Stalls beyond the Malt-Crofs.

BESIDES the *Malt-Crofs*, there are two others the *Hen-Crofs* and the *Week-day-Crofs*. The firft ftands Eaft of Timber Hill, and almoft in the Center between four Streets which here meet; it is a fair Column ftanding on an hexangular Bafis four Steps high, this is the Poultry Market as may be gathered from its Name; hither on Saturdays the Country People brings, all forts of Fowl both tame and wild, as Geefe, Turkeys, Ducks, Pidgeons, &c. alfo Pigs. The Week-day-Crofs is likewife a Column ftanding on an octangular Bafis larger than the former, with four Steps placed almoft in the midft of an open fpace between the *High* and *Middle-pavement*; here the Wednefday and Friday Market is kept, for Butter, Eggs, Pidgeons, wild Fowl, and all kind of Fruit in Seafon; befides on Fridays here are fold, Sea and River Fifh. Near this Crofs ftand other Shambles placed North and South, where all the Week except on Saturdays, the Butchers fell all kinds of Flefh-meat. Over and above all thefe Markets, a Monday Market was lately endeavoured to be eftablifhed, on a Piece of Wafte Ground between the Weft End of St. *Peter's* Church-yard, *Wheelergate* and *Houndgate*, which attempt tho' it did not anfwer the End, becaufe the Country People would not take to it, yet has proved an Advantage to the Town, for this Place which is in the Heart of the Town was a meer Sink before, and dangerous to pafs efpecially in the Night, is now made good and as well paved as any other part of *Nottingham*; the Crofs, with a Roof fupported by four Pillars is now walled in, and proves a very convenient Receptacle for the Town's Fire Engines, and on Saturdays it is the Sheep Market, the Folds, which formerly were placed in the Great Market Place being now removed to this, they ftand along the Weft and North Sides of St. *Peter's* Church-yard and at the Eaft End of *Houndgate*. On the South fide of the *Week-day-Crofs* is the ancient Town Hall, ftanding upon part of the Old Wall, call'd *Mont-Hall*, probably becaufe it is fituated on the Top of the Hill which leads up to the Week-day-Crofs, it has given the Lane going clofe by it down between the two Marfhes the Name of *Mont-lane*, and the ftreet oppofite to it, that of *Mont-Hall-gate*, now called *Blow-bladder* ftreet. This Hall was very lately a low Wooden Building wearing the Badge of Antiquity, the firft Room, and which was anciently all the Hall, is fpacious; in it ufed to be held the Affizes and Seffions for the Town, as has been juft now mentioned, over the Seat where the Judge in the Circuit and the Mayor at other Times ufed to fit, are the King's Arms handfomely painted, on each Side of it are hung up the Arms of nine of the Benefactors to this Town, with Infcriptions under them, (of which more in Sect. VII.) Within this Court there is an handfome Wainfcotted Chamber called the *Council Houfe* (which anciently did not belong to the Hall) where the Mayor and his Brethren with the reft of the Members of the Corporation tranfact the Bufinefs of the Town, and here the Records and all other Writings of the Town are kept, under three Locks and Keys, of which the Mayor for the Time being has one, the youngeft Alderman not being Mayor, the fecond, and the fenior Coroner the third. In this Hall the Burgeffes are chofen who are to reprefent this Town in Parliament. Under it is a Prifon, both for Debtors above and for Felons under Ground. This feems to me to be the old Prifon of which mention is made in the Charter of Confirmation of King *Edward* III. which recites an Inquifition taken and retained in Chancery, whereby it was found, " That the Burgeffes Time out of " Mind, unto the Time of King *John's* Charter and fince, had a Goal in the Town " for the Cuftody of fuch as were taken therein as belonging to the Town." It could therefore not be that which King *John* built about the third Year of his Reign, as Dr. *Thoroton* feems to doubt. This Prifon was lately in very bad Order, efpecially

C

that

that of the Felons, but is now repaired as well as the ancient Hall, (the whole Front of which was in the Year 1744 pulled down, and faced with a Modern one, the Top of which refts upon Tufcan Columns, the Roof of which is probably near 700 Years old, and is framed not unlike that of *Weftminfter*, is perfectly found and therefore preferved.) It is indeed but juft to confider, that tho' the Law confines the Bodies of the Debtors, it does not countenance the Ruin of their Health, and tho' Felons may have deferved Death, yet are they not to be deftroy'd before they have been fairly convicted.

ON the fame fide of the Way and at the upper End of the *High-pavement*, almoft over againft *Mary-gate*, is the *King*'s *Hall*, or the *County* or *Shire Hall*? This tho' within the Town is not within the County of the Town of *Nottingham*, being excepted by the Charter of *Henry* VI, and all the fubfequent Charters. In this Hall the Affizes and Seffions for the County at large, as alfo the County Court are held, &c. here likewife by the Suffrages of the Freeholders the Knights of the Shire are chofen who are to ferve the County in Parliament, and the Coroners of the Shire, as well as the Verderers for the Foreft of *Shirwood*. This Hall was built of Stone, 27 Feet and a half in Front, and 54 Feet deep, the Courts ftood facing one another, the Judge of the Common Pleas looking towards the South, and the Judge of the King's Bench towards the North. * *John Boun* Serjeant at Law, did fome Years before the Civil War, give an Houfe having the Common Hall of the County on the Eaft, and another Houfe, now † Sir *Thomas Hutchinfon*'s, on the Weft fide, to be ufed by the Country People for the more convenient Tryals of *Nifi prius*, it was built with Arches open to the Street as it remains to this Day.

I found a large pannelled Table which formerly was hung up in the Hall, but fince the repairing of the Courts has been taken down, cut in two, and made ufe of to repair the Weft End of the *Nifi prius* Bar; upon this Table were painted 23 Coats of Arms, with the Bearers Names under each, with this Infcription:

Thefe whofe Names and Arms are here fet down, being then in the Commiffion of the Peace for this County, were Contributors to the Building of this Hall. Anno Dom. 1618.

SOME of thefe Arms and Names are rubbed out and thofe I have been able to make out are the following;

" *Lord Cavendifh, Lord Stanhope, Sir Percival Willoughby*, Knt. *Sir John Byron*,
" *Sir George Parkyns*, Knt. *Sir George Lafcelles*, Knt. *Sir Gervas Clifton*, Bart. *Sir*
" *Francis Leek*, Knt. *Sir Thomas Hutchinfon*, Knt. *Folk Cartwright*, Efq; *Hardolph*
" *Waftnes*, Efq; *Robert Pierpoint*, Efq; *Robert Sutton*, Efq; *John Wood*, Efq; *Robert*
" *Williamfon*, Efq; *Lancelot Rollefton*, Efq; *Gervas Trevery*, Efq;

By this Table it appears that this Houfe was given to the County upwards of 24 Years before thofe inteftine Troubles. ‡

Both

---

* *Thoroton*, page 493.   † *This was formerly the Property of Nicholas Kinnerfly, and it continued in the Family of the Hutchinfon's 'till Julius Hutchinfon Efq; fold it to the Juftices of the County of Nottingham, at the Perfuafion of Sir Thomas Parkyns, who then had a Scheme for pulling it down to enlarge the County Hall and Goal.   ‡ It is 40 Feet in Front and about 20 Feet deep.*

A Prospect of ỹ COUNTY HALL as it appear'd in the Year 1750.

T: Pacey Scul

Near the top of Barker-gate

BOTH Courts are at this Time kept in the old Hall, and tho' of late repaired and altered, so that the Judge of the Crown faces the West and the Judge of the Common Pleas the South, yet are they still very inconvenient. The old as well as the additional arched Hall is in a very indifferent Condition, the Stone Work is here and there patched up with Brick, in short 'tis hardly fit to bring any of his Majesty's Judges into, and indeed a certain Judge being very much offended at it, instead of speaking to the Gentlemen of the County in a persuasive manner, laid a Fine upon the County of two Thousand Pounds, but it not being determined how the same should be levied, so far from forwarding the Building of a new Hall, it has rather retarded it; however I would not be suspected to doubt, that e'er long the Gentlemen Justices of the County, will agree on some expedient for the Honour of their Country and in Duty and Regard to his Majesty, (whose Representatives the Justices of Assize are) for erecting a Building worthy of themselves, and suitable for the Reception of the Minister's of Justice. Under the old Hall was the Goal for the Counties of *Nottingham* and *Derby*, as several Charters express, this is most likely, that which King *John*, built. It is now converted into a Brew-house and Cellars, for the use of the Goaler and a new one is built behind the old Hall, leaving a light airy Yard between.

HERE I must not omit to acquaint the Reader, that as after the *Norman* Conquest, this Town was divided into two Boroughs of separate Jurisdiction; so there were also two Town-Halls, of which that hitherto not mentioned seems to have been the best Building, *viz.* of Stone, it stood in the French Borough, on the spot where now the *Feather's* Inn is, some Ruins of the old Stone Work is still visible about the Stables. The Street leading from this House up to the Castle, commonly called by the People *Frier-lane* is in all Leases term'd *Moot-hall-gate*.

IN this Town there are Streets, Lanes, Courts, Rows, &c. besides Yards, to the Number of 90. the which for the Ease of the Reader I have disposed alphabetically in the following Table, where the curious will find the Name of each, in the first Column, the Number of Houses in the second, and that of Souls in the third Column.

An

An Alphabetical Table of the Names of Streets &c. and Number of Houfes and Souls in each.

Streets.	Houfes.	Souls.	Streets.	Houfes.	Souls
Angel-Row — —	22	130	Frier-Lane See Moot-Hall-Gate — —		
Back-Lane — — —	9	57	Frier-Row — — —	28	132
Back-Side — — —	214	1313			
Barker-Gate — — —		174	Goofe-Gate — — —	21	96
Bearward-Lane — —	34	145	Gray-Frier-Gate ——	16	80
Beck-Lane — — —	16	91	Gridle-Smith-Gate —	32	
Beck-Barns — —	8	46	Hallifax-Lane common ly called Jack Nut-tal's-Lane — —	2	9
Beller-Gate — — —		83			
Boot-Lane — — —	9	40			
Bottle-Lane See Lin-by-Lane — —			Hen-Crofs — — —	6	31
			High-Pavement — —	48	240
Bridge-End — — —	28	78	High-Street See Sad-ler-Gate — —		
Bridlefmith-Gate —	77	331			
Brightmore-Hill com-monly call'd Gardi-ner's-Hill — —	3	18	Hockley-Hole — — —	25	106
			Hound-Gate — — —	66	332
			St. James's-Lane —		
Broad-Lane — —	17	97	Jew-Lane — — —		14
Broad-Marfh — —	36	162	Johnfon's-Court — —	15	81
Byard-Lane — — —	3	6			
			Linby-Lane — — —	13	59
Carter-Gate — — —	16	104	Lifter-Gate wrongly call'd Grayfriergate	17	85
Caftle-Gate — — —	92	445	Long-Row — — —	63	487
Chandlers-Lane — —	20	47	Low-Pavement — —	18	115
Chappel-Bar — —	25	135			
Chappel's-Court — —	14	58	Malin-Hill — — —	7	27
Chefterfield-Lane —	25	82	St. Mary's Church Side	33	158
Coalpit-Lane — —	4	20	St. Mary's-Hill — —		
Cow-Lane — — —	19		St. Mary's-Gate — —	56	210
Cuckftool-Row — —	13	80	Marfden's-Court —	11	61
			Middle-Pavement —	18	97
Fair Maid's-Lane vul-garly call'd S — n-Lane — — —	4	21	Mont-hall-Gate now Blowbladder-Street	19	89
Fink-Hill-Street — —	15	97	Mont-Lane commonly called Middle-Hill for-merly Medla-Hill	7	30
Fifher-Gate — — —	47	275			
Flefher-Gate by fome Fletcher-Gate —		163			

Mont-

Streets.	Houses.	Souls.	Streets.	Houses.	Souls.
Moot-Hall-Gate *common ly* Woolergate, *wrong ly* Frier-Lane — —	—	11	Short-Hill — — —	33	137
			Smithy-Row — —	13	55
			South side of St. Peter's -	10	47
Millstone-Lane — — —	—		South side of the Leen —	16	105
			Spaniel-Row — —	8	32
Narrow-Marsh — — —	—	535	Stephen's-Court — —	14	93
Newarke-Lane — — —	—		Stony-Street — — —	26	126
New-Change — — —	6	27	Swine-Green — — —	14	77
North side of the Leen —	8	34			
			Timber-Hill — — —	22	137
Palavicini's-Row — —	8	40	Trent-Bridge — — —	9	34
Peck-Lane — — —	8	51	Turncalf-Alley — —	9	31
Pennyfoot-Lane *See* Back-Lane — —			Turnbull-Street — —	11	74
Pennyfoot-Row — —	7	32	Vout-Lane *commonly call'd* Drewry-Hill	11	59
Pepper-Street — — —	12	52			
St. Peter's Church-yard -	5	19			
St. Peter's Lane — —	—		Wallnut-Tree-Lane —		
Peter-Gate — — —	23	113	Waste without Chappel-Bar — — — —	18	69
Pilcher-Gate — — —	19	128	Waste over-against the Castle — — —	9	56
Queen-Street — — —	9	35	Warfar-Gate *commonly call'd* Worser-Gate	46	189
Rosemary-Lane — —	14	72	Week-day-Cross — —	15	57
Rotten-Row — — —	10	53	Wheelwright-Gate — —	30	168
Row opposite to Pecklane	9	38	Woolpack-Lane — —	17	94
Sadler-Gate *now call'd* High-Street	8	36	To these we add the Castle and Brew-House-Yard	18	67
Shamble-Lane — — —	6				
Sheep-Lane — — —	14	70			

This Account of the Number of Souls in the Town of *Nottingham*, was taken in the Year 1739 — Not computing the amount of them by allowing a certain Number in each House one with another; but gathering the exact Number of Men, Women and Children, in every individual House or Tenement.

THE

IN the Number of Houfes within the foregoing Table are not comprized Beadhoufes, Hofpitals, Workhoufes, Goals, nor the Houfe Correction, all which contain upwards of 200 Souls.

THE Origin of the Names of thefe feveral Places is as various as that of the Sirnames of Men. Some are derived from their Situation, as the *High, Low,* and *Middle-pavements,* the *Back-fide, Back-lane, &c.* Some from their Shape and Magnitude, as the *Long-row, Broad-lane, Short-hill, Narrow-marfh, &c.* Some from the Neighbourhood of fome Church, Chappel, Religious Houfe, or the Caftle : as *St. Mary's-gate, St. Peter's-gate, St. James's-lane, Caftlegate, &c.* Some from fome noted Perfon living there, or having a Property in that Place : as, *Marfden's Court, Stephen's Court, Chappel's Court, Barkergate, Bellergate.* Some from the former Condition of the Ground : as, *Rotten-row,* or from what in Times paft ftood there, as *Cuckftool-row.* Some from particular People inhabiting the Place as *Jew-lane,* * or from fome Animals formerly kept there : as *Hound-Gate* and *Spaniel-Row,* where doubtlefs in the Time when our Kings ufed to refide in the Caftle of *Nottingham,* the Hounds and Spaniels of the King, ufed to be kept, and as at this prefent Time Lions are kept at the Tower, fo formerly in the Room of thefe, Bears ufed to be kept, as appears by the Title of the Officer who takes Care of them, (which to this Day) is not the King's *Lion-Keeper* but the King's *Bear-Keeper,* and thence *Bearward-Lane* may have obtained its Name. Some from the frequent Paffage of Cattle and other live Provifions : as *Sheep Lane, Cow Lane, Goofe Gate, &c:* And fome from the particular Trades that ufed to dwell in them : as *Sadler Gate, Fletcher Gate, Smithy Row, Bridlefmith Gate* and *Gridlefmith Gate,* of which two laft my Anonymous Author expreffes himfelf to this Purpofe : " Of the Streets in *Nottingham* I find two very near " in Sound, differing only in one Letter, *viz.* B and G, but very wide in their Deri- " vation, for the firft was fo called by Reafon of the great Number of Smiths dwelling " there, who made Bitts, Snaffles and other Articles for Bridles, of which Trade " there are are fome ftill inhabiting this Street tho' the Major part of them is now " worn out by Smiths of a rougher Stamp, fuch as make Plough Irons, Coulters, Shares, " Stroake and Nayles, Harrow Teeth and the like, of which Trade there are at this " Day fuch Store in this Street, and other parts of the Town, as ferve to furnifh not " only the County of *Nottingham,* but divers other bordering Shires, as *Leicefter,* " *Rutland* and *Lincoln.* The Reafon of which Number I fuppofe, the great Plenty " of Coals got and the great Plenty of Iron made in thefe Parts.

Gridlefmith Gate he turns into *Girdlefmith Gate* and this he derives from the Dialect of the Common People about the Confines of *Derby* and *Staffordfhire,* who call a Girdle a Gridle, and in this Street fuch lived, who made Buckles, Hooks, and other Matters for Girdles.

Not-

---

* *By an Exemplification of the King's ancient Poffeffions in* Nottingham *out of the Pipe Office it appears that there were feveral Houfes of Jews, as alfo a Synagogue in* Nottingham, *until in the* XXth *of* Edward *the* 1ft, *the King granted the fame to* Hugh Putrell *of* Thurmenton *and to his Heirs for ever, paying annually to his Majefty on* Michaelmas Day *by the Hands of the Bailiffs of* Nottingham *one Penny.*

Nottingham has in general one Benefit hardly to be match'd by any other of the Kingdom, to wit: That the Inhabitants are not only well provided with good Barley to turn into Malt and Ale (for which this Town is famed all over England) but that they have also the beft, cooleft and deepeft Rock Cellars, to ftow their Liquor in, many being 20, 24 to 36 fteps deep, nay in fome Places there are Cellars within Cellars deeper and deeper in the Rock; but of all the Rock Cellars thofe which his Honour *Willoughby* not many Years ago caufed to be hewed out, deferve the principal Notice for feveral Reafons, and it is a Queftion whether there be any Rock Cellars to be compared with them in the whole Kingdom. From the paved Yard even with the Brewhoufe, which is about 12 Feet below the Level of the Ground Floor, thefe Cellars are 16 Feet perpendicular in depth, the Paffage leading down to them opens to the North, is arched and has 32 eafy Steps cover'd with Bricks, and receives light enough to make the defcent pleafant; at the bottom you meet with three Doors, that which faces you leads to the greateft Cellar, the other two on each fide give entrance into two leffer Cellars; all three defcribe exact Circles having hæmifpherical Roofs, the Center of each is fupported by a proportionable round Pillar of Rock, the leffer have Bings all round them, and what is peculiarly remarkable is, that in fo large an extent of Rock requifite for three fuch confiderable Excavations there does not appear the leaft Crack or Flaw.

THE fhalloweft Cellars are made ufe of by Tradefmen for Store places to keep certain Goods in; others had large and level Floors in them with Cifterns and Kilns to fteep Barley and dry Malt in, of thefe there were very many even fo lately as the latter part of the Reign of King *Charles* the 1ft, and in fome of thefe fubterraneous Malt Rooms, they ufed to make Malt as kindly in the heat of the Summer, as above Ground in the beft Time of the Winter, and tho' thofe Malt Kilns were much lefs than the Malt Offices at prefent, which are almoft all above Ground, yet the Number of the others and the working of them all the Year round, made the yearly Quantity very confiderable, elfe this Town could never have fupplied with Malt, *Lancafhire*, *Chefhire*, *Shropfhire*, *Staffordfhire* and the *Peak* of *Derbyfhire*, which ufed to be done by Carriers and Hukfters, then commonly called Badgers, of whom thofe of *Chefhire* ufed to make a double Return, by bringing Salt from the Withes, and carrying back Malt.

THE Town of *Nottingham* is about two Statute Miles, and the County of the Town fpreads its Jurifdiction upwards of ten Miles in Circumference, the Boundaries of which they carefully preferve by chufing every half Year a certain Number of Perfons of the Town, headed by one of the Coroners, which are called the *Middleton-Jury*; this Name I take to be a Contraction of *Middle-Town-Jury*, not only becaufe they are fummoned from amongft the Towns People in the Town, but becaufe they not only take Care of the extream Boundaries, but they likewife walk through the Middle and every part of the Town, taking Notice of, and prefenting all Incroachments and Nufances.

SPEAKING of Nufances calls to my Mind what I fhould have mentioned before when I was fpeaking of Building in general, *viz.* my finding fome Time ago in the Statute Books, a Title of a Statute of the 27th of *Henry* the 8th. C. 1. For re-edifying *Nottingham, Gloucefter, Northampton* and other Towns. This put me to a ftand how this Decay fhould come, not having either read or heard of any Fire, Tempeft or War, this Town had fuffered by, I therefore in hopes of fome Information wrote to Mr. *Plumptre*, who likewise not recollecting to have read of any bad Accident of so modern a Date, went and did see the original Statute, and was so good as to transmit to me the Preamble, which tho' it does not relate the Cause, yet tells us the Condition this and other Towns were in at that Time : It is as follows :

" FOR so moche as dyverse and many Howses, Mesuages and Tenements of
" Habitations in the Townes of *Notyngham, Shrwysbury, Ludlow, Bridgenorth,*
" *Quynborow, Northampton* and *Gloucefter,* now are and of long Tyme have been in
" great Ruyne, and Decaye, and specially in the pryncypal and cheif Stretes there
" beyng, in the whiche cheif Stretes in Tymes passed have been bewtiful dwellyng
" Howses there well inhabited, whiche at this Day moche Part thereof is desolate
" and voyde Groundes, with Pyttes, Cellars and Vaultes lying open and unkovered
" very perillous for People to go by in the Nyghte withoute Jeopardy of Lyf, which
" Decayes are to the great impoveryshyng and Hindrans of the same Townes for the
" Remedy whereof it may please the Kyng oure Soveraigne Lorde by the assent of
" his Lordes spiritual and temporal and the Commons in this present Parlyament
" assembled, and by th'authorite of the same that may be enacted &c.

THE enacting part provides that if the Owners of the vacant and decayed Houses and Grounds do not re-edify the same, within three Years after Proclamation for that purpose by the chief Magistrates of the Towns, those vacant and decay'd Grounds, and Houses, shall fall to the Lords of the Manours, and if in three Years more those Lords do not re-edify, then they shall go to the Bodies Corporate of those Towns respectively, and if they do not re-edify in three Years more the, said Grounds and Houses shall revert to their first Owners. And there is then a saving to all Persons under Age, under Coverture, in Prison or beyond Sea, provided they re-edify within three Years after the Disability is removed.

BEFORE I conclude this Section I cannot forbear taking Notice of my Anonymous Author's blameable Partiality for his Native Place, with regard to its Beauty and Cleanliness. He is extremely angry with the Author of a Leomine Distich which he fathers upon some *Stall-fed-Monk,* viz.
Non nisi confingam possum laudare Nottingham,
Gens foetet atque focus sordidus ille locus.
the which he translates thus :
I cannot without Lye and Shame,
Commend the Town of *Nottingham,*
The People and the Fuel stink,
The Place as sordid as a Sink.
If he thinks the Lines to be very old, they could not at all affect the Condition of *Nottingham* in his Time. But since they have so highly provok'd his Indignation, let us see whether the Injustice done the Town by them be so great as he fain would make it.

IN 1641 the Traveller especially in Winter, found the *Trent* Lanes very dirty and after he had passed the *Leen* Bridge, the very Foot of the Town called the Bridge-End, deep and miry. At his first Entrance into the narrow Passage which used to lead between two high Precipices to the upper part of the Town, he was from a parcel of little Rock-houses (if the Wind was Northerly) saluted with a Volley of suffocating smoke, caused by the burning of Gorse and Tanners Knobs. Every Body knows the Fragrancy and Cleanliness of Tanners, Fellmongers and Curriers, many of
which

which were then difperfed all over the Town; the greateft thoroughfare in the Town, *Bridlefmith-Gate* was then lined on both Sides with the rougheft kind of Black-fmiths; the Market Place though fpacious, yet was paved but on one Side, and on the other called the Sands it was very miry. That Place near St. *Peter's* Church where the Monday Market was after Projected, was not paved and part of it was fo boggy that there was a bridge of Planks laid a-crofs it with a fingleRail, 'till of late Years, over which People did pafs not without Danger in the Night Time; all St *Peter's* Church-yard fide was low and dirty, and from the Rock of the Church-yard through *Lifter-Gate* to the Leen, was one continued Swamp and the Ground was not raifed and paved till the Year ****** (‡) when Mr. *William Thorp* and Mr. *Lilly* were Chamberlains. All this is evident by what People remember to have obferved within thefe 40 Years, whence the Reader may judge whether the Author of the Diftich has done any more than deliver'd the naked Truth. To me it is plain that the Improvement of the Town, by mending Roads and raifing and paving Streets as well as beautifying it with fightly Buildings, was a Task left to later Generations, who have indeed now done it effectually, and no Stranger who has taken the Pains attentively to confider the Situation and prefent Buildings, the State of Trade and Manufacture, the Plenty of Provifions brought to the Market, the excellent Malt Liquor brew'd at *Nottingham*, but will gladly fubfcribe to what is faid of them in the following Lines:

> Fair *Nottingham* with brilliant Beauty graced,
> In ancient *Shirwood's* South Weft Angle placed,
> Where Northern Hills her tender Neck protect,
> With dainty Flocks of golden Fleeces deckt,
> No roaring Tempeft difcompofe her Mien,
> Her Canopy of State's a Sky ferene.
> She on her left *Belvoir's* rich Vale defcrys,
> On th' other, *Clifton* Hill regale her Eyes;
> If from her loftySeat fhe bows her Head,
> There's at her Feet a flowry Carpet fpread.
> *Britain's* third Stream which runs with rapid force,
> No fooner Spys her, but retards his Courfe,
> He turns, he winds, he cares not to be gone,
> Until to her he firft has Homage done,
> He chearfully his wat'ry Tribute pays,
> And at her Footftool foreign Dainties lays,
> With Affiduity her favour Courts,
> And richeft Merchandize from Sea imports.
> Ceres her Gift with lavifh hand beftows,
> And Bacchus o'er his Butt of Englifh Nectar glows.
> Thy Sons O *Nottingham* with fervour pray,
> May no inteftine Feuds thy Blifs betray,
> Health, Plenty, Pleafure, then will ne'er decay.

D

SECT. II.

‡ *See* Index.

SECT. II.

PARISHES, CHURCHES, CHAPPELS, MONUMENTS, and MONUMEN-
TAL INSCRIPTIONS in them and the Church-Yards, &c.

NOTTINGHAM is divided into three Parishes: St. *Mary's*, St. *Peter's* and St. *Nicholas's.* —— Of these the first is the largest, including much the greater half of the Town.

THEY are governed after the same manner of those in *London*, by the Minister, two Churchwardens and a proportionable Number of Overseers of the Poor, to the extent of each Parish, except that they enjoy free Vestries, whereas many in the *Metropolis* groan under the Arbitrary Impositions of select ones. Ours in Imitation of *London* have erected Work-Houses, where their Poor are very well maintained at a much easier and cheaper Rate then formerly.

THAT of St. *Mary* is built upon a piece of Waste Ground, situated near to the Clayfield Pound between two Roads, one leading from the Gallow-Hill to Cow-Lane, the other from the same Hill to Broad-Lane, which Ground this Parish holds of the Corporation by Lease dated the 5th of April in the 12th Year of the Reign of King *George* I. 1726, for the Term of 999 Years, at the Yearly Acknowledgement of *One Shilling*, to be paid annually at the Town-Hall on the 29th of *September*.

THAT of St. *Peter*, is built upon that spot, where their share of the *White-Rents* stood, given to the three Parishes by *William Gregory*, Gent. *See* Sect. VII.

St. *Nicholas's* Work-House, stands on a Piece of Waste Ground, over against the Castle of *Nottingham*, held by Lease of the Corporation, bearing Date *June* 27th in the 12th Year of King *George* I. 1726, for the same Term and upon the same Condition, as St. *Mary's*.

THE three Parish Churches stand upon Eminences, St. *Mary's* on the highest, *viz.* 23 Yards perpendicular above the Plain of the Meadows; St. *Peter's* stands on a lower, *viz.* 12 Yards and an half; and St. *Nicholas's* on the lowest of all, to wit, 11 Yards.

THERE appears no certain Accounts when they were built or by whom founded, except concerning the Age of St. *Mary*, a Workman who was employ'd in repairing the West End of the Church (then very much decay'd) informs me that there was found a Date cut out in one of the Timbers, which, tho' he could not precisely remember, yet this he was sure of, that it made the Church then upwards of Eleven hundred Years old. And indeed the oldest part of the Building, bespeaks it of Saxon Original, as well as St. *Peters'*.

AFTER the Conquest in the Reign of *Henry* I. we find them all three mentioned in the Foundation Deed of the Priory of *Lenton*, (a) where *William Peverell* a-

(a) *Thoroton*, p. 218, 490.

mong

mong other Gifts granted to it, (with leave of his Lord *Henry*) the Church of St. *Mary* in the English Borough of *Nottingham*, with Land, Tythe, and Appurtenances, the Church of St *Peter*, and the Church of St *Nicholas*, likewise in *Nottingham*.

THE Church of St. *Mary*, as it is the oldest, so it is by much the largest, standing (as has been said) on the highest Rock of the three. It is built in the form of a Cross with a square Tower in the Intersection, the whole is contrived like a Collegiate Church, with Stalls on both sides of the Quire, which last being very much decay'd in 1625, (Mr. *Hansby* being then Vicar) was put in repair by the Farmers of the Tythes, by Sequestration of the Profits; it was again repaired in the Year 1727, and adorned with a very handsome Altar Piece, of neat Joyners Work, the Rev. Mr. *Disney* Vicar.

ON the North side of the cross Isle, is the Chappel of *All-Saints*, belonging to the Family of the *Plumptre's*, in which are divers Monuments hereafter mentioned. This Chappel has been the Property of that ancient Family, ever since the 23d of *Henry* VII. after *Tho. Page* of *Misterton*, Gent. of whom *Henry Plumptre*, Gent. (a) purchased one Messuage and thirteen Cottages, whereof the Messuage and nine Cottages lay together in the North-side of the Church-yard of St. *Mary*, where now is the Mansion House of *John Plumptre*, Esq; who some years ago had part of it pulled down, and rebuilt by his own Directions, whereby he has joined to the external Beauty of the *Italian*, the inside Conveniencies of an *English* Taste.

TO this, the Chappel or Oratory with a Quire adjoining to it, was an Appurtenance, the which in the Year 1632 was confirmed to *Henry Plumptre*, Esq; *Nicholas Plumptre*, Gent. and *Huntingdon Plumptre* Dr. of Physic, his Sons, and the rest of the Inhabitants of that House, to hear divine Service, pray and bury in, by *Richard* Archdeacon of *York*, under the Hand and Seal of *Francis Whittingham*, M. A. Surrogate of *William Easdale*, Dr. of Laws, Vicar General in Spirituals of the said Arch-Bishop.

OPPOSITE to this Chappel, is another on the South-side dedicated to the Virgin *Mary*, as appears by the Will of *Thomas Willoughby*.

IN this Church were three Chantry's, *viz.* the Chantry of St. *Mary*, St. *James*, and *Amyas* his Chantry, who was a Man of Note in this Town, about *Edward* the 3d. his Time(c): Besides these Dr. *Thoroton*, mentions a Guild or Fraternity of six Priests called the Guild of the Holy *Trinity*, whose House was on the *High-pavement*, called, even in this Authors Time, *Trinity-House*: It stood as I am informed, where now Mrs. *Saville's* Stables are. At the South-West Corner, and close to the Church-yard, stood the Chantry-House, which is at this Time the Property of the Corporation, it being granted to the Mayor and Burgesses by King *Edward* VI. for the repairing of *Nottingham* Bridges.

FORMERLY the Windows of St. *Mary's* were adorned with a great Variety of beautiful Figures stained upon Glass, of which very small Footsteps are remaining. The only whole Figure is that of St. *Andrew* in a Window on the North-side of the

---

(a) *Thoroton*, p. 497. *the 8th of* Edward III.

(d) *he was Mayor of* Nottingham

Quire

Quire.   In the North-Window of the Chappel of All-Saints are ftill to be feen a
Head of the Virgin *Mary* on the Eaft-fide, and two Female Heads, of which one is
that of *Mary Magdalene*.   In the Eaft Window of this Chappel, almoft even with the
top of the new Loft, are the Arms of *Plumptre*.   In the tops of the Windows on the
North Ifle were the Figures of our Saviour (good part of which is ftill remaining) and
the Apoftles, the Heads of feveral of them are left.   On the South fide of this Church
nothing remains that can be made out.

THE Weft End of this Church being in a tottering Condition, a Brief was obtained for repairing the fame, in the Year 1726

THIS Churchhad Organs before the Civil War, as my Anonymous Author informs me, who fays, that a few years before he wrote his Account of *Nottingham*, a
certain Perfon, (then ftill living) when Churchwarden, fold the Organ-Pipes, and
left the empty Cafe in its Place, which was over the Lion and Unicorn, at the entrance into the Quire.   Since that Time there were no Organs till the Reign of
Queen Anne, when about 1704 by the Subfcription of the Parifhioners, Organs were
purchafed ,and fet up at the Weft End of the middle Ifle ; thefe Organs being very
much out of Order, were by Order of the Veftry taken down, and Mr. *Swabrick* of
Warwick an eminent Organ-Maker was employed in 1742, at the Charge of the
whole Parifh, not only to repair the old one throughly, but to enlarge it with a Choir-
Organ, all which he has performed fo Mafterly, that none hears the Inftrument but
commends the Maker.

THIS Church has alfo a Ring of fix very Mufical Bells, the Infcriptions of them
you will fee in the following Table.

THE firft Bell mentions but one Church-Warden, (very likely the other mightthen
be lately dead.) On the 2d and 6th I find three Church-Wardens, which I cannot folve
any other way, then that perhaps the Church Warden elect for the next Year might
be complimented ; there appears no Date on the 6th Bell, but by the modern Language of both Infcriptions, this Bell muft have been caft fince the Reformation. The
Dates of the reft of the Bells fhew them evidently to have been fo.

N. B. *Thelaft Word of the Infcription on the 4th Bell fhould be* infernorum, *this Sentence being taken from the Vulgate Latin Tranflation of the 10th Verfe of the fecond
Chapter of the Epiftle to the Philippians.*

ST. MARY'S CHURCH.

P 20

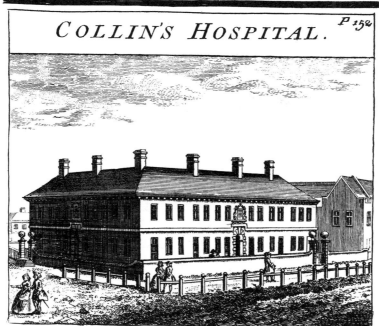

COLLIN'S HOSPITAL.

P 152

A TABLE of the Inscriptions, Dates, &c. upon St. *Mary's* Bells, in *Nottingham.*

1.

Suscito voce pios tu Christe dirige mentes venite exultemus.
Edwardus Sweetapple, Church-Warden, 1699.

2.

Robert Aldrege, Ralph Shaw, Henry Alvie,
𝖂 𝕬 𝕽 𝕯 𝕰 𝕹 𝕾.
1613.

3.

Hec Campana Sacra Fiat Trinitate Beata.

W. Sturrup,   T. Gray, 𝖂 𝕬 𝕽 𝕯 𝕰 𝕹 𝕾. 1690.

4.

Jn noe xsti ihu ome genu flcdat celestm trestm et justorm.

R. A. V.   M G.   1605.

5.

1695.
MADE BY HENRY OULDFIELD.

TV TVBA SIC SONATV DOMINI CONDVCO COHORTES,
RICHARD HVRT MAIOR.

Nicholas Sherwin, Richard Johnſon, **W A R D E N S.**

John Gregory.

Robert Alvie, Peter Clarke, Humphrey Bonner, Richard Morehaghe,
Anker Jackſon, *Aldermen.*

6.

R. Greaves.   I. Combe.

I will ſound and reſound unto thy People O Lord,

With my ſweet Voice to call them to thy Word.

A. Gregory,   H. Greaves,   Tho. Middleton, *Wardens.*

I Tole the Tune that dulful is to ſuch as liv'd amiſs.

But ſweet my ſound ſeem unto them who hope for joyful Bliſs ;

MONUMENTS and MONUMENTAL-INSCRIPTIONS.

DR. *Thoroton* mentions the following Inſcription on a Braſs Plate in the Chancel, which at preſent I do not find there :

Hic jacet Radulphus Hansby, Art. Mr. quondam Socius Johannenſis Cantab. ibidem-que Taxator, hujus Eccleſiæ Vicarius & Bartonenſis in Fabis Rector, Qui Obiit *Novemb*, xx. *Anno Dom.* 1635.

Hansbius hàc cecidit terra lapſum extulit aura,
Quo jacet hìc caſu, ſurgit in aſtro ſuo.

THIS muſt have been pretty near the Communion Table, where ſince the laſtReparation no Grave-Stones are ſeen.

ON the North ſide of the Railes of the Communion Table is a rough Stone with :

J. D.
1729-30
This is the Grave of the Rev. Mr *John Diſney* Vicar of this Church.

who deſired that nothing elſe might be put upon his Stone.

Near

SECT. II.

NEAR the Veſtry Door on a blue Marble Graveſtone,

REV. JOHANNES WHITLOCK
Filius item
Rev. *JOHANNES WHITLOCK,*
Obiit
Ille prid. Non. Dec.
A. D. MDCCVIII. Ætat. LXXXIV.
Hic XVI Cal. Ap,
A. D. MDCCXXIII. Ætat. LXII.

ON the South-ſide of the Chancel on the Wall near the **Communion Table,** on a ſmall but neat Monument of White Marble :

The Honourable Lady *MARY BRABAZON*
a devout and conſtant Attender on God's
Publick Worſhip here, and one of
Exemplary Piety and Virtue
through the whole Courſe of her
Life. Died Jan. 2d. 1737-8.
And lies here interred,
Near her Father
The Right Hon.
Chambre Earl of *Meath*
who departed this Life
April 1ſt. 1715.

Over it: *Quarterly 1ſt. and 4th G. on a Bend O. 3 Martlets S. the 2d and 3d Barry of 10 A. and G.*

ON the ſame ſide againſt the Chancel Wall almoſt even with the Lion and Unicorn, a Monument of colour'd Marble with this Inſcription in Golden Letters :

Johannes Alton in Artibus Mr. ob ſolertiam, prudentiam, experientiam, mediocrum (apud boreales ſaltem partes) facile princeps, uxorem habuit Elizab. Brightman, quæ apprimè modeſta erat fæmina, venerabilis matrona, et pro morum ſuavitate apud omnes gratiſſima, exea duos ſuſcepit liberos, Georgium, et Eleonorum uxorem Thomæ Bray, Armig. matremq; Elizabethæ Bray, quæ nupta Fran. Pierreponto ſummæ pietatis obſervantiæ et gratitudinis ergo, hoc Monumentum in defunctorum memoriam qua fieri poteſt ſempiternam, propriis ſumptibus erigi curavit. Obierunt uterq; circiter annum Ætatis ſuæ octogeſimum; Ille autem 22do. die Febr. Anno Dom. 1629. Hæc decimo Novemb. Annoq; Dom. 1638.

ON a Graveſtone under the Pews :

Johannes Alton & Elizab. uxor ejus chariſſima hîc conſepulti jacent, egregium par amantium, quos una eademq; Domus ut vivos ita mortuos tenet. Diem et Annum utriusq; obitus ſupra poſitum dabit Monumentum.

ALMOST oppoſite to the preceding againſt the North Pier in the Chancel, a beautiful Marble Monument with this Inſcription :

Near this Place
Lyeth interred the Body of THOMAS NEWDIGATE, Eſq;
third Son of Sir RICHARD NEWDIGATE of *Ardbury*
in the County of *Warwick* Bart. Serjeant at Law.

who

who departed this Life
the 24th of January 1722.
Aged 74.

Under it : *G. 3 Lions Paws A. a* for Difference.

ABOUT the middle of the Chancel not far from the Railes of the Communion Table on a blue Grave-ftone :

Exuviæ
Samuelis Hallows Armigeri
Obiit
12 Die - Mar. - -
.Anno Ætatis 82.
1714.

A little more towards the middle Ifle, is a black Marble Grave Stone with two Brafs Plates of this Form :

ON the upper :

A Fefs varry A. & V. between 3 fpread Eaglets. The Creft a Dog ty'd to a Tree.
Anno 1607.
In memoria æterna juftus erit.

THE Infcription on the lower being quite worn out, I muft borrow of Dr. *Thoroton* :

Nicholas Kinnerfley, Efq; and his Mother
Dear Amye their Corps this Stone doth here cover
They live now with Chrift in whom they did truft
Their Bodies do wait the rifing of the Juft.

ON the South fide of the preceeding, upon a rough Stone :

Arms a *Griffin*.
Here lies the Body of ROBIE SHERWIN, Efq;
late Member of Parliament for this Town
who died the 6th of *Auguft* Anno Dom. 1718.
in the 51ft Year of his Age.

Here lies alfo the Body of JOHN SHERWIN
(Brother to the faid *Robie Sherwin*)
Mayor of this Corporation, died 25th
of *November*, Anno Dom. 1718.
in the 53d Year of his Age.

AT the Head of Mr. Sherwin's Grave Stone, upon a black Stone : *Per pale 1ft. a dexter Hand within a Border ingrailed. 2d.*

Here lies the Body of *Thomas*
Manly Efq; who departed this
Life the 11th of *November* 1708.
in the 42d Year of his Age.

Before

BEFORE I leave the Chancel I muſt take Notice of an old Piece of Painting upon the Wall over the Veſtry Door, almoſt effaced, which I have often attentively look'd upon: Of this what is left, and may be diſcover'd without the help of a
ſtrong Imagination, is the Figure of a Man of a Gigantic Size, with his Right Arm
bent upwards and the Hand inwards, the Left Arm and Shoulder is in part worn out but
the Hand is ſo placed in the Side, that without doubt it had been a Kembo; his Face
ſeems to be looking towards his right Side, his Legs ſtanding in Water, to denote
which the plainer (for it was certainly done by a very indifferent Hand) a Fiſh is
painted ſwimming between them; on his Left at a Diſtance are ſtill to be ſeen a few
Houſes, and in the Water there ſeems to appear two Heads of Ships. The Table of
the King's Arms is fixed over the middle of the Body and covers part of the Legs.
On the right Hand there is the Figure of a Fryar looking and holding up ſomething
like a Book in his left Hand.

FROM theſe obſcure Traces I readily concluded that the great Figure was to
repreſent St. *Chriſtopher*, having never met with any Roman Catholick Saint which
is pictur'd as a Giant but the juſt named. Yet being unwilling to decide too precipi-
tantly, and not then able to Account for this Saint's being ſet up in a Church dedicated to St. *Mary*, I placed this Picture in the Number of my printed Queries: But had
not been favoured with any Anſwer till lately by *John Plumptre*, Eſq; who upon reading Dr. *Stukely's* Diſſertation on the Cave at *Royſton*, called to Mind that Piece of
Painting of which I am ſpeaking, and has been ſo kind as to communicate his Thoughts
to me concerning it, which I give the Reader in his own Words:

" IN St. *Mary's* Chancel at *Nottingham* on the North Wall juſt over the Veſtry-
" Door, there are (or were lately) the dim Remains of an ancient Gigantic Picture
" of a Man. I have formerly taken Notice of it, (but not much of late Years) and never
" doubted its being intended for St. *Chriſtopher*. From whence I ſuppoſe, the Chriſt
" (as uſual) was then viſible either in his Arms, or on his Shoulder, tho' I do not now
" remember that Circumſtance. But why St. Chriſtopher ſhould have been ſo gla-
" ringly put there in a Church not dedicated to him, I never could Account for to my
" Satisfaction. Dr. *Stukeley* has now cleared up the Matter to me. Among the Fi-
" gures rudely cut in the ſide of the Cave aforeſaid, there is one much larger than the
" reſt, a manifeſt St. *Chriſtopher*, with the Child Jeſus on his Shoulder, as he always
" has been drawn, and as you frequently may ſee him, even upon Signs at this Day,
" and the Subſtance of the Doctor's ſhort Diſſertation upon it, is this:

St. Chriſtopher *was a Canaanite or Syrian by Birth, he conſidering his great Sta-
ture and Strength, and how he might beſt ſerve God and be uſeful to Mankind, built
himſelf a Cell by a River ſide, where there was neither Bridge nor Boat, and there
employ'd himſelf in carrying over all Paſſengers. Farther this Saint was thought to
have a ſpecial Privilege in preventing Tempeſts and Earthquakes, for which reaſon
we ſee him ſo often painted in Churches.* (a) " And for the ſame Reaſon his Figure
" found a Place in this Cave, which by the ſeveral Religious Sculptures in it, is moſt
" likely was an Oratory; and the Doctor by many very probable Arguments, fixes its

---

(a) *I ſince recollect to have ſeen the Picture of this Saint, over the Weſt Door of the Cathedral Church of* Hamburgh, *tho' the Church is dedicated to St.* Mary.

E

Erec-

" Erection between the Years 1170 and 1189." Within which Time, *viz.* 1185, our Historians record a most terrible Earthquake in England in the Month of March, such a one as was never known before ; many Houses thrown down, even such as were built of Stone ; Lincoln Cathedral split from Top to Bottom.   The first of May following there was an Eclipse of the Sun ; soon after great Thunder and Lightning, many Men and Cattle destroy'd, many Houses burnt.   " This might well induce " Men in those superstitious Times to furnish their Churches with the Image of a " Saint who's peculiar Protection they had been taught to be so necessary against the " the like Calamities ; and the Doctor gives a remarkable Instance, that the neg-" lect of this did not pass unregarded by the State ; he cites an old Record in the " Court of Liveries 32 *Hen.* III. (62 Years after the Mischief) thus : "

The *KING,*

To the Sheriff of *Hampshire*, Greeting.

WE *Command You, that out of the Rents issuing from your County, you cause to be painted in the Queen's Chappel at* Winchester, *upon the Gable towards the West, the Image of St.* Christopher, *who holds in his Arms as usual our blessed Saviour, And the Cost which you lay out on this Work shall be accounted for in the Exchequer.*

Witness the KING *at* Windlesor, *the 7th Day of* May.

" If we may suppose now that our St. *Christopher* was painted about the Time of " the aforesaid general Fright, it may be very consistent with the Age of the Chan-" cel ; for tho' it be evident, by the Stile of its Architecture, that it was not built in " its present Form at the same Time with the rest of the Church, yet there is no rea-" son to suspect its not being as old as the Time we are speaking of ; and I have " heard it reported (whether from Tradition or better Authority, I know not) that " our Chancel is about 600 Years old.   But were it pardonable in me to put on the " Air of an Antiquary, and advance a bold Guess, I should say that we may safely " conclude that the Earthquake which split Lincoln Cathedral from Top to Bottom, " threw down St. *Mary's* original Steeple, upon the original Chancel, and both be-" ing demolished, these new ones we now see were soon after built in the room of " them, and St. *Christopher* was clapt on the Wall to prevent the like Destruc-" tion for the future.   I feel the Imagination strengthen upon me, and I begin to be-" lieve it was really so.

" I know not whether you have ever observed the Picture ; but if you have, I be-" lieve what I have written here, will induce you to make it another Visit and there-" fore I shall here add a few Words more.   In the Cave at *Royston* there is a Figure " of a Cross like a Staff standing upright, from the Top of which some Leaves seem " issuing ; this tho' separated from the Figure of St. *Christopher* by many interven-" ing Figures, Dr. *Stukeley* says belongs to that Saint and proves it thus : He says, *That once on a Time, before a great Assembly of People, St.* Christopher *stuck his Staff into the Ground, and it took Root immediately, and produced Leaves, Flowers and Fruit,* (a) *in token of the Truth of the Doctrine he taught them.* " I pray you to observe whether there be any Traces of such a Staff in our Picture.

                                                                    THESE

(a) *That it was believed as a Truth is farther confirmed by a Relique of his, kept in a certain Village in* Tyrol, *where they shew one of the largest Nails of this Saint, kept in a Case of Palm-Tree, which did grow from his Pole after he had stuck it in the Ground.*   Misson's new Voyage, Vol. 1st. part II. p. 391.

The Tomb of the first and Second EARLS of CLARE in the South Isle of St. MARY'S CHURCH

I. Clee Sculp. 1750.

Arms of the first EARL

Arms of the second EARL

THESE more than probable Conjectures of this Honourable Gentleman have entirely confirmed me in my firſt Opinion, and tho' no Child Jeſus is viſible now, it is full as reaſonable to believe it was placed on the left Shoulder of the great Figure, as to ſuppoſe that this Figure had a left Shoulder, which is now worn out. The Staff 'tis true on the right Side does not appear very plainly, yet does the Poſition of the Arm and Hand which is the ſame as a Man's who holds a Pike or Halbard upright, give ground ſufficient to think that once the Staff was as diſcernable as the Arm and Hand that held it is at this Time.

Under the King's Arms is the following Inſcription :

C H A R L E S by the Grace of God, King of Great-Britain, France and Ireland, and third Monarch of the whole Continent, which Sovereign King the Lord of all Lords and King of all Kings Jehova preſerve long amongſt us, to the Peaceful Go-vernment of the Common-wealth and Building up of his Church. Submit yourſelves therefore unto all manner of Ordinance of Men for the Lords ſake, whether it be unto the King as having the Pre-eminence, either unto Rulers as unto them that are ſent by him for the Puniſhment of Evil Doers, but for the Laud of them that do well, for ſo is the Will of God, that with well doing you may ſtop the Ignorance of fooliſh Men. As free, and not as having the Liberty for a Cloak of Naughtineſs, but ever as the Servants of God. Honour all Men, love Brotherly Fellowſhip, Fear God and Honour the King. I Deut. 2 Chap. 13, 14, 15, 16 and 17 ver. Anno Dom. 1660.

I proceed now to the South part of the Croſs-Iſle, which is our Lady's Chappel, on the Eaſt Side of it is the ſtately Tomb of black and white Marble, in which are de-poſited the Bodies of the 1ſt and 2d Earls of Clare. The Epitaph of the 1ſt Earl is on the Weſt-ſide of the Tomb.

H. S. E.
Johannes Hollies de Houghton Equ. Aur.
Denzillii F. Willielmi N.
in Baronem Houghton, nec non in Comitem Clare per Regem Jacobum erectus, uxorem duxit Annam Thomæ Stanhope de Shelford Equ. Aur. Filiam, è quâ Filios Johannem, poſtea Comitem de Clare, Denzillum in Baronem Hollies de Ifield in comitatu Suſſexiæ per ſereniſſimum Regem Carolum II. promotum, Franciſcum qui cælebs obiit; ac Carolum et Willielmum, et Carolum in cunis de mortuos.
Fillias etiam
Eleonoram, Olivero Vice comiti Fitz-Williams ac Comiti Tyrconnel; Arabellam, Thomæ Wentworth de Wentworth Woodhouſe in Com. Ebor. Baronetto (poſtea vero in Vice Comit. Wentworth et Comitem de Strafford evecto) copulatas ; ac Elizabe-tham ante nuptias defunctam
ſuſcitavit.
Diem obiit IIII Octobris
Anno Dom. MDCXXXVII.

THAT of the ſecond Earl is on the Eaſt-ſide :

H. S. E.
Prænobilis Johannes Comes de Clare,
Johannes F. Denzillii N.

Uxorem duxit Elizabetham Horatii Vere, Equ. Aur. Baronifq; de Tilbury (in re
bellica clariffimi)filiam et Cohæredem è quâ filios Johannem in cunis de mortuum ac
Gilbertum poftea Comitem de Clare.

Filias vero

Annam, Edwardo primogenito Theophili Comitis Lincolniæ; Elizabetham, Went-
worthio Comiti de Kildare; Arabellam, Edwardo Roffeter de Sommerby in Com.
Linc. Equ. Aur. Matrimonis conjunctas.

Mariam in cunis alteram Mariam ante nuptias defunctas; Eleonoram fuperftitem Ka-
tharinam et Margaretam in cælibatu direptas, Sufannam, Johanni Lort de Stackpole
Court in Agro Pembr. Baronetto defponfatam.

Franciscam infantulam exanimem; Dianam HenricoBridges filio et Hæredi Thomæ
Bridges de Keynfham in Com, Sommerf. Equ. Aur. enuptam; Penelopen, Jacobo
Langham de Cotesbroke, in Com. Northampt. Baronetto copulatam. Dorotheam, et
Franciscam in teneri ætate fublatas, procreavit.
Diem obiit fecundo Januarii Anno Dom.
MDCLXV.

ON the South fide clofe to the Wall there is an ancient Tomb in which lies the
Figure of a Man, here are yet to be made out the Arms: *A a Bend between a Mullet of fix Points pierced and an Annulet Gules. Samon.*

Near this under the Pews
- - - - Richardi Samon, quondam Majoris et Aldermanni iftius Villæ, qui obiitXVIII
Die menfis Decembris Anno Dom.
MCCCCLVII.

NOT far from this is the Grave-ftone of *William Greaves*, Alderman, and Re-
gifter of the Archdeaconry of *Nottingham*, has this Infcription:

CONDITUM
hîc eft
Quod Mortale Fuit
GUILIELMI GREAVES, A. M.
D̄no Archidiacono de Nott. ab Archivis
Infra Jur̄nes de Nott. et Bingham
Decani Ruralis
Qui pulcherrimæ hujus Villæ
Prope ab Origine Chartâ Regiâ donatæ
Diu erat inter Patricios
Atque ut Dignitatem Pretoriam
Suftinuit multoties et decoravit
Ita Jura fua municipalia
fideliter tuendo
Bono publico multum profpexit
Nihil fuo
obiit Maji xxx.
Anno Salutis
MDCXCVII.
Ætat: fuæ
LXXVII.

IN the South Iſle about the mildſe, upon a rough Grave-ſtone, on a Braſs Plate:

Here lyeth the Body of *Gowen Knight*, ſometime Fellow of Merton College in Oxford, late Maſter of the Free-School in this Town, Who died Sept. 9th. 1691. In the Year of his Age LVI. Current.

Whoſe Name ſo fully doth his Worth expreſs,
That to ſay more of him were to ſay leſs,

ALMOST over this laſt Stone is fixed to a Pillar a fine Monument of Marble thus inſcribed:

Near this Place lyeth the Body of
THOMAS SMITH, Eſq;
who died Jan. 8th A. D. 1727 Ætat: 45.

He was a Man of exact
Integrity and Skill in his extenſive Buſineſs
by which he acquired a handſome Fortune
and Reputation of Univerſal Humanity and
Benevolence. The Charity intruſted with him
by others, received anIncreaſe from
his Prudence and Generoſity.
Qualities that he readily and heartily exerted in the
Service of Mankind.
And which were returned to him
by a general and moſt ſincere
Love and Eſteem.
He married *Mary* the Daughter of
Thomas Manly, Eſq;
and left behind him 5 Daughters.

He bore: *Or a Chevron cotiſed between 3 Demy Griffins ſable. The Creſt on a Wreath of his Colours, an Elephants Head eraced or charged with 3 Fleur de Lis B, eared G.*

IN the Middle Iſle on a Pillar overagainſt the Pulpit is a Marble Monument with this Inſcription:

Near this Place lyeth the Body of *William Flamſtead*, Gent. late Steward and Town Clark of *Nottingham*, who for his exemplary Piety, eminent parts, and ſingular Fidelity, lived much deſired and died no leſs lamented, the 38th Year of his Age. *Aug.* 24, 1653.

The Memory of the Juſt is bleſſed.

IN this Iſle, and the Body of the Church are ſeveral very large Grave-ſtones, which have been covered with Braſs Plates, but theſe being torn off by the Soldiers during the Civil War, it is not to be known who are buried under them.

IN the North Iſle near Mr. *Plumptre's* Seat, on a Braſs Plate:

Hic

Hic jacet Henricus Farington,
Servus fidelis D. H. Plumptre
qui obiit Jul. 1645.

ON another Brafs Plate not far from the laft:

Exuviæ
Jofephi Gardiner
Med. D.
qui obiit Mar. 4.
1 6 6 9.

ABOUT the Middle of this Ifle on a fmall Brafs Plate:

Hic jacet Johannes Bee
in Medicinis Doctor
obiit 28. Feb. 1719. Ætatis
fuæ 84.

IN the Chappel of All-Saints, in the middle facing the South, there is a large ancient Tomb upon which there have been feveral large Brafs Plates with Figures engraven on them, thefe having had the fame Fate with thofe mentioned in the middle Ifle,
it does not appear who of that Family lye interred in it.

THERE was in Dr. *Thoroton's* Time a Grave-ftone before the faid Tomb with
the Arms of Plumptre, viz. *A. a Chevron between two Mullets, and an Annulet* S:
infcribed:

Domus æterna
John̅s Plumptre
Anno Dom. M D L I I.
defuncti.

but this Stone now lies entire under the Pew, removed thither upon making the Vault.

AT the Eaft End of this Chappel is an Alablafter Tomb, on which lies the Figure
of a Man in a Gown, with wide Sleeves and a Cap on his Head, the Hands in a praying Pofture, it has no Infcription; in the Side which Faces the South are four Figures in Baffo Relievo, the 1ft. and 3d. counting from the left to the right Hand, are
Angels holding each an empty Scutcheon before them, the fecond is a mitred Figure,
and the 4th. feems to be in a fitting Pofture, having a Coronet on the Head.

OVER this, in the Corner, is a Marble Monument in Memory of the eldeft Son
of *John Plumptre*, Efq; on the top are the Arms of the Family.

Here lies interred *Henry* eldeft Son of
John Plumptre, Efq; born 22d. July 1708, deceafed Jan. 3d. 1718-19:
In thefe few and tender Years he had to a great
Degree made himfelf Mafter of
the Jewifh, Roman, and Englifh Hiftory,
the Heathen Mythology and the
French Tongue, and was not
inconfiderably advanced
in the Latin.

SECT. I.

In a fmall Compartment under this:
Animam nati
his faltem accumulem donis,
et fungar inani
munere.

AT the Weft End of this Chappel is a very beautiful Monument of Marble, with the following elegant Latin Epitaph, made by a Relation, his quondam Tutor, at Pembroke in Cambridge, and the Addition for Joyce his Wife was made by another Relation.

Hic infra requiefcit pars terrena
Henrici Plumptre Armig.
mortui 20. Decembris 1693. ætatis 49.
Qualis Vir fuerit fcire aves.
Ab antiqua ftirpe in oppido Nottinghamiæ ortus
Omni genam Eruditionem honeftis moribus adjuxit
Eruditionis finem duxit effe regimen Vitæ
Hinc factâ fibi morum fupremâ lege
Bene volentia univerfali
Pietatis haud fucatæ evafit Exemplar fingulare
Amicus, Civis, Maritus, Pater, miferorum Patronus
Qualem jam exoptare licet vix reperire
Viduam reliquit ejus amantiffimam
Jocofam Henrici Sacheverel Armigeri
De Morley in agro Derbienfi filiam natu fecundam
quæ cum tres filios vivo peperiffet
Johannem, Henricum et Fitz-Williams,
optimi Patris Monumenta
Hunc etiam Lapidem in perpetuam memoriam
Mortuo cum Lachrymis poni curavit.
Hic quoq; demum letho
Confortionem redintegravit interruptam
Illa Jocofa
Verbo omnes complectar Laudes
Conjux illo digna Viro
Functa fato 8 die Novembris
1708. Ætatis 69.

The Arms: *Plumptre impales A. on a faltier B. 5 Waterbougets O. Sacheverel.* — The fame are in a Hatchment placed over the great Tomb.

IN the Body of the Church which is very fpacious are many Grave-ftones among the reft thofe of feveral Aldermen of this Corporation, but as there is nothing very remarkable in the Infcriptions I fhall content myfelf with the two following:

H. I. S.
Robertus Hedges
Armiger, Filius
Gulielmi Hedges
Equitis Aurat.

Mer-

Mercatoris et Aldermanni
Londinenfis
Obiit 14 die Februarii
Ann. { Dom. 1730.
       { Ætat. 49.

ON a Brafs Plate about the middle of the Body of the Church:

Here lie the Bodies of three
Daughters of Richard Mafcie
of Sale in the County of
Chefter, Efq; who was lineally
defcended from the ancient Family of Mafcie Baron of Dunham Mafcie.

Jane, the feventh Daughter aged five Years, died 14th Febr. 1684.

Elizabeth, the fixth Daughter aged eleven Years, died the 4th of March 1688.

Mary, the fifth Daughter aged fixteen Years, died the 30th of June 1689.

IN the Church-yard of St. *Mary* I find nothing worth Notice, but thefe Arms on a Tomb-ftone, *viz*:

A. on a plain Crofs.   G. 5 Efcallop Shells O.   a Mullet for Difference.

the Grave of Mr. *Jacob Villier's*, by this, tho' the Family which continues ftill in *Nottingham*, is employ'd in the Stocking-Manufacture, it appears that they are defcended from a collateral Branch of the Family of the great Favourite of King *James* and King *Charles* I. *George Villiers* Duke of *Buckingham*.

IN the Church of St. *Mary*, Prayers are read twice a Day throughout the Year, two Sermons preached every Lord's Day, and on Wednefdays a Morning Lecture, befides other Sermons on particular Days. *See Sect*. VII.

IT is a Vicarage, which was twenty Marks Value, when the Prior of *Lenton*, was Patron, but now its in the King's Book 10 l. 5 s. value.

A

A LIST of the VICARS of St. *Mary's* Church in NOTTINGHAM,
from the Year 1290.

1290	JOhannes de Ely. —	1504 Richard Travenor. — —
1304	J Robertus de Dalby. —	1534 Richard Matthew. — —
1313	Henricus de parva Haly. —	1535 Richard Wylde. — — —
1317	Johannes de Ludham. —	1554 Oliverus Hawood. — —
1322	Joh. ff. Witti.Coryn. —	1568 Johannes Lowthe. — —
1347	Johannes de Launde. —	1572 Willielmus Underue. — —
1347	Robert de Wakebridge. —	1578 Robertus Aldridge. — —
1348	Richard de Radclyffe. —	1616 Oliverius Wytherington. —
1349	Roger de Nyddingworth. —	1616 Johannes Tolfon. —
1349	Richard de Swanyngton. —	1617 Radulfus Hansby. —
1351	Thomas Pafcayl. — —	1635 Edmundus Laycock. (a) —
1357	Johannes Lorimer. —	1662 Georgius Mafterfon. — —
-----	Johannes de Hoveden. —	1686 Samuel Crobrow. S. T. P. —
1364	Joh. de Stapleford. —	1690 Benjamin Catnfield. A. M. —
1371	Willielmus de Sandyacre. —	1694 Tymothy Carrol. A. M. —
-----	Robertus de Retford. —	1998 Edwardus Clarke. A. M. —
1401	Richardus Chilwell. —	1708 Samuel Berdmore. A. M. —
1409	Willielmus Ode. — —	1723 Johannes Difney. A. M. —
1447	Willielmus Wright. —	1730 Thomas Berdmore. A. M. —
1461	Johannes Hurt. — —	1743 Scroop Berdmore, S. T. P. ?
1476	Thomas Turner. — — —	----- prefent Vicar. — —
1498	Johannes Greve. —	
1499	Simon Yates. — — —	

(a) Mr. *Edmund Laycock* held the Living till 1642 inclufive: From
which Time St. *Mary's* Church had no fettled Minifter till 1651, when
Mr. *Whitlock* was prefented by the Marquis of *Dorchefter*, and his
Friend and infeperable Companion Mr. *Reynolds*, was made Lecturer.
About this Time was built the prefent Vicarage Houfe for the Habitations of both thefeMinifters, it being adapted for two entireFami-
lies.

— In the Year 1693 the Vicarage was vacant.

ST. *PETER's* Church, by what remains of the old Work, seems hardly quite so old as *St. Mary's*: It has suffered very much as is visible by the different Reparations. Among other Casualties in the Civil War, an accidental Bomb falling into the Vestry batter'd all that part of the Building to Peices. Whatever the original Steeple might be, the present is a Spire.

THERE are in this Church two Chappels, one towards the South, which I take to be St. *Mary's*, the other towards the North, which is the Chappel of *All-Saints*. In the Year 1739, in the Month of *July*, Mr. *Abel Smith*, Banker of this Town, caused a Vault to be built for his Family in this Chappel, the Workmen digging to come to the Rock for a Foundation, met with an Arch in the North-Wall about four Feet high, from the Foundation of the Church, which in all is not above five Feet deep, in this Place, and near 10 from the Rock. At the bottom of this Arch, they observed a Stone Trough, part of which advanced into the Chappel, the rest was under the Arch, just broad enough to hold a Coffin, and long enough for the same purpose, in it they found the Bones of a Corps which were all firm and sound, whereof myself was an Eye Witness, and a red Tile glazed with Cross Keys upon it. Diverse were the Conjectures concerning this Tile, when *John Plumptre*, Esq; then one of the Members of the Honourable House of Commons for *Nottingham*, coming soon after from *London*, upon my relating to him the Story, shew'd me a like Tile, which he had found entire, amongst several broken Pieces in the Burial Place of his Ancestors, in St. *Mary's* Church, at his making a Vault there. (a)

IT is a red Tile of a very hard Composition, just four Inches and a half Square, and one Inch thick, the upper Surface of it glazed of a brownish Colour, and on it the Figure of a Bell in Yellow, placed diagonally, and of as large a Dimension as the Tile will admit of, on one side of the Bell the Figure of a Key, and on the other a broad Sword, the Symbols of St. *Peter* and St. *Paul*. Mr. *Plumptre*, with very great Probability is of Opinion, that these Characters shew such Tiles to have been destin'd at their making for the Use of a Church; and that probably these were the original Pavement round the Altar, which was on the East-side of the said Cross Isle, and separated from the rest of the Chappel of *All-Saints* by the Cancelli, which remained standing till the Year 1719 of the same form with those that still enclose the whole Chappel. That the original Pavement was probably in Process of Time broken up for Graves, and the Peices of it thrown negligently in with the Earth, that had been taken out, and that as this Chappel had been dedicated to All Saints, and on this Tile here are the Symbols of two Saints, it is not unlikely that if more of these Tiles had been preserved, the Symbols of other Saints might have appeared thereon.

THE just mention'd Gentleman informed me, that the Bones found in the Arch were the Remains of *John de Plumptre*, Founder of the Hospital at the Bridge-End, who desired to be buried in this Chappel, under the Wall of this Church, and that near this Place *Henry Plumptre*, and several others of the Family were buried. And Dr. *Thoroton*, p. 497. mentions, " That *Henry Plumptre*, (Brother of " the Founder) by his Will dated the 11th of *Henry* IV. 1408, ordered that his Body " should be buried in the Chappel of All-Saints beneath, or in the Church of St. *Pe-* " ter in *Nottingham*.

IN the Church there was a Guild or Fraternity of St. *George*, as appears by the
                                                                                        Guild

St. PETER'S CHURCH. *P.34*

St. NICHOLAS'S CHURCH. *P.42*

Guild-Book, still preserved in the Vestry, wherein the Accounts of the Guild were kept, it beginneth in the Year 1440 and is continued to the Dissolution of Chappels and Chantries. There was also, besides another, the Chantry of St. *Mary*.

IN the West Corner of the South Isle is held the Spiritual Court, which formerly used to be kept in the Chappel of *All Saints*. They meet once a Month, and oftner if Business require it.

ST. *Peter's* has a Ring of 8 Bells but neither so large nor so Musical as those of St. *Mary*.

A TABLE of the Inscriptions, Dates, &c. upon St. *Peter's* Bells, in *Nottingham*.

I.
IN PERPETUAM MEMORIAM SOCIETATIS IVVENVM BOREALIVM 1672.

2.
IN PERPETVAM MEMORIAM SOCIETATIS IVVENVM BOREALIVM. 1672.

3.
GOD SAVE THE KING. 1666.

4.
GOD SAVE HIS CHVRCH. 1635.

5.
GOD SAVE HIS CHVRCH. T. HVNT. I. WILSON, WARDENS. 1685.

6.
IESVS BE OVR SPEDA.

7
aue maria of you charitie for to pray for the sole of magere dubbyseay.

8
ROBERT SHERWIN, IOHN CAWTON, WILLIAM FREEMAN, RICHARD WELLAH, ALDERMEN.

MONUMENTS and *Monumental* INSCRIPTIONS.

IN the Chancel, formerly was a large East Window with many Coats of Arms painted on the Glass, this at present is Walled up, and an Altar-Piece representing the Lord's Supper placed in the room of it.

ON the North Side of the Communion Table under the Figure of *Moses* is the following Inscription:

Tertio die Octobris MDCCXX.
Juxta hunc Locum
Sepulta est Hannah,
Uxor
Alverii Dodsley Genorosi
Qui
Hujus Ecclesiæ Ornatui
Consulens
Ad Altare Cœnam Domini
delineandam
propriis sumptibus curavit.

WITHIN the Rails of the Communion Table on a square Brass Plate :

D. O. M.
Johannes Volusenus Westmonasterii natus
Oxon: educatus S. T. P. Decanusa Ripis BT I.
Petri Westmonast. et B tæ Mariæ Lincoln.
Præb. P ochiæ Ecclesiæ de Bruneston Vic.
et Ecclesiæ de Beedal Rec. hic in Domino
requiescit. obiit Febr. x. 1634.

Here John Wilson sleeps in Trust,
That Christ will raise him from his Dust,
Serve God with Fear thou canst not tell
Whether thy Turn be next, Farewel.
Disce mori.

ON the South side of the Chancel over the Door, was an handsome Monument, with the following Inscription in golden Letters :

Viri apprimè venerabilis Georgii Cotes bo-
narum Artium ferè omniu Thesaurarii :
principis artis et instar omnium Theologiæ
cimeliarchi, gregis egregii Custodis: deniq ;
ut ingenii, ut vitæ cultum instituerint,
omnibus meritó Exemplar.

{ Pectus Pietatis Sacrarium }
{ Lingua Spiritus Tuba }
{ Manus Christi erogatrix }
{ Domus Religionis Schola }
{ Vita morum censura, }

Qui

Qui ut annos quatuor et viginti ſummâ fide
ſum̄ âq; diligentiâ curam hujus Ecclefiæ ſuſ-
tinuerat exantlato labore ad patriam reditu-
rus mortate quod erat ſervandū hîc depoſuit
cœtera perennior ; luctum amicis, & ſui
ingens deſiderium ſuis, adeoq; bonis omnibus relinquens ; è corporis evolavit vin-
culis 3°. Calend. Decembris Anno poſt
natum Chriſtū 1640. Ætatis Autem ſuæ
XLIII.

Cui nepos ejus Samuel Cotes hoc in pii
doloris et perpetuum **juxta** patrui merito-
rum, ſuisq; ſuperſtitis amoris merenti moe-
rens Monumentum.

P.

THIS when the Chancel was repaired, was in taking down broke in Pieces.

ON the North ſide of the **Chancel** a Marble Monument :

Memoria Sacrum.

Pientiſſimæ Conjugis Margaretæ Domini Matthæi Saunderii Shanc-
tonienſes in agro Leiceſtrenſi Equitis Aurati filiæ, quæ cum opti-
mis naturæ dotibus ex inſtinctu prædita, tum virtutibus parentum
curâ diligentiâq? ſummum quâſi ad verſtigium aucta quin-
tum et vigeſimū ætatis annum agens Johanni Lokeo Regienſi in
ſedibus Hertfordianis Generoſo nupta eſt. Quocum ut piiſſimè
conjunctiſſimèq; ſuum uxoris per tres annos conjugale munus obiit
ſera ſibi, citò ſuis carnem depoſitura ſe ad plures penetravit quarto
Idus Septembris Anno Verbi incarnati 1633. Cui officii èt amoris
ergo monumentum hoc maritus ille moeſtiſſimus extruxit.

Eja, age, ſiſte, locum tenet hunc matrona ſacra
Clara, Venuſta, pudens, religioſa gravitus,
Ergò jacent charitas, pietaſq; ſed aſtra viciſſim,
Hâc poterant aliâ non repirere Via
Margarita jacet, non annis dempta ſed anni
Ut Spectes Animū dant obiiſſe ſenem.

ABOVE theſe Inſcriptions are the Arms of *Lockes* and *Saunders* impaled :

*A. a Bend between two Waterbougets S. Locks. Per Chevron S. and A.
3 Elephants Heads eraced counterchanged. Saunders.*

CLOSE by the laſt is another Marble Monument for a ſecond Wife, where
Locke's Arms are impaled with :

*G. on a Feſs A. between three creſcents O. as many Eſcalops azure.
Ellis of Grantham.*

Ad Memoriam fempiternam Janæ fuæ Dom. Thomæ Ellifio de
Grantham in finibus Lincolnienfibus, Equiti Aurato unique à
Confiliis Domino Regi in provincià boreali, minoris natu filiæ,
morum pariter et formæ fpectabilis venuftate, fibiq; poft quadren-
nium interrupti fæliciffimi Conjugii, paribus aufpiciis in fecundi
thori matrimonium collocatæ : cui (ut ferè quæ funt cordi maxime.)
Vertente biennio, Nottinghamiæ accidit humanitus fato præma-
turo cedere, calendis fextilibus; Annoq; jam haud unoviginti
plus habente ad humanæ falutis : MDCXXXIX.

Joannes Lockeus Hertfordienfis de Regia, Generofus, monumentum hoc Defiderii et Conjunctionis ergo confecravit fanctiffi-
mæ Conjugi fuperftes diffidium luctuofe deflet.

> Elifia de Gente redux J. Jana : fed eheu !
>   Cur hæc Lux, quæ dat Gaudia curta daret ?
> Ne Cœlum invidiæ : quanquam juvenifq; vigenfq;
>   Serior optarim, viferet Umbra polos.
> Image chara diem, melior neque munus obivit,
>   Reddita Elifiis ortaque digna tuis.

IN the Chappel of *All-Saints* on a Table facing the Weft :

*A. a Lion rampant queve furche S. Creffy impaling Barry of fix A
nine Mullets G. 3. 33. Jefop.*   And :

> William Creffy Son of Hugh Creffy one of his
> Majefty's Judges of the King's Bench in
> Ireland was married to Elizabeth Daughter of
> George Jeffop of Brancliff in the County of
> York Efq; died the ninth of March 1645.

ON a Brafs Plate :

> Hîc jacet Corpus Johannis Combe, Generofi,
> civitate Exon. nati, olim Comitatus Notting-
> hamenfis Regiftrarii qui ab ⸢hâc (expectans
> meliorem) migravit undecimo die Octobris
> Anno Domini 1667, Ætatis fuæ fexagefimo
> feptimo.

Upon the Stone :

Refurgam.   J. C.

This Stone was taken up (when Mr. *Abel Smith*'s Vault was made) and broke but
the Plate is preferved.

NEAR unto this were on a Grave-ftone thefe Lines :

Lector in hoc tumulo requiefcunt offa Richardi Elkini Medici pluri-
bus haud opus eft.   Obiit Maji 19. Anno Dom. 1650. Ætat. 85.

ON

ON the Wall of the South Ifle, is a Marble Monument with this Infcription :

Near this Place lies the Body of Benjamin Rickards late of this Town Grocer, Son of Arthur Rickards Minifter of Hart-fhorn in the County of Leicefter, who married Elizabeth Daughter of William Parker, late of this Town Apothecary, by whom he had 8 Children, Elizabeth, John, Benjamin, Hannah, Elizabeth, Arthur, Samuel and Arthur, all being now dead except Samuel. He departed this Life Aug. 27, 1675. in the 37th Year of his Age.

Near this Place lies the Body of Alderman Thomas Trigge, Grocer, Son of Matthew Trigge, Minifter of Stretton in the County of Leicefter, who married Elizabeth the Widdow of Benjamin Rickards, by whom he had 6 Children, Elizabeth, Thomas, Matthew, William, Jofeph, Nathaniel, all furviving except Nathaniel. He departed this Life March the 20th 1704-5. in the 52d Year of his Age.

The Above

Thomas Trigge gave by Will 50 Pounds to buy Land for ever, the Rent to pay for Bread to be diftributed to poor Houfe-keepers of this Parifh, by the Minifter and Church-Wardens and Overfeers in two equal parts, one part on Chriftmas-Day, the other on good Friday.

Elizabeth Trigge, in Refpect of her Husbands abovementioned, has erected this Monument to their Memory, and departed this Life 28th of March, 1720.

NOT far from the laft on the fame Wall is a Marble Monument fet up for Alderman Rickards :

Here lyeth,
the Body of
JOHN RICKARDS
late Alderman of this Town
Son of *Benjamin Rickards* late
of this Town, who married *Anne* the Daughter
of *Jofeph Clay*, by whom he had
Iffue three Sons
Parker, Benjamin, and John,
and three Daughters
Anne, Elizabeth and Anne,
Whereof
Benjamin, Elizabeth and Anne,
furvived him
He died the 20th of April
Anno Dom. 1703.

O-

OVER-AGAINST the before-mentioned Monument in the Isle upon a flat Gravestone :

> Here Lye the Bodies of *William Ayscough*, Printer and Bookseller of this Town : And *Anne* his Wife, she was Daughter of the Rev. Mr. *Young*, Rector of *Catwick* in the County of *York* ; he died March 2, 1719 ; she died Dec. 16, 1732.

the above Mr. *Ayscough* is remarkable, for having first introduced the Art of Printing in this Town, about the Year 1710.

IN the Church-Yard which abounds in Grave and Head-Stones, I find nothing remarkable except the following Ioco-serious one, upon a Man who was a great Champion of the High Party in this Town, and who had a strong Influence upon the Mobile, and all this Zeal of his did not proceed in him from any mercenary Views, but his own Choice. He was otherwise, tho' bred in low Life, (for he was a Stocking Needlemaker) a Person of good natural parts, and peculiarly remarkable for his filial Duty to his poor Mother. He died on the Election Day of Members of Parliament for the Town of *Nottingham*, soon after he had seen that Gentleman chaired, in whose behalf he had exerted himself in an extraordinary Manner.

> Here lies *VIN: EYRE*
> Let fall a Tear
> For one true Man of Honour
> No courtly Lord
> That breaks his Word
> Will ever be a Mourner.
>
> In Freedoms Cause
> He stretcht his Jaws
> Exhausted all his Spirit
> Then fell down dead
> It must be said
> He was a Man of Merit.
>
> Let Freemen be
> As brave as he
> And Vote without a Guinea
> *Vin : Eyre* is hurl'd
> To the other World
> And ne'er took Bribe a Penny.
> *Sept.* 6th 1727.

> True to his Friend to helpless Parent kind
> He died in Honour's Cause to Int'rest blind
> Why should we grieve, Life's but an airy Toy
> We vainly weep for him who died with Joy.

A LIST of the RECTORS of St. *Peter's* in NOTTINGHAM:
from the Year 1241.

1241	Joh: de Nottingham.	—
1280	Johannes Cathal. —	—
1287	Richardus de Stapleton.	—
1292	Joh: de Brus de Pykering.	—
1300	Adam de Kyrkby. —	—
1322	Lancelot de Corebto. —	—
1323	Willielmus de Willoughby.	
-----	Robertus Jolan. —	—
1347	Willielmus de Whatton.	—
1349	Henricus de Keyworth.	—
1369	Robertus de Newbald.	—
1375	Willielmus de Rodington.	—
-----	Hugo Martel. — —	—
1426	Johannes Burton. —	—
-----	Johannes Drayton. —	—
1445	Willielmus Gull. —	—
1483	Johannes Mayewe. —	—
1486	Robertus Cotyngham.	—
1499	Willielmus Ilkeston. —	—
1510	Joh: Plough. Kyngsbury.	—
1538	Johannes Plough. *jun.*	—
1550	Nicholaus Cooke. —	—
1578	Johannes Nytter vel Wittie.	
1583	Carolus Aynsworth. —	—
1588	Radulphus Shutte. —	—
1593	Johannes Pare. —	—
1604	Franciscus Rodes. —	—
1606	Roger Freeman. —	—
1610	Johannes Kelle. — —	—
1610	Thomas Low. — —	—
1617	Georgius Cotes. — —	—
1618	Hugo Parke. *Sequestrator.*	
1619	Georgius Cotes. —	—
1640	Johannes Goodall —	—
1642	Johannes Aysthorpe.	—
1667	Samuel Leak. — —	—
1672	Edwardus Buxton. —	—
1680	Willielmus Wilson. A. M.	—
1693	Nathan Drako. A. M. —	—
1704	Timothy Fenton. A. M.	—
1721	James Wilson. A. M. —	—
1725	Edward Chappell. A. M.	—

During the intestine Troubles, there was by the Parliament Party upon the Removal of Mr *John Aysthorpe*, one *Richard Whitchurch*, put in his Room who dying in the Year 1656 was succeeded by Mr. *John Barret*, M. A.

IN the Church of St. *Peter* are preached two Sermons every Lord's Day, and on Wednesdays and Fridays Prayers are read Morning and Afternoon. Besides Sermons on particular Days, *which see among the Benefactions.*

MY Anonymous Author who wrote his Account of *Nottingham* in 1641, speaks of a Sermon or Lecture, preached by the Industry of a religious and worthy Minister every Friday Morning at this Church, by which I take it he means the then Incumbent, which was Mr. *John Goodall.*

ST. *Peter's* is a Rectory which when the Prior of *Lenton* was Patron, was valued at twenty Marks, now in the King's Book, 8 l. 7 s. 6 d. and the King Patron.

THE present Church of St. *Nicholas* is a modern Building, which was finished in the Year 1678, of Brick ornamented with Stone. The old Church sharing in the Civil War the same Fate with that of St. *Edmund of Dudley*, both which were pulled down (by Reason of their Nearness) for the safety of the Castle, it was somewhat larger than the new one, of Stone, the materials were mostly converted to private Uses, the Boxes in the Kitchen of a certain Inn in this Town were made out of some of the Pews, and the Bells were by Order of Col. *Hutchinson*, (who was Governor of the Castle of *Nottingham*) removed to *Outhorpe.* There goes a Tradition among the People of this Town, that St. *Nicholas* is the Mother Church, but for my part I cannot find any Foundation for it unless the Defference was paid to it by way of Compliment, it being in the Kings Demesne before and after the Conquest. Where-ever I find the 3 Churches mentioned, St. *Mary's* is always named first, and St. *Nicholas's* last, nor is it reasonable to suppose that the least of these Churches should be the Mother, and take the Rank before St. *Mary's* who had a Suffragan Bishop, besides all public Solemnities, as the Election of the Mayor, Sheriffs, &c. were, and are, performed at St. *Mary's*, where also the Assize Sermons are preached before the Judges, not on Account of their Lodgings being near that Church, but Time immemorial, when they used to lodge in the Heart of the Town. One might upon much better Grounds conjecture that the Collegiate Church of *Southwell*, was once the Mother Church of our Parishes, because before the Town was made a County of itself, the Corporation was obliged once a Year to make a Procession thither in their Formalites, to hear Divine Service, of which more in Sect. VI.

THIS Church has at present but one Bell besides the Sermon Bell with this Inscription :

Abson, Rector, God Save his Church.
Nevil and Scattergood, *Wardens.*

1726.

MONUMENTS.

NO ancient Monuments are left in this Church, nor any old or new in the Churchyard, except the few following modern ones :

ON

ON a Monument of Marble againft the Wall on the Right Hand of the Communion Table :

Sab. between a Chevron 3 Doves Or.

Near this Place
Lies the Body of *ELIZABETH ALSOP.*
who died *June* 2d. A. D. 1731.
Bleffed are the Dead who die in the Lord,
for they reft from their Labours and their
Works follow them.

ON the left Side oppofite to the foregoing are hung up three Hatchments, *viz.*

1ft.

Gules three Lion's Paws Arg. Newdigate *a Mullet* for Difference impaling. *Arg. a Chevron between three Crefcents Gules. On a Wreath a Flower de Lis.*

2d.

Quarterly fix Coats the 1ft.
Azure a Chevron Arg. between three Cinquefoils Or. The Second,
Arg. within a Border ingrailed a Lion Sable. The Third,
Azure a Chevron Or. in Chief a Lion paffant of the fecond. The Fourth,
Arg. between a Chevron ingrailed 3 croffes forme fiche Sable. The Fifth,
Ermin. on a Bend Gules 3. The 6th,
Per Pale azure and Gules, over all 3 Lions rampant. Arg.
A Scutcheon of Pretence quarterly. Or two Bars and a Canton Gules.
2 Vert a Griffin Sergreant, in chief 3 efcallops Or. The 3d. as the 2d.
the 4th. as the 1ft. on a Wreath of his Colours A Blackmore couped at
the Knees, armed proper, about his Head a Bandage Arg. in his dexter
Hand extended a Goblet cover'd. Or. the dexter Arm a Kembo, Cooper.

AT the South-Weft End of the Crofs Ifle againft the Wall is a beautiful Marble Monument :

Vert. a Griffin Sergreant Or. On a Chief indented Arg.
two Croffes forme z Gul. Collin. impaling : Paly of fix
Or. and Gules a Bendarg. Langford. on a Wreath of
the Colours a Talbots Head.

Near this Place
lies the Body of
JOHN COLLIN Efq;
who departed this Life June 18th 1717.
in the 45th Year of his Age.
He married *Mary* Daughter of *George Langford* Efq;
and *Judith* his Wife, by whom he had Iffue
fix Sons and four Daughters, *Langford, Abel,*
Thomas, John, Samuel, and *George,*
Anne, Mary, Judith, and *Anne,*

F 2

Anne,

Anne, Samuel, and *George,*
died in their Infancy before him
Abel Collin, died *August* 8th 1730.
Judith Collin died *Feb.* 7, 1730-1.

His Widow in Memory of him and his deceased Children has placed this.

NEAR this Monument on the Ground are three Grave-Stones laid close together: On the first is this Inscription:

Here
Lieth the Body of Abel
Collin who departed this Life
the 2d Day of *April*
A. D. 1705.

And also here
Lieth the Body of Thomas
Collin Alderman, who departed
this Life the 18th Day of
January in the 61st Year
of his Age A. D.
1706-7.

ON the Second:

Here
Lieth the Body of
Laurence Collin, who departed
this Life the 9th Day of August
in the 91st Year of his Age,
A. D. 1704.

THE third covers the last Gentleman's Wife.

AT St. *Nicholas's* are likewise preached two Sermons every Sunday, and Prayers read as at St. *Peter's* twice a Week:

IT is a Rectory, when the Prior of *Lenton* was Patron, valued at ten Marks, now in the King's Books 2 l. 16 s. 6 d. and the King Patron.

───────────────────────────────

The above Abel Collin *is the Founder of the New-Hospital.* Thomas *is the Father of* John Collin, *who (tho' his Monument does not mention it) was also an Alderman of this Town.* Lawrence *was the Grandfather of* John, *and the first of the Family who settled in this Town at the End of the Civil War. He had been Gunner of the Castle of* Nottingham, *as appears by a Muster-Roll of the 27th Jan.* 1648. — *But of him more in another Place.*

A LIST of the VICARS of St. *Nicholas* in NOTTINGHAM, from the Year ⸺

----- Will. Bifhop. — — —
1267 Richard de Weremfworth. —
1286 Johannes de Ludham. — —
1317 Herbertus Pouger. — —
1318 Willielmus de Ilkefton. —
1321 Galfridus de Wilford. —
1329 Gilbertus de Ottrington. —
----- Thomas Tutil. — — —
1351 Richardus Kaym de Gotham.
1366 Johannes Templer. — —
----- Johannes Deinby. — —
1367 Thomas Lorday de Stanley.
1371 Willielmus de Bilham. —
----- Roger Bampton vel Mempton
1427 Willielmus Cokker. — —
1432 Willielmus Weftthorpe. —
1435 Johannes Sampfon. — —
1436 Johannes Hopwell. — —
1464 Nicholas Fifh. — — —
1466 Richardus Elkefly. — —
1471 Robertus Echard. — —
1476 Thomas Tewe. — — —
1477 Edmundus Holme. — —
1497 Johannes Dale. — — —

1502 Thomas Reyner. — —
1503 Reynaldus Marfhal. — —
1531 Alexander Penhill. — —
1533 Thomas Ward. — — —
1585 Radulphus Shute. — —
1588 Johannes Lambe. — —
1611 Robertus Malham. — —
1622 Robertus Aynfworth, the laft Incumbent till after the Reftoration.
1663 Joh. Ayfthorpe, Rector of St. Peter's and Sequeftrator.
1664 Blank for Sequeftrator. —
1665 to 1668 vacant.
1669 Samuel Leek to 1872.
1674 vacant to 1681. — — —
1682 Joh. Simpfon.

1715 Johannes Abfon. A. M. —
1749 George Wakefield, A M the prefent Incumbent. — — —

BESIDES the Parish Churches, there are in this Town several Places of Worship of Protestant Dissenters of different Denominations : as,

Presbyterians, who have a Meeting House on the South-side of the *High-Pavement*. These were the first Dissenters which did form a Congregation in this Town, after the Restoration about the Year 1662, when Mr. *Whitlock* and Mr. *Reynold's*, who had been established Ministers of the Parish Church of St. *Mary* from the Year 1651, to that Time, were silenced for refusing to conform to the Act of Uniformity. They were both remarkable Men, especially for unparalell'd Examples of true and constant Friendship, as appears by Dr. *Calamy's* Account of them. Their present Minister is Dr. *Samuel Eaton*.

THE Independents, whose Place of Worship is at the lower End of *Castle-Gate*. Their present Minister is Mr. *James Sloss*, a Scotch Gentleman.

THE *Anabaptists*, these have a Meeting in *Fryar-Lane* near the *New-Hospital*, their Preacher is a Layman, Mr. *George Eaton*. This Congregation is lately divided, the one part adheres to their old Teacher, the other follows one Mr. *Morley*, a Schoolmaster who has obtained a Licence for his Place of Meeting in *Pilchergate*.

THE *Quakers*, have a Meeting in *Spaniel-Row*, facing the North East End of *Collin's-Hospital*, who tho' they seem rather to decrease in Number, have lately rebuilt and enlarged their Meeting-House in the modern Taste, and have adorned the ame with fashionable arched Windows.

THE Tenets of these several Dissenters are so well known, that it would be superfluous to speak of them in this Place. But as the *Philadelphians* had an House in *Brewhouse-Yard*, under the Castle Rock, where they used to meet, and they being now entirely dispersed I will just shortly take Notice of the Origin of that Sect of Men.

THEY obtained the above-mentioned Name, as also the English Name of *Family of Love*, from the Love they profess to bear to all Men, tho' never so Wicked, and their Obedience to all Magistrates, tho' never so tyrannical, be they Jews, Gentiles, or Turks.

THEIR Founder was one *David George*, of *Delpht* in *Holland*, an *Anabaptist*, a Man of graceful Aspect, affable tho' grave, wearing a long yellowish Beard, of a becoming modest and discreet Deportment, who after he had continued in his own Country 40 Years, thought himself not safe any longer there, and sought a Settlement at *Basil* in *Switzerland*, for himself, his Family, and some Companions, 1544, the which, on Pretence of being driven out of his Country for the sake of the Gospel, by his moving Eloquence he obtained from the Magistrates, who made him a Brother Citizen. There he purchased divers Houses, where he and those belonging to him lived in common, he bought besides a Farm in the Country. His diligent Study of Religion, his frequent Exercise of Devotion, Munificence, Alms, and all kinds of good Offices, (for which his Riches enabled him) procured him an universal good Character, and gained him many Friends and Adherents. During this Time, by his Letters, Writings, and Emissaries, he planted and propagated his new Doctrine, not at Home, but through the *Low-Countries*, where it occasion'd great Tumults. However

ever

ever himfelf died in *Auguft* 1556, and was at firft honourably interred, but to the great furprize of his People, to whom he had declared himfelf immortal, or at leaft that he fhould rife again in three Days, neither of which proving true, made many of his Sectaries at *Bafil* difown his Doctrine, but after a ftrict Enquiry into his Tenets his Doctrine was declared Impious, and himfelf unworthy of Chriftian Burial, with a Sentence, *That his Body and Books fhould be burnt, by the common Hangman, in a public Place* ; and accordingly his Carcafs was taken up three Years after his Death, and with his Printed and Manufcript Writings committed to the Flames.

THIS Man was fucceeded by one *Henry Nicholas* of *Amfterdam*, a Difciple of the faid *David George*, who called himfelf the Father of the Family of Love, the Reftorer of the World, the Prophet fent of God. He wrote feveral Tracts, in one of which he mentions, that the Minute of the laft Trumpet was coming, that fhould unfold all the Books of unquiet Confciences, Hell and Eternal Judgment, which fhould be found to have been only Things grounded upon meer Lies, and as all Wicked and high Mifdeeds were hateful and deteftable to God, fo alfo were glorious and plaufible Lies no lefs odious to him.

See more in Dr. Dennifon's *White-Wolf,* Mr. Newftub's *Famlifts Confeffion,* Mr. Jeffop's *and* Alexander Rofs, *his View of Religions.*

SECT. III.

SECTION III.

RELIGIOUS-HOUSES in or near this TOWN before the *Reformation*, and the several *Professions* and *Rules* of the *Regulars*.

DR. *Thoroton* takes Notice, that in the 5th of King *Stephen*, mention is made of the Monks of *Nottingham*, this was before any particular Denomination of Regulars were in this Town, else they would have been called by the peculiar Name of their Profession, but what puts it out of all doubt is, that the *Franciscans*, of which the *Minors* are a Branch, did not come into *England* till 1220, and the *Carmelites* not till 1240, whereas the 5th of King *Stephen* is so early as 1110, it will therefore I hope not be ungrateful to many of my Readers if I here briefly touch upon the Origin of a Monastic Life.

IN the first Centuries of Christianity during the severe Persecutions the Christians indured, several of them to avoid a cruel Death, and the better to give themselves up to Fasting, Prayer and Contemplation, retired by themselves into Desart Places ; such were called Hermits from the Greek Ἐρημος, a Desart-Place, also a forsaken Person or destitute, and likewise solitary, whence Ἐρημίτης, a Person who lives solitary in an uninhabited Place, destitute of many Conveniences of Life, which Persons who live in Community enjoy. Monks from the Greek Word Μοναχος, unicus or solitarius, from a single Life, they were also called Anachorets from their Living separate from other Societies.

THE first of these we read of, was *Paul* of *Theban* about the Year of Christ 260, who having lost both his Parents in the Persecution of *Decius*, and fearing to be betrayed by his Sister's Husband, betook himself to a Cave at the Foot of a Rocky Hill at the Age of 15, where he continued till his Death, at 113 Years old.

THE next I meet with is *Antoninus* who set up this sort of Life in *Egypt*.

THEN *Hillarion* in *Palestina*, and in *Syria Paul* Sir-named the *Simple-Ammon*.

AFTER the Persecutions of the *Christians* were over and the Church enjoy'd Peace, these Hermits by Degrees returned to Towns and Cities, and associating together they lived in Houses called Monasteries, and confined themselves to certain Rules agreed upon amongst themselves.

THE first Monks used to Work when Occasion served, to Eat and Drink soberly, to go decent in Apparel, to Fast and Pray often, to possess all in common, to read, meditate

ditate, preach, and hear the Word of God, to Study Temperance, Continence, Modefty, Obedience, Silence, and other Virtues.

IN thefe primitive Monafteries it does not appear that they were tied to fet Fafts, to the three Vows of *Chaftity*, *Poverty*, and *Obedience*, or to the different Cloaths and Colours, or to ftay in the Monaftery any longer than their own liking.

THERE were alfo primitive Nuns for we read of *Marcella*, *Sophronia*, *Principia*, *Paula*, *Euftochium* and others, who did profefs Chaftity and contempt of the World, and had an earneft Defire of heavenly Things.

THE firft Monks of all were called *Thabenenfii* from *Thabenna*, an Ifland in the Province of *Thebais* about the Time of *Conftantius* the Son of *Conftantine*.

AFTERWARDS the firft we find mentioned who gave a certain Rule to his Difciples to regulate their Conduct by is St. *Bafil*. The Monks of this Saint were gathered by him and lived about *Pontus* ; much about his Time St. *Hyerom* collected a Number of Hermits in *Syria*.

Of the Monks of St. *Bafil*.

THE only abfolute Reftraint their Founder (whofe Rule confifted of 95 Articles) laid them under, was not to return to their Parents Houfes, except to inftruct them, and by their Superiour's Leave.

THE moft material parts of this Rule are thefe.

HE earneftly recommends the love of God and one's Neighbour, together with the Exercife of all Chriftian and Moral Virtues, and denial of the World.

ALL Contention of Superiority at the Table is forbidden, the Monks are to wear plain and homely Apparel, and a Girdle in Imitation of St. *John* the *Baptift*, and that no Man fcorn to wear an old Garment when it is given him.

ALL Things to be in Common, and that tho' in refpect to themfelves they muft not care what they Eat or what they Drink, yet that they may be helpful to others, they muft Labour with their Hands.

OBEDIENCE is enjoyned to their Superiours, but chiefly to GOD.

HE fpeaks of the Behaviour of the Governour, &c.

HE advifes that Men of Eftates beftow on their Kindred what is their due, and the reft to the Poor.

HE preffes his Difciples in Imitation of God and Chrift to love their Enemies.

THAT they who defame, or patiently hear their Brother defamed, be excomunicated.

THAT no Brother alone vifit a Sifter but in Company, and that by Permiffion, and for Edification.

H

THAT

T H A T they labour not for Faith, (as some do) without Charity.

T H A T Children may be admitted into this Order, but not without the consent of their Parents.

T H A T Satan is not the Cause of Sin in any Man, but as he consents to it, therefore the more watchful should every Man be over his own Heart, &c.

T H U S we see that the first Monks were in *Asia*, and that no particular Denomination of Regulars were known in *Europe*, till the latter End of the fourth or beginning of the fifth Century : When the *Benedictin's* were the first, and continued long without any Rival, the *Carthusians* were the next, then the *Augustinians*, after them the *Franciscans*, who were followed by the *Carmelites*, of all these more by and by.

T H E R E were in the Town of *Nottingham* before the Reformation, these several Religious Houses. *viz.*

1st. **T H E** *Brothers of St. John of Jerusalem* : 2d. The *Minorites* or *Minors*, professing the Rule of St. *Francis*, otherwise called the *Gray-Friers*, and 3d. The *Carmelites*, alias called the *White-Fryars*.

T H E first of these, to wit: The Brothers of St. *John*, professed the Rule of St. *Austin*, in the younger Time of their Life they were employ'd in the War against the *Saracens*, they were also called *Knight's Hospitallers*, because their Order obliged them to entertain poor Pilgrims and Travellers, whether Sick or well.

O F these Sir *William Dugdale*, from a Manuscript then in the Custody of *Gilbert North*, Esq; gives us the following Account.

Walter Gray, Archbishop of *York*, A. C. 1241, ordained that the Master and Warden of this Hospital, should take Care that there should be always in it two Priests, to perform Divine Office, that all the Brothers should rise early to sing Mattins, that they might be ended before the break of Day, afterwards to sing the other Hours at the proper Times.

T H A T they should be obedient to their Master, and that none keep any Thing he could call his own, and if any did so, during seven Days, to be then excommunicated. The Master to convert any thing he had of his own to the public Use, and if any one died possessed of any Thing particular, to be denied Christian Burial, and the Brethren to cast on him what he had, saying : *Thy Money be with thee to Perdition.* None to have a Chest locked, unless it belonged to his Office ; all of them to Eat, Cloath and Drink alike, and to eat Flesh only three Times a Week : *viz.* on *Sunday*, *Tuesday* and *Thursday*, without Leave of the Master ; all to eat together in the Refectory in Silence, unless Necessity required them to Whisper any thing. All to lye in one Dormitory in Drawers and Shirts, or such Garment as they used instead of Shirts ; all of them to be Chaste, and Sober, to be temperate in Diet, and apply the Revenues and Alms to the Poor. To wear a regular Habit of Russet and Black-Cloth, not to admit more Brothers and Sisters than are requisite to serve the Sick and look to the Affairs of the House ; any Brother being a Drunkard or lewd, if not mending, to be expelled. No Brother to wander abroad without the Masters leave. To pray for the Dead.   **I T**

IT is not certain by whom this Order is inftitutcd.

THE beginning of the *Hofpitallers* is by fome related in a fabulous Strain, and founded upon Monkifh Miracles, *e. g.* fome derive it from *Simon Maccabee*, who after the Battle with the neighbouring Kings wherein many Jews were flain and difabled, fent to *Jerufalem*, (after the Expulfion of the profane Nations) much Silver and Gold, and with it founded and endowed an Hofpital, ordered that Prayers fhould be put up for the Souls of the deceafed (a) and that for the future that Place fhould be a Receptacle for the unfortunate and an Expiation for the Dead. They fay, that *Jefus Chrift* not difdained the Place, had there all things in common with his Difciples, and it was there he wafhed their Feet, ordained them Priefts, and left the Memorial of his moft precious Body, and that there he gave St. *Peter* the Power and Keys of his Church, &c.

BUT when afterwards the Chriftian Charity had much increafed the Revenue of this Houfe, they hired Soldiers under Brother *Raymund*, (who after inftituted their Rule) to defend the fame and repel the Pagans. That the Soldiers growing infolent and defpifing the Priefts, it was agreed that the Soldiers themfelves fhould be made Members of the Hofpital, and defend the Chriftian Religion, and it was likewife decreed that they fhould wear a Crofs on their Breaft. After the Saracens took *Jerufalem*, thefe Chriftian Soldiers were difperfed, and at firft took Refuge in *Cyprus*, where they were received, and continued there defending the Chriftian Faith. After many Years the *Rhodians* revolting from the *Conftantinopolitans*, who not able to fubdue that Ifland, gave it to the Knights of *Jerufalem*, who foon became Mafters of it, and made thence War upon the Infidels. Sir *William Dugdale*, continues from the fame MSS. that the Hofpital of *John* the *Baptift*, is traced back by others to the Days of *Julius Cæfar*, when one *Melchior* a Prieft having opened the Tomb of *David*, and taken thence a great Treafure, was accufed before *Antiochus*, who then was Governour of *Jerufalem* and refolved to punifh the Prieft, but our Saviour appearing to him in the Night, and declaring to him that he would have an Hofpital built by the Prieft with the Treafure on Mount *Calvary*, and having in a Vifion declared the fame to the faid *Melchior*, *Antiochus* was appeafed and confented that the Prieft fhould build that Houfe to ferve the Poor, as was written in the Book concerning the *Maccabees* ; and that Prince at his Death gave a great part of his Wealth to that Houfe. This Manufcript tells farther, of our Saviour's appearing before his Birth to one *Zacharias* and to one *Julian*, commanding them to go and govern this Hofpital after the Death of the faid *Melchior*. It adds that our bleffed Saviour after his Incarnation was frequently there with his Difciples and wrought many Miracles, and that afterwards they continued there till they were difperfed abroad in the World. After the *Saracens* got Mafters of *Jerufalem*, one *Conrad* kept this Houfe, and diftributed the Alms thofe Saracens gave him, among the Poor. When *Godfrey* of *Bouloigne*, befieged *Jerufalem* and a great Famine being in the Chriftian Army, this *Conrad* ufed to go upon the Wall and throw down Loaves as if he had been cafting Stones at them, and being accufed thereof to the Sultan, he ordered him to be feized and brought before him, with the Loaves, which being done, when he appeared in his Prefence,

---

(a) *The only Plea the Romanift have for that profitable Branch of their Worfhip. The Prayer for the Dead.*

the Loaves were miraculoufly turned into Stones, whereupon the Sultan difmiffed him to throw them at the Chriftians, which he continued to do. After *Godfrey* of *Bouloigne* had taken *Jerufalem*, great Poffeffions were given to him and his Hofpital in Honour of St. *John* the *Baptift*, &c. *Raymond de Puy*, fucceeded *Conrad*, and inftituted the Rule of the Houfe which was obferved, and after confirmed by Pope *Innocent* II. &c. Some fay that about the Year 612 in the Reign of *Heraclius* when the *Turks* were in Poffeffion of *Jerufalem*, fome Italian Merchants of *Amalfi* in *Apulia* obtained of the Governour of the Town, a fpot of Groundon which they built a Church of the *Invocation* of the Virgin *Mary*, with other neceffary Buildings for Monks and Appartments for their Countrymen, and placed an Abbot and Monks of their Country there. Many Women afterwards coming thither in Pilgrimage, the Monks would not receive them for fear of giving Scandal, whereupon the Merchants built there a little Church with Lodgings for the Female Pilgrims and Sifters to ferve them. And as many Pilgrims reforted to this Place, who were ftripped of all they had by the Infidels, before they got into *Jerufalem*, to relieve them, they built a Houfe of God, to entertain the poor Pilgrims in, whether Sick or in Health. They built alfo a Church in Honour of St. *John* the Alms-giver, Patriarch of *Alexandria*. Thefe three Churches had no Revenue, but the Merchants of *Amalfi* made a yearly Collection, with which the Abbot did maintain the Brothers and Sifters of thofe Abbies, and the reft was fpent in relieving the Poor. This was before the Chriftians got Poffeffion of *Jerufalem*. When the Infidels were expelled, an Holy Roman Woman who was Abbefs of the Sifters, and in the Houfe of Men, one *Gerrard* a Brother were found who had long ferved the Poor. From this fmall Beginning this Order increafed and became rich, in-fo-much, that they were Owners of Towns and Caftles. They afterwards got by the Pope difcharged from the Power and Obedience of the Patriarch. They grew infolent and became hurtful to the neighbouring Churches, but no redrefs could be got from *Rome* they having blinded the Eyes of that Court with Gold. Whomfoever the Patriarch or Prelates had excommunicated, they admitted to their Churches to Mafs, and when Dead buried them in their Church-Yards. However they did many Acts of Charity and defended the Chriftians againft the Infidels. The Brothers of St. *John*, after the Eradication of the Order of the *Templars* by Pope *Clement* in the Year 1312, got and enjoy'd moft of the Poffeffions of that Order.

THE Houfe of the *Hofpitallers* in *Nottingham*, ftood without the Wall on the North Side of the Town, near the North Road; this and the Lands belonging to it were after the Diffolution of the Monafteries, by *Edward* VI. granted to the Mayor and Burgeffes of *Nottingham*, who have converted the Building into a Houfe of Correction which at this Time is corruptly call'd St. *Jones's*. (a)

THE *Minorites* or *Minors* had their Convent alfo out of the Town, *viz*. at the Weft Corner of the Broad-Marfh, the Wall which inclofed their Garden reach'd as far South as the River Leen. Thefe Friers commonly called the *Gray-Friers*, were Mendicants, following the Rule of St. *Francis*, At the Diffolution of Abbeys and Monafteries here were found the Prior and feven Friers. (b)

THE

(a) *It is faid to have been in being in the Year* 1215 *and that it was endowed in* 1534 *with* 5 l. 6 s. 8 d. ----- (b) *It is faid to be founded by* Hen. III. *Anno* 1250. *This was granted in the Year* 1548, *to* Thomas Heneage, *furrendred Feb.* 5th 1539, *by* Thomas *laft Warden and* 7 *Friers*. Burnet.

THE *Carmelites* commonly called the *White-Friers*, had an House between *Moot-hall-Gate* and *St. James's-Lane*, in the Parish of St *Nicholas*, which has given the Lane which is formed by the Clofe belonging to that Convent, and fome Gardens on the other fide where now the *Nate-Hofpital*, and the *Anabaptift's* Meeting House, &c. ftand, the Name of *Frier-Lane*, and the Row of Houfes facing the great Market Place between the Corner of *Moothall-gate* and St. *James's Lane*, the Name of *Frier-Row* : (a) Of thefe there were at the Diffolution, the Prior *Roger Copp*, fix Friers remaining, (b) both thefe Monafteries furrendered *Feb.* the 5th 1539. the 30th of *Henry* VIII. The Profeffion of the *Carmelites*, (who were likewife Mendicants) as well as of the *Francifcans*, See hereafter in their Places.

Of the BENEDICTIN's.

ST. *Bennet*, the Founder of the moft ancient Order of Monks in *Europe*, was born at a Town called *Nurfi* in the Dukedom of *Spoletto* in *Italy*, about the Year of *Chrift* 480. of Noble Birth and his Father's Name was *Eutropius*, his Mother's *Abundantia*. He went from *Rome*, (whither he was fent to improve himfelf in Learning, without having made any Progrefs in his Studies) firft to a Place called *Afylum*, then to a Defart called *Sublacum* [*Subiaco*] 40 Miles from *Rome* ; here he met with a Monk whofe Name was *Romanus*, who being acquainted with his Defign, encouraged and affifted him in it, and gave him the Religious Habit. *Benedict* chofe for his Place of abode a very fmall Cave, formed by Nature in a Rock, almoft inacceffible by Men, which is now called the *Holy-Grotte* or Cave, and to this Time is to be feen the Place were St. *Romanus* did from Time to Time let down to him fome Pieces of Bread which he had fpared from himfelf at his Meals, and tied a little Bell to it to give St. *Bennet* Notice to come and take them. After he had been there fome Time, being difcovered by fome Shepherds, who were aftonifhed that any Man fhould live in fuch a Place, the Fame of his Holinefs fpread abroad, he was over-perfwaded to go and be Abbot of the Monaftery of *Vicovare* between *Subiaco* and *Tivoli* ; but thefe Monks not liking the Reftraint he put them to, and deaf to his Reproofs, they attempted to poifon him, which not fucceeding, after a charitable Reproof he left them as incorrigible and returned to his former Solitude which became foon very populous, for many came to be inftructed by him, and became his Difciples, which obliged him to build 12 Monafteries, to ftir up the Religious Men to an higher Pitch of Piety, to ftrengthen the Weak, and to quicken the flothful ; he prefcribed Laws to his Monks after the manner of St. *Bafil*, but it is not certainly known whether he writ his Rule at *Subiaco* or *Monte-Caffno*, an ancient Town were *Apollo* was ftill worfhipped ; this Saint fell prefently to work to abolifh the Idolatrous Remains, he broke the Idol in Pieces, overthrew the Altar, and burnt the fuperftitious Woods confecrated to him, and caufed a Chappel to be built in Honour of St. *Martin*, upon the very Ground of the Temple of *Apollo*, and another for the Invocation of St. *John* the *Evangelift*, on the Place were the Idolatrous Altar had ftood ; in fhort here

H 3

he

(a) Burnet's *Hift. of the Reformation.* p. 146. ----- (b) *In* 1439 John Farewell *was Prior of the* Carmelites. *The Convent of thefe* Carmelites *is faid to be founded by* Reginald *Lord* Gray of Wilton, *and* Sir John Shirley, *in the Year* 1276.

he built a large Monaſtery which was the chief of the reſt, and was richly endowed by *Tertullus* a Roman Patrician, who beſtow'd on it Caſtles, Villages, Lands, and Poſſeſſions.

THIS Order ſoon ſpread all over the Weſtern World, and was brought to *England* by *Auſtin* Archbiſhop of *Canterbury*, in the Year of *Chriſt* 596: And *Trithemius* ſays, *lib.* 4. *chap.* 4. that in his Time there was above 15,000 Abbeys, out of which proceeded Multitudes of *Cardinals*, *Archbiſhops*, *Biſhops*, *Abbots*, and other eminent Men beſides *Popes*.

THE immenſe Riches which they obtained from the vaſt Donations they every where were over-heaped with, cauſed them to ſlacken in the Obſervance of the Severity of their Rule, inſomuch, that after having enjoy'd a flouriſhing State for the ſpace of 400 Years, a Diſcord aroſe amongſt them, which occaſion'd Schiſms, and many Orders ſprung out of this one, who took their Names either from the Places they were ſet up, or from their Leaders.

The Subſtance of the Rule of St. BENNET.

HE begins with the Duty and Qualifications of the Abbot, *viz.* To be careful of his Charge, to be holy, juſt, wiſe and charitable in his Deeds, powerful in his Words, to exhort, correct, reprove, to beware of Partiality and Diſſimulation, and chiefly of Covetouſneſs and Pride, not to do any thing of himſelf without Advice of of the Convent.

HE enjoins all to be obedient, ſilent, humble, to be watchful to Prayer in the Night.

HE preſcribes what Pſalms they are to ſing every Day and Night, and what Pſalms in their Cannonical Hours. That Halleluja ſhould be ſaid continually between *Eaſter* and *Penticoſt*, that they ſhould praiſe God with *David* ſeven Times a Day, *to wit :* In the Morning, at the 1ſt. 3d. 6th. and 9th. Hours, in the Evening, and Completory and at Midnight. Particular Pſalms are appointed for each of theſe cannical Hours. That they muſt pray with all Reverence.

THAT there be choſen Deans in each Monaſtery to eaſe the Abbot.

THAT every Monk have his own Bed to ſleep in, and that a Candle burn by them till the Morning, that they ſleep in their Cloathes girt, that at the ringing of the Bell they may be the more ready for Prayer.

DIVERSE Degrees of Penance are enjoyned according to the Degrees of Offence.

THAT the Abbot do all he can to reclaim the excommunicated Perſon, that the loſt Sheep may be brought home with Joy, and if no Correction will prevail, the obſtinate Perſon to be expelled the Convent, who upon Repentance may be received three Times, but never after the third Time.

THAT

SECT. III.

THAT the Steward of the Monaftery be a Man of Difcretion, Government and Truft.

THAT the Abbot keep an Inventory of all Utenfils belonging to the Convent.

THAT all Things be common among the Brothers, that there be no grudging nor murmuring.

THAT every one ferve in the Kitchen and other Places when his Turn is.

THAT a fpecial Care be had to the Sick and infirm, fo likewife of the Aged and Children.

THAT there fhould be chofen a Weekly Reader, to read in Time of Refection.

THAT each Man be content with a Pound of Bread for a Day, and that only the Sick be permitted to eat Flefh, that Wine be drank fparingly. That from *Eafter* to *Penticoft* the Brothers may have a Refection at the 6th Hour, and their Supper in the Evening.

IN Summer let them Faft every 4th and 6th Day in the Week till the 9th Hour. From the midft of *September* till *Lent* let them have their Refection at the 9th Hour but in *Lent* Time at the Evening, fo it be Day light.

THAT after Completory there be no fpeaking at all.

IF any come late to Prayers or to the Table, he is to ftand a-part by himfelf, and to be laft ferved, and to be fhortned in his Victuals.

IF any for fome great Offence be excommunicated out of the Oratory, he fhall make Satisfaction by proftrating himfelf before the Oratory.

THAT they fhall not only give themfelves to Prayer and Meditation at the appointed Hours, but fhall alfo labour fome part of the Day with their Hands to keep them from Idlenefs.

THAT they obferve *Lent* with all ftrictnefs.

THAT they ufe Strangers with all Reverence and Chearfulnefs, and that the Abbot falute them with a Holy Kifs and wafh their Feet.

THAT none receive Letters or Tokens from their Parents without the Abbots Leave.

THAT no Novice be admitted into the Monaftery without fufficient Trial of his Conftancy and Patience.

THAT if a Prieft defires to enter into a Monaftery, he fubmit himfelf to the Laws thereof, and that he have the next Place to the Abbot.

THAT

THAT Noblemen who offer their Children to God in the Monaftery, fwear, they will never give them any part of their Eftate, but that it be conferred on the Convent.

THAT if a Stranger Monk defire to continue in the Monaftery, he be not denied, fo his Life be not fcandalous.

IF the Abbot defire to have a Prieft or Deacon ordained, let him chufe one of his own Convent.

THAT he fhall be Abbot whom the whole Convent or the greater or better part fhall chufe.

THAT the Provoft or Præpofitus be chofen by the Abbot to whom he muft be Subject.

THAT the Porter be an ancient and difcreet Man, who receive and give An-fwers.   And

THAT the Monaftery be provided with Water and a Mill and other Neceffaries within itfelf, leaft the Brother's fhould wander abroad.

IF the Abbot enjoyn to any Monk Impoffibilities, he muft with Reverence and Submiffion excufe his Inability, if the Abbot urge it, he muft obey, and truft to God's Affiftance.

THAT in the Monaftery none prefume to defend, ftrike, or excommunicate ano-ther, but that they be obedient and loving to each other, that they be zealous for God, and when they are working to be ftill finging of Pfalms.

THE original Monks at *Monte Caffino* had befides thefe, feveral other Rites and Inftitutions.   The Council of *Soiffon* calls this Rule *The Holy Rule.*

THE *Benedictin* Habit is a round Coat or Tunick, a Hood or Cowl called *Cu-culla*, gray, of the colour of a Badger, of whofe Skin it was anciently made, a Scapu-lary (St. *Bennet* himfelf was clad in Skins) the colour of their upper Garment is black under which they wear a white Woollen Coat, with Sackcloth, and they go booted. The Habit of thefe Monks was left to the difcretion of the Abbots, according to the Na-ture of the Countries being either hotter or colder.   In temperate Climates a Cowl and a Tunick was fufficient, the Cowl thicker for Winter and thinner for Summer, and a Scapulary to work in.   Every one had two Tunicks and two Cowls either to change at Night, or to wear one whilft they wafhed the other.   The Stuff they were made of was the cheapeft the Country afforded.

THAT none might have any thing he could call his own, the Abbot found them all with every thing neceffary ; that is, befides the Habit, an Handkerchief, a Knife, a Needle, a Steel Pen and Tablets to write ; their Beds were Mats or Straw-Beds, a piece of Serge, a Blanket and a Pillow.

IN the Year 860 the fecond Council of *Aix-la-Chapelle* took off or at leaft mitiga-ted fome of the Severities of the Rule of St. *Bennet* and allowed the Brethren at
Chrift-

Chriſtmas and *Eaſter* for eight Days to eat the Fleſh of Birds. It was forbid to take any Prieſt or Layman into the Monaſtery except they turned Monks ; they were permitted to have Prieſts of their own, and to receive Tythes, firſt Fruits, Oblations and Donations, as well as others, by *Gregory* the *Great, Boniface* and other Popes·

THEY are not to bow their Knees in *Whitſun-Week* nor Faſt. They are not to kiſs the Lips of any Woman.

Of the CARTHUSIAN Order.

THIS Order which had its Name from the Place where the firſt Monaſtery was founded, *Carthuſia*, in French *Chartreuſe*, in the Province of *Dauphine* in *France*, is the next oldeſt, having for its Author one *Bruno*, born at *Cologne*, and *Profeſſor* of *Philoſophy* at *Paris*, about the Year of Chriſt 1080.

THE Legend makes the following pretended Occurrence, the cauſe of his eſtabliſhing this Order, viz :

Bruno being preſent at the ſinging the Office (a) for his Fellow-Profeſſor then newly dead,(a Man highly eſteemed for his Holy-Life) the Dead Corps ſuddenly ſits up in the Bier, when they were come to theſe Words : *Reſponde mihi, quantas habeo iniquitates:* Anſwer me how many Sins I have. And cries out, *Accuſatus Sum* I am accuſed, upon this the Office was put off for that Time. The next Day at the celebration of the ſame Funeral Office, the Corps roſe a ſecond Time, and cried *Judicatus Sum*, I am judged, which put again a ſtop to the Service ; and the third Day upon attempting it again, the Corps roſe a third Time, and uttered theſe Words, *Condemnatus Sum*, I am condemned. At which *Bruno* was ſo affrighted, and thought that if a Man reputed ſo pious was damned, what would become of himſelf and many more : Therefore concluded there was no ſafety for him, but by forſaking the World ; whereupon he and ſix of his Scholars betook themſelves to the Place already mentioned, which was hedious for dark Woods, high Hills, Rocks and wild-Beaſts, and there built a Monaſtery, having obtained the Ground of *Hugo* Biſhop of *Grenoble*, who alſo became a Monk of that Order. Their Rule is in ſome Meaſure built upon that of St. *Bennet*.

AS to this frightful Story, it is allowed by all, that *Bruno* with his Companions did retire to the Place above mentioned, but it has been as inconteſtably proved by the Doctors of the Univerſity of *Paris*, that the Tale is utterly falſe, there being none of the cotemporary Writers or any that were 200 Years after, who make the leaſt mention of it.

ACCORDING to their Rule the *Carthuſians* ſhould wear Sack-cloth, or an Hair Shirt next their Skin, a long white Cloth Coat looſe, with an Hood and black Cloak over, when they walk abroad. The Lay-Brothers wear a ſhort Coat to their Knees.

THEIR Diſcipline is to eat no Fleſh at all, nor even when they are ſick, to buy no Fiſh, but eat them when offered, to eat branny Bread and drink Wine mixed with Water : On the Lord's Day and the 5th Day of the Week, they feed only upon Cheeſe and Eggs, on the 3d and Saturday, on Pulſe or Pot Herbs, on the 2d. 4th. and 6th. upon Bread and Water only. Every one Dreſſes his own Meat, they eat

but

but once a Day, and are all apart, except on the chief Festivals, as *Christmas*, *Easter*, *Whitsuntide*, *Epiphany*, *Purification*, the 12 *Apostles*, St. *John* the *Baptist*, St. *Michael*, St. *Martin*, and on *All-Saints Day* they eat twice a Day and all together at one Table, and then they may talk together, at other Times they must keep silence, every one having his own Cell, wherein they pray, read, meditate and write Books; in these Cells they observe the canonical Hours, but the Mattins and Vespers they keep in their Churches, and have Mass on the Days they eat twice. None is suffered to go abroad except the Prior and Procurator and that upon the Affairs of the Convent. They are limitted to enjoy a certain Quantity of Land, a certain Number of Sheep, Goats, and Asses, which they must not exceed. They must admit no Women into their Churches, nor were they to have in one Convent above twelve Religious Men besides the Prior and eighteen Converts or Lay-Brothers, with a few Servants, who are not to come within the Quire where the Prior and his Brethren sit, but these are in a lower Quire by themselves.

SINCE these original Rules to which they were tied, they are something fallen off now.

THEY have a Yearly Meeting at *Chartreuse* about their own Affairs, whither out of every Cloyster two Monks are sent who stay fourteen Days.

THIS Order was confirmed by Pope *Alexander* the 3d. 1178. They came into *England* in 1180, just one hundred Years after their first Institution, and settled at *Witham* near *Bath*.

Of the AUGUSTINIANS.

BY this Name go two sorts of Religious Persons, both professing the same Rule.

THE first are an Order of Canons regular, which are ascribed to St. *Augustin*, but it is difficult to prove whether he himself instituted them, or some of his Disciples, as well as others of diverse Denominations who profess to live after his Rule.

THE Habit of these Canons is a white Cloth Coat open before and down to the Feet, this is girded to their Body, and over it they wear a Linnen Surplice to their Knees, and over that a short black Cloak to their Elbows, with an Hood fastened to it, their Crowns to be shaved like other Friers and when they go abroad, they wear a broad Hat or a black corner'd Cap.

THE other Sort of this Order are the *Hermits* of St. *Austin*, who wear a black Coat with a Hood to it of the same Colour, underneath is a white little Coat, their Girdle is of Leather with a Horn Buckle. These were originally diverse sorts of Hermits who lived by different Rules, called together A. C. 1550. by Pope *Innocent* IV. and invited to live under one Head and profess one Rule, *viz*. that of St. *Augustin*. This Pope dying, *Alexander* IV. succeeded and united them in one Order by the Name of the *Hermits* of St. *Augustin*, and dispensed with their former Rules and Observances. About 1290 Pope *Honorius* gave them several Priviledges. The reputed Founder of these two Orders was till the 31st Year of his Age a *Manichæan* and professed *Rhethoric* at *Rome* and *Milan*, but upon reading the Life of *Anthony* the Monk by the persuasion of *Simplicianus*, he became a Convert, and in a Garden with his Friend *Alipius* (as the Legend has it) as he was bewailing his former Life, he heard a Voice accompanied with the Music of little Children, saying

to

to him *Tolle lege, Tolle lege*, that is to say, take up and read; looking about and seeing nobody, he took this for a Divine Admonition, and so taking up the Bible the first Passage he lighted on was this : *Not in surfeiting and Drunkenness, not in chambering and Wantonness, but put on the Lord Jesus, &c.* Upon this he resolved to become a Christian and was accordingly baptized with his Sons *Adeodatus* and *Alipius*, at *Milan*, by St. *Ambrose*, (a) a Bishop of that Place. Having after spent a few Years in Fasting, Prayers, and the study of the Holy Scripture, he was called to *Hippo* in *Africa*, where he was first a Presbyter and then a Bishop of that Place. He lived there with other learned Men as in a College, and thence sent abroad diverse Clergymen for *Hippo* and who were Bishops in other Places.

THE Canons as well as the Monks have three Rules given them (as they say) of St. *Austin. viz.*

THE first, relates to their Eating, Drinking, Cloathing, Admission and Deportment in general, &c. that they possess nothing in Propriety, but have all Things in common, that they be not solicitous what to eat and what to drink and wherewith they shall be cloathed. That none be admitted without Trial, that none depart or carry any Thing out of the Monastery without the Superiours Leave, that no Man maintain any Point of Doctrine without acquainting the Superior with it, that secret Faults, &c. first be reproved and if not repented of, punished. That in Persecution they repair to their *Præpositus.*

THE second, contains the Times and Manner of Praying and Singing, their Times of Working, Reading and Refreshing. It treats of their Obedience, Silence, and particular Behaviour both at Home and Abroad, and how Contumacy must be punished.

THE third Rule contains their Duty more largely as :

THAT they must love God above all Things.

THAT they maintain Unity.

THAT Meat, Drink and Clothes be distributed as Need is.
THAT all Things be common.
THAT there be no Pride, Contempt or Vain-Glory amongst them ; here they are injoyned, Prayer, Reverence, and Devotion, Abstinence, Silence, and Contentment.
TO hear the Word read at Table, to be careful of the Sick and Infirm.
TO be modest in Apparel, Words, Gestures, and in their Look when they chance to see a Woman, to reprove immodesty in their Brethren, to receive no Letter nor Gift without the Superiour's Knowledge, to have their Clothes well kept from Moths.
TO beware of murmuring and repining, that to conceal any Thing shall be accounted Theft.

I 2

THAT

(a) *Near unto the Church of St.* Ambrose, *at* Milan, *is a little Chappel, where St.* Austin *with his little Son and Friend* Alippius, *were baptized, as the Inscription over the Altar denotes. On the other side of the great Church, not far off, is another Chappel, built on the Spot they tell you, where St.* Austin *heard the Voice.*

THAT they be not too nice in washing their Cloaths.

THAT in Sickness the Physician be advised with, that they may bathe sometimes, that the Sick want not any Thing needful for him.

THAT there be no Strife, Envy, or evil Words among them, that the Superiour use not harsh Words in reproving, that he shew good Example to his Brethren in Holy Conversation, that he be wise, humble, and careful of his Charge, and that the Duties here injoyned may be the better performed, these Rules must be read once a Week.

Of the FRANCISCANS.

THE next Religious Order that started up was that of St. *Francis.* Of him the Legend gives us the following Account : That he was an *Italian* and a Merchant, who before his Conversion was called *John,* that he had led a wicked and debauched Life in his younger Years, but was at last reclaimed by a Vision of a Castle full of Arms and Crosses, with a Voice telling him that he was to be a Spiritual Soldier. Afterwards as he was praying, he was warned by a Voice to repair the decay'd Churches or Houses of Christ, which he did by stealing Money from his Father, and bestowing the same on the Reparation of Churches ; whereupon his Father beat him, put him in Prison, and disinherited him. He rejoiced in this, stript himself naked of all his Garments, which he deliver'd to his Father, shewing how willing he was to relinquish all for Christ. Within a short while he gathered many Disciples to whom he prescribed, A. C. 1198. a Rule, consisting of a strict Observance of three Vows, *viz.* of *Chastity, Poverty,* and *Obedience,* which he guards in manner following.

Poverty, they are to have neither any Thing in Common, nor in Propriety, to handle no Money, nor a third Person for them.

THAT their Habit be made of a course Woollen Web. They are allowed to mend their Habit with a Piece of Sackcloth or some other course Stuff.

THEY must always walk on Foot, except when they go by Water, they may take the Convenience, as others do.

THEY are to wear no Stockings.

Chastity, they are strictly forbid to converse with Women, nor are they to go into the Monasteries of Nuns. They are forbid all Niceties in clothing, and eating, Conveniencies in Travelling, they are to go barefoot, and to Fast every Friday from *All-Saints* Day to *Christmas,* and from *Epiphany* to *Easter,* besides other Mortifications and penitential Works.

THEY are enjoyned to apply themselves to Prayer, which this Saint prefers before the Study of human Literature.

THEY dare kill no Vermin, nor lye on Feather-Beds.

Obe-

Obedience, they are to be obedient to Chrift, the Pope, and their Superiours, they muft renounce their own Will, follow their Superiours without Referve, or offering any Reafon, in all Things not contrary to the Rule.

IN any fcruple of Confcience, he refers them to their Superiours, to remove their Doubts and fet their Confciences at Eafe.

THAT none be admitted into the Order until they be duly examined and proved.

THAT the Clergy in their Divine Worfhip, follow the Order of the Roman Church, and that the Lay-Brothers fay 24 Pater-nofters for their Mattins, &c.

THAT they enter not into any Houfe till they fay, *Peace be with this Houfe,* and then they may eat what is fet before them.

THAT they help one another, and that Pennance be impofed on thofe that Sin, that they have their public Meetings and Chapters.

HE would not have them call themfelves *Francifcans*, but *Minores*, nor their Governours *Mafters*, but *Minifters*.

HE Orders them to chufe their provincial *Minifters*, and thefe to chufe a general *Minifter* over the whole Fraternity.

THAT they ufe brotherly Admonition, and Correction.

THAT their Preachers be Men of approved Gifts, and that they preach not abroad without Leave from the Bifhop.

THAT none go to Convert Saracens or other Infidels, but fuch as are fent by the Provincial *Minifter*.

THAT they all remain conftant in the Catholic Faith, and that none break the Rule unlefs he will incur the Curfe of GOD, and his two Apoftles St. *Peter* and St. *Paul.*

ST. *Francis* ftrengthned this his Rule by his Will and Teftament, which he injoyns to be read as often as they read the Rule.

THIS Rule was wrote, and approved by Pope *Innocent* III. 1210. Afterwards alfo by the *Lateran Council*, 1215. And again confirmed by Pope *Honorius* III. 1223.

IT is given out that Pope *Innocent's* Approbation, was occafioned by a Vifion of a Palm-Tree growing and fpreading under him, and of a poor Man's fupporting the decaying *Lateran*, after he had tried St. *Francis's* Obedience, which he fhew'd by wallowing in the Mire with Swine, as the Pope had advifed him.

ST. *Francis*, who wore a fhort Coat of the natural colour of the Wool, and inftead of a Girdle, a Cord, not leaving any Direction about the Form, Meafure, and Colour of their Habit, it occasioned a great deal of Altercation among his Followers, until at last it was referred to Pope *Paul* the 22d. who leaves it at the Discretion of the General and Provincial Ministers.

THE *Minorites* at this Day wear a long Coat with a large Hood of gray or hair Colour, they go barefooted and girded with a Cord, whence the *French* call them *Cordeliers*.

THE *Franciscan* Garment has been held in such Esteem, and of such Virtue, that divers Princes have called it the *Seraphic* Habit, and have desired to be buried in it, thinking thereby to be safe from the Devil, tho' St. *Francis* himself died and was buried naked, because he would imitate Christ who died naked on the Cross. *Francis* Marquis of *Mantua*, *Robert* King of *Sicily*, and even the Emperour *Charles* V. have been buried in this Habit.

THERE are also Nuns, who observe the Rule of St. *Francis*, but not quite to that Degree of Severity as the Men. These from St. *Clara* the Sister of St. *Francis*, are called *Clarissæ*, in English *poor Clares*.

DURING the space of 169 Years, *i. e.* from 1211 to 1380. this Order increased to 1500 Monasteries, which is attributed :

1st. TO the Sedulity and Diligence in making Proselytes.

2d. THEIR Priviledges.

3d. THEIR pretended Sanctity and Mortification : And

4th. THE incredible Miracles and Visions attributed to this their Saint, *viz.* The five Wounds Christ impressed on his Body. His bearing Christ in his Arms. His Mansion in Heaven next Christ, and many more Things which they obtrude to the Belief of the Populace.

THIS Order came first into *England*, A. C. 1210. about the 4th of King *Henry* III. when Brother *Agnellus* the first Provincial of the *Franciscans* shew'd his Commission to the King, who in respect to St. *Francis*, who was then still living, placed the *Franciscans* at *Canterbury*, and soon after, the King made *Agnellus* one of his Privy Council.

THE *Franciscans* as well as the *Benedictin*'s, through the considerable Relaxations crept in, by Degrees became divided amongst themselves, and gave Birth to different Sects, who all profess the Rule of St. *Francis*, tho' some take a greater Latitude than others.

THEY behaved so ill about the latter End of the 12th Century, that the Order was condemned in *England* in 1307. but was again advanced by *Peter Tuxbury*, a *Franciscan* Minister, and allowed in the Chapter of *London*.

Of

Of the Order of CARMELITES.

THESE were originally a fet of Hermits, whofe Habitations were in Caves and among Rocks within Mount *Carmel*, noted for the Prophets *Elias* and *Eliſha*, by whom thefe Friers pretend their Order was inftituted, and have even by fome means or other obtained feveral Bulls of diverfe Popes to confirm their Antiquity, among other. that of *Pius* IV. 1477. fays, they are defcended from *Elias*, *Eliſha* and *Enoch*, which laft, the *Carmelites* fay, is one *Enoch* of *Amathim*, Difciple of St. *Mark* the Evangelift. About the End of the laft Century a very great Conteft arofe between them and the *Jeſuits*, which was carried on with great Heat and Scurrility, about the Antiquity of this Order. But the *Carmelites* making Application to the Popes *Innocent* XI. and XII. and *Charles* II. King of *Spain*, the *Jeſuits* who were an over Match to them, were filenced by a Brief of Pope *Innocent* XII. bearing Date *Nov.* 20, 1698.

ALL agree that thefe Friers followed the Rule of St. *Baſil*, but the Accounts of their Inftitution and by whom till the 11th Century, are full of Obfcurity and Contradiction. Some Writers fay, that A. C. 1160, and fome 1121, *Almericus* Patriarch of *Antioch*, and the Popes Legate, came thither and gathered thefe difperfed *Anchorets* into one Body, and built them a Monaftery on the top of Mount *Carmel*, near the Well of *Elias*, by which ftood an ancient Chappel of our *Lady*, whence probably the *Carmelites* were called the *Virgin's-Brothers*.

IN the Time of Pope *Alexander* III. whofe Popedome without *Anti-pope* began in 1170. they had a Latin Governour one *Bertholdus Aquitanus* fet over them; fome will have it that this Order was not inftituted till 40 Years after in the Papacy of *Innocent* III Their 2d. Governour was *Brochard* of *Jeruſalem*, who made them a Rule much after the Rule of St. *Baſil*, which was abridged 1198, and confirmed by *Albert*, the Latin Patriarch of *Jeruſalem*, who tied them to Fafting, Silence, and canonical Hours, and the Lay-Brothers to *Peter* the Hermit's Beads or Prayers, and to our Lady's Pfalter, they were tied to no Vow but to that of Obedience to their Governours which was A. C. 1204 according to *Lezana*, or 1209. according to Papebroch. This 1ft. Rule among other Things confines them to little Cells where they are to ftay and employ themfelves Night and Day in Prayer, unlefs they are otherwife lawfully employed, they are prohibited having any Property, they are to hear Màfs every Morning in the Oratory, they are injoyned Fafting from the Feaft of the Exaltation of the Holy-Crofs, till *Eaſter*, except Sundays, Abftinence from Flefh is commanded at all Times. The Order obliges them to manual Labour, they are to keep ftrict Silence from the Vefpers to the Hour of Tierce the next Day. They are to refpect their Prior. They were fome Time after the Publication of this Rule difturbed on Account of their following a Rule not known in Europe. The Decree of the Council of *Lateran* held in 1215. prohibiting the erecting of any new Orders without the Confent of the Holy See; in the Year 1224. they pray'd Pope *Honorius* III. to approve the Rule given them by the Patriarch *Albert*. When the *Carmelites* came over to Europe and had founded Convents, they found there were fome Things in the Rule which wanted correcting and mitigating, wherefore they apply'd to Pope *Innocent* IV. who fent a Commiffion, which he impowered to examine the Rule, and to make fuch Amendments as fhould be judged fit. The Commiffioners were *Hugh*

Cardinal of St. *Sabina*, of the Order of St. *Dominic*, and *William* Bishop of *Antrada* a City in *Syria*.

THESE thought proper to add to the 1st. Article, which treats of the Obedience the Brethren owe to the Prior, that they should also keep Chastity, and have no Property, and as some of the Anchorets believed, they were only to reside in Desarts; the Commissioners to remove these Scruples, declared that they might have Monasteries in Solitudes, and in such other Places as should be given them, provided that Regular Observance might there be maintained. The Patriarch absolutely prohibited eating Flesh at any Time, except in Sickness and extreme Weakness.

THE Commissioners left out the Words *at any Time* and *extream*, to the End that the *Carmelites* might not be burthensome to those that entertained them, they ordained, that when they travelled they might eat Herbs, boiled Flesh, and even eat Flesh at Sea. They prescribed Silence only from Compline till after Tierce the next Day, they also allowed them to eat in a common Refectory, whereas till then, they were to eat apart in their Cells. They also made some Regulations relating to divine Office and granted them Leave to have Asses, Mules, and to keep Cattle for their Use.

THIS Rule with Amendments was approved by Pope *Innocent* IV. 1247.

I have placed the *Carmelites* after the *Augustinians*, because the last came into Europe 34 Years before them.

THE Habit of the *Carmelites* was a striped Mantle of Party Colours, which they pretend was used by the Prophet *Elias*. *Gregory* IX. forbad them any Possessions or Revenues, but to beg from Door to Door. *Honorius* IV. took from them this Habit and instead thereof gave them a white Cloak and a white Hood, and under it a Coat with a Scapulary of Hair Colour. (a) This Pope will have them called instead of *Carmelites*, *Brothers* of the *Virgin Mary*, and exempts them from the Jurisdiction of Kings and Princes.

THE use of the white Cloak was confirmed by his Successors *Nicholas* IV. *Alexander* V. allowed them Prisons to punish their Apostates, and *John* XXIII. took them into his immediate Protection, and was (as they say) warned by a Vision, to keep them out of Purgatory. To enter into this Order is deemed meritorious, and three Years Indulgence is promised to them who at any Time call them *Brothers of the Virgin Mary*.

MANY of the *Carmelites* falling off from the Strictness of the last mentioned Amendment of the Rule, they were divided into two Sects: Those who adhered to the Rule were called *Observants*, the others who obtained a farther Mitigation are called *Non-Observants* or *Conventuals*, this Mitigation was obtained of the Popes
Eu-

(a) *In the Year* 1290 *all the Friers of this Order throughout* England *changed their Habit, putting on white Cloaks in the room of their Party-coloured Mantles.*

Eugenius IV. and *Pius* V. thefe laft have changed their Hair coloured Coat for Diftinctions fake into black.

A N D thefe five were the original Orders which were fucceffively fettled in *Europe* within the fpace of 681 Years, of which, that of the *Benedictines*, being the 1ft. enjoy'd all the Reverence, and thence arifing large Donations upwards of 530 Years alone without any Competitor. Whence they became fo exceedingly rich, that fumming up the Revenues of all the feveral Monaftic Congregations in *England*, the *Benedictin's* or black Monks only, enjoyed as much as all the reft together. Thefe Monks poffeffed in *England* at the Reformation, 60668l. Sterling per Ann. which Lands, improved proportionably with others, muft now at leaft be worth 606680l. per Ann. which is ten Times the original Value; I fpeak within Compafs, for the Rents of that parcel of Lands of the diffolved Priory of *Coventry*, which was bought by Order of Sir *Thomas White*, of the then Value of 7ol. per Ann. is now increafed to above fourteen Times the original Value. Thefe feveral Orders, except the *Carthufian*, have by Degrees branched themfelves out into confiderable Numbers of feparate Sects of Friers taking their Names, fome from their Leaders, others from the Place where they firft fettled, &c. as appears by the following Lift.

Benedictin's.	Auguftinians.	Francifcans.	Carmelites.
Benedictin's ftrictly fo called.	Auguftinians ftrictly fo called.	are called Minors.	Obfervants.
Cluniacks.	Regular Canons.	Fratres Obfervantiæ.	Non-Obfervants or Conventuals.
Camaldulenfes.	Scopetini.	Fratres Gaudentiæ.	
Fratres Vallifumbrofæ.	Lateranenfes.	Capucines.	
Ciftertians.	Of St. George in Alga.	Minimi.	
Bernardines.	Dominicans.	Collectanei.	
Coeleftrines	Brigidians.		
	Jefuati.		
	Cruciferi.		
	Brothers of St. Peter the Confeffor.		
	Servants of the bleffed Virgin Mary.		
	Hieronomites.		
	Antonians.		
	Præmonftratenfes.		
	Trinitaries.		
	Brothers of St. John of Jerufalem.		
	Brothers of the Lord's Sepulchre.		
	Hermits of St. Paul.		

THE *Carthufians* are indeed the only Monks who have not fuffered any Separation, but tho' they make it their boaft, that have never been reformed fince their firft Inftitution; yet if we may take a Pattern of their prefent way of living from their chief Convent the Great *Chartruefe* near *Grenoble*, as it is defcribed by the Author *of the Frauds of the Romifh Monks and Priefts*, they have as great Occafion for a thorough Reformation of their notorious Irregularities, as any other Regulars of the Church of Rome, the juft named Author p. 35. in his firft Letter gives us this Specimen:

K

" Thefe

" THESE new Buildings (a) were brought to Perfection, with a Magnifi-
" cence very unbecoming the Modefty of Hermits, and more becoming the Palace
" of a King, then the Cells of fuch who pretend to have forfaken the World. As
" for their Manner of living, they ftill retain fomething of their firft Inftitution, as in
" particular their Abftinence from Flefh ; but the Diverfity and Abundance of Fifh,
" Herbs and Eggs, and other fuch like Things wherewith they are ferved, is far
" more pleafing and agreeable to Senfe, than any fort of Flefh-Meat, and much
" more coftly. The Father Purveyor of the Houfe affured us, that the Expence of
" every Religious amounted at leaft to five hundred Crowns a Year; they have a way
" of extracting the Subftance and as it were the Quinteffence from feveral great
" Fifhes, whereof they make Jelly Broths, that are extremely nourifhing. Their
" Bread is of an extraordinary Whitenefs, and the beft Wine that can be got for Love
" or Money, is afforded them without Meafure. Befides this, every Religious has in
" his own Apartment a Refervatory, ftored with Fruit and other Neceffaries, fo that
" they may eat and drink when-ever they pleafe, and entertain their Friends who
" come to vifit them. Every *Carthufian* has his feparate Apartment which confifts
" of five or fix fair Rooms, very neatly furnifhed and adorned, with a neat Garden
" which feparates one Apartment from another, all which Gardens have a Door that
" opens into the Cloifter, &c.

HOW does all this agree with living in a fmall Cell, dreffing one's own Victuals, eating branny Bread, living three Days in the Week upon Bread and Water,
and with eating the major Part of the Year but once a Day, and drinking no Wine
except with Water ?

EACH of thefe above-mentioned Orders, to raife in the People the greater Reverence for their Saint, and procure the larger Benefactions to themfelves, have u-
fed their utmoft Skill to fet off their Founder in the moft brilliant Manner, bringing
many Inftances to prove him the peculiar Favourite of Heaven, and vie with one a-
nother, who fhall produce the longeft String of the moft incredible Miracles wrought
by him and even fome of his Difciples. What I have already faid of St *Francis* fhall
fuffice for a fample, nor will I tire the Reader's Patience with the miraculous Cures
faid to be performed by St. *Auftin*'s Girdle, tho' there is not any folid Proof that he
wore one. And as to St. *Bennet*, who ever reads his Life wrote by Pope *Gregory* the
Great, will readily grant, that his Panegyric of that Saint is not to be exceeded by
any Pen ; He with others recounts many Legerdemain Tricks the Devil play'd at
Monte-Caffino, when St. *Bennet* built his 1ft and largeft Monaftery there, and then
goes on in the Rehearfal of a large fet of Miracles, but not content with thofe, his
Saint worked himfelf, he farther fhews the extent of the Power granted him, in the
Relation of divers Miracles performed by one *Maurus* a Difciple of St. *Bennet*, by his
Mafter's Commands, &c.

HOW far the Reader may be induced to give his Belief to thefe bold Affertions
I will not pretend to fay. But the Sentiments of feveral Roman Catholic Writers
have caufed me to fufpend mine. For *Canus* calls the Author of the *Golden Legend*, a
Man of a brazen Face and a leaden Heart. *Efpenceus* upon II *Tim.* 4. fays the Legends

---

(a) *The Great Chartreufe at Grenoble.*

gends are full of Fables, and *Cajetan Digr.* 12 *Opufc. de concept. Virg.* C. 1. plain-ly tells us, that it cannot be infallibly known, that the Miracles the Church Grounds the Canonization of Saints upon be true, becaufe the Credit depends on Men's Report who may deceive others, and be deceived themfelves.

IN Order to fhew that *England* is not left without a Saint of its own, and a Found-er of an Order, I cannot pafs by St. *Gilbert,* a native of *Sempringham* in *Lincolnfhire,* who inftituted an Order of Monks and Nuns, whofe Statutes confifted of a Collection out of the Rules of St. *Bennet* and St. *Auftin,* they were after their Founder's Name, called *Gilbertines,* their Rule was confirmed by Pope *Eugenius* the 3d. and their chief Monaftery was at *Sempringham,* built both for Friers and Nuns, of the latter there were in it at one Time 1100, and of the former 700. I have de-fignedly made no mention of thefe Regulars after the *Auguftinians* (where accord-ing to Time they fhould have been placed) becaufe they are not one of the Cardinal Orders, nor in the Lift of the Subaltern or fecondary Orders, becaufe they do not profefs any one particular Rule, but a Compound out of the two moft ancient.

BEFORE I take my leave of this Subject, it may not be amifs to bring it near Home, in giving a Catalogue of all the Monafteries in the County of *Nottingham* at large, at the Time of the Diffolution.

There were of the BENEDICTIN Order.

THE Priory of *Lenton,* dedicated to the *Holy Trinity,* they were *Cluniacks,* founded by *William Peverel* in the Time of *Henry* I.

THE Monaftery of *Rufford,* dedicated to St. *Mary,* thefe were *Ciftertians,* founded by *Gilbert de Gaunt,* in the Time of *Henry* II.

THE Priory of *Blythe,* dedicated to St. *Mary,* thefe were *Benedictin's* ftrictly fo called, founded by *Roger de Bufsly* and *Muriel* his Wife, in the Reign of *Henry* I.

THE Priory of *Walling-Wells,* dedicated to the bleffed Virgin and called St. *Ma-ry of the Park,* they were *Benedictin* Nuns, and founded by *Ralph de Chevrolcurt,* the Man or Tenant of *Roger de Bufsly,* in the Reign of *Henry* I.

Of the Order of St. AUGUSTIN.

THE Priory of *Thurgarton,* Canons, dedicated to St *Peter,* founded by *Ralph d' Ayncourt,* in the Time of *Henry* I.

THE Priory of *Newfted,* Canons, dedicated to St. *Mary,* founded by *Henry* II.

THE Priory of *Felley,* alfo dedicated to St. *Mary,* founded by *Ralph Annefley* and his Son *Reynold,* in the Reign of *Henry* II.

Workfop, dedicated to St. *Cuthbert,* Canons, founded by *William de Luvelot* in the Time of *Henry* II.

Shelford, not mentioned to whom dedicated, Canons, founded according to *Dug-dale,* by *Ralph Haunfelyn* in the fame Reign.

Wel-

Welbec, not mentioned to whom dedicated. These Canons were *Præmonstraten-ses*, founded (as *Thoroton* has it from the Register of *Welbec*) by *Ralph de Bellafago*, whose Gifts to this Monastery were confirmed by King *Stephen*.

Brodham, dedicated to St. *Mary*. Here were both Canons and Canonesses of the *Præmonstratenses*, founded by *Ralph de Albeniaco* in the Time of *Henry* II. or the. beginning of *Richard* I.

Of the CARTHUSIAN Order.

THE Priory of *Beauval*, this was in the Park of *Griesly*, founded by *Nicholas de Cantilupo*, for a Prior and twelve Monks, in the Reign of *Edward* III.

Of the GILBERTINES.

THE Priory of *Mattersey*, I find not to whom this was dedicated; but that it was founded by the Family of *Marsey*'s in the Reign of King *John*.

THESE are all the Monasteries we have an Account of in the County of *Nottingham*, of which none claims greater Antiquity than King *Henry* I. nor none has been founded later than *Edward* III. since whose Reign till *Henry* VII. in the heavy Civil Wars, occasioned by the Contest between the Houses of *Lancaster* and *York*, the Nobility had neither Time for founding new Religious Houses, nor Lands to spare to endow them with, (the Property of their Estates almost entirely depending upon the Fate of the Wars) and from *Henry* VIII. to *Edward* VI. his Reign, the immoral Lives of the Monks of almost all Orders were so glaring, that far from inducing any Body to increase the Number of Convents, they rather proved greatly instrumental in bringing about a Reformation in *England*, which was considerably advanced in the Reign in *Edward* VI. and notwithstanding the Interruption by Queen *Mary* I. happily accomplished in the long and glorious Reign of Queen *Elizabeth*.

WHEN the Authority of the See of *Rome* had received a considerable Shock, by the Loss of so many Kings and Princes, who having considered the haughty and insolent Behaviour of former Popes, and the Luxury and Irreligion of the Popes in their Time, (a) as well as of all the Clergy both Secular and Regular, had lately forsaken the Romish, and were (by taking their Refuge to the Holy Scriptures) return'd to the true Apostolic Church: Pope *Paul* III. who came to his Papacy in 1534. did use all his Endeavours to muster up what Forces he could to strengthen the sinking Power of the Holy See. To which End, he in the first Place called the famous *Council of Trent*, in the next Place caressed and cherished the Mendicant Orders, of which the *Dominicans*, by establishing the *Inquisition*, were to padlock the Tongues of Men in all Places, where this Tribunal was received, the others, who make up a very

---

(a) *The Reformation began in the Papacy of* Leo X. *He gave* Henry VIII. *the Title of* Defender *of the* Faith, *on Account of the Book this King had wrote against* Luther. *This Pope was the very Man who used to boast how much Money the See of* Rome *had got by the Fable of* Christ.

very numerous Army, being every where among the People, were to gain the Belief of the Populace in Matters of Religion, by the outfide fhew of Humility and Sanctity, and in the third Place, he confirmed a new Order of Monks, inftituted by *Ignatius Loiola* a Spaniard, which call themfelves the *Society of Jefus*, that thefe by having obtained, on Account of their Learning, the Management of the Education of almoft all the Youth of the Romifh Church, might have it in their Power to inftil fuch Principles, into their Pupils, as were moft agreeable with, and conducive to the Intereft, and confiftent with the Papal Authority. However, tho' thefe means were moft artfully concerted, and the Jefuits greatly influence the Councils of Princes, yet it is evident by daily Occurrences that thefe Romifh Princes ever fince that great Event the *Reformation*, are very little terrify'd by any Storm that threatens from the *Vatican*, and that the Popes of the laft and prefent Century are obliged to make ufe of the Fox inftead of the Lion.

A N D now hoping the Reader will excufe this long Digreffion, I proceed to the next Section.

SECT

SECTION IV.

The Neceffaries, Conveniencies and Superfluities of Life this Town is furnish'd with, taking in the Natural HISTORY of this Place and Parts adjacent.

THE Reader has been informed in Sect. I. not only of the desirable Situation of the Town of *Nottingham* : But also of the convenient as well as ornamental Buildings, for the comfortable and pleasurable Reception of the different Classes of its Inhabitants.

I shall now proceed to examine how the People are provided with such Things as belong either to the immediate Support of Life; or such as contribute to a greater Elegancy and Enjoyment.

UPON the whole, thus much may be said in general, that Nothing is so cheap as to render it contemptible; nor any Thing requisite to a comfortable way of living so dear; but that the middling People in the respective Seasons may have a share.

PROVISIONS of all kinds may be considered under these two Heads, *viz. Immediate Neceffaries,* and *Lefs Neceffaries,* the price of which in their proper Seasons, *communibus annis,* is set forth in the following Table.

Immediate Neceffaries.	d.
Bread Corn p. LondonBuſhel } from 3s. &6d. to 4.	o.
Malt, from 3 s. to - - - -	3 6
Beef Veal Mutton Lamb Pork } per Stone of 14 lb.	3. o
Butter, per lb. fr. 4 d. to - - o.	6.
Cheefe, per lb. - - - - - o.	3.
Eggs, from 10 to 16 for - - o.	4.
Salt-Fiſh, p. lb. from 2d halfpenny to	3.
Beans & Peafe, green p. Peck, fr. 4 to	6.

Lefs Nec effaries.	s.	d.
Fowls, p. couple, fr. 1s. & 4d. to 2.		o.
Chickens, fr. 8 d. to - - -	o.	10
Pidgeons, p. doz. fr. 1s. & 4d. to 1.		6.
A Goofe, { green fr. 6d. to 1. o. stubble - - 1. 6. Christmas fr. 2s. to 2. 6.		
Ducks p. { tame, fr. 8d. to 1s. & 1. 6. couple. { wild, fr. 1s. to - 2. o.		
A Turkey, fr. 2s. to - - - 3.		6.
A Pig fr. 1s. 6d. to - - - 2.		6.
Rabbets, p. couple, fr. 6d. to - o.		8.

Carrots

Immediate Neceſſaries.

Carrots, ⎫
Turnips, ⎬ per Bunch. — s. d. o. 1.
Parſnips, ⎭

Cabbages, Savoys, &c. in proportion.
Potatoes, p. peck, fr. 6d. to — o. 8.
Small Beer, three half-pence p. Gal.
Midling Beer, 2d. — —
Fine and ſtrong Ale p. Quart. o. 4.

Leſs Neceſſaries.

Trent Fiſh.

Carp, ⎫
Tench, ⎬ p. lb. — 1. 0.
Trout ⎭

Pike, ⎫
Perch, ⎪
Barbote ⎬ p. lb. — 0. 6.
Eels, ⎪
Grayling, ⎭

Other ſmall Fiſh, — 0. 4.

Barbel, ⎫
Bream, ⎬ p. lb. — 0. 2.
Chub, ⎭

Gudgeons p. ſcore. 0. 2.

Leſs Neceſſaries.

Sea-Fiſh.

Salmon, p. lb. oft 1s. rarely 4d.
moſtly, — o. 6

Cod, ⎫
Freſh Ling, ⎬ p. lb. 4d.
Lute, ⎪
Haddock, ⎭

Hollybut, commonly called ⎫
Turbut. ⎬ p. lb. 5d. to 8d.
Butts & Plaice, ⎭

Soles,
Smelts,
Lobſters, and Crabs.
Oyſters, a Barrel, — 5. 0.
Lincolnſhire D °. p. ſcore,
4d. to — o. 6.

Muſcles, per peck, 8d. & 6d.
Shrimps,
Cockles,
Broccoli, till within theſe ſix or ſeven Years was only to be met with in Gentlemen's Gardens, but now are ſold in the Market.
Collyflowers, are from 1 to 2d. a Head.
Aſparagus, from 6d. to 8d. per 100.

Sugars, Spices and all ſorts of Grocers Goods almoſt as cheap as in *London.*
Wine and Cyder, as about *London.*
Strong-Beer, 2s. p. Gallon.

Fodder, &c.

Barley at a Medium, 16s. p. Quarter.
Rye, 14s. to 16s. —
Oats, 7s. to 10s. —
Beans & Peaſe, both are fluctuating Commodities, between 16 s. and 1 l. 12 s. p. Quarter.
Hay at a Medium of 1 l. 10 s. tho' ſometimes but 1 l. and ſeldom exceeding two Pounds p. Tun.
Wheat and Rye Straw at 1 d. p. Bottle, *i. e.* a Bundle, two of which will make a Thatch.

Peaſe-Straw, 6d. a ſcore of ſmall Bundles.
Barley-Straw, 1s. p. Flail, that is as much as a Man can Threſh in a Day.
Oat-Straw is ſeldom ſold but given to the Farmer's own Cattle.
Many of theſe Articles are oft cheaper, and ſometimes dearer, eſpecially at their firſt coming in.

THIS

T H I S Table makes no mention of Game, becaufe not brought to the open Market. Neverthelefs this Neighbourhood produces a confiderable Quantity of fundry Kinds, and every Body who is acquainted with *Nottingham*, muft allow, there would be enough for the Sport of all Perfons qualified, were it not for the too great Number of Pochers who neglecting their lawful Bufinefs, employ their Time both Night and Day in invading the Property of others, and notwithftanding the Severity of the Game Laws, they appear as daring as before. Our great Inns are feldom in want of this Sort of Dainties to ferve their Cuftomers with.

T H E Chace, which is as it were at the next Door, is well provided with Fallow Deer, and divers Gentlemen's Parks about *Nottingham*, are alfo well ftock'd, thefe Gentlemen and the Right Hon. the Earl of *Chefterfield*, Ranger, in the Buck and Doe Seafons, annually compliment theiy Friends in this Town with Venifon.

B E S I D E S thefe Provifions for the Neceffity and Elegancy of living, the People here are not without their Tea, Coffee and Chocolate, efpecially the firft, the Ufe of which is fpread to that Degree, that not only the Gentry and Wealthy Traders drink it conftantly, but almoft every Seamer, Sizer, and Winder, will have her Tea, and will enjoy herfelf over it in a Morning, not forgetting their Snuff, a Pinch or two of which they never fail of regaling their Noftrils with, between every Difh ; and even a common Wafher-woman thinks fhe has not had a proper Breakfaft without Tea and hot buttered white Bread.—To conclude this Article of Tea, being the other Day at a Grocer's, I could not forbear looking earneftly and with fome Degree of Indignation, at a ragged and greafy Creature, who came into the Shop with two Children following her, in as difmal a Plight as the Mother, asking for a Pennyworth of Tea and a Halfpennyworth of Sugar, which when fhe was ferved with, fhe told the Shop-keeper : Mr. *N. I do not know how it is with me, but I can affure you I would not defire to live, if I was to be debarred from drinking every Day a little Tea.*

T H E next Things to be confidered are the Conveniencies, Nature and Art has furnifhed this Town with, for Exercife, which is as neceffary for the Prefervation of Health, as Food is for the Support of Life, it being impoffible for a Perfon long to enjoy an uninterrupted State of Health, if the Exercife he takes does not in a great Meafure counterballance his Way of living, I mean his eating and drinking : And it is obfervable that fewer People who have where-withal, eat to live, than live to eat. Perfons therefore whofe Birth and Fortune have exempted them from the bufy part of Life, or whofe Profeffion or Trade obliges them to fit much, require fome other means to promote a due Circulation of the Juices, and thereby the neceffary Secretions and Excretions, requifite to preferve the Body in Health and Vigour ; the principal of which are Walking and Riding : For this purpofe here are feveral pleafant Ways; as a Walk to *Colwick-Spring*, a Mile from *Nottingham* ; by the Trent-fide toward *Beefton* Meadows, where on the right there is a Profpect of *Wollaton-Hall*, and on the left the Eye is feafted with the gay view of *Clifton* Hills ; to St. *Anne's Well*, about a Mile from Home, the Walk to which is pleafant, the Refrefhment agreeable, and the Ufage obliging and reafonable ; here in the Summer Seafon you may either be entertained with a Concert of Aereal Muficians in *Nottingham* Coppices, or on Mondays and Wednefdays join in Company with thofe who ufe the Exercife of Bowling.

NEAR

NEAR this Well, which has been mentioned in Sect. I. and which is frequented by many Persons as a cold Bath, and reckoned the 2d. coldeft in *England*, there ftood anciently a Chappel dedicated to St. *Anne*, whence the Well obtained the Name it bears, tho' before this Chappel was built, it was known by the Name of *Robin Hood's* Well, by fome called fo to this Day. The People who keep the Green and Public Houfe to promote a Holy-day Trade, fhew an old wickered Chair, which they call *Robin Hood's* Chair, a Bow, and an old Cap, both thefe they affirm to have been this famous Robber's Property; (*a*) this little Artifice takes fo well with the People in low-Life, that at *Chriftmas*, *Eafter* and *Whitfuntide*, it procures them a great deal of Bufinefs, for at thofe Times great Numbers of young Men bring their Sweethearts to this Well, and give them a Treat, and the Girls think themfelves ill-ufed, if they have not been faluted by their Lovers in *Robin Hood's* Chair.

OF the Chappel I find no Account; but that there has been one in this Place is vifible, for the Eaft Wall of that *quondam* Chappel fupports the Eaft fide of the Houfe, which is built on the Spot where that Place of Worfhip ftood. In the Room of the Altar is now a great Fire-place, over which was found upon a Stone the Date of the building of this Chappel, *viz.* 1409, which whilft legible one Mr. *Ellis* a Watchmaker took down into his Pocket-Book, and communicated to me; by this it appears that it was built in the Reign of King *Henry* IV. 335 Years ago, and who knows whether it might not be founded by that King, who refided about that Time at *Nottingham*; it did not ftand much above 200 Years, for my oft mentioned Anonymous Author does not remember any of the Ruins of the Chappel, who wrote his Account in 1641, which however he might plainly have feen, had he taken Notice of the Eaft Wall of Stone, when all the reft of the prefent Houfe is a Brick Building.

ST. *Anne's* Well was about a hundred Years ago, a very famous Place of Refort, concerning which take the above Author's Account in his own Words.

" AT the Well there is a Dwelling Houfe ferving as an Habitation for the Wood-
" ward of thofe Woods, being an Officer of the Mayor. This Houfe is likewife a
" Victualling Houfe, having adjoining to it fair Summer-Houfes, Bowers or Arbours
" covered by the plafhing and interweaving of Oak-Boughs for Shade, in which are
" Tables of large Oak Planks, and are feated about with Banks of Earth, fleighter-
" ed and covered with green Sods, like green Carfie Cufhions. There is alfo a
" Building containing two fair Rooms, an upper and a lower, ferving for fuch as re-
" pair thither to retire to in Cafe of Rain or bad Weather. Thither do the Townf-
" men refort (*b*) by an ancient Cuftom beyond Memory.

" THIS Well is all Summer long much frequented, and there are but few fair
" Days between *March* and *October*, in which fome Company or other of the Town,
" fuch as ufe to Confort there, ufe not to fetch a walk to this Well, either to dine or
" fup, or both, fome fending their Provifion to be dreffed, others befpeaking what
" they will have, and when any of the Town have their Friends come to them, they
" have given them no welcome, unlefs they entertain them at this Well. Befides

L   " there

(*a*) *See Sect.* XIII.   (*b*) *See Sect.* V.

" there are many other Meetings of Gentlemen, both from the Town and the Coun-
" try, making Choice of this Place rather than the Town for their Rendezvous to
" recreate themselves at, by Reason of the sweetness and openness of the Air, where
" besides their Artificial, they have Natural Music without Charge; in the Spring by
" the Nightingale and in the Autumn by the Wood-Lark, a Bird whose Notes for va-
" riety and sweetness are nothing inferiour to the Nightingale, and much in her Tones,
" which filled with the Voices of other Birds like inward parts in Song serve to dou-
" ble the melodious Harmony of those sweet warbling Trebles. Here are likewise
" many Venison Feasts, and such as have not the Hap to feed the Sense of Taste
" with the Flesh thereof when dead, may yet fill their Sight with those Creatures
" living, (*a*) which all Summer long are picking up Weeds in the Corn-Fields and
" Closes, and in Winter and hard Weather, gathering Sallets in the Gardens of such
" Houses as lie on the North-side of the Town.

" AMONG other Meetings I may not omit one Royal and remarkable Assem-
" bly at this Place, whereof myself was an Eye Witness, which was that it pleased
" our late Sovereign King *James*, in his Return from Hunting in this Forest, to Ho-
" nour this Well with his Royal Presence, ushered by that Noble Lord *Gilbert* Earl
" of *Shrewsbury*, and attended by many others of the Nobility, both of the Court
" and Country, where they drank the Woodward and his Barrels dry."

BUT to proceed to other Walks or Rides; there cannot be any thing more a-
greeable, then to go over *Wilford* Ferry, and so by the *Trent* Side to *Clifton*, three
little Miles from *Nottingham*; nor to those who love Bowling, to *Basford* on a Tuesday, two Miles; or to *Holm-pierpoint*, three Miles from our Town on a Thursday,
in both which Places he will find good Company, and a plentiful Ordinary, and the
Green of the latter, is accounted as large and as fine as most Bowling-Greens in
England. Other Persons of this Town who cannot be spared so far from Home, may
have the Opportunity of Bowling in the Town Green any Day in the Week.

TO these Conveniencies for Exercise, let us add the Opportunity the People of
this Town have to use the wholsome Exercise of Hare-Hunting: For there is a Pack of
Hounds kept in this Town by Subscription; the Honourable *Rothwell Willoughby*, Esq;
keeps a Pack, and the Right Honourable the Lord *Middleton*'s Hounds are out several Days in the Week.

HAVING now enumerated the several Invitations our Situation gives to Men
for the Preservation of Health, we will see in the next place what is provided for the
Ladies.

SUCH of the Fair-Sex as do not chuse to go at a Distance from the Town, they
may take a pleasant Tour in the Green Court of *Nottingham* Castle, or if they like
a somewhat keener Air, in the paved Yard above, where in Case of Rain or too much
Wind, they may Walk under Shelter. (*b*)

FOR

(*a*) *So much seems my Author to enjoy in describing this Place, that he forgets himself
when he reckons among the Delights, the Deer's frequenting the Cornfields and
Gardens. Every Body is sensible what wretched Gardeners they are, and Owners
of Cornfields are convinced by sad Experience what Weeders they are, for they
Weed very clean, picking up Corn and all. Sure my Author had neither Cornfield
nor Garden on the North side of the Town.* (*b*) *See Sect.* IX.

FOR those who are more Active, St. *Anne's* Well is by no means an improper Walk, for as it is a Mile from the Town, there is a resting Place, where they may refresh themselves, (as they do at Home in an Afternoon) with Tea, and return in the Evening.

OR such as are early Risers, may after Breakfast take a turn the Field-Way to *Sneinton-Wood,* and create themselves an Appetite by running the Shepherds Race ; I have mentioned *Sneinton* Wood, which bears this Name from what it once was, but is now entirely bare and by the Gift of the Family of *Pierpoint* become a Common to *Sneinton,* upon this Common which lies pretty high, and about half a quarter of a Mile East of St. *Anne's* Well, there is a kind of a Labyrinth cut out of a flat Turf, which the People call Shepherd's-Race : This seems to be a Name of no old standing, probably occasion'd by its being observed that those who look after the Sheep on this Common, often run it for an Airing. It is made somewhat in Imitation of those of the ancient *Greeks* and *Romans* who made such intricate Courses for their Youth to run in to acquire Agility of Body : Dr. *Stukeley* in his Itinerary speaks of one of *Roman* Original still in being at *Aukborough* in the County of *Lincoln,* called *Julian's Bower,* which comes pretty near ours ; he says it is a kind of Circular Work, made of Banks of Earth in the Fashion of a Maze or Labyrinth, and that the Boys to this Day divert themselves with running in it one after another : That which I mentioned, differs from the Doctor's, in that it pretends to no *Roman* Origin, and yet is more ancient than the Reformation, as is evident from the Cross-croslets in the Centers of the four lesser Rounds ; and in that there are no Banks raised but circular Trenches cut into the Turf, and those so narrow that Persons cannot run in them, but must run on the top of the Turf. Nobody can at this Time give any Account when it was first made, nor by whom, neither is it known whose Business it is to keep it in Repair ; but might I offer my Conjecture, I should think this open Maze was made by some of the Priests belonging to St. *Anne's* Chappel, who being confined so far as not to venture out of Sight or Hearing, contrived this to give themselves a breathing for want of other Exercise.

THOSE of the Fair Sex who like the Water-side, have a very agreeable Way to it over *Nottingham* Meadows, where in Summer Evenings they do not want Conveniencies at the *Trent* Bridge to bath themselves unseen.

I should not have omitted till now to speak of that delightful Walk to *Colwick* Hills, whither in the Summer Season, the cool Shade and the Music of the Birds used to invite a great Number of young Ladies ; but that since these Hills are walled in, this pleasure is only allowed to them whom *Mundy Musters,* Esq; (whose Property they are) is pleased to favour with a Key.

AT *Nottingham* are also two Monthly Assemblies contrived for the Interview of of the genteel Part of the Town of both Sexes, where the younger divert themselves with Dancing, whilst the senior or graver Part enjoy themselves over a Game of Quadrille or Whist.

ONE of these places of Meeting, is on the *Low-pavement,* built purposely for this Use, consisting of a handsome, lofty and spacious Room, with a Gallery for the Music at the upper End, the Room is 67 Feet long and 21 Feet broad, to this belong two withdrawing Rooms and a Place where a Person attends who sells all kinds of Refreshments. This is called the Ladies's Assembly.

L 2

THE

THE other called the Tradefmen's Affembly, is held in a large Room 70 Feet long and 20 Feet broad, where the Wealthy Tradefmen, their Wives and Sons and Daughters meet for the fame Recreation. This is at *Thurland* Hall in *Gridlefmith-gate*.

THE ufual Days of thefe Affemblies are: That of the Ladies the firft Tuefday, and that of the Tradefmen every 3d Tuefday in the Month. When in the Evening there is in both a numerous Appearance. In both thefe Places there are held Affemblies extraordinary in the Affize-Week, Election Time, and at the Horfe-Race; of this laft I fhall fpeak next.

Nottingham is one of the twelve Towns where the King's Guineas are run for, befides other Money or Plates.

THESE Races are kept in *July*, the Courfe which formerly was four Miles round, is at this Time but two Miles. It is one of the beft in *England*, and is never out of Order for running be the Weather what it will.

HERE is a fine Valley for Coaches, Chariots, &c. to pafs and repafs, and for the Accommodation of the Nobility and Gentry who come to the Races. This *Nottingham* Courfe could once have vyed with any Courfe in the Kingdom for a grand Appearance of Nobility, neither *Newmarket* nor *Banftead-Downs*, boaft of better Company nor Horfes, but fince the great Increafe of Horfe-Races it has rather dwindled, however the late Act of Parliament has been of fome Service to it, and there feems a very great likelihood that in a Number of Years it may recover its former Luftre.

DURING the Race a Company of Comedians always are in the Town, who Act at a Theatre built for that purpofe in St. *Mary* Gate.

IN *Nottingham* are kept upwards of 400 Saddle Horfes, above 130 Coach, Chaife and Team-Horfes, 11 Gentlemen's Coaches and Chariots, a confiderable Number of Chaifes and Chairs, befides 5 Hackney Glafs Coaches, one Chariot, and feveral Chaifes and Chairs.

HERE is alfo an Hackney Sedan, the firft ever ufed here for Hire, which ferves to carry Perfons who are taken Sick from Home, and ancient Ladies to Church and Vifiting, as alfo Young ones in rainy Weather.

I will now proceed to examine how the Elements favour our Town and 1ft.

Of the HEAVEN and AIR.

THE Heaven in thefe Parts is feldom ruffled by violent Tempefts, and for ought I can learn has been fubject to as few uncommon and frightful Appearances as any where.

I meet with no Account in my Reading, of any extraordinary Tempeft, but that

which

which *Stow* Records (*a*) to have happened in the Year 1558, in the 6th of Queen *Mary*, about four Months before her Death, *viz.* " On the 7th of *July* within a Mile of *Not-* " *tingham*, was a marvellous Tempeft of Thunder, which as it came through two " Towns, (*b*) beat down all the Houfes and Churches, the Bells were caft to the out- " fide of the Church-Yards, and fome Webs of Lead 400 Feet into the Field, wri- " then like a Pair of Gloves. The River *Trent* running between the two Towns, " the Water with the Mud in the bottom, was carried a quarter of a Mile and caft " againft the Trees, the Trees were pulled up by the Roots and caft twelvefcore " Foot off : Alfo a Child was taken forth of a Man's Hands, two Spear Length high, " and carried an hundred Foot and then let fall, wherewith his Arm was broke and " fo died ; five or fix Men thereabout were flain, and neither Flefh nor Skin perifh- " ed. There fell fome Hailftones that were 15 Inches about.

BUT what is ftill frefh in People's Memory, is a Tornado blaft, which hap-pened in the Year 1731, *February* 11th, coming from the South, hafted *in* a Line with the utmoft Force and Swiftnefs Northward, and coming to Thorny-Wood, there made a Lane of feveral Feet wide and a confiderable length, leaving the firft Lodge a little to the Right, tearing all the Trees in its Way up by the Root, and fplitting fome of each fide from Top to Bottom, I myfelf did obferve in the Year 1737, fome few Haffels and Crab-Trees, (which had only felt a fide Force of that Whirl-Wind) fplit in two, and twifted as one might twift a Wifp of Straw.

ANOTHER Phænomenon more familiar to Sailors then Inland Perfons, is what the Sailors call Spouts, very common in the Weft-Indies and happening fometimes in the Mediterranean Sea, but more uncommon in Places diftant from thofe great Wa-ters : Of this kind was obferved one by *Langford Collin*, Efq; at *Shelford* in the County of *Nottingham*, four Miles from this Town, in the Year 1730, fometime in *Auguft*, which he related to me thus : " That Walking with his Lady in the Gar- " den of the Parfonage Houfe (where he then lived) about One o'Clock in the Af- " ternoon, he faw a large Column of Water, upwards of fix Yards in Breadth, as it " feemed to him at a quarter of Mile's Diftance, reaching from a Cloud down to the " River *Trent*, which coming down with great Violence, had forced the Water in " the River, (which was there not quite two Feet deep) above 300 Yards beyond its " Bank, as he found, going afterwards to the Spot where it fell, where he met with " a Boatman, who told him, that he had a narrow efcape, being in his Boat but a " few Yards from it."

THE moft common Appearance, and which is almoft become familiar with the People, is the *Aurora Borealis* of *Gaffendus*, or North-Lights : This in the Winter Seafon is very frequent, and the lucid Tracts of it fo numerous and bright, that the Light they give by their Vibration is often equal to that of the Moon.

THE Air is here very wholefome, being generally clear and dry, and as *Not-tingham* ftands at a juft Elevation above, and Diftance from the Rivers, it is freed from the crude, chilly, aguifh Vapours, which the too near Neighbourhood of Cur-rents always is accompanied with, fo that this Town is feldom in Winter much an-

---

(*a*) *Sum. Chron. p.* 500.   (*b*) *The two were* Lenton *and* Wilford, *this on the South, the other on the North-fide of the* Trent, *exactly oppofite.*

noyed with thick and ſtinking Fogs, whence in Proportion to the Number of Inhabitants, Agues are rare, few Men Hypochondriacal, few Women afflicted with Hyſ-
terical Diſorders, nor do we meet with many Rainbow Complexions, to the Prevention of which, I muſt own our Females contribute their part, in uſing more Exerciſe,
than in many other Towns.

THIS Healthfulneſs of the Air will beſt appear if we take a View, 1ſt. of the
Births and Burials in this Town for the ſpace of ſeven Years, ſet forth in the following Table, and in the 2d. Place take Notice of the great Number of Perſons in this
Town who live to a very advanced Age, many exceeding the ultimate Term of the
Pſalmiſt, (a) and ſome outliving 93, the Age of St. John the Evangeliſt : Of ſuchI
have here annex'd a Liſt, wherein I have confin'd myſelf to the Town, and the Compaſs of four Years, and none are contained in the ſaid Liſt who are or were under 80,
not thinking it worth while to take Notice of Perſons from 70 Yeàrs to fourſcore, they
being ſo numerous, that it would have been an eaſy Matter for me to fill up a Catalogue of between 500 and 600 : I ſpeak within Compaſs, and the following Liſt is
far from being a compleat one of all who are living, or who have died during four
Years from 80 and upwards ; but judging that the Number here collected, will be a
ſufficient Teſtimony of the Longevity of the People of Nottingham, I have forbore
making a very ſtrict Enquiry.

A TABLE of Births and Burials in the Town of Nottingham, ex-
cluſive of the fatal Year 1736, for 7 Years, from 1732 to 1739.

In St. Mary's Pariſh.				In St. Peter's Pariſh.				In St. Nicholas's Pariſh			
Years.	Bap.	Bur.	Inf.	Years.	Bap.	Bur	Inf.	Years.	Bap.	Bur	Inf.
1732	242	221	94	1732	48	52	10	1732	49	66	28
1733	210	175	89	1733	50	67	30	1733	58	48	21
1734	234	140	73	1734	52	51	23	1734	59	53	29
1735	252	187	98	1735	69	59	31	1735	67	62	30
1737	255	211	95	1737	78	74	43	1737	63	60	25
1738	243	236	124	1738	59	70	36	1738	72	60	27
1739	282	192	96	1739	54	60	31	1739	74	82	39
Total	1718	1362	669	Total	410	433	204	Total	442	431	199

The Total Number of Baptiſms in the 3 Pariſhes is — 2570.
Among the Preſbyterian, —
Among the Independents. — 0054.
Births of Baptiſts. — 0070.
Births of Quakers. —

Summa Summarum. — 2694.

The Total Number of Burials in the 3 Pariſhes is — 2226.
Preſbyterians. —
Independents. — 0046.
Baptiſts. — 0059.
Quakers. —

Summa Summarum. 2331. Births

(a) Pſalm. 90. v. 10. The Days of our Years are threeſcore Years and ten; and if by
reaſon of Strength they be fourſcore Years, yet is their Strength Labour and Sorrow,
for it is ſoon cut off, and we flie away.

Births in 7 Years.	—	—	—	—	2694.
Burials in 7 Years.	—	—	—	—	2331.
Increase of Souls in 7 Years.		—	—	—	363.
Total of Infants buried in 7 Years.		—	—	—	1072.

A LIST of Aged Persons from 80 Years and upwards, who are either now Living or Died since 1740.

Living.		*Dead.*	
Alcocke ( )	81.	Arnald (Mary) *H. H. d.* 1743.	81.
Andrews (Alice) *N. H.*	89.		
Allen (Richard)	83.		
Boroughs (Mary) *N. H.*	80.	Beardsley ( )	—
Boroughs (Joseph)	80.	Banks (Joseph) 1741.	86.
		Blag (Robert) 1741.	93
		Bridgeford (Anne) *N. H.* 1742.	82.
Chetham (Anne)	84.	Cox (Anne) *B. H. d.* 1740.	83.
Cockup (Mary)	84.	Challands ( ) *d.* 1744.	93.
Clay (Joseph) Gent.	82.	Crampton ( ) *N. H.* 1740.	100.
Clay (Mary) his Wife.	84.	Crofts (Stephen) *B. H. d.* 1740.	90.
		Crofts (Thomas) *d.* since.	86.
Derry (Jane) *N. H.*	80.	Draycot (Philip) *d.* 1744.	80.
Elby (Mary)	85.	E	
F.		Freeland ( ) *d.* 1741.	99.
		Fuller ( ) *d*	86.
Garland (Sarah)	—	Green (Benjamin) *d.* 1742.	87.
Gedling ( )	84.	Goddard (Dorothy) *d.* 1740.	95.
Gedling ( ) his Wife.	91.		
Gregory (Mary) *N. H.*	80.		
Hatheway (John)	90	Henson (Anne) *d.* 1742.	87.
Hollis ( )	80.	Haywood ( ) *d.* 1742.	89.
		Hazard (Zachary) *d.* 1743.	84.
		Hilton (John) *d.* 1740.	93.
Jackson ( )	80	James (Nathan) *d.* 1740.	84.
Jalland (Thomas)	81.	Johnson (John) *d.* 1741.	82
		Johnson (Sam.) *d.* 1744.	84
Killingly (John)	84.	K.	
Launder (Philip) Gent.	81.	L.	

Living.		Dead.	
Metcalfe ( )	84.	Miller (George) d. 1744.	82.
Martinel ( ) N. W.	89.		
Marshall (Elizabeth)	82.		
Oliver ( )	81.		
Onion (Samuel)	81.		
P.		Paramour (Jonathan) d.	—
		Paul (Mary) d. 1743.	89.
Ridley (Mary)	89.	Radford (William) d. 1741.	80.
		Radford (Roger) d.	
		Ryley (Mary) M. W. d. 1739.	100.
Selby (Lydia)	80.	Smallpage ( ) d. 1741.	90.
Shawe ( ) H. H.	80.	Smith ( ) Widow, 1741.	82.
Sheers ( )	84.	Smith (Anne) d. 1741.	81.
Southern (Robert) L. H.	80.		
Stone (John)	82.		
Strey ( )	82.		
T.			
V.		Tacy (George)	100.
White ( ) Widow	85.	Vickers (Mary) d. 1740.	89.
Wildboar (John)	84.	Wag (Hannah) d. 1744.	83.
Wood (Elizabeth) Midwife.	88.	Ward (Henry) d. 1736.	109
Wood ( ) by St. Peter's Church.	82.	Weston (Robert) d. 1742.	84.
Wright (Mary) on the Long Row.	82.	Weston (Elizabeth) d. 1744.	84.
Wright ( )		Wig (John) Gent. d. 1743.	84.
		Wildboar (Samuel) d. *	

This List was taken in June 1744.

Some Remarks on several Aged Persons.

1st. Mrs. *Freeland* had all her Faculties and was strong and hearty to the last; she died of no Distemper, but went to sleep at Night and never wak'd after. She was Aunt to Mr. *Ellison*.

2d. Mrs. *Chalands*, Mother of Mrs. *Ellison*, second Wife of the just-named Mr. *Ellison*, Distiller in this Town : She lived at the Time of her Death at *Edwalton*, about

---

* *Explication of the Capital Letters in the List.* N. H. *New Hospital.* B. H. *Bilby's Hospital.* M. W. *St. Mary's Workhouse.* H. H. *Hanley's Hospital.* N. W. *St. Nicholas's Workhouse.* L. H. *Labourer's Hospital.*

bout two Miles from this Town ; was noted for her Dexterity in fetting broken and diflocated Bones, whereby fhe was very helpful to the Poor, to whom fhe never refufed her charitable Affiftance, even when fhe was near her End ; for about fix or feven Weeks before her Death, fhe fet a broken Arm of a Child of four or five Years old, and took Care of it till it was well. It was remarkable of her that fhe lived to fee the 6th Generation.

3d. *Madam Fuller* managed all her own Affairs with the utmoft exactnefs to her Death ; fhe was bleffed in her old Age with a peculiar Cheerfulnefs, and enjoy'd a great fhare of Health. She was Mother of *Mundy Mufters,* of *Colwick,* Efq; but lived and died at *Nottingham.*

4th. Mr. *George Milner* of this Town, was till within two Years of his Death, one of the Stewards to the Earl of *Chefterfield,* and was as able to do Bufinefs as ever.

5th. Mr. *Haywood,* was a ftrong lufty Man, and followed his Bufinefs of Malting to the laft.

6th. *Mary Vickars,* was at her Wheel Spinning, but three Days before fhe died.

7th. Mr. *Wig,* Brother of the Relict of the late Alderman *Green,* had fo young a Countenance that he feemed to be not above 60 ; he walked well, and in the Seafon till within fix or feven Months before his Death, never fail'd once a Week to go to St. *Anne's* Well, a Mile from the Town, and back again, after he had bowled all the Afternoon.

8th. Mrs. *Green* juft mentioned, after fhe had enjoyed a great fhare of Health for many Years, died at the Age of 87. Her Husband who died fome Years before her, was 83.

9th. *John Hilton,* had all his Senfes perfect to the laft.

10th. *Stephen Crofts,* was a labouring Man, and myfelf have feen him do a tolerable Day Work at Hedging and Ditching when 86 Years of Age.

11th *Goody Ryley,* till within three Years of her Death, being in St. *Mary's* Workhoufe, if fhe was not pleafed with her Ufage, would every now and then, take a Ramble on Foot to *London,* where fhe had fome of her Children fettled, and if, they gave her the leaft Offence, fhe would as readily trot down again to *Nottingham ;* fhe was above 100 Years of Age, but there was not the fame circumftantial Proof to believe fhe was fo old as fhe pretended, *viz.* 110 Years, tho' her Daughter now living is upwards of 80.

12th. I may be allowed to add two Perfons of above an hundred Years of Age, tho' they do not come within the compafs of four Years : The firft is *George Tacy* who died in the *New-Hofpital,* he drove a Water Cart when he was 100.

13th. The 2d. is *Henry Ward,* who was in good Health at the Age of 106, when he was made a Burgefs of *Nottingham,* to which he had a Right, having ferved feven Years in *Nottingham,* where he was alfo born; he had fpent the moft confiderable part of his Life at *Nottingham,* tho' he died two Miles off, upon the Foreft, in

Bas-

Basford Parish, by his own Confeffion he had drank pretty freely for many Years, during which he kept a Public Houfe.

Among thofe who are living, all which I have met with in the Hofpitals, are in tolerable Health.

14. 15. 16. 17. 18. 19. Of the genteel part of the Town, Mrs. *Jackfon*, Mrs. *Metcalf*, Mrs. *Wright*, Mother of Meff. *Wright* on the *Long-Row*, with Mr. *Clay* and his Spoufe, whofe joint Ages make up 160 Years : As alfo Mr. *Launder*, who Walks well, and can Ride on Horfeback as well as ever, and during the Summer Seafon, Bowles every Week at St. *Anne's* Well ; are fingular Inftances of an healthful old Age.

21. Mr. *Hathaway* is a lufty Man and enjoys good Health, and at 80 married a fecond Wife.

22. Mr. *John Killingley*, Reads without Spectacles, has hardly a grey Hair on his Head ; he ufed till within a very few Years, to Walk to *London* on Foot and backagain, works now for his Amufement in the Stocking-Frame.

23. 24. 25. ----- *Hollis*, *Samuel Onion*, and *Robert Southern*, the firft a Joyner, the fecond a Sadler, and the third a Stocking-maker, Work all at their refpective Trades. Of the laft it is remarkable that he was married to one, and his only Wife, 53 Years wanting five Days.

26. *Goody Gedling*, without *Chapel-Bar*, fells Ale, fhe Walks about, brews herfelf, and Spins, is extremely nimble Tongued, and has a Voice very fhrill, by her Countenance one would judge her not to be above 70.

Lydia Selby, is likewife in good Health, and Walked the 15th of this prefent *Auguft* in the Forenoon, to *Gedling* and back again, which is full fix Miles.

Of all the reft none is Bed-rid, (except three or four) and are hearty and well.

AS healthful as *Nottingham* is, there moftly happens once in five Years fome Diftemperature in the Air, which either brings along with it fome Epidemical Fever, (tho' feldom very Mortal,) or renders the Small-Pox more dangerous than at other Times, of this laft, the Year 1736, was a fatal Inftance, for from the latter End of *May* to the beginning of *September*, this Diftemper fwept away a great Number of Souls, (but moftly Children,) and in the fingle Month of *May*, there were buried in St. *Mary's* Church and Church-yard only, 104 ; in fhort, the Burials exceeded that Year the Births by above 380, whereas otherwife there is *communibus annis*, an increafe of about 65 ; a Mortality, the like I have not been able to difcover in looking back into the Church Regifters for above 30 Years, and I much queftion whether there has been the like fince the Plague, which vifited this Town in 1667, and made a cruel Defolation in the higher part of *Nottingham*, for very few died in the lower, efpecially in a Street called the *Narrow-Marfh*, it was obferved, that the Infection had no Power, and that during the whole Time the Plague raged, not one who lived in that Street died of it, which induced many of the richer fort of People to crod thither and hire Lodgings at any Price ; the Prefervation of the People
ple

ple was attributed to the Effluvia of the Tanners Ouze, (for there were then 47 Tanners Yards in that Place) befides which they caufed a Smoak to be made, by burning moift Tanners Knobs.

LET me add to this Prefervation, feveral Prefervations of another kind, I mean wonderful Efcapes of fome Perfons in this Town from Death.

I have met with a very fingular Cafe of one *Cicily Ridgeway*, who in the Reign of King *Edward* III having fafted forty Days in clofe Prifon at *Nottingham*, obtained the King's Pardon : For a more particular Account of which, I refer my Reader to the XIIIth Section. I fhall here only mention fome few Efcapes within our Memory.

IN the Year 1709, one *William Lees*, who when he had been drinking was always like a Perfon diftracted, came in one of thefe Fits of Madnefs to the *Week-day-Crofs*, there jumped into a Well between 23 and 24 Yards deep, and was thence pulled out by his Brother without having received the leaft Hurt.

IN the Year 1720, in the Month of *July*, when his Grace the Duke of *Newcaftle* kept open Houfe at the Caftle of *Nottingham*; one *John Chambers*, a Gingerbread-Baker, and the firft of the Trade in this Town, being extremely Drunk, went out from the paved Yard upon the Rock, but being Top heavy, fell backwards headlong down the Precipice, into a Gardiner's Ground near the *Leen*, without receiving any other Hurt than beating off fome of the Skin of the Knuckles of his Fingers. The perpendicular Height of this Rock is 133 Feet.

ABOUT the Year 1719, one *Charles Beck*, was employed to clean the Well, at the *Cock* in the *High-Pavement*, which is 30 Yards deep; the Apprentice and Son of the Houfe, who were to draw the Bucket as the Man at the bottom filled it, through Heedleffnefs let go the Rope, and the Bucket came down with fuch velocity, that the Barrel about which the Rope was wound, was by the violence of the Motion torn off, and fell after the Bucket, the Lads frighted run away and thought the Man was killed, but it proved otherwife, for he had the Prefence of Mind to ward off the Bucket from his Head with both his Arms, which were thereby very much bruifed, and the Barrel falling fideways, tho' it very much wounded him, yet did it not give him any mortal Hurt.

IN the Year 1742, another Accident of like Nature with the firft, happened in the Month of *May*, to one *John Rollefton*, then of *Wollaton*, Taylor, who happened to lie ill of a Fever, in a back Garret in *Barkergate*, being delirious flung himfelf out of the Garret Window, run through a Neighbour's Yard down the Street, at the bottom of which he jumped into a Well. He being foon miffed, it was thought he was run Home to *Wollaton*, where the People went to fee for him, but miffing of him there they returned, and fomebody telling them that fomething groaned in the Well which was covered, they lifted up the Lid and found the Perfon they wanted, who now had ftood above an Hour there, almoft up to the Neck in Water, he had not fo much as a fcratch on his Skin when he was taken out, and being got into a Bed well warm'd, he foon came to himfelf, and grew well in a fhort Time, and about three Months after, he married a young Woman who lived over againft the Place where the Accident happened; he lives now in *Goofe-gate*.

AS

AS furprifing an Accident befel a Child about 4 Years old in 17   which falling into a Well at the End of the *Narrow-Marfh* a Man went down but could not find the Child, whereupon the Child's Father went down himfelf by a long Ladder, and finding his little Babe, he took it in his Arms but was fo hurried and furprized, that (fhaking and trembling) before he was got half up the Ladder, he let it fall ; upon this he went down again, and took it up as before, but when he had got almoft to the top of the Ladder, he let it drop a fecond Time ; then the Standers by would not fuffer him to try any more, but another Perfon went and brought the Child out alive, but not fenfible ; however, being put into a warm Bed, the Child by the next Day was entirely recovered, and had received no hurt about its Body, but a little Bruife upon one of its Cheeks.

IN *June* 1744, the Boot-catcher of the *Crown* Inn in *Nottingham*, being in Liquor and otherwife fubject to rife in his Sleep, got up about 11 o'Clock at Night and fell out of a Window four Stories high (meafuring 12 Yards) upon the hard Pavement. The Miftrefs hearing fomebody groan in the Yard came out with a Candle, with fome other Perfons then in the Houfe, who having difcovered the Matter, fent immediately for a Surgeon to examine his Condition, who coming, found neither Fracture nor Laxation of any part, he that Night opened a Vein, the Fellow was fo ftunned with the Fall, that he was not fenfible for feveral Days, and when he came to himfelf he knew not what had happened to him, but complained of being fore and weary, attributing it to his Walking fo far, which probably he dreamt when he had this Fall. He recovered in lefs than a Week's Time, and had no bad Symptoms nor Harm, but that of being bruifed which was unavoidable.

TO thefe let me add an Inftance of Rafhnefs which might have been attended with Death, *to wit* : One *John Branfon*, a Frame-Work-Knitter, in the Year 1736, in the Month of *July* (there being then fo great a Flood at *Nottingham*, that the Planks between the *Leen*-Bridge and the *Chainy*-Bridges which are threefeet high were overflowed,) laid an inconfiderable Wager, that he could Walk from the *Leen*-Bridge to the other, upon the Railes, which are ftill four Feet higher than the Planks, and about 294 Yards long : He accordingly fet about it, but by the Time he had got two thirds of his Way, a Woman with a Milk-pale on her Head coming from *Bridgeford* towards *Nottingham*, met him, and to fave her Milk-pale, pufhed him with her Hand from the Rails into the Water ; he being got out with fome Difficulty, run Home, fhifted his Clothes and returned to the Place, not willing to allow that he had loft, he attempted the Railes a fecond Time, and won his trifling Wager.

AFTER the feveral Efcapes from Death, I fhall here take Notice of fome particular Warnings, fome Perfons have had of the Death of fome of their Family : as will appear by what follows.

IN 1727-8, in the Month of *February*, at which Time *Langford Collin*, Efq; liv'd at *York*, one Night coming Home, he immediately, and very fpeedily undreffed himfelf, and went to Bed to his Lady, who being awake, he fpoke to her, asking her concerning fomething he thought fhe could inform him of, but he had hardly exchanged fix Words, when he was furprized at a fudden Knock given to the Street Door, fo loud, as if it had been done with a great Sledge-Hammer, which made him as fuddenly rife up out of his Bed, and with a pair of Piftols in his Hand he hafted acrofs the landing Place to the Dining-Room, but before he could reach the

                                                                                                    Door

Door of it, he heard a second Knock, full as loud as the firſt, at which impatient, and fearing it might injure his Lady then pregnant, and near her Time, he with all Expedition did run to the Window, during which a third Knock was heard, not only by himſelf but ſeveral of his Family ; but throwing the Saſh open, he ſaw No-body, neither at the Door nor on one ſide or other of the Houſe, tho' it was clear Moon-Light, and nothing to obſtruct his Sight either Way for a conſiderable Space ; ſtill thinking it was done by ſome unlucky Perſons out of Game or Wantonneſs, he diſcovered the next Morning his Uneaſineſs at ſuch Uſage at the Coffee Houſe, declaring with ſome Warmth how highly he would reſent it, could he come at the Knowledge of that rude Perſon who had been guilty of that ridiculous Action : Nor did he change his firſt Opinion till the next Poſt brought him a Letter which informed him of the Death of his Couſin, *Thomas Smith* of *Nottingham*, Eſq; who died at *London*, at the very Time the ſaid knocking was heard.

ABOUT three Years after that, the ſame Gentleman, ſitting up with his next Brother, Mr. *Abel Collin*, heard from 12 o' Clock at Night, till it ſtruck One, a continual Noiſe of driving Nails into a Coffin, in the Work-ſhop of *John Baker*, a Joyner, which abutted upon their Yard, at this he was much offended as thinking it very unkind from an intimate Acquaintance of the Sick Perſon, when ſoon after he heard a Noiſe as if two or three Men were landing a Coffin in the Room over his Head, which made him ſuſpect it to be a Forerunner of his Brother's Death, who departed this Life exactly at One o'Clock the next Day.

I could produce many Inſtances of the like Nature accompanied with very ſurpriſing Circumſtances, communicated to me by Perſons of reputed Veracity, but I rather wave being prolix on this Head, leaſt I ſhould be charged with a ridiculous Credulity by thoſe who disbelieve every Thing of this kind, and indeed I may fairly claim a Right to ſuſpend my Belief, ſince neither myſelf nor any of my Relations as far as I ever could learn, have at any Time experienced any ſuch Fore-bodings of Death.

WHAT has been ſaid concerning the general Salubrity of the Air of *Nottingham*, leads me naturally to the Conſideration of the Waters about this Town, for upon theſe depend very much the goodneſs and badneſs of the Air. And firſt, the *Trent*, beſides its convenient Diſtance, has a Courſe ſo rapid as will always preſerve its Sweetneſs, and prevent any noiſome Vapours to riſe from it. Between this and the River *Leen*, we have two Pools, the ſmallneſs and diſtance to which can no ways be injurious. As to the *Leen* which runs cloſe by *Nottingham* Caſtle, it lies at the Foot of the Town, and tho' it is ſlower in its Motion then the *Trent*, yet are not the Vapours thence ariſing capable of becoming hurtful, not only on Account of the great Height the Town ſtands above it, likewiſe becauſe of the Openneſs of the Ground below, which readily admits the Ventilation of the Wind to diſperſe all noxious Particles, and the few boggy Incloſures between this River and its back-Water, are by the prudent Care of the Corporation raiſed and made good Land. The Springs in general, of which, beſides the two principal ones taken Notice of in another Place, there is a very good one in a Cloſe called *Trough-Cloſe*, near *Mapperley* Hill, ſpringing out of the Side of a Rock, and two more in the two Coppices, there has alſo lately been diſcovered a pleaſant Spring under one of the Arches of the Town-Bridge. There is alſo a very good one in a Cloſe over againſt the Caſtle Rock. Theſe I ſay in general do participate very little of Salts or Sulphur, a Milky ſoftneſs which appears

by

by the Waters boiling and cooling almoſt as readily as any River Water, and alſo lathering with Soap. This Softneſs of the Springs in all Probability has in a greatMeaſure been the Cauſe why the *Nottingham* Tanners, have never been ſo much famed for Sole Leather as in ſome other neighbouring Places, where the Springs are harder. Of Springs impregnated with Medicinal Virtues, this Town is not altogether deſtitute, there is one call'd the *Nottingham* Spaw; this Spring riſes on the South-ſide of the River *Leen*, not far from the Engine Houſe; it has a ſtrong Chalybeat Aſtringency, and is a very heavy Water. There are beſides this Martial Water, two other Springs on the North-ſide of the Town, the one in a Cloſe called the *Beycroft*, the other in the next Cloſe beyond it, this laſt lies ſomewhat lower, and never fails, whilſt the firſt mentioned is ſometimes dry in Summer; both theſe have been very much cryed up, and have been frequented by Multitudes of People as excellent Eye-Waters. There were formerly, nay till within theſe 30 Years above 300 Wells in the Town of *Nottingham*, both public and private, of which tho' many of the publick ones, have ſince been ſtopped up, there are yet upwards of 200 in Uſe, and of great Service to the Town, (the Water of divers of theſe Wells is conſiderably harder than that of the Springs before mentioned,) eſpecially for Malting and Brewing. But that *Nottingham* might be more conveniently ſupply'd with River-Water, which was then brought up in Water Carts, and alſo with Pales, a Water-Engine was ſet on Foot by a private Company of Proprietors, this whole Undertaking being divided into 32 Shares. The Original Sharers, as in all new Projeĉts, met with many Difficulties, and found it very expenſive for ſome Years, before they could rightly bring it to bear, but of late is brought to a competent Perfeĉtion, ſo that they are in a Condition of ſupplying any part of *Nottingham*; the Eaſt-part of the Town has the Water immediately from the Engine, whilſt the Weſt-part receives it from a large Reſervoir made in that part of *Butt-Dyke* where the ancient Poſtern ſtood, mentioned in *Seĉt.* I. beſides this, leaſt at any Time, there ſhould be want of Water on Account of the River *Leen* being low, the Company Rent of his Grace the Duke of *Newcaſtle*, a large Pond in the Park, lying cloſe by the River, to which they have fixed Flood-Gates, ſerving in Time of Floods to let the Water in, and in Time of Scarcity, to furniſh Water enough to ſet the Engine to Work.

SO much for the Quality of the Waters, and the Conveniency they furniſh this Town with. As to the Courſe of the two Rivers, the Store of Fiſh they furniſh, and eſpecially what Advantage the *Trent* affords to the Trade of this Town, is reſerved for the 6th. and 7th. Seĉtions.

BEFORE I conclude this Article of Waters, I ſhall juſt touch upon what extraordinary Appearances, relating to them have happened here.

STOWE, in his ſummary of Chronicles p. 126, informs us: " That in the Year " 1110, the Water of the River *Trent* was dried up, at *Nottingham*, from One o'Clock " till Three : " And *Henry Knighton* Canon of *Leiceſter* ſays, " from the Morning " to Three o'Clock in the Afternoon." This laſt is quoted to very good purpoſe by Dr. *Plot*, in his Hiſtory of *Staffordſhire*, in ſupport of his well grounded Opinion : " That Springs are neither all, nor only, produced by Rains, but ſupply'd by the " Sea by ſubterraneous Meanders, and that by tranſcolation in their Paſſages, the " Water is filtrated and becomes freſh." He (*Knighton*) ſays: " This River " which riſes in *Staffordſhire*, did become dry of a ſudden at *Nottingham*, &c. and no " Queſtion, adds the Doĉtor, but it was ſo at other Places, which could not have hap-
" pened

" pened, had not the Springs been fupply'd by fubterraneous Paffages, which be-
" ing cafually ftopt by the Fall of Earth, could not furnifh Water, 'till fuch a Time as
" it could work its Way through the fallen Earth, or find fome other Paffage."

IT has been faid above, that the Luxuriance of *Nottingham* Meadows, is in great part owing to the Overflowing of the two Rivers which encompafs them, and that with very great Truth: But it muft be confeffed that Fortune feldom beftows her Favours in fo high Perfection as to leave no Room for Wifhes or Fears, fo has this o-therwife, great Benefit, been fometimes attended, tho' feldom, with Inconvenien-cies, I mean unfeafonable and great Floods: as in the Year 1713, and within my Time, in 1736, when the Flood was fo high in the Month of *July* at *Nottingham*, that in many of the Parlours in the Houfes near the *Leen*, the Water did rife upwards of 2 Feet above the Floor; this Flood carried away a great deal of Hay, fpoiled the reft and did otherwife a confiderable Damage

WE will now proceed and fee what kind of Ground there is about *Nottingham*: As the general Diftinction of the Land of the County is into Sand and Clay, as be-ing predominant, fo that of *Nottingham* is the fame, tho' there is all forts of Ground befides. The Meadows we have already been fpeaking of, and the Fields are fo plentifully enriched by the great Quantity of Dung and Afhes the Town affords, that there is no need to look for Marle and other kind of Manure. But as *Nottingham* receives a great Supply not only of Fewel and Materials for Building from its Neighbourhood, both by Water and at eafy Land Carriage, I hope it will not be thought altogether Fo-reign to my Purpofe, to take a View of what the County of *Nottingham* produces in the compafs of 12 Miles round about its Capital.

AND firft Pit-Coals, fince the almoft univerfal Deftruction of Wood in the Fo-reft, is become the only Fewel ufed here, for which End there are Coal-Mines within 3, 4, 6, & 7 Miles, North-Weft and Weft of this Town, which being work'd, furnifh to it Plenty of Coal, at a reafonable Rate, for they are never above 4d. to 6d. per Hundred unlefs when a wet Winter Seafon has made the Roads very bad, for which great Advantage *Nottingham* owes an everlafting Gratitude to the Memory of the Late, and the Perfon and Family, of the Right Honourable the prefent Lord *Middleton*.

THE Coals of this Country, tho' they do give Way to thofe which come from *Newcaftle* to *London*, in durablenefs, and confequently are not altogether equal to thofe for culinary Ufes, yet for Chambers and other Ufes, they exceed them, ma-king both a fweeter and a brisker Fire, and confidering the difference in Price, thefe are divers ways preferable: A Chaldron of Coals which fhould weigh full a Tun Weight, is at the cheapeft at *London*, in the Pool, 1 *l*. 3 *s*. befides Carriage, where-as the deareft, *i. e.* at fix-pence per Hundred, we have a Tun of our Coals brought to the Door for 10 Shillings. The Coak or Cynder which is ufed in the drying of Malt, and which is fold at 1 *s*. and 4 *d*. per Horfe Load is much fweeter than that made of the *Yorkfhire* Coal, which appears in that the *Nottingham* Malt has hardly any of that particular Tafte, which the *Yorkfhire* Malt communicates to the beft of their Ale.

AS

A S to Materials for Building, the Clay-Land about *Nottingham*, has caufed many Brick-Kilns to be fet up, fo near the Town, as to make the Carriage not to exceed 3 *s*. and 6 *d*. per Thoufand, and yet at a Diftance fufficient to give no Annoyance to it. Thefe Kilns afford :

Common Brick, at 10 *s*.   ⎫
Dreffed Brick, at 17 *s*.   ⎬ per 1000.
Flat Tiles, at 15 *s*.   ⎪
Pan Tiles, at 1 *l*. 10 *s*.   ⎭

T H E Freeftone ufed here, is moftly fetched from *Mansfield*, 12 Miles from hence. But there is Stone at *Gedling*, 4 little Miles from *Nottingham* not unlike the *Bath* Stone, for it is foft and works fine and eafy, and ftands well in the Air, where it hardens, and is rather nourifhed than decay'd by it : Notwithftanding all this, not much of this *Gedling* Stone, is employ'd in the Buildings of this Town.

LINBY, Papplewick, Bulwell, Nuthall, &c. of which the moft diftant does not exceed fix Miles, furnifhes Plenty of Lime, burnt of the gray Lime-ftone. [*a*]

CROPWELL, Ratcliff, and *Gotham,* at no greater Diftance, afford a kind of Plaifter, little inferiour to the Plaifter of *Paris*, which ferves to make very good Plaifter-Floors, very much in Ufe here.

T H O S E whofe Affluence of Fortune will allow them to decorate the infide of their Houfes with Marble, may be fupply'd with divers forts of almoft all Colours, by our Neighbour the County of *Derby*, which in fome Places falls little fhort of the Foreign, and comes cheaper beyond Proportion.

O A K-Timber, tho' at this Time it will not allow the People to be fo lavifh as to wafte it as former Ages have done, yet according to the prefent manner of Building, we want not a neceffary Quantity about us, the Property of private Gentlemen, of whom it may be purchafed at reafonable Rates, and as to what Wood is ufed of Foreign Product the *Trent* conveys hither by the way of *Hull*.

T H E R E is a great Quantity of Iron-Stone in this Neighbourhood, but as the Iron Manufacture is fhifted from hence, very little Oar is now got, to what there was a Century or two ago ; however there is ftill one Forge a going at *Bulwell*, about 4 Miles from *Nottingham*.

P A V I N G-Stone, which formerly ufed to be got out of the *Trent*, is now plentifully brought hither from *Keyworth*, and other parts not far diftant.

A M O N G this kind of Stone there are frequently found in the Road and upon the Foreft, fome which are diverfify'd with two or more Colours, and mark'd with a
beau-

[*a*] *There has alfo Limeftone been difcovered lately, fo near as* Wollaton, *as alfo a kind of ftrong Potter's Clay, and between this Town and* Efply, *fome Chalk, not common in this County.*

beautiful Variety of Spots and Veins, this has been lately taken Notice of by some Persons of Leisure, who by their Example have considerably increased the Number of Stone Admirers, and this new Fancy, is within these two Years, grown upon several of them to that Degree, that it may be called a *Lithomania*.

A S to formed Stones, this County must give way to *Staffordshire*.

I F we cast an Eye on the Vegetables, which Nature here spontaneously produces, the Soil about *Nottingham* may justly be called a Physic Garden, abounding in great Variety of useful Plants, as may be easily seen by the *Catalogus Stirpium*, published by me in the Year 1738, to which I shall refer my Reader, I shall in this Place only set down what scarce Plants, both of the imperfect and perfect kind are met with hereabout, more frequently than elsewhere.

FUNGUS's.

Fungoides clavatum coloris aurantii: not in the *Synopsis*. It is exactly of the shape of the *Pistillum* of *Aron*.

Fungoides clavatum compressum summitatibus luteis: not in the *Synopsis*. This has white and somewhat flat Foot-stalks, the Tops of which are of a pale Yellow, are spread thin and wrinkly, the whole is of a soft spungy Substance.

Fungoides minimum fusco luteum dignitatum apicibus obtucis albis: not in the *Synopsis*. It is not quite an Inch long of a brownish Yellow Colour, sending forth very short Branches, which terminate in round white Knobs.

Fungi Clathroides nigri pediculis donati. *Dr. Dillenius*: Not in the *Synopsis*. These grow in Clusters, are of the Size, Shape and Colour, of Mouse-Turds, having on the Top a little oblique Awn, and at the Bottom, a short Foot-stalk not much thicker than an Horse-Hair.

Fungus favaginosus. *Syn.* 11 *Park*. *Rugosus vel cavernosus sive merulius*. J. B. The *Morel*.

Fungus Phalloydes. *Syn.* 12. J. B. *Virilis Penis arreoti facie*. Ger. *Stink Horn*.

Fungus pulverulentus coli instar perforatus cum volva Stellata Dood. Syn. 28. *Stelliformis Merr. Pin. Lycoperdon vesicarium Stellatum Inst.* R. H.

Byssus aureus Derbiensis humifusus. Syn. 56. found in the Stone Wall of *Colwick* Church. Saffron colour'd silken Stone-moss.

Byssus fusco-purpuria petræa gelatinam referens. Not in the *Synopsis*.

Byssus petræa galatinam referens nigerrima. Not in the *Synopsis*.

Ulva marina tenuissima et compressa. Syn. 63.

Lichenoides crustaceum peregrinis velut literis in Scriptum. Syn. 71.

Lichenoides crustaceum nigerrimum e meris papillis conflatum. Not in the *Synopsis*.

N

Lich.

Lichenoides fufco nigricans membranaceum gelatinofum majus folus latioribus Lichenis inftar difpofitus. Not in the *Synopfis.*

Bryum trichoides aurium capfulis pyriformebus nutantibus. Dr. *Dillenius* to whom I fent it ; this Mofs is mentioned by Nobody that I know of ; I found it in *Nottingham* Park, growing to the Roof of one of the Rock-Holes, it bears Heads in *May.*

Caryophyllus minor repens noftras. *Syn.* 335,

An Virginius Ger. Common here.

Lychnis fylveftris, alba nona Clufii. Syn. 339. Wild white *Catchfly* ; on the Wall of *Nottingham* Caftle-Yard, and on the Rock at *Sneinton* Hermitage plentifully.

Colchium commune. Syn. 373. *Meadow Saffron,* in *Nottingham* Meadows, efpecially on the Rye-Hills, and on both fides the Foot-path, going to *Wilford*, in Abundance.

Gramen tremulum medium albis glumis non defcriptum. In a hollow Lane between *Pleafley* and *Mansfield.*

Verbafcum pulverulentuno flore tureo parvo. J. B. Syn. 287. On a Wall in *Sheep-Lane, Nottingham*, alfo on the outfide of the Garden Walls on the Rock of the *High-Pavement.*

Petafites major floribus longis pediculis infidentibus. Syn. 179. In the Mill-Yard at *Lenton,* in the Road to *Wollaton.*

S E C T.   V

SECTION V.

Of the TRADE and MANUFACTURIES of this Town, in former, as well as the prefent Time ; a particular Account of the *Stocking-Manufactury*, to which is added a LIST of all the *Handicrafts* and other *Employments* exercifed in *Nottingham*.

IT appears plainly by *Doomfday-Book*, that the River *Trent* was Navigable before the Conqueft, whence there is no doubt, but that a good Share of Trade, was carried on, between *Nottingham* and other Places by Water, Time immemorial, the which, after the Conqueft has been increafing proportionably to the Increafe of Trade in general, 'till this prefent Time, when this Town is plentifully fupply'd by the *Trent* at a moderate Freight with Bar-Iron, Block-Tin, Wines, Oyls, Grocer's Goods, Salt, Pitch, Tar, Hops, Hemp, Flax, Dye Drugs, Deals, Norway Oak, and all forts of other Foreign Wood ; whilft *Nottingham* fends down the River, Coals, Lead, Timber, Corn, Wool, Potter's-Ware, and large Quantities of *Chefhire*, *Warwickfhire*, and *Staffordfhire* Cheefe.

THAT the Trade to and from this Town by Land-Carriage is confiderably advanced for this laft Century is manifeft in this, that in the Year 1641, there were but two, and now there are nine Carriers in this Town, befides thofe who pafs through it.

OUR *Nottingham* Shopkeepers till within thefe 60 Years laft paft, did not venture to go long Journies, but depended upon the great annual *Martin-mafs* Fair at *Lenton*, (a) a Village about a Mile diftant from *Nottingham*, where they ufed to buy

their

N 2

(a) *The ancient Fair of* Lenton, *was granted to the Monaftery of the Holy-Trinity of* Lenton, *by* Henry I. *to be held at the Feaft of St.* Martin, *and to laft eight Days : That No-body fhould buy or fell in* Nottingham *during that Time, and returning, every one fhould be free from Law Procefs or Plaints.* Thor. *fr.* Reg. Lent. p. 218.

The Manor of Lenton, *with the Fair and all the Royalties and Priviledges, Rents and Services was purchafed by* William Gregory, *the 6th* Car. I. *for* 2500 l. *referving the Fee Farm Rent of* 94 l. *per Annum to the faid King and his Heirs and Succeffors, who by Letters, Patents, dated* Dec. 16, *in the 13th Year of his Reign, among other Things, did grant the faid Fee-farm Rent of* 94 l. *per Ann. to the Right Noble* James Stuart, *Duke of* Richmond *and* Lenox, *who by his In-*

den

their Mercers, Drapers, Grocers, and all sorts of Goods they wanted, brought thither by the *Londoners*, and others ; and when first they attempted to Travel to *London*, they would take Leave of their Relations and Friends (as I am informed) in as much Form as if they were never to see them more, and many before they set out, did settle their Houses and make their Wills : But now they are no more concerned at going to the Metropolis and other distant Trading and Manufactury Towns, then they were formerly to go a Journey of 12 or 20 Miles. This late Spirit has given them an Opportunity of buying their Commodities at the best Hand, and contributed much to the Increase of the Number of Wholesale Dealers in *Nottingham*, whilst *Lenton* Fair is dwindled to a very inconsiderable Market. Besides the Country Grocers, or as they were wont to be called (Mercers) from *Mansfield, Loughborough, Mountsorrel, &c.* who used to fill a good part of our Spice-Chamber every Saturday, finding that the Grocers of *Nottingham*, were not only in a Condition to supply our Town and County, but able to furnish several neighbouring Shires, have since thought it needless to bring their Goods hither.

THE first Manufacture which flourished in the Town of *Nottingham*, was established before the Reign of King *John*, who encouraged by his Charter bearing Date *March* 19, 1199, wherein all Persons within 10 Miles round *Nottingham*, are forbidden to Work Dy'd Cloth but in the *Borough*.

THIS Manufacture took its Progress from Time to Time, till the Removal of the Staple of Wool to *Calais*, after which Time it obtained its greatest Lustre, and gave Rise to many considerable Families in the Town and County, as the *Bugges*, the *Bingham*'s, the *Willoughbies, Tannesley, Mappurley, Thurland, Amyas, Atlestree, Samon's, Plumptre's* the *Hunt's*, and others, all Merchants of the Staple of *Calais* ; in this prosperous State the Woollen Manufacture continued till the Reign of Queen *Mary* I. when *Calais* was lost, and then it gradually went off, till at last it entirely left this Place. *(b)*

THE Malting Business, may reasonably be conjectured to be in this Town as early as in any part of *England* equally well seated for it ; since the greatest and best part of *Nottingham*, was from the beginning of the Conquest inhabited by *Normans*, who were the first that introduced Malt-Liquor into this Kingdom, as well as the making of Cyder. How extensive and profitable this Branch of Trade has been for several Ages to this Town, who enjoy'd it long without any Competitor, in the Midland part of this Realm, I have already hinted in another Place. Dr. *Thoroton*, expresses himself of the State of the Malt Trade in his Time thus : " *p. 492. col. 1.* " Since the late Civil War there are many Houses new built, and the greatest part of
the

---

denture bearing Date Feb. 20, 1651, *for the Sum of* 1460 *l. sold the same to* John Gregory, *Son and Heir of the said* William Gregory, *and to his Son* George Gregory, *who in the* 15*th* Ch. II. *Nov.* 9. *obtained Letters, Patents, for another Fair, to be kept at* Lenton, *every Year on the Wednesday after Penticost, and to last six Days.* id. p. 219.

(b) *The Merchants of the Staple, were one of the most ancient Companies of Merchants in* England, *incorporated by King* Edward III. *the Wool Staple being then at* Calais. *They bore for their Arms* : Nebule *of six Pieces* A. *&* Az. *on a Chief* G. *a Lion of* England. Guilim's *Heraldry.* Edit. 6.

" the good Barley which grows in the Vale of *Belvoir*, and the Parts adjacent, are
" there (at *Nottingham*) converted into Malt, yielding thereby, (as I fuppofe) more
" Profit to the Place, than ever Wool did heretofore. ——And tho' of late Years, the
modern Improvement of Land has made fome Neighbouring Towns Sharers, yet may
it be faid with Truth, that even now, this Trade is not inconfiderable, the Malt-
fters of *Nottingham* only, paying one Sitting with another, One Thoufand Pounds
Excife.

B U T the Doctor is greatly miftaken, when in the fame Page and Column, he
affirms, that *Nottingham*, fince the Decay of the Cloth Fabrick, has had no beneficial Trade ; for the Tanners were once, a wealthy and powerful fet of Men in this
Town, and of a long ftanding, which I Conjecture to be upwards of two hundred
Years at leaft, in which I am confitmed by a Deed bearing Date *February* 18, in the
37th Year of King *Henry* VIII. whereby, " The Mayor and Burgeffes oblige them-
" felves to *William Sharpington*, *James Mafon*, *John Renell*, *John Gregorie*, and
" *Thomas Sibthorpe*, Tanners, to pay to them and their Succeffors, Tanners of *Not-*
" *tingham*, for ever, an Annuity of Forty Shillings.

T H E Tanners were once very numerous here, and their Habitations as well as
their Pits, were formerly difperfed all other the Town, both in the higher and lower Parts, within and without the Wall ; I will give but one Inftance, of the Truth of
which any one may be eafily fatisfied, *i. e.* That the Houfe of Mr. *Thomas Coates*,
Attorney at Law, in St. *Peter's* Church-yard, was formerly inhabited by a Tanner
the Marks are yet vifible. Our Tanners were long famed for the beft Upper Lea-
thers for Shoes and Boots, as alfo Harneffes, and for covering Coaches and Chaifes.
The Mafters of this Trade, were in 1641, ftill 36 in Number ; in the Year 1664,
they were 47, and even within thefe 40 Years, to wit, 1707, there were 21, fince
which Time they are dwindled to the Number of three who follow Bufinefs. It is a
difficult Matter to Account for this fudden decreafe of the Men of this Occupation,
fome lay it upon the fcarcity of the Bark near the Town, but this compared with the
advanced Price of Leather, to what it was, when there was more Plenty of Bark in the
Neighbourhood is not a Reafon fatisfactory enough ; others with more Probability al-
ledge : That the Tanners holding together, like the *London* Melters of Tallow and
Hornes, againft the Butchers, to fet the Price of Hides and Skins at their own Rate,
has invited thofe of other Towns and Counties to come to our Market, and give a
better price for that Sort of Goods, and has even made it worth while to our Butchers to carry their Hides and Skins into fome parts of *Leicefterfhire* and *Derbyfhire*,
and that this has been the chief Caufe of the fhifting of this Trade to other
Places.

B E F O R E the Cloth Manufacture was quite decay'd, *Vulcan* fet up his Office
in this Town, and the Plenty of Coals and Iron-Oar, invited Plenty of all forts of
Workmen in Iron to fettle here, efpecially fuch as made Articles for the Ufe of Sad-
ers, and alfo afterwards Inftruments of Husbandry, (as my *Anonymous* of *Nottingham*
informs me) who liv'd near the middle of the laft Century, and fays, that that Manufacture was ftill in fome Degree carried on in his Time : And the Names of feveral
Streets in *Nottingham*, denote the Artificers that formerly inhabited them, fince this

Trade

Trade has moved its Seat to *Birmingham* and *Sheffield*, it has been succeeded by a much cleanlier Employment.

THE Bone-Lace Trade, by which great Numbers of Females were constantly employ'd, 'till within these 35 Years, when all these Hands were more advantageously taken up by a fresh Manufacture, which has ever since comfortably maintained, besides these Females, above thrice their Number of Men; I mean the Manufacture of Frame-worked Stockings: Of which, as it is at this Time of the greatest Importance to this Town, and as it well deserves it, a more particular Account shall be given, after I have laid before the Reader a Table which represents to his View the Increase and Decrease of all the Trades and Employments exercised in this Town since the Year 1641.

A TABLE of Trades and Employments, exercised in the Town of *Nottingham*, with the Numbers of Masters of each, compared with a List of the Year 1641.

A	List.	Old.	New.
Apothecaries.	—	4	5
Attorneys.	—	—	15
B.			
Bakers.	—	22	40
Bankers.	—	0	1
Barbers.	—	6	30
Basket-makers.	—	6	4
Bell-Founders.	—	2	1
Bird-Cage-makers.	—	0	1
Bleachers of Linnen Cloth.	8	1	
Bleachers of Cotton Hose and Gloves.	—	0	2
Booksellers.	—	2	3
Brass-Founders.	—	0	2
Brasiers.	—	3	3
Bricklayers.	—	—	11
Butchers.	—	61	—
Button-makers.	—	0	3
C.			
Cabinetmakers & Joyners.	7	24	
Carpenters and House-Joyners.	—	7	7
Carriers.	—	7	9
Chandlers.	—	14	10
Clothworkers.	—	4	0
Coach-makers.	—	0	1
Collar-makers.	—	4	3

	List.	Old.	New.
Confectioners.	—	0	1
Coopers.	—	4	7
Cork-cutters.	—	0	1
Counsellors.	—	—	1
Curriers.	—	6	4
Cutlers.	—	3	3
D.			
Distillers.	—	0	3
Drapers { Woollen.	3	3	
Drapers { Linnen.	—	2	
Druggists.	—	0	3
Dry-Salters.	—	0	1
Dyers.	—	3	3
F.			
Fellmongers.	—	9	2
Fishmongers. See Ironmongers.	—	—	
File-cutters.	—	0	1
Flax-dressers.	—	—	
Fletchers.	—	1	0
Framesmiths.	—	0	14
Framework-Knitters.	—	2	50
Free-Masons.	—	3	—
Fruiterers.	—	4	—
G.			
Gardiners.	—	5	20
Glaziers.	—	14	9

Glass-

	Lift. Old	New		Lift. Old	New
Glafs-makers.	0	1	Rope-makers.	13	2
Glovers & Breechesmakers	17	12	**S.**		
Goldfmith-Shops.	1	3	Sadlers.	4	7
Grocers.	4	—	Setters-up of Frames.	0	8
H.			Shoemakers.	26	30
Haberdafhers of Hats.	4	4	Silk-Weavers.	2	0
Haberdafhers of Hardware	0	3	Sinker-makers.	0	5
Hair-pickers.	0	4	Skinners.	1	0
I.			Fire-Smiths.	0	3
Inn-holders.	14	41	Soapboylers.	0	4
Iron-Founders.	0	1	Stay-makers.	0	4
Iron-mongers.	16	4	Stocking-makers. See }	0	
L.			Framework-Knitters. }		
Leadworks } Red. } White.	0	1	Stocking-needle-makers.	—	12
M.			Stocking-Trimmers.	0	1
Maltfters.	60	40	Stone-Cutters.	0	1
Mafons. See Stonecutters.	—	—	Spurriers.	3	0
Mat-makers.	1	2	Surgeons.	0	3
Mercers.	4	12	**T.**		
Millers.	0	1	Tanners.	36	3
Milliners.	0	3	Taylors.	28	52
N.			Tinmen.	0	2
Nailers.	0	1	Tobacco-pipe-makers.	1	4
Needle-makers.	0	1	Toy-fhops.	0	3
P.			Turners.	2	3
Printers.	1	2	Tile- and Brickmakers.	4	10
Painters.	2	3	**V. U.**		
Parchment-makers.	4	0	Vintners.	6	—
Paviours.	0	2	Upholders.	3	2
Phyficians.	0	6	**W.**		
Pin-makers.	4	1	Weavers of Linnen Cloth.	19	5
Plaifterers.	7	12	Wheelwrights.	5	2
Plumbers.	4	*	Wooden-heel-makers.	4	2
Point-makers.	2	0	Woodmongers.	1	—
Pot-makers.	1	2	Wool-combers. *	0	3
Pot-houfes or Ale-houfes.	—	91			
R.					

The New Lift was taken
in the Year 1739.

* The Glaziers are alfo Plumbers
here

* The Woolcombers alfo employ Frames.

Some Remarks on the preceeding TABLE.

THE old Lift counts four Apothecaries, at prefent there are five, who notwith-ftanding the Inhabitants are increafed fome Thoufands, make a fhift with three Sur-geons to ferve the whole Town, hardly leaving room for one Phyfician to gain gen-teel Bread, tho' there are fix of that Profeffion in the Town. Dr. *Thoroton*, p. 498. fpeaking of Alderman *John Parker*, the Apothecary, fays : "Of which Trade, (*viz.* "Apothecaries) there were lately above twenty more than formerly have been, "when the Gains and Employments were greater." Indeed I have known Seven, within thefe five Years, but according to the Doctor, there muft in his Time have been four or five and Twenty, if fo, it is furprizing how fo great a Number could gain a Livelyhood ; when the Town was much lefs peopled than at prefent.

THE above Lift does not mention Phyficians, tho' at the Time it was made, there was at leaft one, whom the Author names on a very particular Occafion, *viz.* Dr. *Atkinfon*, but there was alfo Dr. *Alton* in his Time, fucceeded by Dr. *Jofeph Gar-diner*, who died in 1669 ; neither do I find Counfellors inferted, tho' this Town has feldom fince his Time been without one or more. Attorneys are alfo omitted, tho' it feems very unlikely that fuch a Trading Town of *Nottingham* fhould have been defti-tute of fome of this Fraternity ; the Author's not taking Notice of them, makes it probable that there were but few in his Days, however they are very much increafed fince.

NO Bricklayer is mentioned in the old Lift, whether there was none at that Time in the Town, (Brick-Buildings being then not common,) or whether the Plai-fterers did what little of that fort of Work was to be done, I will not prefume to de-cide, but I conjecture that when he fpeaks of Free-Mafons, he does not mean what we now call your Free and accepted Mafons, but either Mafons or Stone-cutters, be-caufe it was then newly come into Fafhion, to have Stone Window Frames, or elfe Bricklayers, who very likely worked both in Brick and Stone, as they now in this Town, all do.

THE Basket-makers are indeed decreafed in this Town, but many live in the neighbouring Villages, who make not only common Work, but are fam'd all over *England* for the curiofity of their Workmanfhip in Wicker-Ware.

THAT the People of *Nottingham* have always been great Eaters of Flefh, ap-pears, in that, the Butchers are not much increafed within thefe hundred Years, but keep pretty near to the Number, which is (I muft own) fufficient to furnifh the Mar-ket with Meat for five Times the People, which come to Market ; nor can it be af-firmed that the Country Butchers which frequent the Saturday Market, make an Ad-dition, for they ufe to come formerly as well as now. The Butchers here have great Advantages, as being Burgeffes, in point of Tolls, and alfo Common for Sheep, &c. many begin with very little, yet being induftrious, they live well, and get a comfor-table Maintainance.

I

I have already mentioned the Carriers, here I fhall name them particularly, and the Days of their going out and coming in : And firft there are three Waggons which Weekly fet out from hence, early on Tuefday Morning, for *London*, and return on Friday inthe Evening.

THE *York*-Carrier, goes out on Tuefday and comes in on Saturday.

THE *Leicefter*-Carrier, goes out on Monday and comes in on Tuefday, and goes out again on Thurfday and returns on Friday.

THE *Mansfield*-Carrier, comes in on Wednefday and Saturday, and returns back the fame Days.

THE *Derby*-Carrier, comes in on Wednefday and Friday, and returns the fame Days.

THE *Melton*-Carrier, comes in on Friday and returns on Saturday.

THE *Loughborough* Carrier, comes in on Wednefday and Friday, and returns the fame Day.

THE *Southwell*-Carrier, comes in on Wednefday and Friday, and returns the fame Day.

THE *Leeds*, *Sheffield* and *Chefterfield*-Carrier, comes in on Tuefday, and returns on Wednefday.

THE *Lincoln* and *Bofton*-Carrier, goes out on Monday and returns on Tuefday, and goes out again on Friday.

THE *Alfreton*-Carrier, comes in on Friday and returns on Saturday.
THE *Manchefter*-Carrier comes in on Friday and returns on Saturday.
THE *Briftol* Carrier, comes in on Wednefday and returns immediately.

THE *Birmingham*-Carrier, comes in on Wednefday and returns on Thurfday.
THE *Bewdley*-Carrier, comes in every other Wednefday and returns on Thurfday.

CURRIERS and Fellmongers are decreafed, probably for the fame Reafon mentioned concerning the Tanners.

BY Fifh-mongers, whom the Lift alfo calls Iron-mongers, are meant Wholefale Dealers in Salt-Fifh, which was a branch of Trade chiefly purfued by the Iron-mongers.

THERE were very few Gardiners more, after the Reftoration than before the Civil-War, and all thofe but very indifferently fkill'd in their Art, till after the Arrival of Marfhal Count *Tallard*, and the reft of the French Prifoners of War, (who were Perfons of Rank) in *Nottingham*, when Encouragement was given to Men of Induftry to render themfelves ufeful, by raifing all kinds of Garden Stuff, in which now they are come to a competent Perfection, and notwithftanding they are increafed to above four Times the Number they were formerly, yet can they all get their

O

Bread

Bread, and in Summer Peafe and Beans would be hardly fold at a reafonable Rate, were it not that the *Newark* Gardiners think it worth their while to come to this Market, twelve long computed Miles.

OUR Bakers have likewife reaped the Advantage of making French-Rolls, as well as they are made in *London*.

AS the old Lift takes no Notice of Linnen-Drapers, I judge that the Mercers then dealt alfo in Linnen.

THERE are no Skinners at prefent in *Nottingham*, tho' it is manifeft, that fome of that Bufinefs did formerly live here, from the Form of the Bridge-Mafters paffing their Accounts, where among other Articles which they receive for the Repairs of the Bridge there is to this Day fet down the following :

Upfets of ⎰ Mercers.
⎱ Taylors.
⎰ Skinners. &
⎱ Cordwainers.

Perfons of that Trade deal in Skins dreffed with the Hair or Wool on, and all kinds of Furs, and I am apt to believe they ufed to live in a Street called *Pilchergate* ; this Name I take to be derived from the Teutonick Word *Peltz*, which fignifies a Fur-Gown or a Fur-Lining ; this might eafily be corrupted into *Pelch*, (as we have an Inftance in the Word *Leafe*, which the Town's People here commonly pronounce *Leafh*) thence *Peltzer* or corruptly *Pelcher*, a Dealer in thefe Goods, and as the found of an *i* before two or three Confonants is nearly the fame with that of an *e*, the Orthography may infenfibly have altered in one Letter, and turned *Pelchergate* into *Pilchergate*.

OF Smiths I have already fpoken above, and taken Notice that the Manufacturing of Iron, is the next oldeft to that of Cloth and Malt, extending not only to the rougher Sort of Workmanfhip, but being famous for the moft curious Part of that Manufacture, which probably may have given Birth to the Proverb : *The little Smith of Nottingham, that does the Work that no Man can.* Mr. *Ray* accounts for it in Manner following :

(*a*) " WHO this little Smith and great Workman was, and when he lived, I
" know not, and have caufe to fufpect that this of *Nottingham* is a Periphrafis, of
" *nemo ꝛτιϛ*, a Perfon who never was. By way of Sarcafm it is apply'd
" to fuch who being conceited of their own Skill pretend to the Atchievement of
" Impoffibilities."

Mr. *Ray*, very probably might not be informed that this Town was once as famous for Hard-Ware of all kinds, as *Birmingham* and *Sheffield* are at prefent, and that therefore very likely, there might be a little Fellow in *Nottingham*, who might fo far excel others in his Branch of Work as to give occafion to this Proverb, which at firft may have been apply'd to Perfons excelling many others in their refpective Handycrafts, tho' it is now ufed by way of Sarcafm, nor is this the only Proverb which

(*a*) *Ray's Proverbs.*

THE STOCKING FRAME

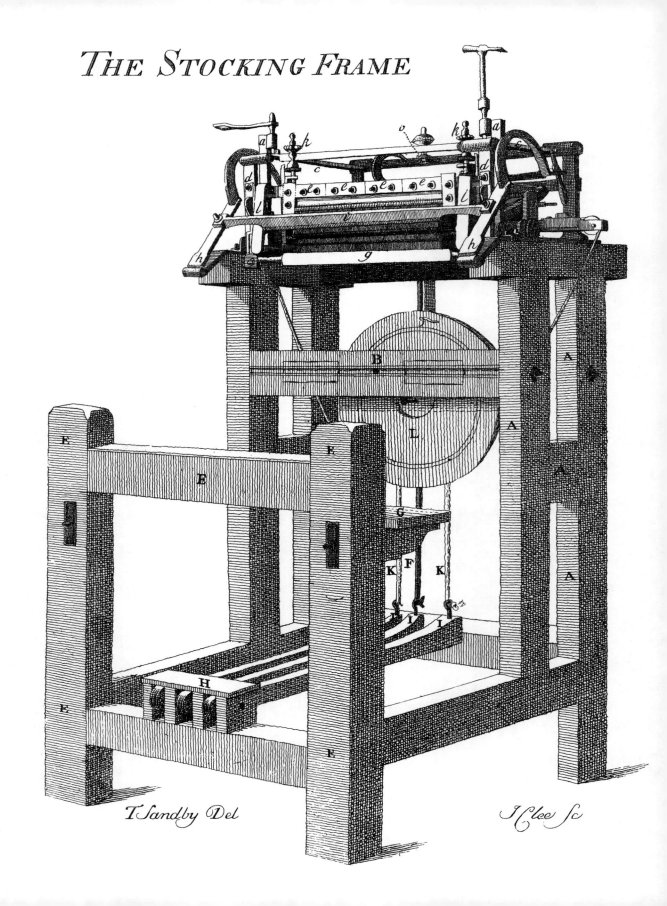

T. Sandby Del.   I. Clee Sc.

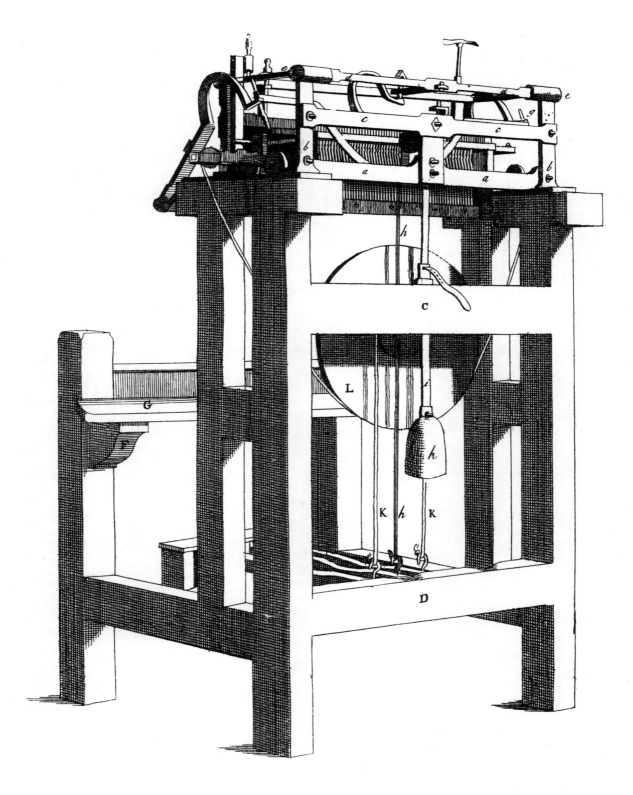

which at this Time is made Ufe of in a contrary Senfe, for we fay: *He has din'd with Duke Humphrey, i. e.* he has had no Dinner at all, altho' the Prince who occafion'd the Proverb, was univerfally allowed to be the moft hofpitable Perfon in all *England.* The Proverb of the little Smith muft be of feveral hundred Years ftanding, fince it is upwards of an hundred Years ago, that the Iron Manufacture has ceafed to be the principal Manufacture of *Nottingham:* However even at this Time, this Town affords extraordinary Workmen, fubfervient to the Stocking-Manufacture, I mean Frame-Smiths, which tho' they have not been able to add any effential Article to that Machine, yet have they greatly improved the fame, by finishing it to a greater Truth, and altering feveral of the conftituent Parts of the Stocking-Frame, for the greater Eafe of the Workmen, and the better Performance of the Work.

AS to *Spurriers* there have (as ancient People affure me) not been any in *Nottingham* thefe Forty Years.

TILERS and *Brickmakers* I have joined in the Lift together, as being properly one Bufinefs, and the Author of the Old Lift, calling them Tilers, wasbecaufe the making of Tiles was in his Time the principal Article of that Trade.

AT this Time we have no Vintners properly fo called, and yet I cannot help thinking, that confiderably more Wine is drank in *Nottingham* than was an hundred Years ago, for we have two Wine Merchants in the Town, three Wine Vaults who fell by Retail, and befides thefe all the great Inns fell Wine as well as other Liquors.

Of the Origin, Progrefs, and Prefent State of the MANUFACTURE of *Frame-work'd Stockings,* and other Goods wrought in a FRAME.

THE Inventor of the Stocking-Frame was one Mr. *William Lee,* M. A. of St. *John's* College, in *Cambridge,* born at *Woodborough,* a Village in *Nottinghamfhire,* about feven Miles from the Town of *Nottingham.* He was Heir to a pretty Freehold Eftate; of whom the traditional Story fays: That he was deeply in Love with a young Townfwoman of his, whom he courted for a Wife, but fhe whenever he went to Vifit her, feemed always more mindful of her Knitting, than the Addreffes of her Admirer; this flight created fuch an Averfion in Mr. *Lee,* againft knitting by Hand, that he determined to contrive a Machine, that fhould turn out Work enough to render the common Knitting a gainlefs Employment: Accordingly he fet about it, and having an excellent mechanical Head, he brought his Defign to bear, in the Year 1589; after he had worked a while, he taught his Brother and feveral Relations to Work under him. Having for fome Years practifed this his new Art, at *Calverton,* a Village about five Miles from *Nottingham;* either himfelf or his Brother *James,* worked before Queen *Elizabeth,* in order to fhew an Experiment of this Kind of Workmanfhip, offering at the fame Time this Difcovery of his to his Countrymen, who inftead of accepting the offer, defpifed him, and difcouraged his Invention: Being thus difcountenanced by his Native Country, and foon after invited over to *France* with Promife of great Rewards, Priviledges and Honour, by King *Henry* IV. he embraced the feeming fair Opportunity, and went himfelf, with nine Workmen his Servants, and as many Frames, to the City of *Roan* in *Normandy,* where

they

they wrought with so great Applause from the *French*, that in all Likelihood the Trade was to have been settled in that Country for ever, had not the sudden Murder of that Monarch disappointed Mr. *Lee*, of his expected Grant of Priviledge, and the succeeding intestine Troubles of that Kingdom, delay'd his renew'd Suit, and at last frustrated all his Hopes, at which seized with Grief, he ended his Life at *Paris*. After his Death seven of his Workmen, (being left to shift for themselves) returned with their Frames to *England*, two only remaining behind.

THESE seven with one(*a*) *Afton*, who had been an Apprentice to Mr. *Lee*, and by him was before left at Home, and who also added something to his Master's Invention, did lay the Foundation of this Manufacture in *England*, and in the space of Fifty Years, this Art was so improved, and the Number of able Workmen become so great; That the Heads among them thought it necessary for the better regulating their Members, and keeping this valuable Business from spreading Abroad, to petition *Oliver Cromwell*, to constitute them a Body Corporate, which however, for what Reason I cannot tell, they did not obtain at that Time. Their Petition is wrote in the Language of the Time, but with so much Strength, and giving so good an Account of the Usefulness and publick Advantage of this Manufacture, that it deserves perpetuating, wherefore I have given it a Place in my *Appendix*.

KING *CHARLES* II. after the Restoration granted them at last a Charter, by which their Jurisdiction extended to Ten Miles round *London*.

IN process of Time, when the Trade spread farther into the Country, they also in proportion stretch'd their Authority and established Commissioners in the several principal Towns in the County where this Trade was exercised, there they held Courts, at which they obliged the Country Framework-Knitters, to Bind and make Free, &c. whereby, they, (for many Years) drew great Sums of Money, till some Person of more Spirit than others in *Nottingham* brought their Authority in Question and a Trial ensuing, the Company was cast, since that Time the Stocking Manufacture has continued entirely open in the Country.

NOR did these large Sums do the Company any Service as a Body, for as they got the Money illegally, so they spent it as lavishly, and instead of growing rich, the Company became very poor; and many of their Heads having got a Taste of highLiving and neglecting their Business also dwindled to nothing. To which add that within these thirty Years last past, the Merchants and Hosiers in *London*, finding they could be fitted from the Country with as good Work at a cheaper Rate than the *London* Framework-Knitters could afford; the Bulk of that Trade has since shifted from thence, and the chief Dependance they had left, was upon what is called Fashion-Work, it being for many Years the Mode to wear Stockings of the same Colour of the Cloaths, and this also, being by Degrees left off, what remains now in *London*, does hardly deserve the Name of Trade.

THERE are besides the Capital of *England*, ten Towns in the Country where this Manufacture is carried on : *viz.* In

Not-

(*a*) *This* Afton, *was sometime a Miller at* Thoroton, *near which Place he was born.* Thoroton. *p.* 297.

Nottinghamfhire	{	Nottingham,
		Mansfield.
In Leicefterfhire	{	Leicefter,
		Mount-Sorrel,
		Loughborough,
		Hinckley, &
		Afhby-de-la-Zouch.
In Northamptonfhire,		Towcefter.
In Surrey		Godliman.
In Derbyfhire,		Derby.

OF all thefe none comes in Competition with *Leicefter* for Quantity of Goods, but even this very Town, tho' it may boaft of its large Concerns, yet muft confefs, that its beft Goods are made at

Nottingham, where by far the greateft part of the richeft and moft valuable Commodity, whether of Silk, Cotton, Thread or Worfted, is wrought, and it feems this fo profitable Employment, as it were by a magnetical Force, is in the Height of its improved State, drawn towards the Place of its Birth, in order to make it ample Amends for deferting it in its Infancy. Thus much fhall fuffice for the Hiftory of Framework-Knitting, which having brought me Home, I fhall now endeavour to fhew of what Importance it is to *Nottingham*.

THERE are, as per Lift, Fifty Manufacturers, Employers of Frames, or as they are commonly call'd Putters out, who all Trade directly to *London*, befides thofe who only deal with *Leicefter* : Both together occupy above 3000 Frames, of which upwards of 1200 are employ'd in *Nottingham*, and the reft in the Villages about, who buy their Provifions and other Neceffaries in this Town : Upon the juft mention'd Frames entirely depends, the Mafters, 3000 Workmen, and a confiderable Number of Winders, Sizers and Seamers ; Woolcombers, Frame-fmiths, Setters up, Sinkermakers, Stocking-Needlemakers, not reckoning thofe Trades who in part get their Livelihood by this Manufacture, as Joyners, Turners, &c. in the whole upwards of 4000.

SECTION VI.

The GOVERNMENT, Ecclesiastical, Civil and Military, Charters, Grants. Liberties, Priviledges and Customs.

NOTTINGHAM is under the Ecclesiastical Jurisdiction of the See of *York*, had formerly a Suffragan Bishop, who governed this County, under his Grace the Archbishop, the last I read off, was *Richard Barnes*, in Queen *Elizabeth's* Reign, (a) mention'd by Mr. *Drake*, in his Antiquities of the City of *York* : At this Time the only Church Dignitary of these Parts, is the Arch-Deacon of *Nottingham*, at present the Reverend *Robert Marsden*, S. T. B. an Aged and Learned Gentleman, who by his exemplary Life sets a fit Pattern to the Clergy committed to his Care. (b)

THE whole County is divided into four Deaneries, viz. *Nottingham*, *Bingham*, *Newark* and *Retford*, of which the first contains Forty one Parishes, (c) of these the Town of *Nottingham* has three ; St. *Mary's*, St. *Peter's* and St. *Nicholas's* : Here the Archbishops use to hold their triennial, and the Arch-deacon holds his annual Visitation of the Clergy in St. *Mary's* Church, where in the Forenoon after Divine Service, and a Sermon preach'd on the Occasion, a Charge is given to the Clergy.

IN this Town is also kept the Spiritual-Court, which meets once in every Month and oftner in St. *Peter's* Church, they used formerly to sit in the Chapel of *All-Saints*, in the North-Isle of that Church, but at present the Court is held in the West End of the South-Isle ; in this Court presides the Official, at present the Reverend Mr. *William Milner*, A. M. Rector of *Barton*, an Ornament to his Cloth as a Clergyman, and as Official, a Gentleman of singular Moderation. The Register is Mr. *Thomas Bennet*, a Person of Probity, and who does Honour to his Post.

BEFORE I mention the present Form of Government in this Town, it will
not

(a) *He was consecrated Suffragan Bishop,* of Nottingham *in the Year* 1558. *More of him in* Section XI.

(b) *The present Archdeacon,* [1749] *is the Rev. Mr.* Thomas.

(c) *There are in all the County,* 182 *Parishes and Chapelries, within the Jurisdiction of the Arch-Deacon of* Nottingham ; *there is besides, the Jurisdiction of* Southwell, *consisting of* 28 *Parishes and Chapelries ; and the Jurisdiction of the Dean and Chapter of* York, *of seven Parishes and Chapelries, and the peculiar of* Kinolton, *the Vicar of which is collated by the Archbishop of* York, *and has Ecclesiastical Jurisdiction belonging to it, of which the Vicar is Commissary.*

not be amifs to look back, and fhortly lay before the Reader, by what Steps the Town of *Nottingham* is come to the prefent Dignity it enjoys.

THAT it was an ancient Borough by Prefcription, long before the Conqueft, is paft all doubt, if we confider that it was a Town fortify'd and encompaffed with a ftrong Stone Wall, above 150 Years before the Norman Invafion, which I fuppofe induced Mr. *Camden*, to call it a City, and after the Conqueft by a general Survey of *Doomf-day-Book*, (which is an authentic Record) it is not only proved to be fuch, but a Borough of no fmall Confideration, in that the Burgeffes had divers Houfes, Lands and Poffeffions, with Priviledge of Fifhing in the Water of *Trent*, &c. and what farther Supports the Truth is, that no Charter in being, of which the oldeft is that of *Henry* II. directed [*Burgenfibus de Nottingham*] mentions its firft Incorporation, but all imply it to be a Body Corporate before.

THIS Borough was firft governed by a Reeve or Bayliff, (*Prepofitus*) for above the fpace of 200 Years reckoning no farther back than the Conqueft; in the mean Time, *Henry* III. Son of King *John*, gave them Coroners of their own, and King *Edward* I. his Succeffor, by his Charter, granted, that in the Town of *Nottingham* they fhould have a Mayor, and that they fhould chufe two Bayliffs, one out of each Borough, according to the different Cuftom or Ufage of the Inhabitants of the fame Boroughs, from the Conqueft till within thefe Forty Years, the Diftinction of the two Boroughs (*a*) fubfifted by the Names of the *Englifh* and *French* Borough, of which more by and by. In this State and with the Title of Mayor and Bayliffs, our Corporation continued 130 Years. Then King *Henry* V. made the Mayor, Recorder, and four others whom the Mayor fhould chufe, Juftices of the Peace, and difcharged the Juftices of the County from intermedling thereafter with the Affairs of the Town, and with this additional Power they held their old Title 36 Years longer, till King *Hen.* VI. incorporated the Town by a new Name, *i. e.* Mayor and Burgeffes, and feparated it for ever from the Body of the County of *Nottingham*, and caufed it to be ftiled, the County of the Town of *Nottingham*, changed their Bayliffs into Sheriffs, and gave Power to the Burgeffes to chufe out of themfelves, feven Aldermen, one of which always to be chofen Mayor of the Town, and that fuch Aldermen fhould all be Juftices of the Peace, and wear Scarlet Gowns of the fame Fafhion as the Mayor and Aldermen of the City of *London* ufe to do.

THIS Charter has from Time to Time been confirmed to *Nottingham*, by the fucceeding Kings and Queens of *England*, *Edward* IV. *Henry* VII. *Henry* VIII. *Edward* VI. *Philip* and *Mary*: The Infpection of all thefe being carried on in the Charter of Queen *Elizabeth*, dated at *Weftminfter*, *February* 7th. *fecundo Regni*, confirmed afterwards by King *James* I. in the 20th of his Reign over *England*, *France*, and *Ireland*, and the 56th of *Scotland*.

IN all thefe Charters nothing is added or altered, neither are the Burgeffes, by the Charter of *Henry* VI. nor any other before, confined to any Number of Counfellors to reprefent them, fo that the Council of a felect Number of Men, takes its original

(*a*) *The Diftinction laft ufed, was that of the Eaft and Weft Town or Divifion, which had their feparate Juries at the Quarter Seffions, &c.*

ginal Beginning, from the Confent and Choice of all the Burgeffes, for the better Management of the Revenues of the Corporation and Difpatch of fome ordinary Affairs.

FROM the Time of *Henry* VI. the Burgeffes enjoyed in Peace all the Advantages which they had beftow'd upon them [by the Crown, till the Reign of King *James* the 1ft. when a difpute arofe, between the Aldermen and the Council, becaufe the former, had lately taken upon them, without the Confent of the Burgeffes, to fit in the Hall as Members of the Council, and to give their Vote, in fetting and difpofing of the Corporation, Bridge and School-Lands ; which Encroachment, caufed the Burgeffes to apply to the Lords of the King's Privy Council, who referred the Affair to the Judges Examinations : Thefe, after mature Confideration, of the Charter and other Matters in Difpute, gave in Certificates of their Opinion, which produced an Order of the Privy-Council, whereby the Aldermen were excluded Voting as Counfellors, and the Numbers of thefe laft was limited to Twentyfour, of which fix were chofen by the Burgeffes at large out of themfelves, who had not ferved the Office of Chamberlain and Sheriff. *(a)* Thefe with the Mayor only, taking unto them the Chamberlains, Bridge-Mafters and School-Wardens, refpectively, as their Places for the Lands within their feveral Offices fhould require, were to have Power to fet and difpofe of the Corporation, Bridge and School-Lands.

THINGS now continued pretty quiet, till after the Reftoration, when King *Charles* II. endeavoured to bring all the Corporations in the Kingdom, by artful Management, to make a voluntary Surrender of their Charters and Liberties, which fucceeded in many Places without much Difficulty, but in *Nottingham* it did not go on fo fmoothly, and when that Affair was abruptly propofed, by the then Mayor, ————— , the legal Majority was againft the Surrender, and even the Votes as they ftood, were but equal, notwithftanding all this, Mr. *Mayor*, had the Seal put to the Inftrument, which was fent up accordingly. But the Surrender being by it made to the Earl of *Hallifax*, and Mr. *Leolin Jenkins*, which was not judged good in Law, another Inftrument was convey'd to the Mayor, who upon the Refufal of the fenior Coroner, to deliver to him his Key to the Seal, without the Mayor's calling a Hall, he found it feems another Method of coming at the Seal, which he privately put to the fecond Inftrument, on the 12th of *Auguft* 1681 : And tho' the Burgeffes made a great ftruggle, prefenting a Writing to the Mayor, on the 4th of *Auguft*, expreffing their Diffent from any Surrender, figned by above 400 Burgeffes ; lodged three Caveats, one at the Lord Chancellor's, one at the Lord Privy-Seal's, and a third in the Signet-Office, againft the Surrendering of the Charters of the Town, or paffing any new Charter, without the Privity, Confent, and Hearing, of the faid Burgeffes, &c. and moreover petitioned my Lord Chancellor to the fame Purpofe ; a new Charter neverthelefs was fent down, on Michaelmafs Day following. *(b)*

THIS occafion'd fome ftir, and two Mayors were chofen that Day ; the New Char-

---

(a) And this was their firft Sanction for chufing fix Junior Counfellors as they Term them.   *(b) Of this whole Affair, the Reader will find a clear and fatisfactory Account in* Mr. Sacheverell's *Cafe of the Corporation of* Nottingham ; *to which I have given a Place in my* Appendix.

ter Men chofe *William Toplady*, the Old Charter Men chofe *William Greaves*, which laft according to Cuftom, had been nominated on the 14th of *Auguft* preceeding, both were proclaimed, and the Matter was carried on with fo much Heat, that a Tryal enfued, before the Lord Chief Juftice *Jeffreys*, at *Weftminfter*, on the 2d. Day of *May* 1684, upon an Information againft *William Sacheverel*, Efq; *George Gregory*, Efq; *Charles Hutchinfon*, Efq; and others, for a Riot, in which Mr. *Sacheverel* and the reft were caft, fined, and bound to their good Behaviour for twelve Months, *(a)* and thus the New Charter Men, came to enjoy their new Bargain. *(b)* But this did not laft long, for in the Year 1687-8, King *James* refolved to compafs his Scheme of an equal Liberty of Confcience, by an Act of Parliament, did determine to new model the Corporations, and to gain the Diffenters, by putting them into the Magiftracy, which among other Towns was done likewife at *Nottingham*, whither he fent his *Quo-waranto*, which put the Town upon frefh Application and Expences, to obtain another Charter of that King. There were two Perfons commiffioned, and called Regulators, one *Timothy Tomlinfon*, and the other *Caleb Wilkinfon*, who had Power to difplace any one belonging to the Corporation, whom they fufpected would not be for the King's Purpofe. King *James* not content with the Advantages his Brother had taken, infifted at firft, upon depriving the Burgeffes at large of the Right of Voting at the Election of Capital and other Counfellors, and tho' he was prevailed upon to let that Point remain as it was, yet did he referve to himfelf the placing and difplacing any Member of the Corporation at his Pleafure. But the Revolution being brought about before this Charter had paffed the Broad-Seal, it never took Place. At laft after their Majefties King *William* and Queen *Mary*, were fully informed of thefe Proceedings, both in King *Charles* and King *James's* Reign, and that the Town of *Nottingham* was ftill a Corporation when the New Charter came down to them, the Surrender not being filed before the faid Charter was fent. Their Majefties moft gracioufly granted to the Town of *Nottingham*, a Charter of Confir-

P

mation

(a) *They were Fined as follows :*

William Sacheverel,	—	500 Marks.	John Sherwin, —	100 Marks.
George Gregory,	—	300 D°.	William Wilfon, —	100 D°.
Charles Hutchinfon,	—	200 D°.	Samuel Smith, —	20 Nobles.
John Greaves,	—	20 Nobles.	Thomas Trigge, —	20 Marks.
William Greaves,	—	20 Marks.	Richard Smith, —	—
Samuel Richard,	—	20 —	John Hoe, —	20 Nobles.
Robert Green,	—	20 —	William Smith, —	20
Francis Salmon,	—	5 Nobles.	Jofeph Turpin, —	100 Marks.
Arthur Riccards.	—	20 Marks.	Nathaniel Charnel, — 100	—
Ralph Bennet,	—	20 —	Jofeph Aftlin, —	5 —

(b) By the Surrender, had it been properly filed, the Corporation would have been entirely diffolved, and by the New Charter have become a new created Body and confequently would have loft all its prefcriptive Rights with other Advantages from Donations and Bequefts. The King indeed confirms the Council of 24, but then by his new Title Mayor, Aldermen, *and* Burgeffes, *he gives to the* Aldermen, *a Power they had not before ; befides he referves to himfelf, the Approbation or Refufal of the* Recorder, *and* Town-Clerk. *and they to hold their Places during the* KING's *Pleafure.*

mation of that of King *James* I. which is the same with that of *Henry* VI. By these last Letters Patents, the Burgesses had their ancient Form of Government, Rights, Priviledges, and Immunities restored to them, the two last Charters being set aside. The Mayor has an Officer called the Town Clerk, who is also Clerk of the Peace for the County of the Town. The Sheriffs have also an Officer called the Steward, (as being Steward of the King's Court of Record, holden before the Mayor and Sheriffs) with whom they advise about Matters relating to the Offices of Sheriffs, as the Mayor does with the Town-Clerk.

THE Mayor has a Serjeant at Mace, and a common Serjeant, which is commonly called the Mayoress's Serjeant.

THE Sheriffs have also each a Serjeant at Mace.

THERE are several inferior Servants of the Corporation who wear the Town's Livery: As the Cryer or Bellman, and the Master of the House of Correction; these have red Liveries, with blew Cuffs trim'd with Silver-Lace.

THE Pindar and Woodward, both have green Liveries, with Silver-lac'd Cuffs.

THERE used to be a Scavinger and Common Paviour, these Officers proving remiss in their Duty, it is now left to the Chamberlains, to hire such as they think will best answer the End.

THERE used to be a Beadle, which Office is now performed by the Master of the House of Correction, who is also one of the Constables.

THE Mayor and Sheriffs had formerly an Officer called a Bill-Bearer, at present that Office is not known.

THERE was likewise a common Cook kept, as long as hot Entertainments on the Mayor's Day, and annual Venison Feasts were in Vogue.----Long since left off.

OF late there is a new Office established, by the Name of the Town's-Husband, whose Employment is to go about and examine what wants Repairing, and to make a Report of the same, and to see that the Publick Work be well and honestly done.

The Election of the MAYOR and other OFFICERS.

ON the 14th of August, the Mayor for the Time being, calls a Hall, and there puts up one of the Aldermen, to be his Successor, upon which every Member gives his Vote, for whom of the Aldermen he pleases, and the Person who has the Majority is nominated Mayor for the Year ensuing.

NB. *It is customary if an Aldermen dies, he who is elected in his Room before the Nomination Day, is the Person named and chosen the Michaelmas following to be Mayor.*

ON the 29th of *September* in the Morning, the Aldermen, and all those who are upon the Cloathing, (*i. e.* all who have served the Office of Chamberlain or Sheriff,
or

or both,) affemble at the old Mayor's Houfe, who entertains them, befides Tea and Coffee, with a cold Collation, (formerly with hot roafted Geefe,) about Ten of the Clock they all go in their Formalities to the Church of St. *Mary*; the Waits with Scarlet Cloaks lac'd with Silver, marching and playing before them, where they attend Divine Service, and hear a Sermon preach'd upon that Occafion by one of the Minifters of the three Parifhes who take their Turn as Chaplains of the Corporation, each of them receiving annually, a free Gift of 20 *l.* by the Hands of the Chamberlains.

DIVINE-Service ended, the whole Body goes into the Veftry, where the old Mayor feats himfelf in an Elbow-Chair, at a Table covered with black Cloth, the Mace being laid in the middle of it, covered with Rofemary and Sprigs of Bay, (which they Term burying the Mace,) then the Mayor prefents the Perfon before nominated to the Body, and after it has gone through the Votes of all the Cloathing, the late Mayor takes up the Mace, kiffes it, and delivers it into the Hand of the New Mayor, with a fuitable Compliment, who propofes two Perfons for Sheriffs, and two for the Office of Chamberlains, thefe having alfo gone through the Votes, the Mayor and the reft go into the Chancel, where the fenior Coroner adminifters the Oath to the New Mayor, in the Prefence of the Old one, next the Town-Clerk gives to the Sheriffs and Chamberlains, the Oath of their Office. The Ceremony being thus ended, they march in Order as before, to the New Hall, attended by fuch Gentlemen and Tradefmen, as have been invited by the New Mayor and Sheriffs: In their Way at the Week-day-Crofs, over againft the ancient Guild-Hall, the Town-Clerk proclaims the Mayor and the Sheriffs, and the next enfuing Market-Day, they are again proclaimed, in the Face of the whole Market, at the Malt-Crofs.

IN former Times, as I am credibly informed, hot Entertainments, very expenfive to the Mayor and Sheriffs, ufed to be made, and each at his refpective Houfe, ufed to Feaft his Friends, the one ftriving to outdo the other in Splendor; but of late Years thofe Extravagancies are laid afide, and the Guefts, at the joint Expence of the Mayor and Sheriffs, are welcomed in the long Room over the Shambles, with Bread and Cheefe and Fruit in Seafon, Pipes and Tobacco, with plenty of Wine, Punch, and Ale if call'd for. At laft the Sheriffs prefent every Gueft with a large Piece of rich Cake, made for that Purpofe.

THE Coroners are chofen by the Hall, and unlefs they are made Aldermen, hold that Place for Life.

THE Bridgemafters and School-Wardens, are likewife chofen by the Hall annually, but are fometimes rechofen, efpecially the former.

TO prove what has been faid concerning the ancient and prefent Form of Civil Government, what Power the Governing part, and what Grants Liberties, Franchifes, and Priviledges, the Burgeffes have from Time to Time obtained, and what they now enjoy, by Virtue of Letters Patents, from the feveral Kings of *England,* it will be proper to look into the Charters themfelves, but as that of King *Henry* VI. fpecifies all the preceeding, and confirms them, and as nothing is added to what that King has granted, by any of the fucceeding Kings and Queens; I will hear give the Subftance of that Charter, referring the Reader to a true Copy of the Latin Charter at Length, which he will find in the *Appendix.*

Subftance

Subftance of the Charter of HENRY VI.

THIS Charter relates that the King had infpected the Charter of *Henry* V. the Father of the faid King, whofe Charter relates the Infpection of:

THE Letters Patent of *Richard* II. which relates the Infpection of

THE Charter of *Edward* III. his Grandfather, which relates the Infpection of

THE memorable Charter of *Edward* II. his Father, which relates the Infpec-on of the Charter of Confirmation

OF *Henry* III. his Grandfather, unto the Burgeffes of *Nottingham*, which relates the Infpection of

THE Charter of King *John* Father of *Henry* III. made to the Burgeffes of *Nottingham*, in *hæc Verba*:

THIS laft mention'd Charter, grants and confirms to the Burgeffes of *Nottingham*, all free Cuftoms which they had in the Time of *Henry* I. and *Henry* II. as is teftify'd by the Charter of *Henry* II. to wit.

THOLL (a) *Theam* (b) *Infongethef* (c) *Theolonia* (d) from *Thrumpton* to *Newark*, and of all Things paffing over the *Trent* as beneficial as in the Borough of *Nottingham*, and on the other fide from the Wold or Down in le Brooke beyond *Rempfton* unto the Water of *Radford* in the North, and of *Vickersdike*.

THE Men of *Nottinghamfhire* and *Derbyfhire*, ought to come to *Nottingham*, on Fridays and Saturdays, with their loaded Waggons drawn by a Team, and with their Horfe Loads.

NO one to work dyed Cloth within ten Miles round *Nottingham*, but in the Borough.

IF any from whence-foever he comes, fhall abide in the Borough, a Year and a Day, in Time of Peace, without being claimed, he fhall be free from all Subjection.

ANY

(a) Tholl, *is a Liberty as well to take as be free from Toll.* (b) Theam, *is a Royalty granted to the Lord of a Manour, for having and Judging in his Court, all the Generations of his Villains and Bondmen,* &c. *with their Suits and Cattle.* (c) Infongethef, *a Priviledge fays* Blount, *or Liberty granted to the Lord of the Manour, to judge any Thief taken within their Fee.* (d) Theolonia, *a Writ to free them from Toll, againft the Officer of any Town or Market, who would conftrain them to pay Toll of their Merchandizes contrary to their Grant and Prefcriptions.*

(*a*) A N Y Burgefs who fhall have bought Land of his Neighbour, and fhall have poffeffed it for a whole Year and a Day without its being claimed by the Kindred of the Seller, if at that Time they be in *England*, he fhall thenceforth poffefs it quiet-ly, neither fhall any one be obliged to Anfwer to the Reeve of the Town in a penal Caufe, unlefs there be a Profecutor.

O F whatever Demefne any one be, who fhall abide in the Borough, he ought to pay his Share of the Taxes with the Burgeffes, and to fupply the Deficiencies of the faid Borough.

A L L who fhall come to *Nottingham* Market, may not be deftrained of, from Fri-day Evening to Saturday Evening, unlefs for the King's Tribute.

A N D that the Paffage of the *Trent* fhall be free for navigating, as far as one Perch fhall reach on either Side of the Stream or Courfe of the Water.

T H E Merchant Guild, granted and confirmed.

T H E Burgeffes are freed from Toll, throughout the whole Land, within and without Fairs,

T H E Y may in the End of the Year, make whom they will of themfelves, their Reeve or Bailiff, who may for them Anfwer the King's Tribute, but if fuch Reeve fhall difpleafe the King, the King may remove him, and they fhall fubftitute ano-ther at the King's Pleafure.

T H E Reeve or Bailiff, fhall pay the Tribute of the Borough, at the King's own Exchequer, where-foever he fhould be in *England*, at two Terms, to wit, half at the clofe of *Eafter*, and half on the octave of St. *Michael*.

W H E R E F O R E the King confirms the faid Cuftoms, the faid Burgeffes had in the Time of *Henry* the King's Great-Grandfather, and *Henry* the King's Father together with the Increafe of Priviledges by him granted.

A N D forbids any one to Trouble them contrary to this Charter, on Forfeiture of Ten Pounds, as by his reafonable Charter when Earl of *Morton*, had been con-frmed.

T H I S Charter of King *John* is witneffed at *Clypfton*, the 19th of *March* in the 1ft Year of his Reign. (*b*)

THEN

(*a*) *That the Reeve of* Nottingham *had at that Time no Power, by Charter, to take Cognizance of Civil Caufes is true ; but it is as certain that the Bailiff held a Court of Pleas by Prefcription, as appears by the Records above, which was af-terwards confirmed to the Mayor and Bailiffs, and left of all, to the Mayor and She-riffs, by the Charter of* Henry VI. *and what is more, the Power of the Court, neither was nor is, limited to any Summons. This is enough to make fuch a Claufe neceffary.*

(*b*) *King* John *began his Reign* Apr. 6, 1199, *fo this Charter bears date,* March 19, 1199.

THEN the above Donations of King *John* are related to be confirmed by the said Charter of *Henry* III. and then

HENRY III. farther confirms the 1st 52 *l.* Crown Rent to be paid at the Kings Exchequer at two Terms, to wit, 26 *l.* at the close of *Easter*, and 26 *l.* blanch, on the octave of St. *Michael*, and that the Burgesses and their Heirs should hold the Town of *Nottingham*, by the said Rent.

THE said King farther grants for himself and his Heirs, to the said Burgesses, that they shall take Tronage, *i. e.* Toll, for weighing Wool, &c. in the Town of *Nottingham*, of Merchandizes depending on Weight, as other Boroughs and Cities are accustomed to do in *England*.

ALSO that they shall have of themselves Coroners in the said Town of *Nottingham*.

WHEREFORE and for rendring the said Rent, of 52 *l.* as aforesaid, the King Wills and Commands, that the said Burgesses and their Heirs, shall have and hold of the King's Gift, the said Liberties and Customs, peaceably and quietly, and that they shall take the said Tronage, and have Coroners of themselves, in the said Town as aforesaid. Witnessed and given by the Chancellor at *Westminster*, the 24th of *February*, in the 14th Year of *Henry* III. (*a*)

THEN Secondly:

ANOTHER Charter of *Henry* III. the said Grandfather of *Edward* II. is related to be inspected, whereby is granted to the Burgesses of *Nottingham*:

THAT they and their Heirs, should throughout the whole Land, and where the King had Power, have this Liberty, to wit: That neither their Persons nor Goods should be stopped or arrested for any Debt, for which they either are not bound, or of which they are not principal Debtors themselves, unless perhaps those very Debtors are of their Commonalty, and have it in their Power to satisfy such Debts, either wholly or in part, and that the said Burgesses have refused to do Justice to their Creditors, and that the same can sufficiently be known.

HE (the King) grants also to the Burgesses, the Return of all Exchequer Writs for ever.

THIS Charter is dated, *Nottingham*, the 20th Day of *July* in the 39th Year of *Henry* III. 1255.

THEN Thirdly:

THE Charter of *Edward* II. carries on its Inspection further, into the Charter of *Edward* I. *in hæc verba*:

WHERE-

(*a*) Henry III. *began his Reign* October 19th. 1216. *so the Charter of Confirmation beareth Date the* 24th *of* February, 1229.

WHEREAS for certain Tranfgreffions of the Burgeffes and Commonalty, the Liberties had been feized, and for three Years and longer, detained in the King's Hands.

THEY are all again reftored, and the Burgeffes and Commonalty are from henceforth to hold and enjoy them, in the fame Manner as at the Time of the Seizure.

ON Payment at the Exchequer Yearly 52 l. and 8 l. advance Yearly.

AND for raifing the State of the Burgeffes, and of other Men of the Town, the King grants that in the faid Town, they fhould have a Mayor.

AND fhould chufe one Bailiff of one Borough, and another of the other Borough, according to the different Ufage of the Inhabitants of the fame Boroughs.

THE King grants the Burgeffes, a new Fair, to laft fifteen Days, to begin on the Eve and the Day of the Feaft of St. *Edmund* the King and Martyr.

GIVEN under the Hand and Seal of King *Edward* I. at *Lincoln*, the 11th Day of *February*, in the 12th Year of his Reign, 1283.

ALL confirmed by *Edward* II. *viz.* the two Charters of *Henry* III. and the Charter of *Edward* I.

THEN *Edward* II. further grants that the faid Burgeffes and their Succeffors, fhall hereafter fully enjoy all the faid Liberties, altho' their Predeceffors may not have ufed fome of them.

AND to fhew farther Favour, the King grants, that none fhall plead or be impleaded out of the Borough, for Tenements in the Borough, or for Trefpaffes, Contracts, or Matters there arifing ; but before the Mayor and Bailiffs of the faid Borough, for the Time being, within the Borough, unlefs the Pleas concern the King or his Heirs, or the Commonalty of the faid Borough.

AND that no Sheriff or other Minifter of the King, fhall enter to execute Procefs, unlefs the Bailiffs for the Time being, make Default in doing it themfelves.

AND further that the faid Burgeffes, and their Heirs fhall for ever, throughout the Kings Dominions, be quit of Murage, Pavage, Stallage, Tarrage, Kaiage, Laftage, and Paffage.

GIVEN under the Hand of King *Edward* II. at *Weftminfter*, the 16th Day of *March* in the 7th Year of his Reign 1313.

WHICH Grants, Confirmations and Reftitutions aforefaid, are ratified and confirmed to the faid Burgeffes, by King *Edward* III.

THE Town and Liberties feized by the King's Juftices Itinerant are likewife reftored.

THEN

T H E N reciting the Priviledge of Return of Writs, claimed by the Charter of *Henry* III. Great-grandfather of *Edward* III.

A N D that the Burgeffes under pretext of the faid Priviledge of *Henry* the 3ds granting, had had all the Returns of his fucceeding Progenitors and his Writs too, to indemnify them, therefore,

T H E King confirms to them the Return of all Writs, and that no Sheriff or other Officer fhall exercife his Office within the Town, but in Default of the Bailiffs.

T H E N this Charter recites an Inquifition, taken and retained in Chancery, whereby it was found, that the Burgeffes Time out of Mind, unto the Time of King *John*'s Charter, and fince, had a Goal in the Town, for the Cuftody of fuch as were taken therein, as belonging to the Town. And grants them for ever the Goal and Cuftody thereof.

T H E N confirms the Market to be held on Saturday every Week, with all Liberties and free Cuftoms belonging to a Market of the like Sort, and that they fhall have no Trouble about their Market.

T H E N grants a Freedom from Pontage throughout the Kingdom.

A L L which feveral Matters, the King Commands, that the faid Burgeffes and their Succeffors fhall hold for ever.

G I V E N under the King's Hand at *Woodftock*, the 1ft. Day of *May*, in the 4th. Year of his Reign, 1330.

A L L which Grants, Confirmations, and Reftitutions, are ratify'd by the Letters Patents of *Richard* II. Witnefs himfelf at *Weftminfter*, the 8th of *April*, in the firft Year of his Reign, 1378.

T H E N *Henry* V. by Charter ratifies all and every the faid Grants, &c. Dated at *Weftminfter* the 18th Day of *November*, in the firft Year of his Reign, 1413.

T H I S King further grants, that tho' they have not ufed fome of their Liberties, yet they fhall continue to hold them without Difturbance.

M O R E O V E R for a ftill greater Favour, by Affent of Council, the King grants and confirms, to the faid Mayor, Bailiffs and Burgeffes, that they, their Heirs and Succeffors, fhall for ever, have Cognizance of all Pleas, by the Mayor and Bailiffs of the faid Town, or whom they depute, as well of Lands, &c. as of Trefpaffes, &c. within the Liberty of the Town. And alfo of Pleas of Affizes, &c.

T H A T the Mayor, Bailiffs, and Burgeffes, and their Succeffors, fhall have for ever, the Chattels of Felons and Fugitives.

A N D all Fines for Trefpaffes and other Offences, alfo Poft-Fines, and Amerciaments, &c.

AND

AND the Return of all Writs and Summons of the Exchequer, and Attachments, and the Execution of the same.

ALSO the Benefit of all Purpreſtures by Land and Water, and all the Waſtes within the Bounds of the Town, in Support of the Corporation thereof.

AND Power to enquire, hear, and determine, by the Mayor and Recorder and four others whom the Mayor ſhall chuſe, of all Matters belonging to Juſtices of the Peace, of Labourers and Artificers.

THE Juſtices of the County hereafter, not to intermeddle with the Affairs of the Town.

BUT the Mayor not to proceed to try Felony, without the King's ſpecial Mandate.

THE Mayor, Bailiffs and Burgeſſes, to have all Fines ariſing before the Juſtices of the Town, as is granted to *Coventry*, by Charters before the 6th of *April*, in 22d of *Richard* II.

AND no arm'd Forces ſhall be raiſed by any Commiſſion within the ſaid Town, unleſs the Mayor be joined in Commiſſion for that Purpoſe.

THEN *Henry* V. confirms all other Grants, Confirmations, &c. to the Mayor, Bailiffs and Burgeſſes of the ſaid Town, and their Heirs and Succeſſors.

EXEMPLIFY'D at *Leiceſter*, the 24th Day of *May* in the 2d. Year of *Henry* V. 1414.

THEN followeth a Confirmation of all, by King *Henry* VI.

HE incorporates the ſaid Town by a new Name : To wit, *Mayor and Burgeſſes of the Town of Nottingham*, on the Date, to wit, 28th of *June* 1449.

THE Town from the 15th of *September* 1449, viz. the 28th of *Henry* VI. to be ſeparated for ever from the Body of the County of *Nottingham*, except the Caſtle and the King's Hall, wherein is the County Goal : And to be for ever called the *County of the Town of Nottingham*.

AND inſtead of two Bailiffs, to chuſe two Sheriffs, who ſhall continue from the 15th of *September* till *Michaelmas*-Day next, and till two new Sheriffs ſhall be choſen for the then next Year.

THE Mayor and Burgeſſes on *Michaelmas*-Day Yearly, ſhall chuſe two Sheriffs, as they were wont to do Bailiffs, who ſhall take their Oath of Office before the Mayor, who ſhall the Sheriffs Names return, under his Seal, within twelve Days after the Election.

THE Mayor ſhall be the King's Eſcheator, in the ſaid Town, and no other.

AND that the Mayor and Sheriffs, and their Succeſſors, ſhall have for ever in the

Q

said Town, the Power, Jurisdiction and Authority, that other Escheators and Sheriffs have, elsewhere, in the Kingdom of *England*.

A N D that all Writs, &c. which before had been wont to be executed by the Sheriffs of *Nottingham*, or Bailiffs of the Town, within the same, shall after the said 15th Day of the Month of *September* aforesaid, be directed to the Sheriffs of the said Town.

T H E Sheriffs to hold their County Court for the said Town, on Monday, from Month to Month.

T H A T the said Burgesses and their Successors, shall for ever, have a Court there at Pleasure, of all Contracts, Covenants, Trespasses against the King's Peace, or otherwise, and of all other Things, Causes, or Matters arising within the said Town and Precincts, from Day to Day, in the Guild-Hall of the said Town, to be holden before the Mayor, or his Deputy, and the Sheriffs.

A N D that the Mayor for the Time being, or his Deputy, and the Sheriffs, shall after the said 15th Day of *September*, 1449, the 28th of *Henry* VI. have Power and Authority, to hear and determine in that Court, all manner of Pleas, &c. as well in the King's Presence as in the King's Absence.

T H E Sheriffs to have the Profits of the Court.

T H E Mayor and Sheriffs, yearly to Account before the Treasurer of the Exchequer, by their Attorney.

E V E R Y Escheator, immediately after his Election, to take the Oath of his Office before the Coroners.

W I T H I N twelve Days after the choice of the Mayor, the Name of the Escheator is to be certify'd into the Exchequer, under the Mayor's Seal.

T H E Burgesses to have the Chattels of all convicted of Felony, Murder, &c. all Amerciaments, Post-Fines, Issues of Pledges, and Bail, tho' they hold of the King, and in all other Courts whatsoever, and before all Justices and Ministers of the King, as well in his Presence, as in the King's Absence.

T H E Burgesses may from Time to Time, chuse out of themselves, seven Aldermen, one of which may be always chosen to the Mayoralty, and be Mayor of the Town, and to continue Aldermen for Life, unless at their own special Request, or for some notable Cause, they be removed by the Mayor and Burgesses.

T H E Mayor and Burgesses may have full Power, on the Death, Departure, or Removal of an Alderman, to chuse from themselves another Burgess to be an Alderman. So from Time to Time for ever.

T H E Aldermen for the Time being to be Justices of the Peace, within the Liberties of the Town, and Seven, Six, Five, Four, and Three, of which, the Mayor to be one present, have Power to punish all Felonies, Murders, &c. as fully as other Justices of the Peace have, or hereafter shall have.

T H E

THE Burgeffes to have all Fines, &c. fet by the Mayor and Aldermen or any of them.

THE Burgeffes to levy thefe Fines by their own Servants, towards defraying the Charges incumbent on the Town.

THE Burgeffes to have the Forfeiture of all Victuals.

THE King's Steward, or Marfhal of his Houfhold, not to exercife their Office within the faid Town.

THE Aldermen to have Licence to wear Gowns, with Collars and half Sleeves, of one Form and Livery, with Furs, Facings, and Robings, when they affemble in Manner and Form, as the Mayor and Aldermen of the City of *London* are ufed to do. Any Statute againft wearing of Cloaths notwithftanding.

THE Efcheator and Sheriffs to accompt by their Attorney before the Treafurer and Barons of the King's Exchequer, and of all fuch Things, (not in the Charter afore excepted;) which were before accounted for by the Efcheator and Sheriffs of the County of *Nottingham*.

THE Burgeffes not to be barred any former Rights or Priviledges, by their Acceptance of thefe Prefents.

THE King will's, that the Burgeffes fhall have and ufe all the Jurifdictions and Franchifes, &c. herein expreffed, or in any former Grant, wholly, and without any Moleftation, &c. Notwithftanding there is not exprefs mention there, of the Value of the Chattels, Amerciaments, Iffues, Fines, or other the Premiffes.

THE Charter of Confirmation granted by the fucceeding Kings and Queens abovementioned, incluſive of that of King *James* I. neither alter nor add any Thing New.

AND now to conclude the Bufinefs of the Charters, I will here fubjoin that part of the Charter of King *William* and Queen *Mary*, which fets afide the Charter of King *Charles* II. and reftores to the Burgeffes their old Charter, and pardons and indemnifies them for what is paft.

CHARTA GULIELMI & MARIÆ Regis & Reginæ.

Dat 19º. Octobris 1692.

GULIELMUS & MARIA Dei Gratia, *Anglie, Scotie, Francie* et *Hibernie*, Rex et Regina, Fidei Defenfores: Omnibus ad quos prefentes Littere noftre pervenerint falutem.

Infpeximus quafdam Litteras Patentes fub magno Sigillo *Anglie*, geren-
tes datum apud *Weftmonafterium* 12 °. die Februarij anno Regni nuper Regis *Jacobi*
Anglie, Francie et *Hibernie*, XX °. et *Scotie*, LVI °. factas et conceffas Majori et
Burgenfibus Ville *Nottingham*, in hec Verba.

JACOBUS Dei gratia *Anglie, Scotie, Francie* et *Hibernie* Rex Fidei Defenfor,
&c. Omnibus ad quos prefentes Littere noftre pervenerint falutem.

Infpeximus quafdam Litteras patentes Domini *Henrici* nuper Regis *Anglie* fexti
Majori Ballivis et Burgenfibus Ville de *Nottingham* factas dat. 28 °. die Junii, anno
Regni fui XXVII °. in memorandos fcaccarii noftri apud *Weftmonafterium* videlicet:
In originalio de eodem XXVII °. anno dicti nuper Regis *Henrici* VI. Rotul.
XXIII. ex parte rememoratoris Thefaurii noftri in dicto fcaccario noftro remanentes
et exiftentes, in hec Verba :

Rex omnibus ad quos &c. &c. &c. &c.

Nos autem premiffa omnia et fingula ad requifitionem et inftantiam nunc Majoris et
Burgenfium dicte Ville noftre *Nottingham* fub figillo Scaccarii, noftri tenore prefentium duximus exemplificanda. In cujus rei teftimonium has Litteras noftras fieri fecimus patentes tefte predilecto et fideli Confanguineo et Confiliario noftro *Lionello* Comite *Middlefexie* fummo Thefaurario noftro *Anglie* apud *Weftmonaft.* 12 °. die
Februarij Anno Regni noftri *Angl. Fran. & Hibern.* XX °. et *Scotie* LVI °.

Nos autem (viz. *Guilielmus* et *Maria*) omnia et fingula Francheses, Libertates,
Privilegia, Quietantias, Immunitates, Conceffiones, Confirmationes et Reftitutiones predicta, rata habentes et grata, pro Nobis et Heredibus et Succefforibus noftris
quantum in Nobis eft acceptamus approbamus et ratificamus omnia et fingula Fran-
chefes, Libertates, Privilegia, Quietantias, et Immunitates predicta, et dilectis nobis Majori Burgenfibus Ville predicte et Succefforibus fuis, tenore prefentium concedimus et confirmamus, ficut Carte predicte rationabiliter teftantur, et prout iidem
Major et Burgenfes ejufdem Ville *Nottingham* vel Predeceffores fui unquam Franchefibus, Libertatibus, Privilegiis Quietantiis et Immunitatibus predictis uti et gaudere debent, potuerunt feu debuerunt. Licet dicti Major et Burgenfes ejufdem Ville et Predeceffores fui Franchefibus, Libertatibus, Privilegiis, Quietantiis, et Immunitatibus predictis vel eorum aliquo vel aliquibus abufi vel non ufi fuerint. Cumq;
datum eft Nobis intelligi, quod pretextu cujufdam inftrumenti vel fcripti ad quod
commune figillum Majoris et Burgenfium Ville predicte per combinationem paucio-
rum, ejufdem Ville appofitum et affixum fuerat gerentis datum 18 °. die Septembrris
Anno Dom. *Caroli* fecundi nuper Regis *Anglie* Anteceffris noftri felicis memoriæ
trigeffimo quarto et in curià Cancellariæ ejufdem nuper Regis de Recordo irrotulati
purportantis fore conceffionem factam per prefatum Majorem et Burgenfes eidem nuper Regi et Heredibus et Succefforibus fuis de omnibus et fingulis, maneris, meffu-
agis, terris, tenementis, reditibus et hereditamentis, cum pertinentis quibufcunque de vel
in quibus dicti Major et Burgenfes ad tunc vel ad aliquod tempus ante tunc fuerunt a-
liquo modo feifiti, poffeffionati, vel intereffati, in Jure incorporationis fue, vel ca-
pacitate fuà incorporatà aliquibus modis quibufcunq; ac etiam purportantis fore conceff-
fionem et furfum redditionem per prefatum Majorem et Burgenfes eidem nuper Regi
de

de omnibus Franchefiis, Cartis, Litteris Patentibus incorporationis, Poteftatibus, Libertatibus, et Immunitatibus quibuscunque ad aliquod tempus vel tempora conceffis ad, vel gravifis per eofdem Majorem et Burgenfes, vel Predeceffores fuos vel aliquos eorum aliquibus viis aut modis vel per aliquod Nomen five Nomina quecunque. Nec non quod tunc ratione predicte pretenfe conceffionis et furfum redditionis quam pretextu fue Colore diverfarum Cartarum five Literarum Patentium incorporationis predicte per nuper Regem *Carolum* fecundum ac per *Jacobum* fecundum nuper Regem factarum et conceffarum, fue mentionatarum, fore conceffa, poft datum dicti inftrumenti vel pretenfe furfum redditionis, diverfa dubia, queftiones, et controverfia orta fuere, de, et concernentia Libertates, Franchefias, Confuetudines, Terras et Poffeffiones Majoris et Burgenfium Ville predicte ac etiam de et concernentis Electionem et Continuationem quorundam officiariorum Ville predicte.

Sciatis igitur quod Nos pacem, tranquilitatem et bonam Gubernationem ejufdem Ville et Burgenfium et inhabitantium ejufdem gratiofe affectantes, et omnia dicta dubia queftiones, et controverfias in hâc parte auferre defignantes de Gratia noftrâ fpeciali et ex certâ fcientiâ et mero motu noftris, de advifamento privati confillii noftri affignavimus, nominavimus, ordinavimus, conftituimus et confirmavimus ac per prefentes pro Nobis, Heredibus et Succefforibus noftris affignamus, nominamus, ordinamq; conftituimus et confirmamus *Willielmum Greaves*, Generofum, qui fuit Major Ville *Nottingham* predicte tempore ejufdem pretenfe furfum redditiones fore et effe prefentem et modernum Majorem Ville predicte continuandum in eodem Officioâ dato prefentium ufque ad ufuatum tempus pro Electione Majoris pro eâdem Villa in Fefto Sancti *Michaelis* Archangeli quod erit Anno Dom. 1693°. fi dictus *Willielmus Greaves* tam diu vixerit. Et ulterius volumus ac per prefentes pro Nobis, Heredibus et Succefforibus noftris Majori et Burgenfibus Ville predicte et Succefforibus fuis concedimus, Poteftatem et Authoritatem ad aliquod vel aliqua tempus vel tempora intra fpatium duorum mentium proximè poft datum prefentium eligere, nominare et conftituere aliquod Burgenfes ejufdem Ville ad Officium de Communi Confilio Ville predicte, ac fore et effe de Communi Confilio ejufdem Ville tam ex iis qui Officium Vicecomitum Ville predicte fervierunt five habuerunt, quam qui Officium illud non fervierunt vel habuerunt quos Majori et Burgenfibus Ville predicte vel majori parti eorum melius expediri videbitur, ad complendum numerum octodecim de Communi Confilio Ville prædicte toties, quoties neceffe fuerit intra dictum fpatium duorum menfium proxime poft datum prefentium.

Et ulterius volumus ac per prefentes pro Nobis, Heredibus et Succefforibus noftris concedimus et confirmamus Majori et Burgenfibus Ville predicte et Succefforibus fuis, quod poft hujus modi Electionem et expirationem duorum menfium predictorum proximè poft datum prefentium ut prefertur liceat et licebit, Majori et Burgenfibus Ville predicte et Succefforibus fuis de tempore in tempus ad omnia Tempora in perpetuum eligere, nominare et conftituere, idoneas perfonas ad Officium de Communi Confilio Ville predicte et fore et effe de Communi Confilio ejufdem Ville in tali modo et formâ prout in eâdem Villâ affuetum et confuetum fuit ante diem dati predicte pretenfe furfum redditionis, viz. predictum decimum octavum Diem Septembris, Anno Regni Domini nuper Regis *Caroli* fecundi trigefimo quarto vel ad aliquod tempus preantea.

Provifo femper et volumus quod dictus *Willielmus Greaves* antequam ad Executionem Officii Majoris Ville predicte admittatur, preftet Sacramentum fuum corporate pro debitâ executione Officii Majoris Ville predicte ac etiam Sacramenta per quendam

dam

dam actum in Parliamento noftro apud *Weftmonafterium*, anno Regni noftri primo tento editum et provifum, appunctuata.

Fore capta et preftita coram *Thoma Trigge* et *Radulpho Bennet*, Generofis, aut altero eorum quibus *Thome Trigge* et *Radulpho Bennet* vel altero eorum dicta feparalia Sacramenta adminiftrandi plenam poteftatem et authoritatem damus et condecimus per prefentes.

Et de uberiori gratià noftrâ fpeciali ac ex certâ Scientiâ et mero motu noftris pardonavimus remiffimus et relaxavimus et per prefentes pro Nobis Heredibus et Succefforibus noftris pardonamus remittimus et relaxamus Majori et Burgenfibus Ville predicte omnia et fingulares, materias, contemptus, crimina et Offenfas et tranfgreffiones quecunque per fe ipfos facta commiffa five perpetrata de, pro, in, vel concernentia executionem aut malam executionem aliquorum officiorum infra Villam predictam et limites vel precinctus ejufdem ad aliquod tempus five tempora poft predictum decimum octavum diem Septembris, Anno dicti nuper Regis *Carolo* fecundi trigeffimo quarto fupra dicto.

Ac etiam pardonavimus remiffimus et relaxavimus ac per prefentes pro Nobis Heredibus et Succefforibus noftris pardonamus, remittimus et relaxamus omnibus et fingulis Burgenfibus Ville de *Nottingham* predicte omnia et fingula, res materias, contemptus crimina, offenfas et trangreffiones quecunque per ipfos vel aliquem vel aliquos eorum feparatim vel conjunctim facta, commiffa vel perpetrata de, pro, vel in executione alicujus Officii vel aliquorum officiorum infra Villam predictam, limites vel precinctus ejufdem, Colore five Pretextu aliquarum Litterarum Patentium Predictorum nuper Regis *Caroli* fecundi et *Jacobi* fecundi vel alterius eorum ad aliquod tempus five tempora predictum decimum octavum diem Septembris Anni dicti nuper Regis *Caroli* fecundi trigefimi quarti fupra dicti.

Et ulterius de uberiori gratià noftrâ fpeciali ac certâ fcientia et mero motu noftris, dedimus, conceffimus, reftituimus, confirmavimus, approbavimus, et ratificavimus, ac per prefentes pro Nobis Heredibus et Succefforibus noftris damus, concedimus, reftituimus, confirmamus, approbamus et ratificamus Majori et Burgenfibus Ville *Nottingham* et Succefforibus fuis omnia et omni moda, maneria, meffuagia, molendinas, redditus, terras, tenementa, decimas, prata, pafcua, pafturas, communias, ferias, nundinas, mercatus et tot, tanta, talia, eadem et hujus modi poteftates, prefcriptiones, libertates, privilegia, francheses, immunitates, jurifdictiones, Cartas Literas Patentes incorporationis, confuetudines, proficua officia, officiarios exemptiones, quietancias, vafta, vacua funda, commoditates emolumenta, bona catallos et heraditamenta quecunque quot quanta, qualia et que per dictas Literas Patentes gerentes datum dicto duodecimo die Februarii Anno Regni Regis *Jacobi* I. *Anglie*, *Francie*, et *Hibernie* viceffimo et *Scotie* quinquagefimo fexto conceffa eft confirmata fuerunt, vel mentionata fore conceffa et confirmata aut per aliquas alias predictas Literas Patentes conceffa vel mentionata fore conceffa aut confirmata Majori et Burgenfibus Ville predicte five que Major et Burgenfes Ville predicte vel predeceffores fui per quodcunque nomen feu quecunque nomina incorporationis ante dictum decimum octavum diem Septembris Anno Regni nuper Regis *Caroli* fecundi trigefimo quarto fupra dicto, habuerunt tenuerunt, ufi vel gavifi fuerunt aut occupaverunt, aut habere, tenere, uti vel gaudere, debuerunt aut potuerunt, fibi et Succefforibus fuis ratione aut pretextu predictarum feparalium Litterarum Patentium vel earum aliquarum vel alicujus vel aliarum Cartarum conceffionum aut Literarum Patentium quarumcunque per aliquem Progenitorum

genitorum aut Anteceſſorum noſtrorum nuper Regum vel Reginarum *Anglie* quomodo factarum, conceſſarum, ſeu confirmatarum ante dictum decimum octavum diem Septembris Anno Regni nuper Regis *Caroli* ſecundi trigeſimo quarto, aut quocunq; alio legali modo, jure ſive titulo, conſuetudine, uſu, ſive preſcriptione, ante datum preſenſium legitime uſitatorum, habitorum, conſuetorum, ſive gaviſorum. Cumque datum Nobis ſit intelligi, quod quedam perſone inhabitantes predicte Ville et Burgi *Nottingham* poſt tempus predicte pretenſe ſurſum reddicionis, ſuſcipientes ſuper ſe fore corpus corporatum per nomen Majoris Aldermannorum et Burgenſium Ville de *Nottingham* in Comitatu ejuſdem Ville pretextu ſue colore quarundam Litterarum Patentium per dictum nuper Regem *Carolum* ſecundum et *Jacobum* ſecundum confectarum, diverſas dimiſſiones vel pretenſas diſmiſſiones diverſis perſonis, diverſarum terrarum tenementorum et hereditamentorum ad Majorem et Burgenſes Ville de *Nottingham* tempore predicte pretenſe ſurſum reddicionis ſpectantium et pertinentium fecerunt, et diverſas denariorum ſummas pretextu dictarum dimiſſionum habuerunt et receperunt. Et quod nolumus quod hujus modi perſone quibus tales dimiſſiones vel pretenſe dimiſſiones bonâ fide et provaluabilibus conſiderationibus facte fuerant de hujus modi firmis ſuis aliqualiter deprivari ſeu fruſtrari ; de gratiâ noſtrâ ſpeciali ac ex certâ Scientiâ et mero motu noſtris conceſſimus et confirmavimus ac per preſentes pro Nobis, Heredibus et Succeſſoribus noſtris concedimus et confirmamus, omnibus et cuilibet hujuſmodi perſone vel perſonis vel quibus aliquis talis dimiſſio vel pretenſa dimiſſio, ſive alique dimiſſiones vel pretenſe dimiſſiones facta fuerat vel facte fuerant de aliqualibus terris, tenementis ſeu Hereditamentis predictis, quod quelibet hujuſmodi perſona et perſone deinceps reſpective habeant, teneant et gaudeant, et habere tenere et gaudere, valeant omnibus terris, tenementis et hereditamentis eis vel eorum alicui vel aliquibus pro valuabilibus conſiderationibus bona fide ſic dimiſſis vel pretenſis fore dimiſſa, pro reſiduo reſpectivorum terminorum in quâlibet hujuſmodi dimiſſione limitatorum, ſub annuali redditu, conditionibus convenſionibus et agreamentis in hujus modi dimiſſionibus ſpecificatis, et juxta verum purportum dictarum dimiſſionum vel pretenſarum dimiſſionum.

In cujus rei Teſtimonium, has Litteras fieri fecimus patentes, teſtibus Nobis ipſis apud *Weſtmonaſterium* decimo nono die Octobris anno Regni noſtri quarto.

PIGOTT.

per breve de privato ſigillo,

J. TREVOR. *C. G.*
W. RAWLINSON. *C. G.*
G. HUTCHINSON. *C. G.*

Pro fine in Hanaper. Viginti Marc :

B Y

BY the foregoing Account of the several Charters, it appears undeniably that the Town of *Nottingham* has an undoubted Title to all its Lands, Possessions, Rights, Tolls, Profits, &c. having ever paid, and still annually paying to the Crown a Consideration for the same, for from the Time of King *John* to *Edward* I. the King received 52 l. blanch *per annum*, and the last mentioned King's farther raisin r the State of the Burgesses, and granting them a new Fair, the annual Consideration was increased to Sixty Pounds, a great Sum in those Days, which they continued to pay till the 28th of *Henry* VI. when an Act of Resumption of Lands, &c. passed, at which Time, for a saving to the Town of *Nottingham*, for certain Franchises, the Consideration was augmented to 13 s. & 4 d. more than what they already yearly paid to the Crown.

THIS King's Answer to the Petition of the Commons in Relation to that Act, taken from a Discourse upon Grants and Resumptions, printed in *London* 1700, will perhaps not be displeasing to the curious, if I give it a place here. *viz.*

" THE Kyng by the Advyse of the Lords Spirituel and temporel in this present
" Parlement assembled, and by the Aucthoritie of the same, agreeth to this Petition
" of Resumption and the same accepteth and establisheth. Alweys foreseyn, that
" all Exceptions, Moderations, Foreprizes and Provisions by him granted, or-
" deined, and admitted and put in Writing in this same Parlement upon the Pre-
" misses, be and stand good and available in Law after the Fourme and Effecte of
" the Contynue of the same Exceptions, Moderations and Provisions ; And that all
" Letters Patentes of the King made to oney Persone or Persones named in oney of
" the same Exceptions, Moderations, Foreprizes, and Provisions, be good and effec-
" tual, after the Fourme and Contynue of the same Letters Patentes, the said Act
" and Petition of Resumption or oney Thing conteined therein notwithstanding.

" THESE that followen been the Exception, Moderations, Foreprizes and
" Provisions by the Kyng graunted, ordeined and admitted, and in this same Parle-
" ment upon the Premisses, put in Writing : The Savings were in Number one hun-
" dred and eighty five.

                                            Rot. Parl. 28. *Henry* VI. *N.* 53.

THE Mayor, Sheriffs, (formerly Bayliffs, and after the Mayor and Bayliffs,) hold and did hold, a Court of Pleas, which sits on Wednesday every Fortnight by Prescription, as appears by the Records. This Court has been confirmed by the several Charters, and what is worth Notice, the Power of the Court is not limited to any Sum.

THE Sheriffs hold their County Court, also on Wednesday every Month, which used to be held on Monday from Month to Month.

THE Normans divided *Nottingham* into two Boroughs, *viz.* the *French* and the *English* Borough, each of which had its peculiar Customs.

THEY were parted almost by a straight Line running North and South, beginning beyond *Boot-lane*, and passing through that, *Cow-lane*, *Sadler-gate*, *Bridle-smithgate*, *Vault-lane*, and through *Turn-calf-Alley*, across the Meadows to the *Trent*,
info-

infomuch that the Eaft part of the Town, Meadows, and Fields, were in the *Englifh*, and the Weft part of the Town, Meadows and Fields, including the Caftle, belong- ed to the *French* Borough, and the Houfes on the Eaft-fide of the Streets which di- vided the Town were in the *Englifh*, and thofe on the Weft-fide in the *French*, which moved my Anonymous Author to take Notice that it fo fell out, that the Houfes in fome Streets were on one Side in one Borough, and on the other fide in the other Borough. This Diftinction of two Boroughs, did not only continue after the Town was made a County, but was not difufed till 1714, in the Mayoralty of *John Collin* Efq; and a feparate Jury ufed to be impannel'd for each Borough ; but fince that Time one Jury ferves for all Occafions, and that Diftinction is almoft entirely forgot.

HOW much the Blood of a *Norman* was valued above that of an *Englifhman*, will appear by the following Cuftom, which was called cafting the Blood.

IF in a quarrel Bloodfhed was committed in any part of the Town, four Confta- bles were called and Sworn before the Mayor, or fome other Juftice of the Peace, be- fore thefe the Witneffes of both Parties were to be heard upon Oath, which done, the faid Conftables were to determine which of the contending Parties drew the Blood, and in which of the Boroughs the Mifchief was done. If in the *Englifh*, the Offender was to pay to the King 6 *s* and 4 *d*. but if in the *French* Borough, eighteen Shillings. And this Cuftom my afore-mentioned Anonymous Author fays, was ftill in his Time, *to witt*, in the Reign of King *Charles* I. but how long it continued af- ter I cannot learn.

Dr. *Thoroton* from a Plea Roll of Common Pleas, M. 5. *Edward* II. informs us of a Cuftom in the *Englifh* Borough of *Nottingham*, that Infants of Fifteen Years old may fell their Land as if they were at full Age. *p*. 491. *col*. 1.

THE prefent Divifion of the Town is into feven Wards anfwering the Number of Aldermen, each of thefe having one of them committed to his Care, tho' he is not confined to live in it, and as Juftice of the Peace, his Power extends throughout all the Liberties of the Town.

I have here for the Satisfaction of the People of the Town, fet down the Limits of every Ward, and for Diftinction fake, have given to each a Name, by which they will be eafily known.

CHAPEL-WARD.

THE Compafs of this is from the North-Eaft Corner of *Moot-hall-gate*, common- ly call'd *Frier-Lane*, acrofs the Market Place, leaving the Malt-Crofs on the Right, along the Weft-fide of *Sheep-lane*, and taking in the Weft part of the *Back- fide*, and the *Bowling-Green-Houfe*, returning by the extreme parts of *Toll-Hill*, and fo proceeding Southward as far as the Refervoir or Ciftern, thence by *Derry-Mount* towards St. *James's-lane* and along the South-fide of *Frier-Clofe*, and the Weft of *Frier-lane*, to the Point where we began.

CASTLE-WARD,

THIS begins at the *Feather's-Inn*, runs by the South-fide of *Frier-lane*, to the

R.   End

End of the Small-Clofe over againſt the Caſtle, thence down the Road to the *Leen*, and taking in the *Engine-Houſe*, croſſes again the *Leen* cloſe by the Wall of the *Gray-friers*, continuing on the Weſt-ſide of *Gray-frier-gate* and *Liſter-gate*, croſſing the *Low-pavement* including St. *Peters-lane*, all the Houſes in *Pepper-ſtreet* and the Eaſt-ſide of St. *Peter's Church-Yard*, and from the Porch'd Houſe there down St. *Peter's-gate* taking in *Peck-lane* as far as the Coffee or News Houſe, then proceeding through *Wheeler-gate* it terminates at the Weſt corner of *Timber-Hill*, over againſt the *Feathers*.

MARKET-WARD.

RUNS from the Weſt to the Eaſt-Corner of *Timber-Hill*, there croſſing over and paſſing along *Rotten-row* and taking both ſides of *Sadler-gate*, now called *High-ſtreet*, proceeds on the Weſt-ſide of *Cow-lane* and *Boot-lane*, thence Southward to the *Mansfield* Road and croſſing over to *Sheep-lane*, continues along the Eaſt-ſide of it, whence it goes by the Eaſt ſide of the *Malt-Croſs* till it reaches the Weſt Corner of *Timber-Hill*.

NORTH-WARD.

TAKES the Eaſt-ſide of *Cow-lane* and *Boot-lane*, deſcends beyond St. *Mary's Workhouſe*, thence round on the Left, takes in St. *Anne's-Well*, *Nottingham-Coppice*, and all the Fields on that ſide of the Town, whence returning it includes *Hockley*, and paſſing upwards on the North-ſide of *Barker-gate* into *Stony-ſtreet*, all which belongs to it, it again deſcends down St. *Mary's-Hill*, and taking *Short-Hill*, and paſſing along the South-ſide of St. *Mary's Church Yard* it turns up St. *Mary-gate*, claiming both Sides, then ſtretches from the North Corner of the Eaſt-ſide of St. *Mary-gate* to the Corner of *Stony-ſtreet*, and having taken in the North-ſide of *Swine-green* and *Gridleſmithgate* it ends where it begun.

BRIDGE-WARD.

FROM the *Charity-School* it paſſes down *Brightmore-hill*, reaches up *Vault-lane*, as far as the third Houſe, takes in its way, all the *Broad-Marſh*, paſſes along the *Frier-*Wall, croſſes the *Leen*, and encompaſſes all the Meadows belonging to the Town, and having reached *Trent-Bridge*, it continues by the *Eaſt-Croft* to *Pennyfoot-Stile*, along the *Back-lane*, and croſſing the Road goes up the South-ſide of *Barker-gate* through *Beller-gate* and the *Hollow-ſtone*, towards the *Bridge-End*, and turning to the Right, mounts *Malin-hill* and paſſes by St. *Mary's Church-ſide*, whence it takes in both Sides of the *High-pavement*, till it again rerurns to the *Charity-School*.

MIDDLE-WARD.

REACHES from the *Blackmoor's-Head*, along the Eaſt-ſide of the *Hen-Croſs*, up *Chandler's-lane*, on both ſides, the South-ſide of *Swine-green*, and turning at the farther End, paſſes up the North-ſide of *Worſargate* till it comes to the North-End of St. *Mary-gate*, then it takes both ſides, as alſo of *Bottle-lane*, thence it goes along the Eaſt-ſide of *Bridleſmith-gate*, to the South-Eaſt Corner of the ſame, and

re-

returning back on the Weft-fide, and paffing *Cuckftool-Row*, terminates at the New's-Houfe in *Peck-lane*.

MONT-HALL-WARD.

IT goes down on the Weft-fide of *Brightmore-Hill*, commonly *Gardiner's-Hill*, and up *Mont-Lane* commonly called *Midah--Hill*, all the Weft End of the *Weekday-Crofs*, all the *Middle* and *Low-Pavement* and *Voult-Lane*, down to the *Welfh-Harp*, the Eaft fide of *Lifter-gate* and the Weft fide as far as the Gully-Hole, the North and Eaft fides of the *Weekday-Crofs*, as far as the *Charity-School*, all *Mont-hall-gate*, alias *Blowbladder-ftreet*, all *Pilchergate*, *Hallifax-Lane*, commonly called *Jack Nuttal's-Lane*, *Byard-Lane* and *Flifher-gate*

TO thefe feven Wards belong thirty Conftables, a Number more than fufficient for a Town of this Extent, whilft too few Watchmen are kept, the bare Number of four, and thefe fo remifs m their Duty. that they feldom give the Hour above twice in a Night, whereas if a fufficient Number of able bodied Men were employ'd, and the Watch fet at proper Hours both Winter and Summer, and they obliged to take their Rounds every Hour in the Night, thofe Attempts of breaking open Houfes and Shops, of late fo much complained of, would effectually be prevented.

THIS leads me to a Cuftomary annual Watch which ufed to be kept in this Town, even fo lately as the Reign of King *Charles* I. of this my Anonymous Author gives the following Account.

" IN this Town by an ancient Cuftom they keep yearly a general Watch every
" Midfummer Eve at Night, to which every Inhabitant of any Ability fets forth a
" Man, as well Voluntaries as thofe who are charged with Arms, with fuch Muni-
" tion as they have ; fome Pikes, fome Muskets, Calivers, or other Guns, fome
" Partifans, Holberts, and fuch as have Armour, fend their Servants in their Ar-
" mour. The Number of thefe are yearly, almoft two hundred, who at Sun-fetting
" meet on the Row, the moft open part of the Town, where the Mayor's Serjeant at
" Mace gives them an Oath, the Tenor whereof followeth in thefe Words :

" *They fhall well and truly keep this Town till To-morrow at the Sun-Rifing ;*
" *You fhall come into no Houfe without Licence or Caufe reafonable. Of all Manner of*
" *Cafualties, of Fire, or crying of Children, you fhall due Warning make to the Par-*
" *ties, as the Cafe fhall require you. You fhall due Search make of all Manner of Af-*
" *frays, Bloodfheds, Outcrys, and of all other Things that be fufpected. You fhall due*
" *Prefentment make of the fame, either to Mr. Mayor, the Sheriffs or other Officers.*
" *If any Stranger come to the Town, well and demeanably to behave yourfelf to them*
" *courteoufly, and to entreat them, and to bring them to their Inns, and well and fe-*
" *cretly keep the Watch, and other Things that belong to the fame Watch, well and*
" *truly do, to your Cunning and Power.* So help you God.

" WHICH done they all march in orderly Array, through the principal Parts
" of the Town, and then they are forted into feveral Companies and defigned to fe-
" veral parts of the Town, where they are to keep the Watch, until the Sun dif-
" mifs them in the Morning.

" ONE Reason besides the Points in the Oath rendered for this Custom is, to
" keep their Armour clean and fair, with all their Accoutrements, fit and ready to
" Use upon any sudden Occasion.   In this Business the Fashion is for every Watch-
" man to wear a Garland, made in the Fashion of a Crown Imperial, bedeck'd with
" Flowers of various Kinds, some natural, some artificial, bought and kept for that
" Purpose, as also Ribbans, Jewels, and for the better garnishing whereof, the
" Townsmen use the Day before, to ransack the Gardens of all the Gentlemen
" within six or seven Miles about *Nottingham*, besides what the Town itself affords
" them, their greatest Ambition being to outdo one another in the Bravery of their
" Garlands."

TO me this Custom seems to be of no greater Antiquity than the Reign of Queen
Elizabeth, brought in here in Imitation of *London*, where such a Watch was commanded to be kept as *Stow* informs us, occasioned by the Armourers petitioning the
Queen more to promote their own Interest than to serve her Majesty.   His Words are
these :

" IN the Year 1564, the 6th of Queen *Elizabeth*, through the earnest Suit of
" the Armourers, there was on the vigil of St. *Peter*, a Watch in the City of *Lon-*
" *don*, which did only stand in the High-streets of *Cheap, Corn-hill*, and so forth to
" *Aldgate*, which Watch was to the Commons as chargeable, as when in Times
" past it had been commendably done. This Watch was also kept the next Year, and
" in 1667, on *Midsummer* Eve.   *Summar. Chron.* p. 513."

THAT this was farther continued appears by what he says, *ibid. p.* 524.

" IN the Year 1569, a standing Watch at St. *John's Even* at *Midsummer*, and
" Sir *John White*, Alderman, rode the Circuit as the Lord Mayor should have
" done."

THIS Custom is quite left off, as well as another much more ancient, *i. e.* The
Corporation's going once a Year to *Southwell*. The Account of which as transmit-
ted to me by the late Rev. Mr. *Samuel Berdmore*, who took it literatim out of the
Register of *Southwell*, is thus :

" THE Maiore of *Nottingh*. and his Brethren and all the Clothing in likewise
" to ride in their best Livery at their Entry into *Southvill*, on *Wytson Monday* and
" so to procession *te Drum*, without the Maior and oder thick the contrary because
" of Foulenefs of Way, or distemperance of the Weder.

" ALSO the said Maiore and his Brethren and all the Clothing in likewise to
" ride in their Livery when they be comyn home from *Southvill* on the said *Witson*
" *Monday* through the Town of *Nottingh*. and the said Justices of Peace to have
" their Clokes born after them on Horseback at the same Time through the Town.

" This is copyed out of the Leiger of
" *Nott* : Town by me *Fran. Leek*,
" *Preb. de Woodborough.*

THIS

THIS shews a greater Likelihood that the Church of *Southwell* was formerly acknowledged by *Nottingham* as the Mother Church, than St. *Nicholas's* in *Nottingham*.

IN Section IV. an Account has been given of St. *Anne's Well* and House, how it was formerly as well as at present, the same Author tells us, " That by a Custom " Time beyond Memory, the Mayor and Aldermen of the Town and their Wives " have been used on Monday in *Easter* Week, Morning Prayers ended, to march " from the Town to this Well, having the Town Waits to play before them, and " attended by all the Clothing and their Wives, *i. e.* such as have been Sheriffs, *and* " *ever after wear Scarlet Gowns,* together with the Officers of the Town, and ma- " ny other Burgesses and Gentlemen, such as wish well to the Woodward, this " Meeting being at first instituted, and since continued for his Benefit.

FORMERLY the Woodward had the House built out of the Ruins of the Chapel allow'd him to live in, who kept a Victualling House there. This Custom is likewise dropt.

THE Butchers in Times past, when ever they had a Mind to kill a Bull, they were obliged first to bait him in the Market-Place, for which Purpose there used to be a Ring fix'd in the Ground, and Mrs. Mayorefs was to find a Rope, for which she has the Consideration of One Shilling, of every one who takes up his Freedom of the Town. At this Time the Bull-baiting is disused, and instead of it the Butchers pay to the Lady of the Mayor 3 s. and 4 d. called Pin-Money, for every Bull they kill.

THE Burgesses have free Common in the Meadows, except the East-Croft (where they pay an Acknowledgement to the Chamberlains,) from Midsummer to Candlemas, and in both the Sand and Clay-Field, all other Inhabitants as well as the Burgesses enjoy Common Right from Lammas to the 1st of *November* ; however the Common is stinted to three Head of Cattle, whether Horses, Cows, &c. or four-score Sheep ; these last are not to be put into the Meadows till Martinmass ; but the Common of the Lordship of *Nottingham* is open all the Year round without stint.

THERE are upwards of 290 Burgesses Parts belonging to the Freemen of this Town from 3 *l.* to 20 *s.* annual Value, which not only they in their Turn of Seniority enjoy during their Life, but their Widows after them, as long as they continue single, and live in the Town ; and tho' a Burges should die, before one of these Parts falls to his Share, yet if his Wife survive him and continue a Widow, she is entituled to his Turn.

THERE is a Close called the *Over-Trent Close,* divided among the seven Al-
R 3
dermen

(a) *By this it seems the Sheriffs used to wear Scarlet as well as the Aldermen ; and an old Person informs me, that Mr.* John Sherwin, *in King* Charles *the* 2 ds. *Reign, claimed when Sheriff, the wearing of a Scarlet Gown, but gave Offence in having it made, not like the Sheriffs, but in the Fashion of an Alderman's Gown.*

dermen, (and on that Account is as commonly called by the Name of the Aldermen's Parts) which they have allotted to them from the Time of their Election, during their Life, and the Widows after their Decease have the Option of the first Burgess Part that falls.

OTHER considerable Advantages which the Burgesses have a Right to, you will find in the next Section.

IN this Town the Assizes are kept by his Majesty's Judges twice a Year, not only for the Town and County of the Town of *Nottingham* at the *Old-Hall*, but likewise for the County at the *King's Hall* or *Shire Hall*, to wit, the *Lent Assize* and the *Midsummer-Assize.*

FORMERLY the Counties of *Nottingham* and *Derby*, until the 10th of Queen *Elizabeth*, had one common High-Sheriff, (*a*) who used to hold their Courts and Torns at *Nottingham*, till the Reign of *Henry* III. when (a certain Author (*b*) says,) " The Burgesses of *Darby* obtained of King *Henry* III. for a Sum of Money, that the " King's Justices Itinerant, should hold their Assizes at *Darby*, for the two Counties, " and likewise that the Sheriffs of *Nottingham* and *Darby*, (for these Counties then " had but one Sheriff) should hold the County Court and their Torns there, and not " at *Nottingham*, as before was accustomed, to both Shires, which was a great Loss " to this Town (meaning *Nottingham*) and much regretted by the Inhabitants." This Author neither gives us his Authority whence he had this Removal, nor the Year when the Assizes, &c. were removed to *Derby*, they were still held at *Nottingham* the 16th of *Henry* III. as appears in *Thoroton*, (*c*) from the Register of *Thurgarton*. However I find that in the 53d. of *Henry* III. the Assizes were held at *Derby* and also the County Court, for there *John Cousel* offered himself in a Plea against *Peter de Monford*, (Lord of *Gunthorp*) and others, demanding by what Right they exacted Common in his Land at *Hoveringham*, seeing he had none in theirs, and they did no Service to him for it: but it seems the *Derby* Men did enjoy their Priviledge, not much, if any longer then the Life of this King, for the 8th of *Edward* I. his Son and Successor, the Assizes were again held at *Nottingham*, and were continued ever after, except that I read of one single Instance *viz.* the 30th of *Edward* III. that the Assizes were then held both at *Nottingham* and *Derby*; nevertheless the Goal for both Counties has always been at *Nottingham*, till the 23d of *Henry* VIII. (*d*) since which Time *Derby* has had a Goal, and since the 10th of Queen *Elizabeth*, an High-Sheriff of its own.

NOT

(*a*) Anno decimo *Eliz.* Chapt. XVI. *An Act that in diverse Counties there shall be but one Sheriff in one County. The Counties of which two then had but one Sheriff, were these:* Surry *and* Sussex, Essex *and* Hertford, Sommerset *and* Dorset, Warwick *and* Leicester, Nottingham *and* Derby, Oxon *and* Berks. *This Act was at the first made but for three Years and took Place the* 1st. *of* November 1567; *afterwards in the* 13th. *of* Eliz. *it was made perpetual saving for the Sheriff of* Surrey *and* Sussex.

(*b*) Magna Britt. Antiq. & Nov. Vol. IV. *p.* 7.   (*c*) *p.* 191. ibid. *p.* 190.

(*d*) Anno 23°. *of* Henry VIII. Chapt. II. *In an Act for making of Goals within the*

NOTTINGHAM was till the ninth of *Edward* II. within the Jurisdiction of the Honour of *Peverel*, the Court of which was held in this Town in a Chapel dedicated to St. *James*, and which has given the Lane, (about the middle of which it stood) the Name of St. *James's* Lane. This Chapel the said King did grant by Charter to the Friers *Carmelites*, (to the back part of whose Convent it was adjoining) in the aforesaid 9th Year of his Reign, at which Time he discharged *Nottingham* of that Burthen. There goes a Tradition that whilst the Court was held here, the Mace which is now carried before the Mayor, used to be carried before the Steward of the *Peverel* Court. There are no ancient Records to be met with in the Offices above, which gives room to conjecture, that as King *John*, whilst Earl of *Nottingham*, held this County and the Honour of *Peverel*, in a kind of a Regal Manner, the Records of that Honour might be kept separate from any other of the Kingdom, but as these Records are not to be found any where in this County at present, they are generally supposed to have been destroy'd in the late Civil War ; neither have we an Account of the Succession of the High-Stewards of the Honour of *Peverel*. The Jurisdiction of this Court, extended to the Hundreds of *Rushcliff*, *Bingham*, *Newark* and *Basset-lowe* in *Nottinghamshire* and to a great part of *Derbyshire*, and a Town or two in *Leicestershire*, but this Honour, not including every individual Town of the several afore-mentioned Wapentakes in *Nottinghamshire*, I have given a Place to the *Nomina Villarum* in the Appendix. This Jurisdiction the 23d of *January*, and the 25th of *Charles* II. received the Addition of *Thurgarton* and *Lee* and *Broxtow* Hundred in this County.

IN the 5th of Queen *Anne*, (e) her Majesty granted a Patent to Sir *Thomas Willoughby* Bart. after Lord *Middleton*, whereby he had the Grant of the High-Stewardship, to him and his Heirs, and the Right Honourable *Francis* the present Lord *Middleton*, is High-Steward at this Time, and *Edward Wilmot*, Esq; Counsellor at Law, is his Steward for the said Court.

SINCE the Court has been removed from *Nottingham* it has been kept in several Towns, being in the Power of the High-Steward to have it held were he thinks fit, within his Jurisdiction. It seems now to be fixed at *Basford*, where Mr. *William Thorp*, Deputy Steward, attended every Tuesday throughout the Year ; on his Decease Mr. *John Farnsworth*, was appointed Deputy Steward.

An

---

the Realm, *where none be, or where they be weak, there is this Clause* : " Be it " further enacted by the Authority aforesaid, that like Provision in every behalf " be had for a *New-Goal* to be made within the County of *Derby*, in like Form " as is provided in other Shires aforesaid.

(e) *Queen* Anne's *Patent to Sir* Thomas Willoughby, *bears date* June *the* 2d. Anno Regni Regine quinto.

An imperfect List of the MAYORS of NOTTINGHAM from the Years
1302 to 1598.

A. D		A. D.	
1302	Johannes fil de le Paumer.	1471	Thomas Lockton.
1314	Robert Ingram. —	1475	Thomas Hunt.
1330	Nicholas de Shelford. —	1486	William Hyggyn.
1332	Lawrence Le Spicer. —	1487	Richard Ody. —
1334	William de Amyas. —	1506	Richard Melleurs.
1334-5	Roger de Botchal. —	1507	Richard Pykerde.
1340	Ralph de Wolaton. —	1522	Thomas Mellors.
1367	John Samon. — —	1544	John Plumptre.
1370	John Saumon. — —	1548	Robert Lovat.
1379	John de Plumptre. —	1551	Thomas Cockayne.
1382	John Samon. —	1557	William Atkynson.
1384	John Samon. — —	1571	John Gregory.
1389	John de Crowshagh. —	1574	Robert Burton.
1390	John de Croweshawe. —	1576	Henry Newton.
1391	Henry de Normanton. —	1577	Richard James.
1303	William Huntsman. —	1578	William Scot.
1394	John de Plumptre. —	1580	Robert Alvey.
1399	John de Tannesley. —	1581	Robert Burton.
1404	Robert Glade. — —	1584	Peter Clarke.
1412	Robert Glade. — —	1585	William Scott.
1415	Thomas Kay. — —	1586	John Gregory.]
1422	Thomas Poge. —	1587	Robert Alvey.
1425	William Stokes. —	1588	Robert Marsh.
1427	John Plumptre. —	1590	John Brownlow.
1429	William Brodhelm. —	1591	Peter Clarke.
1437	John Plumptre. —	1592	William Scott.
1438	William Webster. —	1593	William Trott.
1441	William Hallifax. —	1594	Robert Alvey.
1444	Thomas Alastre. —	1595	Richard Hurt.
1447	Guaitrid Knyveton. —	1596	Richard Morehaghe.
1449	Thomas Thurland. —	1597	Peter Clarke.
1458	Thomas Thurland. —	1598	Anker Jackson.
1467	John Hunt. — —		
1469	Thomas Alestre. —		
1470	Robert Englishe. —		

A

A more perfect Lift of the MAYORS of *Nottingham*, from the Year 1600 to this prefent Time.

A. D.			A. D.		
1600	Humphrey Bonner.		1639	William Gregory.	—
1601			1640	William Drury.	—
1602	Richard Hurt.		1641	John James.	—
1603	Richard Morehaghe.	—	1642	Richard Hardmeat.	—
1604	Richard Welfh.	—	1643	William Nix.	—
1605	Anker Jackfon.	—	1644	The fame.	—
1606	William Freeman.	—	1645	Thomas Gamble.	—
1607	Humphrey Bonner.	—	1646	John James.	—
1608	Robert Staples.	—	1647	William Drury.	—
1609	Richard Hurt.	—	1648	William Richards.	—
1610	Richard Morehaghe.	—	1649	William Nix.	—
1611	Richard Welfh.	—	1650	Thomas Gamble.	—
1612	Anker Jackfon.	—	1651	Richard Dring.	—
1613	William Freeman.	—	1652	William Drury.	—
1614	Marmed. Gregory.	—	1653	Francis Toplady.	—
1615	Robert Staples.	—	1654	John Parker, Mercer.	
1616	Thomas Nix.	—	1655	Thomas Huthwaite.	—
1617	Leonard Nix.	—	1656	William Richards.	—
1618			1657	Thomas Gamble.	
1619	Anker Jackfon.	—	1658	Richard Dring.	—
1620	Marmeduke Gregory.	—	1659	William Drury.	—
1621	Richard Parker.	—	1660	Francis Toplady.	—
1622	Robert Staples.	—	1661	John Parker, Mercer.	—
1623	Robert Sherwin.	—	1662	Chriftopher Hall.	—
1624	Leonard Nix.	—	1663	William Greaves.	—
1625	Stephen Hill.	—	1664	Ralph Edge.	—
1626	Peter Parker.	—	1665	William Jackfon.	—
1627	John James.	—	1666	Richard Hodgekins.	—
1628	Richard Parker.	—	1667	Jofeph Wright.	—
1629	Alexander Staples.	—	1668	John Parker, Mercer.	—
1630	Robert Sherwin.	—	1669	Chriftopher Hall.	—
1631	Leonard Nix.	—	1670	William Greaves.	—
1632	William Gregory.	—	1671	Ralph Edge.	—
1633	Robert Parker.	—	1672	William Jackfon.	—
1634	John James.	—	1673	Richard Hodgekins.	—
1635	Richard Hardmeat.	—	1674	Jofeph Wright.	—
1636	William Nix.	—	1675	John Parker, Grocer.	—
1637	Robert Sherwin.	—	1676	Chriftopher Hall.	—
1638	Robert Burton.	—	1677	William Greaves.	—

S   1678

A. D.			A. D.	
1678	Ralph Edge.	—	1709	John Peake.	—
1679	John Parker Grocer.	—	1710	Samuel Smith.	—
1680	Gervas Rippon.	—	1711	Benjamin Green.	—
1681	Gervas Wyld.	—	1712	William Barke.	—
1682	William Toplady.	—	1713	John Collin.	—
1683	Christopher Hall.	—	1714	John Shipman.	—
1684	William Petty.	—	1715	(b) Thomas Hawksley. —	
1685	Robert Wortley.	—		— Samuel Watkinson.	—
1686	John Parker Grocer.	—	1716	John Sherwin.	—
1687 (a)	Gervas Rippon. John Sherwin. George Langford.		1717	Thomas Trigge.	—
			1718	Marmaduke Pennel.	—
1688	George Langford.	—	1719	Richard Bearn.	—
1689	Charles Harvey.	—	1720	William Bilbie.	—
1690	John Hawkins.	—	1721	Benjamin Green.	—
1691	Joseph Turpin.	—	1722	Alexander Burden.	—
1692	William Greaves.	—	1723	Thomas Trigge.	—
1693	Thomas Trigge.	—	1724	Marmaduke Pennel.	—
1694	Arthur Rickards.	—	1725	Richard Bearn.	—
1695	John Hoe.	—	1726	William Bilbie.	—
1696	Francis Samon.	—	1727	Joseph Walters.	—
1697	Samuel Leland.	—	1728	Benjamin Greene.	—
1698	William Greaves.	—	1729	Alexander Burden.	—
1699	Thomas Collin.	—	1730	William Trigge.	—
1700	Samuel Watkinson.	—	1731	Thomas Trigge.	—
1701	John Rickards.	—	1732	John Huthwaite.	—
1702	John Peake.	—	1733	Thomas Langford.	—
1703	Samuel Smith.	—	1734	William Bilbie.	—
1704	William Barke.	—	1735	Benjamin Green.	—
1705	John Shipman.	—	1636	Alexander Burden.	—
1706	Francis Samon.	—	1737	William Trigge.	—
1707	William Drury.	—	1738	John Newton.	—
1708	Samuel Watkinson.	—	1739	James Huthwaite.	—

1740

(a) This Year came King *James* II. his *Quo Waranto* to this Town, when *Gervas Rippon* and the five preceeding were turned out, and the following put into their Room, viz. *John Sherwin, George Langford, Charles Harvey,* —— *Hyde* and —— *Crisp,* which two last did not live to be Mayors, *John Sherwin* dying during his Mayoralty in the Month of *May, George Langford* was placed in the Chair, and continued Mayor the succeeding Year.

(b) Alderman *Hawksley,* was displaced *March* the 20th, in the Year of his Mayoralty.

1740 (*c*) Thomas Langford. — | 1745 Henry Butler. —
1741 Alexander Burden. — | 1746 James Huthwaite. —
1742 William Trigge. — | 1747 Thomas Langford. —
1743 John Hornbuckle. — | 1748 William Trigge. —
1744 John Burton. — | 1749 John Hornbuckle. —

SECTION

(*c*) Of this Gentleman it is obfervable, that he was chofen Alderman whilft he was ferving the Office of Sheriff: That in his firft Mayoralty, one *Ward*, Aged 106 Years was made Burgefs: And that when he was Mayor a fecond Time, he was alfo High Sheriff of the County of *Nottingham*, and acquitted himfelf with great Applaufe.

SECTION VII.

Public DONATIONS, CHARITIES, FREE-SCHOOL, CHARITY-SCHOOL, HOSPITALS and other ALMS-HOUSES.

O F all the Benefactions this Town has from Time to Time received, none is better calculated for the perpetual Increase to the Advantages of the Burgesses of this and the rest of the Towns concerned in it, than that of Sir *Thomas White*, commonly known by the Name of the *Coventry-Charity*, of which the following is a particular Account.

THIS Benefactor was an eminent Merchant, by Company a Merchant Taylor in *London*; an Alderman of that great City, and Lord Mayor of the same in the Year 1553 the 1st of the Reign of Queen *Mary* I.

HE gave to the Mayor, B. and C. of the City of *Coventry* 1400 Pounds (a) to be laid out in a Purchase of Lands, &c. for the Relief and Preferment of the Common-Wealth of the said City; and accordingly the Mayor, &c. purchased with the same of King *Henry* VIII. (as appears by his Grant dated at *Walden*) Lands, &c. parcel of the late dissolved Priory of this City, for the Sum of 1378 *l*. 10*s*. 6*d*. the annual Rent of 7 *l*. 13 *s*. 2 *d*. being reserved to the said King his Heirs and Successors.

AFTERWARDS there was an Indenture made and Executed between the Mayor, &c. of the one part, and the Master and Wardens of the Merchant-Taylors in the City of *London* of the other Part, reciting, that the Mayor, &c. did purchase of King *Henry* VIII. Lands, &c. of the yearly Value of about 70 *l*. (as appears by a Schedule annexed) by the only Procurement, Aid, and Help, of *Tho. White*, Merchant-Taylor of *London*, who to relieve and prefer the Common-Wealth of the City of *Coventry*, then in great Ruin and Decay, gave the said Mayor, &c. the Sum of 1400 *l*. — In Consideration thereof, and at the Request and Mediation of certain Friends of the said Mr. *White*, the said Mayor, &c. do covenant and agree with the said Master, Wardens, &c. that they the said Mayor, &c. and their Successors, shall for ever after the Decease of the said Mr. *White*, yearly distribute and deliver of the Rents, Issues, and Profits of the said Lands, &c. the Sum of 70 *l*. in Manner and Form following.

TO twelve poor Men Inhabitants of this City, being Householders, and no common Beggars, in free Alms on the 10th of *March*, or within six Days after the same, the Sum of 24 *l*. to each 40 *s*. — Provided that they of the said poor Men which shall

have

(a) *Account of the many great Loans, Benefactions and Charities, belonging to the City of* Coventry. *p.* 448.   *From another Authority we are assured that Sir* Thomas White *gave only* 1000 *l*. *to the City of* Coventry, *and that the Corporation raised the rest of the Money mentioned.*

have the said Alms one Year, shall not be admitted thereunto again within five Years next following, unless it shall be as charitable to help them as to help any other Persons. —— That the said Mayor, &c. shall, after one full Year determined next after the Decease of the said *Tho. White*, yearly upon the 10th of *March*, or within three Months after, pay and deliver by way of Free-Loan, during the space of ten Years, of the yearly Rents,&c. of the said Lands, the Sum of 40*l*. to four young Men of good Name and Thrift, who have been Apprentices in *Coventry*; to each 10*l*. to have the Occupation thereof for nine Years, putting in Bond and Security for the Re-payment of the same, after the nine Years are expired. —— That the said Mayor, &c. after the Return and Re-payment of such Sums, as shall have, in the space of ten Years, been delivered by them in Loan, as aforesaid, shall pay the same to other young Men in like Manner and Form, from nine Years to nine Years for ever. ——That the said Mayor, &c. after the End of the said ten Years shall, during the space of thirty Years, deliver and pay the Sum of 40*l*. coming and growing as aforesaid, to two other young Men of *Coventry* of good Name and Condition; to each 20*l*, to have the Occupation thereof for the Term of nine Years, finding Sureties as aforesaid, for the Repayment of the same. ——That the said Mayor, &c. shall after the Re-payment of the said several Sums, deliver out the same to two other young Men in like Manner as is before express'd for ever. —— That the said Mayor, &c. shall after the above-nominated thirty Years are expired, pay and deliver in free Loan, the Sum of 40*l*. due and growing of the Premisses, in the first Year after the said thirty Years, to one several young Man of *Coventry*, of good Name and Condition, to have the same for nine Years, upon Security as aforesaid. —— And after Re-payment thereof to another young Man, &c. and so from nine Years to nine Years for ever. —— That the said Mayor shall in the second Year next ensuing the Term of the thirty Years aforesaid, deliver, or Cause to be delivered the Sum of 40*l*. which shall be due and growing of the Premisses to the Mayor, B. and C. of *Northampton*, to be by them immediately delivered by equal Portions, to four young Men, Inhabitants of the said Town, &c. to have the Occupation of the same for the Term of nine Years, finding Security as aforesaid:

The Third }
The Fourth } Year 40*l*. to { *Leicester*,
The Fifth } { *Nottingham*, (a) *Warwick*,

To be disposed of in those Towns respectively in like Manner and Form as aforesaid. —— That after the five Years after the above-said thirty are expired, the said Mayor, &c. of *Coventry*, shall in the sixth Year deliver the Sum of 40*l*. arising as before, to one several young Man of the said City from nine Years to nine Years, and so circularly to other Towns for ever. —— That the 40*l*. be given to the other four Towns, shall for one hundred Years be disposed of, to four Men in each Town; and after the End of those hundred Years to one Man from nine Years to nine Years for ever. —— That the Money shall be delivered without Charge. —— That the four Towns shall give Security to the City of *Coventry*, to deliver out the Money as aforesaid. —— That the said Mayor, &c. shall ever more, after the Decease of the said *Thomas White*, yearly at the Feast of St. *Bartholomew*, or within twenty Days after, pay to the said Master and Wardens, &c. at their Hall 20*s*. for their Labour. —— That the Moneys

(a) *The Sum now paid by* Coventry *to* Nottingham, *can never be ascertained, varying of Rents, Taxes, Repairs, loss by Tenants, and divers unavoidable incidents, make it impossible to fix the Sum for any Town, 'till the Years Rent is collected. In* 1749, Nottingham *received* 450*l*.

Moneys lent ſhall be repay'd within one Month after the nine Years are expired, or within one Month after the Death of any Perſon to whom it has been delivered——— That the twelve poor Men ſhall be yearly choſen by the Mayor, Aldermen, and Reſidue of the Council of the ſaid City. — That the Mayor, Recorder, &c. and ten Aldermen of the ſaid City ſhall have 6 s. 8 d. a piece, and the Clerk 20s. for making the Bonds — That the ſaid Mayor, &c. for Neglect of performing thoſe Conditions and Payments, ſhall pay to the ſaid Maſter and Wardens, &c. for the firſt Year 20l. for the ſecond Year 30l. &c. to be raiſed by Diſtreſs of the ſaid Lands,&c.

THERE is alſo from Time to Time, two Books kept, one by the Corporation of *Coventry*, and the other in the Veſtry of St. *Michael's* Church within the ſaid City of *Coventry*, and therein is entered in the firſt Place, Copies of the Schedules of the Securities, and other Books, Papers, Deeds and Writings, and the Names and Places of Abode of the ſeveral Perſons and their Sureties who ſhall receive any part of the Charity or Loan Money; and that two other Books are kept in like Manner, wherein is entered at firſt an Abſtract of the ſeveral Leaſes now in being of any part of the Charity Lands, expreſſing the Parcels, the Name, and Place of Abode of the Leſſee, the Term, and the Rent; and afterwards like Abſtracts of ſuch Leaſes as ſhall from Time to Time be made of the ſaid Charity Lands or any part thereof: And as to ſuch of the ſaid Books as are to be kept by the Corporation, the ſame are from Time to Time put into the Cheſt with the Writings belonging to the ſaid Charity; Saving that the Books at any Time in preſent Uſe for making ſuch Entries, and the Book uſed laſt before that in preſent Uſe, is kept out of the Cheſt for the more eaſy Recourſe thereto; but no more than two Books for the Entrys of Loans, and no more than two Books for the Entrys of Leaſes at one Time are kept by the Corporation out of the Cheſt; and the Books directed to remain in the ſaid Veſtry, are likewiſe kept in a Cheſt there under three different Locks, the Key of one to be kept by the Vicar of the ſaid Pariſh of St. *Michael* aforeſaid for the Time being, another by the Church-Wardens, and the third Key by the Overſeers of the ſaid Pariſh for the Time being: And that any of the Parties, or of the Inhabitants of the City of *Coventry*, or of the Towns of *Northampton, Leiceſter, Nottingham* and *Warwick*, are at Liberty from Time to Time to reſort to the Court, for ſuch further Order as Occaſion ſhall require.

Mr. *Perkes* (Lottery 13 *July* 1620) at his going from this Town, he gave 5l. to the Poor, and 30l. more to lend to ſix young Men Burgeſſes of this Town at 5l. per Man, by way of free Loan for ſeven Years, and ſo after ſeven Years are expired, to ſix others, to have the ſaid Money as before for ſeven Years, and ſo to ſix others from ſeven Years to ſeven Years for ever; they putting in ſufficient Security for Payment thereof accordingly.

THE ſaid ſix Burgeſſes to be nominated by the Mayor, Aldermen and Town-Clerk of the Town of *Nottingham*, for the Time being. The following were the third ſet which had this Loan:

William Newcombe,	*John James,*	To pay the ſame
Robert Gambol,	*William Calton,*	the 3d. of *November,* 1648.
William Scattergood,	*Thomas Chapel.*	

Robert Staples, p. Indent. dated *February* 8th. the 6th. of *Caroli* 1631. did give to the Mayor and Burgeſſes of the Town of *Nottingham* and their Succeſſors for

ever

ever 40 *l.* to remain and be lent to eight young Men and Burgesses of the said Town of *Nottingham*, and Inhabitants within the same Town by equal Portions at 5 *l.* a Man and for six whole Years, freely, without Interest, they putting in such Securities for the Payment thereof, as the Persons who are to nominate the said Burgesses shall appoint, and after they have held it six Years, then other eight Burgesses of the said Town to have the same 40 *l.* at 5 *l.* a Man, for six Years, putting in Security as before, and so to six more for ever.

THE same eight Burgesses from Time to be nominated by *Alexander Staples*, Alderman, and *Robert Greaves*, now Town Clerk of the same Town, during their Lives, and the Life of the Survivor of them, and after by the Mayor, Recorder, Aldermen and Town-Clerk, or the greater part of them :

Edward Slater,	*Thomas Single,*	Bound to Mr. *Greaves*
Edward Green,	*James Mould,*	for the Payment of it
Will. Charles Mason,	*Robert Jerman,*	on the 1st, of *March,*
Richard Harrison,	*Thomas Brentnal.*	1642.

These two last Loans, I found among Mr. John Town's *Papers, now in the Possession of the Reverend Mr.* Chappell, *Rector of St.* Peter's Nottingham.

Other GIFTS and CHARITIES.

Sir *Thomas Mannors*, by Indenture bearing date the 30th of *June* in the 4th of *Elizabeth* in the Year of our Lord 1562, grants a Rent Charge of Five Pounds per Annum, out of a Messuage or Tenement in *Wilford*, to certain Trustees in the said Indenture mentioned, for the Use and Maintenance of the Poor in *Nottingham*, to be disposed and given by the Discretion of the Parsons, Vicars, or Curates and Church-Wardens of all the three Parishes.------*From the Vellum Book in the Vestry of St. Mary.*

William Willoughby, of *Noneaton* in the County of *Warwick*, by his Will bearing Date the 3d. of *October* 1587, gave to the Poor of the Town of *Nottingham* every 5th Year, *viz.* to four Poor, Aged, Weak and Needy Persons for ever, Frize Gowns, ready made, about the Price of 10 *s.* a Piece, and unto six honest Men of Occupations or Husbandmen, 6 *l.* of current Money of *England*, and to a godly and learned Preacher to instruct the People on the Day of this Distribution, *i. e.* on *Whitsunday* 6 *s.* 8 *d.* He lies buried at *Normanton* upon *Soar*, in the County of *Nottingham*.

Roger Mannors, Esq; by Indenture quadripartite, gave and granted the yearly Rent of 5 *l.* to be distributed among the Poor, Aged and impotent Persons, and such other poor People inhabiting in *Nottingham*, as shall have most need thereof.

IN the Old Town Hall is a Table whereon are 16 Coats quartered, of which the 1st. *Or, two Bars azure on a chief quarterly, two Flower de Liz of France, and one Lion of England.* The second *Gules 3 Waterbougets's Arg. &c.* the Earl of *Rutland's*, under it is this Inscription :

Rogerus Mannors *vir illustris, serenissimæ Reginæ Elizabethæ Somatophylax dignissimus, Comitis* Thomæ Rutlandiæ *filius, in perpetuam Eleemosinam*

leemoſinam, huic Villæ Nottinghamiæ *quinque minas dedit per Annum. In cujus tam largi muneris Major, Fratresq; hic ejus affixerunt inſignia, Anno Dom.* 1601.

ON another Table in the old Town-Hall : *Or : two Barres and a Lion paſſant in Chief Azure.* William Gregory, Gent. ſome Time Town Clerk of *Nottingham,* did by his laſt Will and Teſtament in the Year of our Lord 1613, give and ----------- eleven ſmall Tenements with the Appurtenances, called the *White-Rents,* ſituate at *Houndgate* End, within the ſaid Town of *Nottingham,* for poor aged People to dwell in, Rent free, and 40 *s.* yearly for ever, towards the Reparation of the ſaid Tenements, &c.

Robert Sherwin, late of *Nottingham* Mayor, by his Will dated the 28th of *September* 1638, gave the one half of the Rent of a Meſſuage or Tenement called by the Name of the *Bell* in *Nottingham,* ſituate on the *Angel-Row,* to be equally divided into three parts and delivered to the Churchwardens of the three Pariſhes in *Nottingham,* who are on every *Michaelmas* and *Lady-day* or within fourteen Days after, to diſtribute to every poor Man or Woman 2 *d.* each, as far as their reſpective 3d. part will reach.

Anthony Acham, Gent. late of *Holborn, London,* by his Will dated the 27th of *June* 1638, left a Rent Charge of Five Pounds per Annum upon ſeveral Lands in *Lincolnſhire,* to the Mayor and Commonalty of *Nottingham,* to be diſtributed at ſix ſeveral Times in the Year at 16 *s.* and 8 *d.* every Time.

IN the old Hall I find on a Table the Arms of Sir *George Peckham. Sable a Chevron Or, between three Croſs-croſlets fitche Arg. quartering ſix Coats more :* with this Inſcription :

THE Arms and Atchievements of Sir *George Peckham* late of *Denham* in the County of *Bucks,* Knt. who out of his noble Diſpoſition to Works of Charity and Piety, by his laſt Will and Teſtament gave to the Town of *Nottingham* one hundred Pounds of lawful Engliſh Money the Uſe and Benefit to be yearly diſtributed to the poor Inhabitants there, by the Diſcretion of the Mayor and Aldermen of the ſaid Town for the Time being, and departed this Life the 23d Day of *July,* 1635.

THIS well meaning Gentleman for ſome Time practiſed Phyſick in this Town, he was a mighty Man for Judiciary *Aſtrology,* as far as relates to the Diſcovery of Diſtempers to which the human Fabric is Subject. He was a Roman Catholick and an implicit Believer of the Romiſh Legends, with Relation to the Miracles wrought by Saints and the Power of Interceſſion, which in a great Meaſure appears by his Death, which happened to him by too eager an Act of Superſtitious Devotion. This *Lilly* the Aſtrologer in his own Life gives us an Account of, after his rough Manner :

" IN the Year 1634, I taught Sir *George Peckham,* Knt. Aſtrology, that part " which concerns Sickneſs, wherein he ſo profited that in two or three Months he " would give a very true Diſcovery of any Diſeaſe, only by his Figures. He prac-

" tiſed

" tifed at *Nottingham* but unfortunately died in 1635, at St. *Winifrid's* Well (*a*) in
" *Wales*, in which he continued fo long mumbling his Paternofters and *Sancta Wini-*
" *freda or a pro me*, that the cold ftruck into his Body, and after his coming forth of
" the Well he never fpoke more."

Mary Wilfon, has left to the Parifh of St. *Mary* and St. *Peter*, a Rent Charge of
30 s. per Annum upon a Clofe called *Trough-Clofe*, to be laid out in Cloth for two
Gowns to be given alternately to two poor People of St. *Peter's* and to two of St. *Ma-ry's* Parifh.

Henry Martin of this Town Baker, fettled in the Year 1689, a Rent Charge of 3 *l.*
Yearly for ever upon a Houfe in St. *James's-Lane*, to be equally divided amongft
the three Parifhes and applied with the Approbation of the Mayor for the Time being, towards putting out a poor Boy an Apprentice in each Parifh.-----*From the Tables of the Charities in St.* Mary's *and St.* Peter's *Church.*

William Robinfon, of *Hull*, Gent. by Indenture tripartite, bearing Date the 14th
of *October* 1703, covenanted, that the Corporation of *Nottingham*, in Confideration
of one hundred Pounds paid to the faid Corporation, fhould pay an Annuity of fix
Pounds per Annum, free of all Deductions, to *William Pierpoint* and *George Gregory*,
Efqrs; to be by them paid to the Vicar of St. *Mary's*, 3 *l.* to the Rectors of St. *Peter's* and St. *Nicholas's*, each 1 *l.* 10 *s.* to be given in Bread, as is fpecify'd in the
Indenture.

Mr. *Abel Collin*, late of the Town of *Nottingham*, Mercer, by his laft Will dated
the 4th of *February* 1704, left 20 *l.* to St. *Mary's* and St. *Nicholas's* Parifh, and
15 *l.* to St. *Peter's*, to ferve for a perpetual Fund to buy Coals in Summer, at the
cheapeft Rate, and to be fold in Winter to the Poor of each refpective Parifh, at the

T   fame

(*a*) Polyolbion, *p.* 166. Illuftrations. *At* Haliwell, *a Maritime Village near* Bafingwerke *in* Flint, *is this* Winifrid's-Well, *whofe fweetnefs in the Mofs, wholefomenefs
for Bath, and other fuch ufeful Qualities have been referred to her Martyrdome in
this Place ; but Dr.* Powel *upon* Girald, *in Effect thus :* Henry II. *in his Welfh
Expedition fortify'd the Caftle of* Bafingwerke, *and near by, made a Cell for* Tem-
plers, *which continued there until their Diffolution under* Edward II. *and was after converted to a Neft of lubberly Monks, whofe Superftitious honouring her more
than Truth, caufed this Dedication of the Fountain (fo much to their Profit into a
kind of Merchandize, then, too fhamefully in Requeft) that they had large Guerdons
(it belonging to the Cell) of thofe which had there any Medicine, befides increafing
Rents which accrued to them Yearly out of Pardons to fuch as came thither in folemn Pilgrimage : This Title of Exaction they purchafed of P.* P. Martin V. *under*
Henry V. *and added more fuch gaining Pretences to themfelves in the Time of* Henry VII. *by like Authority ; nor until the more clear light of the Gofpel, yet continuing its comfortable Beams amongft us, diffipated thofe foggy Mifts of Error
and Smoakfelling Impofture, ended thefe collected Revenues. The Author follows the
Legend ; but obferve Times compared, and you will find no mention of this Well, and
healthful Operations of it, until long after the fuppofed Time of St.* Winifred's
Martyrdome.

same price they were bought in at. He left also 100 *l.* to the Poor of *Nottingham*, 20 *l.* to be distributed soon after his Decease, the Residue by 10 *l.* annually on the 2d. of *February*, 'till the whole is distributed. Also 20 *l.* to put out eight poor Boys Apprentices.

Mr. *Thomas Saunderson*, Gent. by his Will dated *February* 2d. 1711, left to the Poor of *Nottingham* 40 *s.* per Annum for the space of seven Years, one Moiety to the Parish of St. *Mary*, the other to be equally divided between St. *Peter's* and St. *Nicholas's*, and after the Expiration of that Term, he left the Rents and Profit of his two Messuages or Tenements in *Pilchergate* in *Nottingham*, together with the Stables and Gardens thereto belonging, (except 40 *s.* per Annum) to the poor Housekeepers of the three Parishes, to be distributed in like Proportion as abovesaid.

Gifts and Charities belonging to St. *Mary's* only.

Thomas Willoughby, by his last Will dated the 4th of *September*, 1524, and prov'd the 11th of *May*, 1525, left to his Wife and Children in Trust and after the Death of his Executors, to the Churchwardens of St. *Mary's* for ever, a Close in *Fishergate* and two Gardens in *Moot-hall-gate*, the Rents and Profits thereof to be employed in the Reparation of his Alms Houses on *Malin-hill*, and if Repairs be not wanting, to be bestow'd on Fuel for his said Bead-folk; out of this each Churchwarden to have six-pence for his Trouble.

THIS Legacy consists in two Gardens in *Moot-hall-gate*, and a Close near *Fisher-gate*; one of the Gardens which is converted into Stables, was by Lease dated *May* 10, 1727, let to *William Cook*, Gent. to whose Freehold the *Feather's* Inn, it is contiguous, at the yearly Rent of 40 *s.* for the space of 21 Years; the other Garden was in the Year 1704, let for the same Term of Years to *Joseph Baker*, Joyner, at 50 *s.* per Annum for 21 Years. The Close is bounded on the East by a little Lane called *Back-Lane*, on the West by a Street called *Cartergate*, on the South by a Street call'd *Fishergate*, and on the North by some Lands and Houses belonging to the Hospital of *John Plumptre*, Esq; There stood in this Place eight little low Houses, when *Richard Hooten*, Plaisterer, obtained a Lease for 50 Years bearing date *April* 5th 1705, for the yearly Rent of 5 *l.* This *Hooten* did sell part of the Land in his Lease, for the whole Term, to *George Merring*, who built three Tenements upon it. After about 15 Years Possession the said *Hooten* sold his remaining part of his Lease-hold and his whole Time in it to *Joseph Hart*, Tallow-Chandler, who having (first built one Tenement upon the Premisses) managed Matters so, as to obtain in the Year 1720, of the then Churchwardens, a fresh Lease of 60 Years to come, beginning the 16th of *April* 1720, only for the part he held, but after the Expiration of the old Lease, the whole Premisses, excluding the poor Man who had built upon the Ground, or his Heirs, to have the Refusal of renewing the Lease of his or their part.

THE whole Rents belonging to *Willoughby's* Bead-Houses for five Poor Widows, are at present 9 *l.* 10 *s.* Besides this, *William Willoughby*, Grandson of the Founder left to the Beadfolk on *Malin-Hill*, an annuity of 10 *s.* a Year to be laid out in Wood or Coals.

A

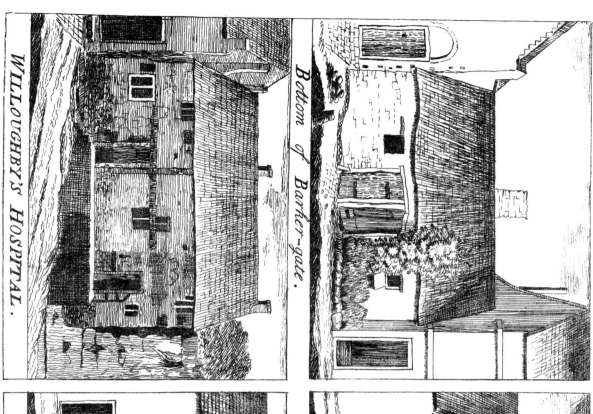

Bottom of Barker-gate.

WILLOUGHBY'S HOSPITAL.

Middle of Pilcher-gate.

In *Warsor-gate.*

A Copy of the Accounts given by the Churchwardens to the Parish of St. Mary *of the Rents of the Alms-House on* Malyn-Hill.

Alms Houſe ſup. Maleyn-Hill in Villa Nott. } COmput. Joh̄ is Gregory et Joh̄ is Browneley gardianorum eccte beate Marie Ville Not. faƈt. pro domo elimoſine ſituat ſup Mayleyn-Hill infra parochiam diƈte ville Not. coram parochianis ejuſdem ecctie in feſto beate Marie Virginis Anno Regnor. Philipp. et Marie Rex et Regine pd. quart et quinto de omnibus reditibus prediƈt. recept. pro dica domo elemoſine tempore *Witti Atkynſon* Majoris diƈte Ville Not.

Comput. de Reddit. unius Clauſure exiſtend in Fiſhergate, et de duobus Gardinis in Mote-hall-gate eidem domo elimoſine conceſs. et plin. prouno anno elapſo XIs. VId. Et de Arreragiis ſup ultimū comput.

ut patet ex pede ejuſdem. ————— ————— iiij s. vi d.

Sunᵃma   XVI s.

I T is now tho' not ſo well improved as might be, 9 l. 10 s. which is near twelve Times the Value.

L A N D eſpecially within Towns is greatly improved ſince the Reign of King *Charles* the 1ſt. as may appear by Indenture bearing date 1645, the 21ſt of *Charles* I. of *Vault-Hall,* mentioned in Seƈt. I. being ſold to *William Drury* the elder, Alderman of *Nottingham,* by *Richard* and *John Martin,* for the Sum of 103 l. *Vault-Hall* in this Indenture is ſaid to ſtand South of the *Low-pavement,* and between *Parkyn's-Lane* on the Eaſt, (a) and a Tenement then *William Burrow's* on the Weſt, and an Orchard in Poſſeſſion of *William Bayley* on the South, and a Tenter Ground in the Tenure of *Anthony Wild,* Sheerman, belonged to it. This in the Year 1733, was by *William Drury* Gent. Grandſon of the above-mentioned Alderman *Drury,* ſold to Mr. *Gauthorn* for 500 l.

Thomas Woolley, late of *Nottingham* Gent. by his laſt Will bearing date the 14th of *April,* 1647, gave to the Pariſh of St. *Mary,* two Cottages and Appurtenances, ſituated in a Place call'd *Beck-lane,* the one to be divided into two Tenements, ſo that both might hold three poor Perſons to be placed therein at the diſcretion of the Miniſter, Churchwardens, and Overſeers of the Poor for the Time being. He alſo left a Rent Charge of 40 s. per Annum, to provide two Gowns yearly of 20 s. Value each, for the Bead-folk, and if there be no need, to employ the Money in the Repairs of the Bead-Houſes. Theſe 40 s. are at this Time paid by Mr. *Clifford Harriſon,* 13 s. 4 d. and by Mr. *Featherſtone,* 6 s. 8 d. half yearly. This is an airy wholſome Place and the Pariſh has built two Appartments over the old ones for two poor People more.

John Patten by his nuncupative Will dated the 8th of *October* 1651, leaves one *George Arnall* and *Stephen Hill,* in Power to receive all the Money that ſhall be

T 2   found

(a) *This Lane was anciently call'd* Voult-Lane, *then* Parkyn's-Lane, *probably from ſome of that Family living in that Houſe for ſome Time, as it is now called* Drury-Hill *from the ſubſequent Purchaſer.*

found and come in his Life Time, or after, upon Bond, Bill, or any lawful Witness, as they shall see Occasion, and that the Use thereof shall be distributed to the poor of the Parish of St. *Mary* in *Nottingham*, so much as shall come to their Hands, at two several Feasts in the Year, that is, on St. *Thomas's* Day next before *Christmas*, and on Friday next before *Easter* for ever, by them and their Successors. And he farther leaves a little House standing in the upper End of *Barkergate*, and the Goods in it for the Use of *Anne Awtoft* and *Margery Rook*, during the Life of the First, and *Margery's* continuing single, and to their Successors, to be appointed by the said *Stephen Hill* and *George Arnall*, and their Successors, and so to be continued a perpetual Alms-House, and the Rent of the respective Houses in which the two Executors then lived, should be employ'd in the Repairs of this Alms-House, and if any be over, the surplus to be employed towards buying Coals for the Poor in this Alms-House.

THIS *Patten* was a Brick-maker, and *Arnall* and *Hill*, whom he left Executors were his Workmen and Tenants. These after his Death, paid only to the Poor in the Alms-House 6 s. each; *Arnall* dying, his Widow sold the House and Ground where she lived, to her Son-in-Law *John Johnson* a Carpenter, for 40 l. who built another House upon the spot, where now a Pipe-maker lives, and at first paid the 6 s. a Year; but being refused upon a Vacancy to put in a poor Person by the Successor of *Hill*, he declared he would pay no more, and to the Day of his Death he never paid one Farthing. The Premisses which this Man bought, are now claimed as the Property of one *Dun* a Shoemaker. At present there is but one poor Body in the Alms-House, who receives 6 s. a Year, paid by Mrs. *Bark*.

William Gregory, Gent. gave to the Poor of St. Mary's, 12 d. a Week for ever, to be given in Bread to twelve poor People of the Parish of the blessed *Mary*, in the Town of *Nottingham*, out of the Rents of four Messuages in *Barkergate*, in the same Town, as appears by the Codicil annexed to the Will of

John Gregory, who added 12 d. a Week more to be paid out of the Rents of the four Messuages. Upon the two middlemost of the four Houses in *Barkergate*, are fixed in the Front two Stones, the one with this Inscription:

William Gregory and John his Son, in Anno 1650, gave the Sum of 5 l. 4 s. yearly for ever, towards the Relief of the Poor of St. Mary's Parish, in Rents, to be paid out of these four Tenements, to be bestowed in Bread every Sunday 2 s.

Hannah Metham, left a Rent Charge of 20 s. per Annum upon a Messuage and Bakehouse, &c. to be disposed of in Bread to the Poor of St. *Mary's*, upon every *Christmas* Eve, the which Bread is to be taken up at the said Bakehouse.

Elizabeth Metham, left an additional Rent Charge upon the same Premisses, in *Spread-Eagle-Court* on the *Long-Row*, of 30 s. per Annum, to the Churchwardens and Overseers of St. *Mary's*, to be distributed in Bread to the Poor of St. *Mary's* on every 11th Day of *November*.

John Parker, Alderman of *Nottingham*, left by his Will bearing date the 26th of *October*

October, 1693, 20 *s*. to be paid to the Minister of St. *Mary's* upon every *Easter-Eve*, upon Condition the said Vicar shall preach or cause to be preached in the said Church a Sermon upon Christian Love and Charity, upon *Good-Friday* in the Afternoon, and the said *John Parker* farther left 20 *s*. to lay out in Two-penny Loaves, to be distributed among such ancient poor People of the said Parish as shall be at the said Church at the preaching of that Sermon.

William Thorpe, Clerk, late of *Blidworth*, by his Will dated the 26th of *May*, 1721, gave 10 *s*. per Annum to the Vicar of St. *Mary's* for an anniversary Sermon on the 29th of *May*, the Day of the Restoration. *From the Table of Benefactions in St.* Mary's *Church*.

William Burton of *Halam*, Gent. left to the Poor of St. *Mary's*, 100 *l*. for which Money the Parish pays Five Pounds per Annum to the Poor. *From the same*.

MY Anonymous Author in his Account of this Town makes mention of some charitable Legacies left to be paid Yearly to divers poor Widows in *Walsergate*, *Barkergate* and *Pilchergate*, but by what Benefactor the same were given, is not certainly known, saving that for some probable Reasons, it is supposed that the Benevolence to those in *Walsergate* was given by *William Scot*, sometime Alderman of this Town.

I find four Tenements in *Walsergate* for the Habitation of four poor People, as also four in *Pilchergate* for the same Use, filled by the Churchwardens of the Parish of St. Mary.

AT the upper End of *Barkergate*, are five thatcht Alms-Houses belonging to the Corporation; the Bridgemasters present to them. There live in these Tenements at present five poor Families, who have no other Allowance, except that they receive 2 *s*. on St. *Thomas's* Day annually.

THESE three answering the three Streets my Author speaks of, may I presume be the Legacies he mentions. Probably the Rents of these Habitations were ordered at first to be distributed among the poor Widows.

Thomas Roberts, Fellmonger, left an annual Legacy of 10 *s*. to the Churchwardens, for the use of the Poor of St. *Mary*, charged upon a House in the *Narrow-Marsh*; payable the 7th Day of *September*, by *Samuel Roberts*, of *Horseley*.

CHARITIES belonging to St. *Peter's* only.

Luke Jackson of the City of *London*, gave two thirds of the Tythes of *Horsepcol* in the County of *Leicester*, (the whole Profits to be equally divided in three parts) to the use of the Church and Poor of this Parish for ever, invested in the Hands of five Trustees for that purpose, *viz.* 40 *s*. yearly to the Rector, for preaching two Sermons, one upon the 28th Day of *July*, being the Day of our Deliverance from the *Spanish-Armada*, the other on the 5th of *November* being the Day of our Preservation from the *Gunpowder-Treason*; and the Residue to be disposed of among the poor People of the said Parish.

Robert Sherwin, Son of Alderman *Sherwin* late of *Nottingham*, by his Will dated the 19th of *June*, 1660, and proved *March* 24th 1662, has given to the Parish of St. *Peter* in *Nottingham*, 26 Shillings a Year, six-pence a Week for six-penny Loaves for six poor Widows, upon a Sermon or Lecture-Day, in the Church of St. *Peter*, to

be

be paid by him who has the Lands, and for want of Payment of the 26 Shillings a Year a diftrain upon any part of the faid *Robert Sherwin's* Lands in or about *Nottingham*. There is now 26 Shillings a Year paid by *John Sherwin*, Efq; but is all diftributed at once on *Candlemas-Day*.

William Greaves, Clerk, Rector of *Nuthall* in the County of *Nottingham*, settled in 1639, a Rent Charge of 20 Shillings yearly for ever upon one House in *Bridlefmithgate*, then in the Occupation of *Cartwright Shaw*, Glazier, in this Town, to be paid to the Church-Wardens of St. *Peter* for the Use of the Poor. *This was never paid.*

William Drury of this Town, Gent. charged two Leys of Land in the Rye-Hills, the yearly Rent of 35 Shillings, within the Liberties of the faid Town, with the yearly Payment of 20 Shillings for ever to be diftributed in fix equal parts to fix poor Widows in the Parish of St. *Peter*, of his Heirs own chufing, the last Week in *January*. BUT in Failure of this, 26 s. 8 d. shall be diftributed to eight poor Widows of this Parish, by the Overfeers, and the Overplus of the Rent of the faid Land, be paid to the Minifter to fee it performed, 1676. *From the Table of the Benefactions in St. Peter's Church.*

William Skeffington Efq; charged a House at the North End of the East-side of *Bridlefmithgate* in *Nottingham*, with the yearly Payment of 20 s. for ever, to be diftributed in Bread to the Poor of St. *Peter's* Parish, upon the Thurfday before *Eafter*.

Mr. *Thomas Trigge*, Alderman of *Nottingham*, gave 50 l. to buy Land, for ever the Rent of which to be laid out in Bread, to be diftributed among the poor Houfekeepers of this Parish by the Minifter, Churchwardens and Overfeers of the Poor upon *Chriftmas-Day* and *Good-Friday*, in two equal parts.

Jonathan Paramour, Gent. purchafed an Acre of Land in *Nottingham* upper Meadows and settled it upon the Rector for the Time being, and his Succeffors, for preaching two Sermons, the one upon *Afh-Wednefday*, the other upon *Afcenfion-Day*, for ever, 1730. *From the Table of Benefactions in St. Peter's Church.*

John Barker of *Nottingham* left 50 l. to buy Land, or to be put out upon good Security, (the Deeds to be made to the Rector and Churchwardens) the produce thereof to be apply'd once in two Years to the putting out a Boy of this Parish an Apprentice. 1732. *ibidem.*

Margery Mellors, Widow, who alfo left fome Meffuages for the Repairs of *Trent-Bridge* by her Will bearing Date the 9th of *June* 1539, four Cottages on the *Low-pavement* to the Mayor of the Town of *Nottingham* and the Parfon of St. *Peter's* and his Succeffors for ever, [the then Parfon was *John Plough*, jun.] with the Appurtenances, to fix poor Women of honeft Name, and they to be appointed by the faid Mayor and Parfon for ever. She left to the finding and building of four Cottages, one Garden and a Stable on the *Low-pavement*.

Mary Lawton, Widow, by her Will dated *January* 24th. 1632, gave two little Houfes in *Liftergate*, to her Sifter *Alice Leeming*, for her Life, and after her Death, gave them and another Houfe, being the corner House, to *Robert Nichols* and *Urfula* his Wife, for their Lives, and after their Deaths, to *Robert Nichols's* Heirs, paying 20 s. a Year for them at *Midfummer* and *Chriftmas*, for the Use of the Poor of St. *Peter's* Parish. This and the preceding were never paid.

CHARITIES belonging to St. *Nicholas's* only.

THIS Church had doubtlefs fome ancient Charities peculiar to itfelf as well as the

the two others, but I find as little Account of them as of the old Church and the ancient Monuments, of which there were no doubt a confiderable Number, befides thofe of the *Plumptre's*. The only mention I meet with of a Charity before the Civil War, is that of *William Collinfon*, which was but for a Term of Years long fince expired. It was as follows :

HE by his Will dated *November* the 14th, 1632, gave after the Deceafe of Mrs. *Parker*, his Mother, to the needful Poor of St. *Nicholas's* Parifh, 20s. per Annum, to be beftow'd in Bread and diftributed half yearly, and to begin the fame Day 12 Months wherein fhe fhould die, and fo to continue twenty Years by 10s. every half Year : And a Sermon to be made the fame Day wherein the faid Bread fhall be diftributed, in St. *Nicholas's* or St. *Peter's* Church, and the Preacher to have for every Sermon 10s. all which to be iffuing forth of his Lands in *Nottingham*. His Will is amongft the Writings in the Town's-Hall.

Elizabeth Bilby, late Widow *Tibfon*, by her laft Will gave 20l. to the Corporation, they to pay 20s. the Intereft thereof, yearly to the Churchwardens and Overfeers of the Poor of the Parifh of St, *Nicholas* in *Nottingham*, for the ufe of thirty ancient Men and Widows of the faid Parifh, to be paid 10s. at *Chriftmas* and 10s. at *May-Day* for ever.

Dr. *Gray*, a Phyfician in this Town, who died in the Year 1705, at *Bilborow*, a Village three little Miles from *Nottingham*, and was buried there, by his laft Will and Teftament, left 20l. the Intereft of which to be diftributed by two equal Portions at *Chriftmas* and *Eafter*, to the Poor of St. *Nicholas*, at the Difcretion of the Rector and Churchwardens.
N. B. This Charity through the diligent Application of the Rev. Mr. *Abfon*, prefent Incumbent of this Parifh, in favour of the Poor, is now encreafed to 30l.

IN the Year 1714, *Anthony Walker*, a Perfon who ufed to Travel much, and by that means fee the Accounts of the Benefactions to the Poor, made his Will, and thereby gave two Cottage Houfes and fix Acres of Land, being a Copyhold Eftate lying at *Matlock* in *Derbyfhire*, to the Poor of the Parifh where he fhould die, and departing this Life about three Years after in the Parifh of St. *Nicholas* in *Nottingham* : *Francis Newdigate*, Efq; and Mr. *John Elfe*, the then Churchwardens, claimed the faid Eftate for the Ufe of the Poor of this Parifh, and after fome Conteft in the Year 1720, obtained a Surrender thereof to them and their Heirs, to the Ufe aforefaid. By the Will the Eftate is computed at 6l. per Annum, and fpecifically divifed to buy twelve two-penny Loaves for the Poor every Sabbath Day throughout the Year for ever. *On a Table in St.* Nicholas's *Church*.

Jacob Tibfon, by Indenture bearing Date *March* the 13th, the 3d of King *George* II. 1729, did give to the Poor of the Parifh of St. *Nicholas*, a Meffuage divided into two or more Tenements, with Cellars, &c. fituated in *Liftergate*, the Rent thereof to be diftributed half yearly to a Number of poor Houfekeepers as fhall be judged proper Objects by the faid Minifter and Churchwardens, not exceeding 5 Shillings each.
N. B. The Premiffes are but in a bad Condition, and therefore not extraordinary well Tenanted ; the prefent Rent is 4l. 11s. almoft one half of which goes in Repairs. The fame Mr. *Tibfon* about three Years before his Death, gave to the Rector and
Church-

Churchwardens 30 *l.* the Intereſt of which to be given to poor Houſekeepers at 5*s.* a piece. The Money is now in the Hands of one of the Pariſhioners at 4 per Cent. A Year after he farther gave 10 *l.* for the ſame Purpoſe, which 10 *l.* together with the 30 *l.* of Dr. *Gray*, are let to the Overſeers at Five per Cent. for which they have given Bond to the Rector and Churchwardens of the ſaid Pariſh.

Other BENEFACTIONS.

Margery Doubleday, who gave the 7th Bell of St. *Peter's*, left ſome Land, of the Value of 20 *s.* per Annum, to be paid to the Sexton for Ringing the ſame every Morning at Four o'Clock. This Woman was a Waſher-woman, who made this Gift out of a public Spirit to her Siſter Waſher-women, whom this Bell was to call to their Work.

SHE alſo left to the Uſe of the Guild of St. *George* in St. *Peter's* Church, a Cloſe at the Woodſide of 26 *s.* 8 *d.* by the Year, to help to uphold Preſt to ſinge for her Huſband's Soul and hers, and a Dirge and a Maſs to be ſungen once in the Year to the Preſts and Clerks. The Will bears date the 20th of *June* 1544.

THIS Cloſe is in the Poſſeſſion of the Corporation, and did let in Mr. *Town's* Time for 4 *l.* per Annum.

Robert Staples, Gent. by his Will dated the 3d of *June* 1630, did give to ſome godly learned Preacher, to preach two Sermons yearly for ever, one on the Sabbath-day before *Chriſtmas*, the other on the Sabbath-day before *Whitſuntide*, exhorting the Hearers to good Hoſpitality, and relieving the Poor, 10 *s.* at each of the ſaid Days, to be iſſuing out of the Rents of his two Shops in Shoemaker-Booths, (*a*) then in the Tenure of Mr. *Watſon*.

ex autograph. Johannis Town.

Henry Handley, Eſq; by Indenture bearing date the 3d Day of *October* 1646, gave 20 *l.* per Annum for a Lecture to be preached Weekly at the Pariſh Church of St. *Mary* in *Nottingham*, in the Forenoon, by ſome pious and orthodox Miniſter or Miniſters for ever.

THIS Lecture is now preached every Wedneſday Morning by the Vicar of St. *Mary's* and the Rector of St. *Nicholas's*, alternately.

THE ſame *Handley*, gave by the ſame Indenture, to the Priſoners of the County Goal or Goals, the Sum of Four Pounds per Annum, to be equally divided amongſt them at four ſeveral Days in the Year, *viz.* on the Day of St. *Thomas* the Apoſtle, on the Feaſt Day of the *Annunciation*, St. *John* the *Baptiſt*, and of St. *Michael* the Archangel. This is at this Time regularly paid by a Tenant of *John Sherwin*, Eſq; who holds the Lands.

ON a Table in the Old Town-Hall is this Coat of Arms: *Ermin a Gryffin Sergreant queve*

(*a*) *They are now the Property of Mr.* Joſeph Burrow, *who pays the Rent Charge.*

P. 145

The Hospital of the Blessed Virgin Mary, near the end of the Leen Bridge, commonly called Plumptre's Hospitall as it appeard in 1750.

J. Cte. Sel et Sculpt.

queve nowe gules, Grantham, impaling *Arg.* on a *Chevron fable* 3 *Buck Heads ca-
bofed Or.* under it the following Infcription :

> The moft pious and virtuous Lady *Lucy*, Wife of
> Sir *Thomas Grantham*, did of her Charity give two
> hundred Pounds at feveral Times to the Town, the
> Ufe thereof to be employ'd to the fetting forth poor
> Burgeffes Children Apprentices for ever.
> *William Greaves*, Mayor 1671.

John Parker of *Nottingham*, Alderman, by his Will bearing Date the 26th of
October, 1693, gave among other Things 9 *l.* every other Year, to be employ'd in putting out three Boys Apprentices, not under 13 nor above 15 Years of Age, and to
thefe Lads when out of their Time 3 *l.* a piece more, to fet them up in their refpective Trades.

Abel Collin, left by his Will to the poor Debtors of the two Goals in *Nottingham*,
viz. for the Town and for the County at large, to each 1 *s.* per Week, to be paid on
every Saturday for ever.

B E S I D E S *Willoughby's, Woolley's*, and *Patten's* Alms-Houfes, with the *White-
Rents*, already mentioned, there are the following Provifions made for the Habitation
and Support of Poor People.

PLUMPTRE'S HOSPITAL.

T H I S is the moft ancient of all the Hofpitals in *Nottingham* now in being, having
for its Founder *John de Plumptre* a Merchant of the Staple of *Calais*, living in *Nottingham* in the Reign of King *Richard* II, of whom he obtained Licence, dated at
Nottingham the 16th of *Richard* II. the 8th of *July* A. D. 1392, to found and endow
within the faid Town, an Hofpital or Houfe of God, confifting of two Chaplains,
whereof one fhould be the Mafter or Guardian [*Magifter & Cuftos*] of the faid Hofpital, and thirteen old and poor Widows. Accordingly the faid *John de Plumptre*,
did build an Hofpital and a Chapel adjoining thereto, as appears by the Inftrument
of Foundation dated at *Nottingham* the 12th Day of *July* 1400, which was confirmed
by *Richard* Archbifhop of *York*, the fame Year *July* 22d. In which Inftrument having firft given Thanks to God for having vouchfafed unto him to build [*conftruere*]
an Hofpital [*Hofpitale*] at the End of the Bridges of *Nottingham*, for the fupport of
13 poor Women to the Honour of God and the Annunciation of his Mother the bleffed
Virgin, *&c.* he proceeds to the Foundation, and Wills and Ordains, that from thenceforth for ever there fhould be a Chantry within the Chapel, which had been built
near the faid Hofpital. This Chantry was to be Supply'd by two Chaplains, who were
daily to celebrate Divine-Service at the Altar of the Annunciation of the bleffed Virgin *Mary* within the faid Chapel, for the welfare of the King whilft living, and of
his Soul after his Deceafe, and of the Founder, and *Emma* his Wife, whilft they
fhould live, and of their Souls when Dead, and for the welfare of the whole Community of *Nottingham* ; as alfo for the Souls of his Succeffors, and all thofe from
whom he had received any Benefit, and of all thofe for whom we are bound to pray,
or to do Works of Charity, and of all the faithful departed, *efpecially of fuch as at their
Death fhould bequeath any Thing to this Hofpital, and for the Support of the Poor
Widows dwelling therein.*

U

ONE

ONE of these two Chaplains he appoints to be Master and Guardian, the other to be secondary Chaplain. The first two Chaplains were *Thomas Tawburn*, primary Chaplain and Master, and *John de Coventry*, secondary Chaplain. And for the Suftentation of them both, and of 13 poor Widows, he affignes a certain Messuage in *Nottingham* for their Habitation, and ten other Messuages, and two Tofts in the said Town, and an hundred Shillings per Annum to each of the said Chaplains, out of the Rents and Profits of the same.

AS to the Support and Maintenances of these poor Women; such was the high Opinion this pious Founder had of, and placed in the Spiritual Men, that he left the Manner of providing for them wholly at their Difcretion, giving them only this general Charge, *viz.* To Support and maintain [*fupportabunt et manutenebunt*] the poor Women to the beft of their Power, and to inftruct them in their Creed and Catholic Faith, [*et in ipfarum fymbolo et fide catholica informabunt ipfas*] not to fupply them unduly out of the Rents, Profits, or other Incomings, granted or to be granted for their Support, nor convert their Habitations into any other Ufe or Ufes, nor cause, nor fuffer them to be converted, but that they, to the utmoft of their Power, fhall refift and hinder any fuch Alteration.

THIS Foundation Deed makes mention of 13 poor Widows, to be maintained in the aforefaid Hofpital, but it does not appear by any Remains that there were ever fo many placed in it, but the contrary may be rather inferred from feveral Documents.

FOR in the Will of *Anne Plumptre* the Wife of *John Plumptre*, dated the 12th of *September* 1403, by which fhe leaves a Legacy(*a*) to thefe Poor, no Number is taken Notice of. In the Will of *Henry Plumptre* elder Brother of the Founder, made in 1408, there is a Legacy (*b*) of 12 *d.* to every Bed in the faid Hofpital that fhall be then occupy'd, &c. by which it fhould feem, that the Founder, who was yet alive, had not then fully compleated the Number of the Foundation. And it is no obfcure Intimation, that the Founder was in Hope of an increafe of his Charity from other well minded Perfons, and that there wanted ftill a fufficient Support for the Poor, when he directs his Chantry-Priefts *to pray* (among others) *for the Souls of thofe who at their Death fhall have bequeathed any Thing to this Hofpital, and for the Support of the Poor in it.*

BUT what puts the Matter out of all Doubt, is, that this *John de Plumptre*, after 15 Years Experience, finding his Expectation not anfwered in the concurring Charities of others, and being fenfible that the Provifion he had made was infufficient for the Maintenance of the propofed Number, having referved to himfelf a Power to make Additions to, and Alterations in the Foundation, as he fhould fee expedient; he made another Inftrument bearing Date the Monday after the Feaft of the Conception

---

(*a*) Lego viduis habitantibus in Hofpitale ad finem Pont. Nott. I. Dozein de panno laneo dividend. inter eas pro indumentis fuis.

(*b*) Lego *cuilibet lecto occupato* in Hofpital. Annunciationis beatæ Virginis Mariæ ad finem Pont. de Nottingham 12 *d.* Item lego totum illud lectum in quo moriar Hofpitali prædicto, ad ufum Mulierum ibidem degentium.

tion of the bleffed Virgin, A. D. 1415. the 3d of *Henry* V. the which was confirmed by *Henry* Archbifhop of *York*, *February* 5th. A. D. 1415.

BY this he confirms the Chantry of two Priefts, augments the Stipend of the chief Mafter to 6*l.* p. Annum, limits the Number of poor Widows to feven, [*pro fuftentatione feptem pauperum mulierum, &c.*] and gives as an Addition to the faid Chantry, his Dwelling Houfe (*a*) in *Cuckftool-Row*, at the Corner of the Lane leading from the Saturday Market to St. *Peter's* Church, (fince called *Peck-Lane*) after his Death and the Death of *Thomas Plumptre*, Chaplain, his Kinfman. The two Priefts were at that Time *Thomas Tawburn*, Mafter, and *John Tawburn*, fecondary Chaplain, in all other material Points, this laft Inftrument agrees with the former, wherein the Founder referves to himfelf the Prefentation of the Chaplains in Cafe of any Vacancy, but after his Death he ordains that the remaining Chaplain fhall elect another fit fecular Prieft, [*fecularem non religiofum*] to be Chaplain of the faid Chantry, within ten Days after Notice of fuch Vacancy, and acquaint therewith by Letter, feal'd with his Seal, the Prior and Convent of *Lenton*, and withal intreat them to prefent that Chaplain fo e-lected, to the Diocefan of the Place, if the See be full, but if vacant, to the Vicar General in Spirituals [*cuftodi Spirituali*] of the Diocefe of *York*. And that the faid Prior and Convent prefent the faid Chaplain within fifteen Days including the afore-faid ten Days, as has been directed. But if the faid remaining Chaplain, fhould not be willing to nominate a fit Perfon within ten Days after fuch Vacation, then fhall for that Turn, the Prior and Convent of *Lenton*, have Power to elect and prefent one, and if they alfo refufe fo to do within fifteen Days, it fhall be lawful for the faid re-maining Chaplain, to elect and prefent another difcreet and fit Prieft [*prefbyterum*] to the faid Chantry, *&c.* he leaves the Direction concerning the Support of the Poor as they were in the firft Deed.

THE Founder did not long furvive this his Regulation as appears by his Will dated in *December* 1415, in which he leaves a Legacy of 20 *s.* to each poor Wo-man. (*b*)

IT is not known how this Charity was managed from this Time for 130 Years, but in the 37th of *Henry* VIII. the Commiffioners for the Survey of all Chauntries, Hof-pitals, Colleges, Free-Chapels, Fraternities, Brotherheds, Guylds and Salaries of ftipendary Priefts, within the Counties of *Nottingham* and *Derby*, certify'd that at that Time there were no poor Widows in this Hofpital, but that the Revenue thereof was employ'd in the living of the two Chantry Priefts there, *Peter Burdefel* and *Wil-*

U 2

liam

(*a*) Item tenementum meum in quo habito in dato prefentium fup le Cuckftole-Rowe fup Corneram venelle que ducit â foro Sabbati ufq; ad Ecclefiam Sancti Petri ex parte occidentali et tenementum predicte Cantarie in quo manet Johannes Philip ex parte orientali, cum omnibus Edificiis ibidem conftructis et fuis pertinentiis qui-bufcunq, tam terraneis quam fubterraneis do et concedo poft terminum Vite mei et terminum Vite *Thome Plumptre* Capellani cognati mei predicte Cantarie infra dictum Hofpitale p. me conftructe fine fine permanfurum.

(*b*) Lego cuilibet Vidue infra Hofpitale ad finem Pont. Nott. p. me fundatum ma-nenti ibidem Deo fervienti et pro me oranti 20 *s.* exinde fua propria commoda faci-end. fecundum ordinationem et fupvifionem Executoris mei.

liam Browne. (*a*) About two Years after this, in the 2d of *Edward* VI. there having paſt a freſh Law for ſeizing into the Poſſeſſion of the Crown, all Colleges, Free-Chapels, Chauntries, &c. The ſaid King iſſued another Commiſſion of Survey, the Commiſſioners of which (*b*) (as the former) certify'd their Survey into the Court of Augmentations, by which it appears that no Poor were in this Hoſpital, but that a Prieſt *Peter Burdeſale,* had the whole clear Income. From this Time ſeveral Perſons ſucceſſively obtained Patents for the Maſterſhip of this Hoſpital, as one *Edmund Wyſeman, Edward Suthworth, William Ball* and *Richard James,* but we don't find that any one of theſe put in any Poor, but it rather ſeems that they converted the whole Profits to their Uſe, as may be inferred from what Dr. *Thoroton* ſays, p. 494 *Antiq. Nott.*

" A F T E R diverſe Patents of the ſaid Maſterſhip, *Nicholas Plumptre,* of *Not-*
" *tingham,* the 24th of *Elizabeth* obtained one, and with the Fines he received, made
" ſome Reparations and brought in ſome Poor."

A F T E R the Death of the ſaid *Nicholas Plumptre,* his Son *Henry* being then a Minor, and married to the Daughter of *Richard Parkyns,* Eſq; the ſaid Mr. *Parkyns* obtained a Patent for the Maſterſhip of this Hoſpital, which he deſigned to Surrender to his ſaid Son-in-Law, when he ſhould attain his full Age. But upon the ſaid Mr. *Parkyns's* Death, before he had ſo ſurrendred, his Son *George Parkyns* Knt. procured a Patent for himſelf, and held the Maſterſhip for his Life. (*c*) After that, *Nicholas Plumptre,* eldeſt Son of the ſaid *Henry,* obtained the Maſterſhip, by a Patent dated the 26th of *June,* the 2d of *Car.* I. A. D. 1626 ; in his Time the Poor had for their Allowance 1 *d.* a Day ; he dying without Iſſue, his Brother and Heir *Huntingdon Plumptre,* had a like Patent dated the 11th of *May,* the 20th of *Charles* I. A. D. 1644, who in 1645, raiſed their Allowance to 2 *s.* 10 *d.* a Month each, with 6 *d.* a Peice over on every *New-Years-day,* and after in 1650, having improved the Rents of the Hoſpital, he alſo increaſed the Poor's Allowance to 5 *s.* a Month each, with the additional 6 *d.* in the Month of *January,* which Allowance has been continued and regularly paid to them every Calendar Month to this Day. This *Huntingdon* dyed while his eldeſt Son *Henry* was yet a Minor, and then by Conſent and Deſire of the ſaid *Henry* and his Mother, (who was his Guardian) *George Cartwright,* Eſq; petitioned for the ſaid Maſterſhip, in order to Surrender it unto the ſaid *Henry* when he ſhould come of full Age, and he obtained a Patent accordingly, the 10th of *July* in the 12th of *Car.* II. Anno Dom. 1660 ; but the ſame was never ſurrendered, the ſaid *Henry* contenting himſelf with the Power allow'd to his Mother and afterwards to himſelf, by the ſaid *George Cartwright,* to govern the Hoſpital and manage its Eſtate at their own Diſcretion. But after Mr. *Cartwright's* Death, the ſaid *Henry Plumptre,* obtained a Patent to himſelf, dated the 5th of *Sept.* the 24th of *Car.* II. A. D. 1672, and he alſo dying during the Minority of his eldeſt Son *John Plumptre,*
Charles

(*a*) *Commiſſioners were* Sir John Markham, Knt. William Cowper, Nicholas Powtrell, Eſqrs. *and* John Wiſeman, Gent.
(*b*) *The Commiſſioners of the laſt Survey, were* Sir Gervaſe Clifton, Sir John Herſey, Sir Anthony Nevil, Knts. William Bowle's Eſq; *and others.*
(*c*) *During the Maſterſhip of* Richard *and* Sir George Parkyns, *both the Hoſpital and Tenements belonging to it, grew into great Decay.* Thor. p. 494.

Charles Hutchinson of *Owthorp*, Efq; apply'd for and obtained a Patent the 10th of *Feb.* the 5th of *William* and *Mary*, A. D. 1692, with the like View of Friendſhip to the Minor as Mr. *Cartwright* had had for his Father, but Mr. *Hutchinſon* dying alfo before the faid *John* became of Age, *Robert Sacheverel*, Efq; of *Barton*, procured to himſelf a Patent with the fame friendly Intention, and both he and Mr. *Hutchinſon* left the whole Management of the Hoſpital to the Mother, (Guardian) of the faid *John*, and after the faid *John* had attained his full Age, Mr. *Sacheverel* furrendered his Patent, and a new one was granted to the faid *John Plumptre*, Efq; the prefent Maſter, on the 29th of *Feb.* the 2d of Q. *Annæ*, A. D. 1703-4, who befides the Allowance laſt mentioned has added a Tun of Coals p. Annum to each of the feven poor Widows.

T H E Hoſpital Eſtate ever fince the Maſterſhip is returned to the Family of the pious Founder, has been improving, the farther Fruits of which will appear in due Time, when the advanced Rent ſhall have cleared off the great Debt incurred by numerous Expences in repairing and rebuilding many of the Houfes gone to Decay and utter Ruin by length of Time, and when a Fund ſhall have farther arifen, fufficient to put in Execution the Defign of the prefent Maſter, to extend, (if poſſible) the Charity to poor Widows, to be anfwerable to the firſt Intention of the Founder, and to the Royal Licence thereupon.

B Y what remains of the old Work it appears, that the original Fabric was Stone, 74 Feet in Front which looks towards the Weſt, and 63 Feet in depth. In the Centre of the Building are at prefent four Rooms opening into a common Paſſage, over which are built four others, at the End of the Paſſage a back Door opens into a little Square Garden, terminated by the Weſt-Wall of the Chapel. On the North and South Sides there are ſtill to be feen in each, two Window-Frames, now bricked up, which looked into the Garden, over thefe it feems were other Rooms. The Wings of the prefent Building, ſtand on twice the Ground of the other Apartments, thefe, not improbably, may have been the Lodging of the two Prieſts; thefe Wings have at this Time a raifed Roof with Gable Ends, and the Center is a flat Roof leaded, which covers all thofe who receive the Charity, which according to the Founder's fecond Inſtrument are feven in Number, the eighth Room being turned to a common Coal Place : Adjoining to this Hoſpital there is ſtill vifible part of the Chapel Wall facing the North, with a Door, over which there is a Niche, wherein was probably placed a Reprefentation of the Annunciation, here are alfo the Remains of a Window. At the South End is likewife left part of the Chapel-Wall, with a Doorſtead, exactly oppoſite to the North-Door, both thefe are bricked up. This Chapel was 58 Feet long and 32 Feet in Front.

T H E prefent Frame of this Hoſpital ſtands indebted to the Care of *Huntingdon Plumptre*, above mentioned, Doctor of Phyfick, as appeared by the Infcription over the Gate, which not being legible at this Time, I have borrowed of Dr. *Thoroton*.

> Xenodochium hoc cum facello adjuncto in honorem Annunciationis
> B. Virginis Mariæ pro 13 pauperiorum Viduarum et 2 Sacerdotum Alimonia *Johannes Plumptre*
>
>   fu‾davit

fundavit A. D. 1390 (*a*) Quod
(temporis diuturnitate jam pene
confectum) inftauravit denuo, et
hâc qualicunq; Structurâ fe fibi
reftituit *Huntingdonus Plumptre*
ex Familiâ Fundatoris Armiger
et ejufdem Hofpitii Magifter
A. D. 1650.

BEFORE I proceed to other Charity Houfes it may not be amifs to give the
Reader a very juft Obfervation of *John Plumptre*, Efq; upon the Inacuracy of Dr.
Thoroton, in Relation to *Plumptre's* Hofpital.

" THE Doctor in his Dedication to *William Dugdale*, Efq; takes Notice that Mr.
" *Pigot*, of *Thrumpton*, had produced fome fhort Notes of Serjeant *Boun's*, on the part
" of Doomfday-Book which relates to *Nottinghamfhire*, and towards the Conclufion
" of the Doctor's Preface, he fpeaks of his Father-in-Law Serjeant *Boun's* Collections.
" The long Quotations taken from thefe Collections, fhew, that they were fome-
" thing diftinct from the fhort Notes before mentioned ; but with how little Care and
" Acuracy they were compiled, may be inferred from the Inftances in one fhort Pa-
" ragraph p. 491, which the Doctor in kindnefs to his Father-in-Law, might as well
" have fuppreffed.

" THE Paragragh fpeaking of the Hofpital by the *Leen-Bridge*, fays it was
" founded about *Edward* the 3ds Time, for divers poor Men. Both which Afferti-
" ons are directly and rightly contradicted by the Doctor in p. 494, where he fhews
" that it was founded in the 16th Year of *Richard* II. and not for Men but 13 poor
" Widows. But it is ftrange too here that the Doctor fhould have taken up with a
" fecond hand Authority, *viz.* the *Monafticon Anglicanum*, which he cites in the
" Margin for this, when it appears in the fame Margin that he had the Perufal of Mr.
" *Plumptre's* Papers, among which then was, and ftill is, an Exemplification, under
" the great Seal of King *Richard's* Licence, of the 16th Year of his Reign, to *John*
" *Plumptre*, Efq; for erecting the faid Hofpital for poor Widows : And in this very
" page it falls out that the Doctor himfelf furnifhes an Inftance of the Danger there is
" in following thefe fecond-hand Authorities. *Dugdale* in the Abftract of the faid
" *John Plumptre's* Inftrument of Foundation of his faid Hofpital, fays, that the Pre-
" fentation to the Chantry there, was after the Founder's Death, to be in the Com-
" munity of the Town of *Nottingham* and the Prior of *Lenton*; for this he quotes
" the Regiftry in the Archbifhop's Court at *York* ; whereas the faid Founder by that
" Inftrument ftill extant, in the faid Regiftry, gives the Prefentation folely to the
" Prior and Convent of *Lenton*, in thefe Words : ―――― Poft obitum vero meum, volo
" quod ad Priorem et Conventum de *Lenton*, quicunq; pro tempore fuerint, pertineat
" Prefentatio ejufdem in perpetuum. ― And the Blunder in the *Monafticon* the Doc-
" tor has roundly transferred into his own Book ; in Truth the Doctor acknowledges
fairly

(*a*) *This Infcription might perhaps be fomewhat worn in* Thoroton's *Time, fo that he
might eafily miftake the round part of the 2 for a cypher. The Licence being obtained in* 1392.

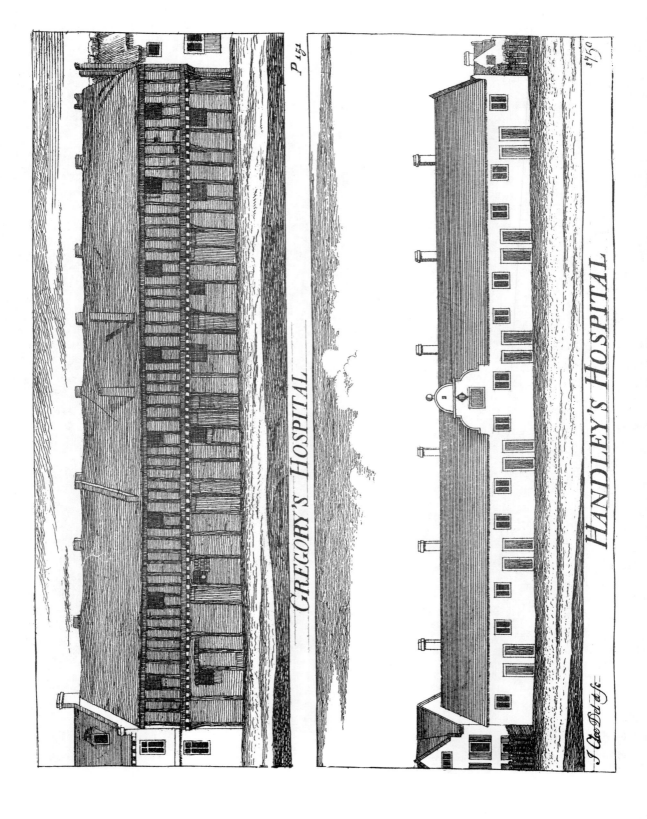

GREGORY'S HOSPITAL

P.454

HANDLEY'S HOSPITAL

450

" fairly in his Preface, that he never infpected the Archbifhop of *York's* Regiftry,
" norhad had it infpected to any Purpofe for him, and yet undoubtedly it would have
" afforded much Light to his Work.   There is alfo another great Fund of Informati-
" on, which he never apply'd to, and that is the *Record-Office* of the Court of Aug-
" mentation of the Revenues erected by *Henry* VIII. upon the Diffolution of Monaf-
" teries, &c. in which there are particular Surveys of all the Church-Lands taken
" into the Hands of the Crown, and many other valuable Documents for fuch a Work
" as the Doctor's."

Henry Handley's Alms-Houfes are in *Stony-ftreet* ; over the middle of the Building are his Arms : *Arg. Feffe Gules between three Goats in Courfe fable, horned,*
bearded and hoofed, Or.

Under it :

Henry Handley, Efq; whofe Body is interred
in the Church of *Bramcote* in the County of
Nottingham, caufed this Alms-Houfe to be e-
rected for 12 poor People, and did give one
hundred Pounds yearly, forth of his ancient Inheritance, Lands at and near *Bramcote* aforefaid, for pious and charitable Ufes, to continue
for ever. Namely XL *l.* for the Maintenance
of the faid 12 poor People ; XX *l.* for a Weekly Lecture in this Town ; XX *l.* for a Preaching and refiding Minifter at *Brámcote* ; V *l.*
for the Poor of *Bramcote* ; V *l.* for the Poor at
Wilford ; XX *s.* to the Poor of *Beefton* ; XX *s.*
to the Poor of *Chilwell* ; XX *s.* to the Poor of
Attenborow and *Toton* ; XX *s.* to the Poor of
Stapleford ; XX *s.* to the Poor of *Trowell* ;
XX *s.* to the Poor of *Woollaton* ; and IV *l.* to
the Poor Prifoners in the Goals for the County
of *Nottingham* yearly for ever, and one third
Bell to the aforefaid Church of *Bramcote.* ——
This pious, moft charitable, and at this Time
moft feafonable Donation, as it defervedly per-
petuates his Memory to be honoured by all Pofterity, fo it gives a moft worthy Example for
Imitation.   He died the 10th Day of *June*
1650.

THESE Habitations of the 12 Poor have been for Years in a very indifferent
Condition, and tho' the Corporation moved by the late two hard Winters, has caufed
the Tiling to be fomewhat Repaired, yet it is to be feared they will in Procefs of
Time, (unlefs fome expedient be found out) be fuffered to tumble down ; becaufe the
Corporation having only their Turn in placing a poor Perfon in, and not one Farthing being left towards repairing the Premiffes, do not think themfelves any more
bound to be at all the Charge of the Repairs then any other fingle Truftee, notwithftanding the Founder in his Will, fixes the whole Charge of the Repairs upon the
Town of *Nottingham.*

Bar·

Barnaby Wartnaby, in his Life Time founded an Alms-House at the Corner of *Pilchergate*, by his Indenture bearing date *October* 30th, 1672, the 24th of *Car*. II. This Alms-House is for the Maintenance of six People, three Men above and three Women below, each of which is to have a Gown every two Years, and annually a Cart-Load of Coals, for which purpose he gave two Houses adjoining to the Alms-House, also two Tenements in *Woolpack-lane*, the Rents whereof to be disposed of for Cloathing, Coals and Repairs. These Rents either increasing or decaying, are really to be employ'd for the Support of the Alms People. If any of the Poor should prove a drunken or debauched Person, the Mayor and major part of the Trustees are impowered to put out such a one and place another in their Room. The Mayor and Trustees are to meet once in two Years to take an Audit of the Rents that are raised, and the Allowances of the Alms-People and Charges of Repairs, and what Stock Remains, at which Meeting 5 s. are allow'd to be spent.

The following is the Inscription upon the Alms-House.

As God above out of his Love
    Has given to me store,
So I out of my Charity,
    Give this House to the Poor.
Let's pray for one another
    So long as we do live,
That we may to God's Glory go,
    To him that this did give.

Barnaby Wartnaby, 1665.

AT his Death he left in his Will bearing date *October* 30, 1672, to each of his Bead-folk 5 s. in Money, and 9 l. to buy them new Gowns, and the Surplus to remain in the Hands of his Trustees for this House.

HE also left 10 l. to be distributed in Money or Bread to the Poor of *Nottingham* at his Funeral, and 40 s. to him who should preach his Funeral Sermon.

Mr. *Abel Collin*, by his Will dated *February* 4th, 1704, left the Remainder of his Personal Estate, (after all Legacies and Bequests were satisfied) to his Nephew Mr. *Thomas Smith* in Trust for his Building and endowing of Alms-Houses, all which the said Gentleman like a good and trusty Steward, has faithfully performed to the utmost, in building an Ornamental, yet at the same Time suitable Fabrick, for the Habitations of 24 poor Men and Women in *Fryer-lane* in the Year 1709, commonly called the *New-Hospital*. These Poor have besides two decent Rooms and as many light Closets, 2 s. a Week paid to them duly every Saturday Morning, and annually a Tun and a half of Coals. On the North Front of this light and airy Building is this Inscription :

This

LABOURER'S HOSPITAL *Derby Road rebuilt* P.152

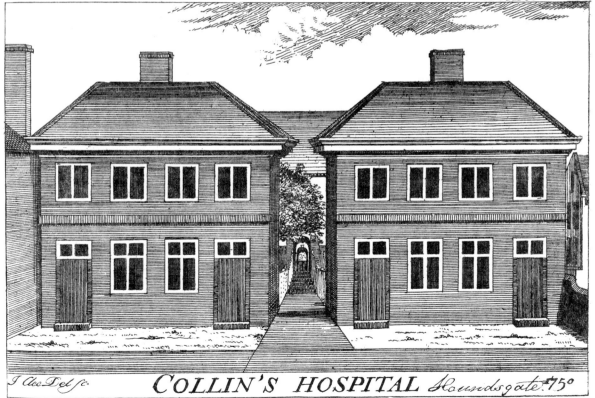

J Ace Del Sc.

COLLIN'S HOSPITAL *Houndsgate* 75°

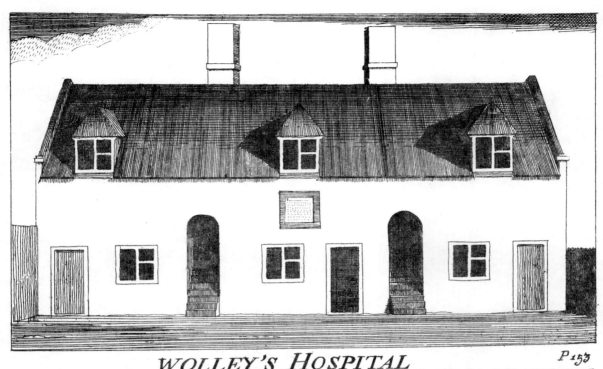

WOLLEY'S HOSPITAL

P 153

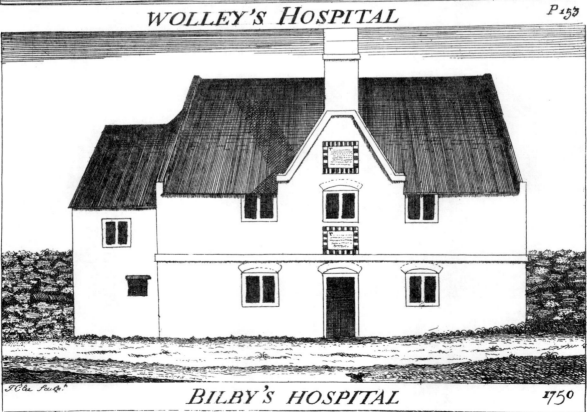

BILBY'S HOSPITAL

1750

This Hofpital
By the Appointment of *Abel Collin* late of
Nottingham, Mercer, deceafed ; who in
his Life was of an extenfive Charity to the
Poor of all Societies, and at his Death by
his laft Will and Teftament, left a compe-
tent Eftate for erecting and endowing the
fame ; was by his Nephew and Executor
Thomas Smith begun and finifhed in the
Year 1709.

ΑΠΟΘΑΝΩΝ ΕΤΙ ΛΑΛΕΙΤΑΙ.

William Bilby, of this town, by trade a fhoemaker, did build in *Coal-pit-lane* an
alms-houfe for eight poor perfons to live rent-free in, each has a two-penny loaf a
week and yearly a tun of coals, befides every new-years-day they have a public dinner, when Mr. Mayor, &c. fits at table with them, after which each man receives one
fhilling and his fhare of the remains of the victuals. All this proceeds out of the
rents of fome houfes in *Goofe-gate*. On the front is this infcription :

The ftarry Science I profefs,
And Surgery withal,
The Chymical among the reft,
And Phyfick rational ;
God gave and blefs'd
What I poffefs'd,
And part of it I lent
Unto the Poor
For evermore
So rais'd this Monument.
Ye Men of Wealth
Whilft now in Health,
Hearken to the Cryes,
The Poor redrefs
And God will blefs
Your Evening Sacrifice.

By *William Bilby*, in the 63d Year of his Age 1709.

Jonathan Labourer, was a ftockingmaker, who left his fortune in truft to *Thomas
Smith*, Efq; banker in *Nottingham*, for charitable ufes, at his difcretion, who caufed
habitations to be built for fix decay'd frame-work-knitters, who receive every friday
11s. i. e. 1s. and 10d. each. And being informed of a near female relation of the teftator
who was marriageable and had no provifion made for her, he looked upon her as juftly
intituled to a part of the charity and therefore gave her 200 l. to her portion. Thefe
houfes ftand by the road fide without *Chapel-bar*.

Dr. *Thoroton*, p. 492. col. 2. takes Notice that the lepers of the hofpital of St. *Leonard* at *Nottingham* the 10th of *Henry* III. had reafonable eftover of dead wood to be
gathered in the foreft of *Nottingham*, and I find in a foreft book written in the 30th
of *Elizabeth*, by *William Marfhall*, ferjeant at mace, for the ufe of his mafter *Robert
Alvie*, then mayor of *Nottingham*, *John Nodyn* and *Nicholas Sherwin*, fheriffs, 1588.

X THAT

" THAT *William Chaundeler*, of *Nottingham*, keeper of the houfe of St. *Leo-*
" *nard* of the fame Time, *viz.* the 31ft. of *Edward* III, made one preprefture of half
" an acre of ground in the king's demains within the court of the town of *Notting-*
" *kam* in the ermitage that is call'd *Owfwell*, and it belonged to the hofpital of St.
" *Leonard* of *Nottingham*."

I have made all the enquiry I was able, to learn where this hofpital might have
ftood, but could not get any intelligence concerning it; I therefore confidering that
this kind of hofpitals were never placed within the walls of towns; after moft diligent fearch about the out-parts of *Nottingham* I did not fee any foot-fteps which
feemed likely to have been fuch a houfe, except the ruins of a ftone building at the
fouth-weft end of the *Narrow-marfh*, which is without the confines of the ancient wall
of the town. My anonymous author not mentioning this hofpital, makes me judge that
in his time, *viz.* 1641, the foot-fteps were full as obfcure as at prefet.

The FREE-SCHOOL.

THE town of *Nottingham* has alfo the advantage of a free grammar fchool.
This was founded by one *Agnes Mellers*, a vowefs, often called lady *Mellors*, fhe was
widow of *Richard Mellers* a wealthy bellfounder in this town, and obtained a licence
to erect a free-fchool of one mafter and one ufher in the parifh of St. *Mary*, bearing
date *November* 22, the 4th of king *Henry* VIII. A. D. 1513.

Her Indenture by which fhe fettles the FREE-SCHOOL is as followeth

TO all chriftian people, to whofe knowledge this prefent writing triplicate indented fhall come to be feen or read, *Agnes Meller*, widow and vowefs, fend-
eth greeting, in him that is the root of *Jeffe*, produced to the falvation of all
people.

WHEREAS the moft excellent and famous prince king *Henry* VIII. of his
right bleffed difpofition and meer mercy, by his letters patents fealed under his great
feal, has licenfed, authorized and granted, to his well beloved counfellor *Thomas Lo-*
vel, knight, treafurer of his moft honourable houfhold, and me the faid *Agnes*, and to
our executors, and to every one of us, licence, power and authority, to begin, found
and erect, unite, create and eftablifh, one free-fchool, of one fchoolmafter and one
ufher perpetually to be kept in the parifh of our lady in the town of *Nottingham*, for
evermore to endure after the ordering, inftitution and will of us the faid *Thomas* and
me the faid *Agnes*, or one of us, our executors or affignes, or the executors of either of us
hereafter to be made, and further things, as in the fame letters patents more plainly
appeareth.

KNOW ye, that I remembring how the univerfal faith catholick by clergy and
commons moft firmly corroborated, and by learning the public weale commonly is governed, ardently have defigned to the honour of almighty God, laud and praife to the
elect and chofen mother of mercy and virgin, our lady St. *Mary*, to accomplifh the
faid virtuous and bleffed Grant, and by force thereof, begin, erect, found, create, eftablifh and make one free-fchool, of one mafter and one ufher, to teach grammar,
ever-

THE FREE-SCHOOL

J. Clee f.

BARNABY WARTNABY'S BEAD HOUSE

1750

everlaftingly to endure, and to be kept in the parifh of our bleffed lady St. *Mary* the virgin within the town of *Nottingham*, willing, ordaining and eftablifhing, that the faid fchool be evermore called the free-fchool of the town of *Nottingham*. And *John Smith* parfon of *Bilborow* I make fchoolmafter of the fame, as long it fhall feem to me and the mayor of the faid town of *Nottingham* for the time being convenient. And to my right trufty friends Mr. *William English* and *William Barwell*, I make deputies, and ordain guardians, keepers and furveyors of the faid free-fchool during their lives : I will alfo, ordain and eftablifh, that the mayor, aldermen and common-council of the faid town of *Nottingham* and their fucceffors, after the deceafe of the faid *Williams*, fhall yearly from year to year on the feaft of the tranflation of St. *Richard* the bifhop, chufe two difcreet perfons, burgeffes, to be chamberlains, guardians, keepers and furveyors of the lands and tenements and poffeffions, pertaining and bequeathed, given, or hereafter to be given and bequeathed and belonging to the faid free-fchool, to rule, govern and fupport, the charges, payments and bufinefs, of the fame, from the fame feaft of tranflation, to the faid feaft of St. *Richard* next following, at which feaft or within eight days then next following, I will that the faid guardians, now by me named, or hereafter to be named, made and elected, fhall make account to the faid mayor and aldermen, and their fucceffors, of all things by them received or taken to the ufe of the faid foundation, and after their accounts fo made and finifhed, new guardians, or elfe the fame, by the advice and difcretion of the faid mayor and aldermen to be elected and chofen, and that the fame guardians, keepers and furveyors, by the name of the guardians of the free-fchool of *Nottingham* may plead and be impleaded before all judges of every court, and alfo writs and actions maintain and have. Moreover I will that the faid mayor, aldermen and common-council of the faid town of *Nottingham*, with the guardians that now be of the faid fchool, or hereafter fhall be, or eight of them at the leaft, whereof the mayor and guardians of the fame free-fchool, I will, fhall be three, after the deceafe of the faid Mr. *John Smith*, parfon of *Bilborow*, or after fuch time as it fhall fortune that the faid Mr. *John Smith*, fhall leave or be removed from the faid office of fchoolmafter, fhall conduct and hire one other able perfon of good and honeft converfation, to be fchoolmafter of the faid free-fchool, and one ufher, at fuch time, and as foon as the lands and poffeffions given to the faid free-fchool, will fupport the charge thereof, and the fame fchoolmafter and ufher, for good and reafonable caufes, or either of them, to amove and expel, and others in his or their ftead, to take, retain, and put in, from time to time, as often, and when they fhall think requifite and neceffary.

AND furthermore I will and ordain, that the fchoolmafter for the time being, and his ufher, or one of them, fhall daily when he keeps fchool caufe the fcholars every morning in their fchool-houfe e're they begin their learning, to fay, with an high voice the whole *credo in deum patrem*, &c.

ALSO I ordain and eftablifh, that the guardians of the faid free-fchool for the time being and their fucceffors, fhall yearly on the feaft of the tranflation of St. *Richard*, which is the 16th of *June*, keep or caufe to be kept and done folemnly in the church of St. *Mary* in *Nottingham*, the *obiit* of the faid *Agnes Mellers*, my husband's and mine after my deceafe, and give, pay and expend, of the rents, iffues and profits, given and bequeathed, pertaining and belonging to the faid free-fchool, for our foul's health 20 s. in form following : That is to fay, to the vicar of the faid church, perfonally being prefent, from the beginning of the dirge and mafs of the fame *obiit* to the ending thereof, for his attendance, and for his lights at that time burning 3 s. and if he occupy by deputy, then to have but 2 s. and to every prieft of the fame church

and

and either of the clarks of the said parish there also being, for such like time 4 *d.* and also to the mayor of the town of *Nottingham*, for the time, being personally present at the beginning and ending of the same mass and dirge, 6 *d.* and to every alderman of the same town, there also being present, for such like time, 4 *d.* and the mayor's clark and his two serjeants being and attending on their master and aldermen at the beginning of the said mass and dirge, and for serving such things as shall be prepared for them at the said *obiit.* to each of them 2 *d.* and to the parish clarks for the great bells ringing eight peals, and after the accustomable length, 3 *s.* and that the said guardians shall retain and keep in their own hands for either of them for their own use ——— —— for their business and attendance, in providing bread, ale and cheese, and towels, cups, pots, and necessary things at the said *obiit* ; and there shall expend in bread, to be sent to the aldermen &c. according to the custom in the church 2 *s.* in cheese 8 *d.* in ale 16 *d.* and the residue remaining over this mine ordinance and will performed, if any be left, I will shall be distributed to the poorest scholars of the said free-school, to pray for our souls and all of our friends.

I will also, ordain and establish and strictly enjoin, that the schoolmaster and usher nor any of them, have, make nor use, any potations, cockfightings, nor drinking, with his or their wife or wives, hostess or hostesses, but once or twice in the year, nor take any other gifts or vails, whereby the scholars or their friends should be charged, but at the pleasure of the friends of the scholars.——Wages to be paid by the said guardians.

AND here if it fortune the said mayor, aldermen and common-council, to be negligent and forgetful in finding and choosing of the schoolmaster and the usher, forty days next after such time as it shall fortune him to be amoved, or deceased, keeping and doing the *obiit* yearly, in manner and form above expressed in such like time ; or the lands and tenements or hereditaments, and other possessions, or the yearly rent of them into other uses than finding of the said free-school, to convert ; then I will, ordain and establish, that the prior and convent of the monastery of the holy trinity of *Lenton*, for the time being, and their successors, shall have as a forfeiture, the rule, guiding and oversight, of the said lands, tenements, or hereditaments, &c. schoolmaster, with all other things to the premisses in any wise appertaining, to the intent above expers's'd, in as ample and large wise as the mayor and burgesses have or should have had the same, by this my present constitution and ordinance.

ALSO I do ordain and establish, that the ordinances, statutes and establishments and constitutions, for the good governance and rule of the said free-school, by me made in my life, under my seal, by me determined, everlastingly to be kept, and each one of them stedfastly shall be holden, observed and kept for ever, without any diminution or abridgement, or changing of them or any of them any wise, and that it shall be lawful to the said mayor, aldermen and common-council and their successors at all times hereafter, from time to time, at their liberty, other constitutions, statutes, and ordinances for the good governance and continuance of the said free-school to make, them or part of them by their discretion to repeal, and admit at their pleasures as often and whensoever they shall think it most necessary and convenient, so that such constitutions, statutes and ordinances, of new to be made, nor any of them, be in any wise contrary or repugnant to the statutes and establishments and ordinances by me, in my life, under my seal, made, written and determined. In witness whereof, &c. &c. &c.

BESIDES

BESIDES the lands and houfes of a good value fettled upon the free-fchool by *Agnes Mellers*, it has received confiderable addition by the bounty of other benefactors.

Robert Mellers, fon of the foundrefs, alfo a bell-founder, by his will bearing date the 16th of *July* 1515, gave a clofe which he bought of *William Page*, lying in *Basford-wong* and an houfe in *Bridlefmithgate* which he bought of the fame perfon, or the money that fhould be gotten for it ; but if the fchool fhould not be kept according to the foundation as it was granted, his heirs fhould re-enter and have the faid clofe with the appurtenances again. He was burgefs in parliament for *Nottingham*. *Thoroton* p. 497.

Thomas Mellers, another fon of *Agnes*, by his will bearing date the 16th of *Auguft* in the 27th of *Henry* VIII. 1535. *It* : I bequeath and give all my lands, tenements and hereditaments, in the town and fields of *Basford* in the county of *Nottingham*, to the ufe of the free-fchool lately founded in the faid town of *Nottingham* by dame *Agnes Mellers*, my mother, deceafed, for ever. This man was mayor of *Nottingham*, A. D. 1523, as appears by a fchedule annex'd to a promiffary note of *Henry* VIII.

In the old town-hall :

Arg. a chevron between 3 garbes fable, 3 eftoiles of 5 points of the 1ft impaling gules and arg. divided by a pale ingrailed or. between 4 lions rampant counter-changed.

Under it :

They be the arms of *John Waft* and *Winifred* his wife, late brewer of *London*, which has given to the maintainance of the free-fchool of this town of *Nottingham*, three tenements in the city of *London*, (fituate in *Black-fryers*) 5 *l.* by the year : On whofe foul *Jefus* have mercy.

N. B. *Thefe where fold to defray the charges of a law-fuit between the corporation and* Mr. Richard Johnfon, *mafter of the fchool.*

John Hesky, alderman, by his will bearing date *feptember* 29, 1558, gave the property of all his tythes in the meadows and fields of the town of *Nottingham*, to the mayor and burgeffes in truft, as alfo a meffuage on *fwine-green*, to be employ'd towards the augmentation of the falary of the fchool-mafters of the free-fchool for ever, and 10 *s.* yearly on the anniverfary of the *obiit* of *Agnes Mellers*, the foundrefs, to be diftributed among the poor, fick, fore and needy.

Mr. alderman *John Parker*, whofe name has been twice mentioned above, did lay a foundation for a library for the ufe of the mafters and fcholars of the free-fchool.— There is alfo another legacy belonging to the free-fchool, of 2 *l.* 13 *s.* 4 *d.* paid by Mr. *Keys* of this town. See *Appendix*.

FROM *John Smith*, parfon of *Bilborow*, the firft fchool-mafter, I find no fucceffion in the books of call, or any where elfe, till 1626, fince which time the following have been Mafters.

A List of the MASTERS and USHERS of the Free-School in *Nottingham*.

MASTERS.		USHERS.	
The Rev. Mr. Tibbald's		The first usher I meet with is:	
—— Mr. Thomas Leek, - -	1630	The Rev. Mr. William Bradshaw,	1669
—— Mr. Balston, - - -	1641	—— Mr. ——— Vroyne,	1672
—— Mr. Henry Pits, - -	1663	—— Mr. John Littlefeare,	1681
—— Mr. Samuel Birch, -	1664	—— Mr. Samuel Birch,	1686
—— Mr. Jer. Chudworth, -	1673	—— Mr. John Lamb,	1708
—— Mr. Gawen Knight, -	1690	—— Mr. John Clarke,	1709
—— Mr. Edward Griffith,	1692	—— Mr. John Peake,	1709
—— Mr. Richard Johnson,	1707	—— Mr. George Bettinson,	1714
—— Mr. ——— Woamack,	1720	—— Mr. John Henson,	1724
—— Mr. John Swaile,	1722	—— Mr. George Wayte.	1732
—— Mr. John Henson.	1731	—— Mr. Thomas Nixon.	1747

THE first reparation of the school is perpetuated by the following inscription in the front :

> This School founded in the Reign of
> *Henry* 8th. by *Agnes Mellers*, and by
> Injury of Time much decay'd was re-
> paired *Ann : Dom* : 1689.
> *George Langford*, Major.
> *John Aste*, *James Huthwaite*, School-wardens.

FARTHER repairs and additions appear by the inscription on the stone in the wall facing the North :

> Pars hæc postica ædium
> Præceptoris Grammatices
> Vetustate labefactata & tantum
> non collapsa, instaurata est
> et superiore conclavium ordine
> amplificata, pecuniâ ex
> oppidano Ærario depromptâ
> *Gulielmo Drury*,
> Arm : Prætore,
> *Matthæo Hoyland*, ⎫
> *Francisco Smith*. ⎬ Scholæ Procuratoribus.
>
> *Richardo Johnson*, Moderatore.
> Anno Dom. 1708.

HERE is likewise a charity-school maintained by the voluntary contribution of several worthy gentlemen and substantial tradesmen of this town for the instruction of fifty poor children, in the principles of religion, spelling and reading. Forty of these are cloathed in blue.

Mr.

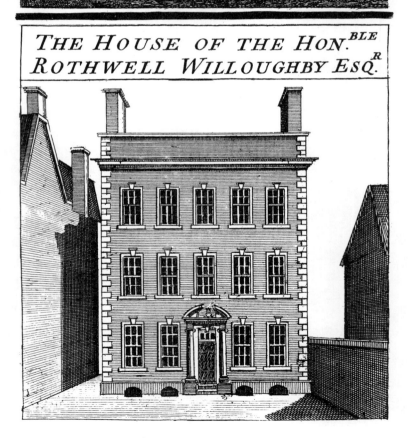

THE CHARITY SCHOOL. P.159

THE HOUSE OF THE HON.BLE
ROTHWELL WILLOUGHBY ESQ.R

Mr. *Thomas Saunderson*, some time register of the spiritual-court in this town by his will dated the 2d of *february*, gave to the charity-children belonging to the charity-school at *Nottingham*, 20 s. p. annum, and after the expiration of seven years, 40s. p. annum, as long as the said charity-school shall continue.

THE school-house is a decent building on the *high-pavement*; the ground on which it stands was given by *William Thorp*, gent. attorney-at-law.

BESIDES this, there is a school in St. *Mary's* parish where thirty poor children are instructed in like manner, for which the master receives 13 l. p. ann. paid to him by the churchwardens out of the sacrament money.

A society of good and well meaning persons, which meet every wednesday and sunday evenings in the vestry of St. *Mary*, pay yearly 6 l. 8 s. for the instruction of sixteen more poor children; and about six are put to school by the charity of private persons.

SECT. VIII.

SECTION VIII.

RIVERS, POOLS, BRIDGES, ROADS, and the Foreſt of SHIRWOOD.

NOTICE has been taken in ſection the 1ſt. that *Nottingham* has the advantage of two rivers, both which are ſo placed that this town receives all the benefits which can be expected from any, without the inconveniencies the too nearneighbourhood of currents generally brings along with it.

THE largeſt of the two is alſo the remoteſt from the town and is one of the four great rivers of *England*, (*a*) navigable at preſent ſo far upwards as *Burton* upon *Trent*, (the name of this river) but has been frequented by veſſels of burthen as far as *Nottingham*, time immemorial, and that it was ſo before the conqueſt appears clearly by *doomſ-day-book*, where it is ſaid, that the water of *Trent*, the ditch and the road to *York*, was kept by *Nottingham*, inſomuch, that if any one ſhould hinder the paſſage of veſſels, plough, or dig an hole, within two perches of the king's highway, he ſhould pay a fine of 8 *l.*

THIS River does in ſome meaſure divide the kingdom in the north and ſouth part, and Dr. *Inx*, in a ſermon preach'd before king *James* I. at *Newark*, calls it the *Metwand* of *England*, this diviſion is frequently found in the old records in the words of *citra* and *ultra Trentam*, and of the two lords chief juſtices in eyre, the one is ſtiled lord chief juſtice in eyre on this ſide *Trent*, the other beyond *Trent*.

NOR does it only divide the kingdom into north and ſouth, but it does this county in a more particular manner, for it is divided into ſix wapentakes or hundreds, of which three, *viz. Ruſhcliff*, *Bingham* and *Newark*, are on the ſouth-ſide, and three, *Broxtol*, *Thurgarton & Lee*, and *Baſſet-lowe*, on the north ſide.

THE origin of the name *Trent*, authors are not agreed about, ſome will have it that it receives it from the abbey of *Trentham*, becauſe it has not any name before it reaches to this place, tho' it riſes ſeveral miles farther up, in two heads, which join below *Norton*, ſo go to *Hilton*-abby, *Bucknal*-church, receiving above *Stoke* the
Foul-

(*a*) - - - - - - - - - - That now they all began
To liſten to a long told prophecy, which ran,
Of Moreland, that ſhe might live proſperouſly to ſee,
A river born of her, who well might reckon'd be,
The third of this large Iſle. ——
Drayton Poly Olbion, Song 12. *p.* 207.

Foulbrook-water, which comes thither from *Tunstall* by *Shelton*, and making a confluence, pass to *Hanfleet*, where they meet with another on the same side that descends from *Newcastle-under-line.* (*a*) This derivation seems to me no ways satisfactory, it being ridiculous in the nature of things, that a current of water, which is at least supposed to be as old as the flood, should receive its name from a little religious house, not founded 'till some thousand years after. Others derive it from the french word *trente* which signifies thirty, maintaining that this river yields thirty different kinds of fish.

I F they mean that it breeds so many they are grosly mistaken, for not much above half that number are properly the produce of the *Trent* ; if they mean such fish as are fit for food, none can make out the number, and if they take in all that comes under the denomination of fish, they exceed the number of thirty. Wherefore I can't allow this to be a fair deduction, and I am ready to think that this last Opinion is founded upon a barbarous old latin version. *viz.*

Limpida sylva focum Triginta dat mihi piscem.

Sherwood my hearth and *Trent* my fish supplies.

N A Y *Drayton* goes farther, when not content with allowing our river thirty kinds of fish, he affirms in the following lines that it receives thirty streams and had thirty large abbies near its banks :

Who (*b*)   bearing many springs which pretty rivers grew,
She could not be content until she fully knew,
Which child it was of her's (born under such a fate)
As should in time be rais'd unto the high estate.
(I fain would have you think that this was long ago,
When many a river that now fluxuously doth flow,
Had scarcely learnt to creep) and therefore she doth will,
Wise *Arden* from the depth of her abundant skill
To tell her which of these her rills it was she meant
To satisfy her will, the wizard answered *Trent*,
For as a skilful seer, the aged forest wist,
A more than usual power did in the name consist,
Which thirty does import, by which she thus divin'd,
There should be found in her of fishes thirty kind,
And thirty Abbies great in places fat and rank,
Should in succeeding time be builded on her bank,
And thirty several streams from many a sundry way,
Should unto her greatness their watry tribute pay.
Poly Olbion Song 12 p. 207.

Y   FOR

(*a*) *This* Leland *takes to be the very* Trent *itself when he says that it arises in the hills above* Newcastle.
(*b*) *The Morelands.*

FOR my part I shall not mifpend my time in any farther fruitlefs etymological enquiry, but take the faxon name from Mr. *Cambden* which is *Treonta*. This might very eafily in procefs of time loofe the *o* and become *Trenta*, which is the name I find in all charters and records wherefoever this river is mentioned. (*a*)

BUT to proceed in the defcription of the courfe of our river *Trent*, (wherein I chiefly follow *Hollinfhed*,) not far from *Trentham* our river croffes a rivulet the name of which my author knows not, and thence going to *Stone-Afton*, *Stoke*, *Burton*, the *Sandons* and *Wefton*, a little above *Subborn* and *Hawood*, upon the foutherly bank it receives the *Sow*, a great channel increafed with many waters, hence it runs to little *Harwood*, meeting by the way one rill at *Oufely-bridge*, another fouth of *Riddlefley*, thence by *Hauksberry*, *Mavefone*, *Ridware*, and fo towards *Yoxhall*, in its way hither it receives two ftreams, the one and leffer by fouth from *Farwell*, the other by weft a fair ftream increafed by two brooks, this enters *Trent* directly weft of *Yoxhall*, hence it goes ftraightways to *Catton*, where it meets with the *Tame*, which comes out of *Staffordfhire* and empties itfelf about a mile above *Rempfton* into our river, which grown to fome greatnefs proceeds to *Walton*, *Darklow*, and there croffing a water that comes by *Newbold-hall*, it runs to *Stapenel*, *Winfhull*, *Whitmere* and *Newton*, where it receives two channels within a fhort fpace, the firft, *viz.* the *Dove*, (which divides *Staffordfhire* from *Derbyfhire*) above *Newton-fouch*, the *Trent* being thus farther enlarged, goes onward with its courfe, and between *Willington* and *Repton* receives two waters, one on each fide, the one falling in by *Willington*, rifes by *Dawberry-Lyes*, and paffes by *Truffeley* and *Afh*, &c. the other which enters above *Repton*, comes down from *Hartfhurn*, &c.: The *Trent* having paffed thefe hafteth to *Twiford*, *Ingleby*, *Staunton*, *Wefton*, *Newton* and *Afton*, and foon after meets with the *Derwent*, a river which arifeth in the edge of *Derbyfhire*, and runs near the *Welles* into our ftream, which goes hence to *Sawley*, and north of *Thrumpton* takes in the *Sore*, which rifeth in *Leicefterfhire*. After this the *Trent* proceeds to *Barton* where it takes in the *Erwafh*, which rifeth about *Kirkby*, thence it purfues its courfe to *Clifton* and afore it comes to *Wilford* it meets with a brook that paffes from *Staunton* by *Bunny* and *Ruddington*, and thence the *Trent* runs to *Nottingham*, where it receives the *Leen*, next of all it paffes by *Thorp* and *Farndon*, where it branches and makes an Ifland, and into the fmaller branch goes a brook from *Belvoir-Caftle*, call'd the *Devan*, and from thence runneth by *Bramfton*, to *Knipton*, and beneath *Knipton* meets with a brook that comes by weft of *Croxton*, and thence holds on with its courfe, between *Wellethorpe* and *Belvoir-Caftle* aforefaid, and fo to *Bottesworth*, *Normanton*, *Killingfton*, *Skilton*, there receives the *Snite* from the fouth, whofe head is near *Claufton*, and e're long another coming from *Bingham*, and *Sibthorpe*, thence it runs to *Coxam*, *Hawton*, *Newark*-caftle, and fo to *Winthorpe*, where the branches are reunited, and thence goes on by *Holm* to *Cromwell*, and foon after taking in a brook coming from *Bilfthorpe*, to *Carlton* and to *Sutton*, there making a little Ifle, then to *Grinton*, where it touches a ftream on each fide, whereof one cometh from *Morehoufe* by *Wefton* and *Grefthorpe*, &c. the other from *Langthorpe*, by *Collingham* and *Bofthorpe*, &c. From thence likewife it paffes to *Clifton*, *Newton*, *Kettlethorpe*, *Torkfey*,

---

(*a*) Mr. Baxter, *in his gloffary p.* 9. *gives us the roman name* Troventio *and fays* Ravennas *calls the* Trent, Troantia.

fey, Knath, Gainsborough, Waltrith, Stockwith, and leaving *Axholm* on the left, it takes with it the *Hogdike*-water out of the Ifle, and fo goes forth to *Wildfworth, Gaftferry, Trufhworth, Burringham, Gummeis, Hixburgh,* and beneath *Burton-ftather,* at a place call'd *Trent-fall,* (having firft received the river *Donne*) our river and another of the great rivers the *Oufe* coming from *York,* as if it were with joint confent caft themfelves into the *Humber.*

THUS we have traced the courfe of the river *Trent* from its fource to its reception by an arm of the fea, which is in all from *Trentham*   miles, it is navigable for above an hundred miles, from *Burton* to *Gainsborough* by flat bottom'd, and from *Gainsborough* to the *Humber,* by keel built veffels, which navigation fupplies diverfe counties with all forts of merchandizes they have occafion for. *See Section V.*

THO' I do not allow the whimfical derivation of the name of *Trent* from the number thirty ; yet am I very ready to own, that this our river abounds in variety of very good fifh. The fifhery at *Nottingham* only, was once fo confiderable an article to the burgeffes, that it is recorded as matter of complaint in *Doomfday-Book, viz.* That the burgeffes were ufed to fifh in the water of *Trent,* and that they then were forbid the fame.

AND afterwards in the reign of *Henry I. William Peverel* in his foundation deed of the priory of *Lenton,* among other things he grants to the convent, the tythe of fifh of the fifhing of *Nottingham,* and no doubt but there were in thofe days a fet of men who rented the water, and made their bufinefs to catch the fifh for the market, thefe probably lived in the lower part and without the walls of the town, where a certain ftreet ftill retains the name of *Fifhergate* to this day, whilft other perfons were better employ'd, than in mifpending their time in deftroying fifh by unlawful means, (a tranfgreffion too common in our days.)

An Alphabetical Lift of all the Fifh catch'd in the River TRENT.

1	Barbel,	19	Pike,
2	Bream,	20	Roach,
3	Bulhead,	21	Rud,
4	Burbot,	22	Ruff,
5	Carp,	23	Salmon,
6	Chub,	24	Salmon-Trout,
7	Crayfifh,	25	Salmon-Pink,
8	Dare,	26	Sand-Eel,
9	Eel,	27	Shad,
10	Flounder,	28	Smelt,
11	Grayling,	29	Stickleback,
12	Gudgeon,	30	Sturgeon,
13	Lamprey,	31	Stream-Pink,
14	Lampern,	32	Tench,
15	Loach	33	Trout,
16	Minow,	34	Whitling.
17	Mufcle,		
18	Perch,		

SOME

SOME of thefe come from the fea, as high and often higher then *Nottingham,* *viz.* Sturgeon, Shad, Salmon, and Flounders, which two laft fpawn in the river. Smelts are feldom catch'd higher than *Gainsborough.*

SOME are forced into the *Trent* by floods from other rivers, brooks, ponds and ftews, as Trout, Tench, Eels, Carp, &c. Cray-fifh, are not very common in this river. Lamperns are a lefs fpecies of Lampreys chiefly catch'd for baits.

CONCERNING the bottom of the *Trent,* fee the account of my anonymous native of *Nottingham* in his own words.

" THIS river from the head thereof, fome four miles above *Stoke* in *Staffordshire,*
" to the midway between *Newark* and *Gainsborough,* runs upon gravel, pebbles and
" boulders, with which it feems, efpecially with boulders, to be naturally paved, that
" being the moft excellent paving ftone that is, for it will never break, nor in any
" reafonable time wear with iron bound carriages. There are in the channel of this
" river divers hurfts or fhelves, which in fummer time lye dry, from whence the bor-
" dering inhabitants gather great ftore of thefe boulders, as they have occafion, and
" with thefe the whole town of *Nottingham* is paved."

I remember to have obferved in *Fifhergate* and on the upper part of the *Low-pavement* when workmen have dug for foundations, an old pavement, under the prefent, of a fmall kind of paving ftone, which might probably be the kind my author fpeaks of. At this time they ufe no ftones out of the *Trent* for paving, but have them moftly brought to *Nottingham* from *Keyworth* and elfewhere.

THERE was a bridge over the *Trent* above an hundred years before the conqueft, built by the order of king *Edward* the elder, in the year 1683, *(a)* when the ice tore away part of this bridge; it had only ftone piers and the bridge itfelf was wood, built in the fame manner as the two fmall bridges are between this and the town-bridge. Since which time it is entirely rebuilt of ftone fupported by twenty arches, at the expence of the corporation, who alfo take care of the repairs of it by their officers the bridgemafters. For which purpofe the burgeffes have obtained divers grants from the crown of houfes and lands, befides many gifts and legacies, the whole amounting even at this day, clear of all charges and payments of burgeffes parts, to upwards of one hundred and thirty pounds per annum, exclufive of what they occafionally receive by the toll of milftones and upfets of mercers, taylors, cordwainers, &c.

FROM the foot of this bridge there goes a ftrong caufway, well fecured with brick-work, and covered with flat ftones leading to the higher part of the meadows, and from thence acrofs the lower parts there are planks raifed a foot, a foot and a half, and in fome places two feet high from the ground, upon which in flood times people may go dry from *Heathbeth*-bridge to feveral parts of the town; all thefe are taken care of and repaired by the before mentioned bridge-mafters.

THIS

(a) This fevere froft happened in the beginning of September *and lafted till the 5th of* February.

THIS ancient bridge bears in all writings the name of *Heathbeth*-bridge, tho' differently spelt, for the etymology of which name I am indebted to *John Plumptre*, Efq; a Gentleman happily furnished with all kinds of learning; the following are his own words:

"IN Dr. *Thoroton's* antiquities of *Nottinghamshire*, p. 492. he quotes an escheat-
" roll of the 30th of *Edward* I. in which the bridge now called *Trent-bridge*, is men-
" tioned by the name of *Heathbethe-brigg*. He also quotes in the same page, a pa-
" per of ferjeant *Boun's*, where this name of the bridge is spelt *Heathbet* (a) and in
" fome ancient writings it is writ (more rightly as it should seem) *Hebethe*; all
" which come to the same point, (for orthography in those elder times was very un-
" certain)and plainly shew the word to be faxon, *heath* in that language fignifies *high*,
" and *heath*, *highth*, and *bæth* fignifies a *bath* or wafhing place, fo that in modern
" *Englifh* it would found *Highbath-bridge*, a name it undoubtedly received from
" fome near adjacent place then noted for the refort of perfons to bathe and fwim in.
----- So far Mr. *Plumptre*.

THIS derivation feems to me to be highly probable, and that the word *high* was to denote fuch bathing place to have been above bridge, and on the higher part of the *Trent*, where at this very day, there is a box (as I may call it) made of wood, on the fouth bank of this river, built over the water upon piles, also another below bridge on the north bank, contrived for the conveniency of bathing unfeen, whither in the fummer the ladies frequently take a walk and bath themfelves.

Dr. *Thoroton* takes notice of a chapel upon this bridge, for a proof of which he quotes the above-mentioned escheat-roll of the 30th of *Edward* I. *viz.* " That the " jury found it not to the king's lofs, if he granted licence to *John le Paumer*, and to " *Alice* his wife, (who was fifter and heir of *Hugh de Stapleford*, fon of *Robert de* " *Stapleford*, of *Nottingham*) to give 6 *l.* 13 *s.* 5 *d.* rent with the appurtenances " in *Nottingham*, to a certain chaplain, to celebrate divine offices for the fouls, &c. " in the chapel of St. *Mary* on *Hethbeth-brigg*:" where in the doctor's time there was an arch, which went ftill by the name of chapel-arch, but at this time is not re-membred by any body I have met with, infomuch that it cannot certainly be known whether the faid chapel ftood at the fouth or north end of the bridge, tho' one might conjecture that it might have been placed near the road, and that this chapel might poffibly have given, (to a fpot of ground which is the fartheft boundary to the eaft be-yond the *Trent*, of the county of the town of *Nottingham*) the name of *Lady-bay*.

WHITLOCK, in his memorials, mentions a fort on *Trent*-bridge in the time of the civil-war, of which I cannot difcover the leaft footfteps, neither on, nor clofe by the bridge, I am therefore induced to think that this fort was raifed at fome diftance in the meadows, where I meet with a high fpot of ground between the bridge and the caftle, which even in the greateft floods remains uncovered, in which opinion I am confirmed by the name it goes by, *viz. Hooper's-fconce*, this laft word being a cor-
Y 3   ruption

(a) *In an Exemplification concerning the* Leen bridge, *that name is fpelt* Heyegh-beythe-Brugge. *See* Appendix.

ruption of the german word *fcantz* or the danifh *fcantze*, both which fignify a fort or place built for the defence of a river, pafs, &c. (*a*)

THE leffer of the two rivers is called the *Leen*, which rifes in the foreft of *Sherwood*, above *Newfted*, formerly a houfe of canons regular of St. *Auftin*, founded by king *Henry* II. but fince the 32d of *Henry* VIII. the poffeffion of the ancient family of the *Byrons*. [See *Section* XII.] Hence it paffes by *Papplewick, Hucknal, Bulwell, Basford, Radford*, to the town of *Lenton*, which receives its name from it *quafi Leen-town*; at *Lenton*-bridge it ufed before the conqueft to turn towards the fouth and empty itfelf into the *Trent* over againft *Wilford*-church; but the prefent channel, which is an artificial, tho' not a modern one, runs from the juft-mentioned bridge, almoft in a line by the foot of the fteep rock, on which the old caftle of *Nottingham* ftood, and the prefent is erected, along the fouth fide of the town of *Nottingham*, and laftly turns off at *Sneynton*-meadows, and feparating the jurifdiction of *Nottingham* from the parifh of *Sneynton*, difcharges itfelf into the river *Trent*.

THE antiquity of this laft mentioned channel appears by the perambulation of the foreft of *Sherwood*, in the 16th of *Henry* III. wherein it is expreffed " That the " boundaries of the foreft came down according to the courfe of the *Leen* to *Lenton*, and " from thence as the fame water was won't of old time to run into the water of *Trent*. This plainly fhews, that the *Leen* was turned long before this king's time, and confequently it muft feem moft probable, that the occafion of this alteration was the conqueror's building *Nottingham* caftle, to which the bringing the river *Leen* muft have been of very great fervice, as well as it has ever fince proved to the town. This entirely overfets the opinion of thofe who affirm that the prefent courfe of this river is not above two hundred years ftanding, whereas it is 526 years fince *Henry* III. began his reign.

OUR *Leen* is a Trout brook, and about *Newfted* it produces Cray-fifh of a large fize, which are carefully preferved for the ufe of my lord *Byron's* family. This river affords befides very good Eels, and many other forts of fifh, of which the Gudgeons for bignefs exceed thofe of the *Trent*.

OVER the *Leen* between *Narrow-marfh* and *Fifhergate*, is built a long ftone bridge of twenty arches, this is called the *Leen* or town-bridge. Dr. *Thoroton*, p. 492, fays the reparation of the bridge of *Nottingham* the 10th of king *John*, was undertaken by the brethren of the hofpital of St. *John* the *Baptift* in *Nottingham*. In the next place he quotes from ferjeant *Boun's* papers, that this bridge is to be repaired at the charge of the town and the whole county, which he grounds upon an eyre roll called *Ragman* of the 3d of *Edward* III. where he finds this prefentment: *Pons de Nottingham vocatus Tunebridge in defectu ville et totius comitatus* : He breaks off fhort here without telling us what proportion of charge the town and the county are to be at; neither does he confider that the record he cites, bears date 112 years before *Nottingham* was created a town and county by itfelf, which ought to have induced him to enquire whether this matter ftood ftill upon the fame foot as before, or whether any alteration was made in relation to that bufinefs in the reign of *Henry* VI.

(*a*) There is ftill vifible fome obfcure foot-fteps of lines raifed in the edge of the Ryehills, *between* Trent-bridge *and the* Caftle, *made in the civil-war*.

VI. or any fubfequent reign, and he could eafily have informed himfelf that there was an exemplification of an inquifition about the *Leen*-bridge to be found among the records in the town-hall of *Nottingham*, of fo late a date as the 36th of *Henry* VIII. wherein it is expreffed that the faid great bridge over the *Leen*, has time immemorial been upheld and repaired by the town of *Nottingham* and the feveral *Wapentakes* or *Hundreds* of the *County* and that in proportion as follows :

T H E town of *Nottingham* is to repair the north end of this bridge, and the two arches next adjoining to the fame, containing in length 46 feet and a half.

B R O X T A L L-hundred, the three adjoining to the juft-mentioned two arches, containing 81 feet and a half, and the middle column between the two arches, is to be upheld and repaired at the joint expence of *Nottingham* and *Broxtall*.

T H U R G A R t O N a L Y G H E, is to repair the five next adjoining to the three arches, containing 135 feet and a half, the middle pillar between them and the three foregoing is to be repaired at the common charge of *Broxtall* and this hundred.

B A S S E T L O W E-hundred, is to repair the five arches next beyond the five before-mentioned, containing in length 169 feet and a half, which is as much as anciently fix arches contained, and the middle column between thefe ten arches, is to be repaired in common by this hundred and the preceding.

N E W A R K hundred repairs the three arches next adjoining to the laft five, and the middle column between thefe three and aforefaid five, this hundred is to repair in common with *Baffet-lowe*.

B Y N G H A M-hundred repairs a certain parcel of this bridge containing 105 feet, and the middle pillar in common with *Newark*.

R Y S C L I F F hundred is to repair two other arches next to the aforefaid parcel, and the fouth end of the faid bridge, containing in length 57 feet and the middle pillar between thefe two arches and the faid parcel is to be repaired in common by the two laft mentioned wapentakes.

B E T W E E N the two principal bridges, *i. e.* the *Trent* and *Leen*-bridge and about the middle, betwixt the *Trent*-lanes, are two confiderable pools of water, not without good fifh in them, around which is the common paffage for horfes and wheel-carriages, except in times of a flood, in which cafe, two bridges built over thefe pools, give paffage to horfes, coaches, waggons, &c. to avoid the danger of driving or riding into one of thefe pools ; thefe bridges at other times have chains a-crofs them, whence both thefe pools and the bridges have obtained the names of *Chainy-bridges* and *Chainy-pools*, a corruption of chained. There are farther between the *Leen*-bridge and thefe juft named bridges, very high planks and rails, reaching from the one to the other, over which when the waters are out people may walk on foot dry to *Chainy*-bridges, and thence over the higheft part of the meadows and the above-mentioned caufeway to *Trent*-bridge, which is a meafured mile. Thefe planks and rails are likewife kept in repair by the bridge-mafters.

H A V I N G now done with the rivers and bridges, we will turn an eye towards the roads, and begin with the road to *London*, concerning which it muft be confefs'd

that

that till within thefe few years between *Nottingham* and *Loughborough*, it was fo very bad, not to fay dangerous, that by travellers it was deemed next to impoffible to make it good, efpecially that part of it which is called *Codlingftock*, commonly *Coftock-lane*, naturally a blew, ftiff and greafy clay, in which the original curfe feems to center, for it is neither fit for culture nor paffage. However upon proper application an act of parliament was obtained, which took place in *May* 1738, when the commiffioners went about it with great vigour and expedition, having firft taken care to be provided with the true fpur to all expeditious works, I mean a fufficient ftock of money; they employed the late alderman *Cooper* of *Leicefter*, a man who underftood the nature of ordering this kind of affairs fo well, and managed them with fo much integrity, that if he did not outdo moft others he at leaft equalled the beft; thus provided the work went on brifkly, and in a furprizing fhort time the road between this town and *Loughborough*, called nine miles, but being fourteen meafured, is now as firm and good as any turnpike road in *England*, and travellers are put to a ftand which to admire moft, the expedition or goodnefs of the performance; to this I muft add, that the corporation in the year 1740, made the fouth entrance into *Nottingham* very convenient, which was a narrow paffage cut out in the rock on which the town ftands, where but one coach or waggon could pafs at a time, as it were between two high cliffs, but now is fo open, light and fpacious, that in fome parts three or four carriages can eafily give way to each other: They were animated thereto by an act of generofity of the right honourable *Francis* lord *Middleton*, who the year before had at his own coft and charges, levelled part of the fand-hills, and thereby much enlarged the coming to the town from the weft, having before done the fame between thefe hills and *Lenton*, infomuch that the road to *Derby* between *Nottingham* and *Woollaton* is very pleafant, and equally good in winter and fummer.

THE road to *Mansfield*, a foreft town, twelve computed miles from *Nottingham*, affords at all times eafy travelling for foot paffengers as well as others.

THE road to *York* is no more the fame it was, before, at, and for fome reigns after the conqueft, I mean upon the *Foffe* by *Lincoln*, &c. but fince the high foreft is become fo bare of wood, travellers have room enough to make their way to that city eafy and pleafant.

THE horfe road over the foreft to *Newark* from *Nottingham*, is likewife feldom inconvenient, but on the contrary for the moft part, efpecially in fummer furnifhes the horfemen for eight miles with a moft pleafurable journey, by the north bank of the river *Trent*, whilft he rides on a green lawn and enjoys the moft delightful view of the high and fteep hills near the oppofite fide of the river, plentifully adorned with all kinds of fpring wood, which frequently tempts the judges in the fummer affize, to chufe this road, and make their entrance into the town on horfeback.

THERE remains now before I clofe this fection, to take notice of the foreft of *Sherwood*.

THIS Foreft is one of the ancient ones, confiderably older than the conqueft, as moft others except the *New-Foreft* in *Hampfhire*, and *Hampton-Court* foreft in *Surrey* and *Middlefex* made by *Henry* VIII. the 31ft of his reign, by act of parliament.(*a*)

MY

(*a*) Blount's *Law Dictionary*

MY anonymous of *Nottingham* divides it into the high-foreſt and thorny-woods, or (which would have been as well) the chace, (a) " this laſt tho' conſiderably leſs " than the former, contains notwithſtanding the bounds and territories of nineteen " towns, of which *Nottingham* is one, (tho' not in view or regard.) That part call'd " the high-foreſt was anciently moſt richly provided with ſtately oaks, in tallneſs " and ſtraightneſs of the bole, hardly giving way to the firs in the northern parts of " *Europe*, quite freed from any thorns or other underwood, where now ſays my au- " thor, (above an hundred years ago) is nothing to be ſeen but oves and boves *et* " *prova campi*, grafing upon a green carpet, without ſo much as a buſh for a nightin- " gal to reſt in, yet are there ſome footſteps or reliques of the ancient beauty of this " foreſt in the parts of *Belhaigh* and *Birkland*, tho' thoſe alſo be ſhrewdly gelded " and pruned." Dr. *Thoroton* in 1675, complains that in his time ſo many claims have been allowed by the deputies and lieutenant of the lord warden, that he fears there will ſhortly not be wood enough left to cover the bilberies, which every ſum- mer were won't to be an extraordinary great profit and pleaſure to the poor people who gathered them and carried them about the country to ſell. The part of thorny-wood took its name from the plenty of thorns, beſides other underwood; in this harbour the kings fallow deer, whilſt the red deer entirely keep in the high-foreſt, tho' very barren. Anciently the extreme ſeverity (b) of the foreſt laws under the norman kings and ſome others were very burthenſome to the ſubjects, eſpecially to thoſe whoſe lands and poſſeſſions did border upon the foreſt; but in king *John's* reign, a charter was obtained to mitigate ſome hardſhips then complained of, and in the reign of his ſon *Henry* III. a farther charter was granted to his people, relating to the liberties in the foreſt the 16th of his reign, as appears by the exemplification of a perambulation, whereby the boundaries of the foreſt were determined and diſtinguiſhed from that part which was then diſ-foreſted. It bears date *July* 15th in the 16th of *Henry* III. and may be ſeen in the *Appendix*, as alſo a perambulation made *Auguſt* 26th, the 21ſt of *Henry* VII. with mention of a perambulation made the 19th of *September* the 35th of *Henry* VIII.

Z SECT. IX.

(a) Manwood's *difference of a chace from a foreſt is* : 1ſt. In that a chace has no par- ticular that are proper for a chace only ; for all offenders in a chace are to be puniſh- ed by common-law, and not by any law peculiar only to a chace. 2*dly*. A chace has no ſuch officers as a foreſt has, *viz*. Neither verderers, foreſters, regarders or re- giſters, but only keepers and woodwards. 3*dly*. A chace has no court of attachment, ſwanimote, or juſtice ſeat, as a foreſt has. *Ibid*.

(b) William *the* Conqueror *cauſed the eyes of a man to be put out who took either a buck or a boar*. William Rufus *would hang a man for taking a doe, and for a hare he made him pay* 20 *s. and* 10 *s. for a coney. The ſame* Rufus *cauſed fifty rich men to be apprehended and accuſed them for taking and killing his bucks, which they de- nying were to clear themſelves by fire ordeal.* Henry IV. *made no diſtinction be- tween he who killed a man and he who killed a buck, and puniſhed thoſe who de- ſtroyed the game (tho' not in the foreſt) either by forfeiture of their goods or loſs of limb ; but* Henry II. *made it only impriſonment for a time. His ſon* Richard I. *re- vived the old laws for puniſhing thoſe who were convicted of hunting in the foreſt : viz. that they ſhould be gelt and have their eyes pulled out, but the ſame king after- wards aboliſhed this puniſhment, and appointed ſuch convicts to abjure the realm, or be committed, or pay a fine.* Edward I. *appointed the ſame puniſhment, but that they ſhould be free life and limb.* Blount's Law-Dictionary.

SECTION IX.

A Defcription of the Caftle of NOTTINGHAM, with a fhort Account of the Governors of it.

AT the fouth-weft end of the town of *Nottingham* there is a fteep rock, the fouth-fide of which, where the river *Leen* runs clofe by, defcends in a precipice, and is quite inacceffible ; (*a*) on this part of the rock ftood an ancient ftrong tower, wherein the *Danes* in the time of the heptarchy, held out a fiege againft *Buthred* king of *Mercia*, king *Alfred*, and *Ethelred* his brother, king of the weft *Saxons* ; but none of our hiftorians informing us when or by whom this fortrefs was built, it may fafely plead its antiquity.

SOON after the conqueft king *William* the *Conqueror*, either repaired this ancient faftnefs, or elfe built quite a new caftle, on the fame fpot where the old tower ftood : (*b*) For hiftory tells us, that when *Edwyn* earl of *Chefter* and *Morcar* his brother earl of *Northumberland* had raifed an army in the north and revolted, king *William* I. drew his forces together with the utmoft expedition and marched againft them, in his march he fortified the caftle of *Warwick* ; this was A. C. 1068, in the fecond year of his reign ; at this very time he alfo built the caftle of *Nottingham*, to fecure a retreat in cafe of neceffity, and to keep the town in awe.

THOROTON fpeaks varioufly concerning the founder of this caftle, one while he fays doubtfull y that it was built by *William Peverel*, or elfe by *William* I. (*c*) his father ; in another place (*d*) he tells us, that he does not certainly find when this caftle was built, but doubtlefs it was by *William Peverel*. Here he plainly fhews, that certainly he never looked into *Holinfhed*, *Camden*, *Stow*, and others, but blind-foldly copied his father-in-law's manufcript. In the fecond column of the fame page, he proceeds : " It feems the *Conqueror* or one of his *Sons*, gave the dominion of *Not-*" *tingham* and the foreft, to his *baftard* fon." If we believe him, that *Peverel* was the founder of our caftle, we muft alfo believe that he had many lands and poffeffi-ons in thefe parts before he did erect it, for it would be ridiculous to think that he would build a fortrefs where he had nothing to loofe. Our above-mentioned hifto-rians agree, that *William* I. committed the cuftody of this caftle to his natural fon *William Peverel*, the fecond year of his reign, *i. e.* the very year it was built in. It is therefore as weak to imagine that *Peverel* was the founder, as that one of the con-queror's fons fhould give to him what he was poffeffed of already.

THIS

(*a*) *Its perpendicular height is* 133 *feet*
(*b*) Rapin, *Vol.* I. p.   (*c*) p. 488.   (*d*) 490.

T H I S castle was greatly enlarged and received vast additions both of strength and beauty by *Edward* IV. who on account of *Nottingham's* having proved very lucky to him, had ever after a great value for it : But he did not live to see all the work compleated, for he began a stately and magnificent fabrick of stone, of which he finished one large tower of three heights, and raised up the rest of the building from the foundation to the laying of the first floor, (says *Leland*). His perfidious and unfortunate brother who after murdering his nephews placed himself on the throne, by the stile and title of *Richard* III. made round windows of timber above those of stone, and did finish all the rest.

T H I S additional part of the castle was commonly called the new-tower, but *Richard* III. who but a very little while before the fatal battle of *Bosworth* resided in it, called it the castle of care, of which, as well as that erected by the conqueror, from *Leland*, who saw it in the time of *Henry* VIII. *Camden*, who saw it in queen *Elizabeth's* reign, an anonimous manuscript author a native of *Nottingham* who lived on the spot in the reign of king *James* and part of king *Charles* I. together with the ruins of the outer bastions remaining, and with the help of a plan of the ancient work, taken by Mr. *Smithson* in the years 1617, I gather the following description.

T H E works of the castle of *Nottingham* were distinguished into the old and new tower. The first built on the highest and steepest part of the rock, was that which *William* I. caused to be erected; the other which had in it much larger and more beautiful buildings, as well as one extraordinary strong tower, stood north of the former, was begun by king *Edward* IV. and finished by *Richard* III.

" T H E bass court (says *Leland*) is large and mighty strong, and there is a stately " bridge (with pillars bearing beasts and giants) over the ditch into the second ward, " the front of which at the entrance is exceeding strong, with towers and port-cul- " lices." (*a*) " Within is a fair green court fit for any princely exercise. The " south-east parts of the castle are strong and well towered, within the old tower there " is another court tho' somewhat less then the last mentioned," (*b*) " in the midst " whereof there is a stair-case of stone, about six or seven feet above ground, in " which there is a door to enter and steps to lead, (of late much worn) through the " main rock to the foot thereof and the bank of the river *Leen* ; by this passage (the " keepers say) *Edward* the 3ds band came up through the rock and took earl *Mor-* " *timer* prisoner." " The dungeon or prison stands by south and east, and is extra- " ordinary strong *et natura loci et opera*. " (*c*) In the first court we go down many " steps with a candle lighted into a vault under ground, and rooms cut and made out of " the very stone, in the walls whereof the story of *Christ's passion* and other things " are engraven, by *David* king of *Scotland*, (as they say) who was kept prisoner " there." *Leland* makes mention of three wells and as many chapels. Dr. *Thoroton*, informs us, " that the castle was a rectory of 6 *l.* per annum, but that now nothing is " to be found concerning it." There is also a tradition of a college of secular priests in the castle. *Brown Willis*, Esq; informs me from bishop *Tanner's Notitia Monas-tica*, of a chapel of St. *Mary*, in the time of *Henry* III. in the rock under the castle.

Z 2

TO

(*a*) *Anonymous Mss.* (*b*) *id.* (*c*) *Camden's Britt.*

TO the caftle did belong according to the account of *Geffry Knyveton*, confta-ble of it and clerk of the foreft, the 25th of *Henry* VI. which I have taken *literatim* fro m a foreft book wrote for the ufe of the mayor of *Nottingham, Robert Alvie*, by his ferjeant at mace *William Marfhall*, in the year 1588 the 30th of queen *Elizabeth, John Nody* and *Nicholas Sherwin* being fheriffs. *fol.* 55.

The accompte of Geffry Knyveton *from the feaft of St.* Michaell *tharchaungle in the* xxvth. *yeare of kinge* Henry *the fixth unto the fame feafte next followinge by one whole yeare for the caftle of* Nottingham.

1ft. He gives accompte of xii *l.* 8 *s.* cominge of xxiiii acres of meadow, lying in a meadow belonging to the caftle of *Nottingham* called the *king's-meadow*. The price 3 *s.* 2 *d.* fo letten this yeare.

And of xiv *s.* the latter agiftment of the fame meadow betwixt *Michallmas* and *Mar-tlemas* happeninge.

And of liii *s.* iiii *d.* of the farme of the clofe called caftle-appleton.

And of xxxvi *s.* 8 *d.* for the farme of another clofe called the conftable-holme, fo letten to the men of *Nottingham*.

And of xxiv *s.* of the farme of a pece of meadow called the milne-dame.

And xiii *s.* of the farme of two peces of meadow lyeinge by the king's-bridge and the rocke-yard.

And viii *s.* of the caftle-hills without the caftle-walls.

And xx *s.* of the farme of the pindage of the caftle fo letten to the men of *Not-tingham*.

And of x *s.* of the farme of the outward, within the caftle walls.

And of the profit of the dove-cott nothing this year, but it was wont to give 3 *s.* 4 *d.*

And of   for the caftle-miln.

And of the 13 *s.* 4 *d.* of the farme of the coneygarth of the caftle this year &c.

This furvey was taken three years before Henry VI. *made the town of* Nottingham *a county by itfelf, in which charter he excepts the* King's-Hall, *and the* Caftle *of* Nottingham, *both which remain at this day in the county at large.*

IN the reign of *Henry* VII. the king finding caftles prejudicial to him, demolifh-ed fome and rendered others ufelefs, this our caftle was fuffered to go to decay, info-much that in the time of *Henry* VIII. when *Leland* view'd it, great part of the in-ner ward as the hall and fome other buildings lay in ruins. " But the whole became " (*a*) far more ruinous in the poffeffion of *Francis* earl of *Rutland* in the latter end " of whofe time, many of the goodly buildings were pulled down and the Iron and o-" ther materials fold."

NOTWITHSTANDING all this, it appeared ftill a place of defence in the year 1642, elfe king *Charles* I. would hardly have thought it a fit place for fet-ting up his royal ftandard, nor would *Oliver Cromwell*, (*b*) after the civil war, have occafion to fend orders and money to captain *Poulton*, the then governor, to demolifh it fo far as render it unferviceable for war.

HA-

(*a*) *Thoreton* p. 490.   (*b*) *ibid.*

HAVING thus collected from others what I could find towards a description of this our castle, I will endeavour to draw what farther light I am able, from such footsteps as time the consumer of all things, has not yet entirely destroyed, and begin with the above-mentioned vault, which from the court of the old tower does lead through the body of the rock to the bank of the river *Leen*, called *Mortimer's-hole*.

THIS vault undoubtedly must have been in a much better condition in *Leland's*, *Camden's* and even in my anonymous author's time, than at present, wherefore I cannot help wondering at their incurious inspection of it, which has led them into diverse errors concerning the name it bears. This way through the rock was provided with no less than six gates, besides a side one on the left hand going down; the first was above ground leading from the turret down to the second, the place where the turret stood is now covered by part of the modern fabrick, and the passage to the second gate is filled and the gate itself walled up with stone, to this leads a new passage cut out of the rock since the building of the present castle, without the wall of the paved yard. The distance between the first and the second gate I take to have been about 16 yards; from this we step down 14 yards and meet with the marks of another, and 15 yards lower was a fourth; about 45 yards below this on the left hand we observe a gate bricked up, which with seven or eight steps did lead up into some works of the old tower, (as the late Mr. *Jonathan Paramour* informed me) in whose time it was bricked up; about eight yards below this stood a fifth, and the sixth and lowest which opened into the rock-yard and is now also bricked up is still about nine yards lower, so that the whole length of this once well secured subterraneous passage from the court of the old tower to the foot of the rock is 107 yards or 321 feet: This vault is 7 feet high and six wide, had all the way down broad steps cut in the rock, the which are at this time almost entirely worn out in the middle, but may plainly be perceived at the sides; there are all the way down till within 15 or 16 yards of the bottom, openings in the side of the rock to convey light into this passage, and to serve the soldiers to shoot their arrows through upon the enemy, in the the upper part are cut out several regular port-holes, which shew, that during the civil war, cannons were planted there, which commanded all the meadows; there are besides in this part of the vault observable, many holes or excavations about a foot in height, breadth and depth, these seem to have been made to lodge cannon-balls in, to prevent their rolling to the bottom.

BY this account taken from the present appearance of this place, it may easily be judged, that it was contrived for a much weightier purpose than to carry on a love-intrigue, as a certain author will have it, *viz.* that *Mortimer* ordered this passage to be cut out, for a private way to come to the queen's appartments, and that from thence it got the name of *Mortimer's-hole*. A very ill grounded conjecture. What occasion had he to come privately to the queen, when the posts and employments the earl was in, during the minority of the king, not only furnished him with frequent opportunities of going publickly to her, but the urgency of affairs made it indispensably necessary that he should often attend her majesty.

HAD Mr. *Camden* been more exact in observing the place we are speaking of, he would hardly have fallen into the error of imagining that it got its name, " because " *Mortimer* had it made to hide himself in, being afraid of himself out of a consci-

X 3

" ousness

" oufnefs of his own guilt." Is it not reafonable to fuppofe, if the earl of *March* had ordered this place to be made for his concealment, he would likewife have taken care that it fhould have been made convenient for that end, whereas the whole vault is one continued ftair-cafe without fo much as one fingle fhelf in the fide of the rock for a perfon to fit down upon.

BESIDES if we lay afide the confideration of the ftructure of this paffage, the opinion of Mr. *Camden* will hardly be approved by any thinking perfon, that that noble-man, generally known to live in the caftle with the queen, fhould chufe to hide him-felf in a rocky cave, when at the fame time he could be in the royal appartment, and and that with full as much fafety, for the queen had the keys of the caftle delivered to her every night, and laid under her pillow ; moreover the earl of *March* when the place was furprized, was not found there but in the apartment of the queen ; (*a*) in fhort had the earl defigned this vault for his fecurity, it muft be fuppofed he would have taken more particular care that it fhould be fufficiently guarded againft any fudden furprize, whereas it feems no extraordinary care was taken of it, elfe it would have been out of the power even of the governor to have given king *Edward* the opportunity of coming into the caftle that way.

BUT there juft now comes to my hand a manufcript *Englifh* chronicle, which by the language feems to be wrote in the reign of king *Henry* VI. this pofi-tively affirms, that neither *Mortimer* nor the queen knew any thing of this paffage ; thefe are the very words : *Chap.* 222.

" AND in haft ther came unto kyng *Edw.* Sir *William Montague*, that he was in
" his caftell and pryvelyche told him, that he ne none of his companions fhulde not
" take the *Mortimer* without counfaile and helpe of *William Eland*, conftabill of the
" fame caftell. Now certis quod kyng *Edward* I leve you full well, and therefor I
" counfaill you that ye goo unto the faide conftabill, and commaunde him in my
" name that he be your frende and your helper for to take the *Mortimer*, all things
" left uppon peyne of lyfe and lymmbe. Sir quod *Mountague* my lorde graunte mer-
" cye. Tho went forth the faide *Mountague* and come to the conftabill of the caftell
" and told him the kyng's wille, and he anfwered, the kyng's wille fhulde be done
" in all that he myght, and he wolde not fpare for no manner of deth and fo he
" fwhore and made his othe. Tho faide Sir *William Mountague* to the conftabill in
" herynge of all them that were helpyng to the quarrel. Now certis dere ffrendes
" us behoveth for to worche and done by your Queyntyfe to take the *Mortimer*, fith
" ye be the keeper of the caftell and have the kayes in your warde. Sir quod the
" conftabill woll ye underftonde that the yats of the caftell beth loken with lokys,
" and queen *Ifabell* fent hidder by night for the kayes thereof, and they be layde un-
" der the chemfell of her beddis hede unto the morrow, and fo I may not come into
" the caftell by the yats no manner of wyfe, but yet I know another weye by
" an aley that ftretchith oute of the ward under the earthe into the
" caftell that gooth into the weft, which aley queen *Ifabell*, ne none of her meayne,
                                                                                      ne

_____

(*a*) See Section XIII.
(*b*) This account is the fame with that in the Cambridge *Mfs.* be done which Arthur
      Collins quotes in his peerage. Vol. I. p. 270.

" ne the *Mortimer* ne none of his companye knowith it not, and fo I fhall lede you
" through the aley, and fo ye fhall come into the caftell without afpyes of any man
" that beth your enemies, &c.

I T is therefore much more probable, that as the king and his band came up this
paffage on purpofe to feize *Mortimer's* perfon, and as the earl after he was taken
prifoner, was brought out of the caftle through this very fame paffage, it was in remembrance of this event call'd *Mortimer's-hole*. There is no account when this
vault was made which I have met with, except what *Collin's* in his peerage quotes
from *Drayton's* barons war, *viz.* " This wonderful paffage had been hued and dug
" during the *Danifh* Invafion by fome of the *Saxon* kings for the better fecurity in
" cafe of a fiege. For my part if I confider how ftrongly this place was provided
with gates, I cannot help thinking that it was defigned to relieve the caftle with men
and provifions, in cafe an enemy fhould be in poffeffion of the town, the opening of
it being both without the town and caftle walls, and the rock yard being covered
with two round baftions, in the outer wall of the caftle facing the fouth, of which a
good part is yet ftanding, and that after the *norman* conqueft, it was made ufe of in
time of peace to convey the meal and beer, which was ground (efpecially after the
Leen was brought to run by the caftle) and brewed for the garrifon, the neareft way
into the caftle.

T H E rock-yard into which the laft and loweft gate in *Mortimer's-hole* opens, is
called in old writings the brewhoufe of the caftle, and indeed it had no other houfes
in it but fuch as ferved for the conveniency of brewing for the garrifon ; until king
James I. by a particular grant under the broad feal, feparated it from the caftle.

T H I S grant was made to one *Edward Ferres*, of *London*, mercer, and *Francis
Philips*, of *London*, gent. exemplify'd to *John Mitten*, and *William Jackfon*, bearing
date the 18th of king *James of England*, and the 55th of *Scotland*, anno dom. 1621 ;
fince which time a pretty many houfes have been built in it, efpecially in the clofe,
which in the grant is called *Dovecoat-clofe*. In this yard ftood alfo the mill of the
caftle, which ufed to grind all the corn for the fupport of the garrifon.

F A R T H E R weft in the yard within a piece of ground now turned into a kitchen garden, are to be feen the remains of a ftair-cafe, opening to the eaft and leading up into the rock, wherein feveral rooms are formed with pretty even floors. Here
formerly was the malt-office belonging to the caftle, as appears plainly by the kiln,
which to thisday is to be feen.

T H E brewhoufe-yard was lately part of the jointure eftate of Mrs. *Collin*, relict
of the late *John Collin*, Efq; alderman of *Nottingham*, and mother of *Langford Collin*,
Efq; one of his majefty's juftices of the peace for the county of *Nottingham* : the kitchen garden and an houfe on the right hand going into *Brewhoufe-yard*, only excepted, which houfe and garden were given by Mr. *Peacock*, to a fociety of people who
formerly ufed to meet here and called themfelves the *Family of Love* ; (*a*) thefe

pre-

(*a*) See Section II.

premifses are at this time in the pofsefsion of mafter *Ring*, an infant, and grandfon of the late *Thomas Smith*, Efq;

I T is a conftablery which Dr. *Thoroton* with *Mfs. J. M.* is pleafed to call a recep- tacle for fanaticks, and other like people, who would not live conformable to the laws. This cenfure feems to me too fevere, inafmuch as it not only favours of a perfecuting fpirit, but is founded on a falfe fuppofition, as if this place (being in the county at large) were any more exempt from the obedience to the laws of the land, than any o- ther place in the county, and that in a reign where no vifible corner of the kingdom could fhelter any number of perfons from the rigorous execution of that coercive law the *Act of Uniformity*.

F R O M the baftion of the eaft corner of the *Brewhoufe-yard*, the ruins of the outer walls of the caftle run north, and over againft a ftreet called *Caftlegate* are feen the ruins of the largeft round baftion, in the middle between this and the outer gate in the wall which bends a little weftward, a low gate is obferved, which I dare ven- ture to fay was a fally-port. The main gate is placed between two Baftilles: From hence the wall almoft due weft to the park, there, makes an angle, and extending it- felf in a line northward did join the poftern, of which notice has been taken in *Section* I.

T H E outer-ward within the outer-wall, is fpacious, on the right hand of which was the pindage of the caftle, and on the left where now a garden and nurfery of trees is planted was the dove-coat, as I am informed by the above-mentioned Mr. *Jo- nathan Paramour*, who lived with duke *William* when the foundation of the new caftle was laid.

T H E ditch round the caftle was a dry mote of a confiderable depth and breadth, as may eafily be difcovered even at this time.

O N the other fide of the ditch at the farther end of that part of the rock where- upon the new tower ftood, there was till within thefe 18 or 20 years, an hole opening fomewhat towards the eaft, called by the common-people *James Scot*'s hole, which as the tradition goes, did lead acrofs the park, under ground, quite to *Lenton*, a good mile in length; this being a vulgar error, I will here take an opportunity of clearing up the matter. Had fuch a pafsage ever been made, it would be hard to find out a ufe for it adequate to fuch an herculean labour, and whofoever confiders how low the va- ley is between the caftle rock and the high hill where *Lenton*-ftile is placed, will with much ado allow it pofsible to be done, but hardly deem it probable that fuch a piece of work fhould ever have been undertaken: To be fhort let the reader but caft an eye upon the plan of the old caftle here annexed, and he will readily be convinced that the truth of the matter is this: When by order of his grace *William* duke of *Newcaftle*, the old works of the new tower were clearing, the labourers by flinging fome pretty large ftones down the fide of the rock, beat in the ground and made ac- cidentally this hole, which fhew'd the curious a way into the rock, this turning at firft

a

_____

(*a*) *See more of him in Section* VII.

a little to the right and the quantity of rubbiſh rendering the going far into the rock very difficult, has made them fancy that paſſage went directly weſt and conſequently to *Lenton,* tho' nobody has ever offered to ſhew any opening at *Lenton,* to anſwer this pretended ſubterraneous way, and the above mentioned plan clearly ſhews, that the hollow in that place was nothing elſe but a way into a range of cellars under the ſe-veral royal apartments and buildings on the north and weſt part of the rock. The name of *James Scot's* hole proceeded from a miſtake of the *Scottiſh* king *David* II. who is ſaid to have been priſoner in this caſtle, which moves me to examine how far the ſtory related of that king is well or ill-grounded.

THE dungeon or priſon of the caſtle was widely diſtant from the hole we have been ſpeaking of, for according to *Leland* it was ſouth from the hole, *i. e.* under the firſt ſteps which lead up to the paved court of the preſent caſtle. That there were ſuch rooms as Mr. *Camden* ſpeaks of, many ſteps deep in the rock, into which per-ſons were obliged to go with candle light, and that theſe ſteps went from the firſt court, as alſo that the paſſion of our Saviour *Chriſt* and other things were engraven on the walls of thoſe rooms, we may credit him who relates it as an eye-witneſs ; but that thoſe figures were made by *David* king of *Scots,* is not quite ſo clear : For that great antiquarian does not aſſert it directly, but with theſe cautionary words, (as they ſay). I will not deny that that king might be a priſoner in the caſtle of *Nottingham,* tho' *Stow* takes notice that he was brought to *Weſtminſter* the 2d of *January* 1147, and thence in the ſight of all the people conveyed to the tower and there lodged in the black nuck near the conſtable's guard, and that he was afterwards removed to *Ol-diſham* caſtle, where he remained priſoner till ranſomed ; becauſe as he was taken priſoner the 17th of *October* 1146 according to the ſame author, and could not be brought to *London* with the reſt of the priſoners on account of his wounds in the head; it is very probable that he was brought to *Nottingham* and remained confined in the caſtle till he was able to travel : But all this is ſtill ſo far from proving that king the author of the above-mentioned figures, that it rather creates a ſuſpicion to the contra-ry, becauſe his wounds in the head would not admit of ſuch a work if they diſabled him from travelling.

ON the north-ſide of the caſtle without the wall, is a cloſe which takes in the major part of the caſtle-hills and went from thence by the name of the hill-cloſe, in the middle of this on a flat and round ſpot was ſet up king *Charles* the 1ſt. ſtandard, ſince which time it bore for many years the name of ſtandard-cloſe, 'till of late ſome of the *Nevil's* having rented it, the town's people call it *Nevil's-cloſe* ; where the ſtandard was fixed there ſtood a poſt for a conſiderable number of years, in the room of which when pulled up, the father of *John Nevil,* Eſq; to perpetuate the memory of that remarkable event, planted ſeveral elms ſucceſſively, none of which eſcaped the unrulineſs of the lads of the town.

IT is a commonly received error, that the royal ſtandard was erected on a place called *Derry-mount,* a little farther north than the juſt-mentioned cloſe ; for it is an artificial hill raiſed on purpoſe for a windmill to ſtand upon, which formerly was there ; beſides this hill is not within the juriſdiction of the caſtle.

THIS our caſtle when in its glory (ſays *William* of *Newborough,*) was made ſo ſtrong both by nature and art, that it was eſteemed impregnable except by famine, if

A a

it

it had a sufficient garrison in it, (a) that it had never undergone the common fate of great castles, being never taken by downright storm; once it was besieged by *Henry* duke of *Anjou*, but in vain, at which time the garrison had burnt down all the buildings about it; (b) it was once also taken by surprize, by *Robert* count de *Ferrariis*, in the barons war, who burnt the town and deprived the people of all they had.

THERE remains now to add what I have met with concerning the governors of *Nottingham* castle, from the conquest to the end of the civil war. The first governor we read of since the conqueror built it is,

WILLIAM PEVEREL, natural son of *William* the 1st. who gave his mother, daughter to *Ingelric* in marriage to *Ralph Peverel*, who attended him into *England*. She obtained of her husband, that this son whom she had by the king, should bear the name of *Peverel*. This *William* was intrusted, (as has already been mentioned) with the custody of the castle of *Nottingham*, the second year of the reign of king *William* I. A. D. 1068. The peerage of *England* places him in the front of the earls of *Nottingham*, but *Glover* in his catalogue of *Honour*, makes no mention of him as such, and *Camden* says: (c)" *William* sir-named the *Conqueror*, made his natu-" ral son *William Peverel*, ruler of this county, [*Nottingham*] not by the title of earl, " but lord of *Nottingham*." (d) He at the general survey held 162 lordships in *England*, was a great soldier, and one of the chief commanders at the famous battle at *North-allerton* (e) the 7th of the reign of king *Stephen*, fighting stoutly on the part of that king at the battle of *Lincoln*; he was taken prisoner with the king in the contest between the empress *Maud* and king *Stephen*.

THE next who was possessed of *Nottingham* castle was:

RALPH PAGANEL or *Paynel* one of *Maud's* captains. This man instigated *Robert* duke of *Gloucester* to come to *Nottingham* to demolish and burn the town. (f) His grandfather possessed in *William* the *Conqueror's* time 45 lordships, the which his father *Fulk Paganel* augmented with good part of the lands of *Fitz Ansculph* in com. *Bucks*. (g) He got possessed of *Dudley* castle, which *Henry* II. after his decease ordered to be pulled down, because his son *Gervas Paganel*, who after his fathers death had manned several castles against king *Stephen*, turned tail and sided with king *Henry* the younger. *Ralph* was not long master of our castle, for the year following, the soldiers of *William Peverel*, did after their commanders enlargement recover it by stratagem, (not unlikely by that passage which obtained afterwards

---

(a) Camden's Brit. *p. m.* 432. ——— (b) Roger Hoved. *p.* 307.
(c) Camden's Brit. *p. m.* 484. ——— (d) Peerage *Vol.* II. *part* II. *p.* 90.
(e) *This war was called* Bellum de standardo *or the standard of war, for this Reason: Because* Walter d'Espec *and* William earl of Albemarle, *who were the chief commanders and had entrenched themselves at* Alverton *expecting the enemy there; they set up a mast at the top of which they placed a silver pix with consecrated host, and the banners of* St. Peter *and* St. John of Beverley, *to serve as an ensign, where they were to meet and rally in case of need.* Rapin, *Vol.* I. *p.* 203.
(f) *The town was burnt by accident. See Section* XIII.
(g) Peerage *Vol.* II. *part* II. *p.* 87, 88.

wards the name of *Mortimer's* hole) and from this time *Peverel* held it to the day of his death, and was fucceeded in his honours and poffeffions by his fon (as the peerage will have it) or his grandfon if we believe *Camden*, who fays, *p. m.* 484.

"*WILLIAM PEVEREL* lord of *Nottingham* had a fon of the fame " name, who died during his father's life time, and he had likewife a fon *Wil-* " liam deprived of his eftate by *Henry* II. for combining with the wife of *Ranulph* " earl of *Chefter*, who was youngeft daughter of the earl of *Gloucefter*, to poifon the " faid earl her husband." This happened the firft of *Henry* II. This *William Pe-verel* fearing the rigour of the king, he betook himself *(a)* firft to a monaftery at *Len-ton*, (*not of his own foundation as this author will have it, but his grandfather's*) not thinking himfelf fafe there, he quitted the habit he had newly taken upon him and fled, the king feized the major part of his poffeffions, and among others of his caftles that of *Nottingham*, which he firft granted to *Ranulph* earl of *Chefter*, *(b)* but foon after had that and the reft of *Peverels* lands in his own poffeffion again, and kept them in his hands a confiderable number of years, during which time it feems, *(c)*

REGINALD de LUCY had this caftle in keeping for the king (the peer-rage fays he held it for *Henry* the younger, *Vol.* II. *part* 2. *p.* 131.) till *Robert* earl of *Ferrers* and *Derby* in the war between the two *Henry's*, father and fon, took it in behalf of *Henry* the fon and drove *Lucy* out of it, plundered the town and diftributed the fpoil among his foldiers. After the death of king *Henry* the younger, the king gave the caftle to

JOHN earl of *MORETON*, his fourth fon. This prince was governor of it during the remainder of his father's life, and was alfo left in poffeffion by his brother *Richard* I. when he went into the holy land. In the abfence of the king earl *John* being fufpected of a defign *(d)* of mounting his brothers throne, *William Longchamp*, chancellor and bifhop of *Ely*, being conftituted protector of the kingdom, difpoffefs'd him of *Nottingham* caftle. At which time

WILLIAM MARESCHAL, earl of *Pembroke*, took poffeffion and the cuftody of the caftle upon him for the king, and put in *Alan de Lee* and *Peter Rovan-court* for his Deputies.

THIS nobleman tho' the caftle did not long remain in his hands made a very great figure in his time, and well deferves our notice, *(e)* he obtained by the kings favour, for his wife, *Iffabella* the heirefs of *Richard Strongbow* earl of *Pembroke*. Upon *Richard* I. his coming to *England*, after the death of his father *Henry* II. and being thus advanced, he bore the royal fcepter of gold with the crofs upon the head of it at his coronation; he was appointed one of the juftices in the government of the realm at the king's going into the holy land; he was likewife a truftee for the per-formance of what king *Richard* agreed upon with the *French* king for their joint en-gaging in that war. The 1ft of king *John* he was fent out of *Normandy* to keep peace in *England* till the king's coming, and obtained feveral of the poffeffions of *Giffard*
Aa 2 earl

(a) Magna Brit. & Hibern *Vol.* IV. *p.* 5. --- *(b)* ibid. --- *(c)* See Thoroton *p.* 489 ----- *(d)* Stow Sum. *p.* 165. ----- *(e)* Peerage, *Vol.* II. *part* 1. *p.* 281.

earl of *Bucks*; the 6th of king *John* he had other lands granted to him; the 9th of this king he obtained the whole province of *Lemster* by grant; the 15th, king *John* made him governor of *Caermarthen*, *Cardigan*, and *Gowther*; the 16th of king *John* he was constituted with *Nicholas* the pope's legate, a commissioner for restoring what had been taken from the king's subjects by reason of a late interdict; also the same year he was intrusted with *William* earl of *Warren* and others for giving safe conduct to such rebel barons as would implore the king's pardon at *Northampton*; and the next year when the barons met at *Brackley* in an hostile manner, he was sent by the king to know their demands, by whom they returned answer, " That if the king " would not ratify their laws and liberties they would constrain him to it," which being refused by the king, they formed an army; upon the death of king *John*, he convened many of the nobility, and setting young *Henry* in the midst of them said: *Behold your king*: Whereupon his coronation was appointed. (*a*) He resided at *Nottingham*, whither the earl of *Chester* retired to him, after he was forced to quit the siege of *Mount-Sorrel*: (*b*) And this earl the short time he had to live, proved as faithful to this king as he had been to his father, being the principal person who had fixed the crown on his head, and was made guardian by the rest of the lords. He reduced his own sons who had been in arms, which much weakened the rebel party. He laid siege to *Mount-Sorrel, in com Leicester*, one of the strongest holds of the barons, and soon after encountered them at *Lincoln*, gained the victory and then went to *London* and besieged it; and through his skilful conduct peace was brought about with the adverse party. The second of *Henry* III. he was sheriff of *Essex* and *Hertfordshire* and died the 3d of that king full of age.

A N D now to return from this long digression, earl *John* mustered up what forces he could, and finding those intrusted by *Pembroke* not altogether incorruptible, he soon got possession of the castle of *Nottingham* again, and made himself master of divers other castles, which he fortified for his own use; however the unwearied opposition of *Longchamp* obliged him at last to make peace, and by articles to surrender *Nottingham* castle; notwithstanding all this, we find him at the return of king *Richard* after he was released from his captivity, that this castle was held for earl *John*, by

ROGER MONTBEGON, who according to the peerage, [*vol.* II. *part* 2. *p.* 147.] sustained a siege against the bishop of *Ely*, vicegerent of the realm, and upon the king's return and his besieging in person, he after some days resistance submitted himself, paying 500 marks to make his peace. I read in another place, that at this very time *William Vendeval*, held out three days against king *Richard*, and then surrendered at discretion; it is not unlikely that this *Vendeval* might be deputy constable of the castle. Since this time it mostly continued in the crown, for after the death of king *Richard*, it was in king *John's* hands, who the 6th of his reign commanded

REGINALD de CLIFTON, (*c*) in whose custody it then was, that immediately upon sight of his letters, he should deliver to

RO-

(*a*) Matthew Paris. ----- (*b*) Peerage *ibid*. ---- (*c*) Thoroton, *p.* 489 *from* *pat.* 6 *John. m.* 7. ----- (*d*) Peerage *vol.* ii. *p.* 2. *p.* 52.

ROBERT de VETERIPONTE, the caſtle of *Nottingham*. (d) This *Robert Vipount* was a man of conſiderable note, he held before of king *Henry* II. eight knights fees of the honour of *Totneys* and accounted 85 *l*. of the honour of *Tickhill*. In the 4th of king *John* he was with the king in *France*, and probably in the memorable battle of *Mirabel*, and for his ſervices there had a grant of the caſtles of *Appleby* and *Burgh* with other privileges the year following, which grants included the barony, tho' not the borough of *Appleby*, which had been before granted to the burgeſſes there. This *Robert* the 5th of king *John* had the cuſtody of *Windſor* caſtle and that of *Bowes* in *Weſtmorland*; and in the 6th of the ſaid reign he became conſtable of the ſaid caſtle as has been ſaid, as he did, ſheriff of *Nottingham* and *Derbyſhire*: 1ſt. jointly with *Richard de Beauchamp*, after by himſelf the year following. In the reign of this king we meet with another chatelain:

(a) *PHILIP MARCH*, who in the king's greateſt difficulties proved to him a faithful and truſty ſervant, after the pope had abſolved all his ſubjects from the oath of allegiance.

THIS king upon concluſion of a peace with the barons, agreed among many other articles, that the caſtle of *Nottingham* ſhould be put under the poſſeſſion of the barons, and that the conſtable of the caſtle ſhould be ſworn to be faithful to them; but this conceſſion the king ſoon repented of, and the war between him and the barons revived again. I find not any more governors mentioned in this reign, but it appears ſtill to have been in the crown, for in the 10th of *Henry* III. ſon of king *John*,

(b) *RALP FITZ NICHOLAS* was warden of the caſtle of *Nottingham*.

(c) *HUGH FITZ RALPH*, was alſo in the fore part of this king's reign, ſheriff of *Nottinghamſhire* and *Derbyſhire*, and governor of the caſtle of *Nottingham*.

(d) *WILLIAM BARDOLF*, was likewiſe governor of *Nottingham* caſtle in the time of *Henry* III. who firmly adhering to him was taken priſoner at the battle of *Lewis*. He died the 4th of *Edward* I.

(e) *HUGH de SPENCER*, one of the greateſt barons of that time, taking arms with other nobles in defence of their ancient priviledges, was choſen by them the 42d year of *Henry* III, one of the twelve, who with twelve others choſen by the king were to amend and reform what they ſhould think amiſs. The 44th of *Henry* III. he was preferred to that great office of fines juſticier of *England*. In the battle wherein the king was taken priſoner the barons made him governor of *Oreford* caſtle, in com. *Suffolk*, of all the caſtles of the *Devizes* in *Wiltſhire*, of *Bernard*-caſtle in the biſhoprick of *Durham* and *Nottingham*. (f)

Aa 3

AF-

(a) Magn. Brit. & Hibern. *Vol.* IV. *p.* 12. ------ (b) Thoroton, *p.* 489. ------ (c) Peerage, *Vol.* II. *part* 2. *p.* 189. ----- (d) *ibid. p.* 173. ----- (e) Collin's *peerage, Vol.* I. *p.* 207. ----- (f) *He was killed at the memorable battle of Eveſham, where prince* Edward *got the day.* Peerage, *Vol.* II. *p.* 2. *p.* 65.

(g) AFTER the battle of *Lewis* king *Henry* III. determined the strife between him and his barons, delivered *Edward* his eldest son for a pledge, who after he was freed from that custody, had the castles of *Dover*, *Bamburgh*, *Scardeburgh*, *Nottingham* and *Corff* committed to him as hostages for five years, by the king his father, the 49th of *Henry* III.

(h) *ROBERT TIBETOT*, son of *Henry Tibetot*, who had a grant of *Edward* III. of the forfeited lands of *Adam de Paynel* for his good services to the king, was governor of *Dorcester*-castle, and being a trusty servant to king *Edward*, attended him to the holy-land. He was after made governor of the castles of *Nottingham*, *Caermarthen* and *Cardigan*, and being the king's lieutenant in *Wales*, took *Rees ap Meridith* their prince prisoner. His son *Pain* was warden of the forests beyond *Trent* and governor of *Northampton* castle, &c.

(i) *REGINALD de GREY*, (whose father *John de Grey*, besides many posts and honours he possessed, was the 49th of *Henry* III. after the battle of *Evesham* made by that king sheriff of *Nottingham* and *Derbyshire*) was the 6th of *Edward* I. appointed sheriff of the same counties, and governor of *Nottingham* castle, and the next year governor of the castle of *Northampton*, in the 9th of this king he was justice of *Chester*, (which post his father had formerly enjoyed) and merited so well from the king, that he had part of the honour of *Monmouth* given him, and in farther consideration of his services, obtained from the king the castle of *Ruthyn*, with other lands, He was appointed assistant to prince *Edward* in the government of the realm during the king's absence, and the 31st of *Edward* I. he was in the king's army in *Scotland*. He died the 1st of *Edward* II. Of this branch of the *Greys* was descended the lady *Jane Grey*.

JOHN SEGRAVE, son of *Nicholas Segrave*, (who was about the 45th of *Henry* III. one of the ringleaders of the rebellious barons of *Nottingham*) was in his father's life time warden of the forests beyond *Trent* and constable of *Nottingham* castle, in the reign of *Edward* I. In the 24th of that king he was made constable of the *English* army in *Scotland*; this was the year after the death of his father. He had after the principal command at the battle of *Faukirk*, and was soon after made governor of *Berwick*, in which command he was wounded and taken prisoner by the *Scots*, but being released he attended the king into *Scotland*, was at the siege of *Caerlaverock*, and upon the king's return he was left lieutenant there. Nor was he less in power and favour with king *Edward* II. for in the first year of his reign, the king made him justice of all the forests from *Trent* northward, and governor of *Nottingham* castle, and the next year warden of all *Scotland*. He was again in the wars of *Scotland* and taken prisoner at the unfortunate battle of *Bonnocksbourn*, but the 18th of *Edward* II. the king having conceived a displeasure against him for the escape of *Roger* lord *Mortimer* out of the tower, sent him with *Edmund* earl of *Kent* into *Gascoygne*, under colour of defending those places, where there being a mortality, he died, having had summons to parliament from the 14th of *Edward* I. to the 18th of *Edward* II.

R O-

(g) Thoroton, *p.* 490. (h) Peerage *Vol.* II. *part* 2. *p.* 206. (i) *ibid* 235.

(k) *ROBERT de CLIFFORD*, was one of the peers in parliament at *Lincoln* the 22d of *Edward* II. who subscribed that letter to the *Pope*, declaring king *Edward's* right to the superiority and dominion of the realm of *Scotland*, against which country he valiantly served that king, who made him justice of all the forests beyond *Trent* and governor of *Nottingham* castle.

WE have already mentioned that *Segrave* was made governor of *Nottingham* castle in the first year of the reign of king *Edward* II. and in the 4th of this reign, 1311.

PIERS GAVESTONE, the great favourite of this king, who was earl of *Cornwall*, was appointed constable of *Nottingham* castle and warden of the forests on this side *Trent*, and enjoyed many other estates and honours. The many extraordinary grants the king bestow'd upon this *Gascoign* gentleman, greatly displeased the nobility and the people. He was banished this same year and returned the next, *viz.* 1312, surrendered himself and *Scarborough* castle on condition he might see the king and be tried by his peers according to the usual form. The earl of *Pembroke* undertook to carry him to the king and restore him to the barons, and intended that the king should come and see him at the castle of *Wallingford*, and coming to (l) " *Deddington* in *Oxfordshire*, he left him in custody of his servants, and himself " and lady lay at a neighbouring place :" But the earl of *Warwick*, violently against the interview of the king and *Gavestone*, came in the night and took him away by force ; the next day in the morning the same earl with some others the most violent of that party, after a quick tryal ordered his head to be cut off, which was done in the presence of the earls of *Lancaster*, *Warwick* and *Hereford*, on *Blacklow-hill* near *Warwick* the 19th of *June*.

THE next governor of our castle I meet with is :

(m) *RICHARD de GREY*, of *Codnovre*, of the senior branch of the *Greys*, present dukes of *Kent*. He was made governor of *Nottingham* castle the 19th of *Edward* II. and the last of this king's reign. This nobleman was very much employ'd, for in the 4th of *Edward* II. he was sent into *Scotland*, and two years after he was appointed seneschal of *Gascoigne* ; in the 8th of this king he obtained the wardship of *Ralph* the son and heir of *Richard Basset*, for the sum of 800 *l*. and received command at the same time to advance with horse and arms to *Newcastle* upon *Tyne* and other parts of the marshes of *Scotland*, for the king's service. In the 12th and 13th he was again in the wars of *Scotland*, and the 17th of that king he was constituted steward of the dutchy of *Aquitain*, being sent the next ensuing year together with his brother *Nicholas* and many other great men with an army to seize that dutchy into the king's hands, in regard the king of *France* refused to do homage to king *Edward* for the same. He was governor when king *Edward* III. surprized the earl of *March* in the castle of *Nottingham*; his deputy constable was Sir *William Eland*; he was continued

tinued governor the 1ft of *Edward* III. in this year he was fent to guard the marches of *Scotland* and died in this king's fervice the 9th of his reign.

WHO was governor during this long reign, I have not been able to difcover except that the foreft books mentions one, (*n*)

STEPHEN RUMBYLOWE, to have been conftable of *Nottingham* caftle the 31ft *Edward* III. he was probably but deputy conftable to fome great perfonage. Nor do I find who was governor in the reign of *Richard* II. but in the 8th of *Henry* IV.

(*o*) *RICHARD GREY*, great-grandfon of the former *Richard*, was conftable of *Nottingham* caftle and chief ranger of the foreft of *Shirwood* for term of life. In the 14th of this king he was conftituted governor of the caftle of *Frounfac* in the dutchy of *Aquitain*, the fame year being lord chamberlain to the king, he was joined in commiffion with *Thomas* bifhop of *Durham* and others, to treat with the ambaffadors of *John* duke of *Burgundy*, for a marriage between prince *Henry* and the lady *Anne*, daughter of that duke ; and after when the prince attained the crown, in his fecond year, he was again commiffioned with the bifhop of *Durham* to treat with the french king, about a marriage betwixt *Catherine* the daughter of the faid king and king *Henry* V. He was likewife employed to treat with the *Scots* about a truce by fea and land. In the 4th of this reign he was made warden of the eaft-marches. In the 5th of the fame king, governor of the caftle of *Argentines* in the dutchy of *Normandy*, but died the year following. This great man was twice in the wars of *France* in the reign of *Richard* II. *viz.* the 17th and 21ft. The fecond of *Henry* IV. he was firft made admiral of the king's fleet northward, and afterwards conftituted jointly with Sir *Richard le Scroop*, governor of the caftle of *Roxborough* in *Scotland*, and next year he was fent into *France* upon the king's fervice, and was the 5th of *Henry* V. made juftice of *South-Wales*.

FROM the 6th of *Henry* V. to the 23d of *Henry* VI. I find no mention made what perfon or perfons had the cuftody of our caftle, and then

(*p*) *RALPH CROMWELL*, obtained a grant from the crown to himfelf and his heirs, of the office of conftable of the caftle of *Nottingham* and fteward of the fame, as alfo the wardenfhip of the foreft of *Shirwood*, with the parks of *Beskwood* and *Clypfton*, to hold by fealty only for all fervices. The 25th of *Henry* VI. mention is made of

JEFFRY KNYVETON, as conftable of this caftle and clerk of the foreft. This man could only be deputy under *Cromwell*, who then was ftill alive, tho' afterwards he died the 34th of *Henry* VI. without iffue. There was in the 25th of *Henry* VI. one *Guelfrid Knyveton*, mayor of the corporation of *Nottingham*, whom I take to be the fame man.

THE next governor I meet with is,

                                                                 R I-

---

(*n*) Section VIII.   (*o*) Peerage *Vol.* II. *p.* 2. *p.* 232.   (*p*) *ibid. page* 207.

RICHARD HASTINGS, Efq; who the 10th of *Edward* IV. with *Joan* his wife, daughter and heir of *Richard Welles* knight, lord *Welles* and *Willoughby* had fpecial livery of the caftles, lordfhips and lands of her inheritance, and the 15th of *Edward* IV. was made deputy conftable of *Nottingham* caftle, and warden of the forefts and chaces north of *Trent*, in the abfence of *William* lord *Haftings*. In the 22d of *Edward* IV. and the 1ft of *Richard* III. this gentleman was fummoned to parliament by the title of lord *Welles*.

(q) Sir *JOHN BYRON*, knight, he received the honour of knighthood *September* 22, in the firft of king *Henry* VII. who the fame year made him conftable of *Nottingham* caftle and porter of the fame, fteward and warden of the foreft of *Shirwood*, of *Billay*, *Birkland*, *Rumwood*, *Oufeland*, and *Fulwood*, with 40 *l.* &c.

HENRY earl of *RUTLAND*, fon and heir of *Thomas* the firft earl of *Rutland* of that family, in the firft of *Edward* VI. facked *Haddington* in *Scotland* with 3000 men ; the fecond of the fame reign he was made conftable of the caftle of *Nottingham* and chief juftice of the foreft of *Shirwood*, as alfo warden of the eaft marches and middle marches towards *Scotland*, and two years after he accompanied the marquis of *Northampton* in *France*, who then went upon a folemn embaffy to that king. In the 3d of *Philip* and *Mary* he was made captain general of all the forces then defigned for the feas, and likewife of the whole fleet ; but ferved only as general of the horfe at St. *Quintin* in *Picardy*. In the firft of queen *Elizabeth* he was conftituted lieutenant of the counties of *Nottingham* and *Rutland*, and foon after lord prefident of the council of the northern parts of the realm, as alfo inftalled knight of the garter ; he died *September* the 17th 1563, the 5th of *Elizabeth*.

JOHN, after his brother *Edward's* death without iffue male, became the 4th earl of *Rutland* of this family in 1587 the 29th of *Elizabeth*, and was made the fame year conftable of the caftle of *Nottingham* and the next lieutenant of *Nottinghamfhire*. He died without iffue male 1588,[fays the peerage]and was fucceeded by his brother: But *Wright* tells us that *John* had three fons, *Roger*, *Francis* and *George* ; this *Roger* therefore was fon and not brother of *John* earl of *Rutland*.

ROGER earl of *RUTLAND*, who after three years travels went voluntary the Ifland voyage, was colonel of foot in the *Irifh* wars, and the 24th of *Elizabeth* conftable of the caftle of *Nottingham*, and chief juftice of the foreft of *Shirwood*, In the firft of *James* I. he was conftituted lieutenant of *Lincolnfhire* and fteward of the manour of *Stoke* and *Grantham* ; he was alfo fent the fame year ambaffador to *Denmark*, to the chriftening of that king's firft fon, and with the order of the garter to the king himfelf. He died 1612.

FRANCIS earl of *RUTLAND*, who fucceeded his brother *Roger*, was juftice of all the forefts north of *Trent* and knight of the moft noble order of the garter ; to him king *James* granted the property of the caftle of *Nottingham* to him and his heirs. He died without iffue male *December* 17, 1632, the 8th of *Charles* I. and his only daughter and heir was mother to *George Villiers* fecond duke of *Buckingham* of that family.

B b

AF-

(q) Peerage *Vol. p.* 128. ----- (r) *Hiftory* Rutlandfhire, *p.* 7.

AFTER the restoration the said duke claimed the castle of *Nottingham* in right of his mother, then sold it to *William Cavendish*, marquis and afterwards duke of *Newcastle*, who notwithstanding his great age, *viz.* 82, in the year 1674, employ'd many hands in clearing the foundation of the old castle and lived so long as to see this present fabric raised about a yard above ground, which was finished in the time of *Henry* his son and successor in his estates and honours, as appeared by the inscription on an oblong square white marble table, in the wall over the back-door, now not legible, but preserved and communicated to me by the late Mr. *Jonathan Paramour*, once a servant in that most noble family. *viz.*

This house was begun by *William* duke of *Newcastle* in the year 1674, (who died in the year 1676) and according to his appointment by his last will and by the model he left, was finished in the year 1679.

THE founder of this modern castle designed it to be one of the compleatest and best finished in *England*, for which end that most honourable lord ty'd the revenue of a considerable estate to be employ'd for that purpose, until the accomplishment of the whole according to his Intention.

THE building is on a rustic basement which supports in front a *Corinthian* order, with a double stair-case landing at the grand apartment. The architect was one *March* a *Lincolnshire* man, who with Mr. *Richard Neal* of *Mansfield-Woodhouse*, one of duke *William*'s stewards, Mr. *Mason* of *Newark*, the duke's solicitor, and Mr. *Thomas Far*, steward both to duke *William* and duke *Henry*, was made joint trustees for finishing the work. *⁎*

OVER the door of the north east front is placed an equestrian statue of the founder with the face to the north, carved out of one single block of stone, brought from *Donnington*

in

⁎ An Account of what *Nottingham*-Castle cost Building, beginning *February* the 12th 1680, and ending *April* the 14th 1683.

	His grace the duke of *Newcastle* paid with 500 h. of wood.	4731*l.* 11*s.*	5*d.*
	And his grace *Henry* duke of *Newcastle*, Oct. 16th 1680.	7259 6	7
Feb. 5th. 1680.	To Mr. *Wright* for cedar wood. - - - - -	120 0	0
	To d°. for marble chimney peices. - - -	52 0	0
	To packing them. - - - - - - -	3 13	4
12th.	To d°. for a saw for the cedar. - - - -	1 10	0
	More paid from the 12th of *Feb.* 1680, to the 20th of *Aug.* 1681.	351 13	6
	More paid from the 20th of *August* 1681, to the 12th of *November* following.	552 14	5
	More paid from the 12th of *November* 1681, to the 18th of *February* following.	253 2	11
	From the 18th of *February* 1681 to the 14th of *April* 1683.	677 5	7

Total. 14002 17 11

in com. *Leicefter* ; the ftatuary's name was *Wilfon*, an ingenious artift, of whom it is remarkable, that foon after this performance of his, he was for a time fpoiled for a ftatuary ; becaufe a *Leicefterfhire* widow lady, the lady *Putfey*, who was poffeffed of a very large jointure, falling deeply in love with him, got him knighted and married him ; but he living up to the extent of his apron-ftring eftate, and his lady dying before him, Sir *William* returned to his former occupation, and the publick recovered the lofs of an eminent artift. The eaft, fouth and weft fides of the building are encompaffed with a yard paved with broad ftones, and fecured by a breaft wall of ftone ; here the ladies and gentlemen in this town walk and take the air both in winter and fummer, to which they are more particularly invited by a convenient arcade under the fouth fide of the caftle, where in rainy or windy weather they may walk under fhelter ; on the north fide there is a fpacious green court, much larger than that mentioned in the old works, becaufe the ftructures of the new tower took up a great part of this ground, which is likewife encompaffed by a ftone wall, not fo high as to hinder any profpect ; in this court facing the middle of the north front, is a wooden door opening into the park ; about twenty odd yards weft of this, there was a door leading by a ftair-cafe cut in the rock, into the great and ftrong tower built by *Edward* IV. which tower was half an octagon, the walls of which were upwards of 12 feet thick ; this paffage Mr. *Paramour* remembred very well ; befides the bridge which goes over that part of the ditch where the ancient fortified bridge once ftood, another was built acrofs the mote more directly oppofite to the old gate of the outer ward, after this new palace was finifhed for the more convenient driving a coach up to the caftle, but the foundation of this was fo badly fecured that the north fide of it fell down fome few years after ; this has lately been made good with earth and is railed on each fide and covered with green fods, and is now become a pleafant way into the green court between which and the north front of the caftle there are many fteps leading from eaft to weft down into a paved yard, by which, when his grace and family are here, the trades people who ferve the houfe with provifions can go into the kitchen and other offices under the main building ; at the weft end of this yard there goes a door out of the rock where his grace the prefent duke in the year 1720, caufed a convenient flaughter-houfe to be built, whither oxen, fheep, deer, &c. were brought immediately from the park, and when drefs'd, by the juft-mentioned door through this lower yard into the kitchen and ftore places ; at the eaft end of this yard is to be feen a place walled up with brick, this opened the way into the dungeon of which *Leland* fpeaks, and alfo Mr. *Camden*, where thofe figures we have fpoken of before were engraven on the walls. His grace when at *Nottingham* in the year 1720, as I am informed, had this place opened, in order to fee whether any thing of them was yet to be found, but it being almoft entirely filled up with rubbifh, no difcovery could be made.

TO this caftle belongs a fmall adjoining park, which till after the year 1720 was well ftocked with deer : It was alfo for its bignefs, till the civil war, pretty well provided with timber trees, when it was fequeftred and the trees cut down. If this is the fpot, (as Dr. *Thoroton* with ferjeant *Boun* fuppofes) which *William Peverel* had licence to enclofe for an orchard, and which in *Knyveton's* furvey is called the *Conygarth, i. e.* the warren, it now is enlarged to almoft twice that extent, containing at prefent upwards of an hundred acres.

IN the park a good way weft of the caftle, near and facing the river *Leen*, we fee the ruins of an ancient pile of building, not erected upon, but cut and framed in the

rock

rock, concerning which, for want of any written account, various have been the conjectures of the learned in antiquities, Dr. *Stukeley*, who in his *Itinerarium curiosum*, gives us a very lively representation in a copper-plate, of these ruins in *Nottingham*-park, commonly called the rock-holes, allows his antiquarian fancy a more than sufficient scope in this description.

" O N E may easily guess (says the doctor) *Nottingham* to have been an ancient
" town of the *Britains* ; as soon as they had proper tools they fell to work upon the
" rocks, which every were offer themselves so commodiously to make houses in, and I
" doubt not here was a considerable collection of colonies of this sort ; that which I
" have described in plate 39. *will give us an idea of them* ; 'tis in the duke of *New-*
" *castle*'s park: *What is visible at present, is not of so old a date as their time,*
" *yet I see no reason to doubt but it is formed upon theirs.* —— This is a ledge of per-
" pendicular rock, hewn out into a church, houses, chambers, dove-houses, &c. The
" church is like those in the rocks of *Bethlehem*, and other places in the holy-land ;
" the altar is natural rock, and there has been painting upon the wall, a steeple I
" suppose where a bell hung, and regular pillars ; *the river winding about makes a*
" *fortification to it, for it comes at both ends of the cliff,* leaving a plain in the mid-
" dle, the way into it was by a gate cut out of the rock, and with an oblique entrance
" for more safety ; without is a plain with three niches, which I fancy their place of
" judicature, or the like ; there is regularity in it, and it seems to resemble that
" square called the *Temple* in the *Pictish* castle, plate 38. in *Scotland.* Between this
" and the castle is an hermitage of like workmanship."

I have chose this description of Dr. *Stukeley*, it being pretty accurate as to what remains of this old fabric, but as to his own remarks and conjectures I shall here examine them as briefly as I can.   And

1st. W I T H relation to the doctor's guess work, that *Nottingham* has been an ancient town of the *Britains*, I refer the reader to my introduction, and leave the decision to himself.

2dly. He calls it a colony ; if I understand the word, it signifies a certain number of families who fix upon some tract of land to settle their abode there, and cultivate (*qui terram colunt*) the same for their sustenance ; such different families we observe among all nations, in all ages and countries, to have been found to live in separate habitations, huts or houses ; but the ruins of this place clearly appear to be the remains of one single large frame of building or appartments, having communication with each other ; it therefore can only have been contrived for the habitation of one large family or else society of men or women.

3d. T H E doctor will needs have it a *British* colony, and promises by his plate of these excavations, to give the curious an idea of that kind of colonies or british villages. For my part I have very frequently and very coolly and deliberately inspected this ruinous place, but cannot after the nicest observation find the least mark of *British* original ; the whole which is still left plainly demonstrates the *Gothic* taste ; and indeed the doctor sufficiently oversets his own opinion when in the same paragraph he honestly owns, that *what is visible at present is not of so old a date as their time,* and what is invisible, (I say) can convey no idea : However he in the same breath repents of his concession, saying: *He sees no doubt but it is formed upon*
theirs

A View of the Rock Holes *in the* Park *near* Nottingham (*belonging to* His Grace) *the* Duke *of* Newcastle

C Dubosc Sc

P 108

theirs. We will suppose there had been excavations in this ledge of rock, fit for habitations made by the *Britains,* and the *Saxons* afterwards had enlarged, altered and framed them after their own way and taste of building; would such a transformed fabric be capable of giving the curious (perhaps a thousand years after) the least idea of what is entirely changed ? The most then that he can mean by this last expression is, that he believes that the *Britains* made this piece of rock hollow after their manner, before the people in the succeeding ages made it convenient for their use, which I will not dispute with him : Besides what makes the doctor's strong conjecture still more improbable, is his confessing *there is regularity in these ruins,* especially in the pillars in the church as he calls it, when *Cæsar* plainly tells us, the *Britains* observed no regularity in the building of their habitations, nor did they make so much as any regular streets in their colonies or villages.

4th. O U R antiquary seems to please himself in the richness of his imagination, when he proceeds : *The river here winding about makes a fortification to it for it comes to both ends of the cliff.* I am satisfied the doctor never asked one question about the water, else he might soon have been undeceived, for it is not very many years ago since a small part of the river *Leen* was brought on the west end within the pales of the park, for the conveniency of watering horses and cows, which since it has been disparked are here agisted, and by this water so running in the park, the most western part of this rocky frame, by far the most ruinous, is so filled with it that there is no passing around the rock, a poor fortification, which annoys and in some measure destroys that which it should strengthen, and the water which comes into the park near the south east part of the castle rock, and forms a large pool, reaching pretty near the cliff he speaks of, is of the same date with the water works in this town, and is rented of his grace by the proprietors for a reserve of water ; moreover the very channel of the *Leen* itself, running from *Lenton* bridge close by the castle, and passing by *Sneinton* meadows, in order to discharge itself into the *Trent,* is an artificial channel, and cannot be proved more ancient then the conquest, much less traced back to the *Britain's* time, or even to the time when these rock habitations were framed, for it is easy to be discovered that the front of this structure looked towards the south (where the river runs by) and came a great deal more forward then what is now to be seen of it ; some ancient people still remember that these ruins were much larger, reaching nearer to the *Leen,* and an old man lately deceased, *John Hilton* by name, upwards of 90 years of age (who enjoyed his senses perfectly,) told me that he had heard his father say : " That in the time of the civil war, the *Round-heads* (for so he called " the parliament party) had demolished a great part of the *rock-houses* in the park " under pretence of their abhorrence to popery." so far *John Hilton.* What seems to confirm in some measure the truth of this assertion is, that this place is by the people in general to this day, as commonly called the *Popish houses* as the *Rock holes.*

I F after what has been said in this place, it be allowed that the front of this ancient building stood south, and that it came considerably farther out towards the *Leen* it may reasonably be supposed, that it was made before the *Leen* was brought to run by the castle, *i. e.* before the conquest. (*f*) For no persons would ever have been so foolish as to build the front of their houses so near the water, (whatever they might
their

Bb 3

(*f*) *See Section* VIII.

their back parts)that they could not ſtep out of their door but muſt ſtep into a river. Beſides tho' I have no reaſon to induce me to believe theſe rocky remains *Britiſh*, yet even
this pleads their antiquity: That we have had divers buildings belonging to this tow n
which are either moſtly or entirely worn away by injury of time, the names of which,
(and of ſome the places were once they ſtood) are ſtill known, *e. g.* St. *Anne*'s chapel,
St. *Michael*'s, St. *Lawrence*'s hoſpital, &c. but of the ruins in the park we may ſafe-
ly ſay, that time has obliterated the very name of them, which confirms that of *Au-*
ſonius : Mors etiam ſaxis nominibusq; venis.

    I N all likelihood this might once be a monaſtery where a certain number of *An-*
chorets had placed themſelves, before monks of any particular denomination or order
were known in *England.* Dr. *Thoroton p.* 491 ſays, " That in the firſt of *Henry* II.
" (rather the 5th of *Stephen*) there is mention made of *Monachi de Nottingham*" :
whence he firſt infers, " That the houſe of the *Carmelites* was before *Henry* the 2ds.
" time a religious houſe of monks : " He continues in the ſame paragraph, " which
" muſt either be the monks of *Lenton* or ſome religious perſons here."

    I do not ſee how the friers of *Lenton* could be called *Monachi de Nottingham*, who
had no convent within the territory of *Nottingham*, and it is certain that at that time
there were no friers of any particular denomination in this town ; for the *Minors* did
not come into *England* till the 4th of *Henry* III. about the year of *Chriſt* 1220, and
according to biſhop *Tanner*'s *Notitia Monaſtica*, did not reach *Nottingham* till 1250,
the 34th Year of *Henry* III. the founder of their convent ; and the *Carmelites* had
no convent till the 4th of *Edward* I. 1276, the founders of which are ſaid to be the
lord *Gray* of *Wilton* and Sir *John Shirley* ; I ſhould therefore think it moſt probable,
that the monks inhabiting theſe rocky dwellings were meant, who afterwards, not
unlikely, might take upon them the rule of the *Carmelites*, and might by their founders be removed into the town, to the place which is ſtill known by the name of
White-friers.

    Dr. *STUKELEY* talks of an hermitage near to theſe ruins of like workman-
ſhip more towards the caſtle. There is indeed an oblong ſquare arched place, not a
great way eaſtward of the ſaid ruins cut out in the rock, which has nothing obſervable
in it denoting the abode of an hermit, but ſeems very well ſuited for a ſtable to ſhel-
ter a cow or two in, which moſt of the communities uſed to keep, were the place admitted of it. So much of the rock holes in the park at *Nottingham.*

    I N this part of the park is the moſt clear and moſt perfect echo I ever met with
any where ; for ſtanding with one's back againſt the park pales facing theſe caves,
and raiſing one's voice to no higher pitch then common converſation, the echo re-
peats every word diſtinctly, tho' beginning with a conſonant, unleſs it be with an *M,*
N, S, or *V.*

    B E F O R E I conclude this ſection, I think it will not be diſpleaſing to the rea-
der if I preſent to his view a table ſhewing the ſucceſſion of the ſeveral dukes of
Newcaſtle and annex to it a ſhort account of the honours conferred upon them as rewards of their merit, and ſingular ſervices done to their king and country.

T H E

THE 1ft. duke of *Newcaftle* and founder of the prefent caftle of *Nottinham* was *William Cavendifh*, fon of Sir *Charles Cavendifh*, (younger brother of *William* the firft earl of *Devonfhire*) and *Catherine* daughter and heir to *Cuthbert* baron *Ogle*, married to him the 4th of *Car.* I.

THIS *William* had a brother Sir *Charles*, who died without iffue.

HE was the 8th of *James* I. made knight of the *Bath* at the creation of *Henry* prince of *Wales*. King *Charles* I. made him governor of the prince his eldeft fon.

IN the year 1642 upon the great defection of the king's fubjects the 18th of *Car.* I. he firft manned and fortified the town of *Newcaftle* and the caftle of *Tinmouth* for the king's fervice, and afterwards levying other forces in the midft of winter, routed the greateft part of thofe rebels that had made head in *Yorkfhire*, taking moft of the ftrong holds in that county. His victories at *Gainsborough* in com. *Linc. Chefterfield* in com *Derb. Piercy-brigg, Secroft, Tankerfley, Tadcafter, Sheffield, Rotheram, Tarum, Beverley, Cawood, Selby, Halifax, Leeds,* and *Bradford*, all in *Yorkfhire*, teftify'd his courage and conduct, in the laft of which, having vanquifhed their greateft northern army, (himfelf leading on) he took 22 cannons and many colours.

IN 1642 he received the queen at her landing at *Bridlington* in com. *Ebor.* who brought with her fupplies of arms and ammunition, and conducted her fafely to the king at *Oxford*, for which fervices he was by letters patents bearing date at *Oxford* the 19th of *Car.* I. created marquis of *Newcaftle* and baron *Cavendifh*.

AFTERWARDS he ftoutly defended the city of *York* for three months fpace againft three powerful armies, and at laft upon the depreffion of the royal intereft in *England* followed king *Charles* II. into banifhment, during the continuance of the ufurpation, by whom he was created knight of the garter, and foon after the reftoration *viz.* the 17th of *Charles* II. *anno* 1664, advanced to the title of duke of *Newcaftle* and earl of *Ogle*.

HE married two wives, 1ft. *Elizabeth* daughter and fole heir to *William Baffet* of *Blore* in com. *Stafford* Efq; widow of *Henry Howard*, a younger fon of *Thomas* earl of *Suffolk*, by whom he had iffue,

CHARLES, who married ------, daughter to *Richard Rogers* of *Brianfton* in com. *Dorfet*, and died without iffue in his father's life time.

HENRY his fucceffor and three daughters. *viz.*

JANE, wedded to *Charles Cheney* of *Chefbam-beys*, in com. *Bucks*, Efq;

ELIZABETH, to *John Eggerton* earl of *Bridgwater* ; and

FRANCES, to *Oliver St. John*, after earl of *Bolinbroke*.

HE married to his fecond lady *Margaret* daughter to *Thomas Lucas*, of St. *John's* near *Colchefter* in *Effex*, Efq; a very learned lady and philofopher, but by her had no iffue. THE

THE second duke of this family was

HENRY CAVENDISH, duke, marquis and earl of *Newcastle*, earl of *Ogle*, viscount *Mansfield*, baron *Cavendish* of *Bolsover*, *Bothal* and *Hepple*, also baron *Ogle* and knight of the garter. He was in the reign of *James* II. one of the privy council and governor of *Berwick*, and lord lieutenant of the counties of *Northumberland* and *Nottingham*, and died 1691.

HE married *Frances* daughter of *William Pierepont*, second son of *Robert* earl of *Kingston*, by her he had issue:

HENRY CAVENDISH, stiled earl of *Ogle*, his only son, (of the privy council to king *Charles* II.) who married *Elizabeth* daughter and heir to *Joceline Piercy* earl of *Northumberland*, whereupon he assumed her title and bore her arms, but died without issue at *London* 1680.

THE late duke thus deprived of male issue, the ducal estate devolved to

JOHN HOLLES, fourth earl of *Clare*, in right of his wife *Margaret*, 3d. daughter of *Henry* duke of *Newcastle*. This nobleman appeared with a spirit like his noble ancestors, and that with the earliest, in the just assertion of the liberties of these nations from the bondage of popery and tyranny; in consideration of which he was in the 6th year of king *William* and queen *Mary* 1694, advanced to the dignity of marquis of *Clare* and duke of *Newcastle*, having been before sworn of their majesties most honourable privy council; also in the 10th of king *William* III. 1698, installed knight of the most noble order of the garter.

IN the year 1700 when the lords in parliament framed and passed an act for authorizing certain commissioners to treat of a union with *Scotland*, his grace was then nominated for one of them, but the treaty at that time not having its desired effect, he was in the 5th year of queen *Anne* 1706, by commission under the great seal of *England*, again appointed of that number, under whose management that great and remarkable work was accomplished. By another act passed in the 4th of queen *Anne* as lord privy seal, he was appointed one of the lords justices, 'till the arrival of a successor, and in the 7th of queen *Anne*, upon the unhappy loss of *George* prince of *Denmark*, was appointed one of the lords commissioners for holding the first parliament of *Great-Britain*, having before been constituted lord privy seal, and sworn of her majesty's most honourable privy council; he was also lord lieutenant of the county, and of the county of the town of *Nottingham*, lord warden of the forest of *Shirwood*, lord lieutenant of the east and north ridings of the county of *York*, and governor of the town and fort of *Kingston* upon *Hull*. He had by his lady one only daughter, the lady *Henrietta*, now countess dowager of *Oxford* and countess of *Mortimer*. This duke having likewise no issue male, settled the ducal estate upon his nephew

THOMAS lord *PELHAM*, eldest son of *Thomas* lord *Pelham* and *Grace* his second lady, youngest sister of *John* duke of *Newcastle*, was born the 21st of *July* 1694. He had this large estate left him by the last will of his uncle, bearing date *July* 15th 1711, and that he should bear the name and arms of *Holles*.

THE

J. Chee. Del. Sc.

The remaining Part of the old Front of Thurland Hall in Gridlesmithgate Notting=ham. The Possession of his Grace the Duke of Newcastle 1750

THE *Pelhams* are an ancient and renowned family; they took their name from the lordship of *Pelham* in *Hartfordshire*, and mention is made that the said lordship in the 21st of *Edward* I. was part of the possessions of *Walter de Pelham*; in the reign of king *Edward* III. *John de Pelham* gained great fame, being with that king at the battle of *Poictiers*, which was fought on monday *September* 19, 1356, the 30th of *Edward* III. He was competitor with Sir *Roger de la Warr* in taking *John* king of *France* prisoner in the battle, and tho' above ten other knights challenged the taking of that king, yet it was found that Sir *Roger* and Sir *John de Pelham* were most concerned, wherefore in memory of so signal an action, and that king's delivering his sword to them, Sir *Roger* had the champet or chape of his sword, for a badge of that honour, and *John de Pelham* afterwards knighted, had the buckle of a belt as a mark of the same honour, which was sometimes used as a seal manual, and at others on each side a cage, being the emblem of captivity of the said king, and was therefore born for a crest; the buckles were likewise used by his descendants; and the second coat in his grace's atchievement is charged with two belts having buckles to them.

THE son of this Sir *John* of the same name, was no less famous than his father, who for his honourable exploits in the service of king *Henry* IV. was by him rewarded with honour and possessions; he was at the coronation of that king created a knight of the *Bath*, and he also had granted to him for term of life, the honour of bearing the royal sword before him, in all places and at all times requisite. He was in the 5th of king *Henry* IV. made constable of *Pevensey* castle, and filled up several eminent posts; he had the duke of *York* committed to his keeping, as also afterward *Edward* earl of *March* and his brother, sons of *Roger* earl of *March*; the king granted to him for his good services the manors of *Crowehurst*, *Burwash* and *Benylham*, with the appurtenances, as also the rape of *Hastings* in *Sussex*, with all franchises, &c. in as full and ample a manner as *John* duke of *Britain* and his ancestors enjoyed them, or the king's father *John* duke of *Lancaster* deceased. He was in no less favour with king *Henry* V. who in the first of his reign sent him one of the ambassadors to treat of a peace and conclude of a marriage, between him and the princess *Catherine*, daughter to *Charles* the *French* king; in the same year Sir *John* had granted to him the guardianship and government of *James* king of *Scots*, with an allowance of 700l.p. ann. for his diet and to find him in necessaries, in such a place or places as should be agreed on by his majesty's council and the said Sir *John Pelham*; the 6th of *Henry* V. he attended the king in his expedition i to *France*; at the siege of *Rohan* the king committed to his custody queen *Joan*, last consort of king *Henry* IV. and mother-in-law of *Henry* V. who was arrested by the duke of *Bedford* the king's lieutenant in his absence and committed to the castle of *Leeds*, there to abide the king's pleasure, being accused of conspiring with frier *Randell* her confessor, by sorcery and necromancy, to destroy the king, and being ordered into Sir *John's* custody he appointed nine servants to attend her and to bring her to his castle at *Pevensey*; he was also at the head of affairs in the reign of *Henry* VI. and was one of the ambassadors sent to treat with *William* bishop of *Glasgow* and other ambassadors of *Scotland*, for concluding a peace between both realms, and died the 7th of *Henry* VI. His seal of arms was three pelicans wounding themselves in the breast, and his crest a peacock in his pride, circumscribed *sigil. Johannis Pelham.*

Sir *JOHN PELHAM*, the only son of the last Sir *John*, was with king *Henry* V. in the *French* war; his father granted to him the constableship of *Pevensey*

C c

with the fees and wages thereto belonging, which he had of the grant of *Henry* IV. to him and his heirs male under his seal of the dutchy of *Lancaster*, in confideration that he had took the fame by a ftrong hand at the king's laft arrival in *England*, and held it for his ufe ; whereunto is appendent the feal of the arms and creft of the family as now born, and on each fide of the helmet the buckles of a belt.

THIS Sir *John* was chamberlain of the houfhold of queen *Catherine*, confort of king *Henry* V. which queen by a charter dated at *Hadham* in com. *Hertf.* the 24th of *June* 1434, grants to her thrice dear and well beloved Sir *John Pelham* and *Owen Tyder*, Efq; full power and authority, to remove and difplace the bifhop of *Lifieux* her chancellor in *France*, and to take from him her feal, as alfo the furvey and repair of all her towns, caftles, &c. The name of Sir *John* is here firft mentioned, tho' *Owen Tyder* was then the queen's hufband. He bore on his feal quarterly 1ft. and 4th, three *Pelicans*, and in the 2d. and 3d. ermin on a fefs, three crowns, and for his creft a cage on a helmet, and on each fide the buckles of a belt. King *Henry* VI. confirmed to him his manors of *Crowehurft*, *Burwaffe*, and *Benylham*, with the rape of *Haftings* ; he had alfo the office of mafter of the royalties and forefts which the queen held in dower in *Normandy*. And notwithftanding the king's having annulled the grant of the 27th of *Henry* VI. and given a patent to Sir *Thomas Hoo*, chivaler ; our Sir *John* died poffeffed of them the 36th of *Henry* VI. as appears by his laft will and teftament. He had three fons, *John*, *William* and *Thomas* ; the eldeft dying without iffue male, the eftate came to *William*, who alfo died without iffue male, fo that the eftate devolved to the youngeft brother *Thomas Pelham*.

WHICH *Thomas Pelham*, Efq; was feated at the time of his death at *Buxted* in *Suffex* ; he died *February* the 1ft. the 7th of *Henry* VIII. and had four fons and two daughters.

JOHN PELHAM, eldeft fon of *Thomas* died in his father's time without iffue, fo that

WILLIAM, the fecond fon, came to the eftate in the 16th of *Henry* VIII. in confideration of the expences he had been at in the king's fervice, and of his good and great fervices done him, he obtained a grant to inclofe and impark 500 acres of wood and 200 acres of land called *Hethwode* or the old *Brule* in the parifh of *Laughton* in *Suffex*, and to have free-warren in all his lands in *Laughton*, *Hothlie*, *Chitinglie*, *Waldren*, *Hothfield*, *Rype*, *Challington*, *Helmlie*, and *Arlyngton*, in the faid county, and a feveral fifhery in the faid manours and parifhes, &c. after which he received the honour of knighthood and attended the king the 24th of *Henry* VIII. at his meeting with the *French* king at *Sandingfield*, from whence they rode to *Bologne*. He died the 30th of *Henry* VIII.

WILLIAM PELHAM, third fon of Sir *William*, was one of the moft famous men of his time, being from his youth employed in the fervice of his country.

HE had the command of the pioneers in the army under the duke of *Norfolk*, which was fent to the affiftance of the *Scots* againft the *French* in the third year of queen *Elizabeth*.

HE was one of thofe appointed to confer with the queen regent of *Scotland*, when the forces came before *Leith* ; at the fiege of *Leith*, of which he had the chief direction

tion, he caufed a fort to be built to batter the fouth-fide of the town which had the name of *Mount-Pelham*.

IN the year 1562 he embarked with the earl of *Warwick* general of the army, fent to the affiftance of the proteftants in *France*; he was at the taking of *Caen* in *Normandy*.

AND in the year 1563, he was wounded in defence of *Newhaven*, which endured a long fiege and held out till queen *Elizabeth* expreffed with tears the commifferation of the fad ftate they were reduced to, and by proclamation, (wherein fhe commended the valour of her commanders and foldiers) declare fhe would no longer expofe her braveft men to the fury of two enemies, the ficknefs and the fword, and therefore gave orders to the earl of *Warwick* to capitulate upon honourable terms, who immediately fent Mr. *Pelham* to the marfhal *Montgomerancy* conftable of *France*, to agree upon the articles of furrender, and when they were figned he was one of the four hoftages for the performance of them.

IN 1579 when in *Ireland* fent againft the rebels, he was knighted by the lord deputy, who dying the fame year in *September*, Sir *William Pelham* was by the council chofen the 11th of *October* following, jufticier of *Ireland*, with the authority of lord deputy, till a lord deputy was created; he knighted the fame day the lord chancellor *Gerrard* and young *Edward Fitton*, fon of Sir *Edward Fitton*, prefident of *Connought*, who had performed great fervices againft the rebels.

DURING his government, he conftrained the baron *Lixnaw* to yield; befieged *Carricfoil* in *Kerry*, took it by ftorm and put all the garrifon to the fword; he drove the earl of *Defmond* to lurk in places of fecrecy with his followers, after he had difpoffefs'd him of all his caftles; he continued lord juftice of *Ireland* till the 14th of *September* 1580, when he furrendered the fword to *Arthur Grey* of *Wilton*, knight of the garter and then embarked for *England*. The queen well fatisfied with his fervices, made him mafter of the ordnance and fwore him one of her privy council.

IN the year 1585, when the queen had appointed the earl of *Leicefter* general of her forces in the *Netherlands*, Sir *William Pelham* was likewife conftituted a field-marfhal.

IN the year 1586, he commanded the *Englifh* horfe, ranging all over *Brabant* and taking feveral places; at the fiege of *Dawsborough* he narrowly efcaped with life, and at laft died at *Flufhing* in *November*. the 30th of queen *Elizabeth*.

Sir *NICHOLAS PELHAM*, eldeft fon of Sir *William* was fheriff of the counties of *Surrey* and *Suffex*, the 3d of *Edward* VI. the fame year he received the honour of knighthood at *Weftminfter* with the duke of *Lunenburgh*, Sir *Ambrofe Dudley*, fecond fon of the earl of *Warwick*, Sir *John Parrot* and Sir *Thomas Ruffel*.

HE had the greateft intereft of any commoner in the county of *Suffex*; when the *French* attempted to land at *Seaford*, he gathered fuch a force as fruftrated their defign and obliged them to return to their Ships; he departed this life the 2d of *Eli-*

beth

keth, aged 44 ; he was member for the borough of *Arundel* the 1st of *Edward* VI. and served as knight of the shire for the county of *Suffex* the 4th and 5th of *Philip* and *Mary* ; he was succeeded by

JOHN, his eldest son, who the 13th of *Elizabeth* served in parliament as knight of the shire for the county of *Suffex*, with *Thomas Palmer*, and received the honour of knighthood from her majesty at *Rye* in *Suffex*, on the 12th of *August* 1573 ; he died 1580 and left his son *Oliver* to succeed him, who dying in his minority 1584.

THOMAS PELHAM, brother to the last Sir *John*, succeeded his nephew ; he was returned to parliament with *William Covert*, as knight of the shire for *Suffex*, the 28th of queen *Elizabeth*, was sheriff of *Surry* and *Suffex* the 31st of queen *Elizabeth*.

ON the erection of the dignity of baronets by king *James* I. he was advanced to that degree the 22d of *May* 1611, and was the 7th in order of precedency ; in his creation patent it is recited : " That his majesty calls to mind the good and accepta-" ble services of Sir *John Pelham*, knight, as well to king *Henry* IV. as to our lord " *Henry* king of *England* the 5th, as to his ancestor *James* late king of *Scotland*, the " 1st of his name, as guardian and governor to his said ancestor during his minority " whilst he remained in *England*, as by certain letters patents of the aforesaid *Henry*, " late king of *England* the 5th. plainly appears &c." He died the 2d of *December* 1624, and left his son

THOMAS PELHAM, bart. 27 years old. This Sir *Thomas* was in his father's life time, the 21st of *James* I. elected knight of the shire for *Suffex*, as also in the 1st parliament of king *Charles* I. and in that held the 15th of the same king, and in that which met the 3d of *November* 1640 ; in these parliaments he constantly voted with those who were for preserving the rights and liberties of the subjects, and endeavoured the composing of our differences during the civil wars, without being any ways concerned in the usurpation of the government, for during *Oliver's* usurpation he lived retired, and departed this life in *August* 1654 ; his successor was

Sir *JOHN PELHAM*, bart. his eldest son, who was elected knight of the shire for the county of *Suffex*, in the parliament which met the 25th of *April* 1660, which voted the restoration of king *Charles* II. He was amongst other exemplary virtues, peculiarly famed for his hospitality and moderation ; his great interest in the county appears, in that he was chosen in four succeeding parliaments in the reign of king *Charles* II. and in that of 1678-9, Sir *Nicholas Pelham* his brother was with him chosen knight of the shire for *Suffex*, whilst his eldest son *Thomas Pelham*, Esq; was elected member for east-*Grinstead*, and also for the borough of *Lewis*, an honour whereof few Instances can be given. Being near 80 years old he died in 1702-3, succeeded by his eldest son

Sir *THOMAS PELHAM*, bart. after lord *Pelham* ; he was first elected for the two just mentioned boroughs, in the parliament which met at *Westminster* the 6th of *March* 1679 and for *Lewis*, in all the parliaments after, during the reigns of king *Charles* II. and *James* II. and the convention parliament, wherein he promoted the succession of of king *William* and queen *Mary*, to the crown of these realms.

ON

ON their majesties acceffion. he was firft made one of the commiffioners of the cuftoms, and on the 19th of *March* 1689, conftituted one of the commiffioners of the treafury, which office he voluntarily refigned in 1694 when it was in his power to have continued in the commiffion. He was elected one of the knights of the fhire for *Suffex* in three feveral parliaments, in the reigns of king *William* and queen *Anne*, and for the borough of *Lewis* in all other parliaments whilft he continued a commoner.

IN 1695, the houfe of commons nominated him one of the commiffioners to examine Sir *Thomas Cook*, and to infpect into bribery and corrupt practices, of which, fome of their own members were then accufed.

IN 1701, he was again conftituted by king *William* one of the lords of the treafury; and at length having difcharged thefe trufts with great fidelity, he was advanced to the dignity of a baron of this realm, by the title of baron *Pelham* of *Laughton* in *Suffex*, by letters patents bearing date the 29th of *December* 1706, the 5th of queen *Anne*. His lordfhip died at his feat at *Halland* the 23d of *February* 1711-12, and is fucceeded in honour and eftate, by *Thomas* his eldeft fon. (s)

HAVING now taken a concife view of the ancient and moft valuable family of the *Pelhams*, who have always been couragious and faithful fervants to their king and country; we now return to his grace, in whom not only center all the honours and eftates, but likewife all the virtues of the *Pelham's* and the *Hollefe's*.

IN the year 1714, the 26th of *October*, his majefty king *George* I. was pleafed to advance him to the dignity of the earl of *Clare* in com. *Suffolk*, and vifcount *Haughton* in com *Nottingham*, with remainder to the honourable *Henry Pelham* his brother, and to his heirs male.

HE was on the 28th of *October* 1714, conftituted lord lieutenant of the county of *Nottingham*, and *Cuftos Rotulorum* thereof, the 16th of *November* following.

ON the 10th of *November* 1714, he was conftituted *Cuftos Rotulorum* of the county of *Middlefex*, and lord lieutenant of the faid county, and of the city and liberty of *Weftminfter* the 28th of *December* following; alfo in the fame year he was conftituted fteward, keeper and warden of the foreft of *Shirwood* and park of *Folewood* in the county of *Nottingham*.

AND his majefty farther confidering his great merits and zeal to his fervice, was gracioufly pleafed on the 2d of *Auguft* 1718, to create him marquis and duke of *Newcaftle* with remainder to his brother the right honourable *Henry Pelham*. On the 13th of *April* 1717, he was declared lord chamberlain of the houfhold, and fworn of the privy council the 16th of *April*; alfo at a chapter held at St. *James's* the 31ft of *March* 1718, was elected one of the knights companions of the moft noble

C c 3   ble

(s) *The reader will find a more particular account of this noble family in* Arthur Collin's *peerage of* England, *Vol.* I. *from page* 393 *to p.* 432.

ble order of the garter, and installed at *Windsor* the 30th of *April* following. On the 22d of *July* his grace was one of the peers commissioned by his majesty who signed at the cockpit *Whitehall* in conjunction with the imperial plenipotentiary and others the treaty of alliance between his *Britannick* majesty, the *Emperor*, and the king of *France*, pursuant to a convention between his majesty of *Great-Britain* and the *French* king.

ON the 19th of *May* 1719 he was declared one of the lords justices for the administration of the government, which honour he had likewise in 1720, 1723, 1725, and 1727.

ON the 4th of *June* 1719, being commissioned by the sovereign with *Henry Grey* duke of *Kent*, lord privy seal, and *John* duke of *Mountague* ; they installed at *Windsor*, *Evelyn Pierrepont*, duke of *Kingston*, a knight companion of the most noble order of the garter. He was likewise in commission with the said duke of *Kingston* the 24th of *May* 1720, and installed *Charles Spencer* earl of *Sunderland*, a knight companion of the said order ; on the 2d of *April* 1724, his grace resigning his post of chamberlain of the houshold, was declared one of his majesty's principal secretaries of state, and in the 8th of the same month took his place at the board.

IN *April* 1726 he was chosen recorder of *Nottingham*. At his present majesty's accession to the throne his grace was continued in all his places and sworn of his privy council. In *July* 1737, he was chosen high-steward of *Cambridge* ; and in 1740, he was one of the regents, during his majesty's stay beyond the seas. Also in 1749 he was chose chancellor of the university of *Cambridge*.

NOTHING can be a greater testimony of his graces inheriting all the virtues of his noble ancestors, than what is said in his preamble of his patent of earl of *Clare* : to witt :

GEORGE R. &c.

CUM regii muneris et dignatis sit nobissimos juvenes ad majorum merita non solum imitanda sed suis etiam virtutibus superanda exhortari nullus sane inter proceres eo nomine commendatior nostro que favore dignior, quam per quam fidelis et dilectus noster *Thomas Holles* dom. *de Pelham* nobis innotuit. Si enim vel â patre vel â matre sibi derivatum sanguinem spectemus hinc *Hollesiorum*, inde *Pelhamorum* series antiquissima tam rerum bene gestarum, quam titulorum numero in signis elucessit ; ille autem utrusque gentis hæres nequaquam indignus, ad avitas virtutes tanquam hæreditatem optimam adeum das imberbis adhuc feliciter contendebat, et dux novicastri, nullum extitisse filium minime dolere videtur cum nepotem tali ingenio præditum in loco filii charissimi habere posset. Qua propter illum tantæ spei juvenem de imperio jam tam bene meritum de patriâ olim quam optime meriturum rerum amplissimarum haredem constituit. Nos autem virum illustrissimum tam animi quam fortunæ dotibus ornatum comitum numero ascribi volumus minime dubitantes quin novæ dignitatis incrementum cumulatius et adhuc insignius virtutum splendore redditurus sit ut ad excelsiorem post hâc honoris gradum invitus licet evehatur quem á nobis ipsi jam oblatum minus ambire mereri quam voluit.

TO

TO conclude, it may be said with truth of his grace, that there are no parties so opposite which do not agree in their esteem and affection for him, and who are not e-qually pleased with all the advancements and posts he has from time to time obtained and long enjoyed.

SECTION X.

SECTION X.

A brief history of all the noblemen who have been dignify'd with the title of earl of NOTTINGHAM, from the conquest to this day, to which is added a list of the members of parliament both for this town and the county at large.

1st. FERRERS.

THIS family owes its original to *Walchelin de Ferriers* or *Ferrariis*, a norman, whose son *Henry de Ferrariis* to whom king *William* the *Conqueror*, gave *Tutbury* castle in com. *Stafford*, also large possessions in that county, *Berks*, *Oxon*, *Wilts*, *Lincoln*, *Bucks*, and *Gloucester*, which *Henry* founded the priory of *Tutbury*. He was succeeded by

ROBERT his third son, (the two elder *Eugenulph* and *William* died during their father's life) he was earl of *Derby*; one of the witnesses to the laws made by king *Stephen* in the first year of his reign; he commanded the *Derbyshire* men at the famous battle at *Northallerton*, where the barons gained a glorious victory over *David* king of *Scots*, for which his service he obtained the earldom of *Derby* but died the year following, 1139, and was succeeded by his son

ROBERT de FERRERS, earl of *Ferrers* and *Derby*, he stiled himself according to *Dugdale*, *Robertus Comes Junior de Ferrariis*, and likewise *Comes Junior de Nottingham*, (*t*) as appears among others by an ancient charter of his bearing date A. D. 1141, in which he confirmed to the church of St. *Oswald of Notle*, whatsoever *Henry de Ferrers* his grandfather, *Eugenulph de Ferrers* his uncle, *Robert* his father or any of their wives or barons had given beforetime to that church: He was a benefactor to the monks of *Tutbury* in com. *Stafford*, to the canons of *Notle*, as has been said, in com. *Ebor*, to the monks of *Geronden*, in com. *Leicester*, and *Cumbermere*, in com. *Chester*; moreover he founded the priory of *Derby*, (which was afterwards translated to *Derley* in that county) and the abbey of *Mereval* or *Murval* in com. *Warwick*. He died the 12th of *Henry* II. 1165, and was succeeded by his only son

WILLIAM de FERRERS, earl of *Ferrers* and *Derby*; he certified the second of *Henry* II. the knights fees he then held to be 79 in number; he confirmed his

---

) Glover's *catalogue of honour. p.* 868. ------ (*v*) *ibid.*

his anceftors grants to the monks of *Tutbury*, and was a benefactor to the knights hofpitallers. (*v*) " He was married to *Margaret* daughter and heir of *illiam Peverel*,
" whofe grandfather was natural fon to *William* the *Conqueror*, (See *Section* IX.)
" The marriage rites of him and his countefs, were performed by *Thomas a Becket*,
" archbifhop of *Canterbury* at *Canterbury*.". He died the 19th of *Henry* II. 1172,
fucceeded by his fon.

R O B E R T de F E R R E R S, earl of *Ferrers* and *Derby*, as heir to his father, and earl of *Nottingham* as derived by his mother, (who died the 19th of *Henry*
II. the fame year and month with his father.) He joined with the rebellious barons
the earls of *Chefter, Leicefter, Norfolk*, and others, taking part with king *Henry* the
younger (whom king *Henry* II. had caufed to be crowned in his life time ;) and
mann'd his caftles of *Tutbury* and *Duffield* againft the father, alfo entered and deftroyed *Nottingham* then held for the king ; but the old king prevailing over his e-
nemies *Robert* made his fubmiffion, rendering up his caftles of *Tutbury* and *Duffield*,
and giving fecurity for his future fidelity ; but the king did fo little truft him that he
forthwith demolifhed thofe forts. He founded the priory of *Woodham-Ferrers* in
com. *Effex*, and died the firft of *Richard* I. 1189. His fon

W I L L I A M de F E R R E R S, earl of *Ferrers* fucceeded him as earl of
Nottingham and *Derby*, but was the fame year outed of thefe two earldoms by *Richard* I. who beftowed them on his brother *John* earl of *Moreton*. This *William* was
at the burning of *Nottingham* when his father made that fpoil there ; he did not continue difpoffefs'd long before his death, for attending the king to the holy-land he
died at the fiege of *Acon* the 3d of *Richard* I. His fon *William* fucceeded him, but
not in the titles of *Nottingham* and *Derby*, nor do I find that any more of this family
were earls of *Nottingham*, tho' the peerage gives that title to four fucceeding earls
of *Ferrers* : However this *William* was in the fucceeding reign of king *John* created earl of *Derby* i. e. the 7th of that king, by a fpecial charter ; he was girt with a
fword by the king's own hand, (being the firft of whom in any charter that expreffion was ufed) having likewife a grant of the 3d penny of all the pleas impleaded before the fheriff, through the county whereof he was earl, to hold to him and his heirs
in as ample a manner as any of his anceftors enjoyed the fame.

2d. PLANTAGENET.

J O H N P L A N T A G E N E T, mentioned already in *Section* IX. was 4th
fon of *Henry* II. to him his brother *Richard* gave the earldom of *Nottingham* and
Derby, and to whom the king his father had before granted the caftle of *Nottingham* and the honour of *Peverel*.

T H I S title of earl of *Nottingham* it feems lay dormant till 1377, when the family of the *Maubrays* obtained it.

3d. MAUBRAY.

J O H N de M A U B R A Y, lord *Maubray* of *Axholm*, by *Elizabeth Seagrave*
his wife, daughter and heir of *Margaret Brotherton* dutchefs of *Norfolk*, was born at
Epworth the 8th day of *Auguft* 1365, and was created earl of *Nottingham* in the year
1377, on the day of the coronation of king *Richard* II. This *John* died without iffue

being scarce 18 years old, after whose death king *Richard* bestowed the earldom on

THOMAS MOUBRAY, his younger brother who was likewise immediately after by the same king created duke of *Norfolk*. He also died young at *London* about the feast of St. *Agath*, the 8th of *February* 1381, the 6th of *Richard* II. and was buried at the friers *Carmelites* in *London*.

THOMAS MOUBRAY, was created earl of *Nottingham* the 9th of *Richard* II. 1382, he was hereditary earl marshal and duke of *Norfolk* the 21st of *Richard* II. 1398; he used to stile himself duke of *Norfolk*, earl of *Nottingham*, *Marshal* of *England*, lord of *Moubray*, *Seagrave*, *Gower* and *Brews*. This gentleman soon a fterhe was created duke of *Norfolk* was banished by king *Richard*, with *Henry* of *Lancaster*; the cause of this banishment was, (a) for that *Henry* duke of *Hertford* one day by chance conferring with *Thomas* duke of *Norfolk* made many complaints unto him against the king's majesty, all which being misunderstood by *Norfolk*, he watched an opportunity to discover all the whole matter to the king, who being very much moved at it called duke *Henry* before him, who stiffly denied the accusation, pronouncing himself not guilty, and that by arms he would retort the fault upon the accusers head, if it would please his majesty but to grant him leave. On the contrary *Moubray* maintained what he had before affirmed; in the heat of this contention the day was assigned wherein the combat should be tried; but the king considering it was only for words (if any such were spoken) was advised by his council to forbid the combat, and seeing there was no certain proof in whom the fault rested, and that neither might be held free, they were both banished; *Henry* had most favour for he was banished for ten years, and after it was decreed but for six years, and at last before one year came about, was called home by the nobles, and caused to take upon him the crown; but *Thomas* was longer exiled and farther off, first travelling into *Italy*, afterward to *Venice* where with grief (b) he died *September* the 27th the first of *Henry* IV. He was first married to *Elizabeth Strange*, his first wife, *August* 23, -----, she died without issue, and was daughter to Sir *John Strange*, son and heir of *John* lord *Strange* of *Blackmere*. The second lady was *Elizabeth* eldest sister and coheiress of *Thomas Fitz-Alan* earl of *Arundel* and *Surrey*, by her he had *Thomas* earl of *Nottingham*, and *John* duke of *Norfolk*: Also three daughters, *Elizabeth*, *Margaret* and *Issabell*.

THOMAS MOUBRAY, eldest son and heir of *Thomas* duke of *Norfolk*, when the dukedom was bestowed upon his father by king *Richard* II. the earldom of *Nottingham* did also belong to him by custom of the land, as his father's eldest son, (c) he also enjoyed the marshalship of *England* as due to him by inheritance. He died in the month of *May* A. D. 1405, in the 6th year of king *Henry*, leaving no children.
This

(a) *The peerage, part* I. *vol.* II. *p.* 235 : *Says he was accused by* Henry *of* Bolinbroke, *for words irregularly spoken of the king*, &c.

(b) *The peerage says he died of the pestilence at his return from* Jerusalem. *It enumerates many posts the king employed him in, and that he was made knight of the garter the* 19th *of Richard* II.

(c) Dugdale *says he never had the title of duke of* Norfolk, *nor any other but that of* earl Marshal.

This *Thomas* had two ladies, the firſt was *Conſtance* daughter of *John Holland* earl of *Huntingdon* and duke of *Exeter* : The ſecond was *Elizabeth* daughter of *John of Gaunt* duke of *Lancaſter*.   The earldom of *Nottingham* was after tranſlated to

JOHN MOUBRAY, brother to this Sir *Thomas*, which *John* in a parliament holden in the third year of *Henry* VI. was reſtored duke of *Norfolk* with his poſterity.   He was the 5th of that name among the barons of *Moubray*.   He died A. D. 1432, and was buried in the abbey or houſe of *Carthuſians*, within the iſle of *Axholm* in the 11th year of *Henry* VI,   His lady was *Catherine* daughter to *Ralph* lord *Nevil*, the firſt earl of *Weſtmorland* and *Jane* his wife, daughter to *John* duke of *Lancaſter*, by whom he had *John* duke of *Norfolk*, *Anne*, married to *William Berkley*, and *Catherine*. (d)

JOHN lord *MOUBRAY*, the 6th of that name of the barons of *Moubray*, duke of *Norfolk*, earl *Marſhal*, earl of *Nottingham*, lord and baron of *Seagrave* and *Gower* ſon and ſucceſſor of *John* the 5th duke of *Norfolk*, in the dignities aforeſaid. " This perſon died A. D. 1461, the firſt of *Edward* VI." and lies buried by the high altar in the abbey of *Thetford*.   His lady was *Eleonora* daughter of *William Bouchier*, earl *Ewe* in *Normandy*, and *Anne* his wife daughter of *Thomas Woodſtock* duke of *Glouceſter* by whom he had

JOHN lord *MOUBRAY*, the 7th of that ſtock and name, he was in the life time of his father created earl of *Warren* and *Surrey*, by king *Henry* VI. and he came after the death of his father by right of inheritance, duke of *Norfolk*, *Marſhal* of *England*, earl of *Nottingham*, baron *Seagrave* and *Gower*.   He died in his caſtle of *Farmingham* the 15th of *Edward* IV. and was buried in the monaſtery of *Thetford*, leaveing only one daughter and heir, who was by king *Edward* preſently married to his younger ſon

D d 2

4th

(d) Peerage *vol.* II. *part* I. *p.* 225. *in the* 3d *of* Henry V. *he was with the king at the ſiege of* Harfleur, *the* 5th *of* Henry V. *at the ſiege of* Cain *in* Normandy, *and continued there till the death of that king.   The* 1ſt. *of* Henry VI. *retained in the king's wars.   The* 8th *of* Henry VI. *retained again in the king's war and made knight of the garter.*

(e) Ibid. *p.* 236.   *He went the* 17th *of* Henry VI. *embaſſador to treat of a peace between* France *and* England, *the* 23d *of* Henry VI. *being confirmed duke of* Norfolk, *he had a grant of a place and ſeat in parliament and elſewhere, next to the duke of* Exeter, *he was alſo knight of the garter* ; *the* 25th *of* Henry VI. *he went in pilgrimage to* Rome ; *the* 35th *of* Henry VI. *he had licence to viſit other holy places, in* Ireland, Scotland, Brittany, Picardy, *and* Cologne, *and the blood of our* Saviour *at* Windiſmark.   *As alſo a ſecond journey to* Rome *and* Jeruſalem, *having vowed to do it for the recovery of the king's health.   In the firſt of* Edward IV. *he was conſtituted juſtice itenerant of all the foreſts ſouth of* Trent.

(f) Anne, *by his lady* Elizabeth *daughter to* John Talbot, *firſt of that family earl of* Shrewsbury. *ibid.*

4th RICHARD PLANTAGENET.

RICHARD PLANTAGENET, of *Shrewsbury,* second son of king *Edward* IV. enjoyed all thefe honours in right of his wife, and was alfo earl *Marfhal* and had the baronies of *Moubray, Seagrave* and *Gower,* together with the vaft inheritance of that family : He was made knight of the garter by his father, but with his elder brother king *Edward* V. was murdered by his uncle *Richard* III. who ufurped the throne under that title 1483. He and his wife both died iffuelefs.

5th BERKELEY.

THE vaft inheritance of the *Moubrays* came next to the *Howards* and *Berkeleys,* in refpect of *Margaret* and *Iffabel* daughters to *Thomas* duke of *Norfolk.* Sir *John Howard* fon of Sir *Robert Howard* and *Margaret* coheir of *Thomas de Moubray,* was created duke of *Norfolk* the 28th of *June* the firft of *Richard* III. as alfo earl *Marfhal* of *England,* and the fame day and year

WILLIAM lord *BERKLEY,* of *Berkley* caftle in *Gloucefterfhire,* fon of *James* lord *Berkley,* by *Iffabell* daughter to *Thomas* duke of *Norfolk* was created earl of *Nottingham* ; king *Edward* IV. in the 20th of his reign had raifed him to the dignity of a vifcount. The *Peerage* vol. I. p. 310, fays, " That he afterwards ad-" hering to the duke of *Buckingham* in his defign of pulling down king *Richard,* he " fled into *Brittany* to *Henry* duke of *Richmond,*" (after king *Henry* VII.) by whom he was conftituted earl *Marfhal* of *England,* the 26th of *October,* the 1ft of his reign, " with limitation of that office to the heirs male of his body."[*Peerage ibid.*]"He was " alfo advanced to the dignity of marquis of *Berkley,* the 4th of *Henry* VII. *January* " 28th. He was famous for his great difpute with *Thomas* vifcount *Lifle,* about cer-" tain lands in conteft between them, who upon a challenge fent him by the faid vif-" count, meeting with others on both fides, the vifcount was flain." He married three wives, but left iffue by none of them, and taking occafion to except againft his brother *Maurice* as his fucceffor, becaufe he had not married with a perfon of honourable parentage, gave all his lands from him, particularly the caftle of *Berkley,* and thofe lands and lordfhips that were the body of that ancient barony, to the king, a good part of which remained in the poffeffion of the crown 'till the death of king *Edward* VI. fo that *Maurice* enjoyed nothing of the honour.

6th FITZROY.

HENRY FITZ-ROY, natural fon to *Henry* VIII. by *Elizabeth* daughter to Sir *John Blount,* knight, the lady *Talboife* ; he was created duke of *Richmond* and earl of *Nottingham.* He was but fix years old when thefe titles were conferred upon him, (g) at which time alfo he was conftituted lieutenant general of the king's forces, north of *Trent,* and warden of the marches of *Scotland,* and foon after admiral

of

(g) Glover's *catalogue of honour,* p. 404. *All in one day viz. the 18th of* June 1525, *the 17th of* Henry VIII. *at the palace of* Bridewell ; *he was alfo at the fame time created duke of* Sommerfet.

of *England*; the 22d of *Henry* VIII. made lieutenant of *Ireland*, Sir *William Skeffington* being conftituted his deputy. He ftudied at *Paris* with *Henry* earl of *Surrey*, there was a great friendfhip between them on the fcore of their education together, which occafion'd our earls intermarriage with *Mary* daughter of *Thomas Howard*, duke of *Norfolk* and fifter of the earl of *Surrey*, but by her had no iffue. He was created knight of the garter (*h*) the 24th of *Henry* VIII. he went bravely attended to meet king *Henry* at *Calais*, at an intended interview between the *Englifh* and *French* kings. He died the 28th of *Henry* VIII. 1536.

7th HOWARD, of *Effingham*.

CHARLES lord *HOWARD* of *Effingham*, fon of *William Howard* head of the eldeft colateral branch of the *Howards*; was in his father's life time one of thofe noble perfons, who by the command of the queen, the 13th of *Elizabeth*, conducted the lady *Anne* of *Auftria* daughter to *Maximilian* the emperor, from *Zealand* into *Spain*, and in the 16th of *Elizabeth* was inftalled knight of the garter. In the 28th of *Elizabeth* upon the death of *Edward* earl of *Lincoln*, lord high admiral of *England*, (being then lord chamberlain to the queen, as his father had been before him) he was conftituted his fucceffor in that great office, whereupon *anno dom.* 1588, the 30th of *Elizabeth* when the *Spanifh* *Armada* threatened an invafion here; he was conftituted lieutenant general of the queen's whole fleet at fea, whofe fuccefs therein fully anfwered the queen's opinion of him, as well knowing him to be a perfon of great knowledge in maritime affairs, difcreetly wary, truly valiant, induftrious in action, and finally, one whom the failors entirely loved.

IN the 39th of *Elizabeth*, when farther danger threatened from the *Spaniards*, who were joined with the rebellious *Irifh*, he was made joint general of the *Englifh* army with *Robert* earl of *Effex*, for the defence of this realm, both by fea and land, viz. *Effex* for the land, and he for the fea. In which year alfo he was made juftice itenerant of all the forefts fouth of *Trent* for life; and not many months after in confideration of his eminent fervices againft the *Spanifh Armada*, as alfo for facking *Cadiz* in *Spain*, and deftroying the *Spanifh-fleet* in harbour there; he was advanced to the dignity and title of earl of *Nottingham*, as defcended from the family of *Moubray*, fome of which had been earls of that county before. In the 41ft. of *Elizabeth*, ftill continuing in high reputation at court, the *Spaniards* again ftirring, he was conftituted lieutenant general of the queen's land forces and in the 44th of *Elizabeth* he was made one of the commiffioners for executing the office of earl *Marfhal* of *England*.

IN the firft of *James* I. preceeding his coronation, he was made *Lord Great Steward* of *England* for that occafion, and the next year upon renewing the commiffion to feven of the great lords, for executing the office of earl *Marfhal* of *England*, he was continued one of that number, but in the 17th of *James* I. he furrendered

C c 3   dered

(*h*) *But died foon after*, viz. *the* 22d *of* July 1535, *in the* 27th *year of* Henry VIII. *in his father's houfe at* St. James *or* Weftminfter. *His body was carried to* Farmingham *in* Suffolk, *and there lies buried.* Glover's Cat. of Hon.

dered his patent for the office of lord *Admiral*, which was given to the marquis of *Buckingham*.

T H I S noble earl's first lady was *Catherine* daughter of *Henry* (*Clary*) lord *Hunsdown*, (*i*) by whom he had issue two sons, the first *William*, who married *Anne* daughter and sole heir, to *John* lord St. *John* of *Bletsboe*, but died in his father's life time, leaving issue *Elizabeth* his only daughter and heir, married to *John* lord *Mordaunt* of *Turvey* in com, *Bedford*, afterwards earl of *Peterborough*.

T H E second was

C H A R L E S, who succeeded him in his honours; he had also three daughters *Elizabeth*, *Frances* and *Margaret*.

T O his second lady he married *Margaret* daughter to *James Stewart* earl of *Murray* in *Scotland*, which *Margaret* was naturalized in the parliament of the 1st of *James* I. by whom he had issue two sons, *James* who died young, and Sir *Charles Howard* knight, and died the 22d of *James* I. having been knight of the garter 52 years, being then 88 years of age.

C H A R L E S, his second son succeeded, (the elder as has been said dying before the father without issue male) he first took to wife *Charity* daughter of --- *White*, and widow of *Leche* of the city of *London*; afterwards *Mary* daughter of Sir *William Cockaine* knight and alderman of *London*, by whom he had no issue; thirdly *Margaret* daughter to *James* earl of *Murray* in *Scotland*, by whom he had issue *James*, who died unmarried.

C H A R L E S succeeding him in in his honours, married *Arabella* daughter of ------ *Smith*, Esq; but died without issue 1681, upon whose decease the barony descended and came to *Francis Howard* of *Great-Buckham* in com. *Surrey*, the next heir male, &c.

8th. F I N C H.

T H E first of this collateral branch raised to the dignity of peerage was Sir *Heneage Finch*, knight, who being a great proficient in the study of the laws in that honourable society of the inner-temple *London*, was upon the happy restoration of king *Charles* II. made solicitor general, and the next year autumn-reader of the before specified inn of court *anno* 1660; in the 12th of *Charles* II. he was by the name of Sir *Heneage Finch*, of *Raunston* in com. *Buck.* advanced to the dignity of a baronet, and in the 22d *anno* 1670, constituted the king's attorney-general. *Anno* 1673, he was made keeper of the great-seal, and shortly after created a baron of this realm, by the title of lord *Finch* of *Daventry*, in com. *Northampton*, (being then owner of that manor) and finally in the 33d of *Charles* II. advanced to the dignity

---

(*i*) *He was the son of* William Clary *by his wife* Mary Bollen, *sister to queen* Anne Bollen.

nity of earl of *Nottingham*. He married *Elizabeth* daughter of *Daniel Harvey*, merchant of *London*, by whom he had issue ten sons : *Daniel*, *Heneage*, (the second son, after lord *Guernsey*) *William*, *Charles*, who died unmarried ; *Edward*, *Henry* and *Robert*, who also died unmarried, *Edward*, *John* and *Thomas*, being before deceased. Also four daughters, *Elizabeth* married *Samuel Grimston*, at that time son and heir to Sir *Harbottle Grimstone* baronet, master of the rolls, *Mary* and *Anne* deceased, and another *Mary*. This earl dying *anno* 1682, was succeeded by

D A N I E L earl of *Nottingham*, he was a person profoundly learned both in the laws and divinity ; distinguished by many eminent posts in the reign of king *William* III. queen *Anne* and king *George* I. " In the year 1720-1, the university of *Oxford* " in a full convocation unanimously decreed, ----- That the solemn thanks of that " university be returned to the right hon. the earl of *Nottingham* for his " noble defence of the christian-faith contained in his lordship's answer to Mr. " *Whiston's* letter to him, concerning the eternity of the Son of God and the Holy- " Ghost, and that Dr. *Skippen* vice-chancellor, *William Bromley* and *George Clark*, " Esqrs. representatives of the university, wait on the said earl, and present to his " lordship the thanks aforesaid of the whole university." ---- Collin's *peerage. vol.* II. *p.* 234-5. ----- In the year 1729, *John* earl of *Winchelsea* dying without issue, that title devolved to his lordship, who departed this life the 1st of *January* 1729-30.

T H I S noble lord was married first to lady *Essex Rich*, 3d daughter and one of the coheirs to *Robert Rich* earl of *Warwick*, by whom he had issue one only surviving daughter, the lady *Mary*, married first to *William Saville*, late marquess of *Halifax*, and since, *anno* 1707-8, to *John* duke of *Roxborough*, of the kingdom of *Scotland*. His second lady was *Anne* only daughter of *Christoffer* lord viscount *Hatton*, (by his first wife *Cicilie* daughter of *John Tufton* earl of *Thanet*) by whom he had issue five sons and nine daughters.

D A N I E L, the present earl of *Winchelsea* and *Nottingham*, *William*, *John*, *Henry*, *Edward* ; the lady *Essex*, eldest daughter ; the lady *Charlotte*, lady *Anne*, who died young, lady *Issabella*, lady *Mary*, lady *Henrietta*, lady *Elizabeth*, lady *Frances* and lady *Margaret*.

D A N I E L, earl of *Winchelsea* and *Nottingham*, was elected one of the knights of the shire for the county of *Rutland* in the 9th year of queen *Anne*, and served for the same county in all parliaments whilst he continued a commoner : On the accession of his majesty king *George*, he was appointed a gentleman of the bedchamber to the prince of *Wales*, at the same time his father was declared lord president of the council, also the 10th of *October* 1715, he was constitued one of the lords commissioners of the treasury, and resigned all his employments on the 29th of *February* 1715. His lordship was made comptroller of his majesty's houshold *May* 24, 1725, which office he voluntarily resigned after he succeeded his father as earl. In the year 1729, his lordship married *Frances Fielding*, daughter of the right honourable *Basil* earl of *Denbigh*, by whom he has issue one daughter, lady *Charlotte*, and her ladyship dying in *September* 1734, at *Wentworth-house* in *Yorkshire* the seat of his brother-in-law *Thomas* earl of *Malton*. He married in *January* 1737-8, *Mary* daughter and coheir of Sir *Thomas Palmer*, of *Ingham* in *Kent*, baronet, by whom he has had also issue, seven daughters, three of which are now alive.

The

The ARMS of the several Earls of NOTTINGHAM.

1st. FERRERS.

Arg. 6 horse shoes sab. 3. 2. 1. nail holes or.

Robert son of *William Ferrers*, bore his mother's arms, *i. e.* the arms of *Peverel*.

vary or. & gules.

2d. JOHN PLANTAGENET, after king of *England*.

Gules 3 lyons passant gardant or. over all a bend az.

3d. MOUBRAY.

Gules a lyon rampant arg. arm'd and langued az.

King *Richard* II. granted to *Thomas Moubray* duke of *Norfolk* and earl of *Nottingham* to bear the arms of *Edward* the *Confessor*, *viz.* Az. a cross patonce between 5 martlets or. as well in his seal as in his banner with two ostrich feathers erected. He bore these impaled with his other of the marshalship of *England*, and on his crest a lyon and two escutcheons collateral with the lyon. *Glover's cat. hon. p.* 870.

The 17th of *Richard* II. the king acknowledging his right to bear for his crest a golden leopard with a white label about his neck, (which right did belong to the king's eldest son) did grant him and his heirs a coronet arg. to be used instead of the label about the neck of the leopard. *Peerage vol.* II. *p.* I. *p.* 268.

4th RICHARD PLANTAGENET duke of *York*.

Quarterly *France* and *England* a label of 3 arg. charged with 9 torteauxes. On an in-escutcheon the arms of *Moubray*.

5th. BERKLEY.

Gules a chevron between ten crosses forme (6 above and 4 below) arg.

6th. FITZROY.

France and *England*, a border quarterly ermin and company arg. and az. a batune sinister of the 2d. an in-eschutcheon quarterly gules and varry or. and vert. a lyon rampant arg. on a chief az. a castle between two buck's heads. cabossed of the last.

8th. HOWARD.

Gules on a bend between 6 croscrosselets fitche arg. an in-escutcheon or. thereon a demy lyon rampant (depicted as the arms of *Scotland*) pierced through the mouth with an arrow. This charge on the bend was an honourable augmentation granted by king *Henry* VII. to *Thomas* duke of *Norfolk* and his heirs male upon routing the *Scots* at the great battle of *Floddenfield*, where *James* IV. king of *Scots* was slain.

9th. FINCH.

Arg. a chevron between three griffins passant sergreant sab.

A Copy from Mr. *Prynne's* fourth part of a Register, &c. of Parli
for the County of *Nottingham*, and the *Burgesses* for the To
IV. of which those Parliaments and names mark'd with an After
Bucks. and generously communicated to me. This List is c

Reign.	Where held.	Knights of the Shire
23 Edw. I. p. ap. Westm.		Gervasius de Clifton. — Johannes de
25 Edw. I. p. ap. Lond.		Willielmus de Stanton. — Willielmus
26 Edw. I. p. ap. Ebor.		Richardus de Bingham. — Richardus
28 Edw. I. p. ap. Linc.		Ranulp. de Waldesby. - (a) Will. de C
28 Edw. I. p. ap. Lond.		Will. de Chadwort. Miles. — Randul
28 Edw. I. p. ap. Westm.		Randulphus de Wandsley. — Will. d
30 Edw. I. p. ap. Lond.		Philippus de Lasseys. — Robertus de
*30 Edw. I. p. ap. Westm.		Johannes de Lysbers. — Robertus de
33 Edw. I. p. ap. Westm.		Thomas Malet. — Hugo de Hersey.
34 Edw. I. p. ap. Westm.		Robertus de Jorts. — Robertus de S
*34 Edw. I. Counc. Westm.		Robertus de Standely. — Robertus d
35 Edw. I. p. ap. Karl.		*Thomas Malet. — *Johannes de Vil
1 Edw. II. p. ap. North.		Walterus Gousle. — Petrus Pycot.
2 Edw. II. p. ap. Westm.		Johannes de Grey. (b) — Willielmus
4 Edw. II. p. ap. Westm.		Walterus de Goushill. — Thomas Ma
5 Edw. II. p. ap. Lond.		*Willielmus Farwell. —
5 Edw. II. p. ap. West.		Thomas Malet. — Hugo de Hercy.
6 Edw. II. p. ap Wind.		Petrus Pycot. — Petrus Foun. Mili
7 Edw. II. p. ap. Westm.		Petrus Picot. — Petrus le Fown.
8 Edw. II. p. ap. Ebor.		Joh. de Charveleys. — Gervasius fil.
8 Edw. II. p. ap. Westm.		
9 Edw. II. p. ap. Linc.		Johannes de Lysorus. — Petrus Fen
10 Edw. II. Counc. Linc.		Laurentius de Chawork. — Hugo de
12 Edw. II. p. ap. Ebor.		Thomas de Longevillers. — Petrus
12 Edw. II. p. ap. Ebor.		Richardus Willoughby. — Petrus
15 Edw. II. p. ap. Ebor.		
17 Edw. II. p. ap. Westm.		Robertus de Jortz. — Richardus de
18 Edw. II. p. ap. Lond.		Reginald. de Aslacton. — Robertus
19 Edw. II. p. ap. Westm.		Johannes Bary. — Robertus Ingram
1 Edw. III. p. ap. Ebor.		Radulphus de Burton. — Petrus Fo
1 Edw. III. p. ap. Linc.		Petrus Foun. — Robertus Ingram.
*1 Edw. III. p. ap. Westm.		Johannes de Annesley. — Willielmu
2 Edw. III. p. ap. Nov. Sar.		Philippus de Calfetoft. — Petrus Fo
2 Edw. III. p. ap. Ebor.		Henricus de Facombery. — Rober
2 Edw. III. p. ap. North.		*Robertus Ingram. — *Petrus Fen

(a) *B. Willis* his List has *Bray* —— (b) *Brown Willis* with good reason suppose

Writs, fo far as it recites the names of the *Knights of the Shire tingham*, from the 23d of EDWARD I. to the 12th of EDWARD ince difcovered by *Brown Willis*, Efq; of *Whaddon-Hall* in com. to the 16th of *Charles* I.

Burgeffes of the Town.

Johannes de Fleming. — Willielmus de Hardeby.

Johannes le Fleming. — Adam. de le Fleming.
Cedula Amiffa.

Johannes de Crophill. — Gualterus de Thornton.
Adam. Fleming. — Johannes Ingram.

John Fitzadam de Morter. — Walter de Thornton.
Johannes Lamboks. — Robertus Ingeham.

Johannes de Nottingham. — Johannes Ingram.
Johannes de Befton. — Johannes de Bere.

Willielmus Gilham. — Johannes Lambok.
Johannes Lamboks. — Richard le Curzun.
Johannes Lambocks. — Richardus de Brumby.

Hugo Stapleford. — Richardus Palmere.
Johannes Bryan. — Robertus de Brundby.
Willielmus Gotham. — Bartholomeus Cotgreve.

Willielmus Buck. — Johannes de Palmere.

Galfridus le Flemyng. — Simon de Folevil.

Robertus de Brunuby. — Alanus Cardoun.
Richardus Curzin. — Johannes le Cupper.
Johannes Bully. — Johannes Widmerpoole.

Nicholas Shelford. — Willielmus de Shelford.

Johannes Peruwyke. — Petrus Briffield.

---

be *Chaworth.* ——

Reign / where held	Knights of the Shire	Burgesses for the T
(a) 4 Edw. III p ap Westm.	Robertus Jorte. (d) -- Johannes Byks. Milites.	Lawrentius Spicer. Ro
*4 Edw. III p ap Wint.	*Petrus Foun.	Johannes Fleming. Ala
4 Edw. III p ap Westm.	Paganus de Villers. ---- Petrus Foun.	
*5 Edw. III p ap Westm.	Johannes de Monteny. --- Willielmus de Eland.	
6 Edw. III p ap Westm.	*Johannes Byke. --- *Rogerus de Verdon.	Willielmus Gotham. Ro
*6 Edw. III p ap Westm.	Johannes Ingram. ---- Johannes de Oxen.	
6 Edw. III p ap Ebor.	Johannes le Brett. ---- Richardus de Strelley.	
7 Edw. III pap Westm.	Willielmus de Eland. ---- Tho. de Rade. Milites.	Joh. de Widmerpoole.
8 Edw. III p ap Westm.	*Richardus de Strelley. ----- *Johannes de Oxen.	Rob. Morewode. Johann
8 Edw. III p ap Ebor.	*Willielmus de Eland. ---- Thomas de Radcliff.	Joh. Wydmerpoole. Jo
9 Edw. III p ap Westm.	Johannes de Brett. ---- Richardus de Strelley.	Joh. de Feriby. Willie
9 Edw. III p ap Ebor.		Joh. de Feriby. Ric. d
*10 Edw. III p ap Westm.	* Joh. de Oxenford. ---- * Richardus de Strelley.	Johannes de Feriby. W
10 Edw. III p ap Westm.	Thomas de Bekeryng. ---- Richardus de Strelley.	
*11 Edw. III Counc Westm.	Willielmus de Eland. --- Ric. de Strelley. Milites.	Will. de Gotham. Rad.
11 Edw. III p ap Westm.	* Johannes de Oxenford. --*Richardus de Strelley.	Rogerus Bothayle. Wil
11 Edw. III p ap Westm.	Willielmus de Eland.---Richardus de Strelley.	Will. Gotham. Robert
12 Edw. III p ap Ebor.		Nicholaus Ingram. Sin
12 Edw. III p ap Westm.	Willielmus de Eland.---Johannes de Oxenford. (e)	Rogerus de Bothale. Wi
12 Edw. III Consf ap North.	Richardus de Willoughby. (f) -- (f) Petrus Foun.	Joh. de Feriby. Rad. I
*13 Edw. III p ap Westm.	Johannes de Vaus. ---Willielmus de Gotham.	
13 Edw. III p ap Westm.	Egidius de Meignill. --- Rogerus de Enington.	Joh. Colier. Will. de
14 Edw. III p ap Westm.	Johannes Darcy. -- Johannes Deyncourt.	Robertus Moorwood. W.
14 Edw. III p ap Westm.	Robertus Jorte. -- Thomas de Asheburne.	Galfridus Fleming. Wi
*14 Edw. III p ap Westm.	Johannes Barry. --- Robertus Jorce.	
15 Edw. III p ap Westm.	Galfridus de Staunton. --- Johannes de Vais. (g)	Will. de Loderham. Simo
17 Edw. III p ap Westm.	Robertus de Jorte. (h)-Richardus de Willoughby.	Rob. Ingram. Ric. Ne
18 Edw. III p ap Westm.	Reginald de Aslacton. (i) -- Robertus le Jortz. (k)	
20 Edw. III p ap Westm.	Thomas de Newmarsh.--Johannes de Kineton.	Rad. Taverner. Ric. l
21 Edw. III p ap Westm.	Johannes de Vaus.--Gervasius de Clifton.	Rad. Taverner. Hugo
22 Edw. III p ap Westm.	Willielmus Trufsbut. Nicholas Bernack (l)	Rad. le Taverner. J. de
*22 Edw. III p ap Westm.	Johannes de Vaus. Gervasius de Clifton.	
24 Edw. III p ap Westm.	Thomas de Bykering. Willielmus del Ker. (m)	Hugo le Spicer. Johann
25 Edw. III p ap Westm.	Thomas de Bykering. Johannes de Wadefsworth.	
26 Edw. III p ap Westm.	Willielmus de Wakebrigg. Willielmus del Ker.	
26 Edw. III (b) p ap West.	(n) Ric. de Grey Miles. *But one kt. by the writs.*	Will. Findern. Thoma
27 Edw. III (c) p ap West.	Richardus de Grey. Miles	Robertus Burnby. Thon
28 Edw. III p ap Westm.	*R. Grey de Landeford. *Will. de Wakebrugg.	Thomas Moorwood. Joh
29 Edw. III p ap Westm.	Ric. de Bingham (o) Rogerus de Hopewell.	†Rog. de Hoppewell, Rc
31 Edw. III p ap Westm.	Richardus de Grey. (p) Johannes Bozoun.	Tho. de Moorwood. Joh
31 Edw. III p ap Westm.		
32 Edw. III p ap Westm.	*Ric. de Grey de Landeford. *Johannes Bozoun.	
33 Edw. III p ap Westm.	Thomas Malett. Hugo de Herty.	
34 Edw. III p ap Westm.	Richardus de Grey. Willielmus Wakebrugg.	Johannes Ingram. Rob
34 Edw. III p ap Westm.	Richardus de Grey. Willielmus Wakebrugg.	R. de Hoppewell, jun. W

(a) All our Historians agree that a Parliament was held at *Nottingham* 1330, 15 days after Michaelmas the 4th of *Edward* III. as also another the 12th of *Eward* III. 1337. (b) B. W. *List* Conf. (c) B. W. *List* Conf.

(d) B. W. *List is* Joyce. (e) B W. *List* Richardus de Strelley. (f) B W. *List* William de Eland. (f) B. W. Johannes de Oxenford. (g) B. W. *List* Vaus (h) Johannes de Vaus (i) Galfridus de Staunton. (k) Johannes de Musters. (l) B. W. *List*, Michael Bernack. (m) B·W. *List*. Johannes de Wadefsworth (n) B W. *List* Richardus Grey de Landeford. (o) B. W. *List names* Byngham *last*. (p) B W. Richardus Grey de Landeford.

† *Senior*

1.	34 Edw. 3 p ap Weſtm.	Richarlus de Grey, Rob. de Morton	Will. Soliere, Thomas Moorwood.
	35 Edw. 3 p ap Weſtm.	Simon de Leek, Will. de Wakebrugg	Will. de Waggbrug, Tho Moorwood
	37 Edw. 3 p ap Weſtm.	Rich. de Bingham, Tho. de Nevil (r)	Rogerus de Hoppewell, Hen Ward.
	38 Edw. 3 p ap Weſtm.	Simon de Leek,- Robertus de Morton	Hugo Spicer, Willielmus Prior
1.	39 Edw. 3 p ap Weſtm.	Simon de Leek, *Robertus de Morton	Hugo Spicer, Rogerus Hoppewell.
	*40 Edw. p ap Weſtm.	Simon de Leek, Robertus de Morton	
	42 Edw. 3 p ap Weſtm.	Simon de Leek, Sampſon de Strelley	Hugo Spicer, Henricus Chamberlain.
r.	43 Edw. 3 p ap Weſtm.	Robertus de Morton, Will. de Strelley	Thomas de Morewode, Petrus Maſon.
1.	45 Edv. 3 p ap Weſtm.	*Rogerus Beler, *Robertus de Morton	Rogerus de Hulme, Henricus Bradmere.
	*45 Edw. 3 Counc. Wint.	Rogerus Beler	Rogerus de Holm.
	46 Edw. 3 p ap Weſtm.	Simon de Leek, Richardus de Grey	Johannes Cropſhull (w) Johannes Bond.
	47 Edw. 3 p ap Weſtm.	Simon de Leek, Joh. de Gateford (s)	
p.	*50 Edw. p ap Weſtm.	S. de Leek, Chivaler. Joh. de Birton	
	(q)50 Ed. 3 p ap Weſtm.	Joh. Auneſley, Joh. de Beckyngham	Robertus German, Willielmus Copper.
r.	51 Ed. 3 p. ap. Weſtm.		Robertus Germayn, Will. Capper.
n.	*1 Rich. 2 p ap Weſtm.	S. de Leek, Chivaler. J. de Anneſley	
d.	*2 Rich. 2 p. ap. Glouc.	J. de Anneſley Miles, W. de Nevil M	
.	*2 Rich. 2 p ap Weſtm.	J. de Anneſley M. J. de Beckyngham	
n.	2 Rich. 2 p ap Weſtm.	Johannes de Anneſley, Joh. Parker (t)	Robertus Germayne, Tho. de Bothale.
	3 Rich. 2 p ap Weſtm.	Samp. de Strelley Miles, R. de Morton	Henricus Cook, Robertus Germayne.
	*4 Rich. 2 p ap North.	Joh. de Gaytford, Robertus Baſely	
	5 Rich. 2 p ap Weſtm.	Simon de Leek, (v) T. de Bampſton M	
n.	*5 Rich. 2 p ap Weſtm.	Samp. de Strelley, Tho. de Rempſton M	
	6 Rich. 2 p ap Weſtm.	Simon de Leek, Miles. Joh. de Burton	
	6 Rich. 2 p ap Weſtm.	S. de Strelley, M. Joh. de Berton (u)	
h:	*7 Ric. 2 p ap new Sarum.	Bert. de Bolynbrok, Tho. de Anneſley	Tho Bochale, (x) Joh. de Tammeſley.
	7 Rich. 2 p ap Weſtm.	Rob. de Baſely, Tho. de Anneſley	
	8 Rich. 2. p ap Weſtm.	Joh. de Anneſley, M. Ric. de Bevercote	Richardus Milford, Robertus Germain.
	9 Rich. 2 p ap Weſtm.	J. de Anneſley, Miles. Joh. de Birton	Johannes Crawſhawe, Will Hunſton.
r.	10 Rich. 2 p ap Weſtm.	Joh. de Anneſley, Joh. de Leek, Milites	Will. Bottiler, Robertus de Henden.
e.	11 Rich. 2 p ap Weſtm.	Joh. de Leek, Joh. de Anneſley, Milites.	
	*12 Rich. 2 p ap Cantab.	Joh. de Anneſley, Rob. de Cokfield, M.	Thomas Meverley, Willielmus Botiler.
	13 Rich. 2 p ap Weſtm.	Joh. de Leek, Johannes de Gaytford	Willielmus Botiler, Robertus Gerney.
	*14 Rich. 2 p ap Weſtm.	Joh. de Burton, Miles. Hugo Creſſy	
	15 Rich. 2 p ap Weſtm.	Rob. Cokeſield, Miles, Tho. Hercy, M	Thomas Mapurley, Willielmus Bottiler.
	16 Rich. 2 p ap Wynt.	*Tho. Rempſton, M. *Joh Gaytford, M	Willielmus Bottiler, Nicholas Alleſtre.
	*17 Rich. 2 p ap Weſtm.	*Will. Nevil, Miles, Nic. de Strelley	
d.	18 Rich. 2 p ap Weſtm.	Tho. de Rempſton, Miles, Nic. Burden	Rob. Germaine, Thomas Mapperley.
n.	20 Rich. 2 p ap Weſtm.	Tho. de Rempſton, Miles Hugo Creſſy	Rob Germaine, Thomas Mapperley.
l.	*21 Rich. 2 p ap Weſtm.	Tho. de Rempſton, M. Rob. de Morton	
n.	1 Hen. 4 p ap Weſtm.	Joh. Gaytford, Willielmus de Leek	Johannes de Plumptre, Joh. Tauntſley.
	*2 Hen. 4 p ap Weſtm.	Joh de Burton, Miles, Joh Knyveton.	
	*4 Hen. 4 p ap Wint.	Ric. Stanhop, Miles, Joh. Clifton. M.	
	*5 Hen. 4 p ap Weſtm.	Ric. Stanhop, Miles, Simon de Leek	
n.	8 Hen. 4 p ap Weſtm.	*Tho Chaworth, M. *Rich Stanhop, M.	(y) Walterus Starcy, Thomas Fox.

(q) B. W. Liſt places Aunſly and Bekyngham in the 51ſt of Edward III.

(r) B. W Liſt Thomas de Roldeſton, (s) B. W Liſt Gaytford. (t) B. W. Liſt Willielmus Parker. (v) B. W. with much more probality Thomas de Rempſton. (u) B. W Liſt Johannes de Burton.

(w) B. W. liſt Croſhull.
(x) Liſt Thomas Bothale.
(y) Walterus Stacy idem.

Reign.	where held.	Knights of the Shire.	Burgesses for the Town.
9 Hen. 4 p ap Glouc.		Johannes Zouche, Miles. Hugo Huffey, Mil.	Johannes Rothell, Johannes Jorr
12 Hen. 4 p ap Weftm.		Willielmus Reginaydon, Thomas de Staunton.	Thomas Mapperley, Johannes
1 Hen. 5 p ap Weftm.		Robertus Plimpton, Henricus de Sutton.	Johannes Tannefley, Thomas M
1 Hen. 5 p. ap Weftm.		Johannes Zouche, Miles. Tho. Rempfton, M.	Robertus Glade, Johannes Tann
2 Hen. 5 p ap Leic.		Robertus Plumpton, Miles. Hen. de Sutton.	
2 Hen. 5 p ap Weftm.		Hugo Hufye, Radulphus Makerell.	Henricus Prefton, Walterus Stacy
3 Hen. 5 p ap Weftm.		Tho. de Rempfton, Miles. Will. de Compton.	Johannes Alleftre, Johannes Bin
5 Hen. 5 p ap Weftm.		Thomas Chaworth, Henry Pierpoint.	Henricus Prefton, Willielmus Bu
7 Hen. 5 p ap Glouc.			Willielmus Stacy, Thomas Fox.
8 Hen. 5 p ap Weftm.		Johannes Zouche, Hugo Hofye.	Thomas Page, Johannes Binghan
8 Hen. 5 p ap Weftm.		Thomas Chaworth, Radulphus Makerell.	
9 Hen. 5 p ap Weftm.		Richardus Stanhop, Henricus Pierpoint.	Thomas Page, Richardus Samon.
1 Hen. 6 p ap Weftm.		Johannes Zouche, Richardus Stanhop.	Thomas Page, Johannes Alleftre
2 Hen. 6 p ap Weftm.		Thomas Chaworth, Henricus Pierpoint.	Johannes Wilford, Thomas Page.
3 Hen. 6 p a p Weftm.		Henricus Pierpoint, Willielmus Merings.	Johannes Alleftre, Johannes Wil.
*4 Hen. 6 ap Weftm.		Gervafius de Clyfton, Norman Babyngton.	Willielmus Burton, Willielmus P
6 Hen. 6 p ap Leic.		Hugo Willoughby, Radulphus Makerell.	Thomas Pogg, Johannes Manche
7 Hen. 6 p ap Weftm.		Richardus Stanhop, Johannes Berwys.	Johannes Manchefter, Johannes
*8 Hen. 6 p ap Weftm.		Richardus Stanhop, Miles. Johannes Bowys.	Johannes Manchefter, Johannes
*9 Hen. 6 p ap Weftm.		Richardus Stanhop, Miles. Norman Babyngton.	Johannes Plumptre, Johannes Ma
11 Hen. 6 p ap Weftm.			Willielmus Halifax, Galfridus K
13 Hen. 6 p ap Weftm.		Richardus Willoughby, Johannes Gower. (a)	Johannes Manchefter, Robertus F
*15 Hen. 6 p ap Cantab.		Thomas Chaworth, Willielmus Plympton.	Johannes Plumptre, Willielmus H
20 Hen. 6 p ap Weftm.		Johannes Zouche, Willielmus Merings.	Thomas Aleftre, Thomas Thurla
25 Hen. 6 p ap Cantab.		Nicholaus Fitz-Williams, Ric. Illingworth.	
25 Hen 6 p ap Weftm.			Thomas Babyngton, Robertus R
27 Hen. 6 p ap Weftm.		Johannes Roos, Armig. Ric, Eftlyngworth.	Thomas Thurland, Thomas Alle
28 Hen. 6 p ap Weftm.		Johannes Stanhop, Miles. Hen. Bofom, Miles.	Thomas Thurland, Thomas Alle
29 Hen. 6 p ap Weftm.		Johannes Waftneffe, Richardus Illingworth.	Thomas Thurland, Thomas Babir
*31 Hen. 6 p ap Read.		Robertus Clifton, Johannes Stanhop.	Richardus Delwood, Johannes Sq
33 Hen. 6 p ap Weftm.		Richardus Illingworth, Johannes Waftneffe.	
*38 Hen. 6 p ap Covent.		Robertus Strelley, Miles. Joh. Stanhop, Armig.	
38 Hen. 6 p ap Weftm.			Robertus Stable, Johannes Serjea
*39 Hen. 6. p ap Weftm.		Robertus Strelley, Miles. Johannes Stanhop.	
*7 Edw. 4 p ap Weftm.		*Defunt.*	Thomas Nevil, Johannes Hunt.
12 Edw. 4 p ap Weftm.		Henricus Pierpoint, Johannes Stanhop.	

(a) B. W. *lift* Bower.

Here Ends PRYNE's Lift.

The next was *Barebones* Parliament, confifting but of 139 Members; it met *July* 4th 1653, and was diffolved
  Cludd, but I find in *Peck's* defideriat. curiofa lib. 5. p. 25. that *Gervas Pigot*, Efq; was required by Writ fro
  jecture that the juft-mentioned Gentleman and *John Odingfells*, were fummoned for the County, and that onl
The Parliament which *Oliver Cromwell* called after he was made Protector, met *September* 3, 1654, it was by
  Members for the Town or County of *Nottingham* in either of thefe two laft.

*17 Edw. 4 p ap Weſtm. | John Byron, Eſq; William Meryng, Eſq; | John Mapully, John Clerk.

N. B. The Writs, Indentures and Returns, from the 17th of *Edward* IV. to the 1ſt of *Edward* VI. are all loſt except an imperfect bundle of the 33d of *Henry* VIII. which wants for the County but thoſe for the Town are, ———— ———— ———— ———— Robert Lovat, Richard Haſyligg.

Reign	where held	Knights of the Shire	Burgesses for the Town
1 Edw. 6 p at Weſtm.		Michael Stanhope, Kt. John Markham, Kt.	John Paſtell, Nic. Powtrell, Rec.
6 Edw. 6 p at Weſtm.		*deſunt.*	Robert Haſiligge, Fran. Colman.
1 Mary 1 p at Weſtm.		John Hercy, Kt. John Hollis, Kt.	Hump. Quarnbye, Tho. Markham.
2 Mary 1 p. at Oxford.		John Conſtable, Kt. Elizeus Markham, Eſq;	Hump. Quarnbye, Fran. Colman.
1 & 2 P. and M. p at Weſt.		Ric. Whalley, Eſq; Elizeus Markham, Eſq;	Nic. Powtrel, Eſq; Will. Markham.
2 & 3 P. & M. p at Weſt.		Richard Whalley, Eſq; Ant. Forſter, Eſq;	Hugh Thornhill Eſq; J. Bateman.
4 & 5 P. & M. p at Weſt.		John Markham, Kt. Hugh Thornhill, Eſq;	Fran. Colman, Ed. Bowne, gent.
1 Eliz. p at Weſtm.		*deſunt.*	*deſunt*
5 Eliz. p at Weſtm.		John Manners, Eſq; John Mollineux, Eſq;	Humph. Quarnbye, gt. J. Bateman.
13 Eliz. p at Weſtm.		Rob. Markham, Eſq; Edward Stanhop, Eſq;	Ralph Barton, Will. Balle, gent.
14 Eliz. p at Weſtm.		Henry Pierpoint, Eſq; Edw. Stanhop, Eſq;	Tho. Mannours, kt. Joh. Bateman, gt.
27 Eliz. p at Weſtm.		Tho. Manners, Kt. Robert Conſtable, Kt.	Ric. Parkyns, Eſq; R. Bateman, gt.
28 Eliz. p at Weſtm.		Tho. Manners, Kt. Thomas Stanhop, Kt.	Rob. Conſtable kt. R. Parkyns, Eſq;
31 Eliz. p at Weſtm.		Robert Markham, Eſq; Brian Laſcells, Eſq;	Geo. Mannors, Eſq; R. Parkyns, Eſq;
35 Eliz. p at Weſtm.		Cha. Cavendiſh, Eſq; Phil. Strelley, Eſq;	Hump. Bonner, gt. R. Parkyns, Eſq;
39 Eliz. p at Weſtm.		*deſunt.*	H. Bonner, ald. Ank. Jackſon, ald.
43 Eliz. p at Weſtm.		Cha. Cavendiſh, Kt. Robert Pierpont, Eſq	Will. Gregory gt. Will. Grayes, gt.
1 James 1 p at Weſtm.		John Holles, Kt. Percival Willoughby. kt.	Ric. Hart, ald. Ank. Jackſon, ald.
12 James 1 at Weſtm.		*deſunt.*	*deſunt.*
18 James 1 p at Weſtm.		Gervaſe Clifton, kt. George Chaworth kt.	Mic. Purefoy Eſq; John. Laſcells Eſq;
21 James 1 p at Weſtm.		G. Clifton, kt. & bart. Rob. Sutton, Eſq;	J. Byron, Eſq; Fran. Pierpont, Eſq;
1 Charles 1 p at Weſtm.		G, Clifton, kt. & bart. Hen. Stanhop, Eſq;	Rob. Greaves, gent. J. Martin, gent.
1 Charles 1 p at Weſtm.		Hen. Stanhop, Eſq; Tho. Hutchinſon kt.	G. Clifton, kt. & bart. J. Byron, Eſq;
3 Charles 1 p at Weſtm.		Ger. Clifton, kt. John Byron, kt.	C. Cavendiſh, kt. H. Peirpoint, Eſq;
15 Charles 1 p at Weſtm.		Tho. Hutchinſon, Eſq; Rob. Sutton, Eſq;	C. Cavendiſh, kt. Gil. Boun, ſer.
16 Charles 1 p at Weſtm.		Tho Hutchinſon, kt. Rob. Sutton, Eſq;	G. Millington, Eſq; F. Peirpont, Eſq;

In the room of theſe laſt in this long parliament In the room of Francis Pierpoint came John Hutchinſon, Eſq; & Ger. Pigot, Eſq; came William Stanhope, Eſq;

The parliaments which did ſit during the inteſtine troubles and the ſucceeding Uſurpation were :

That which king *Charles* called to meet at *Oxford*, *January* 22d. 1642-3, I find no members either for the Town or County of *Nottingham*.

fame year. *Heath* ſays there were but two Members for *Nottinghamſhire*, viz. *John Odingſells* and *Edward Cromwell*, to appear the 4th of *July* 1553, as Member for the County of *Nottingham*, which makes me con- *Edward Cludd* of *Southwell*, was for the Town of *Nottingham*.

ed in 1657. *Richard Cromwell's* Parliament ſat *Jan.* 27th 1659; I have not been able to find who were

This and the two foregoing tables comes in after page **209**.

A Catalogue of KNIGHTS of the SHIRE and BURGESSES who have served for the County, and the Town of NOTTINGHAM from the 23d of EDWARD I. to this present Time.

I hope it will not be displeasing to most of my readers, if I here premise a few words concerning the antiquity of these national meetings taken from some of our best authors.

PARLIAMENTS in *England* are as ancient as the government of the *Saxons*; they called such an assembly of the states of the nation *Witnagemot* or an assembly of wisemen; this was composed of the dignitaries in the church, the *Thanes* or earls, the *Wites* which were the head magistrates of tythings, and burgesses which were some times the chief magistrates, sometimes others chosen by the several boroughs.

AFTER the conquest, the norman parliaments agreed with the *Witna-gemot* of the *Saxons* so far as relates to the ecclesiastics, the nobles and the burgesses, but the conqueror designing to weaken the power of the *Saxon* earls, he in some measure seperated the barons estates from the counties, and made them acknowledge no superior but the crown, by this they became members of the legislature by succession, whereas the *Wites* were chosen to serve the county only for a time. The barons were designed to represent the tenants of their respective baronies, which excused them from paying towards the wages of knights of the shire; in short they had an equal authority with earls in parliament, and as great a power over their vassals, the only difference consisted in the extent of their possessions. This new creation of lords of parliament continued without opposition till the end of the reign of king *Henry* I. afterwards in the civil wars, especially between king *Stephen* and the empress *Maud* and her son *Henry* II. when the barons espoused different interests, each party treated the opposite side as rebels, and as both knew what power the barons had over their vassals, and having many to reward for their good services, they divided the forfeited baronies into lesser tenancies, still holding immediately of the crown, which increased the number of these petty sovereigns (*k*) to that degree, that the kingdom was very unequally represented; this becoming at last an intollerable grievance, a clause was inserted in the *Magna-Charta* of king *John*, that all the greater barons should be summoned severally to parliament, and the lesser barons in general, by which the latter were excluded from sitting in parliament singly and in their own persons, but by this general summons they had a right to chuse from among themselves such as they thought fit to be their representatives, and none had a vote in the election of these, (who from the tenure of their lands and from representing the county for which they served were called *knights of the shire*) but the immediate tenants of the crown (*l*) till the 8th of *Henry* VI. all freeholders of 40 s. *per annum* were permitted to vote for *knights of the shire*; upon this foot it stands to this day. The right of chusing representatives for burroughs differs according to the different places, for in some the burgesses only are electors, in some the burgesses and freeholders, and in others all who pay scot and lot. In the town and county of the town of *Nottingham*, the burgesses and freeholders chuse their representatives.

E e   THE

(*k*) *They were called the lesser barons,* (*l*) *They are chosen in the county-courts.*

THE surviving members of the long parliament which met in *November* 1640, dissolved themselves the 17th of *March*, (or according to *Whitlock*, the 10th.)1659 by an Act made for that purpose, and writs were issued out in the names of the *keepers of the liberties of England*, for another to meet *April* 25, 1660. The speaker was Sir *Harbottle Grimstone* : This proclaimed king *Charles* II. they were by the king constituted a parliament and after making several necessary laws, were by him dissolved *December* 29th 1660.

For the County, 1660.	For the Town, 1660.
William Pierepont.	Arthur Stanhope.
Gilbert lord Houghton.	Robert Pierepont.

THE first parliament called by king *Charles* II. was to meet *May* the 8th 1661, this continued to the 25th of *January* 1678, *i. e.* 17 years 8 months and 17 days; during which time they had three speakers, the first Sir *Edward Turner*, to the year 1672; the second Sir *Job Charlton*, (who desired to be dismissed on account of his ill state of health); and the 3d. *Edward Seymour*, Esq; chosen in his room :

1661.	1661. The same.
⎧ Sir John Clifton,	
⎨ John Eyres, Esq;	
⎩ Sir Scroop How, Kt.	
Sir Francis Leek, kt. & bart.	

THE second parliament of king *Charles* II. met *March* 6th. 1678; they chose Sir *Edward Seymour*, speaker, who was refused by the king, then they chose serjeant *Gregory*; it was prorogued to the 15th of *March*, sat till the 27th of *May* 1679, prorogued to the 14th of *August*, but dissolved by proclamation before that day.

1678. For the County.	1678. For the Town.
Sir Scroop How, Kt.	Robert Pierepont, Esq;
John White, Esq;	Richard Slater, Esq;

THE 3d parliament of king *Charles* II. met *October* the 17th 1679, after a prorogation of ten days, and adjourned to the 30th of that month. This after several prorogations, sat at last *October* the 21st. and continuing sitting till *January* 10, then was prorogued to *January* 20, 1680, but dissolved by proclamation before that time. The speaker was *William Williams*, Esq;

1679. The same.	1679. The same.

THE last parliament of king *Charles* II. appointed to meet at *Oxford* the 21st of *March* 1680-1 : The speaker *William Williams*, Esq; was dissolved the 28th of the same month, upon ordering the second reading of the exclusion bill. It is called the parliament of 1681, because they had entered that year before they were dissolved.

1680-1. The same.	1680-1. The same.

king

KING *Charles* having reigned feveral years without a parliament, and being weary of it refolved to call one, but did not live to do it. But king *James* who came to the crown *February* 1684-5, fummoned a parliament to meet the 19th of *May* 1685. Sir *John Trevor* was chofen fpeaker and approved the 22d. It fat *July* the 2d, adjourned to *Auguft* the 4th, and after feveral adjournments they fat again *November* the 9th; the king made a fpeech and declared he would keep his popifh officers in the army, which being difliked by the parliament it was prorogued on the 20th, to *February* the 15th, then to *April* 28th, next to *November* the 22d, 1686, but diffolved before then by proclamation, dated *July* the 2d.

1685. For the County.	1685. For the Town.
Sir William Clifton, bart.	John Beaumont, Efq;
Reafon Mellifh, Efq;	Sir William Stanhope, kt.

THE king declared *Auguft* the 24th in council, that another parliament fhould be fummoned for *November* the 27th 1688; the writs bearing date *September* the 5th but upon news of the prince of *Orange's* defign were recalled.

THE king declared in council, *November* 29th 1688, that a free parliament fhould meet the 5th of *January*, and *November* the 30th a proclamation was publifhed that all fhould have liberty to fit in parliament notwithftanding their having been in arms, but on the 10th of *December* he ordered the writs not fent out to be burnt, and the fame night on his going away, he threw the great-feal into the *Thames*.

A convention was called by letters of fummons from his royal highnefs the prince of *Orange* to meet at *Weftminfter* the 22d of *January* 1688-9; *Henry Powel*, Efq; was chofen fpeaker. This convention was declared by an act of parliament paffed the 23d of *February* to be a lawful parliament. They continued fitting till the 20th of *Auguft* 1689, then after divers adjournments and a prorogation for two days *viz.* to *October* 23d. they met and fat till *January* the 27th, were prorogued to the 2d of *April* 1690, but before that day were diffolved, *February* 6th 1689, by proclamation, and writs were iffued out for a new parliament to meet the 20th of *March* 1989-90.

1689-90. For the County.	1689-90. For the Town.
John lord Houghton, *made a peer, and*	Hon. Francis Pierepont.
fucceeded by John White,	Edward Bigland, *ferj. at-law.*
Sir Scroop How, kt.	

THE fecond parliament of king *William* and queen *Mary*, met on the day appointed *viz.* the 20th of *March* 1689-90, and chofe for their fpeaker, Sir *John Trevor*, fat till *May* the 2d 1690, and after feveral adjournments and prorogations to *October* the 2d, they fat again till *January* the 5th, then after feveral adjournments and three prorogations they fat a 3d time from *October* the 22d to *February* the 24th, and after one adjournment and feveral prorogations, fat a 4th time, *November* the 4th to *March* the 14th; after feveral proclamations they fat a 5th time, *November* the 7th to *April* the 25th 1694, during which time, *viz.* the 20th of *March*, Sir *John Trevor* was expelled the chair and houfe for taking a gratuity after the act for the benefit of orphans was paffed, and *Paul Foley* Efq; was chofen in his room. Then after three

pro-

prorogations they sat a 6th time, from *November* 12th till *May* the 3d, and after several prorogations were diffolved by proclamation, *October* the 11th 1695.

1690. For the County.	1690. For the Town.
Sir Scroop Howe, kt.	Charles Hutchinfon, Efq;
William Sacheverel, *died.*	Richard Slater, Efq;
John White Efq;	

T H E third parliament of king *William* and queen *Mary*, met *November* the 22d. 1695, of which *Paul Foley*, Efq; was chofen fpeaker. It fat till *April* 27th 1696, and after feveral prorogations fat a fecond time, from *October* the 20th to *April* the 16th 1697. It fat a third time after divers prorogations on the 3d of *December* to *July* the 5th 1689, then was prorogued to the 2d of *Auguft* next following, but was diffolved before that time by Proclamation.

1695. For the County.	1695. For the Town.
Sir Scroop How, kt.	Charles Hutchinfon, Efq;
John White, Efq;	Richard Slater, Efq;
Mr. Hutchinfon dying,	William Pierepont.

T H E 4th parliament of king *William* and queen *Mary*, met on the 24th of *Auguft* 1698, but was prorogued to the 27th of *September*, and after three more prorogations they met on the 6th of *December* when they chofe for their fpeaker Sir *Thomas Littleton*; then adjourned to the 9th, and continued fitting till *May* the 4th 1699; then after divers prorogations they fat a fecond time *November* the 16th 1699, till *April* the 11th 1700, when this parliament was diffolved.

1698. For the County.	1698. For the Town.
Sir Thomas Willoughby, bart.	William Pierepont Efq;
Gervas Eyre, Efq;	Richard Slater, Efq; *who*
	dying Robert Sacheverel, Efq;

T H E 5th parliament of king *William* III. met on the 10th of *February* 1700-1, chofe for their fpeaker *Robert Harley*, who was approved by the king the next day, they continued fitting till *June* the 24th 1701 and after feveral prorogations was diffolved by proclamation *November* the 11th, and a new parliament appointed to meet *December* the 30th 1701.

1700. For the County.	1700. For the Town.
	William Pierepont, Efq;
The fame.	Robert Sacheverel Efq;

T H E 6th and laft parliament of king *William* III. met on the day appointed and chofe *Robert Harley*, Efq; for their fpeaker, who was approved the next day by the king, they continued fitting till *May* the 25th 1702, (the king dying *March* the 8th) by virtue of the ftatute of the 7th and 8th of *William* III. then were prorogued by queen *Anne* to *July* the 7th, but diffolved by proclamation dated *July* the 2d. This parliament was the firft of queen *Anne*.

1701.   For the County.

    Sir Thomas Willoughby, bart.
    Sir Francis Mollineux, bart.

1701.   For the Town.

    William Pierepont Efq;
    Robert Sacheverel, Efq;

THE fecond parliament of queen *Anne* and the firft of her calling, was appointed to meet *Auguft* the 20th 1702, but was prorogued to *October* the 8th, then to *October* the 20th, when they met and chofe *Robert Harley*, Efq; fpeaker. They continued fitting till *February* the 27th, and after feveral prorogations they fat a fecond time *November* the 9th 1703, and continued fitting till *April* 1704; after three feveral prorogations their 3d feffion began *October* the 24th 1704, which continued fitting (under their own adjournment) till *March* the 14th, and then was prorogued to the 5th of *May* 1705, but was diffolved by proclamation dated *April* the 23d.

1702.   For the County.

    Sir Francis Molineux, bart.
    Gervas Eyre, Efq; *who dying*
    John Thornhagh, Efq;

1702.   For the Town.

    William Pierepont, Efq;
    George Gregory, Efq;

THE 3d parliament of queen *Anne* was prorogued on the 14th of *June* 1705, on the day that the writs were returnable, to *September* the 6th, then to *October* the 25th, when the commons chofe for their fpeaker *John Smith*, Efq; one of the privy council, they continued fitting under their own adjournment till *March* the 19th, then were prorogued to the 21ft of *May*, and after feveral prorogations fat a fecond time *December* the 3d. and continued till *April* the 8th 1707, under their own adjournments, then were prorogued to the 14th of *April*, then fat till *April* the 24th, again prorogued to *April* the 30th; then they were difmiffed without prorogation, adjournment or diffolution, the lord keeper declaring the queen's pleafure, that they fhould meet as the members of the parliament of *Great-Britain*, for and on the part of *England*, and the queen fhould fignify the time of their meeting by proclamation.

1705.   For the County.

    Sir Thomas Willoughby, bart.
    John Thornhagh, Efq;

1705.   For the Town.

    Robert Sacheverel, Efq;
    William Pierepont, Efq; *dead.*
    John Plumptre, Efq;

A proclamation dated *April* the 29th 1707, declaring (according to the 22d article of the *Union* between *England* and *Scotland*) that the lords of the parliament of *England*, and the commons of the prefent parliament of *England*, are members of the refpective houfes of the firft parliament of *Great-Britain*, for and on the part of *England*, and *June* the 5th 1707, another proclamation appointed the firft parliament of *Great-Britain* to meet at *Weftminfter* the 23d of *October* next, on which day they met and chofe for their fpeaker *John Smith*, Efq; who was their former fpeaker, adjourned in obedience to her majefty's pleafure to *November* the 6th, and after two prorogations, they on the 15th of *April* were by another proclamation diffolved.

THE third parliament called by queen *Anne* and the fecond of *Great-Britain*, (and the firft fummoned by the queen's writs as fuch) met on the 8th of *July* 1708, was firft prorogued to *September* the 9th and by fucceffive proclamations to *November*

16th when they met and chose for their speaker Sir *Richard Onslow*, they continued sitting till the 21st of   1709. The second session began *November* the 15th, and continued till the 5th of *April* 1710. They were after several prorogations dissolved by proclamation on the 21st of *September*.

1708 For the County.	1708. For the Town.
Sir Francis Willoughby, bart.	John Plumptre, Esq;
John Thornhagh, Esq;	Robie Sherwin, Esq;

THE 4th parliament of queen *Anne's* calling and the 3d of *Great-Britain*, met *November* 21 1710; They chose for their speaker *William Bromley*, and continued sitting till *June* the 12 1711. After several prorogations the second session began *December* the 7th, they sat till *December* the 22d, when the lords adjourned to *January* the 2d and the commons to the 14th. This parliament continued sitting till *June* the 21st 1712, then adjourned to *July* the 8th and after many prorogations sat again and continued till *July* the 16th when they were prorogued to *August* the 28th but dissolved by proclamation before that day on the 8th of *August* 1713.

1710. For the County.	1710. For the Town.
The right hon. Scroop lord visc. How.	John Plumptre, Esq;
William Levinz, Esq;	Robert Sacheverel.

THE fifth parliament of queen *Anne's* calling and the fourth of *Great-Britain* began to sit *February* the 16th 1713, and chose Sir *Thomas Hanmer* speaker, they continued sitting till *July* the 9th 1714, then were prorogued to *August* the 10th, but upon the queen's death on the first of *August*, they met again the 2d, adjourned to the 25th, were prorogued by the lords justices to *September* the 23d, then by commission to *October* the 21st, then to *January* the 13th, but dissolved by proclamation *January* the 5th 1714-15.

1713. For the County.	1713. For the Town.
The hon. Francis Willoughby, Esq;	Robert Sacheverel, Esq;
William Levinz, Esq;	Borlace Warren, Esq;

THIS parliament was the 5th of *Great-Britain* and the first called by king *George* I. It met *March* the 17th 1714-15, *Spencer Compton* was chosen speaker, continued sitting till *September* the 21st 1715, then adjourned to *October* the 6th, and after several farther adjournments, the second session began the 9th of *January*. The septennial act to continue this parliament till *March* the 17th 1722, was passed *May* the 7 1716 continued sitting till *June* the 26th 1716, after several proclamations the 3d sitting but 2d session, began *February* the 20th, they sat till *July* the 15th 1717, and after several prorogations the 4th sitting and 3d session began *November* the 21st, which continued till *March* the 21st then they were prorogued to *May* the 20th 1718, and after three farther prorogations, their 5th sitting and 4th session began *November* the 11th, this continued till the 18th of *April* 1719. Then after five several prorogations, the 6th sitting and 5th session began *November* the 23d, being a busy time (the south-sea year) they continued sitting till *June* the 11th 1720, after several prorogations they sat the 7th time and held their 6th session *December* the 8th and continued to *July* 29 1721, when they were prorogued to *July* the 13th, then they

fat

fat till *August* the 7th, then were prorogued to *October* the 19th, when their 8th fitting and 7th feffion began, and continued till *March* the 7th, at which time the king made a fpeech and prorogued them to the 15th, but on *March* the 10th they were diffolved by proclamation, and writs were iffued for electing a new parliament returnable the 10th of *May* 1722.

1714-15. For the County.	1714-15. For the Town.
The hon. Francis Willoughby, Efq;	John Plumptre, Efq; got an office and re-chofen.
William Levinz, Efq;	George Gregory, Efq;

THE fecond parliament of king *George* I. and the 6th of *Great-Britain*, was prorogued *May* the 4th by writ, from *May* the oth to *June* the 5th, and after feveral prorogations they began their firft feffion *October* the 9th and continued to *May* the 27th 1723; then after feveral prorogations they met a fecond time *January* the 9th, they fat till *April* the 24th 1724, then after divers prorogations their 3d feffion began *November* the 12th and continued till *May* the 27th 1725, when they adjourned on account of the king's birth-day and the reftoration, to *May* the 31ft, were prorogued at feveral times to *January* the 20th, then their fourth feffion began, which continued till *May* the 18th 1726, they were prorogued at feveral times to *January* the 17th when their 5th feffion began ; *May* the 15th they were prorogued to *July* the 21ft, and by feveral prorogations to *June* the 27th, but on the death of the king the parliament met *June* the 15th, and was prorogued by his prefent majefty to the 27th when they met again, and continued fitting till *July* the 17th, then were prorogued to *August* the 29th, this was the 6th and laft feffion, for on the 7th of *August* they were diffolved.

1722. For the County.	1722. For the Town.
The right hon. Scroop lord vifc. How,	John Plumptre, Efq;
Sir Robert Sutton knight of the bath.	George Gregory, Efq;

THE firft parliament fummoned by the writs of king *George* II. and the 7th of *Great-Britain* met *November* the 28th 1727, was prorogued by commiffion to *January* the 11th, then to the 23d, they chofe for their fpeaker *Arthur Onflow*, who notwithftanding his excufes was approved by his majefty on the 27th. The king opened the feffion by a fpeech, they fat till *May* the 28th 1728, was prorogued to *August* the 8th, and by feveral farther prorogations to *January* the 21ft, when they met and fat a fecond time till *May* the 14th 1729. After feveral prorogations they fat a third time on the 15th of *May*, were prorogued at feveral times to *January* the 21ft, when the 4th feffion was opened, and concluded *May* the 7th 1731. After feveral prorogations the 5th feffion began *January* the 13th and fat till *June* the 1ft 1732, prorogued at feveral times to *January* the 16th, when the 6th feffion began, this ended *June* the 13th 1733, and after divers prorogations the 7th feffion began *January* the 7th, and concluded *April* the 16th 1734, and was diffolved by proclamation the 18th.

1727. For the County.	1727. For the Town.
The right hon. Scroop lord vifc. How. *Office.*	Borlace Warren, Efq;
William Levinz, Efq;	The hon. John Stanhope Efq;
Thomas Bennet, Efq;	

The

THE second parliament summoned by king *George* II. and the 8th of *Great-Britain* did meet *June* the 13th 1734, was prorogued to *July* the 16th, and by several other prorogations to *January* the 14th, they chose *Arthur Onslow*, Esq; for their speaker, who was approved by his majesty the 23d, they sat till *May* the 15th. After divers prorogations the 2d session began *January* the 15th and concluded *May* the 20th 1736. The 3d session was opened by commission on account of his majesty's indisposition *February* the 1st. and continued to *June* the 21st. 1737, prorogued at several times to *January* the 24th, when the 4th session was opened by his majesty, this continued to *May* the 20th 1738, then was prorogued at several times to *February* the 1st when the 5th session began and continued to *June* the 14th 1739 By several prorogations the 6th session was deferred to *November* the 15th then sat to the 29th of *April* 1740, was prorogued at several times to *November* the 18th, then the 7th and last session was opened which continued to *April* the 25th, was prorogued to *May* the 12th, but dissolved *April* the 28th 1741.

1734. For the County.	1734. For the Town.
Thomas Bennet, Esq; *dead.*	John Plumptre, Esq;
William Levinz, Esq; *jun.*	Borlace Warren, Esq;
The honourable John Mordaunt, Esq;	

THE 3d parliament called by the writs of king *George* II. and the 9th of *Great-Britain* did meet on the   of   1741. They chose *Arthur Onslow*, Esq; a third time unanimously their speaker.

1741. For the County.	1741. For the Town.
William Levinz, Esq;	Borlace Warren Esq; *dying.*
The hon. John Mordaunt, Esq;	Sir Charles Sedley, bart.
	John Plumptre, Esq;

THE 4th parliament called by the writs of king *George* II. and the 10th of *Great-Britain* did meet   1747

1747. For the County.	1747. For the Town.
The right hon. lord Robert Sutton,	Sir Charles Sedley, bart.
John Thornhagh, Esq;	The right hon. *George* lord visc. *How.*

SECT. XI.

SECTION XI.

Memorable Perſons born in or near this Town, or who have made it their Abode.

AMONG ſuch memorable perſons as have made choice of *Nottingham* for their reſidence, or have occaſionally viſited this town, the firſt rank is due to crown'd heads and ſovereign princes, of whom is remarkable, that to go no farther back then the conqueſt, (regard being had of the great diſtance of *Nottingham* from the metropolis, hardly any inland town in *England* has been viſited or choſen for a place of reſidence more frequently and by more of our monarchs, than this ancient borough.

THAT *William* the *Conqueror* was here both in his march againſt the earl of *Northumberland*, when he ordered the building of *Nottingham* caſtle, and alſo in his return from the north, is beyond all doubt.

KING *Stephen* in the war with the empreſs *Maud* reſided frequently at this caſtle.

HENRY II. was a conſiderable time at *Nottingham* after he had taken the caſtle, and before he was king.

RICHARD I. after his return from captivity came to *Nottingham* and be-ſieged the caſtle in perſon, which was then held for his brother *John*, he alſo held a great council here.

KING *John* reſided much at *Nottingham* both as earl of *Mortayn* and after as king. It was at *Nottingham* he ordered the *Welch* hoſtages to be hanged, and laſtly he died, in this his beloved county, at *Newark*, 12 computed miles from *Nottingham*.

HENRY III. was at *Nottingham* 1252, for it appears that he there granted un-to *Ralph de Freſheville* free warren in all the demeſne lands of his manors of *Boney* in *Nottinghamſhire, Cruch, Scardecliff, Atwoldeſton, Chelardeſton* in *Derbyſhire*, and *Cuswortham* in *Yorkſhire*, which grant is dated *December* the 1ſt the 36th of *Henry* III. He was likewiſe here in the 39th of his reign, as appears by a charter granted to *Nottingham* dated *July* the 20th 1255.

EDWARD I. during his war with *Scotland* was divers times at *Nottingham*.

EDWARD II. and *Iſſabella* of *France* his queen, had their reſidence at this caſtle, and *Iſſabella* whilſt ſhe was queen regent reſided at *Nottingham* caſtle when her favourite was ſurprized there by the king's band.

Mortimer

E D-

E D W A R D III. was at *Nottingham* in the year 1330, where about *Michael-mafs* he held a parliament, he after held a fecond in the year 1337, in which an act was paft in favour of the cloth-trade, and great encouragement was given to foreign clothiers to fettle in *England*.

R I C H A R D II. was at *Nottingham* in the year 1387, and again in the 15th year of his reign, and likewife in 1397.

H E R E alfo lived fome time *Henry* IV. when a combat was appointed betwixt and englifhman and a frenchman, but for fome reafons was not performed. *Anonym*.

E D W A R D IV. was at *Nottingham* in 1470 ; the fame king refided for fome time at *Nottingham* when he was enlarging the caftle with ftrong and beautiful additional buildings.

R I C H A R D III. was at this town in 1483, in the month of *Auguft* when he took his circuit northward, during the execution of that execrable murder of his two nephews and others of their relations ; he alfo refided here in 1685, and from hence went to the battle of *Bofworth*, where he loft his life.

H E N R Y VII. in 1487, was at *Nottingham* caftle, where he held a council of war before he marched to the famous battle of *Stoke* by *Newark*.

M Y *anonymous* of *Nottingham* fays, there goes a vulgar tradition : " That king " *Henry* the VIII. made a fecret boon voyage to the town of *Nottingham*, but that " having no warrantable ground and the occafion unworthy fo great a prince, I pafs " it over in filence." Let this my author think what he will concerning this journey of gallantry, I cannot help being of opinion that the tradition he mentions is not altogether without foundation, when among the records of the town of *Nottingham* I find a promiffary note for 147 *l*. 13 *s*. and 4 *d*. dated *February* the 14th in the fourteenth year of his reign, this was in the year 1523 : He could not then want money for publick ufes, becaufe, but the latter end of the preceding year after cardinal *Wool-fey* had caufed a new furvey to be made all over the kingdom, like that of *Doomfday book* in the *Conqueror's* reign, a general loan was given to the king, of the tenth of his lay fubjects, and a fourth of the clergy, according to the true value of their eftates, befides 20,000 *l*. which he borrowed of the city of *London* in particular ; wherefore, and feeing that the fum of the loan was made up by the voluntary fubfcription of a certain number of private perfons, it fhould feem to have been borrowed for the king's private occafion, tho' the war with *Scotland* and *France* at that time furnifhed a plaufible pretence. Moreover if we confider the extreme livelinefs, not to fay violence, of that monarch's paffion, together with his age, *viz.* not quite 31, at which he was at the height of his ftrength and vigour, the whole feems to ftrengthen the conjecture in favour of the tradition.

T H E fame author informs me that king *James* I. was fix feveral times at *Nottingham*, and appeals to perfons living when he wrote his account. This prince's royal confort *Anne* of *Denmark* as alfo queen *Mary* confort of *Charles* I. have both vifited this town.

THE

THE laſt mentioned king was here twice whilſt prince and four times after he
was king. " In his journey to *Scotland* paſſing through *Nottinghamſhire*, his majeſ-
" ty and all his retinue were entertained by the earl of *Newcaſtle* at his own expence,
" in ſo wonderful a manner (ſays my juſt mentioned author,) and in ſuch exceſs of
" feaſting, as had ſcarce ever been known in *England*, and would ſtill be thought
" very prodigious, if the ſame nobleman had not within a year or two afterwards
" made the king and queen a more ſtupendous entertainment at his return from *Scot-*
" *land*, which happened about the end of *Auguſt* 1632.   The third time this king
viſited *Nottingham*, was when he ſet up his ſtandard here in 1642 ; and the fourth
and laſt time was in 1646-7, after he had been delivered to the *Engliſh* commiſſioners at *Newcaſtle*.

BOTH the *Elector Palatine* and his brother prince *Rupert*, were divers times
at *Nottingham*.

QUEEN *ANNE*, whilſt yet princeſs took her refuge at *Nottingham* at
the revolution.

KING *William* III. was likewiſe at *Nottingham*.

BESIDES the juſt mentioned ſtars of the firſt magnitude, my *Anonymous* adds
a liſt of eminent perſonages, who had before, and in his Time, choſen the town of
Nottingham for their abode, concerning which take his own words :

" HERE have inhabited from time to time divers of the nobility, and others
" of honourable birth and great and ancient families ; here lived in the memory of
" ſeveral perſons yet alive, to omit more ancient times, that noble and wiſe lord *Ed-*
" *ward* earl of *Rutland*, Sir *Thomas Mannors* his brother, Sir *William Courtney* of
" the weſt, after them Sir *Henry Talbot*, ſon to that great and opulent lord *George*
" earl of *Shrewsbury*, Sir *Thomas Stanhope*, Sir *Thomas Willoughby*, Sir *Anthony*
" *Strelly*, Sir *Edward Stanhope*, and after them *Thomas* lord *Scroop*, Sir *Henry*
" *Pierpoint*, Sir *John Buron*, Sir *John Souch*, Sir *Philip Strelly*, Mr. *Henry Caven-*
" *diſh* eldeſt ſon of that wiſe and rich lady *Elizabeth* counteſs of *Shrewsbury*, the
" root and ſtock of ſo many noble families.   And of later time *Henry* lord *Stanhope*,
" Sir *Edward Osburn*, knight and baronet, vice preſident of the north, Sir *Thomas*
" *Peckham*, (who tho' born a ſtranger to theſe parts took ſuch a liking to this town,
" that at his death he gave to it a hundred pounds legacy,) and Sir *Thomas Huet*.
" And at this day here reſides much, that wiſe, ſtout and learned lord the earl of
" *Clare*, and his noble ſon the lord *Houghton*, Sir *Thomas Hutchinſon*, Sir *Thomas*
" *Wamſley*, Mr. *William Stanhope*, Mr. *Richard Buron*, and Mr. *Charles Cotton*, a
" gentleman tho a ſtranger here, of an ancient family and worthy. Beſides other gen-
" tlemen whoſe names for brevity ſake I here omit.   Of this catalogue many have
" travelled not only in this kingdom, but moſt of the foreign parts of the world, in
" which they could not but ſee great variety of countries, cities and towns of plea-
" ſure ; yet after all have made choice of this place for their rendezvous and reſi-
" dence not for any lands or means they have here, or to make any benefit by tra-
" fique or trading but only for their delight and pleaſure."

SECTION XII.

SECTION XII.

A short account of the neighbouring feats of the NOBLEMEN and GENTLEMEN.

KNIVETON.

THIS is a village in the hundred of *Bingham*, fituate near the fouth-bank of the river *Trent* about feven miles fouth-eaft of *Nottingham;* on a confiderable high cliff, where Sir *Charles Mollineux*, bart. who is lord of the manour here and patron of the living has a feat. The late Sir *Francis*, who was a great fportfman, ufed annually to fpend the hunting feafon here.

THE church is dedicated to St. *Peter ;* the vicarage 6 *l.* when the prior of *Newbow* in *Lincolnfhire* was patron, now it is 4 *l.* 9 *s.* and 6 *d.* in the king's books. Not far from hence in the fame hundred is

KIRKETON by SCREVETON .

THIS manour is commonly called *Kirton-hall,* the houfe is fituated in the very divifion of the lordfhip of *Colfton* and *Screveton.* This place was formerly the feat of the *Whalleys* and their progenitors the *Leeks* and *Kirtons.* Of this family were *Edward Whalley* major general on the parliament fide, and *Henry* his brother advocate, who both were advanced by *Oliver Cromwell*, their kinfman on the female fide. It is now the manfion houfe of *Robert Thoroton,* Efq; of the family of Dr. *Thoroton,* who wrote the antiquities of *Nottinghamfhire.*

CARCOLSTON.

IN the fame hundred and a neighbour of the preceding, the feat of *Robert She-rard* Efq; auditor of his grace the duke of *Rutland.* The church is a vicarage, valued at ten marks when the prior of *Wirkfop* was patron ; it is now in the king's book 6 *l.* 10 *s.* and the duke of *Newcaftle* patron.

WIVERTON.

ALSO in *Bingham* hundred, now depopulated. Here Sir *Thomas Chaworth* in the 24th of *Henry* VI. made a park, having the king's licence for it. Dr. *Thoroton* takes him to be the chief builder of that once very grand and ftrong houfe in this place, which after him was the principal manfion houfe of his fucceffors. In the civil war it was made ufe of as a garrifon for the king, which occafioned its ruin ; fince which time moft of it is pulled down and removed, except the old uncovered gate-houfe which ftill ftands as a monument of the magnificence of that family.

LAN-

LANGAR.

THE principal feat of the right honourable the lord vifcount *How* of the king-dom of *Ireland*. This is diftant about fix miles from *Nottingham*, in the fame hundred. Here ftood a very goodly old houfe with a park to it well ftocked with deer. This houfe has fince the death of the late lord *How*, at his government of *Barbadoes*, been very much beautified, by the lady *Pembroke*, fifter of the late lord, who chufing to live at this feat during his prefent lordfhip's minority, has adorned it with a new front of ftone towards the garden, at her own expence.

THE church ftands clofe to the houfe and is dedicated to St. *Andrew*, in it are feveral tombs of the *Scroops* and *Chaworth's* lords of *Wireton* and *Anfley*. The rectory of *Langar* has but one third of the tythes, was 10*l*. and the lord *Scroop* patron, is now 10*l*. 7 *s*. 11 *d*. value in the king's book, and *George* lord vifcount *How* patron.

COLSTON-BASSET.

IN the hundred of *Bingham* feven miles from *Nottingham*, here is one of the feats of the right honourable the earl of *Strafford*. Colonel *Francis Hacker* the great re-publican had a houfe in this place built by *Francis* his father.

THE church dedicated to St. *Mary* ftands in the fields, now all enclofed, and the town thereby depopulated, fays *Thoroton*, *p*. 80. The vicarage was eight marks when then the prior of *Laund* was patron, now 8 *l*. 7 *s*. 6 *d*. in the king's book, and the king patron.

OWTHORP.

ALSO in the fame hundred four miles from *Nottingham*, at prefent the jointure houfe of Mrs. *Hutchinfon* relict of *Julius Hutchinfon*, and defcendant of Sir *Thomas Hutchinfon* by his fecond lady *Catherine* daughter to Sir *John Stanhope*, knight, and half fifter to the firft earl of *Chefterfield*. It is a very good houfe, which was built by colonel *John Hutchinfon*, member of parliament for the town of *Nottingham* in the long parliament and continued in it till the reftoration, he was alfo governor of the caftle of *Nottingham* for the parliament, in difcharge of which truft he was fo faithful to his principals, that he ftood proof againft all temptations ; whofe widow daughter of Sir *Alan Apfley*, fold it together with the greateft part of the eftate, to *Charles Hutchinfon*, eldeft fon of the faid Sir *Thomas Hutchinfon*, by his fecond lady. The colonel was his eldeft fon by the firft, *viz*. lady *Margaret* daughter of Sir *John Byron* knight; he pulled down the old church which was pretty large, and the chancel, both covered with lead, and caufed this prefent fmall one to be built to the north wall of the chancel, in which he made a vault wherein his body now lies, being brought from *Sandown* caftle in the county of *Kent*, where he died a prifoner. Dr. *Thoroton* wrongly fays *Deal* caftle, as plainly appears by the following monumental incription :

Quosq;
Domine

In a Vault under this Wall lieth the Body of *John Hutchinson* of *Owthorpe* in the County of *Nottingham*, Esq; eldest Son and Heir of Sir *Thomas Hutchinson*, by his Wife *Margaret*, Daughter of Sir *John Byron* of *Newstead* in the same County.

This Monument doth not commemorate
Vain airy Glories, Titles, Birth and State,
But sacred is, to free illustrious Grace,
Conducting happily a Mortal's Race,
To end in Triumph over Death and Hell,
When like the Prophet's Cloak the frail Flesh fell,
Forsaken as a dull impertinent,
Whilst Love's swift fiery Chariot climb'd the Ascent,
Nor are the Reliqu's lost but only torne
To be new made and in more lustre worne,
Full of this Joy he mounted he lay downe,
Threw off his Ashes and took up his Crowne,
Those who lost all their Splendour in his Grave,
Ev'n there yet no inglorious period have.

He married *Lucy* daughter of Sir *Allen Apsley*, lieutenant of the Tower of *London*, by his third Wife the Lady *Lucy*, daughter of Sir *John* St. *John's* of *Didiard Eregon* in the County of *Wilts*, who died at *Owthorpe* *October* 1659, and lies buried in the same Vault.

He left surviving by the said *Lucy*, 4 Sons, *Thomas* married *Jane* daughter of Sir *Alexander Radcliff*, buried also in the same Vault, and *Edward*, *Lucius* and *John*; four daughters *Barbara*, *Lucy*, *Margaret* and *Adelia*, which last lies also in the same Vault.

He died at *Sandown* Castle in *Kent*, after eleven Months harsh Imprisonment, without Crime or Accusation, upon the 11th Day of *September* 1663, in the 49th Year of his Age, full of Joy in assured Hope of a glorious Resurrection.

STAUN-

STAUNTON.

THIS is in *Rufhcliff*-hundred; here is a houfe belonging to Sir *William Parfons*, bart. who not many years fince built an handfome dwelling houfe for his place of refidence on the *Short-hill* at *Nottingham*. The Rectory was 46 s. 8 d. and now is in the king's book 2 l. 13 s. 4 d. and Sir *Robert Clifton* patron, as his anceftors have been ever fince the reign of *Edward* III.

WIDMERPOOL.

IN the fame hundred near the borders of *Leicefterfhire*, where is ftill remaining a branch of the ancient family of the *Widmerpools*, of which fee *Thoroton p.* 40. The rectory was 15 l. and Mr. *Pierpont* patron, now 14 l. 16 s. in the king's book and the duke of *Kingfton* patron.

STANFORD.

IN the hundred of *Rufhcliff*. Here the late Mr. *Lewis* had a handfome feat, whofe father rebuilt the church. The rectory was 20 marks and the late Mr. *Ingleworth* patron, now 9 l. 7 s. 6 d. and Mr. *Lewis* patron. This family had it by purchafe, *viz. Thomas Lewis* alderman of *London*. The houfe was built in 1647, by one *Robert Raynes*, whofe fon fold it.

NORMANTON upon SORE.

HERE is the houfe of *John Richards*, Efq; formerly a branch of the *Nottingham Willoughby's* lived in this place, *viz. William Willoughby*, who was buried here A. D. 1581. The rectory was 12 l. when the prior of *Durham* was patron, now 7 l. 11 s. and *Daniel Earl* patron. The church is dedicated to St. *John, Francis Lewis* Efq; patron, 1728.

WILLIAM WILLOUGHBY was buried at *Normanton* upon *Sore*, ann. dom. 1587; he gave out of his lands in *Nottingham* and *Lenton*, 8 l. 6 s. 8 d. to be yearly paid to five towns in courfe, *Normanton, Great-Marlow, Nuneaton, Nottingham* and *Wolvey*.

SUTTON-BONNINGTON.

THE rectory of *Bonnington* was 12 l. value and Mr. *Barkley* patron. The rectory of *Sutton* 7 marks and the prior of *Reppingdon* patron. In the king's Books the rectory of St. *Michael* in *Sutton-Bonnington*, 15 l. 2 s. 1 d. and the rectory of St. *Anne's* there 4 l. 17 s. 6 d. and *Henry Walker* of *Epperfton*, and *Henry Sherbrook* of *Oxon* patrons.

Great-LEAK or Eaft-LEAK.

ALSO in *Rufhcliff*-hundred. Here the late Sir *Thomas Parkyns* of *Boney-park*, bart. did build fome years ago a large houfe defigned by him for his grandfon, which the
country

country people call the lanthorn-house on account of its having windows on all sides but it has never yet been inhabited. The rectory formerly belonged to the prior of *Reppington*, and was valued at 3 *l.* at present the earl of *Huntingdon* is patron, and it is in the king's books 25 *l.* 7 *s.* 4*d.* the Rev. *Granville Wheeler*, Esq; rector. The church is dedicated to St. *Helen.*

Little-L E A K, or West-L E A K.

C L O S E by the foregoing, the family of the *Mansfields* have been lords of this manour ever since the 35th of queen *Elizabeth* and have made it their place of residence, but at the death of the late *Thomas Mansfield* Esq; barister-at-law in the year 1713 the male line being extinct, his eldest sister *Elizabeth* relict of *George Chadwick*, Esq; was for some time in possession of this estate, and lived in the house, and upon her decease in the year 1746 it devolved to her only Son *Evelyn Chadwick*, major of his royal highness the duke of *Cumberland's* regiment of dragoons.

T H R U M P T O N.

I T is in the same hundred, lately the house of *John Emmerton*, Esq; formerly belonging to the family of the *Pigot's*. This house has been very much improved by the last possessor, who left it to *William Westcombe*, Esq; who is still making farther improvements. Of the last Sir *Gervase Pigot* but one, it is remarkable, that being high-sheriff and in mourning for his daughter he gave black liveries with small silver trimming, which happened to suit his men for their last attendance upon their master to his vault, for he died soon after the midsummer assizes 1669 (*a*). In the church are divers latin monumental inscriptions of the *Pigots*, and a very beautiful monument for the 1st Sir *Gervase Pigot.*

C L I F T O N.

T H E seat of Sir *Robert Clifton*, knight-baronet, and knight of the bath. From this lordship the ancient family of the *Clifton's* derive their name; it lies in the hundred of *Rushcliff* on the south-side and close by the side of the river *Trent*, three miles south-west from *Nottingham*; the goodly old house as it had from time to time been beautified, so it has since Sir *Robert's* second marriage with *Hannah* eldest daughter of Sir *Thomas Loom*, gained several considerable additions, among which is a very beautiful summer-house of stone, at the west end of a fine long gravel-walk beyond the bowling-green, which commands a side prospect of *Nottingham*, and looks a great way down the river *Trent*; there is also made several visto's and at the farther end of them an *ha ha.* This house stands on the top of an high and towards the river almost perpendicular cliff, whence probably it took its name, as well as the whole lordship; it enjoys a prospect of many miles whilst it yields a delightful view to those who pass along the opposite side of
the

(*a*) *Thoroton* p. 14.

the *Trent*, which runs clofe by the foot of the cliff ; it looks down upon a carpet of luxuriant meadows on the north fide of *Trent* belonging to its lord, who enjoys alfo *Wilford* lordfhip, which affords him a paffage through his own ground on both fides of the river to the boundaries of the county of the town of *Nottingham*. The provident care of the late Sir *Gervafe*, and the love of planting trees of the prefent Sir *Robert Clifton*, has caufed this lordfhip to be well wooded. The whole eftate is fertile and well tenanted. The *Trent*, of which Sir *Robert* has the royalty on both fides from *Thrumpton* to *Nottingham* lordfhip, does plentifully furnifh him with all kinds of fifh, nay in the feafon with plenty of Salmon and fometimes even Sturgeon, which induced an old fervant of the family to write the following lines, ftill to be feen in the hall, wherein he introduces the *Trent* fpeaking to the lordfhip :

> Thee *Clifton* do I love of all the ftore
> Of ftately buildings that enrich my fhore,
> And fhall be proud to ferve the at thy wifh,
> With my beft choice and braveft kind of fifh.
> My fatteft Pikes I'll caufe to leap on land,
> And betray Salmon to thy fifhers hand,
> And Sturgeons large as prefents will I bring,
> From the vaft empire of our *Trident* king.
> Thee ever frefh and fruitful will I make,
> Whofe flowing ftream fhall ne'er thy cliff forfake.

UPON the whole whether we confider the pleafant fituation of the houfe with its embellifhments, or the fertility of the land, and the trees in the hedge rows, which for the benefit of his tenants the late Sir *Gervafe* caufed to be planted with the beft fort of fruit-trees ; or we take notice of the delightful walk from *Nottingham* to *Clifton*, we muft confefs that the owner poffeffes a pretty paradife, who after a courfe of years will have nothing to wifh for, than that there may never want an heir male to carry the name of this ancient and confiderable family to late pofterity, an earneft of which he has already received in a fon born *June* —— 1744, baptized by the name of *Gervafe*.

THE *Cliftons* have been lords of *Clifton* and *Wilford* ever fince the reign of king *Henry* III. but held lands in them long before, and had been perfons of note and a knightly family for above 600 years in *anno* 1630, as appears by the ftately monument erected in memory of his wives, *Penelope*, *Frances* and *Mary*, by the famous Sir *Gervafe Clifton*, the infcription whereof I have annexed to the end of the account of this feat, as alfo that of Sir *Gervafe*.

Dr. *Thoroton* p. 52, 53, in the pedegree begins with *Alvederus de Clifton*, knight, lord of the manour of *Wilford* and keeper (*guardianus*) of the caftle of *Nottingham*, whofe fon *Robert de Clifton*, kt. lord of *Wilford*, was alfo keeper of the caftle of *Nottingham*, but in the margin he tells us, that he had this from an old fkin of parchment among the collection of St. *LoKniveton*, of dubious authority. However he purfues the fucceffion from this *Robert* lineally, whence it appears he allows the relation, but will not allow that his father and he were lords of *Wilford* and keepers of the caftle of *Nottingham* ; the firft he proves, but as to the latter I fee no improbability of their being entrufted with the care of this caftle under *William Peverel* and his fon, tho' the laft lived in it themfelves.

THERE is a college at *Clifton* begun to be built by Sir *Robert de Clifton* dedicated to the *Holy-Trinity*, but he dying *April* the 9th, the 18th of *Edward* IV. his son Sir *Gervase* accomplished the design of his father, as appears by the inscriptions which were upon their gravestones in the north-isle of the church of *Clifton* which is dedicated to St. *Mary*.

THE rectory of *Clifton* was 22 *l.* and *Wilford* 16 *l.* and now it is 21 *l.* 7 *s.* 6 *d.* and *Wilford* 18 *l.* 7 *s.* 6 *d.* in the king's book, Sir *Robert Clifton* patron, as his ancestors have been ages before.

IN this church are divers ancient monuments, besides the modern one of Sir *Gervas*, the first baronet of this family, and that which is erected for his wives.

THIS Sir *Gervase* succeeded his grandfather in his estate, his father dying before him, and having left Sir *Gervase* an infant of but one year old behind, the only male heir gotten by a consumptive parent, who nevertheless lived to the Age of 80 years, the rest the inscription shews: *viz.*

Hic intus cum patribus et uxoribus suis dormit generosissimus dominus *Gervasius Clifton*, miles, et (primæ creationis sc. *Jac.* 9.) Baronettus qui de patria er tribus regibus in octo parliamentis bene meruit, nec non de *Carolo* I. durante bello in præsidiis *Oxonio* et *Newarka* quem antea cum *Maria* regina in manerio de *Clifton* festive refecerat. Septem uxores duxit quarum tres juxta memorantur. *viz.* 1. *Penelope* filia *Roberti* comitis *Warwic.* 2. *Francisca* filia *Francisci* comites cumbriæ. 3. *Maria* filia *Joh. Etioke* arm. relicta *Francisca Leek*, militis. 4. *Issabella* vidua *Johannis Hodges* alderman. *Lond.* hic sepulta *July* 10, 1637. 5. *Anna* filia *Francisci South* militis, hic etiam condita *Jun.* 1, 1639. 6. *Jana* filia *Anthonii Eyre* de *Rempston* ar. mater *Roberti Clifton*, *Jane* et *Caroli Clifton* obiit *Londini* huc translata *March* 17, 1655. 7. *Alicia* filia *Henrici* comitis *Huntingdon*, marito superfuit sed eodem anno 1666 in ecclesia *Sti. Egidii London* inhumata. Ipse lætus felicem obivit mortem *Jun.* 28 et pompâ decorâ hic repositus fuit *Aug.* 2d. 1666. anno ætat. suæ 80. Hunc secutus est filius ejus dom. *Cliffordus Clifton* miles, &c.

IN the chancel on the side of the vault is the inscription on Sir *Gervase's* first three wives.

Memoriæ conservandæ causa
Dilectissimarum sibi conjugum.

Penelopes filiæ *Roberti* comitis *Warwicensis* et *Penelopes* uxoris ejus, fœminæ tum corporis tum animi egregia pulchritudine conspicua. Quæ cum convixisset marito annos 5. peperissetque ei unicum filium *Gervasium* mortua est et hic conditur obiit 26 die *Octobris* anno salutis MDXIII. ætatis 23.

Franciscæ Francisco et *Grisildæ* comite et comitissæ *Cumbriæ* genitæ nobilissimæ prudentissimæ pientissimæ fœminæ quæ relicta prole, *Margareta garetta, Francifca, Anna Cliffordo* et *Lætitia* migravit ex hac vita die *Novembris* anno dom. 1627, ætatis fuæ 33. et eodem conditur.

Mariæ filiæ *Johannis Egioke* de *Egioke* in comitatu *Wigorniæ* armigeri et *Annæ* uxoris ejus, *Francifci Leek* de *Sutton* in agro *Derbienfi* equitis aurati viduæ, lectiffimæ fœminæ, ætatis in feneçtutem inclinatæ animi in marito liberos materni, mortua eft 19 die *Januarii* anno dom. 1630. Et fepulta in templo divi egidii.

Illis quidem Monumentum
fibi vero meditamentum.

Inter fepulchra majorum fuorum qui per annos plufquam fex centos equeftri dignitate villam hanc incoluerunt pofuit *Gervafius Clifton*, eques auratus et baronettus.

Expecta tot terra meis majoribus orta
Tandem me ejufdem hinc ordinis loci
Et fimilem ; quod fi quifquam concidere nobit
Muneris ecce tibi eft ut fimilem facias.

WOLLATON-HALL.

T H I S noble pile of building is fituated about two miles weft of *Nottingham*, from feveral points of which it prefents itfelf in a very beautiful view, and greets thofe who travel from *Nottingham* towards *Derby* with a very beautiful afpect. It is a grand fabric of ftone, and the front enrich'd with curious mafonry work, and adorned with divers bufto's of great men among the ancients, placed in niches. Over the door facing the fountain is this infcription : *En has* Francifci Willoughbæi *ædes rara arte extructas* Willoughbæis *relictas. Inchoatæ*, 1580. *Finitæ*, 1588. ------ That which exceeds all the reft within, is the beautiful hall, for fpacioufnefs and loftinefs hardly matchable in any of the neighbouring counties. This pompous edifice was built in the reign of queen *Elizabeth* by Sir *Francis Willoughby* kt. at immenfe expence, which perhaps might induce a certain tranflator of *Cambden* to make his author fay, " That Sir *Francis* built it out of oftentation to fhew his riches," tho' I find no fuch expreffion in any of thofe latin editions of *Britannia* which are fallen into my hands. The 3d edition publifhed 1590, fpeaking of the *Leen*, fays, page 433 : " *Fertur proxime (linum fluviolus)* Woollaton Francifci Willoughbæi *villam* " *fummo artificio fummaq; arte nuper conftructam ;*" and the edition of 1600 expreffes the fame paffage thus : " *Linum rivulus fertur proxime* Woollaton *ubi ædco* " *profpectu lætiffimo et fummo artificio fane magnificas maximis impenfis* Francifcus " Willoughbæus *æques auratus noftra memoria extruxit.*" Neither of thefe paffages have any fting in them ; however thus much is certain, that altho' all the ftone was brought from *Ancafter* in *Lincolnfhire* in exchange for pit-coal, yet by that time the houfe was raifed and finifhed, it had funk three whole lordfhips : Indeed in that frugal reign of queen *Elizabeth*, it was looked upon rather as a princely building than the feat of a commoner ; it is highly probable that Sir *Francis Willoughby*, having neither fon nor brother alive, and none but daughters to fhare this great inheritance, would hardly have thought of building, (much lefs of erecting fo expenfive a fabric) had not the profpect of the continuance of his name at *Wollaton*, by a union of his family with a branch of the houfe of *Erefby*, encouraged him to it. This leads me (contrary to my declared intention in the preface, that I would not meddle with pedegrees) to make mention of the defcent of thefe two ancient familíes, induced to it

by

by the grofs miftake of *Arthur Collins* in his peerage publifhed in 1741, in 4 vo-
lumes 8vo. " He calls the family of Sir *Francis Willoughby* of *Wollaton* in com.
" *Nottingham*, another branch of this ancient family (meaning *Eresby*) of the *Willoughbys*
" defcended from Sir *Richard Willoughby* lord chief juftice of *England*, the great-
" eft part of that long and flourifhing reign of king *Edward* III. and the faid Sir
" *Richard* from *William de Willoughby*, younger brother of Sir *Robert de Willoughby*;
" lord *Willoughby* of *Eresby* living in the reign *Edward* I. and *Edward* II. as I have
" before obferved, under the title of *Willoughby* of *Parnham*." What he fays in this
place ought to be a juft caution to all perfons ever to look at the bottom of the page
for this authors vouchers, for what I here quoted *is gratis*, faid without any proof, and
tho' he refers you to the title of the *Willoughby's* of *Parnham*, which is page 48, he
does not tell us how many fons Sir *William Willoughby* had, nor does he there tell us
that Sir *Robert* had any brother at all. He quotes *Thoroton's Antiquities* concerning the marriage of *Bridget Willoughby* of *Wollaton* and Sir *Percival Willoughby*,
and yet by an unwarantable negligence never looked two pages back into the true and
genuine pedigree of the *Willoughby's* of *Wollaton*; befides he gives us the arms of
the lord *Middleton* defcended from the union of the two families, whofe arms he
bears, *viz.* quarterly 1ft. & 4th. *or. fretty az. the* 2d. & 3d. *or. on two bars gul.* 3 *waterbougets ar.* which laft were the arms of Sir *Francis Willoughby* of *Wollaton*, and
of his ancient anceftor *Richard Bugge* of *Willoughby*. The following table will
fet the reader to rights.

B O T H thefe noble families united by the marriage of Sir *Percival Willoughby*,
with *Bridget*, eldeft daughter and coheir of the oft mentioned Sir *Francis*, (by whom
he got both *Wollaton* and the greateft part of his large Inheritance) have had very
confiderable perfonages among their anceftors.

T H E firft having their antiquity as far as the conqueft from *John de Willoughby*
a norman knight, who took his fir-name from *Willoughby*, a lordfhip in *Lincolnfhire*,
which he held by the gift of *William* I. this was the original anceftor both of the
houfe of *Parnham* and *Eresby*, from a younger branch of which laft defcends *Francis* the prefent lord *Middleton* by the father's fide. *viz.* of

T H O M A S W I L L O U G H B Y youngeft fon of *Chriftopher*, who was
created knight of the bath at the coronation of king *Richard* III. which *Thomas* having applyed himfelf to the ftudy of the law, was knighted by *Henry* VIII. and the
22d of the fame reign was conftituted the king's ferjeant, and in the 29th of *Henry*
VIII. was advanced to be chief juftice of the common pleas. His fon *Robert* feated
at *Boerplace* in *Kent*, married (according to *Collins*) *Dorothy* daughter of Sir *Edward Willoughby* of *Wollaton* in com. *Nottingham*, who brought him *Thomas* his fon
and heir.

T H I S *Thomas* had by his lady *Catherine* daughter of Sir *Percival Hart* of the
county of *Kent*, feven fons and three daughters, of which fons the eldeft was Sir *Percival Willoughby*, who married as above.

T H E *Wollaton* family had for its original anceftor *Ralpe Bugge* of *Nottingham*, a man of confiderable note in the town and the anceftor of feveral good families. He lived in the reign of king *Henry* III. He bore on a *fefs* three *water bou-
gets*, which were alfo born by the elder branch of his family, who after took the
                                                                                    na me

name of *Bingham*, whilft *Richard de Willoughby*, being of the younger branch, bore the three boudgets on two bars, the fame as my lord *Middleton* now quarters them. Thefe *Willoughby*'s take their fir-name from *Willoughby* on the *wold*, a lordfhip in the county of *Nottingham*.

Sir *RICHARD de WILLOUGHBY*, grandfon of the abovefaid *Ralph Bugge*, was one of the judges of the king's bench from the 3d of *Edward* III. to the 31ft of his reign, and was fometime chief juftice of *England* when *Galfridus le Scroop* was gone on the king's bufinefs beyond the feas. He was the great advancer of his family, and left *Edmund de Willoughby* by *Joan* his fecond wife, all his children by the firft dying without iffue : Which *Edmund* had a fon of his own name *Edmund*, father of Sir *Hugh Willoughby* knight, who married *Margery* daughter and coheir of *Baldwin Trevil*, for his fecond wife, who brought him *Robert de Willoughby* for his heir ; his children by his firft lady dying young, except Sir *Richard Willoughby* the eldeft. Sir *Hugh* his father was knight of the fhire for the county of *Nottingham* the 6th of *Henry* VI. and *Richard* the 13th of the fame king, Sir *Hugh* and *Richard Willoughby*, Efq; (as we have reafon to believe) were fheriffs of *Nottingham* and *Derby* in the fame reign, the one the 9th the other the 28th of *Henry* VI. as alfo the firft of *Edward* IV. but this Sir *Richard* dying without iffue, the above-mentioned *Robert Willoughby*, Efq; fucceeded him ; he married *Margaret* daughter of *John Griffith* knight of *Wicknor* in the county of *Stafford*, by her he had Sir *Henry Willoughby* knight and banneret, who was fheriff of *Nottingham* and *Derby* the 11th of *Henry* VII. he died 1528, having married four wives, by the firft *Margaret* daughter of Sir *Robert Markham* knight, he had Sir *John Willoughby*, who left no iffue, Sir *Edward*, &c. By the 3d *Elen* daughter and heir of *John Eggerton* of *Wren-hall* in the county of *Chefter* ; he had Sir *Hugh Willoughby* knight the famous navigator, who being of an enterprizing genius, went out in order to difcover the north-eaft paffage, but was with his company found frozen to death. His lady was *Jane* daughter to Sir *Nicholas Strelley*, who brought him a fon, which after his grandfather was named *Henry*.

I return to Sir *Edward Willoughby*, fecond fon and fucceffor of Sir *Henry* ; he had by his lady *Anne* daughter of *William Fi iol*, *Henry Willoughby* Efq; who was kill'd in the commotion at *Norwich* the 27th of *Auguft*, the 4th of *Edward* VI. the year after the death of his uncle Sir *John Willoughby* ; he left by his lady *Anne* daughter of Sir *Thomas Grey* marquis of *Dorfet*, two fons ; *Thomas*, the eldeft died at the age of eight years, much about the time of his father's death, and was fucceeded by his brother Sir *Francis Willoughby*, knight, whofe eldeft daughter *Bridget* was married to *Percival Willoughby* already mentioned above This *Percival* attending king *James* in his paffage through *Nottinghamfhire*, on his acceffion to the crown, receiv'd the honour of knighthood at *Workfop* in that county, and the 20th of *April* 1603 he was elected knight of the fhire for the county of *Nottingham* in the firft parliament called in the reign of king *James* I. Sir *Percival* left by his lady five fons, of which the eldeft was Sir *Francis Willoughby*, who died in the year 1665, and was father by his lady *Caffandra*, of that prodigy of natural knowledge, *Francis Willoughby*, Efq; (whofe valuable memory mention has been made in the preceding fection.) One of our modern hiftorians (*a*) celebrates in the following manner. " *Francis Wil-*

Gg 3   *loughby*

(*a*) Eachard's *hiftory of* England.

" loughby, Efq: a gentleman of *Warwickfhire*, was highly celebrated amongſt the
" greateſt virtuoſi in *Europe* ; he was deſcended from two branches (*a*) of that an-
" cient and famous family of the *Willoughby*'s, and proved a mighty orna-
" ment to both. His rare natural abilities joined with an indefatigable induſtry
" brought him to a very great skill in all ſorts of learning, particularly in thoſe ſci-
" ences which are moſt abſtruſe and uncommon to vulgar capacities, the moſt ſubtle
" parts of the mathematicks and natural philoſophy, and more particularly the hiſtory
" of animals, beaſts, birds, fiſhes, and inſects, in which he diſtinguiſhed himſelf be-
" yond example, and became the glory of the age. In order to which he travelled
" into many countries, (*b*) and left no experiment untried, and laſt of all he was
" ſnatched away in the 37th year of his age, to the great concern of all curious and
" inquiſitive ſcholars, eſpecially of the royal ſociety, and the great loſs of all good
" men who were acquainted with his virtues, and of all learned men who could
" judge of his labours."

HIS hiſtory of birds was not publiſhed till after his death, 1ſt. in latin in *London* in 1676, being reviſed, digeſted and collected into order by *John Ray*, F.R.S. one who had been brought up in the author's family, and been the conſtant companion of his ſtudies ; to compleat this book the more, his relict *Emma*, daughter of Sir *Henry Bernard*, had his fine drawings committed to copper at her own expence. It was afterwards tranſlated into engliſh, with an appendix added to it by the ſame Mr. *Ray*, in the year 1678 : The latin title is, *Ornithologie libri tries in quibus aves omnes hactenus cognitæ in methodum naturis ſuis convenientem redacte accurate deſcribuntur diſcriptiones iconibus elegantiſſ mis et vivarum avium ſimi imis ære inciſis iluſtrantur.* He has alſo written : *hiſtoriæ piſcium libros quatuor &c.* Oxon. 1686, which work was with great pains reviſed and made fit for uſe, and the two firſt books entirely compleated by the ſaid eminent virtuoſo, Mr. *Ray*, and adorned with a very many cuts of ſeveral ſorts of fiſhes, never before known in *England*. He has likewiſe publiſhed a letter containing ſome conſiderable obſervations about that kind of waſps called *Ichnuemones, &c.* dated the 24th of *Auguſt* 1671. See *Philoſophical Tranſactions*, num. 76. p. 2279. ----- And another letter about hatching a kind of bee lodg'd in willows, dated the 10th of *July* 1671. See *Philoſophical Tranſactions*, num. 74. p. 2221. ----- This gentleman died the 3d of *July* 1672, and left by his lady two ſons and one daughter : Sir *Francis Willoughby* created a baronet *April* the 7th 1677 with remainder to his brother *Thomas*, he died unmarried in the 20th year of his age, 1688, leaving for his ſucceſſor in honour and eſtate his brother : *Caſſandra* was married to *James* duke of *Chandois*, and died without iſſue.

Sir *THOMAS WILLOUGBY*, bart. who was afterwards in 1711, the 10th of queen *Anne*, raiſed to the dignity of a baron of this kingdom, by the ſtile and title of *Thomas* baron *Middleton* of *Middleton* in the county of *Warwick*. His lordſhip whilſt a commoner ſerved for the county of *Nottingham* in ſeveral parliaments in the reigns of king *William* and queen *Anne* ; as has his preſent lordſhip, the 12th of queen *Anne*, and the firſt of king *George* I. The late lord died the 2d of *April* 1729, leaving behind him by his lady *Elizabeth*, daughter and coheir of Sir *Richard Rothwell* of *ſtapleford* in the county of *Lincoln*, bart. four ſons.

1ſt.

_____

(*a*) *He miſtakes as well as* Collins. ----- (*b*) France, Spain, Italy, *and the* Low-Countries.

1ft. *FRANCIS*, the prefent lord *Middleton*, who married *Mary* fecond daughter of *Thomas Edwards* of the *Middle-Temple*, *London*, Efq; who has brought his lordfhip two fons : *viz.* *Francis*, now of *Jefus-College* in the univerfity of *Cambridge*, and *Thomas*, ftill at fchool at *Bury-St. Edmund's*.

2d. *THOMAS WILLOUGHBY*, Efq; married *Elizabeth* fole daughter and heir to *Thomas Southerby*, Efq; of *Bridfhall* in the county of *York* ; by her he left iffue five fons and four daughters, and died. He was elected member of parliament for the univerfity of *Cambridge*, the 19th of *December* 1720, and alfo in the fucceeding parliament, and was member in the laft parliament for *Tamworth* in the county of *Stafford*. N. B. Half of *Tamworth* is in *Staffordfhire* and half in *Warwickfhire*

3d. *ROTHWELL WILLOUGHBY*, Efq; this gentleman lives as yet unmarried at *Nottingham*, where he has built himfelf a beautiful and well finifhed houfe. He has a peculiar genius for mechanicks and other parts of the mathematicks, and inherits the tafte of his moft fam'd grandfather for natural and experimental philofophy, together with his focial virtues, which render him beloved by all who have the honour to be acquainted with him.

4th. *HENRY WILLOUGHBY*, Efq; died unmarried the 5th of *December* 1738, aged 33.

BONEY-PARK.

IN the hundred of *Rufhcliff* is the feat of Sir *Thomas Parkyns*, bart. This houfe is remarkable for being built very maffive and ftrong, which was the late Sir *Thomas's* tafte for building. It has a good park well ftocked with deer. The manours of *Boney* and *Bradmere* have been in the family of the *Parkyns* ever fince the reign of queen *Elizabeth*, obtained by purchafe. The church here is a vicarage and was valued at 8 *l.* when the prior of *Ulvescroft* was patron, now it is 6 *l.* 15 *s.* in the king's book and Sir *Thomas Parkyns*, patron ; it is dedicated to St. *Mary* ; at the upper end of the fouth-ifle is the monument of *Humphrey Barlow* ; in the chancel north wall is the monument of *Richard Parkyns*, Efq; juftice of the peace and quorum in the county of *Nottingham*, and recorder of the towns of *Nottingham* and *Leicefter*, and an ancient utter barifter of the inner-temple, &c.

THE late Sir *Thomas* was a great mafter at wreftling and took pleafure in fhewing the art to others, of which he publifhed a book, the which he prefented to his majefty king *George* I. with a manufcript dedication. He was alfo author of a grammer. He gave direction for his monument, which was made during his life time, he apply'd to feveral for a latin monumental Infcription alluding to his being a great wreftler. I fhall give place here to one, befides that expreffed upon the monument, *viz.*

> Sternunt longa dies et in eluctabile lethum
>   Quem britonum invictum eft faffa paleftra decus.
> Sed furgens iterum ducet de morte triuphum
>   Quæ fiet (mundus quo perit igne) cinis.

OR the two last lines might run thus :

>Ille triumphabit victa de morte refurgens
>Illa cadet flamma qua peritura dies.

H. L.

Imitated in english.

>Into this grave death did a wreftler fling,
>The matchlefs champion of the british ring,
>But he shall rife when death subdued and hurl'd,
>Shall mix his ashes with the burning world.

THE monument reprefents him ftanding in a wreftling pofture to encounter death, with this infcription :

>Quem modo ftravifti longo certamine tempus
>Hic recubat britonum clarus in orbe pugit
>Nunc primum ftratus, præter te vicerat omnes
>De te etiam victor quando refurget erit.

THIS has been imitated in english by feveral, of which I will only mention the following two :

>After a patriarch's age in ftruggling paft,
>Into this grave long winded time at laft
>Breathlefs and fpent the british wreftler caft :
>'Tis his firft fall; before no match was found,
>By flight or ftrength to fling him to the ground;
>But when he rifes with frefh youth renew'd,
>Time fhall be conquer'd and the grave fubdu'd.

H. L.

Another :

>At length he falls, the long long conteft's o'er,
>And time has thrown whom none e'er threw before,
>Yet boaft not (Time) thy victory for he
>At laft fhall rife again and conquer thee.

NOT far from *Boney-hall* at a place called *High-field*, this Sir *Thomas* built another houfe, defigned for his fecond lady's jointure houfe, but fhe died a fhort time before him.

TOLLARTON.

IS in *Bingham* hundred, about three miles almoft due fouth from *Nottingham*, is a pleafant houfe, of late very much altered and improved by *John Neal*, Efq; who at prefent lives in it; this lordfhip came to the *Neals* of *Mansfield-Woodhoufe* by
purchafe

purchafe, it is part of the eftate of *Pendock Neal*, as yet a minor, eldeft fon of the juft-mentioned *John Neal*, Efq; the church is dedicated to St. *Peter*; the rectory was 16 *l.* when Mr. *Barry* was patron, is now 15 *l.* 9 *s.* 4 *d.* and *Pendock Neal* patron

HOLM-PIEREPONT.

ONE of the feats of his grace the duke of *Kingfton*. This lies about the fame diftance from *Nottingham* eaftward, as *Clifton* does weftward. The ancient family of the *Piereponts* have been poffeffed of this lordfhip, among others, ever fince the reign of *Edward* I. Here ftands a ftately old palace, part of which was a few years ago pulled down, however there is ftill room enough left for the reception of his grace, whenever he has a mind to vifit it. The bowling-green is as large and as fine as any in the kingdom, in which his grace the late duke of *Kingfton* ufed to take fingular delight. Concerning the antiquity of this noble family, *Collins* tells us, [*Peerage* vol. I. *p.* 382.] from the french pedegree, that *Robert Pierrepont* was a lieutenant general in the *Conqueror's* army; that the *Piereponts* derive their original from the caftle of *Pierrepont* on the confines of *Picardy*. That the faid *Robert* had feveral lordfhips in the time of *William* I. appears by *Doomfday-book*, the which he held of the great earl *Warren*, who accompanied *William* duke of *Normandy* in the victorious expedition into this kingdom.

IN the church which is dedicated to St. *Edmund*, are divers monuments of his graces anceftors, efpecially two very beautiful ones, *viz*: That of *Henry Pierrepont*, who died 1615, and that of *Gartrude* countefs of *Kingfton*, the infcription whereon is this:

Here lyeth the illuftrious princefs *Gartrude* countefs of *Kingfton*, daughter to *Henry Talbot*, Efq; fonto *George* late earl of *Shrewsbury*. She was married to the moft noble and excellent lord *Robert* earl of *Kingfton*, one of the generals of king *Charles* I. in the late unhappy differences, and in that fervice loft his life. She had by him many children, moft dead. There are living, *Henry* marquefs of *Dorchefter*, *William* and *Gervafe Pierrepont*, Efqrs. and one daughter the lady *Elizabeth Pierrepont*. She was a lady replete with all qualities that adorn her fex, and more eminent in them than in the greatnefs of her birth; fhe was moft devout in her duties to God; moft obfervant of thofe to her neighbours; an incomparable wife; a moft indulgent mother; and moft charitable to thofe in want: In a word her life was one continued act of virtue; fhe has left a memory which will never die; and an example that may be imitated but not eafily equalled. She died in the 61ft year of her age A. D. 1649. And this monument was erected for her by her fon *Gervafe Pierrepont*.

IN the church lies alfo buried one of our beft poets, I mean *Oldham*, who died too young at *Holm-pierepont* of the fmall-pocks. He was a great favourite of *William* earl of *Kingfton*, as appears by the following infcription made by the faid earl to his memory:

M. S.

Oldhami poetæ quo nemo facro furore plenior,
nemo rebus fublimior aut verbis felicius audax.
Cujus famam omni ævo propria fatis confe-
crabunt carmina quem inter primos honora
tiffimi *Guilielmi* comitis de *Kingfton* amplex-
us variolis correptum heu! nimis immatura
mors rapuit et in cœleftem tranftulit chorum.
Natus apud *Shipton* in agro *Glouceftrenfi.* In
aula fancti *Edmundi Oxoniæ* graduatus. Obiit 19 *Decembris*, A. D. 1682. Ætatis 30.

S E C T I O N XIII.

SECTION XIII.

Remarkable Occurrences relating to this Town, from the earlieſt Times to the preſent Century.

I N the year of *Chriſt* 868, the *Danes* with an army entered the kingdom of *Mercia*, and came to *Nottingham*. *Buthred* king of *Mercia* having timely notice of it with his nobles intreated, *Ethelred* king of the *Weſt-Saxons* and his brother *Alfred*, that they would aid him in fighting againſt the pagans; they according. ly went with an army of *Weſt-Saxons* as far as *Nottingham*, found the army of the *Danes* who wintered at *Nottingham* in their entrenchments, and beſieged them, but there was not much fighting, for the *Mercians* ſtruck up an agreement with the *Pagans*. (*a*)

STOW (*b*)ſays: " The *Pagans* being munited with a ſtrong tower, and the *Chriſ-* " *tians* having not wherewith to break the wall, there was a peace concluded. (*c*) *Camden* alſo agrees, " That the *Danes* relied on the tower built on an exceeding " ſteep rock."

T H I S was the firſt time of the *Danes* entering *Mercia*, which was occaſioned by (*d*) *Bruern Brocard* an earl being injured by K. *Osbert* of *Northumberland*, he having raviſhed his wife; to be revenged, beſides raiſing an inſurrection in part of that kingdom and cauſing the *Bernicians* to chuſe *Ella* for their king, would have *Osbert* alſo robbed of the throne of *Deira*, went over into *Denmark* and immediatly apply'd to king *Ivar* or *Hinguar*, and related to him the diſtracted ſtate of *Northumberland*, adding, that if he would improve the preſent juncture, he might eaſily make himſelf maſter of the kingdom. *Ivar* was very ready and the more ſo to revenge the death of *Regnerus* his father, who having been taken priſoner in *England*, was thrown into a ditch full of ſerpents, where he miſerably periſhed. He entered the *Humber* in the ſpring 867, and advanced that year as far as *Nottingham*.

(*e*)A. D. 872, *Hubba* the brother of *Ivar* who was gone back to *Denmark*, turned his arms againſt *Mercia*, but *Buthred* knowing he was unable to reſiſt, ſince *Alfred* was bound not to ſend him any ſuccours, thought it the wiſeſt courſe to buy off the *Danes* with a ſum of money. *Aſſer in vit. Alfred*, affirms on the contrary, that *Buthred* apply'd to *Alfred* for ſuccours, who accordingly ſent him a very conſiderable army, that went and beſieged the *Danes* at *Nottingham*, and forced them to make peace.

Hh 2   B E

(*a*) Salmon *from Saxon Ann.* ----- (*b*) Sum. Chron. *p.* 65. ----- (*c*) Britan *p.* 482. (*d*) Rapin, *vol.* I. *p.* 88. ---- (*e*) idem *vol.* I. *p.* 90.

(f) BE this as it will they returned the very next year and were bought off ; but no sooner was the money paid but they fell to plundering and ravaging, and let *Buthred* know, that even his own person was in danger. (g) He retired to *Rome* were he spent the remainder of his days in the *English* college, in the year 874 after he had reigned about 22 years.

AND thus the *Danes* got an opportunity of making themselves masters of this spacious kingdom. A. D. 942 they were possessed of these five considerable places : *Nottingham*, *Leicester*, *Lincoln*, *Stanford* and *Derby*, which they held till the warlike heir of *Edward*, king *Edmund*, in 944 set them free, who gained several other great advantages over the *Danes*, and took several other places of less note. Notwithstanding all this, the whole kingdom of *England* was at last forced to submit to the *Danish*-yoke 1017, when *Canutus* took upon him the empire of the whole.

A. D. 1068 *William* the *Conqueror* with his army went to *Nottingham*, in his march against the earls of *Chester* and *Northumberland*, and there built a castle. See *Section* IX.

A. D. 1140, *Robert* earl of *Gloucester*, got out of *Wallingford* castle, and went and seized *Worcester*, whilst the barons on his side ravaged the counties of *Chester* and *Nottingham*. (i)

(k) THIS same year the earl of *Gloucester* by the instigation of *Ralph Paynell*, who was then in possession of *Nottingham* castle, with great power invaded the town of *Nottingham*, and spoil'd it, the townsmen were taken, slain, or burnt in the churches, whereunto they fled ; one of them more rich than the rest was taken and led to his house by his takers to shew them were his treasure lay, he bringing them into a low cellar, whilst they were busy to break open locks and coffers, he conveyed himself away, shutting the doors after him, and set fire to the house, and so the thieves to the number of thirty were burnt, and by reason of this fire all the town was set on flames. (l)

(m) A. D. 1153. In the 18th of *Stephen*, duke *Henry* son to empress *Maud* after king of *England* by the name of *Henry* II. besieged and took *Stamford* and *Nottingham* castles. This agrees with R. *Diceto* and *Brompton*, by which it appears that *Henry* was master of *Nottingham* castle before he deprived *William Peverel* of his

---

(f) Rapin, *vol.* I. *p.* 90.   (g) Saxon *Ann.*   (h) Stow's *Summ. p.* 109.   (i) Rapin, *vol.* I. *p.* 205.   (k) Stow's *Summ. p.* 135.

(l) *The late reverend Mr.* Hardy, *vicar of* Melton-Mowbray, *in com.* Leicester, *a person of great knowledge in antiquities, told me, that in the course of reading, (but could not readily recollect where) he had met with an account that this Fire, begun at an house opposite to the south side of St.* Mary's *church where lately Dr.* Greaves *lived, formerly known by the name of* Mappurley-Place, *from a considerable merchant of the Staple,* Thomas de Mappurley, *who flourished in* Nottingham *about the latter end of the reign of* Richard II.

(m) Stow's *Sum. p.* 145.

his eftate upon the earl of *Chefter's* account, which happened in the firft of his reign A.C. 1155.

(*n*)A. D. 1189. At the death of king *Henry* II. *John* his 4th fon was poffeffed of the caftle of *Nottingham* and the honour of *Peverel* with the titles of earl of *Mortayn*, *Cornwal*, *Glouceſter*, *Devon* (*o*)and *Nottingham*, and lord of the honour of *Lancaſter*, alfo lord of *Ireland*.   And his brother king *Richard* I. at his going to the *Holy-land*, left the earl in poffeffion of all thefe lands, honours and dignities, the which *John* who moftly refided at *Nottingham*, held in a kind of a regal manner. During the abfence of his brother he afpired to the crown, concerning which *Stowe* expreffes himfelf thus: (*p*) "*John* having an itching to be king, faid he wift not if his brother *Ri-*
"*chard* were alive or not, to whom the bifhop of *Ely*, (*Longchamp* chancellor and
"protector of the kingdom) anfwered, if king *Richard* be yet living, it were an
"untruth to take from him the crown ; if he be dead, *Arthur* the elder brother's
"fon muft enjoy the fame.   About the 4th of *Richard* I. earl *John* hearing of the
"imprifonment of his brother, and having infinuated himfelf to the nobility and
"gentry in the northern parts of *England*, he made war within the realm and took
"by ftrength the caftle of *Nottingham*, (which had been taken from him) the caf-
"tle of *Windfor* and others, in the year 1193.

(*q*)A. D. 1194. King *Richard* being releafed from his captivity, returned to *England* and reduced his brother's party, efpecially fome caftles in the hands of his adherents, of which *Nottingham* caftle was the only one that held out a fiege of fome days and the king befieged it in peffon.

(*r*)UPON this *Richard* called a parliment at *Nottingham*, where the queen his mother fat on his right hand, the archbifhop of *Canterbury* and *York* on his left, with other bifhops earls and barons according to their dignities. In this honourable affembly the king demanded judgment againft his brother *John* and his complices for their traiterous enterprizes againft him and his countries.   Whereupon judgment was given that *John* and the other principals fhould have fummons peremptorily given them for their appearance, and if within 40 days after fuch fummons they came not to anfwer all complaints informed againft them, earl *John* fhould forfeit all whatever he held within the kingdom, and the others fhould ftand to fuch cenfure as was awarded them by the faid parliament.

(*ſ*) *JOHN* not appearing within the limitted time, the king caufed a fentence to be paffed againft him, confifcating all his lands, and declaring him incapable of fucceeding to the crown ; however the very next year 1195, *Richard* being at *Roan*, the queen his mother introduced prince *John*, who throwing himfelf at his feet begged his pardon : The king received him civilly (as he promifed the queen) but intimated to him that he was not fatisfied of the fincerity of his repentance, faying : "I forgive you, (raifing him up) and wifh I could as eafily forget your offences as "you will my pardon."   A. D.

(*n*) Glover's *Cat. of Honour*.   (*o*) *I do not find any where elſe that he had the title of earl of* Devon.   (*p*) Stowe's *Summary p.* 165.   (*q*) Rapin, *vol.* I. *p.* 255. ----
(*r*) Glover's *Cat. of Honour, p.* 115.   (*ſ*) Rapin, *vol.* I. *p.* 255.

(s) A.D. 1215. King *John* sent the archbishop of *Canterbury* and the earl of *Pembroke*, who had before been with the barons, to acquaint them that the king refused to confirm their articles; upon which they gave their host a very plausible name, calling it : *The army of God and the holy-church*, so setting forwards they came to *Nottingham* (t) and besieged it, but being not able to prevail, they raised the siege and came to *Bedford* and lay before the castle there, which Sir *William Beauchamp* commanded, who bearing a part in their confederacy soon delivered the same into their hands.

(v) A. D. 1213. King *John* marched to *Nottingham* with intent to chastise the barons for their disobedience in refusing to assist him in the expedition against *France*, but upon the threats of cardinal *Langton* that he would excommunicate all that should take arms before the relaxation of the interdict; (fearing his troops would desert him) he desisted.

(w) A. D. 1212. After king *John* returned from the outrages of the *Irish*, on a sudden the *Welchmen* began to rush in upon the *English* marches, wasting the country and overthrowing diverse castles; whereupon the king taking in hand to quell the pride of the *Welchmen*, forthwith mustered forces and coming to *Nottingham* hanged up the hostages, which but the year before he had received to the number of 28.

(x) T H I S same year after repeated intelligence of a plot against him, he mistrusted his officers, disbanded his army and retired to *Nottingham*, and shut himself up in the castle, and hired foreign archers for his defence.

(y) A. D. 1216. King *John* not thinking himself and his treasures safe at *Lynn*, being pressed by the barons, he resolved to remove them to a place in *Lincolnshire* where he intended to retire. He narrowly escaped drowning with his whole army in the washes between a place called the *Cross-keys* in *Norfolk* and the *Forsdike* in *Holland* in *Lincolnshire*, where he lost his baggage; he arrived that night at *Swine's head* abbey, where he lodged; his vexation for his loss which was irretrievable in his present circumstances, threw him into a violent fever, which was heightened by inconsiderately eating of peaches and also attended with a flux; on the morrow not being able to ride, he was carried in a horse-litter to *Sleford* castle, from whence the next day he proceeded to *Newark*. Here finding his illness increase, he made his will, and appointed *Henry* his eldest son then but ten years of age, and died the 18th of *October* 1216.

T H E cause of this king's death is by some of our historians attributed to poison, who agree in the place and person that committed the fact, but differ in the manner; *Hemingham* and after him *Highden* and *Knighton*, say, that the abbot perswaded the monk to poison the king, because he would have lain with his sister, and that he did

it

(s) Glover's *Cat. of Honour. p.*129. (t) Matthew Paris, *will have it that they besieged* Northampton 15 *days*. (v) R a p i n, *vol.* I. *p.* 273. (w) Glover's *cat. of Honour*, *p.* 125. (x) *Ann. Waverl. p.* 173. (y) Rapin *vol.* I. *p.* 279.

it by a difh of pears which he poifoned all but three, and then prefenting them to the king, he bid him tafte them himfelf, which he did, eating only the three that he had mark'd, and fo efcaped. Others relate the ftory thus : That the king hearing how cheap corn then was, anfwered he would e'er long make it fo dear that a penny loaf fhould be fold for a fhilling ; at which a monk took fuch indignation that he went and put the poifon of a toad into a cup of wine, and came and drank to the king, which made him pledge him the more readily, but finding himfelf very much out of order upon it, he asked for the monk, and when it was told him that he was dead, *God have mercy upon me*, faid the king, *I doubted as much*. *Speed* and *Baker* have this fame account from *Caxton*. A manufcript hiftory intituled *Brute of Englonde* originally wrote in *Englifh* in the reign of *Henry* VI. without the author's name, relates this action of the monk of *Swynes-head-abbey*, as a meritorious act, and that before he perpetrated it, he went to confeffion and obtained the abbots abfolution, and that upon the death of the monk, there were ordered in the faid abbey five monks to fing for his foul as long as the abbey fhould ftand.

THUS we have ftept a little afide to fee the end of the life and troubles of this great benefactor to the burgeffes of *Nottingham*, in his favourite county.

A. D. 1330, Happened the downfal of that great favourite of *Iffabella* of *France*, queen to *Edward* II. and mother of *Edward* III. *Mortimer* earl of *March*, which was brought about in manner following :

KING *Edward* III. who came to the crown *January* the 25th 1326-7, at the age of 15, chofe the time the parliament was to meet at *Nottingham*, viz. fifteen days after *Michaelmafs* 1330, in the 4th of his reign, for this purpofe, the court being come to *Nottingham*, the queen and *Mortimer* lodged in the caftle with a guard of 180 knights, whilft the king with a fmall retinue lodged in the town. The king iffued out warrants to all fheriffs for apprehending the earl of *March*, Sir *Oliver de Ingham* and Sir *Simon de Bereford*, bearing date *October* the 20th at *Nottingham*, and on the 3d of *November* fummoned all perfons whatfoever, that had any complaints to make againft *Mortimer* and the reft, to come and lay them before the parliament, (a) and the king having gained the deputy conftable, entered the caftle (*Stowe* fays in the night time) through a fubterraneous paffage, (See *Section* IX.) and came into his mother's appartment accompanied by Sir *William Montacute*, (b) afterwards earl of *Salisbury*, Sir *Humphrey de Bohun*, Sir *Edward* and Sir *William* his brothers, Sir *Ralph de Strafford*, Sir *William de Clinton*, Sir *John de Nevil* of *Hornby*, Sir *William Eland*, deputy conftable of the caftle, and others, all bent to loofe their lives in his fervice.

There

(a) Rapin *vol*. I. *p*, 413.
(b) *This* Sir William, *fays* Collin's *peerage of* England, *was the chief perfon that boldly laid before the king, the infolent behaviour of* Roger Mortimer *earl of* March, *who immediately thereupon taking in confideration his own difhonour and damage as alfo the impoverifhing of the people, and revealing his mind privately to* Sir William Montacute, *gave him command to take to his affiftance fome refolute perfons which he did accordingly*. *vol*. I. *p*, 270.

THERE was at first some noise made and two knights (*viz.* Sir *Hugh Tur-plington*, steward of the king's houshold and Sir *Richard*, (according to the *Fœdera*) or Sir *John Monmouth* according to *Dugdale* and *Barnes*) of the guard were killed, who having less regard for the king than their companions offered to resist. The earl of *March* was apprehended, and notwithstanding the queen's cries and entreaties to spare the gallant *Mortimer* (*c*) he was carried out the same way, the king came in, and conducted under a strong guard to *London*, *October* the 19th.

HE was treated with the utmost rigour. His impeachment brought before the parliament, contained divers articles, of which these were the principal:

1st. THAT he had seized the government of the kingdom without authority and contrary to the express regulation of the parliament.

2d. THAT he had placed about the king, spies of all his actions, that he might not be able to free himself from the subjection he was kept under.

3d. THAT he procured the death of *Edward* II. by his express orders.

4th. THAT he had contrived a treacherous plot to take away the life of the late earl of *Kent* the king's uncle.

5th. THAT he had appropriated to his own use the 20,000*l.* paid by the king of *Scotland*.

6th. THAT he had lived in too familiar a manner with the queen mother. (*d*)

FOR all these crimes which were affirmed to be notorious, and for proof where-of no evidences were so much as heard, he was condemned to dye.

HIS sentence which ran that he should as a traitor be drawn and hanged on the common gallows at tyburn on the 19th of *November* was executed without favour, (*e*) and there was this remarkable in his sentence that he was condemned without being heard as he himself served the *Spencers* in the preceding reign: But this irregularity proved advantageous to his family; for *Roger* his grandson who obtained afterwards

-an

(*c*) *Her words were*: Bel fitz, bel fitz ayez pitie du gentile *Mortimer*. *Or as the old manuscript above mentioned,* (*who says nothing of the king's being present*)*has it*: " Now fair sirs I pray you that you do no harm to his body for he is a worthy " knight, our well beloved friend and our dear cozin."

(*d*) *The above-mentioned manuscript history adds this article*: " That by his procure-" ment the charter of *Ragman* was delivered unto the *Scots*, wherein the ho-" mages and fealties of *Scotland* were contained, which the *Scots* should do for e-" ver to the kings of *England* for the realm of *Scotland*." *Capit.* 222.

(*e*) Tyburn *was formerly called the* Elms *which was then in* Smith-fields. Wal-singham *says that his body after having hung two days and two nights was grant-ed to the* Friers Minors, *who buried it in their church now called* Christ-Church.

an act to reverse this sentence as erroneous, and of this family by the female side was descended king *Edward* IV. Upon this event *Rapin* makes the following remark.

" T H A T how great soever favourites and ministers may be who abuse their " power, they must expect to see themselves abandoned by all, whenever their " affairs begin to decline.

A S to the queen mother, he first seized of her exorbitant dower, (which exceeded the two thirds of the revenues of the crown) and reduced it to a pension of three thousand pounds a year. She was at the same time confined to her house at *Risings*, least by her intrigues she should excite new troubles ; in this confinement she lived twenty-eight years [says *Rapin*] (where the king visited her once or twice a year, more out of decency than affection) and blames *Mazeray* for affirming that *Edward* hastened her death.

(*a*) A. D. 1337. A parliament was held at *Nottingham* wherein it was enacted, that whatsoever clothworkers of *Flanders* or of other countries, would dwell and inhabit in *England*, should come quietly and peaceably, and the most convenient places should be assigned to them, with great liberties and priviledges, and the king would become surety for them, till they should be able to gain by their occupation. In the same parliament it was enacted that none should wear any cloth made without the realm, the king, queen and their children, only excepted.

T H E exportation of wool of *English* growth was also prohibited.

(*b*) A. D. 1376. *Peter de la Mare*, speaker of the house of commons, was by order of king *Edward* III. confined in *Nottingham* castle for having spoken a little too freely against *Alice Pierce* the king's mistress, at the time when he presented the petition of the house, for the removal of the said lady, the duke of *Lancaster*, *Latimer* lord chamberlain, and others ; some will have it that he was not speaker, but a considerable knight of *Herefordshire*, both for prudence and eloquence. He was confined till the beginning of the next reign.

A. D. 1387. King *Richard* II. by the instigation of his favourites made a bold attempt upon the liberties of the subject, which if it had succeeded would have established absolute power and terminated in the slavery of the people ; and *Nottingham* was pitched upon for the scene of action, which was conducted in the manner following :

(*c*) T H E year preceeding, the marquis of *Dublin*, created duke of *Ireland*, a great favourite of this king, was in compliance with the parliament's desire removed from the king's person and sent to *Ireland*, with a pension of 3000 marks, or as *Walsingham* has it 30000, his whole estate being confiscated. But before the year's end both he and others, as the earl of *Suffolk*, *Alexander Nevil*, archbishop of *York*, *Robert de Vere*, earl of *Oxford*, returned to the king, and soon stirred him up to re-

Ii   venge

(*a*) Stow's *Summ. p.* 266.---(*b*) Rapin, *vol.* I. *p.* 444.---(*c*) Rapin, *vol.* I. *p.* 464.

venge upon their enemies. This year the duke of *Ireland*, prefuming upon his influence over the king, had the infolence to divorce his wife, daughter of the lord *Coucy* and grand-daughter of *Edward* III. in order to marry *Lancerona* maid of honour to the queen, a *Bohemian* of mean birth. (*a*)

THOUGH this divorce was very injurious to the royal family, *Richard* fhew'd not the leaft concern, but it was not the fame with the duke of *Gloucefter Thomas* of *Woodftock*, his uncle, who highly refented the affront, and declared he would revenge it the firft opportunity. This threat made the duke of *Ireland* refolve to prevent him ; to that end after concerting the means with the king, he feigned to go into *Ireland*, and took the road to *Wales*, where the king was pleafed to accompany him; but this pretended voyage was only to confult more privately how to execute their project of affuming an arbitrary power, of which the duke of *Gloucefter*, the earls of *Arundel*, *Warwick*, *Derby*, and *Nottingham*, were to feel the effects : The refult of this confultation was, that the king fhould raife an army to terrify thefe lords, and then call a parliament, the election whereof fhould be fo managed, that the members fhould be all at his devotion, and that he fhould caufe to be paffed all fuch acts as were neceffary to fecure him an unlimitted power.

AS foon as the plot was contrived, they went to *Nottingham*, where the king fent for all the fheriffs, fome of the principal citizens of *London*, and all the judges : When they were met he communicated to them his defign of raifing an army to chaftife fuch lords as he named to them, amongft whom was the duke of *Gloucefter*, and demanded of the fheriffs what number of troops each could furnifh him with; then he told them to let no reprefentative be chofen, but what was in the lift he fhould give them himfelf.

THE fheriffs made anfwer, it was not in their power to execute his orders : That the people were fo well inclined to the lords he had mentioned, that there was no profpect of levying an army againft them ; it was ftill more difficult, to deprive the people of their right of freely electing their reprefentatives in parliament.

BUT the judges were not fo fcrupulous in what related to them, as :

WHETHER the king had not power to turn out the 14 commiffioners appointed by parliament, and to annul fuch acts as were prejudicial to him ? They reply'd .

THE king was above the law. (*b*)

NEVERTHELESS when they were required to fubfcribe their opinion, fome endeavoured to be excufed, but were compelled to it by the menaces of the favourites. The fix judges were, Sir *Robert Trefilian*, lord chief juftice of the king's bench, Sir *Robert Belknap*, lord chief juftice of the common pleas, Sir *John Holt*,

Sir

(*a*) *Some fay fhe was a* Vintner's, *fome a* Joyner's *daughter.* Walfingham.
(*b*) *There were ten queries put to them to which the anfwer was delivered on the 25th of* Auguft. Knighton's *Collection*.

Sir *Roger Fulthorp*, and Sir *William de Burgh*, with *John Lockton*, serjeant at law. *(c)*

(d) THE opinion of the judges being thus extorted, *Richard* thought he had surmounted all difficulties. He immediately issued out commissions to levy an army, but found so few willing to serve him that he was forced to desist from his project; enraged at this disapointment he returned to *London*, after a fruitless declaration of his designs, which rendered him more odious to the public.

(e) A. D. 1392. In the 15th of *Richard* II. the *Londoners* having proudly denied the king the lending of a thousand pounds which he demanded of them, the mayor, sheriffs and aldermen of that city were summoned to a council at *Nottingham* in the feast of St. *John the Baptist*, and there arrested, and for divers faults laid to their charge, imprisoned, the king disannulling their liberties made Sir *Edward Dalengrige* warden of *London*, anno regni 16°. who, because men said he favoured the *Londoners*, was removed the first of *July*, and *Baldwin Radington*, constituted in his place; the mayor was Sir *William Stondon*, grocer, and the sheriffs *Gilbert Mansfield* and *Thomas Newington*. When the king saw that the *Londoners* sore repented their trespass, he took pity on them, and through the mediation of the duke of *Gloucester* came from *Scheene* in *Surrey* to *London*, with queen *Anne* his wife, who were received at St. *George's* church in *Southwark*, with a procession of *Robert Braybrooke* bishop of *London*, and all his clergy of the city, who conveyed him through *London*, the citizens, men, women and children in order, meeting the king, and doing him honour, attended him to *Westminster*; as he passed through the city, the streets were hanged with cloth of gold, silver and silk, the conduit in *Cheapside* ran with red and white wine, and by a child angelic, the king was presented with a very costly crown of gold, and the queen with another; a table of the *Trinity* of gold, was given to the king valued 800 *l*. and another to the queen of St. *Anne*; by this means the king became more tractable to grant them their liberties again, and then the king's bench from *York*, and the chancery from *Nottingham*, were returned to *London*. *Rapin* says, from *Walsingham*, that the populace of *London* cut an *Italian* merchant to pieces who offered to lend the king the thousand pounds.

Ii 2

A. D.

(c) Knight. *Coll.* Sir Robert Belknap, *said after he had signed:* "Now want I no-
"thing but a ship, or a nimble horse, or an halter, to bring me to that death I de-
"serve; if I had not done this I should have been killed, (for it seems the duke
"of *Ireland*, and the earl of *Suffolk*, threaten'd to kill him if he refused to sign)
"and now I have gratified the king's pleasure I have well deserved to die, for
"treason against the nobles of the land. *idem.*

Of these judges Sir Robert Tresilian, *was drawn through the midst of* London *and hanged at* Tyburn; *the other five had their lives spared but were banished and had their estates confiscated.* Blake *the king's council at law, and* Usk *the under sheriff of* Middlesex *were also hanged upon this account.* Triumph of justice over unjust judges. *p.* 9.

(d) Rapin *vol.* I.

(e) Stow's *sum. p.* 311.

A. D. 1397. *Richard* II. fummoned all the peers of the realm to *Nottingham*, *Auguſt* the 1ſt. (*a*)

A. D. 1461. *Edward* IV. after his landing at *Ravenſpur* in *Yorkſhire*, with 500 men, and having obtained of *Richard*, after duke of *York*, and the lord *Rivers*, about as many more, his little army in his march to *London* came to *Nottingham*, where he hoped to increaſe it ; this ſucceeded to his wiſhes, for ſoon after his arrival here Sir *William Parr* and Sir *James Harrington* with 600 men well armed and appointed, and ſhortly after Sir *Thomas Burgh* and Sir *Thomas Montgomery* with another conſiderable body of men joined him, upon which he cauſed himſelf to be proclaimed by the name of K. *Edward* IV. and having been informed that the duke of *Exeter*, the earl of *Oxford*, and the lord *Bardolf* were lodged at *Newark* ; he with his whole army marched againſt them, but the duke of *Exeter* hearing of his coming did not think fit to expect him but retired in the night ; whereupon *Edward* having notice of it returned to *Nottingham*, and from hence began his march towards the earl of *Warwick*, who had left *London* and was gone into *Warwickſhire*, to levy forces for king *Henry*, which he did and came to *Leiceſter* with 3000 forces, able men, well armed, and extremely well affected to him, ſo as to reſolve to live and die in his quarrel. --- *Magna Britan antiq. et nov. vol.* IV. *p.* 11.

(*b*) A. D. 1470. When the earl of *Warwick* landed in *England* with the *French* auxiliaries, *Edward* IV. gave orders to levy troops and appointed the rendezvous about *Nottingham*, and marched towards that place attended by his brother the duke of *York*, the lord *Haſtings* his chamberlain, the lord *Scales*, &c.

(*c*) A. D. 1483. In this year *Richard* duke of *York*, brother to *Edward* IV. having got poſſeſſion of the crown of *England*, his nephews impriſoned, and their relations executed at *Pomfrete*, made his progreſs by *Windſor*, *Oxford* and *Coventry*, to *Nottingham* ; (during this, the execrable murder of the two young princeswas perpetrated in the tower) and thence he deſigned as far north as *York*, in order for a ſecond coronation in that city ; from *Nottingham* (according to a record among the archieves of *York*) a letter was wrote by his ſecretary, to ſtir up a zeal in the citizens of *York* towards his better reception, in theſe words :

To the gude maſters, the Mair, Recorder, and Aldermen, and
Sheriffs of the cite of York :

" I recommend me unto you as heartily as I can. Thanked be Jeſu the king's grace is
" in good health as is likewiſe the queen's grace, and in all their progreſs have byn
" worſhipfully reſeyved, with pageants and odyr, &c. and his lords and judges in every
" place ſittyng, determinyng the compleynts of pore folkes, with due punicion of offen-
" ders againſt his laws. The cauſe I writ to you now is, forſomuch as I verily know
" the king's mind, and intire affection that his grace beareth towards you and your
wor-

(*a*) Rapin, *vol.* I. *p.* 468. ----- (*b*) Rap. *vol.* I. *p.* 608. ---- (*c*) Drake's *Antiq.* of York. B. 1. *p.* 116.

" worſhipful cite, for many your kynd and lovyn defignings to his grace, ſhew'd
" heretofore, which his grace will never forget, and intendeth therefore foe to doe
" unto you, that all the kings that ever reigned beſtow'd upon you, did they never
" foe much.   Doubt not hereof, ne make ne manner of petition or defire of any
" thing by his highneſs to you to be graunted.   But this I advife you, as laudable as
" your wiſdom can imagin, to receive him and the queen at their coming, difpofe
" you to do as well with pageants, with ſuch gude ſpeeches as can gudely (this ſhort
" warning confidered) be deviſed, and under ſuch form as maſter *Lancaſter* of the
" king's councel this brynger ſhall ſumwhat advertiſe you of my mind in that behalf,
" as in hanging the ſtreets through which the king's grace ſhall come, with cloths
" of arras, tappeſtry work and odyr, for there comen many ſothern lords and men of
" worſhip with them, which will mark greatly your reſayving thar graces.   Me ne-
" ded not thus to advife you, howbeit many things I ſhew you thus of good heart, and
" for the ſingular zele and love which I beer to you and your cite afore all other.
" Ye ſhall well know, that I ſhall not forbeer calling on his grace for your weles, ne
" remember it as Mr. *Lancaſter* ſhall ſhew you, which in part heard the king's grace
" ſpeak hereon, to whom touching the premiſſes it may like you ------ ------- in
" haſte the 23d day of *Auguſt* at *Nottingham* with the hand of your friend and
" lover,

J O H N   K E N D A L, Secretary.

(a) A. D. 1485.   When the duke of *Richmond*, (after king of *England*, by the title of *Henry* VII.) had landed in *Wales* and was marched to *Shrewsbury*, *Richard*
III. was at *Nottingham*, and from that town he marched towards *Boſworth* to give
battle to that duke.

A. D. 1487.   *Henry* VII. before the battle of *Stoke* by *Newark*, was advanced
to *Nottingham* and there held a council of war.   Authors differ in the day of the
month on which this battle was fought; my lord *Bacon*, ſays *June* the 6th, *Hall*, *Stow*
and *Hollingſhed* affirm it to be the 16th, and Sir *John Ware*, will have it the 20th.
This battle was fought at *Stoke*, againſt the earl of *Lincoln*, aſſiſted by *Flemiſh* and
Iriſh forces, undes the conduct of that undaunted captain *Martin Swartz*.   *Rapin*,
[vol. I. p. 659.] like the reſt tells us, that the king being informed that the earl of
Lincoln was advancing towards *Newark*, reſolved to prevent him ; to that end he
marched with ſuch expedition that he encamped between the enemy and *Newark* ;
the earl of *Lincoln* advanced that day to a little village called *Stoke*, where he encamped on the ſide of an hill.

B Y this account it appears that none of the writers who have given an account of
this battle, did ever inform themſelves of the ſituation of the place where the engagement was.   I ſhall therefore to clear up this matter, make uſe of my oft quoted
anonymous author, who being a native of this country knew perfectly well the ſituation of *Newark* and *Stoke*, who ſays : " The truth is, the king did not put himſelf
" between *Newark* and the enemies camp, for which purpoſe he muſt have been on
" the north of *Newark*, and *Stoke* where the battle was fought is two long miles on
the

(a) Rapin, *vol.* I. *p.* 645.

" the fouth of *Newark*, and the battle itfelf was fought on the fouth of *Stoke*, It is
" rather thought that the night before the battle, the king lay entrench'd in *Elfton*
" fields faft by the place where the field was fought, there being to this day an ap-
" parent fign of a large trench there, and it is as truly conftant and undoubtedly tra-
" dition, yet frefh among the aged people in thofe parts, that the night before the
" battle the earl and his army lodged at *Newark*, who having marched through the
" the north parts of *England* without affront or refiftance, and having now at *Newark*
" paffed the *Trent* and fo fet foot on the fouth part of the kingdom, flattered them-
" felves with the deceived hope of fucceeding victory ; in jollity whereof, like the
" foolifh *Trojans*, they fo frolicked and drank all night, as the next morning great
" numbers of them were unfit for the fervice in hand, many of them following the
" main army in fcattered troops, and fome fcarce came out of *Newark* when the bat-
" tle was joined at *Stoke*."

(*a*) I N this battle were flain on the fpot, the earl of *Lincoln*, the earl of *Kildare*,
(or as Sir *James Ware* fays, *Thomas Fitzgerald*, who according to him is erroneoufly
called earl of *Kildare*) and *Martin Swartz*, and moft of the germans killed or
wounded, the *Irifh* took to flight not able alone to refift the *Englifh* ; it is faid there
were at leaft four thoufand killed on the fide of the rebels, and half of the king's
firft line, which fhews with what obftinacy it was fought on both fides : Amongft
the prifoners were found the new king of *Ireland*, become again *Lambert Simnel*,
and the prieft his companion and inftructor.   *Henry* either out of generofity or poli-
cy, was pleafed to give *Simnel* his life, and to honour with the office of turn-fpit
in his kitchen, the' perfon who had boldly afpired to the throne and even worn a
crown.   Some time after he was preferred to be one of the king's faulconers, in which
office he died.   As for the prieft he was immediately committed clofe prifoner, and
heard of no more.

A. D. 1641, *April* the 21ft, a petition againft the hierarchy was prefented to the
parliament by *Nottinghamfhire* and *Lancafhire*.

(*b*) A. D. 1642.   King *Charles* I. came to *Nottingham July* the 10th and fummoned and careffed the freeholders of the county, and promifed to act according to
the proteftation at *York* : The like he did at *Lincoln*.

T H E proteftation was : That he would not exercife any illegal authority, but
defend them and all others againft the votes of parliament, and not engage them in
any war againft the parliament.   *July* the 11th, he fent a meffage of his intention to
reduce *Hull* if it be not rend'red to him, which if they do, he will admit of their farther propofitions, &c.

T H I S fame year *Auguft* the 22d, he erected his ftandard at *Nottingham*.

R A-

(*a*) Rap. *vol.* I. *p.* 659. ---- (*b*) Whitlock's *memorials p.* 57.

SECT. XIII.

RAPIN (vol. II.) says from *Clarendon*, on the 25th, and that the standard was erected by the king's order on a turret of *Nottingham* castle. *Nalson* in his trial of king *Charles* I. mentions the evidence of one *Samuel Lawson*, of *Nottingham*, malt-ster, who deposed that about *August* 1642, he saw the king's standard brought forth of *Nottingham* castle born upon divers gentlemen's shoulders, (who as the report was) were noblemen, that he saw the same by them carried into the hill-close adjoining to the castle, with an herald before it, and there the said standard was erected, with great shouting, acclamations and sound of drums and trumpets, and that when the said standard was so erected, there was a proclamation made, and that he saw the king present at the erecting of it, &c.

THIS difference of time and place may easily be reconciled by the unquestio-nable tradition of persons yet living, who heard their fathers say, that the standard was first erected on the highest turret of the old tower, (which *Thoroton* attests as his own remembrance, to have been the 22d of *August*, in the castle,) but that after a few days, people not resorting to it according to expectation, it was judged that upon the account of the castle being a garrison, where every body had not so free ac-cess to the standard as if it was erected in an open place, it might be more proper to remove it out of the castle, which was accordingly done on the 25th of *August*, into the close adjoining to the north side of the wall of the outer-ward of the castle, then called the *Hill-Close*, and afterwards for many years *Standard-Close*.

ONE remarkable accident happened at the first setting up of this standard in the just mentioned close, *viz*. That the weather grew so tempestuous that it was blown down soon after it was erected, and could not be fixed again in a day or two. This (as *Rushworth*, *Hooper*, and some others take notice,) was looked upon by ma-ny melancholy people as a fatal presage of the war.

THE following other particulars remarkable, happened during the king's stay at *Nottingham*.

(a) THE day after his arrival at *Nottingham* he reviewed his horse, which were 800, and no sooner was this review over but the king received information that two regiments of foot were marching to *Coventry* by the earl of *Essex's* order; where-upon he hasted thither with his cavalry, in hopes of preventing the parliament's forces, and possessing himself of that city, before which he accordingly arrived a day before the two regiments, but the mayor of the city, tho' without a garrison, shut the gates against him, and fired upon his men; the king was very sensibly touched with this indignity, but as there was no remedy he was forced to return to *Nottingham*, leaving the command of his cavalry to commissary-general *Wilmot*; *Rapin* adds from *Clarendon*: that on the 2d of *August* the king imagined that set-ting up his standard at *Nottingham* would draw great numbers of people, thither, but was very much disappointed; he had with him but 300 foot and some trained bands, drawn together by Sir *John Digby*, sheriff of the county; his horse (as has been said) consisted only of 800; his artillery was still at *York*, from whence it was

difficult

(a) Rapin, vol. II.

difficult to bring it, many things being yet wanting to prepare and form it for marching; nevertheless he had given out many commissions and ordered his forces to repair to *Nottingham*; he expected them in that town, tho' not without danger, the parliament having at *Coventry* 5000 foot and 1500 horse.

THE king was certainly in great danger at *Nottingham*, the town was not in a condition to resist long, the king having scarce any forces and the parliament troops were not above twenty miles off, which had they marched directly to *Nottingham*, the king must either have retired with dishonour to *York*, or else have hazarded his being made prisoner; this danger was evident, and yet quitting *Nottingham* could not but be very prejudicial to him: He was therefore advised to send a message to both houses with some overture to incline them to a treaty; the king refused it, was offended at it, and broke up the council; the next day the same motion was renewed, but under a different view, *i.e.* it was advised to send a message to both houses only to gain time, the king was still reluctant, but upon it being represented to him that very likely both houses would reject the offer, they would thereby render themselves odious to the people, who were desirous of peace, and who would be the more inclinable to serve his majesty for his endeavours to procure it, that if the overture was accepted, the king would have an opportunity of demonstrating that the war on his part was purely defensive; in short, that the bare offer of peace would of course retard the preparations of the parliament, because men's minds would be in suspence, whilst the king's levies might be continued by virtue of the commissions already sent out: The king yielded to these reasons and on the 25th of *August* three days after the setting up of the standard [*within the castle*] a message was sent by *Thomas Wriothesley* earl of *Southampton*, Sir *John Culpepper*, the earl of *Dorset* and Sir *William Uvedale*, knight.

THE king's deputies were but ill received, the earl of *Southampton* was called upon by the lords to withdraw, they being offended at his boldness, and ordered him to send his message in writing, and wait for an answer out of *London*. The commons obliged *Culpepper* to deliver his message at the bar, at which the king took great offence.

THE King's message was:

" THAT some persons might be by them enabled to treat with the like num-
" ber authorized by him, in such a manner and with such freedom of debate, as
" might best tend to the peace of the kingdom; and he assured them, that nothing
" should be wanting on his part, which might advance the protestant religion, op-
" pose popery, secure the laws of the land, and confirm all just power and privileges
" of parliament; if this proposition should be rejected he protested he had done his
" duty so amply, that God would absolve him from any of the guilt of that blood
" which must be spilt."

THE Parliament's answer was to this effect:

" THAT notwithstanding their endeavours to prevent the distracted state of
" of the kingdom, nothing had followed but proclamations and declarations against
" both houses of parliament, whereby their actions were declared treasonable, and
" their persons traitors; so that until those proclamations were recalled, and the
                                                                        " standard

" ftandard taken down, they could not by the fundamental priviledges of parliament,
" give his majefty any other anfwer to his meffage.

T H E King's fecond meffage :

" T H A T he never defigned to declare both houfes of parliament traitors, or
" fet up his ftandard againft them, and much lefs to put them and the kingdom out
" of his protection, he utterly profeffed againft it, before God and the world. But
" he promifed that if a day was appointed by them for the revoking of their decla-
" ration againft all perfons as traitors or otherwife for affifting him, he would with
" all chearfulnefs upon the fame day recall his proclamations and declarations, and
" take down his ftandard."

T H E Anfwer of both Houfes :

" T H A T his majefty not having taken down his ftandard, recalled his procla-
" mations and declarations, whereby he had declared the actions of both houfes
" of parliament to be treafonable, and their perfons traitors, and having publifhed
" the fame fince his meffage of the 25th of *Auguft*, they could not recede from their
" former anfwer. That if his majefty would recall his declarations and return to
" his parliament, he fhould find fuch expreffions of their fidelities and duties, that
" his fafety, honour and greatnefs, could only be found in the affections of his peo-
" ple, and the fincere councils of his parliament, who deferved better of his majefty
" and could never allow themfelves (reprefenting the whole kingdom) to be bal-
" lanced with thofe who gave evil councils to his majefty."

I N the mean time both houfes perceiving that the king's aim was to keep the
people in fufpence, by an uncertain expectation of peace, publifhed a declaration pro-
tefting they would never lay down their arms till his majefty had left the delinquents
to the juftice of the parliament.

T H E King on his part fent this third meffage :

" T H A T all the world might judge who had ufed moft endeavours to prevent
" the prefent diftractions, either he who had condefcended to defire and prefs it, or
" the two houfes who had refufed to enter into a negociation. That for the future if
" they defired a treaty of him he fhould remember that the blood which was to be fpilt
" in this quarrel was that of his fubjects, and therefore would return to his parlia-
" ment as foon as the caufes which had made him abfent himfelf from it, fhould be
" removed."

T H E two houfes finding that the King's defign was to render their refufal to
treat, odious to the people, they returned a more particular anfwer to this meffage,
the fubftance whereof was the following :

" T H A T at the very time his majefty propounded a treaty, his foldiers were com-
" mitting numberlefs oppreffions and rapines. That they could not think that his majefty
" had done all that in him lay to remove the prefent diftractions, as long as he would
" admit of no peace without fecuring the authors and inftruments of thefe mifchiefs
" from juftice. That they befought his majefty to confider his expreffions, *That God*

K k   *fhould*

" *should so deal with him and his posterity as he desired the preservation of the just*
" *rights of parliament* : That neverthelefs his intention was to deny the parliament
" the privilege of declaring to be delinquents, thofe they deemed fuch, a privilege
" which belonged to the meaneft court of juftice in the kingdom. That his majef-
" ty has no caufe to complain he was denied a treaty, when they offered all that a
" treaty could produce, fecurity, honour, fervice, obedience, fupport, and fought
" nothing, but that their religion and liberty might be fcreened from the open vio-
" lence of a wicked party ; that if there were any caufe of treaty, *they knew no*
" *competent perfon to treat betwixt the king and the parliament* ; that befides the
" feafon was altogether unfit, whilft his majefty's ftandard was up, his proclamati-
" ons and declarations unrecalled, whereby his parliament was charged with trea-
" fon. That indeed his majefty had often protefted his tendernefs of the miferies
" of *Ireland*, and his refolution to maintain the proteftant religion and the laws of
" this kingdom ; but that thefe proteftations could give no fatisfaction to reafonable
" and indifferent men, when at the fame time feveral of the *Irifh* rebels and known
" favourers and agents for them were admitted to his majefty's prefence with grace
" and favour, nay fome of them employed in his fervice, when the cloaths, munition,
" and horfe, bought by the parliament for the fupport of the *Irifh* war were violently
" taken away, and applyed to the maintainance of an unnatural war againft his peo-
" ple ; that if his majefty would be pleafed to come back to his parliament they
" fhould be ready to fecure his royal perfon, crown, and dignity, with their lives
" and fortunes.

U P O N this the king publifhed the following declaration :

" I N the firft place he alledged the laws in his favour ; he denied that his fol-
" diers had committed any diforder or violence, and affirmed he had never fuffered
" them to opprefs any perfon whatfoever."

" H E recriminated upon the parliament ; he denied that there were any *Irifh*
" about him, and maintained that it was notorious calumny, like that caft upon him
" heretofore by Mr. *Pym*.

" H E faid the artillery horfes he had taken at *Chefter* were few in number and
" of fmall value, and for the cloaths, if the foldiers had taken any that were de-
" figned for *Ireland*, it was done without his order, and tho' he might have feized
" 3000 fuits which were going thither, yet he refufed to do it, and gave order for
" their fpeedy tranfportation."

" T H A T the parliament made no fcruple to employ an hundred thoufand
" pounds particularly appointed for the relief of *Ireland*."

" T H A T of near 500 members of which the lower houfe confifted, there re-
" mained not above 300, the reft having been driven away by tumults and threats, or
" withdrawn themfelves out of confcience from their defperate confultations ; that
" of above an hundred peers there remained but 15 or 16 of the upper houfe."

                                                                        T H A T

" THAT it was not the body of the parliament but the violent leading mem-
" bers were the authors of the war. (*a*)

AFTER this about the 16th of *September* the king perceiving he could no longer remain at *Nottingham* with safety, he marched to *Derby, Stafford, Leicester,*
and so to *Shrewsbury,* where the king had (through the negligence of the parliament in sending instructions to their general) the good fortune to receive safely considerable sums of money, as had been procured by his friends in *London,* together
with all the college plate, very considerable, which the university of *Oxford* affec-
tionately delivered for the king's support, and there he set up a mint, in the latter
end of *September* or beginning of *October.*

1642-3. THE 22d of *January* following the noted *Oxford* anti-parliament met,
which advised the king to borrow an hundred thousand pounds of the richest men
of his party; to that purpose the commons went into their respective counties to take
the number of those who were reckoned money'd men, and make a list, wherein were
set down the quality and ability of each.

THE commons being returned to *Oxford* with their lists, the taxes were pro-
portioned, after which the king sent circular letters to every particular person, to borrow of one an hundred, of another two hundred pounds, &c. promising to repay the
same as soon as he was able, and not forgeting to say in these letters, that this loan
was by the advice of his parliament. (*b*)

THESE letters were printed bearing date *Oxford, February* the 14th, in the
nineteenth year of his reign, 1643; on the top of each was writ with the king's own
hand, *CHARLES R.* they were signed,

{ *Edward Lyttleton,* } the speakers of the two houses.
{ *Samuel Eure,* }

One of these letters fell accidentally into my hands, directed to *Willoughby Manley,*
gent. at *Stafford.*

THE reader I hope will excuse this digression it being only designed to shew
the difference of success and reception his majesty met with almost immediately after
he had been so sorely disappointed at *Nottingham,* and what fund he had in the beginning of the war for the carrying on his military preparations.

(*c*) A. D. 1643. IN *July* captain *Hotham,* son to Sir *John Hotham,* governor of
Hull, being suspected by the parliament was imprisoned in *Nottingham* castle, whence
escaping he underhand treated with the earl of *Newcastle,* and coming to *Hull* he and
his father stood upon their guard. (*d*)

Kk 2

THE

(*a*) *All these messages &c. were taken from* Rushworth. ---- (*b*) *This parliament was
prorogued April 16th 1643.* ---- (*c*) Whitlock, *p.* 62. ---- (*d*) *He was seized by*
Sir John Meldrum. Rushworth.

(*a*) THE same year about *Christmass*, colonel *Hutchinson* governor of *Nottingham* castle, acquainted the parliament with an offer of the earl of *Newcastle* to pay him 10,000*l.* and to make him a lord and governor of the castle, to him and his heirs, if he would deliver it to him for the king, which *Hutchinson* refused.

(*b*) A. D. 1644. IN *June* colonel *Hutchinson* governor of *Nottingham* met with a party of *Newarkers*, flew captain *Thimbleby*, and took 50 of them; the same party from *Nottingham* the next day took more of the *Newarkers*, 20 gentlemen and officers and 60 of their horse and furniture.

(*c*) THE latter end of this year colonel *Thorney* with a party from *Nottingham*, took a garrison of the king's near *Newark*, and in it the master of the house, Sir *Roger Cooper* and his brother, and 50 others prisoners, with their arms.

(*d*) THE same year a party of the king's forces from *Newark* came forth to gather contribution, and took prisoners some countrymen that were in arrears; the committee of *Nottingham* having notice thereof sent forth a party who pursuing those of *Newark* they left their prisoners and five or six of their men behind, and hasted to their quarters; the *Nottingham* men followed them close, and so far, that another party of *Newark* forces came forth upon them, routed them, recovered their prisoners, and took of the parliament party, major *Meldrum*, lieutenant *Smith* and about 28 soldiers with their arms and horses.

(*e*) A. D. 1645. THE committee and the governor of *Nottingham* disagreed so much, that the parliament referred the difference to a committee *April* the 17th, and on the 21st of *April* colonel *Hutchinson*, governor of *Nottingham*, a member of the house, informed them that a party of horse from *Newark* had stormed a fort upon *Trent-bridge* near his garrison, and became masters of it, and put about 40 to the sword. It was referred to the committee of both houses to compose the differences between the governor and the committee, and to take care of the safety of the place.

(*f*) THE 5th of *May* some *Leicester* and *Nottingham* forces marching to regain *Trent-bridge*, the king's forces in it fled away at night, carrying with them what they could and set fire to the rest.

(*g*) THE 20th of *June* the *Scots* army being at *Nottingham* and Sir *Thomas Fairfax* at *Leicester*, it was referred to a committee of both kingdoms, to manage the armies to the best improvement of the public service. (the *Scots* were afterwards ordered to sit down before *Newark*.)

(*h*) THE 30th of *June* colonel *Hutchinson* took 60 horse and 48 prisoners, officers and arms.

THE

(*a*) Whitlock, *p.* 75. —— (*b*) id. *p.* 85. —— (*c*) id. *p.* 116. —— (*d*) id. *p.* 121. —— (*e*) id. *p.* 137. —— (*f*) id *p.* 139. —— (*g*) id. *p.* 147. —— (*h*) ib.

(a) THE 4th of *October* 1000 *l.* was ordered to the *Nottingham* horse who fought gallantly at the late fight at *Chester*, and other sums for others of his forces.

(b) A. D. 1645. *March* the 18th. *Nottinghamshire* having been highly oppressed by the armies lying before *Newark*, the house ordered to take it into consideration.

(c) 1646. *July* 11th. Order for reducement of the forces of *Nottingham*, and for money for that work, and for the losses and damages of that county.

(d) A. D. 1645. *February* the 13th. The king was brought to *Nottingham*, having been the 3d of the same month delivered to the *English* commissioners at *Newcastle*. (e) Sir *Thomas Fairfax* went and met the king, who stopt his horse, Sir *Thomas* alighted and kissed his majesty's hand, and afterwards mounted and discoursed with the king as they passed towards *Nottingham*: The king said to one of the commissioners: *That the general was a man of honour and kept his word with him.*

A. D. 1647. *July* the 15th. The forces in the north and the horse quartered in *Nottingham* sided with the army, and published a declaration of their adherence to the army commanded by general *Fairfax*. (f)

(g) A. D. 1648. *June* the 13th. The parliament was acquainted with a design to surprize *Nottingham* castle, but that the governor captain *Poulton* surprized and took prisoners the complotters, which were Sir *Marmaduke Langdale*, with ten more gentlemen in disguise.

THE 18th of *December* a sheriff of *Nottinghamshire* was chosen. *ibid.*

A. D. 1648. THE 27th of *January*, the garrison of *Nottingham* castle was mustered, by which it appears that then it consisted only of one company of foot, of 100 private men exclusive of drummers, commanded by captain *Poulton*, governor.

AT this time one *Lawrence Collin* was gunner of the castle, of whom 'tis remarkable, that after the garrison was disbanded, he chose to stay at *Nottingham*, in order to follow his former occupation, which was wool-combing, but the corporation offering to give him disturbance he petitioned *Cromwell*, which occasioned the following order to be sent to the governor, which accidentally dropt into my hands, *viz.*

" SIR,

" HIS highness the lord *Protector* having heard the petition of *Laurence Collin*, which is here enclosed, is pleased to recommend it unto you to speak
to

(a) Whitlock, *p.* 160. —— (b) id. *p.* 203. —— (c) id. *p.* 220. —— (d) id. *p.* 235. —— (e) *The commissioners were the earl of* Pembroke, *the earl of* Denbigh, *the* lord Montague, *named by the lords*: *And by the commons Sir* William Armine, *Sir* John Holland, *Sir* Walter Earl, *Sir* John Cook, *Mr.* John Crew, *and major general* Brown. id. *p.* 237.
—— (f) Rap. *from* Rushw. *vol.* II. *p.* 533. —— (g) id. *p.* 253.

" to the mayor and other magiftrates of *Nottingham*, to know the reafon why they will
" not fuffer the petitioner to fet up his trade in the town. And if there be no other caufe
" of exception, but that he is not a freeman, in regard he has faithfully ferved
" the commonwealth, his highnefs does think it fit that he fhould continue in the town,
" and be admitted to follow his calling for the maintainance of himfelf and family.
" (*a*) Which is all I am commanded to communicate to you from his highnefs by the
" hands of

" S I R

Whitehall, this 17th of *July*.   " your very humble

" and faithful fervant,

" *L I S L E   L O N G.*

A F T E R this he lived in quiet and laid the foundation for a thriving family
in *Nottingham*, which at this time is very confiderable, being ftrengthened by the
intermarriage into the family of *George Langford,* Efq; one who had not only been an
eminent furgeon, but alfo bore a commiffion in the parliament army, and was mayor
of *Nottingham* at the revolution. *Laurence* lived to the 91ft year of his age, as appears by his grave-ftone in St. *Nicholas's* church.

(*b*) A. D. 1650. T H E latter end of *May* or beginning of *June*, the general Sir
Thomas Fairfax, his regiment, and the train of artillery were at *Nottingham*, in their
march to the north.

(*c*) A. D. 1656. In *March* colonel *Hacker had apprehended feveral of the con-
fpirators againft *Cromwell* in *Nottinghamfhire* and *Leicefterfhire*, and kept them all
in awe. The confpiracy againft the protector began in march 1655; firft at *Salisbury,* then *Exeter, Northumberland, &c.* a ftrong declaration was publifhed by the
title of :

The Declaration of the free and well affected People of *England* now in Arms againft the Tyrant *C R O M W E L L.*

I T will be needlefs to repeat here at large, that in the year 1682 after a furrep-
tious furrender of the old charters of the town of *Nottingham,* a new charter was fent
down

(*a*) *Thefe laft lines were wrote by a different hand, I fuppofe, the hand of the
fubfcriber.* —— (*b*) Whitlock. —— (*c*) ib. *p.* 602.
(*) *Colonel* Hacker *was a gentleman, a native of the county of* Nottingham, *he attended the king with about* 30 *officers and gentlemen with halberts, to the bar of
the court, he was afterwards commanding officer at the king's execution, and was
on the fcaffold with him, all which at the reftoration coft him his life.*

down by king *Charles* II. and what diſturbance it occaſioned ; nor that king *James* II. by *quo waranto* took away the charter of this town, granted by his brother in *May* 1687, having already taken notice of it in ſection VI. but ſhall proceed to what paſ-ſed ſome time before, and at the revolution, wherein *Nottingham* was particularly concerned.

A. D. 1687. King *James* having found by experience in the late reign, that the ſeverities exerciſed upon proteſtant diſſenters did not produce any advantageous ef-fect, he reſolved to lay aſide the lion's ſkin and make uſe of the foxes tail. He therefore ſent emiſſaries into all parts, to let the diſſenters know, that he intended to take them into his peculiar protection, that he looked upon them as his very loyal and obedient ſubjects, that he would at all events procure to them a full liberty of conſcience, and in order to ſhew he was in earneſt, he publiſhed on the 4th of *April* 1687, his declaration for liberty of conſcience, forgetting how ill his brother's de-claration for the ſame was taken by the parliament, (*a*) nay not thinking the firſt ſufficient he publiſhed a ſecond the 27th of *April* 1688, and ordered the biſhops to ſee it read in all churches and chapels ; how that ſucceeded I ſhall not hear mention leaſt I ſhould be led too far from my purpoſe.

T H E king having by his *quo warranto* taken away the late new charter of king *Charles* II. that he might have it in his power to make ſuch alterations and re-ſervations to himſelf, as might make this as well as other corporations, to be at his en-tire devotion. He ſent down his commiſſion to two perſons of this town, *viz.* *Timo-thy Tomlinſon* and *Caleb Wilkinſon*, by which they were ſtiled regulators, with power to diſplace ſuch members of the corporation as had not acted according to their truſt, or ſuch as would not anſwer the king's gracious deſign, in favour (as was pretended) of the diſſenters, in giving their vote for ſuch perſons to repreſent them in parlia-ment as would be for ſettling liberty of conſcience by a law. King *James*'s above-mentioned intention in taking away the charters, plainly appears by the contents of a letter of Mr. *Nathan Wright*, deputy recorder of *Nottingham*, (who ſollicited for a new charter) to *George Langford*, Eſq; then mayor, dated *June* the 21ſt 1688, wherein he ſays :

" T H A T his majeſty had referred their petition to the attorney-general."

" T H A T he [Mr. *Wright*] had attended upon him almoſt every day ſince, and " that he thinks that the matter is almoſt come to a concluſion."

" T H A T all the preſent members of the corporation are to ſtand, all the cor-" poration's deſires are granted, only in the buſineſs of the elections of officers of the " town, Mr. Attorney General, will not be perſwaded *to let the populace have any* " *vote, as being a matter contrary to his Majeſty's deſign,* and tending to a diſturbance " among

---

(*a*) Charles II. *publiſhed his declaration for liberty of conſcience* March 15, 1672, *the commons not only addreſſed the King on* February *the* 19th *following, but brought a ſecond addreſs againſt it the* 26th *of the ſame month, inſomuch that the king in order to appeaſe them, not only recalled the ſame, but broke the ſeal with his own hands.*

" among themselves (the corporation) and he will limit all elections of mayor, alder-
" men capital-counsellors, counsellors, coroners, sheriffs, chamberlains, &c. to be
" chosen by the mayor, aldermen, and common-council, and no others. This will
" be a new thing to you [says Mr. *Wright*] but it is not to be avoided, nor is it much
" material, for *his majesty referves to himself a power of displacing any member of*
" *the corporation, and also to nominate and appoint others to succeed such as shall be*
" *removed.*"

" T H E S E are the terms upon which all charters are granted at this day, and
" none are to pass without them, &c."

AND here I should be wanting in doing justice to Mr. *Langford* the
mayor, (who was a dissenter) if by suppressing his answer to the above letter, I
should give room to persons of a different persuasion to pass an unfair judgment upon his conduct. This answer dated *June* the 23d 1688, signed by himself and five
aldermen, *viz. Thomas Smith, John Hawkins, Charles Harvey, Thomas Collin*, and
John Hides, is as follows :

        S I R,

" UPON the perusal of your letter we called a hall and are troubled at nothing
" but the exclusion of the popularity or common burgesses in the election of
" the town officers which they have always voted for, (that is to say) in the electi-
" on of head-counsellors and counsellors, higher officers they have not been con-
" cerned in. They will without doubt look upon it as a great infringement of their
" priviledges and have a very ill eye upon us, supposing it is done by our means ;
" or cause them to apprehend ill of the government, which we would by no means
" have them to do : Now dear sir we would intreat you if possible to prevail with
" Mr Attorney General, that they may have their votes as formerly, so they will be
" exceedingly obliged, and we hope his majesty's designs not in the least hindered,
" for his majesty having power to displace and place at his pleasure, we humbly con-
" ceive they cannot be injurious. We must be thankful for any thing the king will
" allow us, but if we had this favour still continued to us, we are very sensible it
" would be much for our peace, and make the government very acceptable to them,
" and much further his majesty's service. Therefore we entreat you once more to be
" very urgent on this point, but if it cannot be obtained we humbly submit, it not be-
" coming us to dispute it any longer, &c."

BOTH these letters as also the three following, are in the possession of Mr.
John Nevil of this town, found among the papers of *George Langford*, Esq; his
grandfather.

NOTWITHSTANDING the difficulties and delays which were
made above with relation to the dispatch of this new charter, frequent letters were
sent down to the mayor, alderman *Harvey*, and others, to keep the dissenters in heart,
and expectation of wonderful great things to be done for them, yet when the king had
signed the calling of a parliament, upon the news of the prince of *Orange's* arrival,
the charter had not passed the great-seal.

                                                                        WHAT

WHAT I have juſt now ſaid concerning the pains that were taken by the government, to the very laſt, to keep the diſſenters ſteadily attached to king *James*, will ſufficiently appear by theſe letters : *viz.*

To Alderman *Harvey*.

SIR,

" I Think it requiſite to direct this to you, Mr. *Tomlinſon* declining any farther
" correſpondence ; the noiſe of the expected invaſion ſtill continues ; I do pre-
" ſume you are alarmed with the rumours of changes in other corporations as well as
" *London*, which we have here no reaſon to expect, notwithſtanding what is publiſhed
" in the gazette, neither can they indeed be ſo reſtored, any more then a dead man re-
" vived again. The experiment at *London* has not anſwered the expectation of
" ſome perſons, for they have this week choſen ſuch aldermen and ſheriffs as are
" of the ſame principles with thoſe lately diſmiſſed, through the diſſenters not ap-
" pearing ; Sir *John Chapman*, the preſent mayor by commiſſion is choſen for the
" year enſuing ; I think it adviſeable for you to appoint ſome perſons to take care
" of your corporation concerns, if you think me capable of it, I ſhall deſire it, I ſhall
" uſe my endeavours to ſerve you. *The King is faſt to maintain liberty for the diſ-*
" *ſenters, and lately ſaid, death itſelf could not work a change of his mind therein.*
" I am &c.

London October 11, 1688.   " EDWARD ROBERTS."

To *George Langford*, Eſq;

SIR,

" H IS Majeſty has taken into conſideration how ready the diſſenters have been
" to ſerve him, and how ſubmiſſive to his commands in the late alteration
" made in the corporations, &c. and that endeavours have and may be uſed to preju-
" dice their minds in reference to the alterations of affairs, as if his majeſty was
" changed in his kindneſs to them. I am therefore commanded by his majeſty, to
" aſſure you from him, that he has the ſame value and eſteem for them he ever had,
" and ſtill owns them for his friends, and will never depart from his declarations,
" but will with his utmoſt endeavours purſue the ſame until liberty of conſcience is
" eſtabliſhed by law ; he has appointed a committee, from whom he expects to re-
" ceive from time to time, an account of what grievances and hardſhips may befall
" the diſſenters, in order to their relief ; if therefore any ſuch thing ſhould happen,
" you are deſired forthwith to ſignify the ſame to me. His majeſty expects that
" the diſſenters continue the ſame affection and readineſs for his ſervice, they al-
" ways profeſſed, and to afford him their utmoſt aſſiſtance on all occaſions, eſpeci-
" ally now in a time of invaſion ; and leaſt you or others may be ſurprized by falſe
" news and repreſentations, which perhaps may be induſtriouſly ſpread for that end,
" you ſhall from time to time have a true account of ſuch public matters as ſhall be
" neceſſary for your information ; I deſire you likewiſe that as matters come to your
" knowledge, or certain information, of any factious news, or of any projects carried on

Ll

to

" to promote fedition, or fecret liftings of men, or rebellion, to give in writing from
" time to time, a true account thereof.   You are defired to confider that *there is*
" *none that promote any fuch thing, or wifh well to this invafion, but is an enemy to*
" *his majefty, as well as to your liberty and intereft; and that they that are other-*
" *wife minded, are for reviving a perfecuting fpirit, and will thereby contract the*
" *blood, mifchief, and guilt, that may be confequent thereon;* it is not a time to halt
" in thefe matters, therefore if you have any love to the king or your own liberty,
" be not flack therein, but ufe your utmoft endeavours to prevent fuch mifchiefs, to
" ftrengthen the hands of his majefty, who will be found firm to you, if you are not
" wanting to yourfelves; this you may communicate to your friends of all forts; if
" there be any with you, which you conceive more proper for what is propofed than
" yourfelf, let me know their names when you have received, and confidered here-
" of; let me as foon as may be, underftand your fenfe and acceptance hereof; di-
" rect your letter according to former directions.   I am

" your affectionate

London 20th *of November* 1688.   " friend to ferve you

EDWARD ROBERTS.

P. S. " By the account from *Salisbury* of this day's date, we are informed that upon
" the mufter of the three regiments that were drawn towards the prince of *Orange,*
" there wanted not above an hundred men; we hear likewife that the lord *De-la-*
" *ware,* with feven other lords in confederacy are raifing forces to join the prince
" of *Orange,* and that they intend to rendezvous at *Nottingham,* of which I thought
" fit to advife you, and to defire you to ufe all your endeavours to prevent the dif-
" fenters concurrence with them; they have hitherto kept themfelves free, and
" 'tis certainly their duty and intereft fo to do; it may be of very ill confequence
" if the magiftracy of your town countenance them; as any thing falls out worthy
" of communication, let me hear from you, as you fhall from me, how matters
" go. I am
" yours as before
EDWARD ROBERTS.

T H E day of the date of this letter, the earl of *Devonfhire* at the head of a great
number of *Derbyfhire* gentlemen, had declared at *Derby* for a free parliament,
agreeable to the prince of *Orange's* declaration, And

T W O days after, *viz.* on the 23d of *November,* the nobility, gentry and commonality, that rendezvoufed at *Nottingham,* fubfcribed there the following declaration:

" W E the nobility, gentry and commonality, of thefe northern countries, affem-
" bled at *Nottingham* for the defence of the laws, religion and properties,
" according to the freeborn liberties and priviledges defcended to us from our an-
" ceftors, as the undoubted birth-right of the fubjects of this kingdom of *England,*
" (not doubting but the infringers and invaders of our rights will reprefent us to the
" reft of the nation in the moft malicious drefs they can put upon us) do here unanimoufly

---

(*a*) *Life of* William III. *p.* 145-6.

" nimoufly think it our duty to declare to the reft of our proteftant fellow fubjects
" the grounds of our prefent undertaking.

" WE by innumerable grievances made fenfible that the very fundamentals of our
" religion, liberties, and properties, are about to be rooted out by a jefuitical privy-
" council, as it has been of late too apparent. 1ft. By the king's difpenfing with all
" the eftablifhed laws at his pleafure. 2d. By difplacing all officers out of all offices
" of truft and advantage, and placing others in their room that are known papifts,
" defervedly made incapable by the eftablifhed laws of this land. 3d. By deftroy-
" ing the charters of moft corporations in the land. 4th. By difcouraging all per-
" fons that are not papifts, and preferring fuch as turn to popery. 5th. By difpla-
" cing all honeft and confcientious men judges, unlefs they would contrary to their
" confciences, declare that to be law which was meerly arbitrary. 6th. By brand-
" ing all men with the name of rebels that but offered to juftify the laws in a legal
" courfe againft the arbitrary proceedings of the king, or any of his corrupt mini-
" fters. 7th. By burthening the nation with an army, to maintain the violation
" of the rights of the fubject, and by difcountenancing the eftablifhed
" religion. 8th. By forbidding the fubjects the benefit of petitioning, and con-
" ftruing them libellers, fo rendering the laws a nofe of wax, to ferve their arbitra-
" ry ends, and many more fuch like, too long here to enumerate.

" WE being thus made fenfible of the arbitrary and tyrannical government, that
" is by the influence of jefuitical counfels coming upon us, do unanimoufly declare,
" that not being willing, to deliver our pofterity over to fuch a condition of popery
" and flavery, as the aforefaid oppreffions do inevitably threaten ; we will to the
" utmoft of our power, oppofe the fame, by joining with the prince of *Orange* (whom
" we hope God Almighty has fent to refcue us from the oppreffions aforefaid) and
" will ufe our utmoft endeavours for the recovery of our almoft ruined laws, liber-
" ties and religion, and herein we hope all good proteftant fubjects, will with their
" lives and fortunes be affiftant to us, and not be bugbear'd with the opprobrious
" terms of rebels, by which they would affright us to become perfect flaves to their
" tyrannical infolencies and ufurpations ; for we affure ourfelves that no rational and
" unbyaffed perfon will judge it rebellion to defend our laws and religion, which
" all our princes have at their coronation fworn to do ; which oath, how well it has
" been obferved of late, we defire a free parliament may have the confideration
" of.

" WE own it rebellion to refift a king that governs by law ; and he was always
" accounted a tyrant that made his will the law, and to refift fuch a one we juftly
" efteem no rebellion, but a neceffary defence ; and on this confideration we doubt
" not of all honeft men's affiftance ; and humbly hope for, and implore the great
" God's protection, who turneth the hearts of his people as pleafeth him beft, it ha-
" ving been obferved that people can never be of one mind without his infpiration,
" which has in all ages confirmed that obfervation : *Vox populi vox dei.*

" THE prefent reftoring the charters, and reverfing the oppreffing and unjuft
" judgment given on the fellows of *Magdalen* college, is plain, are but to ftill the
" people, like plumbs to children, by deceiving them for a while ; but if they fhall
" by this ftratagem be fooled, till this prefent ftorm that threatens the papifts be
" paffed, as foon as they fhall be refettled, the former oppreffion will be put on

" with greater vigour ; but we hope, *in vain is the net spread in the sight of the*
" *birds* : For the papist old rule is, *that faith is not to be kept with hereticks,* as
" they term proteſtants, tho' the popiſh religion is the greateſt hereſy : And queen
" *Mary's* ſo ill obſerving her promiſes to the *Suffolk* men, that helped her to the
" throne, and above all the pope's diſpenſing with the breach of oaths, treaties or
" promiſes at his pleaſure, when it makes for the holy church, as they term ; theſe
" we ſay are ſuch convincing reaſons to hinder us from giving credit to the aforeſaid
" mock-ſhews of redreſs, that we think ourſelves bound in conſcience to reſt on no
" ſecurity that ſhall not be approved by a freely elected parliament, to whom
" under God we refer our cauſe."

THERE are men ſtill living in this town who well remember, that above
ten days before the foregoing declaration was made publick, the duke of *Devonſhire*
the earl of *Stamford,* the lord *How,* and other noblemen, and abundance of gentry of
the county of *Nottingham,* reſorted to this town and went to meet one another at their
reſpective inns, daily increaſing in number, and continued at *Nottingham* till the arrival of lord *Delamere,* with between 4 and 500 horſe ; this nobleman quartered at
the *Feather's* inn, whither all the reſt of the noblemen and gentlemen came to meet
him ; and 'till this time the people of the town were unacquainted with the reſult of
theſe frequent conſultations, when the abovementioned lord, after he had ſtaid a
while in the town, having a mind to try the diſpoſition of the populace, on a ſudden
ordered the trumpets to ſound to arms, giving out that the king's forces were within
four miles of *Nottingham,* whereupon, the whole town was in alarm, multitudes who
had horſes mounted and accoutred themſelves with ſuch arms as they had, whilſt o-
thers in vaſt numbers on foot appeared, ſome with fire-locks, ſome with ſwords, ſome
with other weapons, even pitchforks not excepted ; and being told of the neceſſity
of ſecuring the paſſage over the *Trent,* they immediately drew all the boats that then
were near at hand, to the north bank of that river, and with them, and ſome timber
and boards on the wharf, with barrels, and all the frames of the market-ſtalls, barri-
caded the north ſide of the *Trent.* My lord *Delamere* and his party, well pleaſed
with the readineſs of the people to give their aſſiſtance, his lordſhip ſent his men
and ſome officers to the prince of *Orange,* but himſelf with a few officers ſtaid till
the next day, being ſaturday, which is the principal market-day, when he, the duke
of *Devonſhire,* the lord *How,* &c. appeared at the *Malt-croſs,* and in the face of a
full market, the lord *Delamere* in a ſpeech declared to the people, the danger their
religion and liberty were in under the arbitrary proceedings of the king, and that
providence had ſent his highneſs the prince of *Orange,* under God, to deliver them
from popery and ſlavery, for which reaſon according to the prince his declaration,
they were for a free parliament and hoped their concurrence ; this was ſeconded by
a ſpeech of the duke of *Devonſhire,* and alſo of the lord *How,* which was followed
by the ſhouts of the people, who cryed out *a free parliament ! a free parliament !*
This done lord *Delamere* departed to follow his troops, whilſt the duke and lord
How, made it known that they were for raiſing horſe in defence of their liberty, and
would liſt ſuch as were willing to be entertained, whereupon upwards of an hundred
men who offered themſelves, were entered that ſame day.

IN this month of *November,* princeſs *Anne* privately withdrew from court,
leaving a letter to the queen behind her, to ſhew the reaſons of her retreat, which if
it had not been produced, the king's own guard would in all probability have joined
the

the enraged mob, and have torn the popifh party to pieces, upon a furmife that they had either made away with her or confined her to the tower. This (a) princefs with the lady *Churchill* and the lady *Berkeley*, took coach privately at the bifhop of *London's* houfe and went directly to *Nottingham*, attended by that prelate, the earl of *Dorfet*, and about 40 horfemen ; but there the earl of *Devonfhire* (after fhe had ftaid feveral days in *Nottingham*) gave her a guard of 200, from whence fhe retired to *Oxford*, where prince *George* foon after met her, with a detachment of the prince of *Orange's* forces.

SOME days before her departure it was reported that the queen had treated her very rudely, and proceeded fo far as to ftrike her, which probably might caufe that fufpicion in the mob, and excite them to go to *Whitehall*.

1688.

ON the 3d of *December* was fent another letter, and the laft (as I prefume) figned *Edward Roberts*, directed to *George Langford*, Efq; which follows :

SIR,

" YOU cannot but underftand the ftate and condition the kingdom is now
" brought to, and that there is no way to efcape or preferve it from ruin and de-
" ftruction, and ourfelves in particular from mifery and oppreffion, but by fome heal-
" ing methods in parliament ; if you have therefore any love for yourfelves, the
" king, or kingdom, let it now appear by an active and united heart among diffen-
" ters, by endeavouring the election of men to reprefent them in the approaching
" parliament, who are moderate and men of principle, that will concur with his ma-
" jefty in fettling an *equal* liberty of confcience, as well as eftablifh the proteftant
" religion. Pray therefore be not remifs, but forthwith, with the utmoft, endeavour
" to engage all forts of diffenters, with others, to concur in chufing fuch perfons ;
" and let not noife and rumour difcourage you, wherein you will ferve God, the
" king, and fecure yourfelves, and preferve your country. All parties now pretend
" that liberty of confcience is both juft and reafonable, but it cannot be expected
" it fhould be eftablifhed by law, but only by men of principle ; therefore once
" more be mindful herein, and let me underftand who you have in your thoughts to
" elect ; this is the laft effort, what is not obtained now, is loft for ever, which I
" hope you will confider." I am &c.

ABOUT this time arofe a fudden rumour that the *Irifh* were coming to drive all before them, which threw this town and the whole county for a little while into great confternation, as it had done other places till they were better informed. It
feems

(a) *When queen* Anne (*then princefs*) *did fly from* Whitehall, *the bifhop of* London *brought her fecretly to my lord* Dorfet, *and my lady, who was the bifhop's niece, both who, furnifhed her royal highnefs with every thing neceffary to it, attended her northward as far as* Northampton, *where he quickly brought a body of horfe to ferve for her guard, and from thence went to* Nottingham *to confer with the duke of* Devonfhire. Collin's *peerage, vol.* I. *p.* 576.

seems this frightful report had for its foundation the lord *Feversham's* abruptly disbanding the army in obedience to king *James's* orders, (for which he was greatly blamed) when some *Irish* soldiers of the disbanded troops, finding themselves moneyless and incapable of subsisting in a country where they were so generally hated, resolved to keep themselves from starving by forcibly entering a country house, whereupon a man of the neighbourhood run directly to *London*, crying as he passed, that the *Irish* were up and marching to *London*; firing of houses, and putting men, women and children to the sword. This news immediately flew through the city, and caused a strange pannick fear, and thence spread suddenly all over *England*, without any farther ill-consequence.

A P P E N D I X.

APPENDIX

Ex Rotulo Paten. a' 27. HENRICI 6ti. p. 2. m. 6. Pro Burgenfibus Villæ de NOTTINGHAM de Confirmatione.

R EX omnibus ad quos &c. falutem. Infpeximus cartam domini *Henrici* nuper regis *Anglie* patris noftri factam in hæc verba: *Henricus Dei gratia Rex Anglie & Francie & dominus Hibernie*, archiepifcopis, epifcopis, abbatibus, prioribus, ducibus, comitibus, baronibus, jufticiariis, et vice comitibus, prepofitis, miniftris et omnibus ballivis, et fidelibus fuis falutem. Infpeximus literas patentes domini *Richardi* nuper regis *Anglie* fecundi poft conqueftum factas in hec verba: *Richardus Dei gratia Rex Anglie & Francie & dominus Hibernie*, omnibus ad quos prefentes litere pervenerint falutem. Infpeximus cartam domini *Edwardi* nuper regis *Anglie* avi noftri in hec verba: *Edwardus Dei gratia Rex Anglie dominus Hibernie & dux Aquitanie*, archiepifcopis, epifcopis, abbatibus, prioribus, comitibus, baronibus, jufticiariis, vice comitibus, prepofitis, miniftris, et omnibus ballivis et fidelibus fuis falutem. Infpeximus cartam celebris memorie domini *Edwardi* nuper regis *Anglie* patris noftri in hec verba: *Edwardus Dei gratia Rex Anglie dominus Hibernie et dux Aquitanie*, archiepifcopis, epifcopis, abbatibus, prioribus, comitibus, baronibus, jufticiariis, vicecomitibus, prepofitis, miniftris, et omnibus ballivis et fidelibus fuis falutem. Infpeximus cartam confirmationis quam dominus *Henricus* quondam rex *Anglie* avus nofter fecit burgenfibus de *Nottyngham* in hec verba: *Henricus Dei gratia Rex Anglie dominus Hibernie, dux Normandie et Aquitanie, comes Andegavie*, archiepifcopis, epifcopis, abbatibus, prioribus, comitibus, baronibus, jufticiariis, vicecomitibus, prepofitis, miniftris et omnibus ballivis et fidelibus fuis falutem. Infpeximus cartam *Johannis* regis patris noftri factam burgenfibus de *Nottyngham* in hec verba: *Johannes Dei gratia Rex Anglie dominus Hibernie dux Normandie et Aquitanie comes Andegavie*, archiepifcopis, epifcopis, abbatibus, prioribus, comitibus, baronibus, jufticiariis, vice comitibus et omnibus ballivis, et fidelibus fuis totius *Anglie* falutem. Sciatis nos conceffiffe et hac carta noftra confirmaffe burgenfibus noftris de *Nottyngham* omnes illas liberas confuetudines quas habuerunt tempore *Henrici* regis proavi noftri et tempore *Henrici* regis patris noftri ficut carta ejufdem *Henrici* patris noftri teftatur, fcilicet *Thol* et *Theam* et *Infongethef* et *Theolonia* a *Thurmodefton* ufque ad *Newark* et de omnibus *Trentham* tranfeuntibus ita plenarie ut in burgo de *Nottyngham* et ex alia parte a ducto ultra *Rempefton* ufque ad aquam de *Radford* in le *North* et de *Bykeresdik*. Homines etiam de *Nottinghamfhire* et *Derbyfhire* venire debent ad burgum de *Nottingham*
die

die veneris et fabbati cum quadrigis et fummagiis fuis, nec aliquis infra decem leucas in circuitu de *Nottyngham* tinctos pannos operari debet, nifi in burgo de *Nottyngham*. Et fi aliquis undecunque fit in burgo de *Nottyngham* manferit uno anno et uno die tempore pacis et abfque calumpnia nullus poftea nifi rex in eum jus habebit. Et quicunque burgenfium terram vicini fui emerit et poffiderit per annum integrum et diem unum abfque calumpnia parentum venditoris fi in *Anglia* fuerint, poftea eam quiete poffidebit neque prepofito burgi de *Nottyngham* aliquem burgenfium, calumpnianti refpondeatur, nifi aliquis fuerit accufator in caufa. Et quicunque in burgo manferit cujufcunque feodi fit reddere debet fimul cum burgenfibus *Tallagia* et defectus burgi adimplere. Omnes etiam qui ad forum de *Nottyngham* venerint a vefpere die veneris ufque ad vefperam fabbati non namientur nifi pro firma noftra et iter de *Trent* liberum effe debeat navigantibus, quantum partica una obtinebit ex utraque parte fili aquæ. Preterea concessimus etiam de proprio dono noftro et hac carta noftra confirmavimus eifdem liberis burgenfibus noftris *Guildam mercatoriam* cum omnibus libertatibus et liberis confuetudinibus que ad guildam mercatoriam debent, vel folent pertinere et quod ipfi quieti fint de theoloneo per totam terram noftram intra nundinas et extra, et licet illis quem voluerint ex fuis in fine anni prepofitum fuum facere qui de firma noftra pro ipfis refpondeat. Ita quod fi idem prepofitus nobis difpliceat illum ad voluntatem noftram removebimus et ipfi alium ad libitum noftrum fubftituent, conceffimus etiam eifdem burgenfibus ut quicunque ab eis fubftitutus fuerit prepofitus ejufdem burgi folvat firmam ejufdem burgi ad dominicum fcaccarium noftrum ubicunque fuerit in *Anglia* ad duos terminos, medietatem fcilicet ad claufum pafche et medietatem in octabis fancti michaelis. Quare volumus et firmiter precipimus quod predicti burgenfes habeant et teneant, predictas confuetudines, bene et in pace libere et quiete honorifice et pacifice, plenarie et integre ficut habuerunt tempore *Henrici* regis proavi noftri et tempore *Henrici* regis patris noftri cum augmentis que eis conceffimus, et prohibemus ne quis contra hanc cartam noftram predictos burgenfes vexare prefumat in aliquo, fuper decem libras foris facti noftri, ficut eis conceffimus et rationabili carta noftra confirmavimus dum effemus comes *Moretonie*; his teftibus G. filio *Petri* comitis *Effexie*; *W. Briwere*; *Hugone Bard*: *B.* filio *Rogeri*; *W. de Studevill*; *Henrico de Nevill*; *S. de Pater*; *G. de Northfolk*; data per manum *Simonis* archidiaconi *Wellenfis* et *J. de Gray* archidiacono *Cliveland* apud *Clypfton* die *Martii* regni noftri anno primo. Nos igitur has donationes et conceffiones ratas habentes et gratas, eis predictis burgenfibus pro nobis et heredibus noftris concedimus et confirmamus. Preterea conceffimus de proprio dono noftro et hac carta noftra confirmavimus pro nobis et heredibus noftris eifdem burgenfibus et eorum heredibus quod predictam firmam ejufdem burgi videlicet quinquaginta et duas libras blanc reddant nobis per manum fuam ad fcaccarium noftrum ad duos terminos fcilicet viginti et fex libras blanc ad claufum pafche et viginti et fex libras blanc in octabis fancti *Michaelis* et quod ipfi et eorum heredes habeant et teneant predictam villam de *Nottyngham* per predictam firmam quinquaginta duarum librarum blanc, ficut predictum eft. Conceffimus etiam pro nobis et heredibus noftris eifdem burgenfibus et heredibus fuis quod capiant tronagium in villa de *Nottyngham* de mercandifis que confiftunt in pondere ficut capi confuevit in aliis burgis noftris et civitatibus per *Angliam*. Et quod habeant coronatores ex feipfis in eadem villa de *Nottyngham*. Quare volumus et firmiter precipimus quod predicti burgenfes et eorum heredes habeant et teneant de proprio dono noftro libertates confuetates, et confuetudines predictas bene et in pace, libere quiete et integre videlicet quod reddant nobis per manum fuam fingulis annis ad fcaccarium noftrum ad duos terminos predictos, predictas quinquaginta et duas libras blanc, et

quod

quod ipfi et eorum heredes habeant et teneant predictam villam per predictam firmiam quinquaginta duarum librarum blanc, et quod capiant tronagium predictum et habeant coronatores ex feipfis in eadem villa de *Nottyngham* ficut predictum eft ; his teftibus *J. Bathonieni, R. Dunelmenfi, W. Carliolenfi*, epifcopis, *H. de Burgo*, comite *Kauc* : Jufticiario *Anglie*. *Hugone de Nevil, Galfredo de Lucy, Stephano de Segrave, Radulpho* filio *Nicholai, Henrico de Capella* et aliis, dat : per manum venerabilis patris *R. Ciceftrenfis*, epifcopi cancellarii noftri apud *Weftmonafterium* vicefimo quarto die *Februarii*, anno regni noftri quarto decimo. Infpeximus etiam quandam aliam cartam quam idem avus nofter fecit eifdem burgenfibus in hec verba : *Henricus* dei gratia rex *Anglie*, dominus *Hibernie*, dux *Normandie Aquitanie* et comes *Andegavie*, archiepifcopis, epifcopis, abbatibus, prioribus, comitibus, baronibus, jufticiariis, vice comitibus, prepofetis, miniftris et omnibus ballivis et fidelibus fuis, falutem. Sciatis nos conceffiffe et hac carta noftra confirmaffe burgenfibus noftris *Nottyngham* quod ipfi et eorum heredes in perpetuum per totam terram et poteftatem noftram habeant hanc libertatem videlicet quod ipfi vel eorum bona quocunque locorum in poteftate noftra inventa non arreftentur pro aliquo debito de quo fidejuffores aut principales debitores non exftiterint nifi forte ipfi debitores de eorum fint communia et poteftate habentes unde de debitis fuis in toto vel in parte fatisfacere poffint et dicti burgenfes, creditoribus eorumdem debitorum in jufticia de fuerint et de hoc rationabiliter conftare poffit. Conceffimus etiam et hac carta noftra confirmavimus eifdem burgenfibus, quod in perpetuum retornum brevium noftrorum de fummonitionibus fcaccarii noftri de omnibus ad burgum noftrum *Nottyngham* pertinentibus, ita quod nullus vice comes aut alius, ballivus vel minifter nofter de cetero intromittant fe de hujufmodi fummonitionibus aut diftrictionibus faciendis in predicto burgo nifi per defectum dictorum burgenfium aut ballivorum ejufdem burgi. Quare volumus et firmiter precipimus, pro nobis et heredibus noftris, quod predicti burgenfes et eorum heredes in perpetuum habent libertates prefcriptas ficut predictum eft. Et prohibemus fuper foris facturam noftram decem librarum ne quis eos contra libertates illas in aliquo injufte vexet, difturbet vel inquietet. His teftibus *Rogero le Picot* comite *Norfolkie* marefcallo *Anglie, Radulpho* filio *Nicholai, Johanne de Leffyngton, Richardo de Grey, Willielmo de Grey, Imberto Pu-----, Wankelino de Ardern, Petro Everard, Willielmo Germyn*, et aliis. Dat : per manum noftram apud *Nottyngham* viceffimo die julii anno regni noftri triceffimo nono. Infpeximus infuper cartam quam celebris memorie dominus *Edwardus* quondam rex *Anglie* pater nofter fecit eifdem burgenfibus in hec verba : *Edwardus* dei gratia rex *Anglie* dominus *Hibernie* et dux *Aquitanie*, archiepifcopis, epifcopis, abbatibus, prioribus, comitibus, baronibus, jufticiariis, vice comitibus, prepofitis, miniftris et omnibus ballivis et fidelibus fuis falutem. Cum nos ob certas tranfgreffiones quas burgenfes et communitas ville noftre *Nottynzham* fecerunt ex fiducia libertatum fuarum eandem villam cum omnibus libertatibus ad ipfam fpectantibus ceperimus, et per triennium et amplius detinuerimus in manu noftra volentes eifdem burgenfibus et communitati gratiam facere fpecialem, eandem villam cum omnibus libertatibus quas burgenfes et homines ipfius ville per cartas progenitorum noftrorum regum *Anglie* prius habuerunt, reftituimus eifdem concedendo pro nobis et heredibus noftris quod iidem burgenfes et communitas omnibus eifdem libertatibus eodem modo de cetero gaudeant et utantur quo tempore captionis ville predicte in manum noftram, eis juxta tenorem cartarum predictarum rationabiliter utebantur. Ita quod ipfi et eorum fucceffores reddant de eadem villa nobis et heredibus noftris fingulis annis ad fcaccarium noftrum quinquaginta duas libras in forma qua prius eas inde nobis reddere confueverunt, et quod octo libras de incremento nobis et heredibus noftris inde nihil

ominus

ominus reddant annuatim. Et ad revelationem status burgensium et aliorum hominum ejusdem ville conceffimus pro nobis et heredibus nostris, quod ipsi de cetero habeant in eadem villa unum majorem de seipsis quem congregatis burgensibus utriuf-
que burgi ejusdem ville singulis annis in festo sancti michaelis unanimi assensu et vo-
luntate eligant ut presit ballivis et aliis de eadem villa in omnibus que pertinent ad
utriusque burgi ejusdem ville regimen et juvamen, et quod statim eadem electione
facta eligant unum ballivum de uno burgo et alium de alio burgo pro diversitate con-
suetudinum in eisdem burgis habitantium qui ea que pertinent ad officium suum ex-
equantur, et quod ipsi et eorum successores preter feriam suam per octo dies ad festum
sancti *Mathei* apostoli durantem habeant in perpetuum unam aliam feriam in eadem
villa singulis annis per quindecim dies duraturam videlicet in vigilia in die et in
crastino festi sancti *Edmundi* regis et martyris et per duodecim dies sequentes nisi
feria illa sit ad nocumentum vicinarum feriarum. Quare volumus et firmiter precipimus pro nobis et heredibus nostris quod predicti burgenses et homines et eorum
successores preter feriam suam per octo dies ad festum sancti *Mathei* apostoli durantem, habeant in perpetuum unam aliam feriam in eadem villa singulis annis per quindecim dies durantem, videlicet in vigilia in die et in crastino festi sancti *Edmundi*
regis et martyris et per duodecim dies sequentes cum omnibus libertatibus et liberis
consuetudinibus ad hujusmodi feriam pertinentibus nisi feria illa sit ad nocumentum
vicinarum feriarum sicut predictum est. His testibus venerabilibus patribus *R. Ba-
thoniensi* et *Wellensi* ; et *A. Dunelmensi* episcopis ; *Thoma de Clare, Otone de Gran-
disono, Johanne de Vescy, Roberto de Tibitot, Roberto* filio *Johannis*, et aliis. Dat.
per manum nostram apud *Lincolum* undecimo die *Februarii* anno regni nostri duodecimo. Nos autem concessiones confirmationes et restitutiones predictas ratas habentes et gratas, eas pro nobis et heredibus nostris quantum in nobis est prefatis burgensibus et eorum heredibus et successoribus burgensibus ejusdem ville concedimus et
confirmamus sicut cartæ predicte rationabiliter testantur. Et insuper concessimus
eis pro nobis et heredibus nostris, quod licet ipsi vel eorum antecessores burgenses e-
jusdem ville aliqua vel aliquibus libertatum predictarum hactenus usi non fuerint, ipsi
tamen et heredes ac successores sui libertatibus illis et earum qualibet et sine occa-
sione vel impedimento nostri vel heredum nostrorum, justiciariorum, esceatorum,
vicecomitum aut aliorum ballivorum seu ministrorum quorumcunque de cetero plene
gaudeant et utantur. Preterea volentes eisdem burgensibus gratiam facere ampliorem concessimus eis pro nobis et heredibus nostris ad meliorationem predicte
ville nostre *Nottyngham* et commoditatem burgensium nostrorum ejusdem ville ut eo
tranquillius negotiationibus suis intendere possint, quod nullus eorum placitet aut
implacitetur coram nobis vel heredibus nostris aut aliquibus justiciariis nostris vel
heredum nostrorum extra burgum predictum de terris aut tenementis que sunt in burgo predicto seu de transgressionibus aut contractibus vel aliis quibuscunque in eodem
burgo factis vel emergentibus sed omnia hujusmodi placita que coram nobis vel heredibus nostris aut aliquibus justiciariis nostris de banco vel aliis summoneri contigerit vel attachiari extra burgum predictum placitanda, coram majore et ballivis
burgi predicti qui pro tempore fuerint infra burgum predictum placitentur et termi-
nentur nisi placita illa tangant nos, heredes nostros, seu communitatem burgi predicti et quod non ponantur cum hominibus forinsecis in assisis, juratis, aut inquisitionibus aliquibus, que ratione tenementorum vel transgressionum aut aliorum negotio-
rum forinsecorum quorumcunque coram justiciariis aut aliis ministris nostris vel heredum nostrorum emerserint facienda nec quod homines forinseci ponantur cum ipsis
burgensibus in assisis juratis aut inquisitionibus aliquibus ratione terre vel tenementorum in eodem burgo existentium aut transgressionum contractuum aut aliorum nego-
tiorum

tiorum intrinſicorum que in eodem burgo emerſerint capienda ; ſed aſſiſe ille jurate et inquiſitiones de iis que in dicto burgo fuerint emergentes per burgenſes ejuſdem ville et in eodem burgo ſolummodo fiant niſi res ipſe tangant nos, heredes noſtros ſeu communitatem ejuſdem burgi. Et inſuper cum burgenſes illi per cartas prædictas habeant retorna brevium noſtrorum et ſummonitionum de ſcaccario noſtro de omnibus dictum burgum tangentibus, et quidam miniſtri noſtri et progenitorum noſtrorum predictorum nihilominus burgum predictum hactenus pluries ſint ingreſſi ad diſtrictiones et attachiamenta ibidem facienda que per ballivos ejuſdem ville fieri deberent. Conceſſimus etiam pro nobis et heredibus noſtris quod nullus vicecomes, ballivus, vel alii miniſtri noſtri vel heredum noſtrorum quicunque dictum burgum ingrediantur ad ſummonitiones attachiamenta ſeu diſtrictiones aut alia officia ibidem facienda niſi in defectu ballivorum ejuſdem ville qui pro tempore erunt. Concedimus etiam eiſdem burgenſibus pro nobis et heredibus noſtris quod ipſi et eorum heredes et ſucceſſores predicti de *muragio, pavagio, ſtallagio, tarragio, kaiagio, laſtagio,* et *paſſagio* per totum regnum noſtrum et poteſtatem noſtram in perpetuum ſint quieti. His teſtibus venerabilibus patribus *W.* archiepiſcopo *Cantuarienſi* totius *Anglie* primate, et *W. Coventrienſi* et *Lichfildienſi* epiſcopo, *Adamaro de Valentia* comite *Pembrokie, Humphredo de Bohun* comite *Hereſordie* et *Eſſexie, Hugone de Diſpenſer, Willielmo le Latymer, Theobaldo de Verdon, Johanne Cromwell, Edmundo de Malo Lacu* ſeneſcallo hoſpitii noſtri et aliis. Dat. per manum noſtram apud *Weſtmonaſterium* ſexto decimo die martii anno regni noſtri ſeptimo. Nos autem conceſſiones, confirmationes et reſtitutiones predictas ratas habentes et gratas eas pro nobis et heredibus noſtris quantum in nobis eſt, prefatis burgenſibus et eorum heredibus et ſucceſſoribus, burgenſibus ejuſdem ville concedimus et confirmamus ſicut carte predicte plenius teſtantur. Preterea cum dicta villa *Nottyngham* una cum libertatibus ejuſdem in inſtanti itinere dilectorum et fidelium noſtrorum *Willielmi de Herle,* et ſociorum ſuorum juſticiariorum noſtrorum itinerantium in comitatu *Nott.* quibuſdam certis de cauſis per conſiderationem ejuſdem curie capta ſit in manum noſtram. Nos volentes eiſdem majori et burgenſibus gratiam in hac parte facere ſpecialem reſtituimus eis villam predictam cum omnibus libertatibus predictis habendam et tenendam ſibi et heredibus et ſucceſſoribus ſuis burgenſibus ejuſdem ville in perpetuum adeo plene et integre ſicut eam per cartas predictas tenuerunt, et tenere debuerunt ante captionem ſupra dictam : Inſuper cum in carta predicti *Henrici* regis proavi noſtri contineatur quod predicti burgenſes et eorum heredes in perpetuum haberent retornum brevium ipſius proavi noſtri et heredum ſuorum de ſummonitione ſcaccarii ſui de omnibus ad dictum burgum *Nottyngham* ſpectantibus. Et quod nullus vicecomes aut alius ballivus ipſius proavi noſtri vel heredum ſuorum, quicunque dictum burgum ingrederetur ad ſummonitiones attachiamenta ſeu diſtrictiones aut alia officia ibidem facienda, niſi in defectu ballivorum ejuſdem ville et predicti burgenſes et anteceſſores ſui eo pretextu hucuſque habuerunt retorna omnium brevium progenitorum noſtrorum et noſtrorum tam de ſummonitionibus ſcaccarii quam aliorum brevium quoruncunque eundem burgum qualitercunque tangentium. Nos ſecuritati eorundem burgenſium ne ſuper hoc inquietari poſſint in futurum, providere volentes, conceſſimus eis et hac carta noſtra confirmavimus quod ipſi et eorum heredes et ſucceſſores predicti in perpetuum habeant retorna omnium brevium noſtrorum et heredum noſtrorum tam de ſummonitionibus ſcaccarii noſtri quam aliorum brevium quorumcunque predictum burgum qualiter cunque tangentium. Ita quod nullus vicecomes, ballivus ſeu alius miniſter noſter vel heredum noſtrorum burgum illum ingrediatur ad ſummonitiones attachiamenta, diſtrictiones vel aliqua alia officia infra eundem

undem burgum exercenda et facienda nisi in defectu ballivorum ville supra dicte ficut predictum eft, ad hec cum per quandam inquisitionem per prefatum *Willielmum* et dilectum et fidelem noftrum *Nicholaum Falftolf* de mandato noftro factam et in cancellaria noftra retornatam compertum fit, quod predicti burgenfes a tempore quo non extat memoria ufque ad tempus confectionis dicte carte predicti *Johannis* regis progenitoris noftri eifdem burgenfibus facte et etiam poft modum goalam in dicta villa *Nottyngham* habuerunt pro cuftodia eorum qui in eadem villa capti fuerunt vel attachiati, et quod goala illa fuit in cuftodia eorum qui cuftodiam ville predicte habuerunt tanquam ad eandem villam pertinens, tam dum villa illa fuit in manibus progenitorum noftrorum predictorum ; quam in manibus burgenfium ville supra dicte. Nos pro pleniore fecuritate ipforum volentes eis gratiam in hac parte facere fpecialem, conceffimus eis et hac carta noftra confirmavimus quod iidem burgenfes, heredes, et fucceffores fui predicti in perpetuum habeant goalam predictam in villa predicta pro cuftodia illorum qui in eadem villa ex quacunque caufa capi feu attachiari contigerit infuper cum prefati burgenfes pretextu predictorum verborum in predictis cartis contentorum quod homines de *Nottynghamfhire* et *Derbyfhire* venire debent ad predictum burgum de *Nottyngham* die veneris et fabbati cum quadrigis et fummagiis fuis, habuerint in eodem burgo unum mercatum fingulis feptimanis per diem fabbati ficut dicunt, nos ne predicti burgenfes fuperdicto mercato fuo occafionentur in futurum, volentes eorum fecuritati profpicere gratiofe conceffimus eis et hac carta noftra confirmavimus, quod ipfi et heredes ac fucceffores fui predicti in perpetuum habeant et teneant mercatum predictum fingulis feptimanis per diem fabbati, cum omnibus libertatibus et liberis confuetudinibus ad hujufmodi mercatum pertinentibus. Nolentes quod ipfi vel eorum heredes vel fucceffores occafione mercati illius pro tempore preterito vel futuro per nos vel heredes noftros feu miniftros noftros quofcunque occafionentur, moleftentur in aliquo feu graventur. Conceffimus etiam eifdem burgenfibus et hac carta noftra confirmavimus, quod ipfi, heredes, et fucceffores fui de *pontagio* per totum regnum et poteftatem noftram in perpetuum fint quieti, quare volumus et firmiter precipimus pro nobis et heredibus noftris quod iidem burgenfes et eorum heredes et fucceffores in perpetuum habeant et teneant predictam villam cum omnibus libertatibus, et etiam in perpetuum habeant retorna omnium brevium noftrorum et heredum noftrorum, tam de fummonitionibus fcaccarii noftri quam aliorum brevium quorumcunque et etiam goalam in eadem villa et mercatum per dictum diem fabbati cum omnibus libertatibus et liberis confuetudinibus ad hujufmodi mercatum pertinentibus et quod quieti fint de hujufmodi *pontagio* per totum regnum et poteftatem noftram ficut predictum eft. His teftibus venerabilibus patribus H. epifcopo *Lincolnienfi* cancellario noftro, *Johanne Wyntonienfi* et R. *Coventrienfi* et *Lichfildienfi* epifcopis, *Johanne de Eltham*, comite *Cornubie* fratre noftro cariffimo, *Rogero de MortuoMari* comite *March*, *Willielmo de Monte Acuto*, *Johanne Mautravers* fenefcallo hofpitii noftri et aliis, dat. per manum noftram apud *Woodftock* primo die *Maji* anno regni noftri quarto.

N O S autem omnes et fingulas conceffiones, confirmationes et reftitutiones predictas ratas habentes et gratas, eas pro nobis et heredibus noftris quantum in nobis eft prefatis burgenfibus ville de *Nottyngham* heredibus et fucceffibus fuis burgenfibus ejufdem ville concedimus et confirmamus ficut carte predicte rationabiliter teftantur et prout iidem burgenfes et fucceffores fui libertatibus et quietantiis predictis rationabiliter ufi funt et gauvifi. In cujus rei teftimonium has literas noftras fieri fecimus

fecimus patentes tefte me ipfo apud *Weftmonafterium* octavo die *Aprilis* anno regni noltri primo.

N O S autem omnes et fingulas conceffiones, confirmationes et reftitutiones predictas ratas habentes et gratas, eas pro nobis, et heredibus noftris quantum in nobis eft acceptamus approbamus ratificamus ac dilectis nobis burgenfibus ville predicte heredibus et fucceſſoribus fuis burgenfibus ejufdem ville concedimus, et confirmamus ficut carte predicte rationabiliter teftantur ; preterea volentes eifdem burgenfibus gratiam facere ampliorem, de gratia fpeciali conceffimus pro nobis et heredibus noftris quantum in nobis eft eifdem burgenfibus, quod licet ipfi vel anteceffores fui aliqua vel aliquibus libertatum vel quietantiarum in cartis predictis contentarum aliquo cafu emergente plene ufi non fuerint, ipfi tamen et eorum heredes et fucceffores libertatibus et quietantiis predictis et earum qualibet de cetero plene gaudeant et utantur fine occafione vel impedimento noftri vel heredum noftrorum, jufticiariorum, efceatorum, vicecomitum, aut aliorum ballivorum et miniftrorum noftrorum et heredum noftrorum quorumcunque. Nos infuper volentes nunc majorem et ballivos ac burgenfes ville predicte nec non eorum heredes et fucceffores, fuis multimodis exigentibus meritis favore profequi uberiori, de gratia fpeciali ex certa fcientia noftra et affenfu confilii noftri conceffimus pro nobis et heredibus noftris et hac carta noftra confirmavimus prefatis majori, ballivis et burgenfibus quod ipfi et eorum heredes ac fucceffores in perpetuum habeant infra villam predictam cognitiones omnium placitorum per majorem et ballivos ejufdem ville pro tempore exiftentes feu alios quos ad hoc deputaverint tenend : videlicet tam de terris, tenementis, reditibus infra libertatem ville predicte exiftentibus ; quam de trangreffionibus, conventionibus, contractibus, negotiis, et querelis quibufcunque infra libertatem predictam et precinctus ejufdem ville emergentibus five factis, de quibufcunque tenentibus et refidentibus infra feodum ville predicte ac etiam placitorum, affifarum de tenuris infra eandem libertatem quas coram jufticiariis noftris vel heredum noftrorum ad affifas in comitatu *Nottyngham* capiend: affignand: arrainand: contigerit et quod jufticiiari ipfi cum cognitiones placitorum earundem affifarum ex parte dictorum majoris ballivorum et burgenfium debito modo petite fuerint hoc eis fine difficultate allocent et brevia originalia et proceffus fi qui inde habiti fuerint prefatis majori et ballivis aut aliis ad dicta placita tenenda ut premittitur deputatis faciant liberari, et quod predicti major ballivi et burgenfes ac heredes et fucceffores fui in perpetuum habeant catalla felonum et fugitivorum de tenentibus et refidentibus infra libertatem predictam. Ita quod fi quis eorum pro delicto fuo vitam vel membrum debeat amittere vel fugerit et judicio ftare noluerit vel aliud quodcunque delictum fecerit pro quo catalla fua perdere debeat ubicunque jufticia de eo fieri debeat five in curia noftra vel heredum noftrorum five in alia curia, ipfa catalla fint predictorum majoris ballivorum et burgenfium ac heredum et fuccefforum fuorum et quod liceat eis feu miniftris fuis fine impedimento noftris vel heredum noftrorum vicecomitum, aut aliorum, ballivorum feu miniftrorum noftrorum quorumcunque, ponere fe in feifinam de catallis predictis et ea ad ufum predictorum majoris [ballivorum et burgenfium heredum et fucceſſorum fuorum retinere, et quod habeant in perpetuum omnes fines pro tranfgreffionibus et aliis delictis quibufcunque ac etiam fines pro licentia concordandi ac omnia amerciamenta redemptiones et exitus forisfactos, foris facturas, annum diem et vaftum et ftreppum ac omnia que ad nos et heredes noftros pertinere poterunt de hujufmodi anno, die et vafto et murdris de omnibus hominibus et tenentibus ville predicte in quibufcunque curiis noftris et heredum noftrorum de fcaccario, et coram jufticiariis noftris et heredibus

redibus

redum noftrorum de *Banco*, et coram fenefcallo et marefcallo feu clerico mercati
hofpitii noftri et heredum noftrorum qui pro tempore fuerint et in aliis curiis et heredum noftrorum quam coram jufticiariis itinerantibus ad communia placita et ad placita forefte et quibufcunqne aliis jufticiariis et miniftris noftris et heredum noftrorum
tam in prefentia noftra et heredum noftrorum quam in abfentia noftra et heredum
noftrorum fines facere vel amerciari exitus forisfacere annum diem et vaftum feu forisfacturas et murdra adjudicare contigerit que fines amerciamenta, redemptiones,
exitus, annus, dies, vaftum five ftreppum forisfacture et murdra ad nos vel heredes
noftros poffent pertinere fi prefatis majori ballivis et burgenfibus conceffa non fuif-
fent. Ita quod ipfi per fe vel per ballivos et miniltros fuos, fines, amerciamenta, redemptiones, exitus et forisfacturas hujusmodi hominum et tenentium predictorum, et
omnia que ad nos et heredes noftros pertinere poffint, de anno, die, vafto five ftreppo
et murdris predictis, levare, recipere et habere poffint fine occafione vel impedimento
noftri vel heredum noftrorum jufticiorum, efceatorum, vicecomitum, coronatorum,
aut aliorum, ballivorum feu miniftrorum quorumcunque. Et etiam quod predicti
major, ballivi, et burgenfes ac heredes et fucceffores fui in perpetuum habeant retorna omnium brevium noftrorum ac fummonitionum de fcaccario noftro et heredum
noftrorum attachiamenta tam de placitis corone quam de aliis quibufcunque in terris et
feodis ville predicte ac executiones eorundem brevium et fummonitionum de omnibus que infra libertatem predictam emergent. Ita quod nullus vicecomes aut alius
ballivus feu minifter nofter, vel heredum noftrorum libertatem predictam ingrediatur ad executiones eorundem brevium et fummonitionum feu attachiamentorum de
placitis corone vel aliis predictis aut aliquod aliud officium ibidem faciendi nifi in
defectu ipforum majoris, ballivorum, et burgenfium, heredum et fuccefforum fuorum.
Conceffimus etiam pro nobis et heredibus noftris ex certa fcientia noftra et de affenfu predicta eifdem, majori ballivis et burgenfibus ac eorum heredibus et fuccefforibus quod ipfi fe appruare et commodum fuum facere poffint de omnibus purprefturis tam in terris quam in aquis factis vel faciendis et de
omnibus vaftis infra limites et bundas ville predicte in fupportationem onerum
infra villam predictam indies emergentium. Ac etiam quod ipfi et heredes ac fucceffores fui predicti habeant in perpetuum plenam correctionem punitionem authoritatem et poteftatem ad inquirendum audiendum et determinandum per majorem et
recordatorem ville predicte ac alios quatuor probos et legales homines ville predicte per majorem ejufdem ville pro tempore exiftentem eligendos et fucceffores fuos
in perpetuum, omnes materias, querelas, defectus, caufas, et articulos, qui ad officium jufticiarii pacis, laboratorum et artificum pertinent ac alias res quafcunque infra
dictam villam et fuburbia ejufdem emergentes vel contingentes et qui aliquo modo
coram jufticiariis pacis laboratorum et artificum inquiri poterunt et terminari, adeo
plene et integre ficut jufticiarii pacis laboratorum et artificum in comitatu *Nottyng-*
ham ante hec tempora habuerunt vel exercuerunt abfque eo quod jufticiarii pacis laboratorum et artificum noftri et heredum noftrorum in comitatu predicto in pofterum
aliqualiter de aliquibus rebus, caufis, querelis, materiis defectibus feu aliis articulis
quibufcunque ad jufticiarios pacis laboratorum et artificum fpectantibus five pertinentibus infra villam predictam et fuburb. ejufdem ex quacunque caufa emergentibus five
contingentibus ita quod predicti major et recordator ac predicti quatuor probi et
legales homines ejufdem ville qui pro tempore fuerint ad determinationem alicujus
felonie abfque aliquo fpeciali mandato noftro vel heredum noftrorum quoquomodo
non procedant. Et quod dicti major ballivi et burgenfes ac heredes et fucceffores
fui in perpetuum habeant omnes fines et amerciamenta, exitus, et proficua ----------

jufticiarii

justiciarii provenientia adeo integre ficut major ballivi et burgenfes ville de *Coventre*, hujufmodi fines amerciamenta, exitus et proficua ante fextum diem *Aprilis* anno regni predicti *Richardi* nuper regis vicefimo fecundo virtute cartarum regum *Anglie* eis inde confectarum et per ipfum nuper regem confirmatarum obtinuerunt. Et infuper quod quandocunque aliqua arraiatio hominum ad arma armatorum hobelariorum, aut fagittariorum fiet ex nunc in dicta villa de *Nottyngham* virtute commiffionis feu aliorum mandatorum noftrorum vel heredum noftrorum fub aliquo figillorum noftrorum vel heredum noftrorum, major ville predicte pro tempore exiftens ipfis qui per nos et heredes noftros ad hoc affignati fuerint ad arraiationem illam faciendam per commiffiones et mandata hujufmodi fit adjunctus, et quod fine adjunctione illa nulla arraiatio hominum armatorum hobelariorum aut fagittariorum in eadem villa fiat quoquomodo. Volumus et concedimus pro nobis et heredibus noftris, de affenfu predicto per aliquam caufam aut colorem aliquæ vel aliqua de franchefiis, libertatibus, privilegiis, immunitatibus, quietantiis, feu commoditatibus, præfatis majori, ballivis et burgenfibus de *Nottyngham* et fucceffcribus per progenitores noftros ante hec tempora conceffis et per nos confirmatis erga nunc majorem, ballivos vel burgenfes ejufdem ville de *Nottyngham* feu heredes et fucceffores fuos nullo modo denegentur, reftringantur, minuantur, nec abbrevientur, et quod iidem major ballivi et burgenfes dicte ville de *Nottyngham* ac eorum heredes et fucceffores, habeant teneant et exerceant omnia alia et fingula franchefias, libertates, privilegia, immunitates, quietancias et commoditates, ac confuetudines et eis et eorum quolibet plene gaudeant et utantur de articulo in articulum ac de verbo in verbum et prout major, ballivi et burgenfes predicte ville de *Nottyngham* ac anteceffores et predeceffores fui habuerunt et exercuerunt ex conceffione et confirmatione dictorum progenitorum noftrorum ante hec tempora in perpetuum. His teftibus venerabilibus patribus *Th. Cantuarienfi* totius *Anglie* primate, *R. Eboracenfi Anglie* primate, archiepifcopis, *R. Londinenfi, W. Wyntonienfi, J. Elienfi, H. Lincolnienfi*, epifcopis, *Edmundo* duce *Eboracenfi*, avunculo noftro cariffimo, *Thoma Warwickie, Henrico Northumbrie, R —— de Weftmorlandie* comitibus *Johanne de Scarle* cancellario, *Johanne Norbury* thefaurario noftro, *Willielmo de Roos de Hamelak, Willielmo de Willoughby, Johanne de Cobham, Thoma Erpingham* camerario noftro, *Thoma Rempfton*, fenefcallo hofpitii noftri magiftro *Richardo de Clyfford* cuftode privati figilii noftri et aliis datum per manum noftram apud *Weftmonafterium* decimo octavo die *Novembris* anno regni noftri primo.

NOS autem omnes et fingulas conceffiones confirmationes et reftitutiones, predictas ratas habentes et gratas, eas pro nobis et heredibus noftris quantum in nobis eft acceptamus, approbamus ratificamus ac dilectis nobis nunc majori, ballivis, et burgenfibus ville predicte heredibus et fucceffcribus fuis tenore prefentium concedimus et confirmamus ficut charte predicte rationabiliter teftantur et prout iidem major ballivi et burgenfes ville predicte libertatibus et quietanciis predictis uti et gaudere debent ipfique et anteceffores fui majores ballivi et burgenfes ejufdem ville libertatibus et quietanciis illis a tempore confectionis cartarum predictarum rationabiliter uti et gaudere confueverunt. In cujus rei teftimonium has literas noftras fieri fecimus patentes tefte me ipfo apud *Leiceftriam* vicefimo quarto die *Maji* anno regni noftri fecundo.

NOS autem omnia et fingula franchefias, libertates, privilegia, quietancias, immunitates, conceffiones, confirmationes et reftitutiones predictas, rata habentes et

grata,

grata, ea pro nobis heredibus, et fuccefforibus noftris quantum in nobis eft acceptamus approbamus et ratificamus ac omnia et fingula franchefias, libertates, privilegia,
quietantias et immunitates predicta dilectis nobis nunc majori ballivis et burgenfibus
ville predicte, heredibus et fuccefforibus fuis tenore prefentium concedimus et confirmamus ficut carte predicte rationabiliter teftantur et prout iidem major, ballivi
et burgenfes ejufdem ville *Nottyngham* vel predeceffores fui unquam franchefiis,
libertatibus, privilegiis, quietantiis et immunitatibus predictis uti et gaudere debent,
potuerunt feu debuerunt ipfique vel predeceffores fui franchefiis, libertatibus, privilegiis, quietantiis et immunitatibus illis unquam poft confectionem cartarum predictarum rationabiliter uti et gaudere confueverunt potuerunt vel debuerunt licet
dicti nunc major, ballivi et burgenfes ejufdem ville vel predeceffores fui franchefiis libertatibus, privilegiis, quietantiis et immunitatibus predictis feu eorum aliquo abufi vel non ufi fuerint. *Et ulterius de uberiori gratia noftra ex*
mero motu et certa fcientia noftris, conceffimus et per prefentes confirma-
mus pro nobis heredibus et fuccefforibus noftris, nunc burgenfibus ejufdem ville Nottyngham *que eft et diu extitit villa fub certa forma corporata ac eorundem burgenfium,*
heredibus et fuccefforibus burgenfibus ipfius ville in perpetuum quod villa illa de majore et burgenfibus ex nunc in perpetuum fit corporata et quod iidem major et burgenfes et fucceffores fui majores et burgenfes ville illius fic corporate fint una communitas perpetua corporata in re et nomine per nomen *majoris et burgenfium ville*
Nottyngham habeantque fucceffionem perpetuam, et quod major et burgenfes ville
illius et fucceffores fui predicti per idem nomen fint habiles et capaces in lege ad
omni moda, placita, fectas, querelas et demandas nec non actiones reales perfonales
et mixtas quafcunque per ipfos feu contra ipfos motas feu movendas in quibufcunque
curiis noftris, heredum et fucceffborum noftrorm aut aliorum quorumcunque tam coram
nobis, heredibus vel fuccefforibus noftris ubicunque fuerimus, et coram nobis, heredibus fuccefforibus noftris in cancellaria noftra heredum et fucceffborum noftrorum ;
quam coram quibufcunque jufticiariis et judicibus fpiritualibus et fecularibus, profe-
quenda et defendenda et quod in eifdem placitare poffint et placitari, refpondere et
refponderi et quod major et burgenfes ejufdem ville et fucceffores fui per idem nomen terras tenementa, poffeffiones et hereditamenta quecunque adquirere poffint,
tenere fibi et fuccefforibus fuis in perpetuum. Et infuper de abundantiori gratia noftra ex mero motu et certa fcientia noftris conceffimus pro nobis heredibus et fuccefforibus noftris, predictis nunc majori et burgenfibus ville illius et fuccefforibus fuis
burgenfibus ejufdem ville in perpetuum *quod eadem villa* Nottyngham *ac precinctus*
ejufdem prout fe extendunt vel utuntur qui infra corpus comitatus Nottyngham *jam*
exiftunt et continentur ab eodem comitatu a quinto decimo die menfis feptembris prox-
ime futuro feparati, diftincti, divifi, et in omnibus penitus exempti exiftant in per-
petuum tam per terram quam per aquam caftro noftro *Nottyngham* et meffuagio noftro
vocato le *Kyngeſhall* in quo eft goala noftra comitatuum noftrorum *Nottyngham* et *Der-*
by tantummodo exceptis. Et quod eadem villa *Nottyngham* et precinctus ejufdem prout
fe extendunt vel utuntur exceptis preexceptis, fint ab eodem die comitatus per fe et non
parcella dicti comitatus *Nottyngham* et quod eadem villa *Nott.* et precinctus ejufdem prout fe extendunt vel utuntur exceptis preexceptis, *comitatus ville Nottyngham*
per fe in perpetuum nuncupentur teneantur et habeantur. Et quod dicti nunc burgenfes ejufdem ville et fucceffores fui burgenfes ville illius in perpetuum loco duorum ballivorum ejufdem ville habeant duos vicecomites in eifdem villa et pre-
cinctu *de feipfis eligendos* nec non vicecomitatum ejufdem ville et precinctuum
ejufdem ville prout fe extendunt vel utuntur, exceptis preexceptis ufque diem fancti
Michaelis

Michaelis archangeli tunc proxime futurum, et per eundem diem quoufque in eodem die *alii duo burgenfes* ejufdem ville in vicecomites ville illius et precinctuum ejufdem ville prout fe extendunt vel utuntur exceptis pre-exceptis pro anno tunc proxime futuro per tunc majorem et burgenfes ville illius eligantur et quod ex tunc vice-comites ville illius et precinctuum ejufdem ville prout fe extendunt vel utuntur exceptis pre-exceptis annuatim in perpetuum in fefto fancti *Michaelis* archangeli eligentur et perficientur in forma fubfcripta videlicet : Major et burgenfes ejufdem ville *Nottyngham* pro tempore exiftentes quolibet anno in loco duorum ballivorum ville illius eligent *de feipfis duas perfonas idoneas* in vice-comites ejufdem ville et precinctus ejufdem ville prout fe extendunt vel utuntur exceptis pre-exceptis eodem modo quo burgenfes ville illius in ballivos ejufdem ville ante hec tempora eligi confueverunt et quod burgenfes ejufdem ville in vice-comites illius et precinctuum ejufdem ville prout fe extendunt vel utuntur exceptis pre-exceptis in forma predicta eligendi ftatim poft electionem de fe factam facramenta fua coram majore ville illius qui pro tempore fuerit, ad officium vice-comitum comitatus illius debite et legitime exequendum preftabunt et quod extra eandem villam ad facramenta fua preftanda non tranfibunt quorum quidem vicecomitum nomina fub figillo majoratus illius ville *Nottygham* in cancellariam noftram heredum et fuccefforum noftrorum annuatim infra duodecim dies electionem hujufmodi proxime fequentes mittentur, et quod tam quilibet burgenfis ejufdem ville *Nottyngham* in majorem ville illius in pofterum eligendus, eo ipfo et quam citius in majorem ville illius electus fuerit quam nunc major ejufdem ville, fit ex tunc efcaetor nofter heredum et fuccefforum noftrorum in villa et precinctibus illius durante toto tempore quo aliquis hujufmodi burgenfis in officio majoratus ville illius fteterit et quod nullo tempore futuro aliquis alius efcaetor aut vice-comites in, feu de eadem villa *Nottyngham* et precinctibus ejufdem prout fe extendunt vel utuntur exceptis pre-exceptis quam de burgenfibus ejufdem ville ut predicitur fiend : quovis modo fiant feu exiftant et quod efcaetor et vice-comites ejufdem ville et eorum fucceffores in perpetuum in eadem villa et precinctibus ejufdem prout fe extendunt vel utuntur exceptis pre-exceptis eafdem habeant poteftatem, jurifdictionem, auctoritatem, et libertatem, ac quecunque alia ad officia efcaetoris et vice-comitum pertinentia quas et que ceteri efcaetores et vice-comites noftri heredum et fuccefforum noftrorum alibi infra regnum noftrum *Anglie* habent vel habebunt aut habere debent, feu debebunt, et quod omnia et fingula talia brevia precepta et mandata qualia per vice-comites *Nottyngham* feu per ballivos ejufdem ville, infra eandem villam feu precinctus ejufdem ante hec tempora quovifmodo ferviri feu exequi confueverunt aut debuerunt vice-comitibus ejufdem ville *Nottyngham* ex nunc in futurum pro tempore exiftentibus a dicto quinto decimo die feptembris immediate in perpetuum dirigantur, demandentur, liberentur et quod vice-comites ejufdem ville et precinctuum ejufdem ex nunc in futurum pro tempore exiftentes comitatum fuum comitatus illius ville *Nottyngham* infra eandem villam et precinctus ejufdem ville prout fe extendunt vel utuntur exceptis pre-exceptis per diem lune de menfe in menfem continue teneant in futurum eifdem modo et forma prout alii vicecomites noftri alibi infra regnum noftrum predictum comitatus fuos tenent feu prout alii vice-comites noftri heredum et fuccefforum noftrorum alibi in eodem regno comitatus fuos tenebunt feu tenere deberent et quod iidem nunc burgenfes ville illius et fucceffores fui in perpetuum habeant curiam ibidem ad eorum libitum de omnibus et fingulis contractibus, conventionibus et tranfgreffionibus, tam contra pacem quam aliter factis ac aliis rebus, caufis et materiis quibufcunque infra eandem villam, feu precinctus ejufdem ville prout fe extendunt vel utuntur exceptis pre-exceptis quovis modo emergentibus feu contingentibus de die in diem in guyhalda ejufdem ville coram majore illius

lius

lius ville feu ejus locum tenente ac vicecomitibus ejufdem ville pro tempore exiftentibus tenendam. Et quod major ville illius pro tempore exiftens aut ejus locum te-
nens et vicecomites ville illius pro tempore exiftentes a dicto quinto decimo die
menfis feptembris habeant poteftatem et authoritatem ad audiendum et terminandum in
curia illa omnimoda placita, fectas, querelas, caufas, et demandas, nec non actiones
reales, perfonales et mixtas quafcunque infra eandem villam ac libertatem et precinctus ejufdem ville prout fe extendunt vel utuntur exceptis preexceptis, motas vel
movendas tam in prefentia noftra heredum et succefforum noftrorum quam in abfentia noftra heredum et succefforum noftrorum cum omnimodis proficuis curie illius
ex nunc in futurum qualitercunque contingentibus feu provenientibus vicecomitibus
ejufdem ville pro tempore exiftentibus ad ufum fuum proprium folvendis, fine occafione
vel impedimento noftri heredum vel succefforum noftrorum aut jufticiariorum noftrorum
heredum vel succefforum noftrorum quorumcunque feu senefcalli vel marefcalli hofpitii noftri, heredum feu succefforum noftrorum five efcaetorum vicecomitum aut
aliorum ballivorum vel miniftorum noftrorum heredum feu succefforum noftrorum
quorumcunque. Et quod iidem senefcallus et marefcallus de cognitione placitorum
de hujufmodi contractibus, conventionibus, transgreffionibus, rebus, caufis aut materiis quibufcunque infra eandem villam feu libertatem vel precinctus ejufdem prout
fe extendunt vel utuntur exceptis preexceptis emergentibus vel contingentibus, fe
ex nunc in futurum nullatenus intromittant, nec nullus eorum ullo modo fe intromittat.
Et quod dicti efcaetor et vicecomites ejufdem ville *Nottyngham* pro tempore exiftentes quolibet anno separatim proficua fua facere et computare poffint coram thefaurario et baronibus de fcaccario noftro et heredum ac succefforum noftrorum per
attornatos eorundem, efcaetoris et vicecomitum illius ville ad hoc separatim deputatos et deputandos per literas patentes fub figillis officiorum eorundem efcaetoris et
vicecomitum ejufdem ville tangen : unde computabiles fuerint et quod attornati illi ad
proficua et computa hujufmodi facienda et reddenda loco ipforum efcaetoris et vicecomitum per eofdem thefaurarium et barones juxta vim et effectum iftarum noftra-
rum literarum admittantur, abfque hoc quod dicti efcaetor et vicecomites ejufdem
ville *Nottyngham* feu eorum succeffores aut aliquis eorum extra eandem villam ad
computandum de aliquibus ad officia fua feu officium alicujus eorum spectantibus per-
fonaliter venire compellantur feu teneantur aut eorum aliquis compellatur feu tenea-
tur quovismodo. Et quod quilibet efcaetor illius ville *Nottyngham* qui pro tempore erit
ftatim poft prefectionem fuam preftet fingulis annis in perpetuum in eadem villa et non
alibi facramentum fuum de officio illo bene et fideliter faciendo coram coronatoribus
vel uno coronatorum ejufdem ville pro tempore exiftentibus, abfque eo quod idem
efcaetor illius ville *Nottyngham* vel succeffores fui ad facramenta fua hujufmodi facienda extra eandem villam alibi coram aliquibus aliis feu aliquo alio venire compellatur feu compellantur. Ita femper quod infra duodecim dies proxime poft electionem majoris ville illius fequentes, de nomine efcaetoris illius ville fingulis annis
ad fcaccarium noftrum heredum et succefforum noftrorum fub figillo majoratus ipfius
ville *Nottyngham* certificetur. Conceffimus etiam ex mero motu et certa fcientia
noftris pro nobis heredibus et succefforibus noftris predictis, prefatis nunc burgenfibus dicte ville *Nottyngham* et succefforibus fuis in perpetuum catalla quarumcunque
perfonarum tam ad fectam noftram heredum vel succefforum noftrorum quam aliorum quorumcunque pro aliquibus feloniis murdris aut aliis offenfis damnatarum, con-
victarum aut aliquo modo attinctarum ac aliarum perfonarum quarumcunque ex quacunque caufa ut legatarum tam ad fectam noftram heredum vel succefforum noftrorum
quam aliorum quorumcunque nec non catalladis advocata felonum de fe et deodanda

infra

infra eandem villam *Nottyngham* et precinctus ejufdem ville prout fe extendunt vel utuntur exceptis preexceptis reperta et inventa et quod iidem nunc burgenfes illius ville et fucceffores fui habeant in perpetuum omnia amerciamenta, redemptiones et exitus, forisfactos vel forisfaciendos ac omnes fines pro tranfgreffionibus et aliis delictis, negligentiis, mifprifionibus et contemptibus quibufcunque ac etiam fines pro licentia concordandi et omnia que ad nos, et heredes noftros quovis modo pertinere poterunt de hominibus vel aliquibus tenentibus feu habitantibus ville illius nec non omnia exitus, fines et amerciamenta de quibufcunque plegiis et manu captoribus alicujus perfonæ infra eandem villam *Nottyngham* commorantis feu ibidem integre vel non integre tenentis exiftentis licet perfona illa feu plegii vel manucaptores ille de nobis, heredibus vel fuccefforibus noftris feu de aliis tenuerit vel tenuerint, nec non de omnibus et fingulis burgenfibus ejufdem ville tam refidentibus quam non refidentibus licet illi integre tenentes ibidem non fuerint feu ibidem vel alibi de nobis heredibus et fuccefforibus noftris feu de aliis tenuerint in quibufcunque curiis noftris heredum vel fuccefforum noftrorum tam coram nobis heredibus et fuccefforibus noftris ubicunque fuerimus, quam coram nobis heredibus et fuccefforibus noftris in cancellaria noftra heredum vel fuccefforum noftrorum ac etiam coram thefaurario et baronibus noftris heredum et fuccefforum noftrorum de fcaccario et coram jufticiariis noftris heredum et fuccefforum noftrorum de banco et coram fenefcallo et marefcallo feu clerico mercati hofpitii noftri heredum et fuccefforum noftrorum qui pro tempore fuerint et in aliis curiis noftris heredum et fuccefforum noftrorum quibufcunque, et coram jufticiariis itinerantibus ad communia placita feu ad placita forefte et quibufcunque aliis jufticiariis et miniftris noftris heredum et fuccefforum noftrorum, tam in prefentia noftra heredum et fuccefforum noftrorum quam in abfentia noftra heredum et fuccefforum noftrorum et quod ipfi per fe vel per miniftros fuos omnia fines, amerciamenta, redemptiones, exitus, forisfacturofque hujufmodi et omnia que ad nos heredes vel fuccefforos noftros pertinere deberent fi prefens conceffio noftra facta non fuiffet levare, percipere et habere poffint fine occafione vel impedimento noftri heredum vel fuccefforum noftrorum jufticiariorum, efcaetorum, vicecomitum, coronatorum aut aliorum ballivorum feu miniftrorum noftrorum quorumcunque. Et ulterius ex mero motu et certa fcientia noftris predictis, conceffimus pro nobis heredibus et fuccefforibus noftris predictis, prefatis nunc burgenfibus dicte ville *Nottyngham* ac eorum heredibus et fuccefforibus in perpetuum quod iidem burgenfes ac eorum heredes et fuccefferes de tempore in tempus eligere poffint de feipfis feptem aldermannos quorum quidem aldermannorum unus femper in majorem ville illius eligatur ac major ejufdem ville exiftat. Qui quidem aldermanni fic electi in hujufmodi officiis aldermannorum ejufdem ville durante vita fua permaneant et exiftant, et quilibet eorum permaneat et exiftat nifi ipfi vel eorum aliquis per fuam fpecialem requifitionem refiduis burgenfibus ville illius pro tempore exiftentibus faciendam feu propter aliquam notabilem caufam ab aldermannis fuis feu aldermannia fua per majorem et burgenfes ville illius pro tempore exiftentibus amoti fuerint feu amotus erit, et quod obiente feu qualitercunque decedente vel amoto hujufmodi aldermanno ab officio fuo aldermanie habeant major et burgenfes ejufdem ville pro tempore exiftentes ac eorum heredes et fuccefferes in perpetuum plenam poteftatem et authoritatem tenore prefentium eligendi unum alium burgenfem de feipfis in aldermannum ville illius loco ipfius aldermanni fic obientis, decedentis vel amoti et fic de tempore in tempus in perpetuum obiente decidente vel amoto aliquo hujufmodi aldermanno ville illius in forma fupradicta. Et quod aldermanni ejufdem ville pro tempore exiftentes fint jufticiarii noftri, heredum et fuccefforum noftrorum ad pacem

infra

infra eandem villam ac libertatem et precinctus ejufdem ville prout fe extendunt vel utuntur exceptis preexceptis confervandam in perpetuum, et quod feptem aldermanni illi fex, quinque, quatuor et tres eorum quorum majorem ville illius pro tempore exiftentem unum prefentem effe volumus, plenam habeant proteftatem et auctoritatem ad inquirendum audiendum et terminandum tam omnimodas felonias, murdra, trangrefliones et mifpriffiones, quam omnimoda alia caufas, querelas, contemptus et malefacta ac cetera quecunque que ad aliquos jufticiarios infra regnum noftrum *Anglie* pertinent feu pertinere poterunt feu debebunt in futurum, ad audiendum inquirendum et terminandum vel quovis modo corrigendum infra eandem villam ac libertatem et precinctus ejufdem prout fe extendunt vel utuntur exceptis preexceptis qualitercunque contingentia feu emergentia nec non correctionem et punitionem eorundem adeo plene et integre ficut cuftodes pacis et jufticiarii ad felonias tranfgreffiones et alia malefacta audienda, determinanda affignati et affignandi ac jufticiarii fervientium, laboratorum et aliorum artificiorum in comitatu *Nottyngham* feu alibi infra regnum noftrum *Anglie* extra villam et libertatem predictam habent vel habebunt qualitercunque in futurum.   Conceffimus infuper ex mero motu et certa fcientia noftris predictis, pro nobis heredibus et fucceforibus noftris predictis eifdem burgenfibus ville predicte ac heredibus et fuccefforibus fuis in perpetuum, quod ipfi in perpetuum habeant omnimoda fines, exitus, forisfacturas et amerciamenta coram aliquibus aldermannis et majore ejufdem ville et cuftodibus pacis feu ratione jufticiarie pacis ibidem facta vel facienda, forisfacta vel forisfacienda aut ratione hujufmodi jufticiarie pacis ibidem infra eandem villam ac libertatem et precinctus ejufdem ville prout fe extendunt vel utuntur exceptis preexceptis, qualitercunque provenientia per miniftros fuos proprios levanda et percipienda in auxilium et fupportationem grandium onerum eidem ville indies incumbentium aut in eadem contingentium et emergentium.   Et quod predicti nunc burgenfes ejufdem ville *Nottyngham* eorumque heredes et fuccefores in perpetuum habeant forisfacturam omnium victualium infra eandem villam et precinctus illos per legem *Anglie* qualitercunque forisfaciendorum videlicet panis, vini, et fervifie ac aliorum victualium quorumcunque que ad mercandifas non pertinent.   Et infuper ex mero motu et certa fcientia noftris predictis, conceffimus et per prefentes confirmamus pro nobis, heredibus et fucceforibus noftris predictis, prefatis nunc burgenfibus dicte ville *Nottyngham* ac eorum heredibus et fucceforibus predictis in perpetuum quod fenefcallus et marefcallus hofpitii noftri heredum vel fuccefforum noftrorum ac clericus mercati hofpitii noftri heredum feu fuccefforum noftrorum de cetero nec in prefentia noftra nec in abfentia noftra heredum vel fuccefforum noftrorum non ingrediantur, nec fedeant nec eorum aliquis ingrediatur nec fedeat infra eandem villam aut libertatem et precinctus ejufdem ville prout fe extendunt vel utuntur exceptis preexceptis ad officia fua feu officium alicujus eorum ibidem in aliquo excercendum feu quovismodo exequendum vel faciendum, nec in placitum trahant vel trahat aliquos burgenfes ejufdem ville aut aliquas perfonas infra eandem villam feu libertatem et precinctus ejufdem ville prout fe extendunt vel utuntur exceptis preexceptis refidentes, pro aliquibus materiis, caufis, placitis, querelis, aut rebus quibufcunque coram eis feu eorum aliquo emergentibus feu exiftentibus quoquo modo in futurum.   Conceffimus etiam ex mero motu et certa fcientia noftris predictis, et licentiam dedimus pro nobis, heredibus et fucceforibus noftris predictis, prefatis nunc burgenfibus predicte ville *Nottyngham* et fucceforibus fuis et cuicunque alii burgenfi ejufdem ville pro tempore exiftentibus qui aldermannus ville illius exiftet quod aldermanni ejufdem ville in perpetuum pro tempore exiftentes uti valeant togis capiciis et collobiis de una fecta et una liberata,

berata, fimul cum furruris et linaturis et collobiis illis convenientibus eifdem modo et forma prout major et aldermanni civitatis noftre *Londini* utuntur ftatuto de liberatis pannorum et capiciorum aut aliquo alio ftatuto five ordinatione ante hec tempora edito non obftante. Volumus tamen quod quilibet predictorum efcaetorum et vicecomitum ville illius pro tempore exiftentium prout ad fuum fpectat officium de omni eo infra eandem villam ac libertatem et precinctus ejufdem ville exceptis omnimodis finibus exitibus et amerciamentis predictis coram jufticiariis pacis infra eandem villam et precinctus ejufdem ville prout fe extendunt vel utuntur, exceptis preexceptis ratione jufticiarie pacis ibidem factis feu faciendis, forisfactis feu forisfaciendis qualitercunque provenientibus et exceptis ceteris premiffis, prefatis nunc burgenfibus ville illius et fucceftoribus fuis per nos virtute prefentium ut premittitur conceffis, quod ad nos et heredes ac fucceffores noftros de jure pertinere et de quo efcaetores, et vicecomites noftri dicti comitatus *Nottyngham* feu eorum alter coram thefaurario et baronibus de fcaccario noftro heredum et fucceftorum noftrorum fi prefens carta noftra eifdem nunc burgenfibus facta non exifteret, computare deberent feu deberet coram eifdem thefaurario et baronibus computum fuum per attornatos fuos ut predictum eft reddere teneantur ac nobis et prefatis heredibus ac fucceftoribus noftris inde prout juftum fuerit refpondere teneantur provifo femper quod predicti nunc major et burgenfes dicte ville *Nottyngham* nec eorum fucceffores ad aliqua, libertates, franchefias feu privilegia burgenfibus ville illius feu ballivis et burgenfibus ejufdem ville per antea quovis modo fpectantia feu pertinentia licet eadem libertates, franchefie feu privilegia aut eorum aliquod per prefentes dictis nunc burgenfibus ville illius et fucceftoribus fuis concedantur vel concedatur quoquomodo clamandi et habendi in jure et titulo fuis per antea pertinentibus feu fpectantibus aliquo modo per acceptationem prefentium excludantur, barrentur, aut eftoppentur fed quod bene licet dictis nunc majori et burgenfibus ejufdem ville et fucceftoribus fuis omnia et fingula hujufmodi libertates, franchefias et privilegia burgenfibus ville illius aut ballivis et burgenfibus ville illius per antea pertinentia vel de jure pertinere debentia in jure et titulo fuis, fibi inde ante datum prefentium pertinentia vel fpectantia, clamare, gaudere et habere aliqua conceffione de aliquo eorundem libertatum franchefiarum feu privilegiorum in prefentibus factorum, feu acceptatione prefentium per eofdem majorem et burgenfes vel fucceffores fuos non obftante. Quare volumus et firmiter precipimus pro nobis heredibus et fucceftoribus noftris predictis, quod prefati burgenfes ville noftre predicte ac eorum heredes et fucceffores omnia et fingula hujufmodi cognitiones, franchefias, libertates et immunitates ac omnia alia premiffa prout fuperius fpecialiter expreffantur, habeant teneant et exerceant ac eis et eorum fingulis plene, libere, integre, pacifice, et quiete, in perpetuum gaudeant et utantur abfque impedimento perturbatione moleftatione feu impedimento noftri heredum, vel fucceftorum noftrorum aut aliquorum officiariorum feu miniftrorum noftrorum, heredum, vel fucceftorum noftrorum quorumcunque ficut predictum eft modo et forma fuperius declaratis, aliquo dono five conceffione per nos aut per aliquem progenitorum noftrorum burgenfibus ejufdem ville *Nottyngham* vel predeceftoribus fuis ante hec tempora factis, et quod inde feu de valore catallorum, amerciamentorum, exituum, finium, feu ceterorum premifforum expreffa mentio facta non exiftit, non obftante.

IN cujus &c tefte rege apud *Wynton xxviij junii* per breve de privato figillo et pro quinque marcis folutis in hanaperio.

T H I S is a true copy of the record :

George Holmes.

deputy keeper of the records in the tower of *London. October* 16 1735.

The cafe of the Corporation of *Nottingham,* as it was truly ftated by *William Sacheverel* of *Barton,* Efq;

T H E town of *Nottingham* has always claimed to have been a borough by pre- fcription : And it cannot well be doubted that it has been fo ; for it appears by *Doomfday-Book,* in the time of king *William* I. that the burgeffes of *Not- tingham* then had divers houfes and parcels of land in *Nottingham* ; and the burgeffes of that town were one hundred and feventy three in number, in the time of *Ed- ward* the confeffor.

T H A T town has alfo always claimed to have been a corporation by prefcripti- on : And it is hard to believe it otherwife, becaufe no charter of its firft incorpora- ting could yet be found ; and the charters granted to the burgeffes of that town by king *Henry* the 2d. and king *John,* do imply them as a body corporate before thofe times.

Y E T it appears by the charter of king *Edward* I. that there was no mayor of that town before his reign ; for that he then was pleafed to grant to the burgeffes of that town a privilege, that they then after fhould chufe a mayor out of themfelves annually ; and fome of their former charters as well as that, fhew that for fome time before they had only bailiffs of that town. From the time of *Edward* I. under mayor and bailiffs the town continued till the time of *Henry* VI. who was pleafed to make it a county, and grant them fheriffs inftead of bailiffs, and the privilege of chufing out of themfelves, feven aldermen, and one of them annually to be mayor ; and that the aldermen (as long as they fo continued) fhould be juftices of the peace within that town ; and moreover, that the burgeffes of the town of *Nottingham* fhould for ever be a body corporate, by the name of mayor and burgeffes. Nor has any char- ter fince, nor any bye-law that can be heard of, given the aldermen any more power than they had by that charter, which was then, nothing more, than every burgefs of that town had, except being juftices of the peace and wearing gowns and hoods ; fo that the aldermen, (tho' of late they have taken upon them to fit as members of the council of that town) can neither prefcribe to that power, becaufe there were no aldermen in that town before king *Henry* the 6th's days; nor can they claim to be of the council of that town

by

by force of any charter, for no charter either in *Henry* the 6th's time, or fince, has granted them any fuch authority, nor did they pretend to fit in that council by virtue of any bye-law, tho' their right of fitting and voting there, has been denied in the council by the members thereof.

THE aldermen indeed in king *James's* time began, (tho' they had no right fo to do) to take upon them to be part of the council, and to intermeddle in the town's concerns, and to encroach fo far upon the burgeffes, without their confent, as to pretend to have a right in the fetting and difpofing of the corporation lands, and of the bridge lands and fchool lands ; but the burgeffes were fo far from confenting to their having any fuch power or authority, that they in the year 1605, by their petition to the lords of the council table, complained of the encroachments of the aldermen and prayed redrefs ; upon which the lords of the council referred the examination of the matter in controverfy to the judges of affize that went that circuit, to the end that they might be certified and better informed by the faid juftices, of fuch courfe as upon good advice and deliberation they fhould find in their judgment agreeable to law, and meet to be fet down and ordered in that behalf ; who accordingly entered into confideration of the complaints on both fides and advifed with the reft of the judges touching the charter granted to that corporation, and all other matters meet to be confidered of, concerning the matters in controverfy, and returned certificates of their opinions of fuch order of agreement as they thought fit and convenient to be obferved and eftablifhed, according to law and juftice for the public good and government of the faid town. Wherefore the mayor and parties indifferently fent up to follicit a peaceful end of thofe controverfies, having taken knowledge did confent thereto ; and thereupon by confent of the faid parties, it was among other things ordered ; That there fhould be a council in that town of twenty four perfons only, out of which the aldermen for the time being, fhould always be excepted ; and that the faid council, with the mayor, or the greater part of them, being at fuch affembly, without any other of the faid corporation, fhould fet and let the town's-lands, bridge-lands, and fchool-lands, taking unto them the chamberlains, bridge-mafters and fchool-wardens, refpectively, as their places for the lands within their feveral offices fhould require, as by the faid order and agreement, which the burgeffes have ready to produce when occafion fhall require will plainly appear. So that now all pretences of the aldermen being of the council, or having any thing to do with the corporation-lands, fchool-lands, or the bridge-lands, was adjudged againft, both by the judges, and the lords of the privy-council, and accordingly was wholly laid afide, till of late.

THE cafe ftanding thus, and the mayor, aldermen and burgeffes of that corporation being by their burgefs oath particularly obliged *that the franchifes of the faid town they will maintain, fuftain with their bodies, their goods and their chattels to their power, and them not let neither for love nor dread, without regard of any man, but maintain the laws, good cuftoms, and franchifes of that town*: And divers burgeffes of that town being informed, about the beginning of *Eafter-Term* laft, that the mayor and fome of the aldermen of that town had a defign to furrender the charters of that corporation ; it was fcarce credited by any of the burgeffes, that the mayor, or almoft any of the aldermen, would confent to do any thing fo directly contrary to their burgefs oath ; yet divers burgeffes of the faid town confidering they had taken the faid oath for preferving the rights of the town, thought it but convenient

nient for the prevention of the ill confequences which they well knew muft befal that town if their charters fhould be delivered up, and a new charter taken without the privity, confent, or hearing of the burgeffes of that town, to order four caveats to be entered ; and accordingly in *Eafter-Term*, ordered two to be entered at the lord *Chancellor's*, and two at the *Attorney-General's*, one of which caveats in each place was againft paffing any new charter to the town of *Nottingham*, without the privity, confent, or hearing, of the burgeffes of that town ; the other againft the accepting of any furrender of any charter of that town without the like privity, confent, and hearing. Which faid caveats were entered accordingly.

A N D fo the matter refted till the 25th of *July* laft ; but upon that day the mayor called a council without giving notice what the bufinefs would be, unlefs it was to thofe of his own party and confederacy. But that he had thoughts of furrendering when he came to the hall, will be pretty manifeft from what he did after the queftion was put to the vote and the poll taken : There appeared at the hall the mayor and five aldermen and two and twenty of the council, and Mr. *William Toplady*, (who the laft year by order of *Gervas Rippon*, the then mayor, was fworn in as alderman, tho' Mr. *Sherwin*, who ftood in competition with Mr. *Toplady*, had near twice as many votes ; upon which Mr. *Sherwin* brought his *Mandamus*, and the caufe is yet undecided in the court of *King's-Bench*) after fome bufinefs in the hall was difpatched, the mayor caufed a queftion to be put for furrendering the charters of that town ; and tho' it was declared by fome of the council that the aldermen had no right to vote therein, yet the mayor caufed a poll to be taken and admitted them and Mr. *Toplady* as voters, fave only that Mr. alderman *Edge* fufpended his vote and gave it neither way. The reft voted as followeth : *viz.*

For furrendering the Charter. ——	Againft furrendering the charter.
Gervas Wild, mayor,	*William Greaves*, alderman,
Chriftopher Hall,	*John Greaves*, } coroners,
John Parker, } aldermen,	*Samuel Richards*, }
Gervas Rippon,	*Robert Green*, fheriff,
William Toplady, alderman *de facto*,	*Huntingdon Eyre*,
William Mabbot,	*Roger Riley*,
Edward Mabbot,	*Thomas Walker*,
William Petty,	*Richard Smith*,
Robert Wortley,	*Francis Salmon*,
Hugh Walker,	*Ralph Bennet*,
William Woolhoufe,	*John Sherwin*,
John Whitby,	*Samuel Smith*,
Thomas Lee,	*Thomas Trigg*,
John Unwin.	*William Smith*.

S O that if the aldermen fhould be admitted to have a right to vote in the council, yet there was no majority for the furrender ; but on the contrary, the aldermen having no colour of right either by prefcription, or charter, or otherwife, for the reafons aforefaid, to be of the council ; it is plain there was only the mayor and nine of the council for the furrender, and thirteen of the council againft it ; and confequently that the greater part of the council voted againft the furrender : Nor

can

can it be imagined that the council of that corporation, (being neither settled by prescription, nor vested in by charter, but only brought in by consent and choice of all the burgesses, only for the better managery of the revenues of the corporation, and dispatch of some ordinary affairs, and not intrusted with many rights of that town) can pretend to any power of surrendering the charters and liberties of that town more than any small number of burgesses. So that how the surrender of fourteen men against the vote of the greater number of the council, and will of almost all the burgesses, should be good in law, is not yet well understood. And if the putting of the town-seal to an instrument without the consent of the body corporate, should be said to be sufficient in law to give away the lands and rights of any body corporate, than any thief that can but steal the corporation seal, will have it in his power, tho' he be no member of the corporation, to give up the lands and liberties thereof; which indeed would be a strange piece of law and justice to be owned in any nation that pretends to sense and honesty. Yet Mr. *Mayor*, all this notwithstanding, did as soon as the said vote was over, pull out of his pocket an instrument in writing, purporting a surrender of their charters, and caused the town-seal to be affixed thereto without any further vote. The draught of the instrument as it is commonly said, was first made at *London*, and thence transmitted to an *honourable person in Nottinghamshire*, and by his order conveyed to Mr. *Mayor*. But this report if it were not for one thing, which it's believed will be proved if there be occasion, might seem not to be well grounded, because as it afterwards will appear, this surrender was not thought sufficient, and so another was sealed; which yet one of the aldermen would have to be the very same, word for word, with that which was first sent up sealed to *London*; as if twice sealing would make that effectual which was not so by being once sealed. But it is likely he had not heard what is commonly reported, and perhaps will be proved when time serves, that the first instrument for surrendering that was sealed, was drawn so as to make a surrender, by the *right honourable the earl of Hallifax*, and Sir *Leoline Jenkins*.

AFTER the said vote touching the intended surrender was over, many of the burgesses of *Nottingham* considering their oath, and that there were many customs and privileges, in reference to trade, which the burgesses of the corporation held only by custom and prescription; and that as some lands which that corporation held, was by grant from some of his majesty's royal predecessors, so most of their town-lands, (which are of great annual value) were given by private persons; thought fit to ask advice of counsel in several points.

THE first question proposed to counsel was: " Whether if the charters were " surrendered, and a new one taken, the new grant would not preserve the lands of " the corporation ?

TO which the counsel replyed : " That if the charters of any body corporate, " were lawfully surrendered, then the corporation that held by such charters, was " dissolved; and that if they had any lands which had been given to that corpora-" tion, the heirs of those who gave those lands, would, as soon as such surrender was " compleated, be intituled to the lands, and recover the same. — And they said, " Those lands which had been given to such corporation by any of his majesty's pre-" decessors, his majesty might if he pleased grant them again to the corporation, but " no new charter of his could, as they conceived, give the corporation any title to

" those

" thofe lands which had been given by private perfons, or enable the corporation
" to keep them from the heirs of thofe that gave them, in cafe fuch furrender
" fhould be. — And fo they fay, it was refolved by the judges when the monafte-
" ries were furrendered or diffolved; and that therefore a fpecial act of parliament
" was advifed to be made, and accordingly was made, to veft thofe lands in the king,
" there being no other way to hinder them from going to the heirs of thofe that gave
" them, when by furrender they had diffolved thofe corporations."

T H E fecond queftion propofed was : " Whether if the mayor and burgeffes of
" a corporation, claim any right of common, by cuftom or prefcription upon other
" men's lands, as is the cafe of *Stafford, Derby, Coventry,* and many other corpo-
" rations, they can furrender their charters, and yet by any new charter to be ob-
" tained from his majefty, or by any means, preferve their right of common ?"

T O which it was anfwered : " That if the mayor and burgeffes of any corpora-
" tion, claim fuch common, and afterwards make fuch furrender, and fo diffolve the
" body corporate, their prefcription for common is deftroyed, and tho' his majefty
" fhould pleafe to incorporate them a-new, yet their title to the common will, as
" they conceive, be totally loft."

T H E third queftion was : " Whether the town of *Nottingham,* being one of the
" ancienteft corporations of *England,* and free of tolls in moft places, fhould have
" the fame privilege if they furrendered their charters ?

T O which it was anfwered : " That if the town of *Nottingham* furrendered
" their charters, and fo diffolved their corporation, then in all other places that had
" formerly tolls granted them and kept their old charters they fhould have toll of
" *Nottingham* men, and all fuch corporations as fhall fo furrender, notwithftanding
" any new charter that can be granted them.

T H E laft queftion propounded was : " Whether if the mayor, or any other
" members of a corporation do, without the major part of the body corporate, occa-
" fion the furrender of the charters of that corporation, the particular perfons that
" received damage by that furrender, may not have an action at law for recovery of
" their damages ?"

T O which it was anfwered : " That it was no queftion but that every particular
" perfon that fhould be any ways damaged by fuch furrender, might by actions at
" common-law recover all his damages of thofe perfons that occafioned the furren-
" der."

Y E T it was thought advifeable, as the moft proper way for preventing the
furrendering of the charters, and of thofe inconveniencies and fuits which might be
occafioned thereby, or by taking of a new charter, if obtained by the mayor and a
few burgeffes, without the privity, confent or hearing of the reft; that the major
part of the burgeffes fhould prefent Mr. *Mayor* with their fenfe of his proceedings,
and declare their *diffent from any furrender.* And accordingly a writing was drawn
and figned by betwixt three and four hundred of the burgeffes; and then a fair copy
made and examined with the original, and fo with all the burgeffes names to it that
had

had fubfcribed, was by feveral of the burgeffes, and in the prefence of feveral gentle-men of quality that were no burgeffes, prefented to the mayor on the 4th day of *Au-guft*, as the fenfe of moft of the burgeffes of that town. The writing fo prefented was as followeth, *viz*:

To Mr. *Gervas Wild,* Mayor of *Nottingham.*

S I R,

" WE whofe names are hereunto fubfcribed, being burgeffes of the town of
" Nottingham, and knowing or underftanding, that you and thirteen more of
" the corporation, have without the confent of the burgeffes of this town, and againft
" their will, taken upon you to agree to the furrender of the charters, liberties, and
" franchifes, of this corporation, and to caufe the corporation feal to be affixed to an
" inftrument for making fuch furrender ; and being by our burgefs-oath obliged to
" preferve as far as in us lies, all the rights and privileges of this corporation ; and
" confidering what great damage it muft neceffarily be to the corporation in general,
" and to us and every other particular burgefs of the corporation, if the charters, li-
" berties and franchifes fhould be fo furrendered, have thought ourfelves obliged,
" in order to prevent fo great on evil, to fignify thefe our thoughts on what you have
" done or are about to do ; and that many of your liberties and franchifes, which are
" only held by cuftom and not by charter, will certainly be loft, if you make fuch
" furrender as you have agreed to. We do therefore, hereby declare our diffent
" from thofe your proceedings ; and that we neither do nor fhall confent, or have
" confented, that any furrender of any charter, liberty, franchife, or privilege of
" the corporation of *Nottingham,* fhould be made either by you or any other member
" of this corporation or other perfon or perfons whatfoever ; and that we will by
" all lawful ways and means oppofe and hinder the furrendering or vacating of any
" of the charters, rights, liberties, or privileges of this corporation ; and that in
" cafe you occafion the furrender of any of the charters, rights, liberties, or privi-
" leges of this corporation, we fhall expect from you fuch fatisfaction as the law
" will allow us."

THE burgeffes were alfo advifed, to order, and accordingly did order caveats in the names of fome particular burgeffes, on behalf of themfelves and moft of the burgeffes in the town, to be entered at the lord *Chancellor's,* the lord *Privy-Seal's,* and the *Signet-Office* againft furrendering of any of the charters of that town, with-out the privity, confent, and hearing of the faid burgeffes, and againft paffing of any new charter to that town, without the like privity, confent, and hearing. And the burgeffes have had an account from their agent at *London,* that he had entered fuch caveats, at the lord *Chancellor's,* and in the office of lord *Conway,* and Sir *Leolin Jenkins,* it being commonly reported that the lord *Privy-Seal* had delivered up the privy-feal to the faid Sir *Leolin.*

THE burgeffes were farther advifed to petition the lord *Chancellor* to be heard before any furrender of the charters fhould be accepted, or any new charter to that town fhould pafs the broad-feal; and accordingly a petition was drawn and figned by above three hundred and sixty burgesses, and a copy thereof fairly engrossed, with the names of the burgesses that had subscribed, was sent and presented to the lord *Chancellor* at *Bath*, on thursday the 10th of this instant *August*, which petition was in these words following, *viz:*

To the Right Honourable the Lord High *Chancellor* of *England*.

The humble petition of the Burgesses of the town of NOTTINGHAM, whose names are hereunto subscribed, on behalf of themselves and most of the Burgesses of that Town.

MOST HUMBLY SHEWETH,

" THAT the town of *Nottingham* being a borough by prescription, and an
" ancient corporation ; and the burgesses of that town, (who are a body-cor-
" porate by the name of mayor and burgesses) having many liberties, privi-
" leges, rights and franchises, which they hold by grant and confirmation from his
" majesty and his royal predecessors, and many other rights, liberties, and privi-
" leges which they hold by custom or prescription ; and divers persons having gi-
" ven lands to that corporation of a very great annual value : The present mayor
" with three or four of the aldermen, and nine other burgesses of that corporation,
" have declared that they design to take a new charter, and have taken upon them,
" without the consent of your petitioners, and most of the burgesses of that town, to agree
" to the surrender of the charters of that corporation ; and have taken the town-seal,
" and affixed to an instrument, designing thereby to make an actual and absolute surren-
" der of all the said charters, which if they have power to effect, it will (as your
" petitioners are advised) not only dissolve the corporation, deprive your petitioners
" and other burgesses of that town, of many rights, liberties, and privileges which
" they held by custom and prescription, cause all the lands given to that corporation,
" to revert to the heirs of the donors, and disinherit your petitioners and other bur-
" gesses of that town, of all the said lands, liberties, and privileges which both they
" and their predecessors, as burgesses of that town have inherited and ought to en-
" joy, but also subject your petitioners and their freeholds, against their will, to such
" services, damages, and great inconveniencies, as may be brought upon them by
" the contrivance ef the said mayor and aldermen, in case they can obtain a new
" charter to pass the broad-seal, without the privity, consent, or hearing, of your pe-
" titioners.

" Your petitioners therefore humbly pray your Lord-
" ship to take into consideration the aforesaid mis-
" chiefs, damages, and inconveniences that are like
" to befall your Petitioners and other burgesses of
" that town, in case such surrender should be made
" and accepted and a new charter taken by the said
" mayor and aldermen : And that your lordship
" would

" would pleafe, before fuch furrender be accepted
" or any new charter for that town be paffed the
" broad-feal, to grant your petitioners a day of hear-
" ing, and to order thereupon as fhall be agreeable
" to equity and juftice.

" *And your petitioners fhall ever pray.*

T H E petition being delivered as aforefaid, and Mr. *Mayor* having been acquainted in manner aforefaid, by the generality of the burgeffes, that they neither
had confented nor fhould confent to a furrender, of any of the charters, rights or liberties of the town, and the burgeffes having been advifed by council that no inftrument for making a furrender of the charters to the earl of *Hallifax* and Sir *Leoline
Jenkins* could be effectual in law ; it was hoped that there would not have been any
farther progrefs in the bufinefs, at leaft before the burgeffes were heard upon their
caveats and petition. And it was taken for granted, that no new inftrument in order
to any furrender, could be made and fealed without calling together the council of
that town ; becaufe by cuftom of that town, the town-feal has always ufed to be
kept under the cuftody of three locks and keys, and not taken out but in council, and
thofe three keys kept by three feveral perfons, for better preventing any indirect ufe
of the feal : But contrary to the burgeffes expectaion, it was fignified in the public
prints that came down to *Nottingham* on the 19th of *Auguft*, viz. *That upon the 14th
of Auguft a furrender of Nottingham charters was made to his majefty.* It will
fcarce be a queftion, by what means, or how lawfully Mr. *Mayor* came by the
feal, or how valid fuch furrender is like to be.

T H I S is the true cafe of the burgeffes of *Nottingham*, who are ready to make
good every matter of fact, as herein ftated, whenever there fhall be occafion, and
doubt not, but to prove, if they may either be heard upon their petition or caveats ;
and however queftion not, but by the affiftance of the courts of juftice, they fhall ftill
preferve their rights, notwithftanding all the endeavours that have been ufed to give
up their charters and liberties.

Some

Some remarks of a learned Gentleman relating to the opinion of Dr. GALE, that *Nottingham* has been a Roman Station, occasioned by his perusal of my INTRODUCTION.

CONCERNING *Roman* remains, I have never yet met with any thing to induce me to believe there are any. And Dr. *Gale's* endeavours to fix *Antoninus's Causennæ* at *Nottingham* have not at all been agreed to by later writers, *viz. Baxter, Stukeley, Salmon, Horseley.* His subterraneous cavities you justly disallow to have any of the roman taste in them ; and there are no appearances of a roman road leading from the southward to *Nottingham*, or from *Lindum* (*Lincoln*) northward. Nor perhaps has the doctor any advantage over Mr. *Baxter*, from the number of miles in the *Iter* : If I understand you right, the miles you set down from Mr. *Baxter* are the present computed miles ; and antiquaries by comparing these with miles in the itinerary in places about which there are no doubts, have found that the itinerary miles are to be computed most commonly at 4 to 3, but sometimes at 5 to 4, and according to this last reckoning 105 in the itinerary make 84 computed miles, which is within one of your number from *Baxter.*

IF by the arguments which have been brought against Dr. *Gale, Nottingham* be thrown out of the *Iter*, they will hold equally strong against *Bridgeford's* being in the *Iter.* And as to its having been a station, if ever it was one, it must have been only a *statio æstiva*, as it lies a considerable distance from any military way ; but as there are no indications remaining of any station thereabouts, except the pot of money found at *Wilford* ; the evidence seems too slight to prove one ; and especially considering that Dr. *Stukeley* is a man extremely liable to mistakes. I have not his book here in the country, but I remember three from amongst several, that have fallen accidentally under my observation. In speaking of the garden in *Stoney-street*, he mentions it as belonging to one *Hurst*, a name never heard of there ; he says that at *Chester* there are but four churches, when I was there, I had ten named to me, exclusive (I think) of St. *Oswald's*, which is in a cross-isle of the cathedral, separated from the rest by a slight partition ; and in some editions of *Camden's Britannia* it is expresly said that *Chester* has eleven parishes. In describing the famous inscription on *Julius Vitallis's* tomb-stone at *Bath*, the doctor gives a reading of one part of it, which is not only different from what plainly appears there, but inconsistent with any sense or grammatical construction.

THESE instances shew how superficial an observer he was ; and therefore in this account of the pot of money, I should be glad of a little farther satisfaction, as whether the old man who told him of it, was one who could distinguish roman from any other ancient coin, and indeed whether he named any sort of coin at all, but upon its being found in a pot, the doctor's own strong imagination, full of antiquarian ideas might presently convert the pot into an urn, and the money into roman coin.

UPON which I took the liberty with all due submission to offer to that most judicious gentleman's farther consideration, —— This Reply :

I

I readily agree that Dr. *Stukeley* commits many errors, where he has only cast a transitory eye upon places and things, or not minutely weighed every circumstance. I could mention a number of mistakes, besides those you have pointed out, one only shall suffice at this time, which if it is not a wilful one, shews the utmost degree of indolence. He says p. 113. That below *Rochester*-bridge there lie about 50 of our biggest first rate men of war : when by asking any common sailor he might have been informed, that we have but seven of that rate : Yet in other places where he has bestowed due attention, his observations are not to be slighted, which I take to be likewise your opinion of the doctor, since among other late writers you are pleased to make use of his name against the dean.

FOR my part I always read him with caution, as appears by some of my notes, which probably may have escaped your notice. *So much of the doctor.*

I frankly confess I never yet could find any roman remains at *Nottingham*, (tho' I have seen a considerable number of roman coins, said to be found in the parish of *Plumtre*) but I may notwithstanding be allowed with some eminent antiquaries, Dr. *Plot, Somner,* and others, to be of opinion that distances, and the neighbourhood of military ways are not very slight proofs All antiquaries agree that *East-Bridge-ford* was a roman station ; they also allow that the distance from one station to another is commonly observed to have been 8, 9 to 10 miles, this being granted, would not one reasonably conjecture our *Bridgeford* conveniently situated near the river *Trent* and not quite 5 itinerary miles N. W. of the *Fosse-way,* and between 8 and 9 itinerary miles distant from the other *Bridgeford,* to have also been a station? The distance from the *Fosse-way* ought not to be looked upon as a great one, for the romans did not always place their stations near their roads as is plainly apparent in *Littleburgh,* which lies upwards of 9 computed miles N. W. of the roman highway, and would perhaps not have been made a station had it not been situated so near the river *Trent,* which same reason favours our *Bridgeford,* and if besides the pot of coin Dr. *Stukeley* speaks of, should prove to have been roman, our title will not be so weak as it may at first appear ; nor is it very improbable, if we consider that the roman coins found about *East-Bridgeford* and elsewhere are most of them brass, pretty large, and thick, and the british and saxon coins generally smaller and thinner, and most of the latter silver or mixed metal, and that they are commonly found scattered and in small quantities, and seldom in pots or urns ; to which if we add, that upon finding this pot, doubtless divers people were acquainted with it, and the clergyman of the parish, or some person more knowing than the old man, might have told him that that coin was roman.

AS to what relates to the miles, you will find upon examination that *Gale* and *Baxter* use much the same measure, be they therefore itinerary or computed ones, the dean in this particular holds the same advantage over *Baxter* as before, and consequently it does not clearly appear that *Nottingham* is fairly thrown out of the *Iter.*

IN order to be the better satisfied, which of these two learned gentlemen's conjecture is the best founded, it will not be amiss to let Mr. *Baxter* speak for himself: *p.* 65. he says :

Cantensis :

Cantennis: Ita enim ausus sum reponere in Antonino pro vitioso Causennis vel Gausennis ut edidit simlerus, quod nihil esse necesse est. Solute quis scripserit cant en (vel an) ist, sive ambitus vel flexura aquæ. Hæc urbs hodie Grantham est in majoribus icenis sive Lindensi conventu. Siquidem idem sonat Britannis Grant quod & Cant sicuti supra docuimus in voce ad Tavum: Et Grantham etiam ibrida compositione profertur pro Grant avon. Amnis scilicet curvatura.

N O W having set down the opinions of these two authors in their own words, the case stands thus:

Dr. *Gale* with a very small and allowable alteration, changes *Causennas* into *Caufennas*, and without straining makes the etymology suit *Nottingham*, he supports this opinion by making his distances agree with the Itinerary, besides which it may be said in favour of him, that the station, *East-Bridgeford*, is at a proper distance for *Nottingham* or *West Bridgeford* either, to be likewise one, and that the *Fosse-way* coming from *Lindum* (*Lincoln*) runs at an inconsiderable distance on the left hand of it, not to say one word of the pot of coin.

Mr. *Baxter*, assumes an authority, hardly (if at all) allowable, to make a very considerable alteration in the name, when in favour of his *Grantham* he turns *Caufennas* into *Cantennas*, and from the turning of the river near *Grantham* and no other concurring circumstance, he positively affirms *Cantennas* to be *Grantham*, tho' there be no roman road from *Gormanchefter* to *Grantham*, at the same time that, using the same measure of miles with doctor *Gale*, he is no less than 20 miles short of the Itinerary.

Y O U mention that later writers have not at all agreed with Dr. *Gale*, this (with humble submission) is pleading authority. I would willingly read these modern gentlemen with as little prejudice in their favour as I do those who have gone before them, especially when I find some of them commit grosser errors then their predecessors. I cannot help wondering to see such a palpable mistake as a certain dignified author in his additions to *Camden* makes, about the situation of *Flawford* church; speaking of *Lenton* he says: " At a little distance from hence there stands in a large " field, a church with a spire-steeple, called *Flawford* church, the burying place " of *Ruddington* a great country town above half a mile west from it, &c." whereas *Lenton* lies on the north side of *Trent*, and the church he speaks of stands near three miles south of that river, and that large country town is but a village: Besides talking of *Stanford*, he immediately mentions its neighbour *Clifton*, which neighbour is at least between five and six statute miles distant from it. Another antiquary would fain make *Lenton* (a village a mile distant from *Nottingham*, known only for a priory of *Cluniac* monks) the noted *Lindum* of the romans; I wave bringing any more instances of this kind, tho' it were easy for me to produce a many. Some of the late writers of antiquities are strangely carried away by the fertility of their own imagination, all are highly beholden to the old ones for the solid foundation of their inquiries, and it is too frequently seen that when a new antiquary is at a loss for new discoveries in certain places, rather than be thought a meer transcriber of the labours of others, he racks his brain to advance something contradictory to what has been said by other men.

T H A T

THAT you have obſerved this in the courſe of your reading of authors of this claſs, I dare not doubt. What I have ſaid upon this ſubject will I hope not draw upon me the imputation of being tenacious of my own opinion, for far from deſiring that any one ſhould acquieſce with what I offer unleſs upon good grounds; I am ſo fond of the beauty of truth in any reſpect, that I would at all times gladly embrace it, tho' it ſhould lay open to me the vanity and fruitleſſneſs of my application for ſeven years paſt, and that I do not only fancy myſelf ſo, but am really of that mind, I conclude from theſe ſigns: In the firſt place, that I can look upon things as yet with an unaltered eye, and take in objects as they really appear to the ſenſes; and in the ſecond place, that my imagination hitherto is not over-ſtock'd with antiquarian ideas, and that I ſee myſelf ſtill at a vaſt diſtance from the enthuſiaſm of that ſtudy, which I look upon to be a great happineſs.

I am &c.

Exemplification of Doomſday - Book concerning the town of NOTTINGHAM.

Inter recorda domini regis Caroli *in theſaur. recepta ſcaccarii ſui ſub cuſtodia duorum commiſſariorum pro executione officii theſaurarii et cancellarii ibidem remanentia,* viz. *in libro vocato* Doomſdaie *inter alia ſic continentur ut ſequitur.*

Snotingham-ſcire.

IN burgo *Snotingeham* fuere T. R. *Edwardi* CLXXIII. burgenſes, & XIX. villani, adhunc burgum adjacent VI. carucatæ terræ ad gildam regis et unum pratum, et ſilvæ minutæ VI. quarentenas longæ et quinque latæ. Hæc terra partita fuit inter XXXVIII. burgenſes, et de cenſu terræ et operibus burgenſium reddit LXXV. ſolidos et VII. denarios, et de duobus monetariis XL. ſolidos. Inibi habuit comes *Toſti* unam carucatam terræ de cujus terræ ſoca habebat rex duos denarios et ipſe comes tertium. *Hugo* vice-comes filius *Baldrici* invenit CXXXVI. homines manentes modo ſunt ſedecim minus. Ipſe tamen *Hugo* in terra comitis in novo burgo ſtatuit XIII. domus quæ antea non fuerant apponens eas in cenſu veteris burgi.

IN *Snotingeham* eſt una eccleſia in dominio regis, in qua jacent III. manſiones burgi et quinque bovatæ terræ de ſupra dictis ſex carucatis cum ſaca et ſoca et ad eandem eccleſiam pertinent V. acræ terræ et dimidia, de qua rex habet ſacam et ſocam. Burgenſes habent VI. carucatas terræ ad arandum et XX. bordarios et XIII. carucas. In aqua trentæ ſoliti erant piſcari, et modo querelam faciunt eo quod piſcari prohibentur. Tempore regis *Edwardi* reddebat *Snotingeham* XVIII. libras, modo XXX. libras et X. de moneta.

ROGERUS de BUSLY habet in *Snotingeham* III manſiones in quibus ſedent XI domus reddentes IIII ſolidos et VII denarios.

Qq

WIL-

WILLIELMUS PEVEREL, habet **XLVIII** domus mercatorum reddentes **XXXVI**. folidos et **XII** domus equitum, et octo bordarios.

RADULPHUS de BURUN, habet **XIII** domus equitum in una harum manet unus mercator.

GULBERTUS IIII domus.

RADULPHUS filius *HUBERTI*, habet **XI** domus, in his manent tres mercatores.

GOISFREDUS ALSELYN, habet **XXI** domus et *Arcardus Presbyter* duas domus.

I N crofta *Presbyteri* funt **LXV** domus et in his habet Rex facam et focam, Ecclefia cum omnibus quæ ad eam pertinent valet per annum centum folidos.

RICHARDUS FRELLE, habet IIII domus.

I N foffato burgi funt **XVII** domus, et aliæ fex domus.

WILLIELMO PEVEREL, conceffit rex **X** acras terræ ad faciendum pomerium.

I N *Snotingeham* habuit Rex *Edwardus* unam carucatam terræ cumgilda terræ **II** caru. ibi habet modo rex **XI** villanos habentes IIII carucatas **XII** acras terræ prati, in dominio nihil. T. R. *Edwardi* valuit III libras modo fim.

I N *Snotingeham* aqua trentæ et foffa et via verfus *Eboracum* cuftodiuntur, ita ut fiquis impedierit tranfitum navium, et fiquis araverit, vel foffam fecerit in via regis infra duas perticas emendare habet p. **VIII** libras.

> Exemplificat. p. *Scipionem le Squyre* pro comiff.
> Scaccarii XV *junii* 1635.

Exemplification of the King's ancient poffeffions in NOTTINGHAM in the time of the Civil War.

Parcell poffeff. antiq. Coron. Angl.

Villa Nott. } val.   I N C R E M. reddit. refervat pro fœda firma vill. *Nott.* et pro increment } in   diverfis franchefiis et libertatibus p. litteras patentes *Henrici* infrafcrip }   quondam regis *Anglie* fexti anno regni fui **XXIX**. majori, hominibus et burgenfibus ville predicte **XIII** *fb.* IIII *d.* conceffis five confirmatis p. ann.

I

I find the abovesaid rent of XIII s. IIII d. per annum upon the mayor, men and burgesses of the town of *Nottingham*; became first charged in the annual roll of the exchequer, the 33d year of *Henry* VI. since which time the same rent has continued so charged in the subsequent annual rolls, but the date of the letters patents or the days, time and place when and where the same rent is reserved payable, I cannot certify for that I have not seen the letters patents or any copy or inrollment thereof. (*a*)

vill. Nott. } *val.* } A N N U A L. redit. de censu domorum plurimorum in vill.
redit. infra } *in* } *Nott.* per annum XXIII *sh.* VI *d.* solubit et de *Tostis* mo-
script. } } netariorum cum incremento p. annum IX*sh.* solubit. p. homines
vill. *Nott.* prout p. magnum rotulum scaccarii de anno VII
Johannis quondam regis *Angl.* et annual. rotul. scaccarii subsequend. *viz.* XXXII*sh.*
VI *d.*

I find that the last abovesaid premisses became first charged in the annual roll of the exchequer of the 6th year of *Richard* I.

B U T cannot further explain or set forth the particulars out of which the said XXXII *sh.* VI *d.* p. ann. do arise, neither can I find any grant or further improvement made thereof or therefore.

B U T I find by the annual roll of the 20th year of *Henry* III. that the men of *Nottingham* were discharged of VI *sh.* VIII *d.* p. ann. by the king's writ, for the house of one *William Jourdan*, which the king had assigned to *Reginald* of *Mendec* and *Esolot* his wife in recompence of their house by the ditch of the barbican of the castle of *Nottingham*, and that VI *sh.* VIII *d.* p. ann. should be every year computed to the bailiffs of *Nottingham* out of the XXXII *sh.* VI *d.* p. ann. *de censu domorum*, which has been allowed yearly unto the men of *Nottingham* ever since. But I have not seen the said writ. Whether the same ought to be allowed so hereafter, is offered to consideration.

Ex. Hen. Croke.

Vill. Nott. } *val* } A N N U A L. redit. reservat. de tenemento illo quod fuit *Mosei* de
redit infra } *in* } de *Suabur, Judei* et de tenemento illo in eadem villa quod fuit *Peytengu* quondam *Judei Nott.* et *Elie* filii ejus et de domo illa
script. } } que fuit schola judeorum in eadem villa, p. literas patentes *Eduardi*
quondam regis *Anglie* Imi. gerent. datum quinto die maij anno regni sui XX. *Hugoni Putrell de Thurmeston* et heredibus suis imperpetuum concess. reddend. eidem summam die sancti *Michaelis* p. manus ballivorum *Nott.* qui pro tempore fuer. p. ann. —— —— I *d.*

(*a*) *The letters patents are dated the* 28th *of* June *in the* 27th *of* Henry VI.

I have made thefe five particulars by order from the honourable truftees according to an act of parliament of *March* 1649, for the fale of *Feofarm* rents, &c. belonging to the late King, Queen and Prince.

27th of April 1650.　　　　　　　　　　*Ex. p. Hen. Croke. Cl. Pipe.*

An Account of the Family and Anceftors of the Right Honourable WILLIAM Lord BYRON.

IT is evident from *Doomfday-book* that this family had large poffeffions in the time of *William* the *Conqueror,* as in the weft-ridings and fouth ridings in the county of *Lincoln.*

RALPH de BURON, held divers manours in *Nottinghamfhire* and *Derbyfhire*; this *Ralph* is the direct anceftor of the prefent lord *Byron.* In *Nottingham* town (fee *introduction*). In the county the manours of *Ofcentune, Calun, Hochdale, Rampeftune, Laudecote, Godegrave.* In *Derbyfhire* he held the manours of *Weftune, Horfley, Deneby, Halun* and *Hereby.*

IN the park of *Horfley* there was a caftle, fome of the ruins are ftill vifible, called *Horeftan* caftle, which was the chief manfion of his fucceffors. *Hugh* fucceeded *Ralph* lord of the caftle of *Horeftan.* —— *William Byron*, was in the king's army in *Scotland* in the reign of *Edward* I. — *John de Byron*, received a præcipe the 8th of *Edward* the 1ft. to meet the king with horfe and arms, together with the fheriff of *Yorkfhire,* *William de Latimer* the elder, and *Ralph Fitz-William*, at *Carlifle*, on *Midfimmer-day*, to march againft the *Scots.* In the 25th of the fame reign he had another fummons, (as holding 20 *l.* per ann. land in *Northamptonfhire*) to be at *London* the funday following the octave of St. *John the Baptift*, with horfe and arms, to go on an expedition with the king beyond the fea : And on the 28th of his reign, he was commanded (holding 40 *l.* in the county) to come to *Carlifle* with horfe and arms on the feaft of the nativity of *John the Baptift,* in order to go againft the *Scots* : This *John* was cuftos or governor of the city of *York,* the 24th of *Edward* I. as he had been for five or fix years before of the caftle of *Dover.* Sir *John Byron* his fon fucceeded him, and this Sir *Richard Byron* his fon, who died the 21ft year of *Edward* III. he left Sir *James Byron* his fucceffor, this left iffue Sir *John Byron* and Sir *Richard Byron*, the firft ferved in the war of *France* under king *Edward* III. and was knighted for his valour at the fiege of *Calais*, dying without iffue, his brother Sir *Richard* fucceeded in the eftate the 4th of *Richard* II. This Sir *Richard* married the fecond daughter of Sir *William Colewick,* he died the 21ft of *Richard* II. leaving behind his only fon Sir *John Byron* ; he had three fons *Richard, Nicholas* and *Ralph* ; his eldeft *Richard,* died in his father's life time ; he left a fon *James Byron*, who died without iffue, and was fucceeded by his uncle *Nicholas,* whofe eldeft fon was Sir *John Byron*, who taking part with *Henry* earl of *Richmond,* who knighted him foon after his landing at *Milford-haven,* and was with him at the battle of *Bofworth* where king *Richard* was flain ; when he af-

cended

ceended the throne by the name of *Henry* VII. he was much in his favour and made
conftable of *Nottingham* caftle, &c. as appears from the infcription on a monument
erected to his memory in *Colwick* church in the county of *Nottingham* : *viz.*

> Here lies Sir *John Byron*, knt. late conftable of *Nottingham*
> caftle, mafter of *Shirwood* foreft, cuftos or lieutenant of the ifle
> of *Man*, fteward of *Manchefter*-college. Which *John* died the 3d
> of *May* in the year 1488.
>
> On whofe foul god have mercy. *Amen.*

He dyed without iffue the 14th of *Henry* VII. leaving his brother *Nicholas* his heir,
this was made one of the knights of the *Bath*, at the marriage of prince *Arthur*, 17th
of *November* 1501.

> This memorial of him is at *Colwick* :
> Pray for the foul of the worthy man *Nicholas Byron*, Efq; and of
> *Joan* his confort, who made this window in the year 1496, and the
> 12th of *Henry* the 7th.

He dyed the 13th of *January* the 19th of *Henry* VII. leaving *John* his heir 16 years
old ; Sir *John* was knighted by king *Henry* VIII. he had *May* the 28th the 32d of
Henry VIII. a grant of the priory of *Newftede* with the manour of *Papilwick*, and
rectory of the fame and all the clofes of the priory, and commons in *Ravenfhede*, and
Kygell in the foreft, and all in *Newftede*, *Papilwick*, and *Lindby*, which has ever
fince been the feat of this noble family, having before refided at *Clayton*. He was
fteward of *Manchefter* and *Rochdall*, as alfo lieutenant of the foreft of *Shirwood* ;
he had iffue by his fecond lady four fons, *Nicholas*, *John*, and *Anthony*, all which
died without iffue ; but the 4th Sir *John Byron*, knighted by queen *Elizabeth*, 1579,
married *Margaret* daughter of *William Fitz-Williams*, lord deputy of *Ireland*, had
iffue two fons, Sir *John* and Sir *Nicholas Byron*.

Sir *NICHOLAS* diftinguifhed himfelf in the wars of the *Low-Countries*,
as alfo in the time of the rebellion againft king *Charles* the 1ft. in the battle of *Edge-
hill*, and as colonel general of *Chefhire* and *Shropfhire* and governor of *Chefter*; and my
lord *Clarendon* gives him the character of a perfon of great affability and dexterity,
as well as martial knowledge, which gave great life to the defigns of the well affected there, and with the encouragement of fome gentlemen of *North-Wales*, in a fhort
time raifed fuch a power of horfe and foot as made often skirmifhes with the enemy,
fometimes with notable advantage, never with any fignal lofs.

Sir *JOHN*, the eldeft brother was made knight of the *Bath*, at the coronation of
king *James* the 1ft. he had by his lady, *Anne*, daughter to Sir *Richard Molineux*,
bart. and fifter to *Richard* lord vifcount *Molineux*, eleven fons and one daughter, *Mary.*

1ft. *JOHN*, created lord *Byron.*

2d. *RICHARD*, who fucceeded his brother as lord *Byron.*

3d.

3d. *THOMAS*, died unmarried.

4th. *WILLIAM*, was drowned coming from *Ireland*.

5th. Sir *ROBERT BYRON*, colonel of foot in the civil war in the ser-vice of king *Charles* the 1st. died unmarried.

6th. *GILBERT*, died also unmarried.

7th. Sir *PHILIP BYRON*, who after many singular services in *York-shire*, was killed at the head of his regiment in the general storm made by the parlia-ment forces on *York*; he never went out with his regiment but he would tell them: " That never brave men came to any thing that resolved not to conquer or perish."

THE other sons, *Thomas, George, Charles,* and *Francis,* all died single except *Thomas,* who was knighted, and as my lord *Clarendon* writes of him was a gentleman of great courage and very good conduct; he commanded the prince of *Wales's* re-giment under the earl of *Northampton* in the fight near *Stafford,* (where the earl was killed) and charging with good execution on the enemy, received a shot in the thigh, whereby he was not able to keep the field.

TO return to Sir *John*, created lord *Byron* the 21st of K. *James* I. he was returned knight of the town of *Nottingham*, as also in the first parliament called by king *Charles* I. at whose coronation he was made knight of the *Bath*; the third of king *Charles* I. he was chosen one of the knights of the county of *Nottingham*, and being one of the lords of the bed-chamber to his majesty, and giving proofs of his courage and fidelity was made lieutenant of the tower of *London* in the year 1641, in the room of *Thomas Lunsford*, removed on a complaint of the House of Commons, but the Commons not satisfied with this change, desiring a creature of their own, used all their arts to remove Sir *John Byron*, they even carryed it so far, after the king was remo-ved to *Hampton-Court*, as to cause Sir *John* to appear at the bar of their house, but his answers were so full to all that was ask'd him that they could not but dismiss them, however, they sent again to the king and proposed Sir *John Coniers*, as a man in whom they could confide; at last, notwithstanding the lords disagreeing with them, " as well for that the disposal of the custody thereof was the king's peculiar " right and prerogative, as likewise that his majesty had committed the charge there- " of to Sir *John Byron* a person of a very ancient family, honourable extraction, " good fortune, and as unblemished a reputation as any gentleman in *England*." Notwithstanding the king's repeated refusal, he was surprized, and Sir *John* himself desiring to be freed from the agony and vexation of that place, &c. and con-sented to place in his stead Sir *John Coniers*. Sir *John Byron* had served in the *Low-Country* war and the states committed to him the care of their ordinance and ammunition; he was a very useful officer to his majesty, on the breaking out of the rebellion, he repaired with a good body of men with arms and ammunition to the standard at *Nottingham*, and brought a large sum of money to the king for supply at *Shrewsbury*; from *Nottinghamshire* he passed with some troops to countenance the commission of array, and especially in *Oxfordshire*, to secure the university from the rebels, when assaulted by the forces from *Northampton*, whither marching to

their

their relief with the utmost expedition, he lost his carriages and cabinet; he afterwards commanded the body of reserve at the battle of *Edge-hill*, and the victory of *Roundway-Down* was chiefly owing to the bravery and conduct of Sir *John Byron*, who at the head of his regiment charged Sir *Arthur Hazlerig's* cuirassiers, and after a sharp conflict in which Sir *Arthur* received many wounds, that impenetrable regiment (as *Clarendon* has it) was routed and chased on their other horse, which in half an hour were so totally dispersed, that were not one of them to be seen upon that large and spacious *Down*, every man shifting for himself, with greater danger by the precipices of the hill than he could have undergone by opposing his pursuers.

HE was 1642, the 1st of *November* with other loyalists, made doctor of the civil law at *Oxford*; 1642 *September* 19, in the first *Newberry* fight, he warily and valiantly led on the king's horse, which were so far too hard for the troops on the other side that they routed them in most places, till they had left the major part of their foot without any guard at all of horse.

THE lord *Byron* having given such proof of his courage and military conduct, and being otherwise a person of great ability, and his six valiant brothers also at that time following his loyal example, he was in consideration thereof, advanced to the degree and dignity of a baron of this realm, by the title of lord *Byron* of *Rochdale, in comitatu Lancastriæ* with limitation of that honour, in default of issue male of his own body lawfully begotten, to every his brothers, and the issue of their respective bodies, *viz. Richard, William, Thomas, Robert, Gilbert,* and *Philip*, by letters patent bearing date at *Oxford* 24th of *October* 1643, *anno* 19 *Caroli primi*; he was afterwards made field marshal general of all his majesty's forces in the counties of *Worcester, Cheshire,* and *North-Wales*, and on his uncle's, (governor of *Chester*) Sir *Nicholas Byron's* being taken prisoner, he was governor of *Chester*, whereupon the declining of the king's cause he was besieged, the which he held out to the utmost extremity, and then obtained the most honourable terms of surrender, for himself and the whole garrison that were given in *England*, except those he afterwards obtained at *Caernarvon*, after which he retired beyond sea.

THE king made him governor of the duke of *York*, and being at *Paris* when his majesty was under confinement, he was sent on importunities from *Scotland*, to get as many to declare in *England* in several places, as might distract the army and keep it from an entire engagement against them, also to dispose his old friends about *Chester* and *North-Wales* to appear as soon as might be, thereupon with the help of colonel *Robinson*, he presently possess'd himself of the island of *Anglesey* and disposed all *North-Wales* to be ready to declare as soon as the *Scots* should enter the kingdom; my lord *Byron* waited on the duke to *Brussels* to visit the duke of *Lorrain*, as also when the duke visited his sister at the *Hague*, and from thence returned with him to *Paris*; after this he accompanied the duke when he made a campaign under marshal *Turenne*, and returning to *Paris* he died there in the year 1652 without issue.

RICHARD lord *BYRON* his brother succeeded him, he was knighted by King *Charles* I. was one of those valiant colonels at the fight of *Edge-hill*, who on the first of *November* 1642 was created master of arts at *Oxford*; he was governor of *Appleby* castle in the county of *Westmorland*.—*Lloyd* in his lives of the loyalists, says fays, he deferves to be chronicled, for his government of *Newark*, and many fur-prizes of the enemy about it ; he died 1679, and left by his firft lady, *Elizabeth* daughter of *George Roffel*, Efq; of *Ratcliffe-upon-Trent, in comitatu Nottingha-miæ*, and widow of *Nicholas Strelley*, in the fame county, Efq;

WILLIAM lord *BYRON*, married *Elizabeth* daughter of *John* lord vif-count *Chaworth* in *Ireland*, by whom he had five fons, 1ft. *William*, 2d. *Richard*, 3d. *John*, 4th. *William* lord *Byron*, 5th. *Erneftus*, who all died young excepting *William* the late lord *Byron*, born 1669 ; he was one of the lords of the bedchamber to *George* prince of *Denmark*, married firft, lady *Mary* daughter to *John* earl of *Bridgewater*, and fifter to *Scroop* prefent duke of *Bridgewater*, died in *April* 1703 ; fecond, lady *Frances Williamina*, third daughter of *William Bentinck* earl of *Portland*, by whom he had iffue three fons : 1ft. *George*, born the 15th of *Octo-ber* 1707, died *July* the 6th 1720 ; 2d. *William*, born the 6th of *July* 1709, died in a few days ; 3d. *William Henry*, born the 23d of *October* 1710, died foon after ; 1 daughter, *Frances*, born *Auguft* the 10th 1711, died *September* the 21ft 1724 ; which *Frances* lady *Byron*, died *March* the 31ft 1712, at *Kenfington* ; his third lady, *Frances*, fecond daughter of *William* lord *Berkley*, of *Stratton*, he married in 1720, by whom he had a daughter, *Iffabella*, born *November* the 10th 1721, and five fons.

1ft. *WILLIAM* lord *BYRON*, born *November* the 5th, 1722.

2d. *JOHN*, born *November* the 8th, 1723.

3d. *RICHARD*, born *October* the 28th, 1724.

4th. *CHARLES*, born *April* the 6th, 1725, died *May* the 16th, 1731.

5th. *GEORGE*, born *April* 22d 1730.

THE late lord died, *Auguft* the 8th 1736.

Dr.

Dr. CALAMY's *Account of* Mr. WHITLOCK, REYNOLDS, and BARRET.

MR. *John Whitlock*, M. A. son of Mr. *Richard Whitlock*, merchant of *London*, of an ancient family, studied at *Cambridge* in *Emanuel* college, under *Ralph Cudworth*. He was besides his learning, remarkable for an unparallel'd example of intimacy and friendship between him and Mr. *Reynolds*, which begun at the university, where they were chums and lasted upwards of 50 years.

THEY travelled together they studied together, they lived together, they preached together, until death separated them. They fixed together at *Nottingham* 1651; Mr. *Whitlock* had the presentation of the place from the then marquis of *Dorchester*, and Mr. *Reynolds* was joined with him as lecturer : He had a good estate of his own, and was ready to do good with it ; he was very charitable to poor scholars ; he had one son who succeeded him in the dissenting meeting-house, and a daughter ; he died *December* the 4th 1708, aged 83. His funeral sermon was preached by Mr. *Barret*.

HE published a discourse of keeping ourselves from our iniquities ; two farewell sermons printed anno 1663, on *Rev*. 3. 3. he also published a sermon which he preached at the funeral of *Francis Pierepont*, Esq; and a short account of the life of his endeared friend.

Mr. *William Reynolds*, M. A. born in *Essex*, *October* 28, 1625. went to *Cambridge* was under the tuition of Dr. *Whitchcot* in *Emanuel* college : Mr. *Whitlock* and he were chamber-fellows, both designed for the ministry, where they contracted such a friendship that they seemed but one soul in two bodies. However Mr. *Reynolds* in compliance with his father who sent him to *Rusia* upon business, was with regret for some time diverted from the ministry ; he left *England* 1644, and in 1646 upon his father's death he returned again, he expected a good estate but was disappointed and discouraged ; thereupon he was going to sea to pursue merchandise, but stopped by a false arrest, which was a happy providence, for the ship he had agreed to go in, was never heard of more nor any of the passengers.

HE resumed his former studies and thoughts of the ministry. At the latter end of that year, Mr. *Whitlock* settling at *Leighton* in *Bedfordshire*, persuaded Mr. *Reynolds* to come and live with him, which he did. From this time they never lived asunder till death, being still under the same roof (tho' keeping distinct houses while both were married) studying in the same room and writing at the same table. Not long after their living together, there was a vacancy at *Okingham* in *Berkshire*, they two undertook to supply both *Leighton* and that place by turns ; when *Okingham* was supplied at the end of half a year, they afterwards did the same between *Leighton* and *Aylsbury*, Anno 1649, they jointly refused to take the engagement, altho' they thereby lost the augmentation at *Leighton*, which was the only maintenance there, and exposed themselves to the displeasure of those through whose hands the allow-

ance

ance was to pass that came out of the impropriation of *Aylsbury*, at last by a means unthought of, they removed both to *Nottingham*: The *Nottingham* carrier Mr. *Adrian Cook*, was used to go in his way to *London* through *Stony-Stratford*; but the way being bad in *February* 1650, he left that road to go by *Leighton*, where he lodged, (which he never did before or after.) Hearing in the town that two ministers lived there, who were under discouragement, because they had refused the engagement, he visited them and discoursed with them, told them that St. *Mary's* in *Nottingham* wanted a fixed minister, and pressed them to come and preach there occasionally; which they told him they some time or other in the approaching summer might probably do. When Mr. *Cook* came home to *Nottingham*, he gave an account of what had passed, and all in general that were told of it, were very desirous to hear the two ministers preach; and thereupon drew up an invitation to them to come and spend some time in their town, in order to mutual tryal and acquaintance; it was signed by *Francis Pierepont*, Esq; member of parliament for the town, and several Aldermen and principal inhabitants, and carried to *Leighton* by Mr. *Spencer*, one of the churchwardens of St. *Mary*. At *Nottingham* they were unanimously approved of and fixed. In 1651 they went up to *London* and were ordained at the classis in *Andrew-Undershaft* church, Dr. *Manton* being moderator. After which they returned to *Nottingham* and continued there in peace till 1662. In the latter end of 1660, they were disturbed by indictments for not reading the Common-Prayer, and from the spiritual-court, and Mr. *Reynolds* was excommunicated and put to great expence in journies to *York* and *London* upon that occasion. At last he procured a prohibition, the proceedings against him being directly contrary to the act of indemnity. In *October* 1662, after being silenced, they and their families removed from *Nottingham* to *Colwick-hall*, about a mile off, there they were seized at their meeting in *September* 1663; they were again seized in *August* 1665 and imprisoned for about three months at the marshal's without any cause assigned. When the 5 mile act took place they removed together to *Sherbrook* in *Derbyshire*, where they lived 2 years, but frequently visited their friends at *Nottingham*. In 1668 they removed to *Mansfield*, where they continued 19 years, in which time they were often at *Nottingham*, by turns officiating among their people. In *March* 1684-5, going as freeholders to *Newark* to an election of parliament men for the county, they were seized and sent prisoners to *Nottingham* by eight justices upon the 5 mile act, there they continued 'till *July* 1685, when upon the duke of *Monmouth's* landing they with many others were sent prisoners to *Hull*. Upon the liberty given in 1687, they returned with their families to *Nottingham* in peace, there they continued fellow-labourers 'till by a fever Mr. *Reynolds* was removed out of this life *February* 26, 1697-8 aged 73. Mr. *Barret* minister of St. *Peter's* preached his funeral sermon. He has printed nothing that is known but a funeral sermon for the honourable *Francis Pierepont*, Esq; preached at St. *Mary's* in *Nottingham*, 4to. 1658.

Mr. *Barret*, M. A. was invited to St. *Peter's* in *Nottingham*, upon the death of Mr. *Richard Whitchurch*, 1656, he met with much opposition but was marvellously screened by a special providence, (*a*) he died

H E

(*a*) *This special providence was, that once after the service of the meeting was over*
he

H E publiſhed two farewell ſermons of his, one, on *Phil.* 2. 12. and the other, on
I *Kings.* 18. 21. He publiſhed and printed a treatiſe on the *Covenant of Grace*, 8vo.
Two controverſial treatiſes againſt Dr. *Stillingfleet* in defence of the *Nonconformiſts*
4to. 50 Queries about *Infant Baptiſm* collected out of Mr. *Baxter's* books, 8vo.
A diſcourſe of *Pardon of Sin. Of Secret Prayer.* And two funeral ſermons for
Mr. *Reynolds* and Mr. *Whitlock.*

The Income and Value of all the Priories and other Religious Houſes in
NOTTINGHAM-SHIRE *taken from* STEPHENS's *Hiſtory of Abbies.*

		l.	ſh.	d.
The priory of *Lenton.* — — —	Summa inde	417	19	3
	Summa clara	329	15	10
The priory of *Thurgarton.* — —	Summa inde	359	15	10
	Summa clara	259	9	4
The priory of *Newſted.* — —	Summa inde	219	18	8
	Summa clara	167	16	11
The priory of *Felley.* — — —	Summa inde	61	4	8
	Summa clara	40	19	1
The priory of *Beauval.* — — —	Summa inde	227	8	0
	Summa clara	196	6	0
The priory of *Shelford.* — — —	Summa inde	151	14	1
	Summa clara	116	1	1
The Monaſtery of *Welbeck.* — —	Summa inde	298	4	8
	Summa clara	249	6	3
The Monaſtery of *Rufford.* — —	Summa inde	254	6	8
	Summa clara	176	11	6

R r 2

The

---

*he being in danger of being ſeized and put in priſon, he eſcaped by putting on the
cloaths of one Mr.* Bartley, *a gentleman one of his hearers, who was very like him
both in ſtature and features, and who lived over againſt the place where Mr.* Barret *preached, which was in ſome malt-rooms on the* long row.

The priory of *Workſop.* — — }	*Summa inde* 302 *l.* 6 *ſh.* 10 *d.*	
	Summa clara 239 15 5	
The priory of *Blythe.* — — — }	*Summa clara* 126 8 2	
	Summa clara 113 0 8	
The priory of *Matterſey.* — — }	*Summa inde* 61 17 7	
	Summa clara 55 2 5	
The priory of *Walling-Wells.* — — }	*Summa inde* 87 11 6	
	Summa clara 58 9 10	
Cella in Mariſco. — — — — { *Summa inde* } —	6 7 2	
{ *Summa clara* }		
The priory of *Brodham.* — — { *Summa inde* }	16 5 2	
{ *Summa clara* }		

Sum of the Value of all *per Annum.* { Total — — 2591 8 4

Clear — — 2025 6 10

JOHN POOL, p. ultimam voluntatem datam 27. *Aprilis* 1479,

ITEM do et lego major. vic. burg. et hominibus villæ *Nottingham,* unum vacuum, foliam, five petiam terræ vaſtat. jacentem in *Nott.* prædict. juxta *Guildhall* villæ ſupradictæ inter viam regiam ex parte boreali - - - Ro: *Engliſh* ex parte auſtrali et abutt. ſuper meſſ: ejuſdem Ro: juxta portas ſuas verſus orientem et ſuper *Guildhall* prædict. verſus occidentem. Long. 55 pedes a meſſ. dicti Ro: uſque *Guildhall,* tenend. predict. major. vic. burg. et hominibus *Nottinghamiæ* et ſucceſſoribus &c.

ex autograph. Johannis Town.

An

An ADDRESS or PETITION to the Protector CROMWELL, of the *Framework-Knitters.*

To his Highness the Lord PROTECTOR *of the Commonwealth of* England, Scotland *and* Ireland, *&c.*

The humble representation of the promoters and inventors of the art and mystery or trade of Frame-work-knitting, *or making of* Silk-Stockings, *or other work in a frame or engine ;* Petitioners *to your Highness, that they may be united and incorporated by Charter under the Great-seal of* England, *whereby their just right to the Invention may be preserved from* Foreigners, *the Trade advanced,* Abuses *therein suppressed, the benefit of the Commonwealth by importation and exportation, and otherwise increased, and hundreds of poor Families comfortably relieved by their several* Imployments *about the same, who will otherwise be exposed to* Ruin, *having no other calling to live of.*

May it please your Highness.

AMONG all the civil ways of improvement of a Common-wealth (next to agriculture) merchandise and manufactury (where and whensoever orderly regulated) in all ages and times, have been, and are most securely beneficial and prosperous during their cherishment and retention : But they are apt to become volant, as soon as slighted, or disordered, into neighbouring (*a*) places and regions, always hospitable to so welcome guests as bring with them not only their own entertainment, but also profitable advantages to their protectors. Leaving behind them unto the place of their former residence an over-late and remedyless repentance of such improvidence, and most commonly an irrevocable consumption ; the experience whereof has anciently and generally made it a principal maxim in state, to encourage by all favourable means requisite, the erectors and practisers of trading ; and has notified for one of the greatest errors in state-government, the discountenancing and disordering thereof.

WHENCE in succession of time (from the antiquity of all records) the great variety and multitude of incorporations, overspreading the face of all eminent parts of the civilly governed world, flourishing under the favour and protection of the several princes and estates thereof, each province striving to exceed its neighbours in numerosity

---

(*a*) *Many places have had their vicissitudes of prosperity and decay, occasioned by access or receding of trade, as witnesses (among many other)* Gaunt *in* Flanders, *and those towns from whence the* English *Staple has removed.*

merofity of them, and enlargement of all convenient privileges, and powers granta-
ble unto them, and reaping innumerable benefits at the cheap rate of countenance,
encouragement, and protection of the induftrious labours of the natives; who in retri-
bution unto the ftate for licence and priviledge to earn their own fubfiftancies, do
disburthen the common-wealth (by employment or maintenance) of many poor, keep
themfelves in clofer order and lefs circumference then others in ready ability for
publick fervice, pay all publick charges and impofitions; draw commerce into their
country with profit unto the ftate by importation and exportation, andfurnifh their own
and all others neceffities with ufeful commodities. So (and many ways much more)
profitable is encouraged and well governed induftry, which if difcouraged, and denied order in the practice, profecution and exercife thereof; it fometimes has (and
ever will) moft certainly become a difadvantage, weakening, and impoverifhment
to the common-wealth, and an advancement, ftrength, and enrichment of the neighbours who are, or may prove enemies.

I N prevention whereof, all nations who live not in abfolute flavery to their fove-
reigns, but enjoy a propriety in their eftates and goods, by claiming alfo a right of
propriety in the fruits of their own endeavours (which was never yet denied but to
the great prejudice of the contradictors) have provided and do allow, that as they
feverally and fucceffively arrive to any affured profit, they are included within their
own territories and appropriated unto the particular defervers, with grants in perpe-
tuity of the regulation of affairs in trade, meerly as matter of power, or the immediate minifters thereof, unlefs for juftice againft infringers and invaders of fuch efta-
blifhments as have been to that purpofe obtained. And it has been (and remaineth)
a great part of the felicity of *England*, that by the grave advice and appropriation of
the ftate, it abounds with indulgend prefidents and provifions of this kind, to the great
encouragement and comfort both of prefent and future induftries.

W H E R E B Y the petitioners are emboldened (now at length) to offer to your
Highneffes confideration and grave judgement, the fulnefs of capacity they humbly
conceive themfelves to have been in, to receive the like grant of favour, truft, and
protection, which many other companies have (upon fewer and lefs weighty induce-
ments) obtained; and whereof there is apparent neceffity, their trade being no longer manageable by them, nor fecurable unto the profit of this common-wealth, without it.

W H I C H trade is properly ftiled framework-knitting, becaufe it is direct and
abfolute knitwork in the ftitches thereof, nothing different therein from the common
way of knitting (not much more anciently for publick ufe practifed in this nation
than this) but only in the numbers of needles, at an inftant working in this, more than
in the other by an hundred for one, fet in an engine or frame compofed of above 2000
pieces of fmith, joyners and turners work, after fo artificial and exact a manner,
that by the judgement of all beholders, it far excels in the ingenuity, curiofity and
fubtilty of the invention and contexture, all other frames or inftruments of manufacture in ufe in any known part of the world. And for the skill requifite to the ufe
and manage thereof, it well deferves (without ufurpation as fome others impertinently
have) the titles of myftery and art, by reafon of the great difficulty of learning, and
length of time neceffary, to attain a dextrous habit of right, true and exquifite workmanfhip therein, which has preferved it hitherto (from the hands of foreigners) peculiar

culiar to the *English* nation, from whence it has extraction, growth, and breeding unto that perfection it is now arrived at. Not only able to serve your Highnesses dominions with the commodities it mercantably workes, but also the neighbouring countries round about, where it has gained so good repute, that the vent thereof is now more foreign than domestick, and has drawn covetous eyes upon it, to undermine it here and to transport it beyond the Seas. Of whose sinister workings to that pernicious end, these petitioners (as most interested) standing in the nearest sent, think themselves in the common duty of well-affected persons to your Highness and their country, (besides their own case of necessity) bound to make address unto the wisdom, protection and care of your Highness (as their predecessors in former times have done to the rulers of this nation) speedily to restrain and suppress all attempts, to bring so great a detriment and inconveniency upon the common-wealth.

Now so it is, and may it please your Highness.

THAT the trade of frame-work-knitting was never known or practised either here in *England*, or in any other place in the world, before it was (above 50 years past) invented and found out by one *William Lea* of *Calverton* in the county of *Nottingham*, gent. who by himself and such of his kindred and countrymen as he took unto him for servants, practised the same many years, somewhat imperfectly in comparison of the exactness it is sithence brought unto, by the endeavours of some of these petitioners. Yet even in the infancy thereof, it gathered sufficient estimation of a business of so extraordinary a national profit and advantage, as to be invited over into *France*, upon allurements of great rewards, privilege and honour ; not long before the suddain murther of the late *French* King *Henry* IV. unsuccessfully accepted by the said Mr. *Lea*, (at that time wanting due encouragement at home). And transporting himself with nine workmen his servants (with some frames) unto *Roan* ; there wrought to so great applause of the *French*, that the trade was in all likelihood to have been settled in that country for ever, had not the decease of the said King disappointed Mr. *Lea* of his expected grant of privilege, and the succeeding troubles of that kingdom, delay'd his renew'd suit to that purpose, into discontentment and death at *Paris*, leaving his workmen at *Roan* to provide for themselves, seven of which returned back again into *England* with their frames, and here practised and improved their trade ; under whom, (or the master-workmen since risen under them) most of these petitioners had their breeding and served their apprentiships. Of the other two which remained in *France* only one is yet surviving : but so far short of the perfection of his trade (as it is used here) that of him, or what can be done by him, or his means, these petitioners are in no apprehension of fear, nor have not been (since then) endangered in foreign countries by any that have served out their full time of apprentiship here.

BUT near about that time a venetian embassador gave 500 *l.* for a remnant of time of one *Henry Mead*, then an apprentice to this trade, and convey'd him with his frame from *London* to *Venice*, where altho' his work and the manner of it was for a while admired, and endeavoured to be imitated ; yet as soon as necessity of reparation of his frame and instruments happened, for want of artificers experienced in such

work

work there, and of ability in him to direct them, the work prospered not in his managing ; so that (his bought time of service being expired) affection to his native country brought him home again into *England*. After his departure the *Venetians* grew disheartened, and impatient of making vain trials, they sent his disordered frame and some of their own imitation to be sold in *London* at very low valuation.

A N D within a few years afterwards the trade was greatly endangered by one *Abraham Jones*, who having by underhand courses and insinuations (and not by servitude as an apprentice) gotten both the mystery and skillful practice thereof, did (contrary to the articles with the rest of the company that had taken some jealous notice of him) pass himself with some more unto *Amsterdam*, and there taking some 'Dutch* unto him as servants, erected frames, and wrought for the space of two or three years, until the infection of the plague seized on him and his whole family and carried them all to the grave. His frames also (as things unprofitable to them that could not find out their right use without an able teacher) were sent to *London* for sale at slight rates.

T H E S E preservations and escapes of this trade from transplantation into foreign countries, these petitioners do with thankfulness acknowledge, and ascribe to have been brought to pass by the divine providence, limiting his bounties and administration whither he has been pleased to direct them. For it may well seem marvellous in human judgement, how otherwise this trade should remain (notwithstanding all the covetous and envious attempts to the contrary practised for the space of 40 years, past) an art peculiar to only this our nation : And to the nimble spirits of the *French*, the fertile wits of the *Italian*, and the industrious inclination of the *Dutch*, a concealed mystery unto this day.

Y E T a continued negligence in presumption thereupon, would ill beseem the receivers of so many damageless warnings, and may soon prove of hard consequence unto these petitioners who without intermission are environed with the like or greater dangers. For there are by other means than the way of apprenticeship, so many intruders crept into this trade, that ill work and ill ware is every where offered to sale ; and the ignominy and disparagement thereof, commonly imputed to the whole manufactury, not without much loss, hinderance and interruption of the true and allowable artisans, and tending to their utter impoverishment who in continual workmanship produce the best, finest, and most approvedly merchantable and useful wares ever sold and bought in the memory of men, otherwise the petitioners could not have driven their trade through many oppositions and difficulties, up unto the height it is now brought, and into fair expectation and open way of large increase, if intrusion were barred, and transportation and teaching of the mystery unto foreigners restrained, and none of this our nation, either artisan, apprentice or intruder, be permitted so mischiviously to seek for gain.

A S one here in *London* makes his profession and custom to do ; exposing himself a teacher of this art and trade for any inconsiderable parcel of money, unto all manner of people without distinction, whether native or not, hitherto uncontroulably ; nor to inveigle and corrupt apprentices from their masters, to discover and teach unto them the whole trade ; (and having gotten it) pretend upon scruple of conscience in matters of religion, or some other occasion, to depart your Highnesses dominions, and
set

set it up in practice in a foreign country; as one not long since has done, whom these petitioners are labouring all they may to reduce, and are not hopeless to find prevalent means to recover him back again time enough, if they receive encouragement in this their humble suit. Wherein they farther shew:

T H A T altho' this manufacture may be wrought in any other materials that are usually made up (or can possibly be made up) into the form of knit-work : Yet has it chosen to be practised in Silk, the best and richest of all others in use and wearing, and most crediting the artisans, and of greatest advantage unto this State and Commonwealth, yielding several payments to the use of the state before it passes out of the hands of the traders therein, and increasing merchandise by both the ways of importation and exportation of the self-same material, imported raw at cheap rates, exported ready wrought at the utmost extent of value ; so that the distance of those valuations is totally clear gain to this Commonwealth, and esteemed upwards of six parts in seven of the whole quantity of this material in the highest value thereof, wrought up by this manufacture ; which has vindicated that old proverbial aspersion: ——— *The stranger buys of the* Englishman *the case of the Fox for a groat, and sells him the tail again for a shilling.* And may now invert and retort upon them : —— *The* Englishman *buys silk of the stranger for twenty marks, and sells him the same again for one hundred pounds.*

T H A T this trade encourages and sets on work other artificers also; as smiths, joyners and turners, for the making erecting and repairing of frames, and other necessary instruments thereunto belonging, and has bred up many excellent workmen among them for farther publick service.

T H A T the artisans of this trade, do moreover employ a multitude of hands besides their own about the preparation and finishing of the materials and ware they work : On which do compleatly subsist and thrive : The winders, throwers, sizers, seamers and trimmers thereof : And also the needlemakers totally depend thereon.

T H A T altho' these petitioners seem in the eyes of the world, to be at present under a cloud and every moment ready to be undone by intruders and foreigners, so that many people fear and forbear to bind their children apprentices unto a trade of such instant hazard and irregularity, until a settlement thereof, under a corporation to the great retarding an increase of able artisans, who are therefore but few in number, in comparison of the knitters the way common to other nations ; yet do they subsist by the labours in a more substantial and serviceable degree to the Commonwealth disburthening it of many poor of both sexes. Whereas that common tedious way multiplies needy persons here, rather because the people of other nations, outwork those of this therein, than by any hinderance they receive from the best artisans of this manufactury that bend their endeavours all they can to the foreign vent in general, as well as, in their own particulars most profitable to this nation, leaving the home sale in great part to the common knitters, uninterrupted, unless by the intruders into this art, whose multiplications (if not restrained) will be equally as pernicious and destructive unto them as unto the petitioners ; who only (and not the common-knitters) have shewed unto this Commonwealth, that it is able abundantly to serve itself and *ultra* with all commodities of knit-work, as stockings, calceoons: waistcoats, and

many

many other things, without the help, or rather inconveniency it formerly had of importation of the same in quantities ready wrought from foreign parts.

T H A T this trade is in no kind impertinent or damageable to the Commonwealth, nor driven in trifling, base and unnecessary stuff or ware, seeing all the world (where habits are worn) is in general and permanent use thereof : But to the contrary, it works on the principal of stuffs, and makes commodious and decent ware for the cover of the whole body of men, perpetually unchangeable in the fashion, endeavouring (as much as in the artisan lies) to found an unexhaustible mine within this nation already prepared to become, (if it shall please your Highness to establish it) henceforth the place of sole resort, as to a special mart, of the rich and staple commodities wrought by this manufacture, for the general service of all the great, honourable and better sorts of inhabitants of the whole communicable world.

T H A T the petitioners have made a large and competent probation of the worth of this manufacture in itself, and merit thereof to the Common-wealth, (for the proportion of its growth) far exceeding any other that trades with foreigners in their own materials, extracting from them (to the use of this Commonwealth, and the maintainance of the people of this land, at foreign charge) upwards of fourscore in every hundred *de claro* of the whole value now, or that may be hereafter, upon a regular way of trading, dealt in, and defraying out of the other parcel of the hundred, being less then twenty current, all customs, imposts, and freights, both homeward and outwards, and also reserving the remainder of the twenty, to the manage of the merchant for as much unwrought material. Which eighty, in quick passages and returns of home trade, (by the way twice accounted for unto the officers of excise) suddenly and insensibly diffuses and disperses itself through very many hands, either totally maintaining, or otherwise adding to the subsistences of many other severally (in part) before enumerated trades and professions, besides this manufacture, the prime wheel, gathering only thereby an ordinary ability, to make the rest move: *viz.* merchants, owners of ships, hosiers, dyers, winders, throwsters, sizers, seamers, trimmers, wire-drawers, needle-makers, smiths, joyners, turners, with many other assistants, all having their sufficient contents and inablements to live out of the clear product of the foreign vent, raised and furnished by the labours of the petitioners and their servants ; who have voluntarily among themselves kept order in their trading, according to the duty of probationers (hitherto) without making any request unto the state for particular countenance and protection, until they found themselves now risen into a number not incapable of incorporation ; and their trade into foreign parts of so great and growing increase (were the momentary dangers of utter ruin, for want of regulating power diverted) that it may well be esteemed the most improveable way of benefit and advantage of this kind, apparent to this present age, and (within some late hundreds of years past) offered unto this nation, and presented unto the state, (as this now is unto your Highness) for an inclosure within the boundary of its native soil, where it may receive its proper husbandry.

T H A T if these petitioners had no other inducement to offer, but what every other trade which is (common also to foreigners) in fear to be over-wrought and out-sold by them, has heretofore presented, as motives, and means to obtain charters and privileges, and consequent provisions by statute, upon reasons drawn from conveniencies accrewing by civil education of some youth of the land, employment of idle

persons

perfons, ferving this Commonwealth with commodities better wrought here, than thofe tranfported hither from beyond the feas, and maintaining many of our people at home with the fame money which foreigners did get away from hence for the maintenance of theirs: Yet might the petitioners (in confidence of the right of fubjects) fue for power fubordinately (according to the laws and conftitutions of this land) to regulate their own endeavours in a company and fraternity among themfelves. But thefe petitioners ftand not in the fame fole capacity, that the pin-makers, and others did, at the times of their incorporations. For thefe have (additionally thereunto) an higher merit towards the Common-wealth, who's intereft in all the fore mentioned extraordinary advantages and benefits, and in the further ufes of them is annexed unto the profperity of this manufacture, and wholly depending thereon. Infomuch that the petitioners (in their humble fuit) do plead unto your Highnefs, a general caufe of the Commonwealth in grofs, for an ineftimable concernment to all pofterity, and crave in their own to be but barely to be preferved, as their lawful endeavours have qualified them, the temporary inftruments and fervitours to that public ufe. Which they may reafonably hope, fhall not now (firft of all forts of men, ever petitioning femblable favour) begin to be refufed unto them, who have not been wanting to the Common-wealth in the main fervice thereof, during its late extremities of danger, but have all been faithful to their country in every thing according to their utmoft abilities, and have many of them undergone much lofs of worldly goods, and peril of life, by and againft the common enemy, and fome of them continue in military office to this day.

A N D feeing the miftrefs of knowlege, experience, has taught that the fole proprietary of a generally defired commodity, has a mafter key to command the lock of trading; which whofoever can prudently manage, has no fmall maftery over the wealth of the univerfe; and feeing that this art of frame-work-knitting here in *England* (as *Printing* formerly in *Germany* out-wrought all the manual writers in the world) is likewife able to out-work all the common-knitters among all nations, and make the commodity (without divulging of the myftery) generally defirable and entertained (as that other was here) with grace and privilege of importation (by provifion of ftatute, 1ft of *Richard* III. *cap.* 9.) and feeing this is much more capable of fecreting, than that, by reafon of the great difficulty to attain this with long practice, and the facility of the other to be conceived at firft fight. This arifing in an entire dominion, and that other in a region full of divided principalities. This is endued with a quality retentive, to continue for many ages, if not ever, (altho' the other could not fo in *Germany*) a peculiar in propriety unto this nation of *England*. Therefore it is fit to be owned as a native (by the hand of your Highnefs) eftablifhed in the rank, and as the nonpareil of handicrafts, to be taken into your poffeffion inclufively within your power of command and fpecial protection, who is herein not flightly concerned, becaufe intrufted to husband the Common-wealth, and is the ballance of reafon to diftinguifh between the allegations and aims of good and bad patriots. Some ftriving to fcatter abroad (about all the earth) that harveft, whereof others defire the ftoring in a magazin; and fome urging the fame exploded clamours againft the ufe of engines in trading, which the file and hammer workers of a fingle pin did heretofore, to divert or retard the privileging the company of pin-makers, in oppofition to thofe that now fue and refer themfelves to be confidered according to difcretion at home, for what they might write their own conditions every where abroad; if piety to their native country, as ftrongly reftrained not them, as they im

plore the coercive power of your Highnefs to reſtrain their ill willers from unra-
velling the entrails of the Common-wealth, and giving or yielding opportunity unto
ſtrangers, to gather them up, and make that common to all the world, which is naturally particular in ſole propriety to this nation, and prepared for the management
of your Highnefs in ſuch manner, as in your Highnefs's wiſdom and great favour
ſhall be thought expedient for the beſt advantage of this Common-wealth, ever in
thriving condition and flouriſhing by exportation of commodities, as well artificially
as naturally appropriated unto this iſland not unknown to your Highnefs to have ſuf-
fered ſome late decay in the main ſupport of its foreign trading, which may receive
a great ſupply and increaſe by means of good encouragement of this manufacture,
only in preſent neceſſity of the like protection and privileges, that have been granted, confirmed, and are enjoyed by many others, tho' of foreign invention and uſe,
and never in poſſibility of becoming, as this is ſolely from hence impartable unto all
other nations :

All which is humbly ſubmitted to your Highnefs's
pleaſure, with great hopes that you will gracioufly
patronize and cheriſh the honeſt endeavours of
ſuch as aim at the public good, as well as their
own private intereſt,

And your Petitioners ſhall ever Pray.

Anciently

ANCIENTLY the extream feverity of the foreſt laws were very burthenſome to the ſubjeꞓt, eſpecially to thoſe whoſe lands and poſſeſſions did border upon the forreſt, but in king *John's* reign a charter was obtained to mitigate ſome hardſhips then complained of, and in the reign of his ſon *Henry* the 3d. a farther charter was granted to his people relating to the liberties in the forreſt. The 16th of this king, he diſafforeſted part of *Nottinghamſhire* by commiſſion, and the walk of the remainder was aſcertained as followeth.

HENRY *by the grace of* GOD *King of* England, *lord of* Ireland, *duke of* Normandy, &c. *To all Archbiſhops, Biſhops, Abbots, Priors, Earls, Barons, Knights, Juſtices, Sheriffs, Mayors, Miniſters, and all Bailiffs, and his true liegemen, Greeting. — Know ye us to have granted, and with our preſent Charter confirmed, for us and our heirs for evermore, That the walk made by our truſty and well beloved* Hugh Nevil *and* Bryan *of the* Yle, *and others to them aſſociate by our commandment. The aforeſaid* Hugh Nevil *then being juſtice of the Foreſt betwixt the parts that be diſafforreſted and the parts ſhall remain ſtill in the county of* NOTTINGHAM, *be firm and ſtable and abide for ever. And that theſe parts in the county aforeſaid diſafforeſted, remain by the marks and bound in the walk thereof, made, expreſſed, and hereafter written.*

That is to witt :

THE aforeſaid walk beginneth at the *Forth* alias *Ford* of *Coningſwath* by the highway that goes towards *Wellahawe* unto the town of *Wellawe* towards *Nottingham*, ſo that the cloſe of the town of *Wellawe* is not of the foreſt and ſo from thence unto that place where the river of *Doverbeck* goes on the ſaid way, and ſo from thence as the ſaid river of *Doverbeck* deſcendeth into the water of *Trent*, ſo that that part of *Nottinghamſhire* which is called the *Clay*, and an other parcel which is called *Hatfield* on the northſide of the great highway of *Nottinghamſhire* that goes from the aforeſaid forth of *Coningſwath* towards the ſouth unto that place that the ſayd water of *Doverbeck* goes on the ſaid highway, beginning at the foreſaid forth of *Coningſwath* and extending itſelf until the ſaid river of *Doverbeck* be diſafforreſted by the foreſaid marks towards the north and the eaſt which forſooth parte aforeſaid is called the *Clay* and the parcel aforeſaid that is called *Hatfield* betwixt the river of *Doverbeck* and *Bickerſdike* and *Sherwood* and *Trent*. Alſo the ſaid walk in the ſame county of *Nottingham* beginneth at the aforeſaid forth of *Conningſwath* and aſcending toward the weſt by the water that is called *Mayden* unto the town of *Warſope* and from the ſame town aſcending by the ſame water unto *Hatrebridge* and from thence turning by the great highway of *Nottingham* unto *Milnefordbridge* and from thence unto *Mansfield* and from thence betwixt the fields of *Hardwick* and of *Kirkby* and the moor of *Kirkby* unto the corner that is called *Nunker* and from thence

thence to the affert of *John Bretton* unto *Tharliftie* and from thence unto *Stolegate* and from thence by the great highway under the old caftle of *Anneſley* and from the fame caftle by the great highway unto the town of *Lindby* and from thence through the midft of the town of *Lindly* unto the milne of the fame town upon the water of *Leen* and from thence defcending by the fame water unto the town of *Lenton* and from thence as the fame water was won't of ould time to run into the water of *Trent* fo that the part of *Nottinghamſhire* that is betwixt that water of *Coningſwath* and the town of *Blythe* and alfo all the part of *Nottinghamſhire* that is on the weft part of the water of *Maiden* afcending towards the fouth unto the water of *Trent* betwixt the divifions and the county of *Darby* be difafforrefted, and that which is within the forefaid bounds remained forefte, faving to us and our heirs our hay of *Welley* and all our other demaine woods, in the aforefaid county of *Nottingham* on the weft part, north, and eaft part of the town of *Nottingham* and of the fouth part of the fame town unto the water of *Trente*. That they remain in the forreft we have granted and with our prefent charter confirmed for us and our heirs to all our men of the aforefaid county of *Nottingham* dwelling in the parts aforefaid after the bounds and aforefaid difafforrefted be quiet for evermore of waft and reward of the view of the forrefters and of all thofe things that to the forreft, forrefters, verdurers and rewarders or other minifters appertaineth, and that none of the aforefaid men that dwell in the aforefaid parts difafforrefted or elfewhere who are in the fame county without the forreft nor their heirs at any time by us nor our heirs be made agifters, verderers or rewarders in the forreft aforefaid in the aforefaid county of *Nottingham*, we have granted alfo to the fame men and with this our prefent charter confirmed for us and our heirs. That no man that be of the parts aforefaid difafforrefted fhall come by common fumnions before our juftices at pleas of the forreft, but if he be attacked for any trefpafs of the forreft, or by the pledge of any man that ought to come before the faid juftices to anfwer for any trefpafs of the forreft wherefore we will and ftraitly command for us and our heirs that the aforefaid walk made by marks and bounds and places aforefaid and above expreffed in the county of *Nottingham* ftand firm and ftable for evermore. And that the parts aforefaid as be in the aforefaid walk noted, be difafforrefted for evermore. So that they be quiet of wafte, reward of forrefters, and of all manner of forrefters, verdurers rewarderers or their minifters and that none of the aforefaid men that dwell in the aforefaid parts difaforrefted or elfewhere in the faid county out of the forreft nor their heirs at any time by us or our heirs be made agifters, forrefters, verdurers or rewarders in the aforefaid forreft of our county of *Nottingham* and that none that be of the faid parts difafforrefted come by common fummons afore the juftices to the pleas of the forreft as by the pledge of any other man that fhould come afore the faid juftices to anfwer for any trefpafs of the forreft as is above faid. Thefe being wittinefs &c. the XVth day of *July* in the XVIth year of our reign.

Perambulatio

Perambulatio forreste de S H E R W O O D.

Facta XXVI die *Augusti* anno regni *Henrici* regis septimi XXI. p. *Jo-hannem* G. Armig *Thomam Leake*, Arm. *Thomam Armstrong*, Arm *Jo-hannem Coste, Henricum Plumptre de Nottingham, Hugonem Annesley*, Arm. *Richardum Byngham de Wattnowe*, Arm. *Richardum Kirkby, Radulphum Greenhall, Rogerum Pierponte, Johannem Hoppwood, Johan-nem Boman, Willielmum Bevercotts, Johannem Warren, Willielmum Biton, Alexandrum Mearing, Robertum in Kellum, Alexandrum Leake, Johan-nem Leake, Thomam Hunt, Georgium Palmer, Thomam Calverton, Jo-hannem Barwick, Jacobum Wood, Johannem Meinell, Thomam Rossel, Richardum Parker, Johannem Brinnesley, Richardum Bactroe, Williel-mum Gartswell, et Alexandrum Barwick*, regardatores dicte forreste de SHERWOOD.

QUE quidem perambulatio a castro domini regis de *Nottingham* incipit et deinde procedendo usque le *Kingsbriggs, Meadow-gate* et deinde per le *Trent* usque ad antiquum cursum aque de *Leene* qui est inter le *King's-Meadows* et pratum de *Wilford* et deinde per dictum antiquum cursum aque de *Leene* usque ad pratum vocatum *Carlam* et deinde p. communem viam usque ad pontem sup. *Leen* juxta pomarium priorum de *Lenton* et deinceps ascenden-do p. dictam aquam de *Leene* usque ad bondarium ville domini regis de *Bulwell* et sic circa boscum domini regis de *Bulwell-Rise* usque ad dictam aquam de *Leene* sic ascendendo p. dictam aquam usque molendinum de *Linby* et sic p. medium ville de *Linby* usque ad crucem ibidem, et deinde a dicta cruce p. magnum chiminium quod ducit ad antiquum *Castrum de Annesley* dimittendo predictum castrum ex parte dex-tra ac deinde p. dictum magnum chiminium usque *Scolegate* que ducit versus *Ches-terfield Lidyate* et deinde descendendo aliquantulum versus occidentem p. le *Scole-stigh* ex parte boreali campi de *Annesley* usque quendam venellum qui est inter cam-pum de *Annesley-wood-house* ex parte orientali et quoddam assartum nuper ad *Hen-ricum Brettennuem Tho. Samon* ex parte orientali et sic descendendo per dictam venellam versus boream usque ad quendam angulum vocatum *Nuncar* et deinde per viam inter le *more of Kirkby* et campos de *Hardwick* et tunc p. eandem venellam versus orientem et tunc versus boream p. portas mansionis de *Hardwick* usque *Ma-wenswell-head* et deinde versus occidentem p. sepe de *Hardwick* et sic descendendo versus austrum p. le *Rewarders Meare* inter campos de *Kirkby* et campos de *Sutton* usque ad *Holbrockhaw* et ab inde p. sepe de *Holbeckhaw* usque *Coleyeat* et sic inde intrando p. le *Coleyeat* in boscum domini regis vocatum *Fulwood* circulariter usque venellam de *Normanton* et a dicta venella p. sepe inter campos de *Normanton* et *Fulwood* usque *Hawkswell* et ab inde circa campos de dirty *Hucknal* usque campos de *Sutton* et p. campos de *Sutton* usque magnum chiminium quod ducit ad *Notting-ham. viz.* inter campos et campos de *Skegby* et deinde usque ad crucem ad finem o-

rientalem

rientalem ville de *Skegby* ac deinde p. sepe quod est inter campos de *Skegby* et bundas de *Mansfield* et sic usque *Plesley* et deinde p. aquam da *Maiden* usque vill. de *Warksop* et sic p. medium vill. de *Warksop* usque ad crucem ibidem et sic directe p. viam in campum de *Warksop* et p. illam viam usque ad p dictam aquam de *Maiden* et sic p. dictam aquam versus orientem usque ad vadum de *Mugley* et deinde ascendendo versus boream usque ad le *Hessellgappe* et sic demittendo le *Serowne* ex parte dextra usque sepe inter *Romewood* et *Clowne-field* usque parcum de abbessa de *Wellbeck* et ascendendo p. dictum parcum usque le *Outgate* forest. qui est inter dictum parcum et parcum domini de et dictam *Owtgate* extendendo usque *Boyard-stable* et iterum descendendo versus orientem dict. *Roodgate* usque quendam lapidem ad finem orientis de *Wurdwood* et deinde descendendo aliquantulum versus austrum usque ad quendam *Lapidem in Clumber* et sic ultra vadum de *Clumber* usque ad alium lapidem fixum ex parte orientali de *Elmyeres* et ex parte boreali vie ibidem et abinde directe versus austrum usque alium lapidem quendam fixum juxta viam que ducit a *Mirelbriggs* usque *Awsland.* Et abinde usque quendam le *Hollen* que est prope campos de *Thoresby* et descendendo p. campos dictos. viz. p. le parson *Balke* usque ad villam de *Thoresby* et deinde p. aquam de *Maiden* usque *Cunningbyforth* et deinde p. magnum chiminium de *Blythe* usque *Coningswasforth* ex parte orientali ville de *Wellow* ac deinde p. magnum chiminium quod ducit apud *Nottingham* usque *Blackstone-Haw* et abinde usque rivulum de *Doverbeck* et sic sicut ille rivulus currit p. medium ville de *Cathroppe* et deinde p. dictum rivulum de *Doverbeck* ubi solebat currere ex antiquo tempore usque ad aquam de *Trent* usque dum venitur versus abbathiam de *Shelford,* ita quod dicta abbathia est extra forrestam et deinde p. dictam aquam de *Trent* ubi ex antiquo currere solebat, *viz.* ex parte orientali novi cursus nunc de *Trent* usque ad manerium de *Colwicke* et ibi ubi vetus aqua de *Trent* currere solebat. Ita quod clausura ibidem vocata *Hickings* est infra forrestam, et deinde p. predictam aquam de *Trent* usque ad pontem de *Nottingham* vocatum. *Hethwett-Briggs* et deinde p. australem partem prater. prefatorum de *Nottingham* usque ad castrum ibidem, &c. et sic finem perambulationis.

Perambulatio de *Shirwood* facta nono die *Septembris* Anno H e n. VIII. XXXV. p. *Robertum Brynnesley, Gabrielem Barwick, Richardum Pierpont,* Arm. *Alexandrum Mearing, Christopher Fitz-Randal, Robertum Whitmore, Johannem Walker, Mauricium Orrel, Johannem Garnon, Johannem Palmer,* Gent. *Robertum Lovet, Willielmum Mellers, Robertum Rawson, Johannem Laskow, Johannem Bristow,* et *Robertum North,* regardatores dicte forreste de S h e r w o o d, &c.

QUE perambulatio incipit ut predictum prosequitur ut predictum et finitur ut predictum est — — — — — — — —

Promissary

Promiffary Note of HENRY VIII. *taken from the Original now repofited in the Treafury of the* CORPORATION.

WE HENRY by the grace of God King af *England* and of *Fraunce* defenfour of the faithe and lorde of *Ireland* promife by thefe prefentes truly to content and repay to all and fingly fuch perfons of the town of *Notting-ham* ———— —— within our countie of *Nottingham* whofe names be contayned in a fchedule indented hereunto annexed all and fingular fuch particular fummes of money as have been by thaym and every of thaym lovyngly advaunced unto us by the way of loan, for the maintenaunce of our warres againfte *Fraunce* and *Scotland*, admounting in the hole to the fumme of one hundred fourty feven poundes thirteyn fhillings iiij *dfe*. In witneffe whereof to thefe prefentes we have caufed our privey feale to be fette the xiiijth day of the moneth of *February*, the xiiij yere of our reyne.

By this Sedulle indented appereth as well the Names as the Summes off Money as the Inhabitants within the Towne of NOTTINGHAM *hath lovyngly advanced unto the Kyngs Grace by way of Loone all thes fame Summes.*

	l. fh. d.			l. fh. d.
Thomas Mellers (Mayre)	xii o o		Robert Rofell. — —	iii o o
John Wylliamfon. — —	xxx o o		Wyllyam Stanbank. — —	iii o o
John Roofe. — —	xii o o		Hugh Oldam. — — —	iii o o
Thomas Wylloughby. —	xii o o		Thomas Baynbrygge. —	ii x o
Wyllyam Kyrkby. — —	xii o o		John Aleynfon. — —	vi xiii iiii
John Howes. — — —	ii o o		Thomas Dokker. — —	ii x o
Thomas Stabulles. — —	ii x o		John Doubleday. — —	iii o o
Wyllyam Parmats. — —	v o o		Oliver Jepfon. — — —	ii o o
Robert Ffysfher. — —	ii o o		Richard Halom. — — —	fii x o
Edward Chamberleyn. —	ii o o		Thomas Hobbs. — — —	ii o o
John Dorantt. — — —	ii o o		Wyllyam Mabfon. — —	ii o o
John Sye. — — — —	ii x o		Thomas Dawfon. — —	ii o o
Wyllyam Johnfon. — —	ii x o		Robert Mellers. — —	xii o o
Coftyn Pykerd. — — —	iii o o			

Summe Total of this Sedulle indented. ———— 147 l. 13 s. 4 d.

HENRY ABUTT.

Tt A

A Copy of the last WILL *and* TESTAMENT *of Mr.* THOMAS
WILLOUGHBY, *one of the Aldermen of the Town of* NOT-
TINGHAM.

IN the name of G O D *Amen,* the 4th day of the month *September* in the year of
our Lord God 1524. 1 *Thomas Willoughby* of *Nottingh.* beinge in holle and perfect mind doe make my testament and last Will in manner of theis articles following:

₁ᵗ First I bequeath my soule to almyghty God, and to our Saviour, St. Mary, and all
the company of heaven and my body to be buried within the parishchurch of St. *Mary's* in *Nottingham,* by *Ladies-Chappell* nigh unto my seat, and my principal to be
given after the laudable custom there used.

Item. I will that myn executors shall give unto every priest of the said church
being *at my burial* 6 *d.* and to every estranger priest there being, 4 *d.* and either of
the freers if they come holle to my burial, 3 *sh.* 4 *d.*

Item. I *will have* 13 torches born light at my burial and every torch-bearer 2 *d.*
and all other charges about my burial to bee done by the discretion of myn executors.

Item. I *bequeath* to the high alter for tythes and oblations forgotten, 10 *sh.*

Item. I *bequeath* 28 *l.* to be dispersed in manner following : That is to say, that
myn executors shall have the keeping thereof and to give yearly to a priest to sing
for my soule in St. *Mary's* church of *Nottingh.* for the space of six years next after
my decease and every year 4 *l.* 13 *sh.* 4 *d.* to be given to the same priest. If it fortune my wife to marry and take an husband, then I will that the residue of this xxviii
pound unto the prior and covent of the abby of *Newsted,* there to remain to find a
priest as is aforesaid in the church of saint *Mary's* in *Nott.* and the said prior and
covent to bee bounden to my executors by their covent seale for performeinge of
the said priests findinge.

Item. I *give* 3 *l.* to be divided among my sisters children, being over live to be
given other in money or cloath as myn executors shall think good.

Item. I *give* to my sister *Margaret Banks* every year a garment of the price of
3 *s.* 4 *d.* during her life as need requires and a pair of shoes, a smoke and a kerchief
of 8 *d.* price and every quarter of a year 2 *d.* and a roame in my bede-house like as
other my bede-folkes have.

Item. I *bequeath* to *Elizabeth* my wife all my lands and tenements within the
*town and fields of Nott. with the appurtenances, and also Woodborough and Radcliff
duringe her life if she live sole and do not marry. And if my said wife take an husband then I will that all my lands and tenements with the appurtenances shall be e-
qually divided between my two sons Richard and Thomas, and to their heirs for*

ever

ever except her dower, And if they or either of them *die without issue it shall remain to Elizabeth and Margery and to their heirs for ever.*

Item. I do except for my wife and my children, *a close in Fishergate, and two gardens in Moot-hall-gate* to be disposed of in manner following : That is, *that the profits cominge thereof be bestowed upon fewell* for my bedefolkes and upon theire reparation of myne *Alms-houses* upon *Malin-hill,* and when *reparation need not,* I will the *profits comeinge thereof bee bestowed on fewell for my bedefolks. And after the death of myne executors I will that the church-wardens of St. Mary's church shall bee maisters of my said close and gardens for ever.* And every one of the said wardens to have of the rents of the same close and gardens for their labour either of them six-pence for ever.

Item. I give to *Richard* my son xx *lb.* to *Thomas* my son xx *lb.* in money.

Item. To *Elizabeth* my daughter xx *lb.* in money.

Item. To *Margery* my daughter xx *lb.* in money, my sons portions to be delivered them or to their assignes at their age of xxi years, and my daughters portions at the age of xv years; and if any of them die before they come to their age aforesaid, then I will that their portion or portions bee distributed amongst the children. And the other half among my executors. I will that *Richard* and *Thomas* my sonnes being executors shall not occupy nor meddle with noe portion of my goods as long as my wife lives except their own portions.

Item. I bequeath to *Joan Becket* my daughter 7 marcks of good and lawful money to be payd by the hands of my executors. A general acquittance of her childs parte.

Item. I bequeath to the church of St. *Mary's* xxvi *sh.* 8 *d.*

Item. To the church of St. *Nicholas* 13 *sh.* 4 *d.*

Item. To the *Grayfriers* x *s.*

Item. To the *Whitefriers* 6 *sh.* 8 *d.*

Item. To the covent of *Shelford-Abbey* 6 *sh.* 8 *d.*

Item. To *Hethbeth*-bridge 4 of my best pieces of timber lyinge at the tile houses.

Item. I give the *Trinity-Guild* 6 *sh.* 8 *d.* of 13 *sh.* 4 *d.* that the *Guild* oweth me for paling of the garden in *Cow-lane.* Another 6 *sh.* 8 *d.* I give to the chamber of the town to *Robt. Hesterige* —— —— to be supervisors of this my will; *Elizabeth* my wife *Richard* and *Thomas* myn sonnes executors. The residue of my goods that is not bequeathed I give unto *Elizabeth* my wife whom I make afore all other my chief executrix. Theis being witnesses,

Mr. *Richard Tavernor,* Official. *William Permiter* and *Thomas Gregory.*
THIS I transcribed from a copy in the hands of Mr. *Isaac Wyld* apothecary.

Copy

Copy of a Commiffion to the Mayor, &c. of NOTTINGHAM *to raife and mufter the* MILITIA *in* NOTTINGHAM *dated May 26th, the 15th of* ELIZABETH.

ELIZABETH dei gratia, *Anglie, Francie,* et *Hibernie* regina, fidei defenfor, &c. Chariffimo confanguineo & concilliario fuo *Georgio* comiti *Salopp* ac etiam chariffimo confanguineo et concilliario *Edwardo* comiti *Rutland.* Nec non dilectis et fidelibus fuis, majori ville fue de *Nottingham* pro tempore exiftenti, *Gervafio Clifton* militi, *Thome Stanhop* armigero *Francifco Willoughbie* armig. *Thome Markeham* armig. *Johanni Gregorie, Johanni Bromeley, Henrico Newton, Roberto Alveye, Richardo James* et *Roberto Burton,* aldermannis infra villam predictam falutem. Sciatis quod nos de approbatis fidelitatibus et prudentibus circumfpectionibus veftris plurimum confidentes affignamus et conftituimus vos commiffionarios et deputatos noftros dantes et concedentes vobis duodecim, undecim decem, novem, octo, feptem, fex, quinque, quatuor, tribus et duobus veftrum tonore prefentium plenam et abfolutam poteftatem, facultatem et auctoritatem omnes et fingulos homines ad arma ac homines habites ad arma ferenda tam equites quam pedites et fagittarios ac fclopetarios fupra etatem fedecim annorum ac infra etatem fexaginta infra villam noftram de *Nott.* tam infra libertates quam extra arraiand. in fpiciend. et triand. ac armari et muniri faciend. nec non affignand. equos, arma, et cetera vellica inftrumenta congruentia habilitati et perfone unius cujufque fecundum formam et effectum ftatutorum et ordinationum ante hec tempora inde edita et provifa. Ac omnibus illis tyronibus hominibufque imbellibus et rei militaris ignaris erudiend. inftruend. et exercend. ad ufum predictorum equorum armorum et bellicorum apparatuum fecundum artem militarem, ac diligenter omnia et fingula alia faciend. gerend. et expediend. et fieri caufand. que ad delectum, monftrationem, et infpectionem ac etiam ad eruditionem, inftructionem et exercitationem fubtitorum noftrorum in re militari pro meliori fervitio noftro et defenfione hujus regni noftri maxime confentanea et oppertuna fore putaveritis ita quod iidem homines ad arma et homines habiles ad arma ferenda equites, pedites, fagittarii, fclopetarii ac alii predicti homines defenfibiles fic arraiati infpecti muniti prompti fint et parati ad ferviend. quoties et quando necefte fuit. Affignavimus in fup. quofcunque tres aut duos veftrum ad omnes et fingulos veftrum non exiftentes duos vel pares regni noftri aut concilliarios in privato confilio noftro fimiliter mutuo et fe invicem infpiciend. triand. arraiand. ac in armis et equis bellico apparatui idoniis ordinand. et vidend. ita quod omnes et finguli veftrum in forma predicta, ut predict. infpect. arraiat. et apparat. prompti fint et fitis et continue parati ad nobis fimiliter ut predictum eft ferviend. Et ideo vobis mandamus quod circa premiffa diligenter intendatis ac ea omnia et fingula ad certos dies et loca de tempore in tempus p. veftras difcretiones exequamini in forma predicta damus preterea univerfis et fingulis officiariis miniftris et fubditis noftris quibufcunque tam infra libertates quom extra tenore prefentium firmiter in mandatis, quod vobis et cuilibet veftrum in executione premifforum intendentes, auxiliantes et obedientes fint in omnibus diligenter. Et quod feceritis in premiffis una cum nominibus et cognominibus ac numera tam equitum, peditum, fagittariorum et fclopetariorum

ac

ac omnium armorum et bellicorum inftrumentorum ceterorumque bello idoneorum p.
vos in forma predicta infpectorum et armatorum ; quam parochiarum et wardorem in
quibus habitant ac de diverfitate armature et inftrumentorum bellicorum quibus unus
quifque eorum armatus et preparatus eft nos et confilium noftrum circa perfonam noftram attendens quam citiffime potetis poft datum prefentium in fcriptis fub figillis
veftris vel trium aut duorum veftrum manibufque veftris eifdem fupfcriptis debite
certificetis. Damus ulterius firmiter in mandatis quod pro meliori expeditione et
executione prefentium per omnia et in fingulis faciatis tam fecundum tenorem arti-
culorum et inftructionum his prefentibus annexorum quam aliorum quorumcunque ar-
ticulorum et inftructionum que p. privatum confilium noftrum cum opus fuerit vel
pereorum fex in fcriptis manibus fuis fignatis aliquo tempore poft hac vobis dirigent.

I N cujus rei teftimonium has literas noftras fieri fecimus patentes. Tefte me ipfa apud *Weftmonafterium* vicefimo fexto die *Maji* anno regni noftri quinto decimo.

p. dominum cuftodem virtute warranti regii.

P O W L E.

A Direction for the Commiffioners for the mufters in the Town of
NOTTINGHAM *how they fhall proceed in the Execution of the faid*
Commiffion.

W HEREAS by the Queen's Majefty's commandement, there are fent
jointlie with her majefties commiffion under her greate feale of *England* diverfe articles fubfcribed by us of her privie counfill by way of inftructions to the
commiffioners for the general mufters of the countie of *Notyngham,* as the like are
fent to all other counties of this realme. In which there are diverfe articles that do
containe matters not fo proper for the mufteringe and traininge of fouldiers both on
horfeback and on foote in citties, townes corporatt and other exempt places as in the
fhieres abrode and yet maney of tharticles in the faid inftructions are verie meete
and neceffarie for the muftringe and traininge upp of foldiers in citties and townes
corporatt confideringe upon your humble fute her majefty has graunted that a fpeciall
commiffion fhould be directed under her greate feale for the muftringe and traininge
of all manner of hable perfons within the faid towne of *Nottyngham* where fhe truft-
eth, that you will directlie and earneftlie advaunce the intention of this fervice
without refpecte of anie perfons. Therefore to the intent you maie have knowledge
of fuche parte of the former inftructions, fent to the commiffioners of the body of the
fhieres which fhall feem meete for the place, we have thought meete to directe you
to receave underftandinge thereof particularlie from the commiffioners in the fhire
next to you who have inftructions at good lengh for the like purpofes. And therefore wee will you in the Queen's Majefties name to requier of fome of the faid principal commiffioners the fight or underftanding of fuche parte of the faid inftructions
to them delivered, as by conference with them you maie have out of the fame a note
in writinge under the hands of three or two of them at the leaft of fuch articles of the
faid

said inftructions or of the fubftance of the faid articles as maie be thoughte by them and you proper and convenient for the fervice of her majeftie for the muftringe and traininge of all perfons and the further fervice of her majeftie in that behaulfe within that town which maie ferve to all intents and purpofes as thoughe all the hable perfons within your town fhould have been fpeciallie muftered and trained before the faid commiffioners of the bodie of the fhiere. And by the fhewing to them of this our writinge and advice. We do requier all and every of the faid commiffioners alfo in her majefties name to confer with you and to inftructe and directe you from tyme to tyme how and in what beft forte you fhall procede in the faid mufters accordinge to the intent of the inftructions which the faid commiffioners have. And thereupon to deliver toyou in writinge figned with their hands as before is faid, fuch fpeciall articles to be extracted out of theire general inftructions as fhall feeme meete for that towne and in all other things to give you from tyme to tyme advice and aide for the furtheraunce of this good and neceffarie fervice without delaie. And we will that you diligentlie and faithfullie obferve and to your uttermoft feeke to performe the faid inftructions for advauncement of the fervice thereby intended in like forte as if the fame had byne directed unto you by particular writinge from us.

This direction, doth agree with the Order taken by the lords and others of the Queen's Majefties privie confill.

Copy of a Licence under the Broad-Seal of ENGLAND, *bearing date the 8th of* Auguft *the* 15th *of the Reign of King* EDWARD III. *of* England *and of* France *the 2d. to give and affigne 30 fh. Rent, &c. to a Chapplain of* Colwych *as an augmentation of his Suftenance.*

EDWARDUS Dei gratia Rex *Anglie* et *Francie* et dominus *Hibernie* omnibus ad quos prefentes litere pervenerint falutem. Licet de communi confilio regni noftri *Anglie* ftatutnm fit quod non liceat viris religiofis feu aliis ingredi fœdum alicujus, ita quod ad manum mortuam deveniat, fine licentia noftra et capitalis domini fœdi illius de quo res illa immediate tenetur. Per finem tamen quem dictus nobis *Galfridus de Walfeleys* clericus fecit nobiscum, conceffimus et licentiam dedimus pro nobis et heredibus noftris quantum in nobis eft eidem *Galfrido* quod ipfe triginta folidatas redditus cum pertinentibus in *Lichfeld* dare poffit et affignare cuidam capellano divina fingulis diebus in ecclefia de *Colewych* celebranti ad aumentationem fuftentationis fue, habendum et tenendum eidem capellano et fuccefforibus fuis capellanis divina ibidem ficut predictum eft fingulis diebus celebraturis ad aumentationem fuftentationis fue imperpetuum ficut predictum eft tenore prefentium fimiliter licentiam dedimus fpecialem. Nolentes quod predict. *Galfridus* vel heredes fui aut prefatus capellanus feu fucceffores fui ratione ftatuti predicti p. nos vel heredes noftros inde occafionentur in aliquo feu graventur. Salvis tamen capitali bq. dominis fœdi illius ferviciis inde debitis et confuetis. In cujus rei teftimonium has literas noftras fieri fecimus patentes. Tefte me ipfo apud turrim *London* octavo die *Augufti* anno regni noftri *Anglie* quinto decimo regni vero noftri *Francie* fecundo. p. fine fexaginta folid. Anno 1341.

E

E Registro Curiæ Prerogat. Cantuariensis Extract. Codicillus Testamento sive ultimæ Voluntati LUCÆ JACKSON *defunct. gerent. dat. 26. die mens. Januarii* 1630 *annex. continet sequentia. viz.*

AND whereas I stand seized of certain tythes yearly coming or arising at or near unto *Horsepole* in the county of *Leicester* to me and my heirs for ever the same being near about the yearly value of twenty pounds p. annum.

NOW I do give and devise the same tythes unto my brother *George Jackson*, my brother-in-in-law *George Coats, Robert Wood* of the town of *Nottingham, Richard Glyd*, citizen and tallow-chandler of *London* and to *Richard Mills* citizen and draper of *London* and to their heirs for ever, upon this special trust and confidence, that they and their heirs shall for ever hereafter from and after my decease, not only yearly for ever pay and distribute all the clear rents and profits thereof arising in manner and form following. That is to say two equal 3d parts thereof (the whole profit thereof in three equal parts divided) as followeth : *viz.* forty shillings thereof yearly to be given for two sermons to be preached in St. *Peter's* church in the town of *Nottingham*, upon the twenty eighth day of *July*, and the fifth day of *November*, acknowledging God's great mercy, and giving thanks for the miraculous deliverance and preservation of this land and people at two several times, the one from that invincible *Armada* (as it was termed) which came in anno 1588. And the other from that unmatchable plot of the *Gunpowder Treason* which was intended against this kingdom and state in *November* 1605, and the residue of the said two third parts to be distributed to and among the poor people in the said parish of St. *Peter* aforesaid, at the discretion of the said five feoffees before named, and of their heirs, and the other third part of the clear profits of the said tythes as followeth. *viz.* forty shillings thereof yearly to be given for two sermons to be preached in the parish church of *Thornton*, near *Horsepoole* in the county of *Leiceister* upon the said 28th day of *July* and 5th day of *November* yearly acknowledging there also Gods great mercy in our deliverance and preservation as is afore said, and the residue of the said one third part thereof to be distributed to and amongst the poor people in the parish of *Thornton* near *Horsepoole* aforesaid at the discretion of my said feoffees before named and their heirs and assignes, but also that the survivour of them the said *George Jackson, George Coats, Robert Wood, Richard Glyd*, and *Richard Mills*, shall upon request, conveygh the said tythes to four of the most honest and able persons dwelling in the parish of St. *Peter's*, and to four other of the most honest and able parishioners in *Thornton* aforesaid, and to their heirs and to the uses and confidence afore-mentioned. And that the survivor of them also shall conveigh the same tythes to other four of the most honest and able parishioners of the same parishes in like manner for ever to the uses aforesaid.

Item. I do will and appoint that all such of the said legacies, (certain and not casual) before-mentioned ; the persons to whom they are bequeathed now being above the age of twenty and one years and whereof no time of payment thereof is before limited, shall be payd by my executors within one year next after my decease. And

And that all such other of the said legacies (certain and not casual) before expressed, the persons to whom the same are bequeathed now not being of the said age of twenty and one years, and whereof no time of payment thereof is before limited, shall be payd by my executors at the said age of twenty and one years accomplished and not before.

A N D I do ordain nominate and appoint my said daughter *Anne Jackson* to be my executrix of this my last will and testament, and I do ordain and appoint the said *Richard Glyd*, and *Richard Mills*, to be co-executors with my said daughter in trust during her minority, and to aid and assist her in the execution of this my will. And for their pains therein, I do give to either of them the said *Richard Glyd*, and *Richard Mills* the sum of forty pounds a piece. In witness whereof to every leaf of this my will containing twelve sheets of paper and one half sheet I have subscribed my name, and to this my will have set my seal. The day and year first before written p. me

Lu. Jackson.

Subscribed, sealed and published by the said *Luke Jackson* as and for his last will and testament in the presence of us

Anthony Bradshawe,
George Dunn,
Robert Render,
John Ewen, scr.

Probatum Londini et coram ventili viro Gulielmo Samas *legum Dre. surro &c. ultimo die mensis januarii anno dom.* 1630. *Jurtis* Richardi Glydd, & Richardi Mills, *extor, &c. Quibus, &c. de bene, &c. jurat. reservata potestate &c.*

Linthwait Farrant. — Regist. ar. deputat. assumpt.

This I have taken from a true copy of the codicill drawn out the 17th day of *August* anno dom. 1713, from the register of the prerogative court of *Canterbury* by Mr. *John Town*, attorney, and Mr. *John Town* cl. — The Rev. Mr. *Chappel*, communicated it to me.

Copies

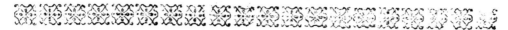

Copies of the DEED *and* WILL *of* HENRY HANLEY, *Esquire, relating to the Alms-houses in Stony-street in* Nottingham *and a Weekly-Lecture in the same Town and several other Charities.*

Deed dated A. D. 1645.
Will dated A. D. 1650.

THIS INDENTURE made the 3d day of October 1645 between *Henry Hanley* of *Brampcoate* in the county of *Nottingham*, Esq; on the one part, and *Francis Pierpont* of ——— —— in the county of —— —— *Gervais Pigget* of *Thrumpton* in the county of *Nottingham*, *Edward Ayscough* jun. of —— —— in the county of —— ——, *Robert Hardy* alias *Harding* of *Gray's-Inn* in the county of *Middlesex*, Esq; *Robert Sommersall* of *Mansfield* in the said county of *Nottingham*, *Walter Edge* and *John Mason* of the town and county of the town of *Nottingham*, gent. *John Foxcraft* of *Gotham* of the said county, *Lawrence Palmer* of —— —— of the said county and *James Brecknock* of *Kegworth* in the county of *Leicester* clerk on the other part, *Wittnesseth*,

THAT he the said *Henry Hanley* as well for the special trust and confidence which he has and reposeth in the said parties, and also for and in consideration of five shillings of lawful mony to him in hand payd by them the said *Francis Pierpont*, &c. the receipt whereof he the said *Henry Hanley* doth hereby acknowledge and thereof doth acquit and discharge them the said *Francis, &c.* their executors, &c. and every of them for ever by these presents. And for the better assurance of a certain rent-charge for ever to be had and issue out of certain lands and tenements of him the said *Henry* hereafter mentioned, to (or to be disposed to) certain charitable and pious uses hereafter in and by these presents declared, and also for the manifestation of his duty which he owes to Almighty God, and the zeal and affection which he beareth to the town and county of *Nottingham* aforesaid, his native country, as for diverse other good causes and considerations him thereunto moving, Hath given, granted, assured and confirmed to them the said *Francis Pierpont, &c.* their heirs and assignes equally without any survivorship, the yearly rent or sum of 120 *l.* of lawful english mony issuing and going, or to issue, be had, and taken, of, in, or out of all other the messuages, cottages, lands, tenements, hereditaments with their and every of their appurtenances whatsoever, of him the said *Henry*, scituate, lying or being within the town, fields, territories, liberties and precincts of *Brampcoate* aforesaid and in *Chilwell* or *Attenborough* in the said county of *Nottingham* or any of them being and only which are the ancient inheritance of him the said *Henry*, and which descended and came to him from his father or any his ancestors, the said lands containing by estimation fourty eight ———— or thereabouts with their appurtenances. To have, hold, receive, and enjoy the said yearly rent of 120 *lb.* of lawful money aforesaid issuing and going forth or to issue be had and taken of, in or out of the manor, messuages, cottages, lands and tenements aforesaid, and all other the afore-mentioned premisses and every of them with their appurtenances to them the said *Fran_*

Uu *or_s*

cis, &c. their heirs and affignes equally without any furvivorfhip for ever. Neverthelefs upon fpecial truft and confidence and to the only ufes, intents and purpofes hereafter following, and to none other ufe, intent or purpofe whatfoever, that is to fay immediately from and after the death and deceafe of him the faid *Henry Hanley,* then for and as concerning 20 *lb.* part of the faid yearly rent or fum to and for the ufe and maintenance of fome pious and orthodox minifter or minifters preaching or to preach a lecture in *Nottingham* aforefaid, that is to fay on every   in the forenoon throughout the year for ever in the parifh church of St. *Mary* in *Nottingham* aforefaid, the faid yearly fum of 20*lb.* to the faid minifter or minifters at four feveral days or times in the year, at the feaft day of St. *Thomas* the apoftle, and at and upon the feaft day of the *Annunciation* of the bleffed virgin *Mary,* and at and upon the feaft day of St. *John* the *Baptift,* and at and upon the feaft day of St. *Michael* the archangel, at or in the fouth porch of St. *Mary's* aforefaid, by even and alike portions yearly for ever to be payd by the then prefent owner or owners, poffeffor or poffeffors of the faid mannor, meffuages, lands, tenements and other the aforementioned premiffes for the time being or fome of them. And the firft payment thereof to begin at fuch of the aforefaid days or times which after the deceafe of him the faid *Henry* fhall firft happen according to the intent and true meaning of thefe prefents. And if it happen the faid *Henry Hanley* do dye without iffue of his body lawfully begotten, or leaving iffue that iffue dye without iffue fo that there is no iffue of the body of the faid *Henry Hanley,* immediately from and after fuch deceafe of him the faid *Henry* without iffue or having iffue immediately from and after the deceafe of fuch iffue for and   of 100 *lb.* part of the faid yearly rent of 120 *lb.* to and for the ufes, intents, and purpofes hereafter, *viz.*

THEN for and as concerning 20 *lb.* part of the faid yearly rent or fum of 120 *lb.* to and for the ufe and maintenance of fome able pious and orthodox minifter or minifters preaching or to preach one other fermon or lecture weekly upon every thurfday in the forenoon throughout every year for ever in the parifh church of St. *Peter's* in *Nottingham,* the faid fumm of 20 *lb.* to the faid minifter or minifters at fuch of the aforefaid daysor times which after the deceafe of him the faid *Henry* without iffue as aforefaid fhall firft happen according to the intent and true meaning of thefe prefents.

AND as for and concerning 40*lb.* part of the faid yearly rent or fum of 120*lb.* immediately from and after the time lately before-mentioned, *viz.* the deceafe of the faid *Henry* without iffue, or having iffue after the deceafe of fuch iffue without iffue as aforefaid, to the ufe and maintenance of 12 poor people which fhall be from time to time elected forth of all or any of the parifhes in the town of *Nottingham* aforefaid or elfewhere, yearly for ever to be diftributed amongft them, to be placed in fome bead houfe or alms-houfe which he the faid *Henry* has pleafed or hereafter fhall pleafe to order and appoint by any writing under his hand or by his laft will and teftament to be erected and founded for that purpofe within the parifh of St. *Nicholas* in *Nottingham* aforefaid or elfewhere the faid fumm of 40 *lb.* to the faid poor people at the aforefaid days and times by fuch even and equal portions yearly for ever in manner aforementioned at or in the faid bead-houfe or almes-houfe, to be appointed as aforefaid, to be payd by the parties before appointed the firft payment to begin as is lately before limited according to the intent and true meaning of thefe prefents.

" A N D

" A N D further it is the intent and true meaning of thefe prefents that as well
" all and every the aforefaid minifter and minifters preaching or to preach the afore-
" faid lectures or fermons, as alfo the faid 12 poor people to be elected as aforefaid
" fhall from time to time and all times hereafter fo oft as occafion fhall require or
" fhall be thought fit, be nominated, elected, appointed and authorizd by the con-
" fent of them the faid *Francis Pierpont*, &c. the Mayor of the town of *Nottingham* a-
" forefaid for the time being and the prefent heir or heirs, owner or owners of the
" aforefaid mannor, meffuages and other the aforefaid premiffes for the time being,
" or by the major part of them the faid parties or perfons according to the true in-
" tent of thefe prefents."

A N D as for and concerning one other 20 *lb.* part of the faid yearly rent of
120 *lb.* immediately from and after the time lately before-mentioned, to the ufe and
maintenance of the moft aged impotent and pooreft people of the town of *Nottingham* aforefaid, to be indifferently diftributed among them with the advice and affiftance of the mayor and aldermen the minifter and churchwardens of the feveral parifhes of the town of *Nottingham* aforefaid for the time being, or the mayor and part
of them whereof fome of every parifh aforefaid as moft need fhall require the faid
fum of 20 *lb.* to the faid poor people   and
at or in the chief market ftreet of the faid town after publick notice given to the faid
inhabitants to be payd by the parties before appointed, the firft payment to begin at
the time lately before limitted according to the true intent and meaning of thefe
prefents.

A N D for and concerning one other 20 *lb.* part of the refidue of the faid yearly
rent or fum of 120 *lb.* immediately from and after the time lately before-mentioned
to the ufes intents and purpofes hereafter following, *viz.*

T O the ufe and maintenance of the poor of the faid town of *Brampcoat* the
fum of 5 *l.* and to the ufe and maintenance of the poor of the town of *Wilford* in the
faid county, the fum of 5 *l.* to the ufe and maintenance of the town of *Beefton* in the
faid county of *Nottingham* the fum of 20*fh.* and to the ufe and maintenance of the
poor of the town in *Chilwell* in the faid county the fum of 20*fh.* and to the poor of
the towns of *Attenborough* and of the poor of the town of *Stapleford* in the faid
county the fum of 20*fh.* and to the ufe and maintenance of the poor of the town of
Trowel in the faid county the fum of 20*fh.* and to the ufe and maintenance of the
town of *Woollaton* in the faid county the fum of 20*fh.* the faid feveral fums laft mentioned to the feveral and refpective minifters and churchwardens for the time being
of the faid feveral and refpective towns at or in the feveral porches of the churches
in the faid towns at the faid days and times by fuch even and equal portions yearly
for ever in manner and form aforefaid to be payd by the faid before-appointed, the
firft payment thereof to begin at the time as is lately before limited according to the
intent and true meaning of thefe prefents, and for and as concerning the fum of four
pounds being the refidue of the laft-mentioned fum of 20 *l.* to the ufe and maintenance of the prifoners in any of his majefty's goals or prifons in the faid county to
be equally diftributed among them the fum of 4 *l.* to the fheriff of the faid county
for the time being or his lawful deputy at the faid days and times by fuch even and
equal portions yearly for ever in manner and form aforefaid at or in the common-hall

for

324

for the said county in the town of *Nottingham* aforefaid to be payd by the parties before appointed the firft payment thereof to begin at the time as is before limited, *viz.* the deceafe of the faid *Henry* without iffue or having iffue the deceafe of iffue without iffue as aforefaid according to the true intent and meaning of thefe prefents.

A N D if it happen that the faid yearly rent or fum of 120 *l.* in and by thefe prefents mentioned or granted or intended to be granted or any portion or parcel thereof at any time or times hereafter to be behind, arrear or unpaid to all or any the aforementioned ufe or ufes intents or purpofes at any the feveral days at which it ought or is intended to be paid contrary to the true intent and meaning of thefe prefents by the time or fpace of 20 days, then next and immediately after the faid *Henry Hanley* for himfelf his heirs and affignes and every of them doth covenant promife and grant to and with them the faid *Francis Pierpont, &c.* their heirs and affignes and every of them, that then and from thence forth, it fhall and may be lawful to and for them the faid *Francis, &c.* their heirs and affignes and every or any of them jointly or feverally according to the intent and true meaning of thefe prefents from time to time and at all times fo oft as need fhall require to enter and deftrain in the aforefaid mannor, capital meffuage, lands, tenements, hereditaments and other the aforefaid premiffes or any part or parcel of the fame and the diftrefs or diftreffes then or there fo found or being, to take, lead, drive, unpound or carry away and to detain the fame till fuch time as the faid yearly rent or fum of 120*lb.* and all arrearage thereof if any fuch be and every part and parcel thereof be fully and truly fatisfied and paid according to the intent and true meaning of thefe prefents, or otherwife to take fuch courfe according to law for the recovery thereof as fhall be moft expedient.

P R O V I D E D always and it is the true intent and true meaning of thefe prefents that if the faid *Francis, &c.* their heirs or affignes or any of them fhall at any time or times hereafter give, grant, convey or affign over the faid yearly rent or fum of 120 *lb.* or any part or parcel thereof, to any perfon or perfons whatfoever that all and every the faid gifts, grants, conveyances and affurances whatfoever fhall be and enure and fhall at all times hereafter be taken, conftrued, deemed and adjudged to be to the only ufes, intents and purpofes in thefe prefents declared or fpecified or intended fo to be and to no other ufe intent or purpofe whatfoever.

A N D it is alfo provided in and by thefe prefents and is the intent thereof, that it fhall and may be lawful to and for him the faid *Henry Hanley* and that he fhall have full power and authority at any time or times hereafter during his life by any writing under his hand or by his laft will and teftament to alter, change, any part or all of the aforefaid ufe or ufes intents or purpofes, and thereby to declare, limit or appoint any part or all of the faid fum of 120 *lb.* to any other ufe or ufes intents or purpofes as he fhall think fit. And that, then and from thenceforth, this prefent indenture or grant and rent-charge fhall be and they the aforefaid grantees or feoffees their heirs and affignes and every of them fhall have perceive ftand and be feized of the faid yearly rent or fum of 120*lb.* or fuch part thereof to fuch ufe or ufes, intents or purpofes as fhall **be** by any fuch writing and will and teftament aforefaid declared limited, or appointed.

A N D laftly it is further by thefe prefents neverthelefs provided and is the intent hereof that it fhall and may be lawful to and for the faid *Henry Hanley* at any time or times hereafter during his life upon tender or payment of 5 *sh.* of — *&c.*

by

by himself or his lawful deputy thereto authorized to them the said *Francis, &c.* their heirs or assignes or any of them (he declaring his intent accordingly) to frustrate and make void these present indentures and all and every thing therein contained and from and after such tender or payment, and declaration of his intent as aforesaid, that then as well they as every thing therein contained as also the said rent charge or sum of 120 *lb.* hereby granted or intended to be granted, shall cease, determine and be utterly void to all intents and purposes whatsoever as if the same had never been made or granted any thing in these presents contained to the contrary in any wise notwithstanding.

IN witness whereof the parties above-named to these present indentures interchangeably have put their hands and seals the day and year first above-written.

The last Will and Testament of HENRY HANLEY.

IN the name of G O D, *Amen.* I *Henry Hanley* of *Bramcoat* in the county of *Nottingham,* Esq; being weak in body but of good and perfect memory praised be God for the same, do hereby make and ordain this my last will and testament in manner and form following :

Imprimis. I bequeath and commend my soul to Almighty God my creator undoubtedly believing that through the mercies of God and the merits of the bitter death and passion of his only son my dear Saviour *Jesus Christ* my soul shall be saved, and my body I bequeath to the earth till the day of resurrection to be buried in the church of *Bramcoat* aforesaid or in the chancel of the same at the discretion of my executors herein after-named.

Item, I give and bequeath to my kinswoman *Mary Bray* the yearly sum, rent or rent charge of 30 *l.* yearly and every year for and during her natural life to be issuing and payable had and taken yearly and every year forth and out of such messuages cottages lands and tenements of mine scituate lying and being at *Bramcoat* aforesaid as are of my ancient inheritance and which came to me by descent, and the said yearly sum, rent or rent charge to be paid unto her the said *Mary Bray* or her assignes yearly and every year forth of my said messuages cottages lands and tenements, to or on the 25th day of *March* and nine and twentieth day of *September* by even and equal portions at or in the south porch of the parish church of St. *Peter* in the town of *Nott.* the first payment thereof to begin at whether of the said days shall first happen next after my decease and for default of payment thereof at any of the several days of payment as aforesaid or within 14 days then next respectively insuing, my will and mind is and I do hereby grant and appoint that there shall be moreover 10 *sh.* a week paid forth of my said messuages, cottages lands and tenements unto her the said *Mary Bray* or to her assignes weekly and every week *nomine pæne* for soe long as the same shall be unpaid after the said 14 days next after the said respective days of payment : And further my will and mind is that it shall and may be lawful to and for her the

said

said *Mary Bray* and her assignes to destrain in and upon the said messuages cottages lands and tenements or any part thereof for the said yearly sum, rent or rent charge of 30 *l*. also for the said weekly sum of 10 *sh*. *nomine pœnæ* from time to time and week to week respectively so often and so much thereof as shall be from time to time arrear and unpaid.

Item. I give and bequeath unto my said kinswoman *Mary Bray* the sum of 100 *l*. of lawful english money to be paid unto her within or at the end of twelve months next after my decease if she be then living otherwise not, and my will and mind is, that if she please she shall make choice of and have 50 *l*. worth of any of the household goods and chattels I shall be possessed of in lieu and satisfaction of the one half of the said 100 *l*. at any time within the said twelve months at a reasonable and just price and value.

Item. Whereas by my deed indented bearing date the 3d. day of *October* in the 22d year of the reign of our late sovereign lord king *Charles*, I did for the consideration therein mentioned grant unto the grantees therein named one annuity or yearly rent or sum of one hundred and twenty pounds to be issuing and going forth of all that my mannor or capital messuage scituate in *Bramcoat* aforesaid and all other my messuages, cottages, lands, tenements and hereditaments with their appurtenances lying and being within the towns, fields, liberties and precincts of *Bramcoat* aforesaid and in *Chilwell* and *Attenborough* in the said county or any of them, which are my ancient inheritance and which descended unto me from my father or ancestors the said lands containing 48 —— or thereabout, yet to and for certain uses and purposes in the said deed expressed, " and 40 *l*. *p. annum* thereof are by the said deed de-
" clared to be for the use and maintenance of two weekly lectures in the said town
" of *Nottingham* that is to say either of the said lecturers 20 *l*. and the other 20 *l*. *p.*
" *ann.* other part of the said yearly rent or sum of 120 *l*. are by the said deed decla-
" red to be for the use of the most aged impotent and poorest people of the said town
" of *Nott.* with power and authority reserved to me in and by the said deed, for me
" at any time during my life by any writing under my hand or by my last will and
" testament to alter change and revoke any part or all of the said use or uses there-
" in mentioned declared or appointed, and to declare limit and appoint any part or
" all the said sum of 120 *l* to any other use or uses, intents or purposes as I shall think
" fit, as by the said deed amongst other things more fully may appear. Now I do
" hereby declare, limit and appoint, that there shall be only one of the said week-
" ly lectures in the said town of *Nott.* and the same to be upon any wednesday there,
" in either of the churches there as my next heir and my executors herein named
" or the greatest part of them or of the survivors of them shall direct and appoint.
" And one of the said 20 pounds to be paid yearly for ever for the same according
" to the intent of the said deed and the place of payment for that 20 pounds to be
" yearly at or in the south porch of the parish church of St. *Mary's* in the said town
" of *Nott.* at the days and times appointed by the said deed, and as for the other of
" the said lectures and the other 20 pounds declared and appointed, and also as to the
" said 20 pounds so declared by the said deed for the use of the most aged impotent and
" poorest people in the said town of *Nott.* my will and mind is and I hereby declare and
" appoint both the same shall be taken off and shall not be, and that the said two se-
" veral 20 pounds appointed and intended by the said deed to have been paid as
" well for the said lecture as for the said poor, for good reasons me thereunto moving

and

" and to me appertaining fhall be taken off and not be paid as by the faid deed are
" limitted and declared, but that the one of the faid 20 pounds fhall be allowed,
" and I do hereby limit, direct and appoint the fame to be and go towards the payment
" of the faid 30 pounds a year to my faid kinfwoman *Mary Bray*, and as for the other
" of the faid 20 pounds my will and mind is and I do hereby give and bequeath and
" declare and appoint the fame to be paid and allowed yearly towards the mainte-
" nance of a preacher or minifter that fhall be refident at *Bramcoat* aforefaid, fo long
" as he fhall preach or be refident there."

A N D *Item*. That if it fhall fo happen that I the faid *Henry Hanley* do dye
without iffue, fo that there be no iffue of my body lawfully begotten remaining, then
my will is and I do hereby give all my houfes lands, and tenements in *Bramcoat* a-
forefaid, whatfoever have been purchafed by me of *John* —— Efq; deceafed and
of *Robert* ———— yeoman or of either of them or of any other, to my executors
herein hereafter named to be fold by them or the furvivor or furvivors of them and
if in cafe any of my executors fhall or do neglect or refufe to take upon him or them
the proof and execution of this my will, then my will and mind is, and I do devife
give and bequeath houfes, lands and tenements laft mentioned to thofe of my
faid executors herein after named who fhall and do take upon them the proof and
execution of this my faid will, to be fold by them or the greater part of them or by
the furvivor or furvivors of them or the greateft part of them with all convenient
fpeed after my death as aforefaid to fuch perfon or perfons as will give the beft price
for them *bona fide* and that the profits of the faid lands till the time of any fuch fale,
fhall be affets in the hands of the faid executors, who fhall take and receive the
fame and the monies thereout or thereunto to be raifed by fuch fale as aforefaid,
fhall be by fuch my faid executors who fhall fell the faid houfes, lands, and tenements laft above-mentioned or by the greateft part of them or by the furvivor or furvivors of them difpofed to the ufes, intents and purpofes hereafter mentioned and
declared, that is to fay firft to procure, purchafe and obtain for ever fome convenient
place within the parifh of St. *Nicholas* in *Nott*. aforefaid or elfewhere in *Nott*. as my
executors or the greateft part of them or the furvivor of them who fhall fo prove this my
will and take upon them the execution thereof, as they fhall think moft convenient, and
therein to found, place, erect and build or caufe to be founded, placed, erected, and
builded one alms-houfe or bead-houfe to be continued for ever in repair convenient at
the charge of the faid town of *Nottingham* for the feveral habitations of twelve poor
people whom I have appointed to be elected and to have yearly allowance for ever
in fuch manner and forme as by my faid deed, indented or granted of rent-charge
above-mentioned is fet forth, ordered, limitted and declared.

Item. If it happen that I the faid *Henry Hanley* do dye without iffue, and having
iffue that iffue do die without iffue as aforefaid then I give and bequeath unto *Francis Pierrepont*, Efq; *Gervas Piggot*, *Edward Ayfcough* and *Robert Hardy*, Efqrs.
Robert Sommerfall and *John Mafon* gent. *John Foxcroft*, *Lawrence Palmer* and
James Brecknock clerke being my feoffees in truft mentioned in my deed indented
or grant of rent-charge for their trouble and care therein feverally to every one of
them or to the feveral heir or heirs of every fuch of them as fhall not be living at
the time of my faid deceafe the feveral fums of 20 *sh*. a-piece.

Item.

Item. My will is and I do hereby devife that the fum of 20 pounds be paid back again by my executors into the hands of the executors of the late *Katherine Charlton*, deceafed, in regard it has pleafed Almighty God to take my fon and heir from me in this life.

Item. I give unto my loving couzin Mrs. *Dorothy Bray* my filver bowl.

Item. I give and bequeath unto my loving couzin Mrs. *Jane Baker* daughter of the faid *Dorothy Bray* my filver can or tankard.

Item. I give and bequeath to my faid couzin *Mary Bray* my gilt bowl.

Item. I give and bequeath to my kind friend *James Brecknock* the fum of 20 *l̶b̶.* to be paid unto him within fix months next after my deceafe in confideration of his pains and many good offices performed and to be performed with me and mine and whom I defire to preach at my burial.

Item. I give for the glory of God and better encouragement of the people to ferve him, one third bell to be provided by my executors and to be hung in the fteeple of the chappel of *Bramcoat* aforefaid which faid bell fhall be bigger than thofe other now there.

Item. I give and bequeath unto Mrs. *Jane Ireton*, widow, the fum of 40*sh.* for and in full of all tythes as have been by me forgotten and unpaid unto her.

Item. I give and bequeath unto every one of my fervants which remain with me at the time of my death the feveral fums of 20 *sh.* a-piece.

Item. I give and bequeath unto my fervant *Joane Searfon* all that my cottage houfe with four acres of land thereto belonging and alfo all commons and profits thereto appertaining fcituate lying and being in *Bramcoat* aforefaid and now or late in the tenure of *Francis Lanfdale* or his affignes any thing herein to the contrary notwith-ftanding, to have and to hold the fame unto the faid *Joane Searfon* for her natural life under the yearly rent of one penny, to be paid yearly the 1ft day of *May* if the fame be lawfully demanded.

Item. I give and bequeath unto my fervant *George Hawkfmore*, all my apparel linnen, woollen and wearing cloathes whatfoever.

Item. My will is and I do devife that my faid executors or the greateft part of them within one year next after my deceafe fhall and do provide, finifh, and lay or caufe to be provided, finifhed and laid, comely and decent grave-ftones for the graves of *Piercival Hanley* my fon and heir lately deceafed, and *Mary Hanley* my daughter deceafed and according to their ranks and qualities lawful and commendable infcriptions thereupon and likewife one tomb or monument for the graves of myfelf and *Margaret* my deceafed wife with the infcriptions as aforefaid.

Item.

Item. I give and bequeath unto every one of my executors and fupervifors here-after named that fhall take care and pains in the proof, obfervance and execution of this my laft will and teftament according to the contents thereof, the feveral fums of 5 pounds a-piece.

Item. That if it fo happen that I the faid *Henry Harley* do dye without iffue as aforefaid, or having iffue, that dye without iffue as aforefaid, then my will is and I do hereby give and bequeath after all the feveral payments, bequefts or legacies hereby given or devifed and all other charges and my funeral expences being firft fatisfy'd and difcharged according to my true intent and meaning, All the reft of the undifpofed money to be raifed by the fale of any fuch purchafe, houfes, lands and tenements aforefaid, together with all my goods and chattels, debts and perfonal eftate whatfoever remaining, unto fuch my executors herein hereafter named as fhall take care and pains and go through with and in the proof, obfervance and execution of this my will according to my intent and meaning.

Item. My will and mind is and I do hereby devife grant and bequeath all my faid manor capital meffuage and other meffuages and cottages, lands and tenements whatfoever with the appurtenances and all the rents, iffues and profits thereof or which fhall be over and above fuch rent-charge and fums of money as are given and payable forth of the fame by this faid will or by the faid deed and alfo the faid cottage houfe and land with the appurtenances fo given to the faid *Joane Scarfon*, for the faid term as aforefaid excepted unto fuch of my executors herein named, and to the furvivors of them as fhall take upon them the proof and execution of this my laft will and teftament, to have, hold, receive and enjoy the fame for one whole year next iffuing after my deccafe for and towards the better payment and difcharge of the gifts, legacies and bequefts hereby given and bequeathed and of the ufes ends and purpofes herein mentioned.

Item. Laftly it is my will and I do hereby nominate, authorize, conftitute, ordain and appoint my trufty and well beloved friends the honourable the faid *Francis Pierrepont* of the town of *Nottingham*, Efq; *John Mafon, William Flamftead* and *Daniel Sulley*, of the faid town gent. and my fervant *George Hawkfmore*, to be the full and lawful executors of this my laft will and teftament hereby defiring them as they tender the honour and glory of God to fee this my faid will obferved according to my intent and meaning, and I do hereby appoint, defire and authorize my loving friends *Gervas Pigott, Jofeph Widmermoole* and *Robert Hardy* alias *Harding* aforefaid Efqrs. and *Huntingdon Harley* the elder, to be my fupervifors and overfeers, and for the true and juft performance of this my will and teftament, trufting that they will be careful as they tender the honour and glory of God to fee it duly executed and obferved according to my intent and meaning.

PROVIDED always that if any perfon or perfons whatfoever fhall go about to act or practife or caufe to be acted or practifed or done either directly or indirectly any thing or things whatfoever any ways to difanul and make void this my faid will or any part of the fame or to hinder the due execution thereof or any part thereof, then it is my mind and will that then and from thenceforth fuch perfon and perfons and every of them fhall thereby forfeit, loofe and be difabled to take or receive

and

any benefit of, in or out of any part of my eftate and goods hereby devifed, intended, limited, appointed or given unto any fuch perfon and perfons then and from thenceforth fhall and remain and is hereby given and appointed to fuch of the reft of perfons herein named who according to the intent, limitation and appointment of this my laft will and teftament intended to take, have and receive the fame, and who fhall take care and pains in the juft execution of this my laft will and teftament, and further it is my will and mind that my aforefaid executors and the furvivor or furvivors of them or the greateft part or any three of them who fhall take upon them the execution of this my will in any fuch or other cafe of oppofition or hindrance of the juft execution of this my will by any other perfon or perfons whatfoever pretending any title to any part of my faid eftate whatfoever, fhall hereby have power and authority (if need require) to fell fo much of any part of my faid eftate lands or goods to them hereby left and devifed to maintain fuite againft all or any fuch oppofer and hinderer thereof, that my will may be truely performed according to my intent and meaning.

P R O V I D E D alfo and my will and mind is, that if any of the faid charitable or pious ufes intents or purpofes to any part thereof hereby or in my faid deed or grant of annuity or rent-charge limited declared or appointed, fhall be at any time any ways obftructed, hindered, mifemploy'd or —— for the fpace of three years, by the perfon or perfons intrufted with the fame, that then the fame fhall ceafe and de-determine and be as if the fame had never been limited declared given or appointed.

P R O V I D E D further and my will and mind is and I do hereby declare that if any perfon or perfons whatfoever fhall endeavour, act or do, or caufe or procure any thing whatfoever to be acted or done either directly or indirectly in any manner whatfoever, to hinder, contradict or interrupt any thing whatfoever by me hereby given, devifed, bequeathed or appointed, or go about or endeavour any ways to crofs my mind and will in any thing hereby declared, that then fuch perfon or perfons fhall thereupon and from thenceforth be for ever barred and for evermore excluded from having or claiming any part or parcel of my lands, tenements, goods, chattels or eftate whatfoever or wherefoever, real or perfonal.

A N D I do laft of all hereby revoke all former wills by me made. In witnefs whereof I have hereunto put my hand and feal this firft day of *May* A. D. 1650.

A

A Muſter-Roll of the Foote Company under the Command of Captain THOMAS POULTON, *Governor of Nottingham-Caſtle.*

T H O M A S P O U L T O N, *Captain.*
John Gillott, *Lt.*
Richard Mortlock, *Enſigne.*

Thomas Lume,
John Allen, } Serjeants.

Henry Grundy,
George Franks, } Corporals.
Robert Barker,

John Cooper,
John Ellis, } Drummers.

Tho. Holt, *Gent. of Arms.*
Lawrence Collin, *Gunner.*
John Pearſon, *Mattroſſe.*

John Rouſe,
William Vincent,
John Barrow,
George Fox,
Robert Breerley,
Henry Wright,
William Wilkinſon,
John Noone,
Francis Walker,
George Coates,
Anthony Hutchinſon,
Henry Gamble,
James Starre,
Robert Wright,
William Wright,
Richard Coursby,
Thomas Campian,
Gervas Waller,
Chriſtopher Barcſey,
John Wilſon,
Robert Barlow,
Francis Smite,
Thomas Hyfield,
John Naylor,
John Cloſe,
Richard Norte,
Robert Lindley,
Mathew Bugge,
John Dickenſon,
Gervas Hallome,

Richard Birche,
Samuel Belcher,
Francis Rayner,
William Smalley,
John Aſton,
Thomas Rayner,
Wm. Claybrooke,
William Chamberlaine,
John Hill,
John Bradwell,
John Trewman,
Robert Clarke,
Thomas Batty,
Rice Jones,
John Howes,
Philip Knight,
Richard Mortley,
Jonathan Newham,
George Faurett,
John Winter,
John Newham,
Nathaniel Chamberlaine,
William Nyles,
George Stoute,
George Kirke,
Richard Baly,
John Hiteerſey,
John Baynett,
James Robinſon,

Richard Hollis,
William Hall,
Thomas Dallowater,
Henry Viccars,
Gervas Johnſon,
Abraham Hextall,
John Brentnall,
Thomas Syfeton,
Robert Croſſe,
Edward Aſhe,
John Lundy,
Samuel Roſe,
Richard Toll,
John Hilton,
John Preſton,
Robert Towneroe,
William Porter,
Richard Fouljam,
John Calton,
Wm. Gent,
Nicholas Colton,
Robert Clarke,
William Walldon,
Edward Harlowe,
George Powell,
Valentine Salt,
John Hutchinſon,
Thomas Patchet,
John Jackſon,
Thomas Moreley,

Xx 2

Robert

Robert Burnett,	John Standly,	Thomas Wright,
James Holborne,	Theoph. Newam,	George Bush,
George Woollett,	Thomas Harrie,	Matthew Livesley.
Robert Chantrey,	Jonathan Saunders,	

January 27th. 1648.

Mustered then in Capt. Poulton's *company Governor of* Nottingham-Castle, *the Capt. Lieutenant, Ensign, two Serjeants, three Corporals, a Gent. of Arms, two Drumers, one Gunner, one Mattrose, and* 100 *private Soldiers.*

Jona. Everard.

Copy of the last Will and Testament of B A R N A B Y W A R T-N A B Y, *taken from a Copy attested by Mr.* James Haynes, *late Register.*

This Will is dated October 30, 1672.

N. B. Queritur 1. *Whether in the original it is not expressed whether the legacies of the executors shall be* 50 lb. *or* 50 sh.

2d. — — — — *Whether it is not mentioned in the original what he leaves his Trustees besides the legacies given them before.*

This is also in the possession of Mr. Thomas Bennet, *Register.*

IN the name of G O D *Amen.* The 30th day of *October* in the year of our lord God one thousand six hundred seventy and two and in the four and twentieth year of our most gracious lord *Charles* the second by the grace of God of *England, Scotland, France* and *Ireland,* King, defender of the faith, *&c.*

I *Barnaby Wartnaby,* of the town and county of the town of *Nottingham* blacksmith, being weak in body but in perfect sense and disposing mind and memory (thanks be given to God Almighty for the same) Do make, constitute and ordain this my last will and testament in manner and form following.

A N D first I give my soul to Almighty God, my maker, and my body I commit to the earth to be buried in the parish church of St. *Mary's* in the said town of *Nottingham* under a stone where my late wife *Ellen Wartnaby* was buried, being at the end of the seat where I the said *Barnaby Wartnaby* used to sit in the said church, at the direction of my executors hereafter named, and for my worldly goods (which God in his mercy has plentifully bestow'd upon me) I give and bequeath the same as hereafter followeth :

AND

A N D firſt I give and bequeath to my loving wife *Iſabell Wartnaby*, all my houſhould goods and plate whatſoever, excepting my money, to hold and enjoy the ſame to her and her executors for ever, from and immediately after my death. Alſo I give unto her the ſum of one hundred and fifty pounds in money, the ſame to be paid unto her by my executors at my deceaſe. Alſo I give and bequeath unto her for and during her natural life, three houſes in *Houndgate* in the town of *Nottingham* in the ſeveral poſſeſſions of *Joſeph Sandal, William Weſton* and *William Burgeſs*, or ſome of them their aſſigne or aſſignes, to fulfill the jointure which I promiſed her on marriage. Alſo I give and bequeath to her all my eſtate, right and title and number of years yet to come and unexpired of and my meſſuage or tenement with their and every of of their appurtenances ſcituate in the town of *Nott.* which I have in leaſe from the mayor and burgeſſes of the ſaid town of *Nott.* now in the tenure or occupation of widdow *Wingfield*, her aſſigne or aſſignes, ſhe paying the rent and performing the covenants from thenceforth on my part and behaulf to be obſerved and performed. Alſo I do further give unto my ſaid wife for and during the terme of her natural life, two tenements with their and every of their appurtenances, in a certain place within the ſaid town of *Nott.* call'd *Wool-pack-lane* now in the ſeveral tenures of *John Cawdron* and *William Watſon*, their aſſigne or aſſignes for the further making up of her joynture and alſo the land made already in joynture, for her life in full of any claim or demand ſhe can have or make out of my ſaid eſtate.

A L S O I give and bequeath to my ſiſter *Frances Preſton* widdow, the ſum or yearly rent of ten pounds p. annum for and during the terme of her natural life, to be iſſuing and payable out of my houſes and lands at *Bobber's-Mill* in the county of *Nott.* the ſame to be payd unto her at *Lady-day* and *Michaelmaſs* by even and equal portions, the firſt payment to begin at ſuch of the ſaid days as ſhall next happen after my death and deceaſe.

Item. I give and bequeath to my brother *Robert Stapleford*, the ſum of five pounds, and to *Margaret Stapleford* the wife of the ſaid *Robert Stapleford* of *Warſop* my ſiſter the ſum of forty pounds of lawful money of *England*.

Item. I give and bequeath to *William Smith* of *Retford* in the county of *Nott.* and his children my couzins and to their heirs for ever two houſes with the appurtenances thereunto belonging ſcituate and being in *Newark* upon *Trent* in the ſaid county of *Nott.* in the poſſeſſion of *Thomas Flear* of the ſame ſtanding near the *Horſe-Market* and the other being in *Mill-gate* now in the tenure of *Original Gabitus* a taylor. And alſo one half acre of meadow land being copy-hold land, lying and being in a place there called *Farnton-Tongue* and in the pariſh of *Farnton*, the ſame to be equally divided among them. And it is my will that the ſame ſhall enure to them and their heirs according to the cuſtom of the mannor, as amply and fully as it ought to do according to the cuſtom of the ſaid court were it put into copy-holders hands otherwiſe for the ſaid uſes.

Item. I give to *Anne* the wife of *Stephen Pickard* if ſhe have any children the ſum of fourty pounds of lawful money of *England* to be put forth and go forward for their uſe and behoof until they ſhall attain the age of twenty and one years, and in the mean time it is my will that my ſaid couzin ſhall have the intereſt thereof to her

own

own ufe ; and in cafe fhe have no children, then it is my mind and will that the fame
fhall go and be payd to *Barnaby Smith* the fon of *William Smith* of *Retford* aforefaid for his and their ufe and behoof.

Item. I give and bequeath to my brother-in-law *John Thornton* of *Eaft-Bridg-
ford* the fum of twenty fhillings.

Item. I give unto *Joan Thornton* my god-daughter the fum of twenty fhillings.

Item. I give and bequeath to my wife's fifter *Alice Goodwin* widdow dwelling
at *Lenton* in the county of *Nott.* the fum of ten pounds, and to her two daughters *He-
fter Johnfon* and *Mary Johnfon* twenty fhillings a-piece.

Item. I give and bequeath unto *Mary Simpfon* the wife of *Jonathan Simpfon* the
fum of ten pounds of lawful money.

Item. I give unto *Thomas Barnes* my couzin fix pounds which he ftands indebted
to me, for the rent of a clofe, and I do alfo acquit him of the fum of four pounds which
I lent him.

Item. I give and bequeath to his two children *Wartnaby Barnes* and *Anne
Barnes* the fum of five pounds a piece.

Item. I give unto my kinfwoman *Rebecca Robinfon* the fum of ten pounds.

Item. I give to my maid fervant *Elizabeth Palmes* the fum of five pounds.

*Item. I give to the poor of the town of Nottingham the fum of ten pounds to be
dealt and diftributed in money or bread at my funeral at the difcretion of my executors.*

Item. I give to him who preaches my funeral fermon the fum of forty fhillings.

*Item. I give to the poor people in my bede-houfe nine pounds amongft them to be
layd forth to buy every one of them a gown: and if any of the faid moneys remain of
that which is to be layd out to buy them gowns the fame to be payd to my feoffees in
truft of my alms-houfe.*

*Item. It is my will and I give to every one of them the fum of five fhillings in mo-
ney, befides the money above-mentioned to be laid out to buy them gowns.*

Item. I give to *Mary* the daughter of *Robert Stapleford* of *Warfop* the fum of 10*l.*

Item. I give to *William Matthew* my wife's brother the fum of forty fhillings.

Item. I give to *Elizabeth Gofs* my couzin the fum of five pounds.

*Item. I give to the poor of the parifh of St. Mary's in the citty of Lincoln the
fum of two pounds to be diftributed by the Advice of Mr. William Hall of the fame
citty and churchwardens of the faid parifh immediately after my funeral.*

Item.

Item. I give to the poor of the town of *Newark* upon *Trent* the sum of ten pounds to be given and distributed at the discretion of the *Mayor* then being and the church-wardens of the same then being, in like manner.

Item. I give the sum of ten pounds to buy funeral rings to be given to my feoffees in trust and other friends hereafter named.

Item. My will is, that if either of my brethren *Thomas Wartnaby* and *Richard Wartnaby*, which went over seas, or both of them shall fortune to come again into *England* they shall have forty pounds a-piece payd unto them forth of the reversion of my lands after the decease of my said wife. And also if my sisters son *Robert Stapleford* which is likewise over the seas shall return again into *England*, my will is and I give and bequeath unto him the sum of twenty pounds forth of the reversion of my lands.

Item. I nominate and appoint my loving friend the said *William Hall* of the citty of *Lincoln*, gent. and my friend *Thomas Greaton* of the town of *Nottingham*, beer-brewer, my executors of this my last will and testament. And I give to either of them the sum of fifty —— of lawful money of *England* a-piece for their pains in seeing it performed according to the contents thereof.

A N D for the rest of my lands tenements and houses in the town of *Nottingham* and the county of the same, and also one messuage and three cottages with all the lands, tenements, rights and titles whatsoever to them belonging, and seven ox-gangs of land lying and being in *Hose* in the county of *Leicester*, my funeral charges, debts and legacies being first discharged, I give and bequeath the same to my executors and their heirs to be sold by my executors, and distributed amongst my relations before-mentioned, to be sold within the space of two years next after my death, and the money to be divided amongst them equally and proportionably, or to so many of them as shall be then living.

A N D whereas I am possessed in fee of three mills with other out-houses, and the grounds, closes and commons thereunto belonging, I leave the same to my executors and their heirs to dispose of them paying the said ten pounds per annum to my said sister *Francess Preston* for her life as I have above given and devised, and the remainder to be paid and employed toward the payment of legacies above recited and mentioned.

A N D whereas I have lately lent to Mr. *George Flower* of *Carburton* in the county of *Nott.* gent. the sum of two hundred and fifty pounds upon the surrender of a paper mill at *Bulwell* with certain closes of meadow and arable land thereunto belonging. My will is that my executors shall have the disposing thereof as to my relations before expressed, the better to enable them to pay my legacies before-mentioned.

A L S O I give to my wife the sum of five pounds to be payd unto her by my executors at my death to give to such nonconformist minister as she shall please.

A N D

AND I do also give to my man *Henry Hawksworth* the sum of forty shillings to buy him a cloak with.

ALSO I do give to Mr. *George Ouldfield*, Mr. *Thomas Burgess*, Mr. *William Petty*, Mr. *John Moreclock*, Mr. *Brownlow Egginton*, and *John Tuffin* all of the town of *Nottingham* my trustees for my alms-house in the town of *Nottingham*, besides the legacies I have given them.

ALSO I give to Mr. *Arthur Rickards* the sum of forty shillings for a legacy to be paid to him by my executors for his pains about my will.

ALL and every my goods and chattels (my debts and legacies being first payd and funeral expences discharged) I give and bequeath unto my said executors.

IT is my will that all my legacies be payd within one year after my death, and those that are under age it is my will that if their parents or guardians give my said executors security that the same shall be payd.

LASTLY I do revoke and make void all former wills and testaments by me made, and do declare this my will contained in four sheets of paper unto each whereof I have written my name and to the last thereof set my hand and seal to be the last will and testament of me the said *Barnaby Wartnaby.*

BARNABY WARTNABY.

SEALED and delivered, published and declared by the said *Barnaby Wartnaby*, to be his last will and testament in the presence of us :

George Ouldfield,
Thomas Burgess,
Arthur Rickards.

vera copia & examinat p. me J. HAYNES.

✛✛✛

Judgment of the Court the 8th of January in the 36th of HENRY 6.
concerning the repairing of the Leen-Bridge.

HENRICUS Dei gratia Rex *Anglie* et *Francie* et dominus *Hibernie*. Omnibus ballivis et fidelibus fuis falutem.

INSPEXIMUS quoddam recordum inter indictamenta noftra de termino ancte trinitatis anno regni noftri tricefimo tertio coram nobis affilato in hec verba, cilicet *Not.* fcilicet : Dominus Rex mandavit dilectis et fidelibus fuis *Radulpho Cromwell,* militi, *Willielmo Babyngton,* militi, *Richardo Byngham, Johanni Portyngton, Thome Chaworth,* militi, *Willielmo Babyngton,* armigero, *Johanni Plumptre,* majori ville *Nottingham, Richardo Samon, Thome Babyngton* et *Richardo Illingworth* literas fuas patentes in hæc verba :

HENRICUS Dei gratia rex *Anglie* et *Francie* et dominus *Hibernie* dilectis et fidelibus fuis *Radulpho Cromwell,* militi, *Willielmo Babyngton,* militi, *Richardo Byngham, Johanni Portyngton, Thome Chaworth,* militi, *Willielmo Babyngton,* armigero, *Johanni Plumptre,* majori ville *Nottingham, Richardo Samon, Thome Babyngton* et *Richardo Illingworth* falutem. Sciatis quod ut plene informamus magnus pons ultra aquam de *Lene* in comitatu *Not.* inter villam noftram *Not.* et pontes vocat. *Heyghbeyth-brugge* in comitatu predicto. p. quem frequens et commune paffagium hominibus, equeftribus et pedeftribus ac animalibus carectis et cariagiis nec non omnibus alliis rebus neceffariis tam ad villam predictam quam extra eandem cariandi in dies habebatur, p. vehementem et infolitam excrefcentiam aquarum pluvialium jam tarde contingentium taliter dirutus fit et confractus quod paffagium hujufmodi totaliter impeditum et ter datum, grave prejudicium et irreparabile dampnum populo noftro generatum et habitum et quod predictus pons, femper, aliqua neceffitate feu periculo eminente p. habitatores wapentachiorum comitatus predicti reparari ac emendari debet et fuftentari et fic a tempore cujus contrarium memoria non habet reparari folebat ac emendari et fuftentari. Nos igitur bonum et aifiamentum populi noftri predicti in hac parte ut condecet affectantes affignavimus vos novem, octo, feptem, fex, quinque, quatuor, tres et duos veftrum quorum aliquem veftrum vos prefatos *Willielmum Babyngton,* militem, *Richardum Byngham* et *Johannem Portynton* unum effe volumus. Jufticiarios noftros ad inquirendum p. facramentum proborum et legalium hominum tam de villa quam de comitatu predictis p. quos reiveritas melius fciri poterit, p. quos pons predictus reparari debet ac reparari, emendari et fuftentari folebat et ad omnes illos et fingulos qui ad reparationem, emendationem et fuftentationem hujufmodi tenentur poteritis in venire, ad pontem illum cum ea celeritate qua commoda fieri poteft reficiendi et emendandi, et eos p. diftrictiones fi neceffe fuit ac alio uno et modis debitis et licitis quibus antiquitus fieri confuevit compellendi et compelli faciendi et ad audiendum et terminandum in hac parte fecundum legem et confuetudinem regni noftri *Anglie.* Et ideo vobis mandamus quod ad certos dies et loca quos vos novem, octo, feptem, fex, quinque, quatuor, tres vel duo veftrum

quo-

quorum aliquem veſtrum vos preſatos *Willielmum Babyngton*, militem, *Richardum Byngham, Johannem Portyngton* unum eſſevolumus, ad hoc provideritis, diligenter ſuper premiſſis faciatis inquiſitionem, et premiſſa omnia et ſingula audiatis et termine-tis ac modo debito et effeɗualiter expleatis informa prediɗa faɗuri inde quod ad juſticiarios pertinet ſecundum legem et conſuetudinem regni noſtri *Anglie* ſalvis no-bis amerciamentis et aliis ad nos inde ſpeɗantibus. Mandavimus enim vice-comiti noſtro comitatus prediɗi quod ad certos dies et loca quos vos novem, oɗo, ſeptem, ſex, quinque, quatuor, tres, vel duo veſtrum quorum aliquem veſtrum vos preſatos *Will. Babyngton*, militem, *Richard. Byngham* et *Johan. Portyngton*, unum eſſe volumus ei ſcire faciatis venire faciatis coram vobis novem, oɗo, ſeptem, ſex, quinque, qua-tuor, tres vel duobus veſtrum quorum aliquem veſtrum, vos preſatos *Will Babyngton*, mil. *Richard. Byngham*, et *Johan. Portyngton* unum eſſe volumus, tot et tales probos et legales homines tam de villa quam de comitatu prediɗ. per quos rei veritas in premiſſis melius ſciri poterit et inquiri.

I N cujus rei teſtimonium has literas noſtras ſieri fecimus patentes teſte me ipſo a-pud Weſtmonaſterium XXIX die *Martii* anno regni noſtri viceſimo quarto, quarum quidem literarium patentium pretextu preceptum ſuit vicecomiti *Nct.* quod non omitteret,&c. quin venire faciat, coram preſatis juſticiaris apud *Notyngham* die *Martis* proximo poſt feſtum ſanɗi *Marci* evangeliſte anno viceſimo quarto ſupradiɗo, XXIIII probos et legales homines de prediɗa villa, nec non XXIIII probos et legales homi-nes de quolibet *Wapentagio* comitatus prediɗ p. quos rei veritas in premiſſis melius ſciri poterit, ad inquirendum et faciendum ea que eis ex parte domini regis in pre-miſſis injungerentur, &c. Et quod haberent tunc ibidem nomina juratorum et pre-ceptum ei in hac parte direɗum, &c. Et vice comes inde faciat executionem, &c.

S E S S I O tent. apud *Notyngham* coram *Richardo Byngham, Johanne Plum-tre*, majore ville *Not.* et *Thoma Babyngton*, juſticiariis domini regis ad inquirendum p. ſacramentum proborum et legalium hominum tam de villa *Notyngham* quam de commitatu *Ntt.* p. quos rei veritas melius ſciri poterit, p. quos magnus pons ultra a-quam de *Lene* in comitatu prediɗo inter villam *Notyngham* prediɗam et pontes vo-catos *Heyghbcythbrugge* in comitatu p. quem frequens et commune paſſagium homi-nibus, equeſtribus & pedeſtribus pred. ac animalibus careɗis et cariagiis nec non omnibus aliis rebus neceſſariis tam ad villam prediɗam quam extra eandem cariandi indies habebatur, et qui p. vehementem et in ſolitam excreſcentiam aquarum pluvialium jam tarde contingentium taliter dirutus et confraɗus eſt quod paſſagium hujuſmodi totaliter impeditum reparari, debet ac reparari, emendari et ſuſtentari ſolebat, et ad audiendum et terminandum in hac parte ſecundum legem et conſuetudinem regni *Anglie* p. literas domini regis patentes ſuperius irrotulatas aſſignatas die *Martis* proxi-ime poſt feſtum ſanɗi *Marci* evangeliſte anno regni regis *Henrici* ſexti poſt con-queſtum *Anglie* viceſimo quarto. Compertum eſt p. inquiſitionem coram prefatis *Richardo Byngham, Johanne Plumptre* et *Thome Babyngton* modo hic captam tam p. ſacramentum *Thome Aleſtre, Roberti Raſyn, Johannis Orgrave, Galfridi Kneton, Johannis Ilkeſton, Johannis Lovet*, ſen. *Johannis Clerk, Henrici Beufroy, Johannis Weſtall, Johannis Bate, Johannis Durham, WilliamBower, RichardWud* et *Nicholas Plumtre*, proborum et legalium hominum de villa *Notyngham* juratorum qui p. ſacra-mentum *Willielmi AlfretondeThoresby, Richardi Baſage de Carlton, Hugonis Padley de Newerk, Thome Gree de Lound, Roberti Woley de Warſop, Johannis Welles de Ever-ton, Nicholai Mable, de Snaynton, Johannis Malthouſe de Newerk, Johannis Turner de de Kellom, Thome Tylling de Holme* juxta *Newerk, Willielmi Glos de Nuthall, Henrici Boney de Stanford, Willielmi Willemot de Hiklyng, Johannis Bosworth de Plumtre, Roberti Hawes de Wilford, Henrici Smyth de Byngham, Roberti Nicholason de Estwayte, Johannis Seylerard de Aslokton* et *Willielme Roger de Kyrkeby* proborum et legalium hominum de wapentagii de *Basset-lowe, Thurgarton* et *Lythe, Newerk, Bingham, Brokstowe* et *Rysclyf*, in comitatu *Notyngham* predicto juratorum quod hominines predicte ville *Not.* debent reparare et fuftentare et a tempore quo non extat memoria reparaverunt et fuftentaverunt caput boreale magni pontis predicti et duos arcus ejufdem magni pontis propinquiores eidem capiti boreali in predicta villa *Not.* qui quidem duo arcus et caput continent in longitudine quadraginta et fex pedes et medietatem unius pedis et quod caput et duo arcus predicti funt defectivi in defectu hominum ville predicte, *&c.* Et quod homines wapentagii de *Brokstowe* debent reparare et fuftentare et a tempore quo non extat memoria reparare et fuftentare confueverunt tres alios arcus magni pontis in predicta villa *Not.* proxime adjacentes dictis duobus arcubus quos predicti homines ejufdem ville ut predictum eft reparare debent ex parte auftrali eorundem duorum arcuum, qui quidem tres arcus continent in longitudine quater viginti et unum pedes medietatem unius pedis. Et quod iidem tres arcus funt defectivi et non bene et reparati in defectu dictorum hominum wapentagii illius. Et quod columpna media inter eofdem tres arcus et predictos duos arcus quos predicti homines dicte ville *Not.* ut predictum eft reparare debent in eadem villa, eft defectiva et non bene reparata in defectu tam dictorum hominum ejufdem ville quam dictorum hominum dicti wapentagii de *Brokstowe* quodque eadem columpna tam p. predictos homines ville predicte quam p. predictos homines wapentagii illius reparari debet et a toto tempore predicto reparari debuit et confuevit in communi, *&c.* Et quod homines wapentagii de *Thurgarton* et *Lythe* debent reparare et fuftentare et a toto tempore predicto reparare et fuftentare confueverunt quinque alios arcus magni pontis predicti in dicta villa *Not.* dictis tribus arcubus quos predicti homines dicti wapentagii de *Brokstowe* ut predictum eft reparare debent ex parte auftrali earundem proxime adjacentes. Qui quidem quinque arcus continent in longitudine centum triginta et quinque pedes et medietatem unius pedis et quod iidem quinque arcus funt defectivi et ruinofi in defectu hominum dicti wapentagii de *Thurgarton* et *Lythe* et quod columpna media inter eofdem quinque arcus et predictos tres arcus quos predicti homines dicti wapentagii de *Brokstowe* ut predictum eft reparare debent in eadem villa *Not.* eft defectiva et non bene reparata in defectu tam dictorum hominum predicti wapentagii de *Brokstowe* quam dictorum hominum predicti wapentagii de *Thurgarton* et *Lythe*, qui quidem homines wapentagii de *Broftowe* et homines wapentagii de *Thurgarton* et *Lythe* columpnam illam reparare et fuftentare debent et a toto tempore predicto debuerunt et confueverunt in communi. Et quod homines wapentagii de *Baffetlowe* debent reparare et fuftentare et a toto tempore predicto reparare et fuftentare debuerunt et confueverunt, alios quinque arcus magni pontis predicti in predicta villa *Not.* predictis quinque arcubus quos homines dicti wapentagii de *Thurgarton* et *Lythe* ut predictum eft reparare debent ex parte auftrali eorundem proxime adjacentes, qui quidem quinque arcus continent in longitudine tantam fpacium quantum fex arcus ex antiquo continuere confueverunt, *viz.* centum fexaginta et novem pedes et medietatem unius pedis et quod iidem quinque arcus funt defectivi ruinofi et non bene reparati in defectu dictorum hominum predicti wapentagii de *Baffetlowe* et quod columpna media inter eofdem quinque arcus et predictos quinque arcus quos predicti homines dicti wapentagii de *Thurgarton* et *Lythe* ut predictum eft reparare debent in eadem villa *Not.* eft defectiva et non bene reparata in defectu tam dictorum hominum ejufdem wapentagii de

Thur-

Thurgarton et *Lythe*, quam dictorum hominum predicti wapentagii de *Baffetlowe*, qui quidem homines wapentagii de *Thurgarton* et *Lythe*, et homines wapentagii de *Baffetlowe*, columpnam illam reparare et fuftentare debent et a toto tempore predicto debuerunt et confueverunt in communi, &c : Et quod homines wapentagii de *Newerk* reparare et fuftentare debent, et a toto tempore predicto debuerunt et confueverunt tres alios arcus magni pontis predicti in predicta villa *Not.* predictis quinque arcubus ejufdem pontis quos predicti homines dicti wapentagii de *Baffetlowe* ut predictum eft reparare debent ex parte auftrali eorundem adjacentes qui quidem tres arcus continent in longitudine fexaginta et novem pedes. Et quod iidem tres arcus funt defectivi et non bene reparati, in defectu hominum ejufdem wapentagii de *Newerk*. Et quod columpna media inter tres arcus illos et predictos quinque arcus quos predicti homines dict. wapentagii de *Baffetlowe* ut predictum eft reparare debent eft defectivo in defectu reparationis tam dictorum hominum wapentagii de *Baffetlowe* quam dictorum hominum wapentagii de *Newerk* qui quidem homines wapentagii de *Baffetlowe*, et homines wapentagii de *Newerk* columpnam illam reparare et fuftentare debent et a toto tempore predicto debuerunt et confueverunt in communi, &c. Et quod homines wapentagii de *Byngham* reparare et fuftentare debent et a toto tempore predicto debuerunt et confueverunt, quandam partem five parcellam magni pontis predicti in predicta villa *Not.* dictis tribus arcubus quos predicti homines dicti wapentagii de *Newerk* ut predictum eft reparare debent ex parte auftrali eorundem adjacentem, que quidem pars five parcella continet in longitudine centum et quinque pedes et eft defectiva ruinofa et non bene reparata in defectu hominum dicti wapentagii de *Byngham*. Et quod columpna media inter partem five parcellam illam et predictos tres arcus quos predicti homines wapentagii de *Newerk* ut predictum eft reparare debent in eadem villa eft defectiva et non bene reparata in defectu tam hominum dicti wapentagi de *Newerk* quam hominum dicti wapentagii de *Byngham*, qui quidem homines wapentagii de *Newerk* et homines wapentagii de *Byngham*, columpnam illam reparare et fuftentare debent ac debuerunt et confueverunt a toto tempore predicto in communi, &c. Et quod homines wapentagii de *Ryfclyff* reparare et fuftentare debent et a toto tempore predicto debuerunt et confueverunt duos alios arcus et caput auftrale magni pontis predicti in predicta villa *Not.* predicte parti five parcelle ex parte auftrali ejufdem adjacentes qui quidem duo arcus et caput auftrale continent in longitudine quinquaginta et feptem pedes et funt valde defectiva ruinofa et non bene reparata, in defectu hominum ejufdem wapentagii de *Ryfclyf*, et quod columpna media inter eofdem duos arcus et predictam partem five parcellam in eadem villa eft defectiva ruinofa et non bene reparata in defectu tam hominum ejufdem wapentagii de *Ryfclyf* quam hominum dicti wapentagii de *Byngham*, qui quidem homines eorundem wapentagiorum de *Byngham* et *Ryfclyf* columpnam illam reparare debent et a toto tempore predicto debuerunt et confuerunt in communi, &c. Per quod preceptum eft vice-comiti quod non omittat, &c. quin venire faciat coram prefatis jufticiariis apud *Not.* die martis in feptimana pentecoftes proxime futura homines predicte ville *Not.* homines dicti wapentagii de *Brokftowe*, homines dicti wapentagii de *Thurgarton* et *Lythe*, homines dicti wapentagii de *Baffetlowe*, homines dicti wapentagii de *Newerk* homines dicti wapentagii de *Byngham* et homines dicti wapentagii de *Ryfclyf*, ad respondendum feparatim domino regi de promiffis &c. Ad quem diem martis coram prefatis *Richardo Byngham, Johanne Plumptre* et *Thoma Babyngton*, jufticiariis, &c. apud *Not.* predict. venerunt predicti homines dicte ville *Not.* p. *Rogerum Brerley* attornatum fuum, et predicti homines wapentagii de *Brokftowe*, p. *Johannem Manchefter* attotnatum fuum. Et predicti homines wapentagii de *Thurgarton* et *Lythe* p. *Ric. Bafage* attornatum fuum, et predicti homines wapentagii de *Baffetlowe* p. *Willielmum Chapman* attornatum fuum, et predicti
dicti

dicti homines wapentagii de *Newerk* p. *Karolum Schawe* attornatum fuum, et predicti homines wapentagii de *Byngham* p. *Thomam Barker* attornatum fuum, et predicti homines wapentagii de *Ryfclyf* p. *Johannem Walley* attornatum fuum, et habito auditu prefentationis predicte dicunt feparatim quod ipfi non poffunt dedicere materias in prefentationibus illis contentas nec quin ipfa dicta capita arcus, columnas, et partem five parcellam magni pontis predicti reparare et fuftentare debent et confueverunt modo et forma prout per prefentationes predictas fupponitur. Ideo confideratum eft quod predicti homines ville et wapentagiorum predictorum diftringantur ad reparationes et emendationes predictas juxta vim, formam et effectum prefentationum predictarum faciendas, &c. Et fint in mifericordia quia reparationes illas prius non fecerunt, &c. Que quidem miferecordie afferantur p. prefatos jufticiarios, *viz.* fup. homines predicte ville *Not.* VI *sfb.* VIII *d.* et fup. omnes cujuflibet wapentagii dictorum fex wapentagiorum VI *sh.* VIII *d.* Et preceptum eft vice-comiti de *Not.* quod non omittat, &c. quin diftringat homines predicte ville *Not.* et homines cujuflibet wapentagii dictorum fex wapentagiorum p. omnes terras, &c. et quod de exitibus, &c. Ita quod ipfi reparationis et emendationes predictas juxta vim formam et effectum prefentationum predictarum fieri faciant nifi prius p. ipfos factae fuerint. Et qualiter, &c. conftari faciat prefatis jufticiariis hic apud *Not.* predict die jovis proxime poft feftum fancti Bartholomei apoftoli proxime futuri, &c. Ad quem diem coram prefatis *Richardo Byngham Johanne Plumtre* et *Thoma Babyngton,* jufticiariis, &c. vice-com. *Not.* retornavit quod caput boreale magni pontis predicti et duo arcus ejufdem magni pontis predicti que predicti homines ville *Not.* ut predictum eft reparare et emendare debent p eofdem homines ejufdem ville *Not.* bene et fufficienter reparata et emendata exiftunt. Et non colupmna media predicta inter eofdem duos arcus et predictos tres arcus ejufdem magni pontis quos predicti homines dicti wapentagii de *Brokftowe* ut predictum eft reparare et emendare debent per eofdem homines wapentagii de *Brokftowe* et predictos homines de villa *Not.* in communi bene et fufficienter reparata et emendata exiftunt. Et quod predicti duo arcus et caput auftrale magni pontis predicti que predicti homines dicti wapentagii de *Ryfclyf* ut predictum eft reparare et emendare debent, p. homines ejufdem wapentagii de *Ryfclyf* bene et fufficienter reparata et emendata exiftunt. Et quod quod columpna media predicta inter eofdem duos arcus & predictam partem five parcellam ejufdem magni pontis quam predicti homines wapentagii de *Byngham* ut predictum eft reparare et emendare debent p. eofdem homines wapentagii de *Byngham* et predictos homines wapentagii de *Ryfclyf* in communi bene et fufficienter fimiliter reparata et emendata exiftunt, retornavit etiam idem vice-comes quod homines cujuflibet wapentagii dictorum wapentagiorum de *Brokftowe, Thurgarton* et *Lythe, Baffetlowe, Newerk* et *Byngham* diftricti funt unde exitus XX *d.* Et quod predicti homines wapentagii de *Brockftowe* manutenentur p. *Adam Say,* et *Alanum Bray* et predicti homines wapentagii de *Thurgarton* et *Lythe* manutenentur p. *Oliverum Olme* et *Galfridum Bond,* et predicti homines wapentagii de *Baffetlowe* manutenentur p. *Thomam May* et *Humfridum South* et predicte homines wapentagii de *Newerk* manutenentur p. *Thomam Thorn* et *Willielmum Morn.* Et predicti homines wapentagii de *Byngham,* manutenentur p. *Matheum Clerk* et *Adamum Smert* ideo ipfi in mifericordia, &c. Et ut prius preceptum eft vice-comiti quod non omittat, &c. quin diftringat predictos homines wapentagii de *Brokftowe.* homines wapentagii de *Thurgarton* et *Lythe,* homines wapentagii de *Baffetlowe,* homines wapentagii de *Newerk* et homines wapentagii de *Byngham* p. omnes terras, &c. et quod de exitibus &c. Ita quod ipfi reparationes et emendationes predictas pro parte fua fieri

faciant

faciant juxta vim formam et effectum presentationum predictarum nisi prius p. ipsos sic facte fuerint, et qualiter, &c. constari faciat presatis justiciariis hic scilicet apud *Not.* predictam die jovis in sancta septimana quadragesime proxime futura ut ulterius, &c. Quod quidem recordum coram nobis habitum duximus exemplificandum.

I N cujus rei testimonium has literas nostras fieri fecimus patentes teste *J. Fortescu,* apud *Westmonasterium* octavo die *Januarii* anno regni nostro trigesimo sexto.

GOGH.

A Copy of a Letter sent from divers Knights and Gentlemen of *Nottinghamshire* to the Knights serving for that County in Parliment. *July* 1, 1642.

———— N. B. *His Majesty's declaration to the Lords and others of the Privy-Council attending his Majesty at* York, *bears date the 13th of June* 1642.

To our much honoured Friends Sir THOMAS HUTCHINSON, *Knight, and* ROBERT SUTTON, *Esq; Knights of the Shire for the County of* NOTTINGHAM.

Gentlemen,

FINDING to our great grief (by divers printed declarations) the unhappy differences betwixt his Majesty and his Parliament and from thence apprehending great fear of farther distractions, we have thought fit to impart our hearts freely unto you, as men chosen by us and intrusted for us to represent us and our desires in your honourable house of Commons : Where in the 1st place, upon all occasions we desire you to tender the acknowledgement of our humble and hearty, thanks for the many good laws which by their care and wisdom together with his Majesty's grace and favour have been obtained for us both for the securing us in the point of our property, and also for the freeing us from the unlimited power of arbitrary government : And herein his Majesty having concurred with you in all that we could expect or can desire both for our persons and estates, and at several times promised to join with his parliament for the reforming and reducing both the doctrine and discipline of the church to the best and purest times since the reformation ; and if this were done, what others would expect we know not, we desire no more.

A N D now we cannot but stand amazed to see the King, the Lords and Commons agree in all that we can think necessary for reformation and for securing us hereafter to be governed according to the good laws of the land in force, and yet such great distraction amongst those three estates.

W E heard long since reports and saw printed papers of the great dangers of papist pifts, and that even in our own country, but believe there was no truth nor ground of any fuch.

WE heard great rumour of a foraigne force from *France* and *Denmark* ; but thanks be to God we fee no fuch danger : And yet under thefe pretences, there is great preparation of putting us in a pofture of defence and a great neceffity pretended of fettling the *Militia* : But we fee more caufe to fear the remedy, than the difeafe, for this pofture (as you call it) of defence does carry a face of war with it, even among ourfelves, and concerning it, we are diftracted with contrary commands. The Houfe of Parliament command one thing, the King forbids that command, and we are at a ftand and yet we are ever ready to yield obedience to all the known laws of the land, and we have ever been taught, that all thofe laws made in parliament confift of three eftates, the Commons, Lords and King, and we think it dangerous to unrwift that triple cord ; and we hold it our greateft privilege that the King and Lords whom we have heard fome time in council joined could not make a law to bind us without our confent in parliament, and by the fame reafon, we cannot expect that the Commons with the Lords fhould make a law or ordinance of the force of a law to bind without the King, efpecially againft the King. And as we do not yield any act of obedience to the King's command fimply but as it is warranted by law, made by his authority with the confent of both Houfes, fo we fhall not conceive ourfelves bound to obey one or both Houfes without the King, but in fuch things as are according to the known laws of the land.

WHEN the King by his writ gave us power to chufe you it was to treat *de quibufdam arduiis, &c:* We never conceived your only votes fhould be our law, nor conceived we had fuch a power to confer upon you, and we require you not to confent to lay any fuch command upon us, nor to engage us in a civil war for the maintenance of fuch votes, under colour of priviledges againft our lawful King, to whom many of us by the appointment of the law have taken the oath of fupremacy, and allegiance, to which all of us are bound. And befide, we have at the command of both Houfes taken the late proteftation, wherein we have vowed to maintain the doctrine of the church of *England*, his Majefty's royal perfon, honour and eftate, the priviledges of Parliament and the liberties of the fubject : And we fhall endeavour to maintain every part and claufe thereof refpectively with our lives and fortunes. And we conceive our beft directions therein to be the known laws, the maintenance whereof we account our liberty and defence. And we account the fureft way to enjoy the benefit of thefe laws, is to join and comply with his Majefty, under whofe protection next under God we can only hope to enjoy the benefit thereof ; efpecially his Majefty having fince this parliament, joined in the making as good laws as ever any King has done, and made fo gracious promifes of his future government according to the laws, and given abundant fatisfaction for fome unhappy accidents in his paft government, that we conceive great caufe to return him cheerful thankfulnefs for thefe laws, and to yield him faithful obedience, and to confide in him for the future.

THIS is the clear expreffion of our hearts, this is that we defire you to confent in for us. And we fhall heartily pray that we might be an example to many others to make the like expreffions. And then we fhould not doubt but this would bring a right underftanding betwixt the King and his people, and take away all fears and jeloufies, and fettle a firm peace amongft us.

W E

WE should gladly and with all humility have petitioned your honourable House, but still to this purpose. And we understand some countries have done so which has been displeasing unto them because contrary to their sense ; and we perhaps through ignorance might fall into the same errour. Yet we hope it will not be displeasing unto you, that we give you our sense freely, for you are us, and we hope you will not be unwilling to follow our sense, so far as you conceive it to be the sense of your county whose you are and for whom you serve. And so we rest your very loving friends and countrymen.

JOHN DIGBY, *High-Sheriff.*

John Byron,	Robert Eyre,	William Needham,
Richard Parkins,	Parke Cresly,	Richard Brough,
William Appleton,	Thomas Houlder,	John Butterworth,
Robert Pilson,	Robert Saunderson,	Tho. Poole,
George Lascells,	John Walker,	John Lee,
Matthew Palmer,	Thomas Fox,	Jo. Worsdale,
Roger Cooper,	John Bolles,	William Shipman,
Isham Parkins,	Gri. Dwall,	Charles Leek,
Jo. Wood,	William Smiths,	William Apsley,
G. Hollis,	Nich. Stoyt,	Francis Cavendish,
Richard Byron,	Thomas Hollwell,	Charles North,
Jo. Nevile,	Richard Draper,	Matthew Palmer,
Edmund Hastings,	Thomas Atkinson,	Richard Holliwell,
Edward Andrewes,	Lancelot Rolston,	Roger Jackson,
Thomas Blackwall,	Thomas Newton,	John Leeke,
William Sandes,	William Wild,	Richard Simman,
Thomas Longford,	Herbert Leek,	Stephen Broome,
Jervas Sanford,	Thomas Brown,	William Colby,
Richard Harper,	William Smythson,	John Newport,
Gabriel Armstrong,	Jo. Gosling,	Edward Holland,
A&. Burnell,	William Oglethorp,	Henry Broome,
Sam. Bolles,	Geo. Lascells,	William Hacker,
Rowland Pand,	John Clay,	James Forbeny,
John Odingsells,	Anthony Gilby,	Job Holden,
Geo. Milford,	Richard Boyer,	William Poclington,
John Caldecott,		Hen. Green.

THE

The following is a Copy of one of the printed Circular Letter of Loan which were sent about and delivered by Troopers. Feb. 1643.

CHARLES, R.

TRUSTY and well beloved, we greet you well.

WHEREAS all our subjects of the kindome of *England* and dominion of *Wales*, are both by their allegiance and the act of pacification, bound to resist and suppress all such our subjects of *Scotland* as have in a hostile manner already entered or shall hereafter enter into the kingdom.

AND by law, your personal service, attended in a warlike manner for the resistance of this invasion, may be required by us, which we desire to spare, chusing rather to invite your assistance in a free and voluntary expression of your affection to our service and the safety of the kingdom.

AND whereas the members of both Houses of Parliament assembled at *Oxford* have taken into their consideration the necessity of supporting our army for the defence of us and our people against this invasion, and for the preservation of religion, laws and liberties of this kingdome, and thereupon have agreed upon the speedy raising of the sum of one hundred thousand pounds by loan from particular persons, towards the which themselves have advanced a very considerable proportion and by their examples hope, that our well affected subjects throughout the kingdome will in a short time make up the remainder, whereby we shall not only be enabled to pay and recruit our army but likewise be enabled to put our armies in such a condition as our subjects shall not suffer by free quarters or the unrulines of our souldiers, which is now in present agitation, and will (we no way doubt, by the advice of the members of both Houses assembled) be speedily effected.

WE do towards so good a worke, by the approbation and advice of the sayd members of both Houses here assembled desire you forthwith to lend us the sum of *twenty pounds* or the value thereof in plate, touched plate at five shillings, untouched plate at four shillings and four-pence p. ounce and to pay or deliver the same within seven days after the receipt hereof to the hands of the high sheriff of that our county, or to such whom we shall appoint to receive the same, (upon his acquittances for the receipt thereof) who is forthwith to return and pay the same at *Corpus Christi* college in *Oxford* to the hands of the earl of *Bath*, the lord *Seymour*, Mr. *John Ashburnham*, and Mr. *John Fettiplace*, or any of them, who are appointed treasurers for receiving and issuing thereof by the said members (by whose order only the said money is to be disposed) and to give receipts for the same, the which we promise to repay as soon as God shall enable us ; this sum being to be advanced with speed, we are necessitated to apply ourselves to such persons as yourself, of whose ability and affection we have confidence, giving you this assurance, that in such farther charges, that the

Yy

necessity

neceſſity of our juſt defence ſhall inforce us to require of our good ſubjeĉts, your for-
wardneſs and disburſements ſhall be conſidered to your beſt advantage.

A N D ſo preſuming you will not fail to expreſſe your affeĉtion herein, we bid
you farewell.

G I V E N at our court at *Oxford* the 14th day of *February* in the 19th year of
our reign 1643.

By the advice of the members of both
Houſes aſſembled at Oxford.

ED. LITTLETON,   } *They were the Speakers*
SAM. EURE.

Stafford,
To *Willoughby Manley*, Gent.

A grant from the Mayor and Burgeſſes of NOTTINGHAM *of forty Shillings a Year to the Tanners.* HEN. 8.

OMNIBUS Chriſti fidelibus ad quos hoc preſens ſcriptum pervenerit, major et burgenſes ville *Nottinghame*, ſalutem in domino ſempiternam.

NOVERITIS nos prediĉti major et burgenſes pro certis cauſis nos moven-
tibus dediſſe conceſſiſſe et hoc preſente ſcripto noſtro confirmaſſe *Willielmo Sharpington, Jacobo Maſon, Johanni Renell, Johanni Gregorie & Thome Sibthorpe,* Lutheoribus ville *Nottinghame* pro nobis et ſucceſſoribus noſtris, unam annuitatem ſive reditum quadraginta ſolidorum annuatim et precipiendam de et in annualem omnibus
terris et tenementis majoris et burgenſium ſeu communitatis ville *Nott.* prediĉte per-
tin. Habendam et percipiendam diĉtam anuitatem ſive annualem reditum quadraginta ſolidorum prefatis *Willielmo, Jacobo, Johanni Renel, Johanni Gregorie* et *Thome Sibthorpe* et ſucceſſoribus ſuis de artificio Lutheorum ville *Nott.* exiſtentibus in
perpetuum ad feſtum annunciationis beate Marie virginis, nativitatis ſanĉti *Johannis
Baptiſte,* ſanĉti *Michaelis* archangeli et nativitatis domini equalibus portionibus p.
manus camerariorum ejuſdem ville exiſtentium annuatim perſolvendam. Ut ſi con-
tingat prediĉtam ſive annualem reditum quadraginta ſolidorum aretro fore in parte
vell in toto poſt aliquod feſtum feſtorum prenominatorum quo ſolvi debeat quod ex-
tunc bene licebit et liceat prefatis *Willielmo, Jacobo, Johanni Renell, Johanni
Gregorie* et *Thome Sibthorp* ac ſucceſſoribus ſuis Lutheoribus ejuſdem ville in omnibus predictis terris et tenementis ſeu quamlibet inde parcellam intrare et diſtringere,
diſtrictioneſque ibidem captas licite abducere et effugare ac penes ſe retinere quo
uſque de predicta annuitate ſive annuali reditu quadraginta ſolidorum una cum arreragiis ejuſdem ſi que fuerint prefato *Willielmo, Jacobo, Johanni Reynell, Johanni Gregorie*

gorie & Thome Sibthorpe ac fucceſſoribus ſuis Lutheoribus ejuſdem ville *Nott.* plenarie fuerint perſolut et integraliter ſatisfact.

E T nos predictus major et burgenſes ejuſdem ville poſſuimus prefatum *Willielmum, Jacobum Maſen, Johannem Renell, Johannem Gregorie* et *Thomam Sibthorpe* in poſſeſſionem predicte annuitatis ſive annualis reditus quadraginta ſolidorum per ſolutionem unius denarii nomine ſeiſie per me predictum majorem die dati preſentis prefato *Willielmo Sharpington* ſoluti in parte ſolutionis annuitatis ſive annualis reditus illius.

I N cujus rei teſtimonium ſigillum commune ejuſdem ville *Nott.* huic preſenti ſcripto noſtro appoſuimus. Datum decimo octavo die menſis *Februarii* anno regis *Henrici* octavi dei gratia *Anglie, Francie* et *Hibernie* regis, fidei defenſoris, et eccleſie *Anglicane* et *Hiberniie* ſupremi capitis triceſimo ſeptimo.

A true Copy of the laſt Will and Teſtament of Mr. ABEL COLLIN, *taken from the rough Draught wrote by the late Mr.* JAMES HAINES *his Fathers own Hand. —— It is now in the Cuſtody of Mr.* Thomas Bennet, *Regiſter.*

I N the name of God, *Amen.* I *Abel Collin,* of the town and county of the town of *Nottingham,* mercer, being under ſome weakneſs of body, but of ſound, perfect and diſpoſing memory thanks be therefore given to Almighty God, doe make and declare this for my laſt will and teſtament in writing, in manner and form following.

Firſt. I recommend my ſoul into the hands of Almighty God hoping through the merits, death and paſſion of my bleſſed ſaviour *Jeſus Chriſt* to have full and free pardon and forgiveneſs of all my ſins, and my body I commit to the earth to be decently buried at the diſcretion of my executor to be hereafter named. And as for my eſtate wherewith it has pleaſed Almighty God to bleſs me, I give and diſpoſe thereof in manner following.

Imprimis. I give and bequeath unto my loving brother Mr. *Thomas Collin,* the ſum of ten pounds to be payd by my executor hereafter named within two years next after my deceaſe.

Item. I give to my loving ſiſter Mrs. *Fortune Smith,* the ſum of ten pounds to be payd within two years after my deceaſe.

Item. I give and bequeath unto every of my brothers and my ſiſters children that ſhall be living at my deceaſe, the ſum of twenty pounds a-piece, of lawful money of *England,* to be payd unto them and every of them by my executor hereafter named within two years next after my deceaſe.

Item.

Item. I give and bequeath to and amongst every of the children and grand children of my unkle *William Collin* late of *Peterborough* deceased, the sum of fifty pounds of lawful money of *England* to be payd unto them and equally divided among them by my said executor, within two years next after my decease.

Item. I give and bequeath unto my couzin *Banks* his children late of *London* carpenter deceased, the sum of fifeteen pounds of lawful money of *England* to be payd unto them and divided amongst them share and share alike, the same to be payd by my said executor hereafter named, within two years next after my decease.

Item. I give and bequeath unto my couzin *Mary Hutchinson* widdow the sum of ten pounds of lawful money of *England* to be payd unto her by my executor hereafter named within two years next after my decease.

Item. I give and bequeath unto *John Stanford* of *Northampton* if he be living at the time of my decease, the sum of fifty shillings or if he be then dead, then I give the said fifty shillings to his widdow if she shall be living at the time of my decease, the same to be payd by my executor hereafter named, within six months next after my decease.

Item. I give and bequeath to the churchwardens and overseers of the poor of the several parishes of St. *Nicholas*, St. *Peter*, and St. *Mary* within the town of *Nott.* and to the executor of this my last will and testament, the sum of twenty pounds of lawful money of *England*, for the binding out and disposing to apprentice or otherwise eight boys, youths or girls, such as shall be approved and liked by my said executor hereafter named and then my said executor to provide the said twenty pounds and payment thereof to be made accordingly within twelve months next after my decease.

Item. I give and bequeath unto the churchwardens and overseers of the poor of the parish of St. *Nicholas* in the said town of *Nottingham*, the sum of twenty pounds of lawful money of *England*, the same to be layd out in buying of coals the next summer after my decease, at the most advantageous time of the summer for buying the same at the cheapest rate, which coals when so bought as aforesaid to be sold to the poor of the said parish in the winter time following, at the same rate they shall be so bought in, so that the said sum of twenty pounds may remain for ever a stock or fund for buying of coals for the use of the poor of the said parish in manner aforesaid and it is my mind and will that the mayor of the said town of *Nottingham* and his successors and also my executor and his heirs for ever shall have power yearly to inspect the accompts of the said church-wardens and overseers, to see the same duly performed according to the true intent and meaning of this my last will and testament.

Item. I give and bequeath unto the churchwardens and overseers of the poor of the parish of St. *Peter* in the said town of *Nottingham* the sum of fifteen pounds of lawful money of *England* the same to be layd out in buying of coals the next summer after my decease at the most advantageous time of the summer for buying the same at the cheapest rate, which coals when so bought as aforesaid to be sold to the poor

of

the said parish in the winter time following at the same rate they shall be so bought in, so that the said sum of fifteen pounds may remain for ever as a stock or fund for buying coals for the use of the poor of the said parish as aforesaid, and it is my mind and will, that the mayor of the said town of *Nottingham* for the time being and his successors, and also my executor and his heirs for ever shall have power yearly to inspect the accounts of the said churchwardens and overseers to see the same duly performed according to the direction of this my will.

Item. I give and bequeath unto the churchwardens and overseers of the poor of the parish of St. *Mary* in the said town of *Nott.* the sum of twenty pounds of lawful money of *England* the same to be laid out in the buying of coals the next summer after my decease, at the most advantageous time of the summer for buying the same at the cheapest rate, which coals when so bought as aforesaid, to be sold to the poor of the said parish in the winter time following at the same rate they shall be so bought in, so that the said sum of twenty pounds, may remain for ever as a stock or fund for buying coals for the use of the poor of the said parish as aforesaid, and it is my mind and will that the mayor of the said town of *Nottingham* for the time being and his successors, and also my executor and his heirs for ever, shall have power yearly to inspect the accompts of the churchwardens and overseers to see the same duly performed according to the intent and meaning of this my last will and testament.

Item. I give and bequeath to the poor debtors in *Nottingham* town goal, or that shall be there, yearly, the sum of one shilling weekly, the same to be payd by my executor and his heirs upon every saturday for ever, the first payment thereof to be made upon the next saturday that shall happen next after my decease.

Item. I give and bequeath to the poor debtors in *Nottingham* county goal, or that shall be there, yearly, the sum of one shilling weekly, the same to be payd by my executor and his heirs upon every saturday, from the first payment thereof to be made upon the next saturday that shall happen next after my decease.

Item. I give unto my couzin Mr. *Thomas Smith,* the sum of 5 pounds to be disposed to such charitable uses as he shall think fit.

Item. I give unto widdow *Thorpe* late of *Brewhouse Yard,* the sum of twenty shillings to be payd by my executor within two years next after my decease.

Item. I give and bequeath unto Mr. *Peter Thompson* of the town of *Nottingham,* glasman, the sum of ten pounds the same to be payd to him by my executor hereafter named, within two years next after my decease.

Item. I give and bequeath unto *John Corks* of the citty of *York* the sum of five pounds the same to be payd unto him by my executor hereafter named, within two years next after my decease.

Item. I give and bequeath unto my couzin *Fletcher's* son of *London,* the like sum of five pounds to be payd by my executor hereafter named, within two years next after my decease.

Item.

Item. I give and bequeath unto *Malell Hunt* the sum of fifty shillings to be by her disposed of amongst such poor people as she in her discretion shall think fit, the same to be payd to her for the purpose before-said by my executor hereafter-named, within two years next after my decease.

Item. I give and bequeath unto my sister *Conway* of *Yarmouth* in the county of *Norfolk* the sum of five pounds to buy her mourning, the same to be payd by my executor hereafter named.

Item. I give and bequeath to my couzin *Elizabeth Conway* of the town of *Nottingham* the sum of five pounds to be payd by my executor within two years after my decease.

Item. I give and bequeath to Mr. *John Egleton* and his wife of the citty of *London* the sum of five pounds a-piece, the same to be payd by my executor hereafter-named within two years next after my decease.

Item. I give unto *Sarah Horowine* and *Rebecca Barraclough* my sister *Smiths* maid servants the sum of twenty shillings a piece if they shall be then living with my said sister at the time of my decease.

Item. I give unto *Bridget* ————, who was my fathers maid servant at the time of his decease the sum of twenty shillings, the same to be payd unto her by my executor hereafter named.

Item. I give and bequeath unto widdow *Parkes* of the town of *Nottingham* the sum of twenty shillings, the same to be payd by my said executor.

Item. I give and bequeath unto widdow *Brittain* living near *Peterborough* the sum of twenty shillings yearly during her natural life, the same to be payd unto her or to such other person as she shall appoint to receive the same upon every *Christmass Eve* by my said executor hereafter-named, the first payment to be made upon the next *Christmas-Eve* that shall happen next after my decease.

Item. I give and bequeath to the poor people of the town of *Nottingham* the sum of one hundred pounds of lawful money of *England* the same to be payd unto them by my executor hereafter named in such manner as is hereafter mentioned, That is to say, the sum of twenty pounds part thereof soon after my decease, and the sum of ten pounds other parts thereof, upon the second day of *February* then next insuing, and the remainder of the said one hundred pounds to be payd by ten pound payments upon the second day of *February*, till the said sum of one hundred pounds be fully paid and discharged. And my mind and will is that the said sum of one hundred pounds before-mentioned and bequeathed shall not be construed or intended to excuse the dole of bread at my funeral.

Item. I give unto Mr. *Samuel Panilcick* and Mr. *William Kirby* my servants the sum of twenty shillings a-piece if they shall be living with me at the time of my decease.

Item.

Item. I give unto *Abel Collin*, fon of my nephew Mr. *John Collin* the fum of twenty pounds over and above the legacy herein before given and bequeathed to him the fame to be payd by my executor hereafter named, within two years next after my deceafe.

Item. I give unto my couzin *John Collin* his wife the fum of five pounds the fame to be payd unto her by my executor here after-named within two years next after my deceafe.

Item. I give unto my coufin *William Clifton* of *Yarmouth* in the county of *Norfolk*, the fum of five pounds, the fame to be payd unto him by my executor here after named, within two years next after my deceafe.

Item. I give unto Mr. *George Langford* the elder two guineas.

Item. I give unto *William Fifhwicke*, my late father's man the fum of twenty fhillings.

Item. Whereas I am executor of the laft will and teftament of my late couzin *Abel Collin* late of the town of *Nottingham*, I do hereby impower and authorize my coufin Mr. *Thomas Smith*, to fee the fame performed as fully and punctually and exactly in every refpect as if I were actually alive and in being to fee the fame performed myfelf.

Item. What truft was repofed in me by my late brother Mr. *Thomas Smith*, touching any lands and tenements in the *Brewhoufe-Yard* in the county of *Nottingham*, I hereby impower and authorize my faid couzin Mr. *Thomas Smith* to act therein as much as I myfelf might or could do if I was alive and in being to act therein myfelf.

Item. Whereas about the eight and twentieth day of *October* laft paffed, *Edward Cropley* at my inftance and requeft did lend unto *William Harvey* of the town of *Nottingham*, fellmonger, the fum of ten pounds upon mortgage, it is my mind and will that if the faid money fhall be loft, and cannot be gotten of the faid *William Harvey*; that then my executor hereafter named fhall pay the fame unto the faid *Edward Cropley* and make it good out of my perfonal eftate.

A N D I do nominate and ordain, conftitute and appoint, my loving couzin Mr. *Thomas Smith* full and fole executor of this my laft will and teftament, and for his pains to be taken in the execution of this my laft will and teftament, I give him the fum of fifty pounds, of lawful money of *England*, provided always and it is my mind and will that the remainder and furplufage of my perfonal eftate after the full performance of this my laft will and teftament, and all matters and things therein expreffed, I do give and bequeath the fame unto my faid executor of this my laft will and teftament to be by him employed and beftowed in the building of fome little houfes and endowing the fame for fome poor men or women to dwell in, belonging to fome of the aforefaid feveral parifhes, together with the feveral legacies of all and every fuch legatee before-mentioned in this my laft will and teftament which fhall happen to die, before the legacy fhall become due according to the true intent and meaning of this my laft will and teftament.

Item

Item. I give to the five children of my said couzin *William Clifton* of *Yarmouth* the sum of ten pounds over and above their said other legacies to be payd by my executor before-mentioned, and it is my mind and will that if any of the said children shall happen to die before his or their legacy shall become due, then the same to be divided among the survivors of them.

I N witness whereof to this my last will and testament contained in one skin of parchment I have set to my hand and seal this 4th day of *February* in the year of the reign of our souveraign lady queen *Anne* and anno domini 1704.

S I G N E D sealed, declared and published by the said Abel Collin *the testator for and as his last will and testament in the presence of us who in his presence subscribed our names as witnesses, &c.*

Copy of a Grant by Queen ANNE *of two new Fairs.*

ANNA Dei gratia magnæ *Britanniæ, Franciæ* et *Hiberniæ* regina, fidei defensor, &c. Omnibus ad quos presentes literæ nostræ pervenerint salutem. Cum per quandam inquisitionem indentat. capt. apud *Guihald.* villæ de *Nottingham* in commitatu nostro villæ *Nottingham* quinto die *Maji* anno regni undecimo virtute cujusdam brevis nostri de *ad quod dampnum* e cancellaria nostra nuper emanat. vice-comit. comitatus villæ *Nottingham* predict. direct. et inquisitionem predict. annexat. p sacramentum proborum et legalium hominum comitatus prædict. compertum sit, quod non esset ad aliquod dampnum vel prejudicium nostri aut aliorum vel ad aliquod nocumentum vicinarum feriarum sive nundinarum si nos concederemus majori et burgensibus villæ de *Nottingham* predict. et successoribus suis quod ipsi haberent et tenerent annuatim imperpetuum apud villam de *Nottingham* predict. unam feriam sive nundinos incipiend. in diem jovis proxim. ante festum pascha et tunc et ibidem tenend. et continuand. durand. octo diebus tunc proxim. sequent. et aliam feriam sive nundinas incipiend. in diem veneris proxime præcedentem primum diem martis immediate post festum epiphaniæ tunc etiam tenend. et continuand. durand. octo diebus tunc proxime sequent. pro emptione et venditione in feriis sive nundinis illis averiorum et pecorum ac omnium et omnimod. bonorum mercimoniorum et mercandizarum quorumcunque communiter in feriis sive nundinis empt. et vendit. et tolnet et profic. inde provenien. et emergen. sibi et successoribus suis percipien. prout per dict. breve et inquisition. in filariis cancellariæ nostræ predict. de recordo remanen. plenius liquet et apparet. Sciatis modo quod nos de gratia nostra special. ac ex certa scientia et mero motu nostris dedimus et concessimus ac p. presentes pro nobis heredibus et successoribus nostris damus et concedimus præfato majori et burgensibus villæ de *Nottingham* prædict. et successoribus suis quod ipsi habeant et teneant annuatim imperpetuum apud villam de *Nottingham* prædict. unam feriam sive nundin. incipiend. in diem jovis proxim. ante festum paschæ et tunc et ibidem tenend. et continuand. durand. octo diebus ex tunc proxime sequentibus et aliam feriam sive nundinas incipiend.

piend

piend. in diem veneris proxim. præcedent primum diem martis immediate poſt feſtum *Epiphaniæ* tunc etiam tenend. et continuand. durand. octo diebus ex tunc proxime ſequent. pro emptione et venditione in feriis ſive nundinis illis averiorum et pecorum omnium et omnimod. bonorum, mercimoniorum et mercandizarum quarumcunq; communiter in feriis ſive nundinis empt. et vendit. unà cum curia pedis pulveriſati tempore feriarum prædictarum, ac cum omnibus tolnet et aliis proficuis prædict. feriis ſive nundinis pertinent ſive ſpectant. habend. tenend. et gaudend. prædict. ferias ſive nundinas et curiam pedis pulveriſati et cæteras premiſſas ſuperius p. preſentes conceſſas ſeu mentionatas fore conceſſas eiſdem majori et burgenſibus villæ de *Nottingham* predict. et ſucceſſoribus ſuis imperpetuum ad ſolum proprium opus et uſum præfati majoris et burgenſium villæ de *Nott.* predict. et ſucceſſorum ſuorum. Et hoc abſque computo vel aliquo alio nobis heredibus vel ſucceſſoribus noſtris proinde reddend. ſolvend. vel faciend. Quare volumus ac p. preſentes pro nobis heredibus et ſucceſſoribus noſtris firmiter injungendo præcepimus et mandamus quod præfatus major et burgenſes villæ de *Nott.* prædict. et ſucceſſores ſui vigore preſentium bene libere licite et quiete habeant teneant et cuſtodiant et habere tenere et cuſtodire valeant et poſſint imperpetuum predictas ferias ſive nundinas uno cum curia pedis pulveriſati et cœteras premiſſis predictis ſecundum tenorem et veram intentionem harum literarum noſtrarum patentium abſque moleſtatione p. turbatione gravanina ſive contradictione noſtri heredum vel ſucceſſorum noſtrorum vel aliquorum vice-comit. Eſceatorum, ballivorum, officiariorum ſive miniſtrorum noſtrorum hæredum vel ſucceſſorum noſtrorum quorumcunque et hoc abſque aliquo alio warranto brevi vel proceſſ. impoſterum in ea parte procurand. vel obtinend. denique volumus ac p. preſentes pro nobis heredibus et ſucceſſoribus noſtris concedimus præfato majori et burgenſibus villæ de *Nott.* prædict. et ſucceſſoribus ſuis quod hæ literæ noſtræ patentes vel irrotulamentum earundem ſint et erunt bonæ firma, valida, ſufficientia, et effectualia in lege eiſdem majori et burgenſibus villæ de *Nott.* prædict. et ſucceſſoribus ſuis ſecundum veram intentionem earundem.

I N cujus rei teſtimonium has literas noſtras fieri fecimus patentes teſte meipſa apud *Weſtmonaſterium* triceſimo die *Auguſti* anno regni noſtro undecimo.

per breve de privato ſigillo

C O C K S.

Zz

Nomina

Nomina Villarum infra Honorem PEVEREL *in Comit.* Nott. &
Derbienſ.

Nottingham.

ADbolton *p. ſe et cum* Cothinſtock·
Aldeſworth *alias* Arſworth.
Anneſley.
Aſpley. Arnold.
Adinburgh.
Aſſert *de* Heywood *in* Foreſt. *de* Sherwood.
Albocton.
Aram *alias* Averham *alias* Arum.

Barton *a Mannor.*
Bridgford *a Mannor.*
Baſſingfield.
Basford.
Brinſley.
Beeſton.
Bramcote.
Bilborow.
Broxſtow *hundred.*
Bulwell.
Barneſton *alias* Bareſtoll.
Blidworth.
Brocton.
Bunney.
Bradmore.
Bingham.
Beavall.
Burton-Jace.
Barnby.
Bagthorp.
Bleasby *cum Membris.*

Clifton.
Conard *alias* Conorde.
Codlingſtoake.
Coſſal *alias* Coteſhall.
Colſton-Baſſet.
Colwick Weſt.
Colwick Eaſt.
Cropſhall *alias* Cropwell-Butler.
Clipſow.

Cleadon *alias* Cleidon.
Carleton *juxta* Nottingham,
Codgrave.
Caunton.
Chilwel.
Cromwell.
Curline.
Carleton North.
Carlton Chelmerton,

Eſtwicke.
Eaſtwood *alias* Eſthwicke.
Eperſtone *alias* Eperſtowe.
Efford.
Edoulton.
Ernesbya.
Eſtwaite.
Eſtnotherwicke.
Edingfield *cum* Halam.

Forreſt of Sherwood.
Flinton *alias* Flintham.
Farnsfield.
Fiskerdow.
Fledborough.

Gunſton *alias* Gunnalſton.
Greaſley.
Gamſton *alias* Gonelſton.
Greſvile *alias* Greſwell.
Glapton.
Gedling.
Geſtock.
Gotham.
Greſthorp *cum* Normanton.

Hucknall.
Hucknall Torkard.
Hempſhall.
Hawkeſworth.
Hickling Mannor.

Hockley *alias* Hochelia.
Hanne *alias* Hulme.
Hubenia *alias* Haverſhaw.
Hovringham Mannor.
Hallowton *cum* Blidworth.

Kingſton *juxta* Ratcliffe.
Kirlington Kirthington *cum* Normanton.
Kimberley. ---- Keyworth.
Kellam-Mannor. --- Kirkbywoodhouſe.
Kirkby in Aſhfield.

Lenton. ---- Langor. ---- Lindby.
Leake parva, ⎱ Mannors.
Leake magna, ⎰
Lambley. ---- Lowdham.

Moore Green.
Morton Muskham Bathley *cum* Holme.
Menenton. - Markham South. -Mark. N.
Markham North and South *cum* Carleton.
Maplebeck *cum* Kneeſal *alias* Kerſal.

Normanton & Kingſton. -- Newbould.
Norwell & Blidworth.
Nuthall *alias* Northall.

Ollaverton *alias* Ollerton. -- Oxton.
Offington *cum* Carleton.

Papplewick. -- Plumptree.

Radford Mannor. -- Ruddington.
Remſon *alias* Rempſton.
Radcliffe *ſup.* Trent.

Sibthorpe. - Staunton. - Stapleford.
Strelley. - Sutton *ſup.* Trent.
Sutton Bonington. - Selſton *alias* Skelſton.
Schreveton. -- Sherwood Forreſt.
Stoke Bardolph. - Sutton Paſſeys.
Sutton Baſſet. - Somervile. - Saxendale.
Stoke *juxta* Newarke. - Slegby.
Shupton. - Suttomeering. - Sierſton.
Southwell in membris. - Stanford.
Stathorp. - Snenton.

Thrimpſton *alias* Thrumpſton. - Toton.
Tithby. - Thorp. - Thorp *jux.* Remſon.
Thorowton. - Trowell.
Towton *alias* Taunton.
Tokeſworth *alias* Tuxford.
Thurgarton â Leigh Hundred.
Thimerton. - Teidſhall.

Upton & Morton.

Wilford. - Willoughby. - Wiverton.
Wyſall. - Weſthorp. - Wollaton.
Watnoll *alias* Watners. - Woodborough.
Widmerpool. - Wanneſley. - Weſton.
Winkborne *cum* Hock.

Derbyſhire.

Aſhford in Peake a Mannor,
Atquathorp,
Alfreton *alias* Alfirton,
Aſhour or Aſhore, - Alſop, - Allernaſh,
Appletree Hundred, —— Alleaſton,
Aſhburne *alias* Eſhburne,

Bollover, - Bradnell, - Baſwell,
Baſtowe, - Burton,
Brakenthwait *alias* Brakenwheat.

Brimington, - Bugnell, - Blacknell,
Brimington *cum* Wilcom Rodithes,
Barlebrough, - Buxton, - Brampton,
Bently Mannor and Hamlet, - Bradley,
Bathorp *alias* Bagthorp, - Baſlow,
Becleſhall, - Belper *alias* Beauſpiere,
Bonſal *alias* Bonteſhall,
Braſſington *alias* Braſſingham,
Bakewell *alias* Bankwell,
Birchwood, - Burton-Lazarus,

Balb-

Balb Forreſt *de* Hopedale,
Brightwiſield *alias* Brightrichfield,
Battfield *alias* Batesfield, a Mannor,
Beckley,
Bouſden *cum* Farneton *alias* Farndlow.

Codnor-Carthalu,
Chatville *alias* Clatvile,
Chatſworth *alias* Chiſtworth, - Calowe,
Crich-Baron, - Cookſey *alias* Cookſley,
Coldlowe, -Cromford *alias* Comford,
Crodecoat, *alias* Croudecoat,
Coldbrook *alias* Caldebrook, - Cotes,
Chadſeden *alias* Chadſden, - Cleyndon.

Dale-Abby, - Darley in the Peake,
Darley-Abby *juxta* Derby, - Dore,
Dernechola, - Dunſton-Mannor,
Denby-Mannor, - Dethick, -Duningſted,
Duckmanton, - Duffield-Mannor,
Deresborow.

Eyme, - Empingham,
Eſhburne *alias* Aſhburne, - Eſtford,
Ederſley *alias* Edrithſley,
Elton-Mannor,
Eſtwall *alias* Etwall *alias* Etoile.

Forton *alias* Foodon, - Forreſt of Peake.
Fairnfield *alias* Fairfield,
Farnlow *cum* Bouden,
Foleſworth *al.* Fawſworth *al.* Foxworth

Greſley Hundred, - Glapwell.

Haddon le Nether, - Hope,
Hopedale Ball. —— Heanor Mannor,
Larlow *alias* Hucklow Mannor deſlumbi,
Hocklow Hamlet, -Haverſeidge Mannor,
Haſſop, - Herlaſton, - Hertherſeige,
Haſland, - Holbrook, - Hunſington,
Hopton, Heare *alias* Heige, - Holland,
Hotſley Caſtle, -Huntington,
Heaſſelbecke, - Habeina, - Hocklia,
Horſepool, - High Peake hun. wholly.
Hayleſyra.
Iball, - Ireton, - Ilkeſton, - Irviceſtrie.

Kilwarmarſh, - Kirtington, - Kinnerſley,

Keeleſton,
Kerelſton *alias* Kedleſton.

Langford, - Longſden *parva*,
Lutton Hamblet *alias* Sutton, - Litton,
Lee and Tanſley, - Langor Mannor,
Langrave Mannor, - Lintot Hamblet.

Matlock Mannor, - Middleton Mannor,
Marton, - Methduplet, - Mapleton,
Malcherba, - Melborne.

Normanton *juxta* Derby, - Normanton.
Normanvile.

Oxcroft, - Overdale Mannor,
Occidental *alias* Ocdental,
Olvaſton in Morley Hundred.

Pinkeſton *alias* Pinſton, - Peake Mines,
Peake Caſt, - Pentridge, - Pilſley,
Parkhall *juxta* Derby, - Pemwick,
Porwich *alias* Powdwich.

Quatford.

Riſley, - Rodeſley *alias* Rodely,
Ripley, - Rowdiches Waſte,
Riſdenden.

Shoreland, - Somercote, - Scarcliff,
Somervile, - Sponden, - Shalton,
Staneley, - Shakethorn, - Starwigge,
Shallcroſs, - Sierſton, - Skegby,
Smitterton *alias* Sinterton, Sirebrok,
Southwood, - Stanton *alias* Staunton,
Stake in the Peake and the Mannor of
    Sandiacre,
Supton *alias* Shupton, - Stalldona,
Stauradale.

Thorp in Glebis, - Tibſhelfe,
Toleberry *cum* Dore *al.* Tolley *cum* Done,
Tidſwall, - Tolvile,
Tanneſley and Lee, - Thimerton.

Underwood.

Waterfield, Walton, Wounhall, | Wirkſworth Hundred, Weſton,
Wingfield North and South, Whitfield, | Wandeſley
Whittington, Wakebridge, Whitwell, | Wymondſall pars in Leiceſterſhire.

A TABLE *of Churches and Chapelries, within the Archdeaconry of* NOTTINGHAM *as the Incumbents and Patrons ſtood in the Year* 1744.

The DEANERY of *NOTTINGHAM*:

CHURCHES & CHAPELS	*Preſent Incumbents.*	PATRONS.
ADdenborough,	Mr. Benj. Cockayne, *V.*	—— Foljambe, Eſq;
Anſley,	Andrew Matthews,	William Chaworth, Eſq;
Arnold,	John Parſons, Eſq; *V.*	
Baſford,	Thomas Beaumont, *V.*	The D. of Devonſhire,
Beeſton,	John Henſon, *V.*	The ſame,
Bilborow,	Will. Goodday, *R.*	Ralph Edge 2 and Mr. Sheppard the 3d turn,
Bramcote Chap. to the P. of Addenborough.	Benjamin Cockayne, *C.*	—— Fouljambe, Eſq;
Bulwell,	Thomas Beaumont, *R.*	The Duke of Devonſhire,
Burton Joice with Bulcote,	John Saunders, *V.*	The Earl of Cheſterfield,
Colwicke,	Thomas Roſe, *R.*	Mundy Muſters, Eſq;
Coſſal Chap. to Wollaton,	Geo. Staunton Brough, *C.*	The Lord Middleton,
Eſtwaite,	Maurice Pugh, *R.*	John Plumptre, Eſq;
Epperſton,	Chr. Rawleigh Seaton, *R*	The Lord Viſcount How,
Gelling 1ſt Mediety, 2d Mediety,	Ric. Chenevix, *V. & R.*	The Earl of Cheſterfield,
Greaſley,	John Cooper, *V.*	Sir Wolſtan Dixie bt. & Sir R. Sutton, alter.
Gonalſton,	John Dean, *V.*	Sir Humphrey Monox, bt.
Hoveringham,	John Roſe, *C.*	John Gilbert Cooper, Eſq
Hucknal Torcard,	Thomas Carter, *C.*	The Lord Byron,
Kirkby in Aſhford,	John Brailsford, *R.*	The Duke of Newcaſtle,
Lamley,	Henry Woods, *R.*	The Lord Middleton,
Lenton,	George Wayte, *V.*	The Lord Chancellor,
Lyndeby,	Andrew Matthews, *R.*	Montague,
Loudham,	Joſeph Brewen, *V.*	The Duke of Kingſton,
Mansfield,	James Badger, *V & R.*	Dean and Chap. of Linc.
Mansfield-Woodhouſe,	William Clarke, *C.*	The Lady Oxford,
Nuthall,	Andrew Matthews, *R.*	Sir Charles Sedley, bart.
		Paplewick,

Church and Chapels.	Present Incumbents.		Patrons:
Paplewick,	Mr. Robert Stanly,	C.	Lady Culloden,
Radford,	George Wayte,	V.	Lord Chancellor,
Selfton,	William Wright,	C.	Sir Wolftan Dixie, bt.
Snenton,	ScroopBerdmore, DD	C.	The Duke of Kingfton,
Skegby,	James Lineham,	C	The Lady Oxford,
Stapleford,	George Bettinfon,	C	Burlace Warren, Efq;
Strelley,	William Goodday,	R	Ralph Edge, Efq;
Sutton in Afhford,			Duke of Devonfhire,
Teverfal,	Edward Wilfon,	R	Sir Charles Mollineux, bt.
Thurgarton,	John Rofe,		john Gilbert Cooper,
Trowel, 1ft Mediety,	Geo. StauntonBrough,	R	{ The Lord Middleton, & Mrs. Mary Hacker,
Trowel, 2d Mediety,	Henry Francis,	R	The fame,
Wollaton	Geo. StauntonBrough,	R	The Lord Middleton,
St. Mary,	ScroopBerdmore, DD	V	The Duke of Kingfton,
Nott. St. Peter,	Edward Chappell,	R	The King,
St. Nicholas,	John Abfon,	R	The King.

The DEANERY of BYNGHAM:

Church and Chapels.	Present Incumbents.		Patrons:
Adbolton,	The Rev. Scroop Berd-more, D D.	R	The Duke of Kingfton,
Barton in Fabis,	Jofeph Milner,	R	The Archbifhop of York,
Byngham,	Henry Stanhope,	R	The Earl of Chefterfield,
Brcughton Sulney,	John Dawfon,	R	Sir Robert Clifton, bart.
Bunney and Bradmore,	Thomas Poynton,	V	Sir Thomas Parkyns, {bart.
Carcolfton,	Robert Manley,		Richard Porter, Efq;
Clifton & Glapton	Will. Standfaft, LLD	R	Sir Robert Clifton, bart.
Cortlingftock,	John Woods,	R	Sir Thomas Parkyns, bart.
Cotgrave 1ft & 2d Pars,	Richard Sterne,	R	The Duke of Kingfton,
Coulfton-Baffet,	Thomas Rofe,	V	Lord Chancellor,
Eaft-Bridgford,	Peter Priaulx, B D.		William Chaworth, Efq;& Mag. College Oxon alter.
Eaft Leek,	Granville Wheler, Efq	R	The Earl of Huntington,
Edwalton,	John Henfon,	C	William Chaworth, Efq;
Elton,	Matthew Bradford,	R	Langford Collin, Efq;
Flintham,	George Butler,	V	Trinity College Cam.
Gotham,	William Bridges,	R	{ Duke of Newcaftle, —— Thorney, Efq; —— Jennings, Efq;
Granby,	Thomas Brádfield,	V	Duke of Rutland,
Hawfworth,	Hamond Turner,	R	The Rev. Hamond Turner
Holm Pierpont,	Scroop Berdmore, D D.	R	The Duke of Kingfton,
Hickling,	John Ward,	R	Queen's College Cam:
Keyworth,	Edward Moifes,	R	Sir Thomas Parkyns, bart

Kneeton

[Churches and Chapels.	Present Incumbents.	Patrons.
Kneeton,	Rev. Mr. Henry Kneeton,	Sir Charles Mollineux, bt.
Kingſton upon Soar,	Edward Moiſes, ſenior, C	Duke of Leeds,
Kynalton,	Richard Hardy, V	The Archbiſhop of York,
Langor & Barnſton,	Bennet Sherard, R	Lord Viſcount How,
Normanton upon Soar,	John Ragdale, R	John Richards, Eſq;
Orſton,	Thomas Wakefield, V	Dean and Chap. of Linc.
Owthorpe,	Richard Hardy, C	Thomas Hutchinſon, Eſq;
Plumtree,	Charles Willatts, R	Lionell Copley, Eſq;
Radcliff upon Soar,	Thomas Poynton, C	Sir Nathaniel Curſon, bt.
Radcliff upon Trent,	Gabriel Wain, V	Duke of Kingſton,
Rempſton,	Robert Marſden, BD R	Sidney College Cambridge
Ruddington,	Job Faulkner, V	Duke of Devonſhire,
Scarrington Chaple in the P. of Orſton,	Thomas Wakefield, C	The ſame as Orſton,
Screveton,	John Roſe, R	Robert Thoroton, Eſq;
Stanford,	Henry Woods, R	Francis Lewis, Eſq;
Stanton upon the Wolds,	Charles Henchman, R	Sir William Parſons, bart.
Stanton-Chaple,	Staunton Degge, C	Job Charlton, Eſq;
Sutton-Bonnington, St. Mic:	Henry Haſcard, R	The Dean and Chapter of Briſtol,
Sutton-Bonnington St Anne	Richard Wenman,	The Lord Chancellor,
Shelford,	Gabriel Waine, C	The Earl of Cheſterfield,
Thorp,	John Cooper, R	Sir Thomas Parkyns, bart.
Tythby & Cropwell,	Thomas Heblethwait, C	William Chaworth, Eſq;
Thoroton Chaple to the P. of Orſton,	Thomas Wakefield, C	D. and Chap. of Lincoln,
Thrumpton,	John Savage, C	—— Emmerton, Eſq;
Tollaton,	Job Faulkner, R	John Neal, Eſq;
Weſt-Bridgeford,	John Stokes, R	Mundy Muſters, Eſq;
Weſt-Leek,	Granville Wheler, Eſq;	The Earl of Huntington,
Whatton,	Thomas Evans, V	Mrs. Shipman,
Widmerpool,	Edward Gregory, R	Duke of Kingſton,
Wilford,	John Woods, R	Sir Robert Clifton, bart.
Wiſall,	Edward Moiſes, V	Sir Arthur Atcheſon,
Willoughby,	Charles Hutchinſon, V	Thomas Hutchinſon, Eſq;

The

The DEANERY of NEWARK.

Churches and Chapels.	Present Incumbents.		Patrons.
A Versham, Barnby, Baulderton,	The Rev. Mr. Ric. Sutton, George Chappell, William Broadhurst,	V V	The Lord Robert Sutton, The Chapter of Southwell, Prebendary of Farndon with Boulderton in the Ch. of Linc.
Coddington Chap. in the P. of Stoke, Cromwell, Cottam, Eykering,	Francis Bainbrigg, Thomas Eastland, —— Goes, Gilbert Mitchel,	C R C R	The Chan. of the Ch. of Lincoln, The Duke of Newcastle, The Lady Oxford, Duke of Kingston and Sir Geo. Saville, alternat.
East-Stoke,	Francis Bainbrigg,	V	Chancellor of the Ch. of Lincoln,
Elston Chaple in the Parish of East-Stoke, Elston Church, Farndon,	The same. George Chappell, William Broadhurst,	R V	The same, Robert Darwin, Esq; The Prebendary of the Ch. of Lincoln,
Flawborough P. of Staunton, Fledborough, Girton,	Staunton Degge, William Sweetapple, John Dalton,	R V	Job Charlton, Esq; Duke of Kingston, Prebendary of the Church of Lincoln,
Hawton, Hockerton, Kelham, Kilvington, Kneesal & Ompton, Langford, Laxton, Marnham,	James Naish, James Gibson, The same, Samuel Leek, Thomas Cooper, William Tomlinson, John Warrel, Farringdon Reid,	R R R R V V V V	Alexander Holden, Esq; John Whetham, Esq; The Lord Robert Sutton, William Cartwright, Esq; The Chapter of Southwell, —— Duncam Esq; The Duke of Kingston, The Lord Viscount Tyr- connel.
Maplebeck, Muskham North a Medity.	John Bracken, —— Leech,	C C	Mrs. Burnell, The Prebendary of it in Ch. of Southwell,
Newark, North Clifton,	Barnard Willson, DD. Nicholas Caffan,	V V	The Lord Chancellor, The Prebendary of it in Ch. of Lincoln,
North Collingham,	Samuel Leek,	V	Dean and Chap. of Peter- borough,
Normanton upon Trent, Ossington, Roleston,	John Lealand, Francis Fothergill, John Abson,	V C V	Duke of Devonshire, George Cartwright, Esq; The Ch. of Southwell, South-

Churches and Chapels.	Present Incumbents.		Patrons.
South Scarle,	Rev. Mr. John Dalton,	V	Prebendary of it in the Ch. of Lincoln,
South Collingham,	Matthew Bradford,	R	The Bp. of Peterborough,
Sutton upon Trent,	Samuel Leek,	V	Sir Edward Hulfe, bart.
Syerston Chapel, P. of Eaft Stoke,	Francis Bainbrigg,	C	The fame as Eaft-Stoke,
Sibthorpe,		C	The Lady Oxford,
Shelton,	George Burghope,	R	The Earl of Salisbury,
Stanton-Church,	Staunton Degge,	R	Job Stanton Charlton, Efq;
Thorney,	John Robinson,	C	
Thorp, nigh Newark,	Edward Chappell,	R	The Lord Chancellor,
Wefton,	Paul Jenkinfon,	R	Sir Robert Clifton, bart.
Winthorpe,	Barnard Wilson, DD.	R	Corporation of Newark,
Winkburn,	John Bracken.	C	Mrs. Burnell.

The DEANERY of RETFORD.

Churches and Chapels.	Present Incumbents.		Patrons.
AUfterfield Chapel in the P. of Blithe,	The Rev. Mr. Matthew Tomlinfon,	C	The fame as Blithe,
Babworth,	Thomas Heald,	R	William Simpfon, Efq;
Bawtrey,	John Fofs,	C	The fame as Blithe,
Bilfthorpe,	Richard Birks,	R	Sir Bryan Broughton,
Blithe,	Matthew Tomlinfon,	V	Trin. Coll. Cambridge,
Bothomfal,	William Bower,		Duke of Newcaftle,
Boughton united to Kneefal	John Cooper,	C	The Chapter of Southwell
Carburton in the Parifh of Edwinftow,	John Meyrick,	C	The fame as Edwinftow,
Carlton in Lindrick,	William Herring,	R	Archbifhop of York,
Clayworth,			
Clarburgh,	Edmund Mower,	V	Duke of Devonfhire,
Cottam P. of South-Leverton,	Nicholas Howlet,	C	The fame as South Leverton,
Eaft Markham and Weft-Drayton,	Thomas Gylby,	V	Duke of Newcaftle,
Eaft Retford,	Thomas Gylby,	C	Duke of Devonfhire,
Eaft Drayton & membris,		V	
Edwinftow,	John Meyrick,	V	Dean and Chap. of Linc.
Egmanton,	Benjamin Clay,	V	John Neal, Efq;
Elkefley,	Henry Stephenfon,	V	Duke of Newcaftle,
Everton,	John Fofs,	V	Duke of Devonfhire,

Finning-

Churches and Chapels.	Present Incumbents.		Patrons.
Finningley,	Rev. Mr. Geo. Flavel,	R	John Harvey of Tikwell in com. Bedford,
Gamston,	Samuel Brook,	R	The Lord Chancellor,
Greanly on the Hill,	Joshua Waddington,	V	The Duke of Rutland,
Grove,	Robert Wright,	R	William Levinz, sen. Esq;
Hayton,	Edmund Mower,	C	Duke of Devonshire,
Haworth,	Matthew Tomlinson,	V	The Lord De-la-war,
Headon & Upton,	Richard Jackson,	R	The Lady Wastiness,
Kirketon,	William Bower,	R	The Duke of Newcastle,
Littleburgh,	Thomas Edwards,	C	John Thorney, Esq;
Mattersea,	John Ludham	V	The Archbishop of York,
Myssen,	John Foss,	V	The King,
Norton Cuckney,	John Richardson	V	The Duke of Kingston,
North Wheatley,	William Standfast, LL.D.		The Lord Middleton,
Ollerton in the P. of Edwinstow,	John Meyrick,	C	The same as Edwinstow,
Ordsall,	Thomas Cockshutt,	R	The Hon. Edward Wortley of Wortley in com York.
Perlethorpe P. of Edwinstowe,	John Meyrick,	C	The same as Edwinstow,
Rossington,	John Jackson,	R	The Corpor. of Doncaster,
Saundby,	John Prinsep,	R	The Lord Middleton,.
Scrooby,	Thomas Fell,	C	The Lady Oxford,
South Leverton,	Thomas Edwards,	V	The Dean of Lincoln,
Sturton,	Bryan Allatt,	V	Dean and Chap. of York,
Sutton upon Lound. & Scrooby,	John Richardson,	V	Lady Oxford,
Treswell, East part, West-part,	Robert Aide,	R	The 1st Mediety D. and Chap. of York, the 2d Mrs. Sharp of Barnby,
Tuxford,	Bryan Birks,	V	Trin. Coll. Cambridge,
Welley,	Richard Jackson,	C	
Wailsby,	The same.	V	Sir George Saville, Bart.
Warsop,	John Moseley	R	Ralph Knight, Esq;
West Burton,	Abraham Sampson,	C	William Levinz sen. Esq;
West Drayton P. of East-Markham,	Thomas Gylby,	R	The same as East Markham,
Walkeringham,	Joshua Waddinton,	V	Trinity Coll. Cambridge,
West Retford,	Thomas Gylby,	R	Bailiff and Burgesses of East Retford,
West Markham,	Thomas Peet,	V	Duke of Newcastle,
Workfop,	John Cook,	V	The Lord Malton.

CHURCHES *and* CHAPELRIES *within the Jurifdiction of the Collegiate Church of* S O U T H W E L L.

Churches and Chapels.	Prefent Incumbents.		Patrons.
BLeasby,	The Rev. Henry Bugg,		The Chapter of Southwell,
Beckingham,	— Richardfon,		The Prebendary of Beck.
Blidworth,	Robert Stanley,	V	The Prebend. of Oxton,
Calverton,	Maurice Pugh,	V	The fame.
Caunton,	— Leach,		Preb. of North Muskham,
Crophill Bifhop,	— Fairfax,	V	Prebendaries of Oxton alt.
Darleton Chapel,	a Ch. belong. to Dunham,		The Vicarage of Dunham
Dunham,	— Cave,	V	The Prebend. of Dunham,
Edingley,	Samuel Abfon,	V	The Chap. of Southwell,
Eaton,	The fame.	V	The Prebendary of Eaton,
Exton *al.* Oxton,	Thomas Cooper,	V	The Prebendaries of Oxton
Farnsfield,	Samuel Bird,	V	The Chap. of Southwell,
Halloughton,	Samuel Bird,		Prebendary thereof,
Halome Chapel,	William Laveroc,		The Chap. of Southwell,
Kirthlington,	-- Crofts,		The fame,
Moreton,	— Fellows,		The fame,
Muskham North a Mediety,	— Leach,		Prebend. of Nor. Muskam,
Muskham South,	— Clark,		Prebendary thereof,
Normanton,	a Hamlet to Southwell,		Prebendary thereof,
North Leverton,	— Hurft,		Prebendary thereof,
Norwell,	John Gregory,	V	Prebendary thereof,
Norwell Overhall,			Prebendary thereof,
Ragnal. Chapel Dunh.	belongs to the V. of Dunham		Prebendary of Dunham,
Rampton,	Nicholas Howlet,		Prebendary of Rampton,
Southwell,	William Laveroc,	V	Prebend. of Normanton,
Southwheatley,	John Richardfon,	V	The Chapter of Southwell,
Upton,	Chappel Fowler,		The fame,
Woodborough,	——		The Prebendary thereof.

A Description of the STOCKING-FRAME.

HAVING before (in number 5.) given the reader an account of that profitable branch of the woollen, cotton and silk manufacture, the *Frame-work-Knitting*, of which the county of *Nottingham* justly claims the first beginning : ——— The curious may perhaps expect a description of the *Instrument* with which so much curious work is performed. Not only because it is the sole uncontested *English* invention, being contrived both by an englishman and at his own native spot ; because it has never yet (as far as I could learn) been attempted by any body. Whether by reason of its being grown so familiar amongst us it has been overlooked by some, or whether the variety of its constituent parts and the difficulty of examining narrowly into the uses of each individual has deterred others from such a task, I do not pretend to determine.

TO oblige therefore the inquisitive, I will here describe this curious machine to the best of my power, and also as intelligibly as I can, the manner after which the work is performed.

THIS invention seems to be a compound of weaving and knitting, and its analogy to the loom appears not only in the use of treddles and slay ; but the slur-box which moves from side to side has no obscure affinity with the shuttle, besides that the work like the web in the loom shews the wrong side upwards.

THE use of needles and the forming of loops exactly the same as are made with the common knitting-needles bespeaks it knitting with this difference ; that in knitting by hand but one stitch or loop is made at a time, whilst by this ingenious contrivance a whole course of the finest goods may be wrought in less time than the swiftest common knitter can make twenty loops.

FIG. 1. *Represents the whole frame with the wood-work belonging to it fronting.*

FIG. 2. *Shews the back part of the same.*

THE constituent parts of the stocking-frame may fitly be divided I. into those of the frame itself and II. into such as belong to the woodwork of the frame.

THE frame itself is by workmen divided into the carcass and the inner parts vulgarly called by the journeymen the guts.

I chuse to divide it I. into the outer and containing, and II. the contained or inner parts.

To

TO the firſt belong: 1ſt. *The ſole Bars* Fig. 1. *a a a a*. Theſe are two ſtrong, thick iron bars which form the ſides of the baſis of the frame, the level part of them is ſcrew'd faſt to the woodwork, the forepart comes ſlanting down beyond the woodwork, about 3 inches in length, at the end each has two joints called the bot-‑tom joints which receive the joints of the preſſer bows.

2d. *The bottom back Bar* is another part of the baſis of the frame ſcrew'd edgeways at right angles to the ſole bars. Fig. 2. *a a*.

3d. *The fore Standards* are two pillars which ſupport the forepart of the carcaſs. Fig. 1. *b b*. F. 3. Fig. 2. *b*.

4th. *The back Standards* are two pillars ſupporting the back part of the carcaſs. Fig. 2. *c c*.

5th. *The middle back Bar* is faſtened to the middle of the back-ſtandards, and to the middle of this bar is fixed —— Fig. 2. *d d d*.

6th. *The Gibbet*, which is a piece of iron of the ſhape of a gibbet, an inch and a half broad and three parts of an inch thick, the longeſt and perpendicular part of it *a*. is ſtrongly faſtened with ſcrews to the laſt mentioned and the bottom-back-bar, with the horizontal parts uppermoſt and pointing inwards — Fig. 4.

7th. *The ſpindle Bar* is octagonal and its round ends enter the holes of the heads of the back ſtandards, and thus form the back-joints. Fig. 2. *e e e*. This bar has in the middle fix'd to it

8th. *The ſpindle Bar-Piece*, Fig. 1. *d*. which is an oblong ſquare piece of iron ex-actly anſwering the gibbet which is under it, between theſe two plates the main ſpring is as it were wedged in, which by a ſtrong ſcrew paſſing through this ſpin-dle-bar-piece is either ſtrengthened or ſlackned to make the frame move with more or leſs facility.

9th. *The main Spring*, is a ſtrong piece of tempered iron repreſented by F. 5.

10th. *The top Arms* are two flat bars cloſely embracing each end of the ſpindle-bar next to the back-joints and in the front of the frame they make a joint with the hanging joints. Fig. 1. *e e e e*.

11th. *The hanging Joints*, Fig. 6. 7. *a a*. are two irons about a foot long and an inch and a quarter broad, they hang by the pin which paſſes through the heads of them and the top arms, and at the bottom the hand-bar is faſtened to them; in the mid-dle of each of theſe hanging-joints facing the workmen is a prominent part (*b*.) called a falſe ſinker (*a*) which in preſſing meets the nuts of the preſſer-bar and thereby

---

(*a*) *Theſe were formerly placed on each ſide at the end of the ſinkers of the exact ſhape of a ſinker but ſtronger and coming out more forwards for the ſame uſe, but this not proving*

thereby prevents that bar's bearing two strongly upon the sinkers, on the lower and back part of these joints is a strong catch, which is received by an Iron knob called a coken, screwed to the sole-bars. —— N. B. *Both the top arm and the hanging joints are held up by the main Spring when the frame is over the arch.*

12th. *The sinker Bar.* Fig. 8. is about two feet three inches long, screwed to the hanging joints, in the middle for about 16 inches, it has rivetted to it a small verge at the lower edge, upon which the sinker-leads rest, to this bar is fastened about half an inch below the edge a peice of iron of the same length of the verge, which is bent square, the perpendicular part is fastened behind to the basis of the sinker-bar, and the horizontal part comes out even with the lower edge of the bar. This stops the heads of the jacks from carrying the sinkers higher than the level of the lead sinkers.

13th. *The sinker Plates.* Fig. 1. *f f f.* are certain iron plates which confine the upper parts of the sinker-leads by screws to the sinker-bar.

14th. *The top Bar.* Fig. 1. *g g g.* is a long flat bar set up edgeways and screwed to the top-arms.

15th. *The hand Bar.* Fig. 9. is as long as the sinker-bar, round at the ends for the greater ease of the workman's hands, the rest of the bar, except about an inch at each end near the round parts, is hollowed before about half an inch deep for the sinkers to rest against, To it

16th. *The facing Bar* is screwed Fig. 1. *h h h.* which makes a channel to receive the lower ends of the sinkers in.

17th. *The needle Bar,* Fig. 10. is screwed fast upon the sole-bars, it is three inches broad and an inch thick, upon the middle part of it for about 16 inches is rivetted a small verge, behind which the needle-leads rest and these are confined by

18th. *The needle Plates,* Fig. 11. which are screwed down upon the needle-leads.

19th. *The presser Bows,* Fig. 1. *i i i i.* The shape of these is sufficiently expressed in the figure, their joint enters into the bottom joints.

20th. *The presser Bar,* Fig. 1. *k k k.* is a long bar fixed at right angles to the flat part of the presser-bows it has a thin edge below, which in pressing bears upon the beards of the needles.

T H E parts contained in the inner parts are:

1st.

---

proving effectual enough there have contrived these strong prominent irons, which tho' they have not the least resemblance of a sinker, do still retain the name. They might more properly be called wards, or guard-sinkers.

1ft. *The back Preffer*, Fig. 2. *f f.* is fingly expreffed by Fig. 12. it is faftened to the flat ends of the curve parts of the preffer-bows by fcrews called the preffer-fcrews, about fix inches long. ⸺ N. B. *Thefe fcrews by touching with their lower ends the fole bars ftop the preffer-bow, from bending too low.* Fig. 1. *l l.*

2d. *The preffer Wire*, Fig. 2. *g g.* is a long flat iron rod hooked to the back-preffer, and faftened below to the middle treddle.

3d. *The preffer-bolt*, Fig. 2. *h h.* is a ftrong flat piece of iron eleven inches long, it is fufpended by the preffer-leather *i i.* which is buckled to it ; it paffes through the preffer-rail, and has at its lower end a weight *k.* of 14 *lb.* hanging to it. The preffer-leather *l.* which is faftened to the arch of the back-preffer runs in

4th. *The preffer Pulley* ; this is a wooden pulley ftrongly fixed to the gibbet. ⸺ Fig. 2. *l.*

5th. *The Jack-Bar*, Fig. 13. *a a a a.* is twenty-five inches long hollow'd like a trough, at the end of the hollow is a long mortice which receives the half-jack-ftaples, *b b.* and the locker ftaples, *c c.* and between them the perpendicular part of the camels, *d d.* at the ends on the out fide of this bar are the carriages *e e e e.* faftened with fcrews, and in the trough part are fet in lead

6th. *The Combs*, Fig. 12. *f f f.* are fquare pieces of brafs about an inch over, and about a 16th thick, Fig. 14. fhews a fingle comb, at the lower end is a narrow foot by which it is fixed with melted lead in the trough of the jack-bar, it has a hole in the middle of its body for the paffage of the jack-wire, there is a fpace left between each comb juft fufficient eafily to receive a jack.

7th. *The Camels*, Fig. 13. *g g.* and Fig. 15. fhews a camel by itfelf ; they are rectangular pieces of iron, of which the thickeft part *a.* goes into the mortice of the jack-bar between the half-jack and the locker-ftaples, the horizontal part of them *b.* is placed parrallel with the carriages, in this part are two mortices, into that neareft the jack-bar is fcrew'd faft the flur-bar, in the other the feet of the fprings, and upon the camels between the two are fcrew'd the feet of the flay.

8th. *The Slay* is an iron-frame, Fig. 12. *h h h.* Fig. 16. fharped almoft like a weavers read, with this difference, thatthe reads through which the threads pafs are flat, and in this through which the jacks pafs to the fprings the wires are round, this as well as the combs ferves to keep the jacks fteady.

9th. *The Springs*, are expreffed in Fig. 17. fhews the fprings together as facing the tails of the jacks, Fig. 18. reprefents a fingle fpring *a.* is the head, *b.* is hollow between two cramps which receives the tail of the jack.

10th. *The Jacks*, Fig. 19. are flat iron plates about nine inches long, at the fore and broadeft part called the head *a.* they are rounded off, which round part is called the crown, which in locking hits againft the falfe rim of the finker bar ; thefe heads have a flit which admits the jack finker *c.* which is loofely rivetted into it ; under

under the head of the jack is a flat shoulder about an inch in length which in the slur-motion drops upon the falling bar behind *d* ; this shoulder is an off-set of a-bout the 6th part of an inch which in bringing the frame forward comes over the falling bar, and makes room for the body of the jack to fall upon the falling bar. About a third part of the length of the jack from the tail of it, is a round hole for the passage of the jack-wire. The tail terminates in a sharp angle, the blunt point of which goes into the hollow of the springs.

11th. *The finkers* are of two forts *jack-finkers* and *lead-finkers*, the shape of both is a-like as appears by Fig. 19. *c*. and Fig. 20. *a* is a lead-finker, *b* is called the catch, *c* the nab, *d* the arch, *e* the belly and *f* the tail, both are of the same use tho' they perform their work after a different manner as will be shewn in describing how a courfe is made ; the leads are flat behind with a little shoulder at the bottom which refts upon the verge of the finker-bar, thefe leads have alfo a flit to receive the finkers who likewife are fo rivetted as to play freely ; the top of the leads is angular and with that part all the leads are faftened to the finker-bar by the finker-plates.

12th. *The half Jacks* are ftrong irons of the shape of a jack cut off a little beyond the hole Fig. 21. they confine the jacks at each end from the jack-bar to the finker-bar, where they form a joint with two oblong fquare plates called the half-jack-pieces.　Figg. 1. *ll*.

13th. *The Cafter Backs and Stays*. Fig.

14th. The *Carriages and Trucks*, Fig. 12. *ee. ee.* they are made very ftrong the bet-ter to bear the weight they carry, upon four iron trucks which runs upon the fole bars.

15th. *The Stars*, Fig. 22. This member of the frame takes its name from only a part of it, which is a brafs head *a*. the circumference of which is divided into fix knobs fomewhat refembling a ftar ; the body is called the ftar-ftandard *b*. which is a piece of iron about feven inches long, at the upper end of it a fmall part is turn'd down at a right angle *c*. about an inch long with a round hole in the middle, through which paffes the ftar fpindle, to the middle of the ftandard is rivetted hori-zontally a piece of iron *e*. with a hollow fcrew to receive the fcrew of the ftar fpindle, at the end of which is fixed the ftar-box *f*. which opens inwards, into this go the ends of the falling bar, which is either raifed or let down lower by the fcrew of the ftar fpindle as the work is to be loofer or clofer.

16th. *The Falling Bar*, Fig. 23. is about an inch broad and half an inch thick, each end of it enters the ftar box the opening of which is wide enough to give room to this bar to go backwards to give room to the jacks to return to their place. It has a fpring on its back edge which when this bar is forced back, forces it into its place again.

17th. *The flur Bar* Fig. 24. *aaaa*. is the longeft bar belonging to the ftocking frame faftned with fcrews into the firft mortice of the camels between the combs and the ftay. It has on each end a box with an iron pulley in it *b b*. in which the flur-line

runs, as alſo in the groove of the greater round of the ſlur-wheel and ſo to the oppoſite pulley of this bar, and the ends of the line are faſtened to the ends of the

18th. The *Slur-Box*, Fig. 24. *c c.* which is about five inches long. It is hollow underneath and its ſides embrace the top and ſides of the flur-bar, yet ſo as to admit an eaſy motion, which is ſtill facilitated by two ſmall pulleys at each end of
this box. In the groove of the leſſer round of the ſlur-wheel runs a cord, the ends
of which are faſtened to the ſide treddles, of which, either the right or left being
preſſed down with the foot cauſes this box to move right or left. In the middle of
the flur-box ariſes an obtuſe-angular knob, which as this box is moved from ſide
to ſide, touches and puſhes every jack out of its place upward.

19th. The *Needles* and *Needle-Leads*, Fig. 25. Theſe commonly are an inch or an
inch and a half long without the reflexed part called the beard, this laſt is bent
convex in the middle *a.* and the end points downwards and dips into the nick of
the needle called the eye, when preſſed by the preſſer-bar. The leads are repreſented in Fig. 25. *b.* the under part of which fits exactly the needle-bar. Fig.
26. ſhews a needle of the full ſize, *a* is the head, *b* the beard, *c* the eye, *d* the
tail by which it is fixed to the lead.

20th. The *Lockers*, Fig. 27. are ſtrong irons the fore part of them *a* is the longeſt
and heavieſt, the head of which terminates in a mixed angle, the upper part *b* being ſtraight and the lower *c* curved, they are placed on the jack-bar next to the
camels and have one common axis with the jacks and half jacks; the ſhorter and
lighter part of the lockers is ſcrew'd at right angles to

21ſt. The *Locker-Bar*, Fig. 28. This bar goes tranſverſally acroſs the jacks between the combs and the ſlay and in the locker motion preſſes the tails of the jacks
into the nicks of the ſprings, at other times it does not touch the jacks the weight
of the fore-part of the lockers bearing it up.

22d. The *Thumb-Plates*, Fig. 1. *m. m.* hang by a looſe joint on each end of the finker-bar, between the half jack pieces and the hanging-joints about ſeven inches
long, and an inch and a half broad, Fig. 29 repreſents the back part of a thumb-
plate, on the middle is rivetted faſt a piece of iron in ſhape of a rectangle-triangle,
except the diagonal *b* curves inward, this when the thumbs of the workmen preſs
the lower ends of theſe plates touches the convex part of the head of the lockers
and puſhes them upwards.

23d. The *Needle* and *Sinker-Moulds*, Fig. 30. Theſe moulds with taking out and
putting in a very few pieces, ſerve to caſt both needle and finker-leads.

TO the woodwork of the frame belong the following parts.

1ſt. The ſide-pieces Fig. 1. *a a a.*

2d The *Box Rail* Fig. 1. *b b.* is ſo called, becauſe there are in it two ſmall boxes
where the workmen puts ſeveral things he has immediate occaſion for.

Bbb

3d·

3d. The preffer-rail, Fig. 2. *a a.* is fo called from the preffer-bow's paffing through it.

4th. The foot rail, Fig. 2. *b b.* is the bottom rail of the back part of the woodwork againft which the workman puts his feet when they are not otherwife employed. Thefe three rails hold together the fide pieces.

5th The back piece is a part of the woodwork againft which the journeyman can lean his back Fig. 1. *c c c.* this has at each end a ftrong piece of wood about a foot long placed in the room of brackets *d d.* called the feat-knobs, upon which a loofe fmooth board is laid called the feat board.

6th. The treddles want no particular defcription, Fig. 2. *c c c.* there are three in number, *viz.* two belonging to the flur, the 3d to the preffer, they move in a box faftened to the back-piece under the feat.

7th. The flur-wheel is made of folid wood, it has two channels, in the greater runs the flur-line and in the leffer the treddle cord.

A L L thefe parts juftly fet together compofe the ftocking-frame. The mechanifm of which tho' it muft have difcovered itfelf already in a great meafure in the defcription of the parts, yet for the clearer conception of it, I will here mention how the four movements (by which the work is done) are performed:

1ft. The flur-movement is put in action by the workman's preffing down either of the fide treddles, which brings the flur-box to one fide or the other by which motion the jack-finkers are brought down upon the falling-bar.

2d. The locker-movement is done by the workman's preffing the lower part of the thumb-plates with his thumbs backwards, this forces the lockers upwards and makes the locker-bar bear down the jacks into their place. This motion is alternate with the foregoing, for whilft that brings the finker down, this raifes them again.

3d. The carriage-movement, this has a double motion, an horizontal one by the workman's taking hold of the two round ends of the hand-bar fo that the backs of his hands are towards the ground and pulling the frame forwards, and a vertical motion by taking hold as before, and pulling the frame downwards, and this movement has the greateft fhare in working a courfe.

4th. The preffer-movement is performed by the workman's bearing down the middle treddle, this makes the preffer-bows to bend, which motion brings the preffer-bar upon the beards of the needles, and makes the ends of the beards dip into the eyes of the needles. By thefe four movement the work is performed thus,

I N the firft place the workmen takes a proper length of filk or worfted, &c. thread, the which he doubles and puts the loop made by doubling upon the extream needle, thence he carries his double thread over three or more needles according to the work, and turning it round upon the laft needle of the three he goes forward paffing it over the two next, then he turns it round the laft and paffes over two more and fo on till he is gone through all the needles, and this method forms the welt.

F I N I S.

AN

INDEX

TO

DEERING'S

NOTTINGHAMIA,

Vetus et Nova.

BY

RUPERT CECIL CHICKEN, F.R.C.S., Eng.,

Surgeon to the Nottingham General Hospital.

NOTTINGHAM:
Printed and Publifhed by Frank Murray,
Regent Houfe, 11, Victoria Street,
MDCCCXCIX.

PREFACE.

IT has often seemed to me that the lack of an Index to Charles Deering's History of Nottingham tends in a measure to lessen the use of the book.

No one can read it and not feel that there is such a vast store of knowledge so buried in its own wealth of facts that its value as a work of reference is in part lost.

There must have been, in its compilation, much patient work done by Dr. Deering, and many an old book and dusty manuscript read to get to a focus so much that, but for him, would have been scattered and forgotten.

So now that by his pains he has put so much within our reach, it is wrong of us to allow its lessened usefulness to continue through the want of an index which he, without doubt, would have made had not his labours been stopped before his work was complete.

It has therefore been a pleasant task to me to employ some spare hours in filling up the gap that Death made in the old man's book.

If, by facilitating reference and so uniting scattered facts, it helps to complete his work my object will have been gained.

June, 1898.

List of Plates.

List of Plates—continued.

To the READER.

A Line printed in Italics refers to the Introduction.

A Page number marked with an Asterisk refers to the Introduction.

As the five extra Sheets containing Prynne's List of the Knights of the Shire and the Burgesses for the Town are not numbered, they have been indexed as 209a, 209b, 209c, 209d, 209e, respectively.

INDEX.

A.

ABBIES in Notts, Revenue of, 299, 300
(fee Priory)
Abbies, Stephens' Hiftory of, quoted,
299
Abby Dale, 356
A'Becket, Thomas, 201
Abfon, Rev. John, 45, 143, 358, 360
Abundantia, Mother of St. Bennet, 53
Abutt, Henry, 313
Accident, Surprifing, in Barker Gate, 83
——— ——— on the Caftle-rock, 83
——— ——— at the Crown Inn, 84
——— ——— on High Pavement, 83
——— ——— in Narrow Marfh, 84
——— ——— at Weekday Croff, 83
Acham, Anthony, 136
Acquitain, Duchy of, 183
Act for the Benefit of Orphans, 211
— — Refumption of Lands, 120
— — ——— — — King's Anfwer
to, 120
— of Uniformity, 46, 176
Adam de Kyrkby, 41
Adbolton, The Village of, 354, 358
Addrefs of the Framework Knitters to Oliver
Cromwell, 301
Aga Radulphus, 1*
Agath, Feaft of Saint, 202
Agelocum : a Roman Station, 5*

Age of Nottingham, 1*, 12*
— — ——— as a Borough, *13*, 103,
278*
— — ——— as a Corporation, 13*,
103, 278
— — ——— as a County, 13*, 103,
113, 272, 279
— — ——— as a Town, 13*, 188
— — ——— *as compared with other
Towns, 12*, 13**
— — Chancel of St. Mary's Church, 26
— — Saint Mary's Church, 18
— — Prefent Church of Saint Nicholas,
42
— — St. Peter's Church, 34
— — Town Wall, 5
Aged Perfons, Alphabetical Lift of, 79
Agnellus, Principal of Francifcans, 62
Ague, Rarity of, 78
Alabafter Tomb in Chapel of All Saints',
St. Mary's Church, 30
*Albanact, Slaughter of Britons at Nottingham
in time of, 2**
Albemarle, William Earl of, 178
Albeniaco, Ralph de, Founder of Brodham
Abbey, 68
Albert of Jerufalem, 63
Albocton, Village of, 354
Alcocke, an Aged Perfon, 79

Aldermen

A

B.

Bark

Beaumont

C

c

D

Faconbery

F

H

Hamelak

Holden, Alexander, 360 (fee Houlden)
———— Job, 344
Hole, Sir John, 243
—— Mortimer's, 173, 178
—— James of Scot's, 176
Holinfhed quoted, *4**, 5, 162, 170
Holland, Conftance, wife of Earl of Nottingham, 203
———— Edward, 344
———— John, Earl of Huntingdon, 203
———— 356
Holles, Margaret, daughter of Henry, Duke of Newcaftle, 192
———— Thomas, Patent of Earl of Clare, 197
Hollins quoted, 245
Hollis (Holles), 209c, 312
—— Denzil, Charles, William, Elenore, 27
—— —— F. William, 27
—— Elizabeth, Sufannah, Dorothea, 28
—— Francis, Arabella, and Elizabeth, 27
—— G., 344
—— Gilbert, Katharine, Diana, Anna, Margaret, 28
—— John, 28
—— —— created Earl of Clare and Vifcount Haughton, 197
—— —— —— Duke of Newcaftle, 197
—— —— Firft Earl of Clare, Tomb of, 27, 192
—— —— Second Earl of Clare, 27
—— Mary (ii.), Frances (ii.), 28
—— Mr., an Aged Perfon, 79, 82
—— Penelope, 28
—— Richard, 331
Hollow Stone, 4, 122
—— —— Portcullice at, 4
Hollwell, Thomas, 344
———— Richard, 344
Holm, 162
—— Pierepoint, 74, 233
—— Pierpont Church, 358
Holme, Edmund, 45
Holmes, George, 278
Holt, Thomas, 331
Holy Grotte, The, 53
—— Trinity, Guild of the, 19
Honour of Peverel, 127
———— —— —— at Lenton, 290

Honour of Peverel, Chapel of St. James of Carmelites of the, 127
———— —— —— conferred on John Plantagenet, Earl of Moreton, 201
———— —— —— Extent of the, 127
———— —— —— held by King John, 237
———— —— —— High Stewards of the, 127
———— —— —— Jurifdiction of the, 127
———— —— —— Names of Villages included in the, 354
———— —— —— Prefent High Steward of the, 127
———— —— —— Removal of Court of the, 127
———— —— —— The Loft Records of the, 127
———— —— —— Tradition of the Mayor's Mace of the, 127
———— —— Potneys, 181
———— —— Tickhill, 181
Hoo, Sir Thomas, Chivaler, 194
Hooper, Mr., quoted, 247
Hooper's Sconce, 165
Hope, 356
Hopedale Ball, 356
Hoppwell (Hopewell), Roger de, 209b, 209c
Hoppwood, John, 311
Hops, Trade in, 91
Hopton, 356
Hopwell, John, 45
Hornbuckle, John, 130, 131
Hornby, 239
Horne, Compte de, 7
Horowine, Sarah, 350
Horfe Market, 7
—— —— at Newark, 333
—— Races, 76
Horfepoole in Leicefterfhire, 141, 315, 356
Horfes, Number of, in Nottingham, 76
———— Saddle, Coach, Chaife, and Team, 76
Horfley, 141
———— Caftle (Horlftan), 292, 356
———— Manor of, 292
———— Mr., quoted, 286
Hofe in Leicefter, 335
Hofiery (fee Framework Knitters)
Hofiery

I

Ipswich

J

K

L

Lateranenſes

Leffer
F

Loan

M

Malt

N

Oak

O

Page

P

Page, Thomas, 209d
—— ——— of Misterton, 19
—— William, 155
Pagnel (Paynel), Fulk, 178
—— Gervas, 178
—— Ralph, 178, 236
Painters, Number of, 95
Palavicini's Row, 13
Palestine, Hillarion of, 48
Palmer, George, 311
——— John, 312
——— Lawrence, 344
——— Mary, 207
——— Matthew, 344
—— Sir Thomas, 207
——— Thomas, knighted, 196
Palmere, Johannes, 209a
——— Ricardus, 209a
Palmes, Elizabeth, 334
Panileick, 350
Pannia Clofe, 4
Papebroch, 63
Papplewick (Paplewick), 88, 166, 355, 358
——— granted to Sir John Byron, 293
——— Limestone, 88
Paramour, Jonathan, 80, 173, 176
——— his Charity, 142
Parapet Walls, 6
Parchment Makers, Number of, 95
Pare, John, 41
Paris, 100, 295
—— Matthew, quoted, 180, 239
Parish of St. Mary, 18, 102, 138, 314, 332, 349
—— — — Mary's, Lincoln, 334
—— — — Nicholas, 18, 53, 102, 138, 348
—— — — Peter, 18, 102, 138, 320, 348
Parishes, Number of, in County, 102
——— ——— — — Jurisdiction of Archdeacon of Nottingham, 102
——— ——— — — ——— — Southwell, 102
——— ——— — — ——— — Dean and Chapter of York, 102

Parishes, Number of, in Jurisdiction of Peculiar of Kinoulton, 102
Park Hall, 356
—— The, 187
Parke, Hugo, 41
Parker, Alderman John, the Apothecary, 96
——— John, 209c, 280
——— —— Grocer, 129, 130
——— —— his Charity, 140, 145
——— —— — Legacy, 157
——— —— Mercer, 129, 140
——— Mrs., mother of William Collinson, 143
——— Peter, 129
——— Richard, 129, 311
——— Robert, 129
——— Will., 209c
——— William, Apothecary, 39
Parkes, Widow, 350
Parkins, Isham, 344
—— Richard, 344
Parkyns Family, 231
——— George, Knight, 148
——— Lane, 139
——— Richard, 148, 209e, 231
——— Sir George, 10
——— — Thomas, 10, 223, 231, 232
——— — ——— Church Patronage of, in Notts., 358, 359
Parliament, Barebone's, 209d
——— Dissensions between the King and, 342
——— held at Nottingham, 209b, 237, 239, 241
——— — — Oxford, 209e, 251, 345
——— of Great Britain, The first, 213
——— — Peers held at Nottingham, 244
——— The Long, 210
Parliaments, Constitution of Saxon, 209
——— ——— — the early, 209
——— in England, Antiquity of, 209
Parmap, Wyllyam, 313
Parnham, Willoughby of, 228
——— ——— Houfe of, 228
Parr, Sir William, 244

Parrott

Piggott, Joſeph, 321, 327, 329

Pigot Family, 224 (ſee Picot)

—— ——— Tombs of the, 224

—— Gervas, 209d, 209e

—— Mr., of Thrumpton, 150

—— Sir George, 224

— Gervaſe, 224

Pike Fiſh, 163, 225

Pilcher Gate, 7*, 13, 46, 98, 123, 138, 141, 152

Pilſley, 356

Pilſon, Robert, 344

Pinkeſton (Pinſton), 356

Pin-makers, Number of, 95

Pipe Office, 14

Pitch, Trade in, 91

Fits, Rev. Mr. Henry, 158

Places of Worship, Ancient Saxon, 7*

Plague, The, in Nottingham, 82

Plaiſter Floors, 5

Plaiſterers, Number of, 95, 96

Plantagenet, John, Arms of, 208

———— Richard, —— 208

———— ——— of Shrewſbury, 204

Plants growing around Nottingham, 89

Plaſter of Paris, 88

Plate, Value of, touched and untouched, in reign of Charles I., 345

Pleaſley, 90

Pleſley, 312

Plot, Dr., quoted (*Hist. of Staffs.*), 5*, 86, 287

Plough, John, Sen., 41

—— —— Jun., 41, 142

Plumbers, Number of, 95

Plumpton (Plimpton), Robertus, 209d

—— Will., 209d

Plumptre Family, Manſion of, 5, 19, 29

—— Henry, 19, 31, 146, 148, 311

—— —— ſon of John P., 30

—— —— de, Tomb of, in St. Peter's, 34

—— Huntingdon, 19, 148, 149

—— John, 30, 34, 128, 149, 150, 165, 213, 214, 215, 216, 337, 338, 340, 341

—— —— de, 34, 128, 209c, 209d

—— —— — his Charity, 143, 145

—— —— — — Abuſe of, 147

Plumptre, John de, Tomb of, in St. Peter's, 34

—— —— Houſe of, 6, 25, 138

—— —— Joyce, 31

—— —— John, Henry, and Fitzwilliam, ſons, 31

—— Mr., 16, 19

—— — Arms of, 20, 29

—— — D. H., 30

—— Nicholas, 19, 148, 338

—— Thomas, 147

—— Village of, 339, 355, 359

—— Wealth of Family, Source of, 92

Plumtre (Plumptre), Ann, 146

—— Arms of, 20, 29, 30

—— Emma, 145

—— Roman Coins found at, 286

Poclington, William, 344

Poge, Thomas, 128

Pogg, —— 209d

Poiays, Humbert, 265

Poictiers, Battle of, 193

Point-makers, Number of, 95

Polyolbion, of Drayton, quoted, 137, 160, 161

Pomfrete, 244

Pontage, Freedom from, 112, 268

Pontus, Monks at, 49

Pool, John, Will of, 300

Poole, Thomas, 344

Pools around Nottingham, 160

Poor of Nottingham, 350

Pope Alexander, 58

—— ——— III., 63

—— ——— IV., 58

—— ——— V., 64

—— Clement, 52

—— Eugenius III., 67

—— ——— IV., 65

—— Gregory IX., 64

—— Honorius, 58

—— ——— III., 61, 63

—— ——— IV., 64

—— Innocent II., 52

—— ——— III., 61

—— ——— IV., 58, 63, 64

—— ——— XI., 63

—— ——— XII., 63

—— John XXIII., 64

Pope

Q

R

T

Therbrook

Trent, Forefts beyond, 182
—— full, 163
—— Hethbeth, Heathbethe, Hebethe, Heathbet, Heth-wett, Heyegh-beythe, or Highbath Bridge, 164, 165, 312, 315, 337, 338
—— Lanes, 16, 167
—— Legacy for Repair of Bridge, 142
—— Paving-ftones obtained from, 88
—— Poems on, 225
—— Timber Trade, 88
—— Villages and Towns upon, 162
—— Waterfpout on, 77
Trente, Trenta, Treonta, Troantia, Trounta, Troventio, 86, 103, 108, 120, 160 et seq., 252, 260, 263, 309, 311
Trentham, 162
—— Abbey of, 160
Trefilian, Sir Robert, 242
*Tresle, Richard, 10**
Treffwell, 362
Treveny, Gervas, 10
Trevil, Baldwin, 229
—— Margery, 229
Trevor, J., 119
—— Sir John, 211
Trewman, John, 331
Trial for Trefpafs or Contracts, 111
*Tribonantes, 2**
Tribute, The King's, 109, 110, 111, 264
—— — increafed, 120, 265
Trigge, Elizabeth, Thomas, Matthew, William, Jofeph, Nathaniel, 39
—— Mr. Thomas, fined, 105, 118
—— Thomas, 130, 142, 280
—— —— Alderman, 105
—— —— —— Bequeft of, 39
—— —— —— Tomb of, 39
—— William, 130, 131
Trinitanes, 65
Trinity Guild, Bequeft of Thos. Willoughby to, 315
—— Houfe Guild, 19
Trithemius, 54
Tronage (Toll by Weight) for Wool, 110
Trott, William, 128
Trough Clofe, 137
—— —— Spring, near Mapperley Hill, 82

Trough Stone found under St. Peter's, 34
Trout Fifh, 163, 164
Trowell, 355, 358
—— Bequeft to the Poor of, 151
—— —— — — —— — by Henry Handley, 151
Trufbutt, Will. de, 209b
Trufhworth, 163
Truffeley, 162
Trufts and Charitable Benefactions of Achan, Anthony, 136
—— —— Barker, John, 142
—— —— Bilby, Elizabeth, 143
—— —— —— William, 153
—— —— Burton, —— 141
—— —— Chaundeler, William, 153
—— —— Collins, Abel, 137, 152, 347-352
—— —— Collinfon, William, 143
—— —— Doubleday, Margery, 144
—— —— Drury, William, 142
—— —— Grantham, Lady Lucy, 145
—— —— Gray, Dr., 143, 144
—— —— Gregory, John, 140
—— —— —— William, 136, 140
—— —— Handley, Henry, 144, 151, 321
—— —— Hefkey, John, 157
—— —— Jackfon, Luke, 141, 319, 320
—— —— Labourer, Jonathan, 153
—— —— Lawton, Mary, 142
—— —— Manners, Roger, 135
—— —— Mannors, Sir Thomas, 135
—— —— Martin, Henry, 137
—— —— Mellers, Agnes, 154
—— —— —— Robert, 157
—— —— —— Thomas, 157
—— —— Mellors, Margery, 142
—— —— Metham, Elizabeth, 140
—— —— —— Hannah, 140
—— —— Paramour, Jonathan, 142
—— —— Parker, John, 140, 145, 157
—— —— Patten, —— 139
—— —— Peckham, Sir George, 136
—— —— Perks' Legacy to Burgeffes, 134
—— —— Plumtre, Anne, 146
—— —— —— Henry, 146
—— —— —— John de, 145
Trufts

U

V

W

War